Reconceiving the Renaissance

Reconceiving the Renaissance

A Critical Reader

EDITED BY

Ewan Fernie
Ramona Wray
Mark Thornton Burnett
Clare McManus

CO-ORDINATING EDITOR
Ewan Fernie

AMERICAN CONSULTANT EDITOR
Dympna Callaghan

OXFORD
UNIVERSITY PRESS

OXFORD

UNIVERSITY PRESS

Great Clarendon Street, Oxford OX2 6DP

Oxford University Press is a department of the University of Oxford.
It furthers the University's objective of excellence in research, scholarship,
and education by publishing worldwide in

Oxford New York

Auckland Cape Town Dar es Salaam Hong Kong Karachi
Kuala Lumpur Madrid Melbourne Mexico City Nairobi
New Delphi Shanghai Taipei Toronto

With offices in

Argentina Austria Brazil Chile Czech Republic France Greece
Guatemala Hungary Italy Japan South Korea Poland Portugal
Singapore Switzerland Thailand Turkey Ukraine Vietnam

Oxford is a registered trade mark of Oxford University Press
in the UK and certain other countries

Published in the United States
by Oxford University Press Inc., New York

British Library Cataloguing in Publication Data

Data available

Library of Congress Cataloging in Publication Data

Data available

ISBN 0-19-926557-7

10 9 8 7 6 5 4 3 2 1

Typeset by RefineCatch Limited, Bungay, Suffolk
Printed in Great Britain
on acid-free paper by
Ashford Colour Press Limited, Gosport, Hampshire

For the Renaissance students of
Queen's University Belfast

Praise for *Reconceiving the Renaissance*:

'*Reconceiving the Renaissance* remarkably succeeds in meeting the ambition of its title. With a thoughtful selection of essays, both clearly organized and usefully introduced, the volume as a whole succeeds not only in conscientiously mapping the field of early modern literary studies but also in generously providing access to its landmarks. The result is a book that compellingly demonstrates how various and exciting contemporary scholarship is, at the same time as it reminds us of how various and exciting are the early modern texts that have provoked it.'

David Scott Kastan, Columbia University

'A one-of-a-kind book: a wide-ranging collection of theoretical and critical approaches to English Renaissance literature. The editors do a superb job of contextualizing and introducing difficult theoretical ideas, and they provide an even-handed diversity of opinions illuminating the crucial critical terms that have dominated the field . . . *Reconceiving the Renaissance* will serve as an indispensable guide to students and teachers of Renaissance literature'.

William Kerwin, University of Missouri-Columbia

'An excellent resource which sets out an impressive array of important materials in a logical, coherent, and engaging manner. The editors' introductions are clear, informative and intellectually stimulating . . . should be required reading for all serious students of Renaissance literature'.

Andrew Murphy, University of St Andrews

'*Reconceiving the Renaissance* is without doubt the most illuminating and comprehensive guide to Renaissance and early modern studies available anywhere today. Together with its indispensable collection of critical texts, brought together for the first time in a single volume, it provides lucid synopses of the most influential developments and a mapping of issues and interconnections that will be invaluable to students and scholars alike. A signal achievement and one that will stand as a guide for many years to come.'

Patricia Parker, Stanford University

Outline Contents

Detailed Contents

Acknowledgements

This is a book that came out of a teaching experience shared by the four editors at Queen's University Belfast. We would each like to express our thanks to our co-editors for their generosity during a long and challenging project. Queen's continues to be fortunate in the enthusiasm and ability of its Renaissance students—our debt to these students is recorded in the dedication. We would also like to thank colleagues, past and present, at Queen's for their shared commitment to the learning experience. Ellen Douglas-Cowie and Adrian Streete have been most supportive of this project, while Fran Brearton, Colin Graham, Nigel Harkness and Peter Stoneley have listened into the night on many occasions and to final good effect. In addition, we want to thank Deanna Fernie, for her careful reading and friendship, and Ewan's new students of Royal Holloway, University of London, who have galvanised and refined some of his contributions. Among his colleagues at the college, Ewan would like to thank Roy Booth, Christie Carson, Martin Dzelzainis, Farah Karim-Cooper, Robert Hampson, Jonathan Holmes, Jennifer Neville, Efi Spentzou, Stephen Regan and, especially, Kiernan Ryan. Ramona is personally grateful to members of the 2004 Shakespeare Association of America seminar on editing, particularly David George, Suzanne Gossett, Bernice Kliman, Sonia Massai, Paul Menzer, Eric Rasmussen and Jesus Tronch-Perez, who offered salient suggestions on how to improve the section on textuality. We all want to express our gratitude to the staff of Queen's University Library, Royal Holloway University of London Library, the British Library, the Folger Shakespeare Library and the Library of Congress. We are very grateful to Oxford University Press for enthusiasm for the project and efficiency in seeing it through. Fiona Kinnear was our first champion at the press; Ruth Anderson brought the book out with energy, meticulousness and good humour. We're also grateful to Matthew Cotton for the cover design. A large debt of gratitude must go to our American Consultant Editor, Dympna Callaghan, who read all the material with conscientiousness, generosity and an enviable theoretical rigour. The anonymous readers at Oxford offered detailed feedback and authoritative counsel: without their contribution, the book would certainly be much the poorer.

1

General Introduction: Reconceiving the Renaissance

EWAN FERNIE

RAMONA WRAY

In Renaissance studies today, theory is everywhere. For the student entering this field for the first time, theoretically inflected thinking is impossible to avoid. The choice to engage with theory, and to interpret Renaissance literature and culture through theory, has, in effect, already been made. From gender critiques and post-colonial investigations to historicist and political explorations, theory is central to the discipline. Since the early 1980s, the transformations enacted in the wake of theory have proved both dizzying and exciting. Pre-theory, in the first half of the twentieth century and beyond, the Renaissance was often imagined as a golden age, its literature and culture a nostalgic repository of all that was 'great and good' about the English nation and its people. Frequently mobilized in reinforcements of this view of the Renaissance was E. M. W. Tillyard's *The Elizabethan World Picture*, first published in 1943. Tillyard's work argued for a fundamental Elizabethan belief in, and commitment to, a 'Great Chain of Being', a hierarchy for everything in existence. Now, however, after the theoretical overhaul which this volume surveys, the notion of an ultimately authoritarian Renaissance has been thoroughly revised. For, in place of Tillyard's fully-fledged and secured physical, social and cosmo-logical system, more recent critics tend to posit a conflicted and constantly renegotiated culture with no essential pattern. Taking over from an older stress on order is an attention to disorder, and usurping the assumption of comfortable consensus is a preference for subversion and dissidence. Consequently, the post-theory twenty-first-century Renaissance has come to be envisaged as an intensely fraught and turbulent period, in which constructions of class, race and gender were negotiated, in which doubts and anxieties freely circulated, and in which the very idea of Englishness was thrown into question by local and newly global perspectives.

The general stress on plurality and change, which is characteristic of this fresh conception of the Renaissance, conditions both the topics and the methodologies of contemporary approaches to the subject. As it is now practised, the discipline of Renaissance studies brings together such heterogeneous themes as transvestism, textual editing and the Shakespeare industry in Stratford-upon-Avon. The Renaissance investigated at the turn of the millennium is at once increasingly specialized (made up of a multiplicity of discrete sub-topics) and promiscuously inter-disciplinary (moving between subjects and methodologies without so much as a 'by-your-leave'). Thoroughly acknowledged as shaped by myriad external circumstances, Shakespeare and other Renaissance authors are explored in terms of multiple relations to history. Juxtaposed with, say, the theology of demonic possession, a developing 'culture of news', provincial ritual practices such as May games and festivals of misrule, and proto-imperial documents by which monarchs laid claim to disputed territories, the Renaissance text has been sucked into the complex swirl of the cultural continuum. This unprecedented commitment to contextualization points beyond the notion of the autonomous work of art and that of the unchanging 'human condition'. It gestures instead towards a recognition of communal concerns among disparate texts and towards a peculiarly Renaissance elaboration of society and the human subject. In turn, since the period is read as both complex and diverse, a bewilderingly detailed array of Renaissances has come into view in the pages of recent criticism.

This transformation in how the period is imagined, and how it is studied, can be traced to considerations outside the realm of pure ideas. The present cultural and political environment, and changes to the constitution of academia, for instance, are important factors. But most significant has been the absorption into Renaissance studies of the theoretical impetus which, since the late 1960s, has altered the humanities and social sciences at large. In the wake of theory, the equipment is available not only to perceive the Renaissance anew but also to accept its variant incarnations. The American poet Wallace Stevens famously formulated thirteen ways of looking at a blackbird; likewise, contemporary critics offer multiple perspectives on a variegated Renaissance, contending that interpretive latitude is the only response capable of accommodating the range and relativism of things and thought.

But if the integration of theory and Renaissance studies can be invigorating, it can also be off-putting to the reader chancing upon criticism of the period for the first time, especially if she or he already is struggling to get to grips with William Shakespeare, Edmund Spenser and Mary Wroth. For too many students, a cursory overview of current criticism presents an apparently unmanageable collocation of perspectives and methodologies, with neither the author nor the book functioning as a stable reference point. The sheer diversity of commentary—together with the engrossing density of much of it—creates difficulty, splintering the field and making it resistant to mapping and navigation. This difficulty is popularly addressed by pigeonholing critical work according to its 'ism' or approach. Thus, the varieties of contemporary Renaissance studies are reimagined as belonging to dogmatically cultural materialist, feminist and poststructuralist schools, to name but three. Inside such a selective procedure, scholars and students are encouraged to separate out essays and critics into their respective groupings, which are recognized as having their own distinctive methods, values and goals. Yet it is often not helpful or even possible to define and place current criticism in this fashion. There is simply too great an abundance of difference under the various rubrics—one feminist critic, for instance, may be at polar opposites from the next—and, equally, there is too pronounced an overlap between the different practices to enable really distinctive definitions. Hence, the different 'schools' within Renaissance studies all borrow liberally from each other. Theoretical separatism prohibits an achieved sense of the discipline as a whole, by precluding an identification of approaches' common characteristics. The predilection for dividing up the field and choosing one 'ism' above the rest has additionally led to new historicism (an approach characterized by its endeavour to return the text to history) being inappropriately foregrounded and spotlighted.

Reconceiving the Renaissance aims to avoid the pitfall of the pigeonhole and to provide a synoptic view of the whole field of contemporary Renaissance studies. Its central premise is that key concerns cut across, and reverberate throughout, criticism of the period. It argues that the profusion of theoretical 'schools' and 'isms' functions within a novel horizon, making it possible to pinpoint a shared theoretical agenda within which contemporary criticism operates. This General Introduction sets out and explains the broad consensus that lies at the heart of the work on the Renaissance being produced today. In doing so, it reveals the pervasive logic of plurality and change, which has resulted in the wholesale transformation of the ways in which the Renaissance is regarded. Of course, the remarks offered here constitute only a starting-point, one that will be built upon incrementally throughout the rest of this book.

The six sections which follow this General Introduction are 'Textuality', 'Histories', 'Appropriation', 'Identities', 'Materiality' and 'Values'. The titles indicate the content and tenor of the sections and offer a sense of their place in the book's overall architecture. Individual section introductions will elaborate how different critics work to complicate and develop the shared theoretical agenda outlined below as well as highlighting the debates active inside particular areas of interest. Each section comprises a range of classic and cutting-edge arguments narratively sequenced and interspersed with shorter extracts. Each section also works as a context for the others, enabling cross-reference, anticipation and culminative knowledge of the field from several points of view. The questions featured at the end of sections constitute an opportunity to test and refine an understanding of the materials and, as it were, talk back to the book.

Altogether, *Reconceiving the Renaissance* provides a rich but coherent map of Renaissance studies in the subject's current state of development. It defines key methodological questions and problems and it also traces the course of debate towards the initiatives of the future.

* * *

The first step towards understanding the new theoretical logic of current Renaissance studies entails acknowledging the instability of all books. Traditional editors of Renaissance texts sought to achieve a text which perfectly recovered the original intentions of its author. But, in our period, the author's original manuscript is, as Stephen Orgel pointed out in 1981, an imaginative 'figment'.[1] Often early modern manuscripts either haven't survived or, as is regularly the case with poetry, they have survived in multiple versions, not as a prelude to print, but as part of a system of manuscript circulation that endured well after the proliferation of print. Moreover, cultural and collaborative theories of artistic production have relegated the author to a position of relative inconsequence. The printed text is strictly the work not of the author but of the publisher to whom it legally belongs; and, in the case of drama, the text isn't an authorial production so much as a changing working script for the theatrical company.

No longer can the book be said to be a coherent object, a transparent window on truth or a vehicle of absolute meaning. To take just one famous instance, there are often significant differences between the freestanding 'Quarto' texts of Shakespeare's plays and the versions in the 'First Folio' of his collected works, printed in 1623. The particular attention given to editing since the 1980s has prioritized textual differences in the form of variant words, passages and editions, and this has worked to underscore the poststructuralist recognition of the inherent slipperiness and treacherous potential of any linguistic utterance. Perhaps the starkest example of this new emphasis on textual difference has been the controversial decision of the Oxford editors to print both the Quarto and Folio versions of *King Lear* (1608 and 1623 respectively) as two distinct plays.

Because the integrity of the book has been thrown into question, critics now prefer to use the word 'text', a term derived from the Latin 'textere', meaning 'to weave'. Texts are permanently unravelling and being stitched up as more-or-less new texts in eclectically different contexts. This is as relevant to the new Arden edition of *Hamlet* as it is to Kenneth Branagh's film version of *Much Ado About Nothing* (1993): the innovative situating and arrangement of both makes them copies and novelties at one and the same time.

Nor is it simply the text that is seen as relative and externally determined: so, too, are the truths it supposedly articulates. The French cultural theorist Michel Foucault captures a flavour of this prismatic textuality when he writes that the book 'is caught up in a system of references to other books, other texts, other sentences: it is a node within a network'.[2] In this sense, meaning becomes a matter of negotiation, and interpretation hinges upon intertextual forms of understanding. A book signifies by means of current conventions of language and style, and in relation to contemporary concerns and debates. Most modern critics would agree that what a book says and does depends entirely, in the words of Jonathan Dollimore, on a threefold process of 'articulation, context and reception'—that is, on what is said to whom, in which circumstances and with what

---

[1] Stephen Orgel, 'What is a Text?', *Research Opportunities in Renaissance Drama* 26 (1981), 3.
[2] Michel Foucault, *The Archaeology of Knowledge*, trans. A. M. Sheridan Smith (London and New York: Routledge, 1991), p. 23.

results.[3] For example, the meaning of *The Sonnets* (1609) is not ultimately constrained by the generic context of the Elizabethan sonnet-sequence, as we might gather from the various gay and queer appropriations of Shakespeare's verse that have flourished since the late nineteenth century. Place a text in an alternative context and a different text will emerge.

The origins of the book, then, cannot be said to enjoy a safe and readily identifiable location; instead, it is necessary to see the book as one in an infinite series of possible editions, all shaped and mediated by history and culture. What emerges from current Renaissance studies in textuality is a Renaissance book insecure in its material form, its sources, its genealogy and its verbal detail.

If the individual book has been destabilized and multiplied, the canon of Renaissance studies has also been thoroughly interrogated and expanded, in ways that are reflected throughout *Reconceiving the Renaissance*. Shakespeare is still a major player in the field, but many writers once judged as minor are now of interest as alternatives to 'the Bard'. In terms of genre, categories have been added to and aided not only by a widening of the dramatic canon but also by a more scrupulous attention to the varieties of Renaissance poetry and prose. Occluded and devalued genres such as travel writing, autobiography and romance have pushed back the borders of contemporary Renaissance studies. Central to this wider focus has been the recovery of writing by Renaissance women. Once a spectral fantasy of Virginia Woolf's, Shakespeare's female contemporaries have since forcefully invaded Renaissance literature, with the effect that women's writing, and the gender politics of writing by men, are aspects of the period that no critic can ignore.

The attention devoted to women represents only one of the ways in which a more thoroughgoing dialogue between literature and history has shaped new criticism of the period. Renaissance women write differently, it has been comprehensively argued, because of the alternative historical environments in which they composed and circulated their texts. In 1986, Jean E. Howard saw the virtues of a 'new historical criticism' as evolving out of a 'widespread attack' on the traditional idea 'that man possesses a transhistorical core of being'.[4] Texts once read in terms of an essentially stable (and paradigmatically male) human condition are taken instead to reveal historically particular understandings and constructions of, say, gender, the self and sexual and political life. Instead of absenting themselves from time better to appreciate the transcendent beauty of the work of art, critics today interpret Renaissance texts as integrally connected to the urgencies of their particular moment. The notion that history is above all 'different' is evident in the methodologies of even the most diluted forms of new historicism. Much current writing reveals the historical distance and embeddedness of early modern literature by demonstrating connections between canonical texts and historical

---

[3] Jonathan Dollimore, 'Shakespeare, cultural materialism and the new historicism', in Jonathan Dollimore and Alan Sinfield (eds.), *Political Shakespeare: New Essays in Cultural Materialism* (Manchester: Manchester University Press, 1985), p. 13.

[4] Jean E. Howard, 'The new historicism in Renaissance studies', *English Literary Renaissance* 16 (1986), 20.

ephemera. Once recovered, the contexts of privileged literary texts function to point up the insufficiency and contingency of purely aesthetic judgements, and to indicate the historical alterity and resistance of familiar texts such as *King Lear* (first performed 1604–5) and *Paradise Lost* (1667). By summoning a range of contexts, the unfamiliar, including a vital substratum of previously derided popular culture, is reinserted as an object of critical attention.

Because of the newly comparable status of the literary text and its environment, and because of the promotion of history from a one-dimensional 'background' to a plural foreground, critics have engaged theoretically with areas previously the remit of historians alone. Hand-in-hand with postmodern historiographers such as Hayden White, work in Renaissance studies has stressed the inevitable fictionality of history. This doesn't mean that history is just 'made up' but rather that it is less complete, less obtainable and more mediated than we once thought. Based largely upon interpretations of incomplete evidence, history, it is now widely acknowledged, can be read differently to reveal different stories. Historical accounts are various, and not only because of the scope for disagreement enshrined in sources that are themselves discontinuous. Current criticism insists that historical difference is always filtered through the different history of the current time. As Thomas Healy puts it, 'Our interest in the past is dictated by our involvement in the present';[5] or, in Benedetto Croce's words, 'All history is contemporary history'.[6] History is written *in history*; it is itself part of, and affected by, a history that is still in process.

This conditioning of the past by the present has been made most vividly apparent in the study of later appropriations of Shakespeare, of other Renaissance figures and texts, and of 'the Renaissance' itself. Such films as Baz Lurhmann's *William Shakespeare's Romeo + Juliet* (1996), an updated 'teen' version of Shakespeare's play, and John Madden's *Shakespeare in Love* (1998), a more historical portrayal of early modern players and playwrights, have readily inserted themselves into the curriculum as proper objects of scholarly enquiry. The poststructuralist notion of 'iterability' is relevant here: like any other sign, the Renaissance text gestures beyond its immediate and subsequent contexts, assuming different significances as it is reiterated across history. In the light of such temporal potential, studies in appropriation offer access to a measure of the new as it is necessarily forged in relation to the old. To cite but one instance: Michael Almereyda's *Hamlet* (2000), concerned as it is with the urban present, late capitalism and forms of technology, reflects upon modern uncertainties via its deployment of a four-hundred-year-old dramatic text.

The open-ended prospects for appropriation show just how widely a Renaissance production may come to entertain a different orientation. Materialist criticism of appropriation records the redeployment of both 'Shakespeare' and the 'Renaissance' as prestige markers in the ebbs and flows of contemporary capitalism—the aura of each has been known to sell anything from academic monographs to beer and pizza. Shakespeare has been radically refigured in terms of queer politics in

---

[5] Thomas Healy, *New Latitudes: Theory and English Renaissance Literature* (London: Arnold, 1992), p. 10.

[6] Benedetto Croce, *History as the Story of Liberty*, trans. Sylvia Sprigge (London: Allen & Unwin, 1941), p. 19.

Gus Van Sant's *My Own Private Idaho* (1991) and even as porn, as Richard Burt's *Unspeakable ShaXXXpeares* demonstrates.[7] Recent studies of post-colonial theatre, film and novels have illustrated the paradox behind Shakespeare's exportation. On the one hand, the imperial project uses Shakespeare to further national interests; on the other hand, it results in a hybridized and differently embedded dramatist. Thus, in a much-cited argument, Ania Loomba demonstrates how an Indian Kathkali appropriation, otherwise utterly indifferent to Shakespeare, 'provisionalizes' the dramatist as a 'suitably weighty' vehicle for its own artistic possibility.[8] But if Shakespeare, as a result of his unrivalled cultural authority, is typically appropriated in the present moment in order to be subtly subverted or turned into profit, there are other Renaissance figures as various as John Dee, the Elizabethan magus, and Moll Cutpurse, the cross-dressing 'roaring girl', who have been appropriated in more straightforwardly radical ways in favour of counter-cultural practices and knowledge.

Figures such as Cutpurse and Dee may resonate with twenty-first-century audiences because of their presumed capacity to overreach social and gender demarcations. Certainly, a broader critical focus on cultural difference across the Renaissance as a whole mirrors increasing toleration and variegation in matters of lifestyle and sexuality in our own postmodern context. In doing so, it foregrounds, in the words of Catherine Gallagher and Stephen Greenblatt, 'groups that in many colleges and universities had hitherto been marginalized, half hidden, or even entirely excluded from the professional study of literature: Jews, African Americans, Hispanics, Asian Americans, and, most significantly from the point of view of the critical ferment, women'.[9] In the drama alone, through a process of critical foregrounding and reappraisal, a range of marginalized and rebellious characters have been reinterpreted in such a way as to highlight the plays' interrogative immersions in religious, racial, national and sexual ideologies. One thinks of figures of religious alterity like Christopher Marlowe's Barabas and Shakespeare's Othello, sexual dissidents like Marlowe's Edward II and Gaveston, and heroines who defy conventional gender constraints like Elizabeth Cary's Mariam and Shakespeare's Lady Macbeth. Accompanying the emphasis upon such differences goes a consideration of class, which is explained in terms of its Renaissance manifestation as status rather than occupation or wealth. Ben Jonson's vagabond magus, Subtle, Thomas Dekker's indigent witch, Mother Sawyer, and Shakespeare's downwardly mobile Prince Hal—all have pressed forward from the Renaissance stage for acknowledgement and reconsideration in these terms.

Such a process is not as simple as it might at first appear. In any historically rich recontextualization, different categories of gender, sexual, racial or national identity

[7] Richard Burt, *Unspeakable ShaXXXpeares: Queer Theory and American Kiddie Culture* (New York: St Martin's Press, 1998).

[8] See Ania Loomba, ' "Local-manufacture made-in-India Othello fellows": Issues of race, hybridity and location in post-colonial Shakespeares', in *Post-Colonial Shakespeares*, ed. Ania Loomba and Martin Orkin (London and New York: Routledge, 1998), pp. 143–63.

[9] Catherine Gallagher and Stephen Greenblatt, *Practicing New Historicism* (Chicago and London: University of Chicago Press, 2000), p. 11.

will always prove internally heterogeneous. With respect to race, Loomba writes, '[t]he outsider in the literature of the period is not always literally of a different colour; after all, the slave population of Europe consisted of Tartar, Greek, Armenian, Russian, Bulgarian, Turkish, Circassian, Slavonic, Cretan, Arab, African (Mori), and occasionally Chinese (Cathay) slaves'.[10] As well as being complexly constructed, categories of difference are also invariably internally fragmented by rival categories. Racial others, for instance, are divided from each other not just by more detailed discriminations of race but also according to criteria of gender, sexuality and class or caste. These caveats notwithstanding, the processes of 'othering' remain structurally similar and connected; hence, Bruce R. Smith's observation that misogyny and racial enmity are combined in the effeminization of the French in *Henry V* (1598–9) is readily understandable.

Smith observes that, in the representation of the war waged between England and France, French effeminacy acts as a foil to English manhood. The characters 'who speak French in the play are women, Princess Catherine and her maid Alice. The French men in their affected speech, as in their exaggerated *politesse* and lack of valour, are allied with women'.[11] Here the literary surface of Shakespeare's play accrues additional levels of meaning through a consideration of its subtexts of race and gender. Smith's work is symptomatic of a more general tendency that insists that a text can never truly be removed from its communicating social and political contexts. To attempt such a removal, the argument runs, both mystifies and naturalizes the ideological work the text inevitably performs.

The investigation of alternative subjectivities has brought feminism, postcolonialism and queer theory to bear on critical debate, and a range of thinkers—from feminists such as Hélène Cixous and Julia Kristeva, to postcolonialists like Homi Bhabha and Edward Said and theorists of sexuality like Judith Butler and Eve Kosofsky Sedgwick—are now commonly quoted in Renaissance studies in ways that facilitate the exploration of cultural difference both inside and outside English Renaissance culture. Here once again a particular constellation of theoretical interests has enabled Renaissance studies to develop into a more richly diverse field. Nor does intellectual energy travel in one direction only. As theory becomes central to Renaissance studies, so, too, does Renaissance studies feed back into theoretical paradigms, allowing a priori formulations a more precise historical purchase. Sexuality is a case in point. Influenced by Foucault, who cautions that homosexual identity (as distinct from practice) did not appear until the nineteenth century, Susan Zimmerman has shown that, in a variety of ways, '[e]arly modern eroticism was fundamentally different from that of today'.[12] Similarly, Alan Sinfield advises that, even if *The Merchant of Venice* (1596–7) and *Twelfth Night* (1601–2) bring out

---

[10] Ania Loomba, 'The colour of patriarchy: critical difference, cultural difference and Renaissance drama', in Kate Chedgzoy (ed.), *Shakespeare, Feminism and Gender* (Basingstoke, Hampshire: Palgrave, 2001), p. 246.

[11] Bruce R. Smith, *Shakespeare and Masculinity* (Oxford: Oxford University Press, 2000), p. 116.

[12] Michel Foucault, *History of Sexuality I: An Introduction*, trans. Robert Hurley (Harmondsworth, Middlesex: Penguin, 1990), p. 43; Susan Zimmerman (ed.), *Erotic Politics: Desire on the Renaissance Stage* (New York and London: Routledge, 1992), p. 7.

GENERAL INTRODUCTION | **9**

of the closet the seemingly homosexual Antonios, we should be cautious about assuming that these characters end up frozen in postures of lovelorn humiliation.[13] What is taken for granted at the present historical juncture, in other words, does not necessarily map easily onto the constructions and practices of earlier epochs. The criticism is salutary, both for a critical practice agitating to reintroduce sexuality to the Renaissance and for a queer studies eager to reinscribe with a gay imprint the differently sexualized body of the early modern 'sodomite'.

A critical concentration around identities is intimately linked to the fact that the body in Renaissance studies has taken centre stage, signalling a shift, which is characteristic of a wider movement in the humanities, from the spiritual to the material. Although its subversive potential is now beginning to be recognized, spirituality has often been conceived by contemporary critics as the internalized affect of a discursive regime which mandates conventional identities and disables resistance. Whereas earlier post-Romantic criticism entertained such unifying abstractions as 'the spirit of the age', the preoccupation of the contemporary Renaissance critic is emphatically to turn towards historical bodies instead.[14] Critics have claimed the Renaissance as particularly 'early modern' in its discovery of the scientific physicality of the human animal which still conditions our own worldview. The 'culture of dissection' played out in Europe's elaborate anatomy theatres, and memorialized in the pages and plates of Andreas Vesalius as well as in Rembrandt's celebrated anatomy paintings, testifies to a new empirical engagement with the spectacular human frame. A fascination with, and an absorption in, the body are also borne out in William Harvey's experiments in, and revolutionary discovery of, the circulation of the blood, and even in John Donne's devotional meditations on his own diseased and dying flesh.

But, if current work has highlighted the Renaissance orientation towards embodiment, it has equally observed that, after Descartes, the modern self is rudely divorced and abstracted from the body.[15] And, if contemporary Renaissance studies has exposed, and sometimes even luxuriated in, human materiality, it has also emphasized, in line with its discoveries concerning the cultural constitution of the subject, the body's surprising volatility. Recent scholarship has explored costume, cosmetics and the surgical refashioning of the body, as well as the extent to which it is moulded by different Renaissance discourses of, say, gender, race and science. And yet, a distinctive power to resist cultural fashioning and appropriation is ceded to the body at the same time. Following the French psychoanalyst Jacques Lacan's argument for a distinctive domain of the 'Real' preceding all language and culture, and the Russian literary theorist Mikhail

---

[13] Alan Sinfield, 'How to Read *The Merchant of Venice* Without Being Heterosexist', in *Alternative Shakespeares 2*, ed. Terence Hawkes (London and New York: Routledge, 1996), pp. 122–40.

[14] Foucault complains about the distortions entailed in the historical category of 'spirit' in *The Archaeology of Knowledge*, p. 22. One non-Foucauldian landmark in the theoretical turn towards the body is Elaine Scarry's *The Body in Pain: The Making and Unmaking of the World* (New York and Oxford: Oxford University Press, 1985).

[15] See especially Francis Barker, *The Tremulous Private Body: Essays on Subjection* (London: Methuen, 1984).

Bakhtin's theories of carnival and the grotesque, the body is simultaneously celebrated and explored as that which exceeds the symbolic order and destabilizes social convention.

In the Renaissance, institutions are often imagined in bodily terms. The Christian church is supposed to be 'the body of Christ'; the nation is embodied in its monarch; the monarch is understood as having 'two bodies', her own natural body and that of her kingdom;[16] America is misogynistically pictured as a woman to be sexually conquered. But the focus on the body sometimes gives way to a new preoccupation with early modern objects. Just as the Renaissance text has been reassessed in the light of its materiality, so, too, have 'things' in general been redrawn according to a heightened awareness of their physical composition and cultural complexion. This trajectory from spirits to subjects to what is thoroughly tangible partly represents an effort to test the limits of ideological evaluations, since it betrays a need to bolster ideas with substance, to complicate abstract philosophizing with 'real' elements, and to defend discursive arrangements with palpable properties.

* * *

This General Introduction has touched so far on new theorizations of textual instability, historical variation, open-ended appropriation, alternative subjectivities, and the varieties of human and non-human physical form. The common denominators here are also the buzz-words of contemporary critical practice— 'diversity', 'difference', 'alterity', 'pluralism', 'relativity', 'change'. One overall descriptor of a critical practice orientated in this direction is 'subversive'; another is 'postmodern', since, in its 'incredulity towards meta-narratives' of truth and progress, postmodernism proclaims a new epoch of unrestricted difference and possibility.[17] It is a small wonder, then, that philosophers of postmodernism of all persuasions—from Jacques Derrida, to Fredric Jameson, to Gayatri Spivak, to Slavoj Žižek—are frequently enlisted in arguments ranging across current Renaissance studies. The invocation of such thinkers attests to the fact that postmodern problematics find a collegial niche in the Renaissance, in part because, as Hugh Grady suggests, the Renaissance stands on one brink of modernity, and we find ourselves in a comparable position at its end.[18] Reconsideration of the Renaissance in relation to the modern and postmodern epochs has, in fact, resulted in its reconceptualization in much recent work as 'the early modern period'. Crucially, if Renaissance studies attests to the ways in which the past is shaped by the present, it also asserts that the postmodern present is shaped by the past. Hence, it is possible, for instance, to trace a narrative of subjection backward, as an influential strain of criticism has done by appealing in the present for justice for those groups

---

[16] See Ernst Kantorowicz, *The King's Two Bodies: A Study in Medieval Political Theology* (Princeton: Princeton University Press, 1981).

[17] See Jean-François Lyotard, *The Postmodern Condition: A Report on Knowledge*, trans. Geoffrey Bennington and Brian Massumi (Manchester: Manchester University Press, 1984), p. xxiv and *passim*.

[18] See Hugh Grady, *The Modernist Shakespeare: Critical Texts in a Material World* (Oxford: Clarendon Press, 1991).

(especially women, the lower classes, other races and homosexuals) who have been subordinated and oppressed by history.

Such a procedure is conducted in terms of pluralism and diversity rather than established standards of 'good' and 'right', which, much like familiar aesthetic values, are typically rejected as securing conservative constructions of home and hearth. Turning the tables of convention, contemporary critics celebrate marginalized and resented individuals and groups as advocates of alterity and dissent that both exemplify the differential nature of identity and foreshadow alternative identities as yet unrealized. Much recent commentary on the Renaissance has teased out, and followed through, this illicit scenario of a voyage into unfettered subjectivity. The rejection of essentialist ideas of the human subject has opened up the prospect of a creative self-fashioning in defiance of traditional notions of gender, sexuality and class. A boy plausibly playing a girl playing a boy in a drama such as *As You Like It* (1599–1600), for example, can now be seen to demonstrate not only that gender is performative but, perhaps more importantly, that it is also possible to perform otherwise. Within the theoretical paradigms which this anthology elaborates, there are no fixed or immutable hierarchies or laws; only artificial orders and injunctions, various and changing, obtain. An important consequence of this is that an appetite for difference and alterity meets no absolute, impassable resistance and thus may initiate genuine, large-scale political change. Positing an anarchic play of differences, which spells the ruin of all domination, Jacques Derrida writes in his classic exposition of deconstruction, 'Not only is there no kingdom of *différance*, but *différance* instigates the subversion of every kingdom'.[19] Moreover, the politics of difference are not just revolutionary but perpetually so, since they are always turned towards a different future.

Many contemporary critics aspire towards this promise of utopian possibilities. Foucault wrote explicitly of historical difference that we might feel the ground moving beneath our feet, while present-day Renaissance studies often envisages the industry of the academic as part-and-parcel of a broader social struggle.[20] Jonathan Dollimore's influential *Radical Tragedy* set the tone for much succeeding criticism of Renaissance texts and culture by vigorously positioning itself against stasis and universals, electing instead to proclaim the need for political action and reformation.[21] Because it is poised at the inception of many of the historical developments that characterize the twentieth century and the new millennium—the most salient being capitalism and empire—the Renaissance instructs us in the origins of our own historical condition. We have seen that the Renaissance can function powerfully as a starting-point for enquiry into the present. The ambitious

[19] Jacques Derrida, 'Différance', in *Margins of Philosophy*, trans. Alan Bass (Chicago: University of Chicago Press, 1982), p. 22. Derrida's neologism 'différance' combines difference with deferral. Since any term or concept operates by differing from all others, it cannot be grasped or referred to directly.

[20] Michel Foucault, *The Order of Things: An Archaeology of the Human Sciences* (London and New York: Routledge, 1991), p. xxiv.

[21] Jonathan Dollimore, *Radical Tragedy: Religion, Ideology and Power in the Drama of Shakespeare and his Contemporaries*, 3rd edn (Basingstoke: Palgrave, 2004), particularly the 'Introduction to the Second Edition', pp. xli–xcix, but also *passim*.

Englishness of many Renaissance texts, to take one more example, is already reverberating with what is currently the most pressing of international issues; during the 2003 season at the National Theatre, London, a production of *Henry V*, brooding obsessively on the responsibilities of leadership and the balancing of rationales for military conflict, offered itself as a timely commentary upon the activation of Anglo-American hegemony on the global stage. As the synoptic view provided by this book suggests, perhaps the most important aspect of the theoretical agenda which contemporary critics share is a sense of Renaissance studies as a vital cultural force, one which has comprehensively reconceived itself the better to confront the limitations and possibilities of today's educational, social and political landscape.

2

Textuality

RAMONA WRAY

In an earlier manifestation, textual studies—the term incorporates the twin disciplines of bibliography and editing—stood outside mainstream Renaissance criticism. Bibliography and editing were seen as peripheral, less important than the 'real work' of literary analysis. One of the gains of the theoretical paradigm which has reshaped the Renaissance in recent years has been to unite these two strands of endeavour: theory has enabled a thorough revision of bibliography and editing, integrating both within the interpretive act and, in the process, transforming the status of textual studies. Significant investigations into the construction of particular Renaissance editions, and discussions of the contemporary and subsequent histories of the early modern book, have given bibliography critical currency. Meantime, the reinvigorating dimensions of theory have transformed editing in such a way as to allow textual studies to shed its specialist image and embrace a centre-stage position. Finding textual studies to possess both relevance and possibility, scholars are turning to bibliographical and editorial undertakings as an urgent priority, increasingly one which must be addressed as a prelude to interpretive licence.

Crucial to the transformation of textual studies has been a new understanding of the materiality of the book. For many years, books constituted the unproblematic basis of English Literature. Generally, there was little questioning of the status of the book as an object; that is, whether its cover, its printing, the nature and extent of its circulation had any bearing on its content. Nowadays, a regard for the physicality of the text, as insisted upon by such critics as Roger Chartier and D. F. McKenzie, means that the content of the book is seen as inextricable from—and dependent upon—the circumstances of its production, reception, and circulation. From printers' marks to records of ownership, and from variant pagination to registers of licence—these are extant historical traces through which the book might be said to reveal itself. All constitutive elements, even the seemingly trivial, play an important role in the emergence and meaning of the book—as Margreta de Grazia and Peter Stallybrass argue here, the very paper making up the Renaissance page can affect the ways in which the text is disseminated and interpreted. The recognition that awareness needs to be focused beyond the words has prompted related work on such matters as marginalia, binding and illustration. The book has come to be seen as a complex assembly of material features, one which signifies not simply in terms of its printed language alone.

An emphasis upon the book as object assists the general contention that the author is only one ingredient in the business of textual production, only one factor feeding into the finished result. Thanks to the scholarship of Leah Marcus, Jeffrey Masten, Stephen Orgel and others, which has been partly mediated via Roland Barthes and Michel Foucault's manifestos about the 'death of the author', widespread dissatisfaction has developed around the anachronistic claim that authorship is emporwerigly singular and and pre-eminently individualized. Beginning with the hypothesis of writers writing together, for instance, Masten broadens out his approach to showcase, under the same banner, a range of participants—actors, directors, censors and printers—who contribute to, and make a mark upon, the final textual creation. His argument—that Renaissance authorship is collaborative, and that more than one individual is involved in production and reproduction— has had far-reaching ramifications. Prior to this interpretive shift, the main task of the textual critic was to adjudicate between competing versions of a particular text, eventually delivering a definitive 'masterwork' that was supposedly closest to the author's 'original intentions'. In the wake of the recognition that making texts is a collaborative process, such an editorial endeavour has become almost untenable: no edition can resurrect the author, since there is no author to resurrect, nor can 'original intentions' operate as a point of reference. All that remain are various incarnations of a text, each of which enjoys a messy and controversial relation to its theatrical source. This recent sea change in critical attention has facilitated fundamental alterations in vocabulary and outlook: most obviously, long-standing formulations about 'foul papers' and 'fair copy' (respectively, uncorrected drafts and final versions), and 'good' and 'bad' quartos (printed versions of varying quality), have been superseded, their judgemental tone proving unsustainable. Here, Laurie Maguire's preference for the formulation 'suspect texts' is exemplary of a newer grammar of multiplicity and difference.[1]

New editorial principles have had a knock-on effect on the ways in which older histories of editing, and editorial histories, are understood. Some of the most important studies of the past twenty years have discovered the ways in which past editorial enterprises are moulded by their own ideological contexts. The power inherent in editing is discovered most forcefully when examined in relation to a political agenda. The trajectory mapped by Andrew Murphy below, for instance, shows how the Shakespearean text has been dismantled and reassembled across centuries of tradition by powerful editors capable of simultaneously closing down

---

[1] Laurie Maguire, *Shakespearean Suspect Texts: The 'Bad' Quartos and their Contexts* (Cambridge: Cambridge University Press, 1996).

and opening up interpretation. Both Suzanne Gossett and Gary Taylor reinforce a historical sense of editorial activity, and conservative ideology, as familiar bedfellows. Their extracts, as well as others dedicated to women writers, suggest illuminating connections between textuality and gender, and queer theory and textual studies, while also pointing up work still to be conducted in this central line of enquiry.

If current criticism is responsive to difficulties with the ways in which the Renaissance text has been edited in the past, what form might a newly theorized editorial practice take? Unsurprisingly, different textual theories sustain different editorial approaches. As Gary Taylor suggests here, a properly self-conscious practice is required to reflect both upon which texts are granted editorial priority and upon their places in history. Concomitantly, there will be the recognition that universal editorial principles are neither possible nor applicable. Women's texts, for example, as several extracted commentators make clear, introduce discrete problems and call for specific, gender-sensitive, editorial solutions. Similarly, it is increasingly recognized that occluded and devalued genres of writing, such as autobiography, travel literature and religio-political polemic, require special editorial knowledge and tact. One obvious route ahead lies with a greater reliance upon parallel texts, including facsimiles. Thus, recent editions of *King Lear* elect to present both contested early versions (Quarto and Folio) side-by-side as a means of celebrating the play's/plays' textual multiplicity, even if an accompanying emphasis upon Shakespeare as author runs counter to recent demythologizing tendencies. More radical would be the 'open text' approach proposed by David Scott Kastan, which privileges proliferation; according to this schema, electronic sources allow an editor to assemble a potentially endless array of materials. A warning note, however, is sounded by Andrew Murphy when he states that the utopian opportunities afforded by the medium of the internet imposes 'more and more constrained selection criteria on what texts get reproduced, and massively increases the rate of textual obsolescence'.[2]

The final selection of extracts suggests some of the ways in which current editors, alive both to the new centrality of their chosen activity and to the theoretical implications of editorial responsibility, approach their tasks. The practical example below from Leah S. Marcus, Janel Mueller and Mary Beth Rose's edition of *Elizabeth I: Collected Works* is particularly useful, since it is explicit about problems and solutions—many textual decisions are passed onto the reader—and fully aware of its necessarily delicate balancing-act. Theirs is a policy which will, no doubt, inspire future interpreters and stimulate as yet unrealized bibliographical and editorial reconceptualizations of the Renaissance book.

[2] Andrew Murphy, 'Introduction', in Andrew Murphy (ed.), *The Renaissance Text: Theory, Editing, Textuality* (Manchester and New York: Manchester University Press, 2000), p. 4.

1 | The book as material object

Margreta de Grazia and Peter Stallybrass, 'The materiality of the Shakespeare text', *Shakespeare Quarterly*, 44 (1993), 280–2.

Perhaps a more helpful way of conceptualizing the text is to be found outside metaphysics, in the materials of the physical book itself: in *paper*. Indeed the crucial quality of paper—its absorbency—eludes the dichotomy. Only because of its absorbency is paper permeable by the black spots of ink. In addition, paper retains the traces of a wide range of labour practices and metamorphoses. In Shakespeare's time paper owed its existence to the rag-pickers who collected the cloth (itself the residue of sheets and clothes) from which it was made. In the sheets of a book, bedsheets began a new life, after the rags had been turned into 'stuff' and then into paper by vatmen, couchers, and layers. And it was commonplace for Elizabethan authors to anticipate another use when the pages of the book were returned to serviceable paper—paper to wrap groceries or to light tobacco.[1]

   The Shakespearean text is thus, like any Renaissance book, a provisional stage in the circulation of matter, a circulation that involved an extraordinary diversity of labours. As an anonymous eighteenth-century poem puts it:

RAGS make paper,
PAPER makes money,
MONEY makes banks,
BANKS makes loans,
LOANS makes beggars,
BEGGARS make RAGS.[2]

And the rags which quite literally composed the works of the National Bard were themselves the heterogeneous products of an international capitalist industry. The rags were vagrant, collected from all over Europe to be processed in the great papermaking industries of France and Italy. The *lack* of paper in England, due at first, no doubt, to the absence of any significant linen industry, meant that the Shakespearean text (like the vast majority of other English Renaissance texts) was a 'foreign' body. It was also, in William Prynne's eye, a luxurious body. 'Shackspeers Plaies', he complained of the Second Folio, 'are printed in the best Crowne paper, far better than most Bibles'.[3] Other, less luxurious 'foreign' bodies were used in the printshop: the words of what was to become a classic text were printed in an ink that mingled not only ingredients like juniper gum, linseed oil, and lampblack but also the residual traces of the urine of the printshop workers, who each night used urine to soak the leather casing of the balls that inked the press.[4] It is these material practices that, even when noted, are ignored in favour of a transcendent 'text' imagined as the product of the author's mind.

*   *   *

Peter W. M. Blayney, 'The publication of playbooks', in John D. Cox and David Scott Kastan (eds.), *A New History of Early English Drama* (New York: Columbia University Press, 1997), pp. 383–422.

Before Elizabeth came to the throne in 1558, the drama had made virtually no impact on the English book trade. A few early printed plays have undoubtedly been lost, and others may have been reprinted more often than we know—but Greg's *Bibliography of the English Printed Drama* lists fewer than thirty pre-Elizabethan plays printed in English. During the 1560s and 1570s there was a noticeable increase, but in neither decade did the number of new titles reach thirty.

For the sake of analysis I shall divide what might be called the Age of the English Printed Play into three twenty-year periods: 1583–1602, 1603–1622, and 1623–1642. The first of those periods (the last two decades of the reign of Elizabeth) saw the first printing of 117 works qualifying for inclusion in Greg's *Bibliography*. The second period (the first two decades of the reign of James I) is represented in Greg by 192 works, and the third (from the First Folio to the closure of the theaters) by 251.

Not all those works, however, are what we would usually call *plays*, and it takes quite a stretch of the imagination to consider Sidney's *Entertainment at Wanstead*, included among the items appended to editions of the *Arcadia* in and after 1598, as a 'playbook' in any realistic commercial sense. I shall therefore subtract all masques, pageants and entertainments, closet and academic plays, Latin plays and translations published as literary texts, and shall consider only plays written for professional public performance (by both adult and juvenile companies). Thus adjusted, the number of new plays published in each of the three periods defined above is respectively 96, 115, and 160.[1]

In the two decades before the accession of James I, then, the average number of new plays published each year was 4.8. In the next two decades it was 5.75, and in the last two decades before the theaters were closed, exactly 8.0. For the same three periods, the chronological index to the revised *Short-Title Catalogue* (Pollard and Redgrave, 3:331–405) lists an average of just under 300, just under 480, and a little over 600 items per year respectively.[2] Not all those items are books, and many of the books are reprints rather than new titles—but it should nevertheless be obvious that printed plays never accounted for a very significant fraction of the trade in English books.

Those figures do not, of course, necessarily reflect demand alone: it could be argued that what they show is how well the players succeeded in withholding their scripts from the press. On the question of supply and demand, the Stationers' Registers provide evidence that is less equivocal. The following table shows the number of plays first registered in 1585–1604.

PERIOD	PLAYS	PERIOD	PLAYS
1585	1	1596	0
1586	0	1597	2
1587	0	1598	3
1588	0	1599	3
1589	0	1600 (Jan.–Apr.)	3
1590	3	May 1600—Oct. 1601	27

PERIOD	PLAYS	PERIOD	PLAYS
1591	3	1601 (Nov.–Dec.)	2
1592	3	1602	4
1593 (Jan.–Nov.)	3	1603	1
Dec. 1593–May 1595	27	1604	5
1595 (June–Dec.)	4		

The most notable features are the two eighteen-month periods during which no fewer than fifty-four plays were registered—as compared with a total of forty in the remaining seventeen years.

If we look at the publication history of the plays registered *outside* the two peak periods, we find that thirty-four (85 percent) were printed in either the year of registration or the following year. Three of the remainder (7.5 percent) were printed within three years of registration, two were newly registered by others six years after (and apparently in ignorance of) the original registration and printed accordingly, and only one (2.5 percent) was never printed. For the plays registered *during* the peak periods, though, the proportions are distinctly different. Only thirty (56 percent) were printed before the end of the following December (1595 and 1601 respectively). Seven others (13 percent) were printed within five years of registration, and one after fifteen years; three were newly registered and printed after eleven, twenty-three, and thirty-eight years respectively, and eleven (20 percent) were never printed. Shortly after each peak period there was a brief but noticeable slump: in 1596 no plays were registered and only two printed; in 1603 only one was registered and two printed. It is difficult to escape the clear implication: in each period plays became available to the book trade in such quantities that the market was temporarily glutted.

The cause of those two flurries of activity is not difficult to guess, but the myth of the reluctant players has tended to obscure the obvious. Even Pollard drew what appears to be the only plausible conclusion—that on each occasion the acting companies themselves offered an unusual number of manuscripts for publication—and suggested that the first peak period was connected with the closure of the playhouses during the plague of 1592–1593 (*Shakespeare*, 9–10; *Shakespeare's Fight*, 41–2). But his suggestion that the players were motivated by financial hardship is less compelling, partly because the peak period happened *after* rather than during the closure and partly because the sums involved would have been relatively small.

Tradition has offered two explanations for the supposed reluctance of acting companies to allow their plays to be printed. One is that they feared losing their exclusive acting rights: that once a play was in print, any other company could perform it.[3] But as Roslyn L. Knutson has shown elsewhere,[4] the London companies seem for the most part to have respected each other's repertories, printed plays included, so there is no obvious reason why any company should have feared otherwise.[5] The second explanation is even less credible: that the sale of printed texts might itself reduce the demand for performance. For that theory to work, the market in printed plays would have to have been lively enough, and the plays themselves deadly enough, to create so many hundred disappointed readers in such a short time that their collective absence from the playhouse was noticeable. I know of no evidence that any player ever feared that those who bought and read plays would consequently lose interest in seeing them performed.

For Pollard, the fact that the first flood of registrations did not begin until the playhouses reopened in late 1593 was a minor difficulty, evaded by implying that there would usually have been quite a long delay between the sale and the registration of a manuscript. To use his own words, 'they had been sold by the players during the time that the theatres were closed and were now being registered as they were got ready for publication' (*Shakespeare*, 9). If we assume that the players thought of performance and publication as mutually exclusive alternatives, it would indeed seem likely that the closure, rather than the reopening, caused the glut. But if we decline to make that assumption, there is a perfectly plausible reason why the reopening itself might have prompted the players to flood the market with scripts. The strategy is known today as 'publicity,' or 'advertising.'

What initiated the second peak period is uncertain. Pollard suggested that it was a Privy Council order of June 22, 1600, that restricted both the number of play-houses and the frequency of performances (*Shakespeare*, 10)—but the beginning of the 1600 landslide can be very precisely dated to the last week of May. Whatever the immediate cause, on this occasion there can be even less doubt that the initiative came from the players.[6] On May 27 the printer James Roberts went to Stationers' Hall and provisionally registered a Chamberlain's play (now lost) called *Cloth Breeches and Velvet Hose*. Roberts held the monopoly for printing playbills and was therefore in frequent contact with the playhouses. But although he occasionally acquired plays and registered them (in most cases only provisionally), after doing so he usually sold them to other stationers rather than taking the financial risk of publishing them himself.

Having written out the registration ('provided that [Roberts] is not to putt it in prynte Without further & better Aucthority' [Arber, 3:161]), the Stationers' clerk, Richard Collins, did something unprecedented. He turned to the beginning of the register, wrote the heading 'my lord chamberlens mens plaies Entred' at the top of a blank flyleaf, and made a brief entry below it: the date, Roberts's name, and the title of the play (3:37). When Roberts provisionally registered a second play two days later, after writing the registration itself Collins turned back to his list and made a second entry below the first. As it happened he did not use the flyleaf again until August and never continued the list in its original form—but what is significant is that he started it at all. Its purpose was probably to keep track of an expected string of provisional entries, so that whenever the required 'Aucthority' for one of the plays was produced, he could use the list as a finding aid. But even its precise purpose is relatively unimportant: what matters is that on May 27 Collins heard something—presumably from Roberts the playbill printer—that made him expect the imminent arrival of enough Chamberlain's plays to make a list desirable. As things turned out, only eight of the plays registered during the second glut belonged to the Lord Chamberlain's Men—but the significance of the list and its heading lies not in the outcome but in the expectation. The single play that Roberts brought in on May 27 was correctly recognized as the first of many.

What I have shown so far is that although comparatively few new plays were published each year, at least twice the supply conspicuously exceeded the demand. But there is more to the question of popularity than the annual number of new works in a genre, and we need also to look at the frequency of reprinting. Once more, however, the facts bear little resemblance to the myth. Of the 96 plays first published in 1583–1602, only 46 (just under 48 percent) were reprinted inside twenty-five years.[7] The percentage is slightly higher for the plays of 1603–1622 (58 out of 115, or just over 50 percent), but in 1623–1642, when the number of new plays per year reached its peak, the number reprinted inside twenty-five years fell back to 46 out of 160, or less than 29 percent. And if an increased number of new texts led to a sharp decrease in the rate of reprinting, it would seem that the overall demand had not greatly increased.[8]

Of the plays that did reach a second edition, a few went through a respectable series of reprintings. Judged by the number of editions inside twenty-five years, the eleven best-sellers were the following.[9]

Play (and year of first edition)	Editions in 25 years
Anon., *Mucedorus and Amadine* (1598)	9
Marlowe, *Doctor Faustus* (1604)	8
Kyd, *The Spanish Tragedy* (1592)	7
Shakespeare, *Henry IV, Part I* (1598)	7
Shakespeare, *Richard III* (1597)	5
Shakespeare, *Richard II* (1597)	5
Heywood, *If You Know Not Me, Part 1* (1605)	5
Daniel, *Philotas* (1605)	5
Suckling, *Brennoralt* (1642)	5
Anon, *How a Man May Choose a Good Wife* (1602)	5
Fletcher, *Philaster* (1620)	5

One point worth making is that if I had included closet and academic plays, Samuel Daniel's *Cleopatra* (1594) would have ranked second (it reached its eighth edition seven years more quickly than did *Doctor Faustus*) and Thomas Randolph's *Aristippus* and *The Conceited Pedlar* (jointly published in 1630), fourth. That would have pushed Shakespeare firmly out of the top five—whether to sixth or seventh place would depend on how the Randolph plays were counted. *Cleopatra* was never published singly and could be purchased only as part of a collection of Daniel's verse. What that means is that the professional stage produced only a single play—*Mucedorus*—capable of outselling Daniel's verse. It is also worth noting that Shakespeare's best-selling work, *Venus and Adonis*, outsold his best-selling play by four editions.

Just in case a final emphasis is needed, let us now compare that list with the performance of some nondramatic best-sellers. The first seven are counted from the date of the first extant edition, and the last four from the editions of 1583.

Work (and year)	Editions in 25 years
Sorocold, *Supplications of Saints* (1612)*	10
Dent, *The Plain Man's Pathway* (1601)†	16
Dering, *A Short Catechism for Householders* (1580)	17
Smith, *The Trumpet of the Soul* (1591)	17
Dent, *A Sermon of Repentance* (1582)	20
Parsons, *A Book of Christian Exercise* (1584)	27
Bayly, *The Practice of Piety* (1612)	36

Work (and year)	Editions in 25 years
The New Testament (English versions published separately from 1583)	34
The Holy Bible (Bishops' and Geneva translations from 1583)	63
The Book of Common Prayer (from 1583)	66
Sternhold and Hopkins, *The Psalms in English Meter* (from 1583)	124

* The first and tenth of the surviving editions describe themselves as the third and twenty-second respectively.

† The sixteenth surviving edition describes itself as the nineteenth.

It is therefore safe to conclude that few early modern stationers ever imagined that the best way to make a quick fortune was to wrest—honestly or otherwise—a play or two from the supposedly protective clutch of an acting company. A demand for printed plays certainly existed, though it was far from insatiable, and a stationer lucky enough or clever enough to acquire the right play at the right time could make a satisfactory profit. Andrew Wise, for example, struck gold three times in a row in 1597–1598 by picking what would become the three best-selling Shakespeare quartos as the first three plays of his brief career.[10] But few of those who dealt in plays enjoyed comparable success. If a printer published a new play for himself, he would expect to break even and begin making a profit when about half the edition had been sold. If he paid someone else to act as wholesale distributor, his higher costs would have taken correspondingly longer to recover. The great majority of plays, however, were published by booksellers,[11] and a bookseller would normally have to sell about 60 percent of a first edition to break even. Fewer than 21 percent of the plays published in the sixty years under discussion reached a second edition inside nine years. What that means is that no more than one play in five would have returned the publisher's initial investment inside five years. Not one in twenty would have paid for itself during its first year—so publishing plays would not usually have been seen as a shortcut to wealth.

At this point it is necessary to define a few key terms. Some of the common misconceptions about the procedures and economics of publication stem from confusion about exactly who was responsible for what. To avoid that confusion we need to use the words *printer* and *bookseller* more precisely than they are often used—more precisely, indeed, than they were sometimes used by the stationers themselves.

The *printer* of a play was the person who owned the type and the press, and whose workmen set the text and impressed its inked image onto the paper. The printer, in other words, physically manufactured the book—and did so in a small factory called a *printing office* or *printing house*. Most printers spent most of their time manufacturing books for others. A typical customer brought in a text, paid to have several hundred copies of it printed, and then took them away. In a transaction of that kind the printer bore no more responsibility for procuring or marketing the text than does a photocopier. Sometimes, indeed, it can be salutary to remember the similarities between a printing house and a copying machine: a text, a heap of clean paper, and the required payment were inserted at one end, and the paper emerged from the other end with the text on it. It is rarely appropriate to hold the machine responsible for the supposed origins of the text it reproduced.

In a few of the larger printing houses the premises probably included a *shop*: a room or annex fronting on the street, from which books were retailed. In such cases it is important to keep the separate functions of the two parts of the premises carefully distinct. Most printers did not retail books to the public, because most of what they printed was not theirs to sell—and a potential reader in search of a book would go to a bookshop, not a printing house. In the early records of the trade the word *shop* always and exclusively means a place where books were sold to the public. Since the modern American *print shop* tends to blur what is sometimes a crucial distinction, it is a term best avoided in historical contexts.

A *bookseller*, obviously enough, was someone who owned or worked in a retail bookshop. But while we can pertinently refer to 'the printer' of a playbook,[12] there was no such thing as 'the' bookseller, and it is therefore necessary to deal briefly with another widespread fallacy. Throughout his career, Greg never gave up the search for new and improved ways of determining who owned the copyright of a printed play at any given time. As part of this quest he spent some time trying to devise what might be called a 'calculus of imprints'—a set of rules for interpreting the various forms of wording found in imprints and colophons.[13] Unfortunately, his discussions of the matter were marred throughout, and partly invalidated, by his belief that any bookseller identified in an imprint was the book's exclusive *retailer*.[14] The assumption was a traditional one, but Greg did more than anyone this century to entrench it.

The primary purpose of an imprint was the same in early modern England as it is today: to inform *retailers* where a book could be purchased *wholesale*. Since virtually all wholesale distributors were also retail booksellers, a potential customer who knew about the imprint might correctly deduce that the distributor's shop would be the one most likely to have copies in stock—but that was merely incidental. Several of Greg's own books were published by the Clarendon Press. We do not therefore conclude that anyone wishing to buy a copy had to go to Oxford, nor should we imagine that the only shop in London selling the first edition of *King Lear* was that of Nathaniel Butter. The goal of whoever handled the wholesaling of a book (either its publisher or a chosen agent) was to sell as many copies as possible, and that meant selling them to as many of England's hundreds of *bookshops* as possible. The idea that anyone could benefit from restricting retail sales to a single shop in a single city is nothing less than absurd.

Any bookseller could buy and sell any book. If we confine our attention to new books published in London,[15] a bookseller who belonged to the Stationers' Company could buy them at loosely controlled wholesale prices from other Company members. Alternatively, a bookseller who had published a book of his or her own might take the shortcut of exchanging small batches with other publishers.[16] Neither London booksellers who belonged to other companies nor booksellers from outside London were entitled to the same wholesale rates,[17] but they could buy books at the usual London retail price discounted by three shillings in the pound (G. Pollard, 'Sandars,' 15). No bookseller, of course, could stock every book that came out—many undoubtedly specialized in books of certain kinds and would tailor their stock to suit their preferred clientele. But although there were probably disapproving booksellers who declined to stock plays at all, any playbook could otherwise have been sold in any shop.

Between the printer and the booksellers stood the prime mover. The person who acquired the text, paid for several hundred copies of it to be manufactured, and sold them wholesale, was the *publisher*. It was the publisher, not the printer who decided that the text should be made public and who would eventually make a profit if it sold well enough during his lifetime.

And by the same token, it was the publisher whose investment was at risk if the public declined to buy the book.

There are two reasons why it is sometimes difficult to keep the terminology precise. The first is that the early modern book trade had no separate word for what we now call a publisher. Once an edition had been printed, the business of distributing it consisted of selling books—and the stationers evidently felt little need to distinguish between selling books wholesale to retailers and selling them retail to the public. Furthermore, when publishers discussed their activities in prefaces, they generally used the word *print* in the sense of 'cause to be printed.' The formulaic heading, 'The Printer to the Reader,' was therefore commonly used by publishers who were not strictly speaking printers at all.[18] And if the publishers themselves could interchangeably call their enterprise 'bookselling' and 'printing,' modern scholars who use the words imprecisely have some excuse.

The other complicating factor is that publishing was not usually thought of as a profession. There were certainly some early stationers who published so frequently that they probably considered publication to be their principal activity—but they were few in number. Most books were published by stationers whose daily trade was bookselling; a few were published by stationers who were also printers. For most of them publishing was a form of speculation, undertaken to augment their regular income rather than to replace it. Since virtually every early modern publisher was also either a bookseller or a printer, it is hardly surprising that the three words are sometimes confused—but even when two of the roles were played by the same person, it is important to keep them distinct.

Whatever his or her regular trade, then, the person who paid for a book to be manufactured was its publisher. If the manuscript had been illicitly obtained, or if any rules of the Stationers' Company were evaded or broken, the responsibility lay with the publisher—not with the printer. In the comparatively uncommon event that the publisher's trade was printing and he manufactured the book for himself, that responsibility was his only by virtue of his role *as publisher*. As printer, he was responsible only for the quality of the printing. If we want to investigate the text of a play—the relationship between what the typesetter saw in the manuscript and what appears on the printed page—we need to study the printer. But if our concern is the source of the manuscript, the reasons why *that* play was published *then*, or the supposed attitude of the players or the playwright to the fact of publication, we must focus not on the printer but on the publisher.

If the publisher had a bookshop of his or her own, that shop would usually be the source of wholesale distribution, so the publisher's name and address would usually appear on the title page. But if a book was published by someone who lacked the facilities for storage and distribution (a printer, or a journeyman book-seller with no shop of his own), that publisher would need to find a bookseller willing to handle the wholesaling. The imprint on such a book would usually announce that it was 'to be sold' by the bookseller in question—meaning 'to be sold wholesale.' It could, of course, be sold to the public by any retailer in England (or elsewhere) who was willing to order one or more copies from that distributor.

Every now and then a particular play would become a cause célèbre, either by virtue of unusual popularity onstage (*Tamburlaine*, *The Spanish Tragedy*, or *Pericles*) or because it fell foul of the authorities (*The Isle of Dogs*, *Eastward Ho*, or *A Game at Chess*). On such occassions one or more stationers might have approached the playwright or the players to ask whether they could buy a text for publication. If the company made it known that a particular play was on offer (or as in 1594 and 1600, a selection of plays), a stationer with a few pounds to invest and nothing more promising in sight might take the hint and approach the playhouse. But since the overall demand for plays was unimpressive it is likely that many of those that saw print were offered to, rather than sought out by, their publishers.

The nature of the manuscript offered to the press would depend largely upon its source. After the first edition was printed, the publisher would usually keep that part of the manuscript on which the authority to publish and the license to print were recorded. What happened to the rest of it might depend on how extensively the printer's workmen had marked or mis-handled it—but the person from whom it had been bought would not usually have expected it back. In special cases, such as some of the plays included in Jonson's *Works* in 1616 or the First Folio of Shakespeare in 1623, a supplier might have lent a printer a manuscript instead of surrendering it, but that was not the usual practice. So if a play still in repertory was offered to a publisher by the players, or by the playwright himself with their consent, the manuscript supplied would not usually have been 'the allowed book' then being used for performance.

One possible manuscript, if it still existed, would be the one from which the allowed book had itself been copied. That might often have been a late draft or 'final' copy in the play-wright's own hand: what the playhouse scribe Edward Knight called 'the fowle papers of the Authors' when he had to copy the extant manuscript of *Bonduca* from them because 'the booke where by it was first Acted from' had been lost (Greg, *Shakespeare*, 107). Or if the current version of a revived play had evolved so much that a new copy had been prepared and allowed, the publisher might have been given an obsolete promptbook. Alternatively, if the players declined to part with any of their existing manuscripts, it would not have cost very much to have one of them (probably the allowed book itself) transcribed.[19] If publication was the playwright's own idea, to which the players had merely consented, he might conceivably have copied out a playhouse manuscript himself. Or, as in the case of Jonson's *Sejanus*, he might have prepared a revised version especially for the press.

Sometimes, though, the person who tried to sell a play to a publisher might have no direct connection with the playhouse at all. A manuscript mislaid by a company might be innocently found by someone else; a player might borrow a manuscript and copy it for a friend; the company might collectively commission a scribal copy for presentation to a patron or benefac-tor. Any kind of manuscript that left the playhouse for any reason might conceivably be copied, more or less expertly, and each new exemplar might itself be transcribed. It is unlikely that there was a very flourishing trade in manuscript plays before the theaters were closed in 1642—that many circulated in manuscript at all, or that there were many copies of those that did—but but extra-theatrical manuscripts certainly existed, and they were sometimes sold to stationers. How closely they resembled their playhouse ancestors would depend on the num-ber and skill of the intervening copyists, and it may often be difficult or impossible to deduce the full history of the manuscript underlying a printed text (supposedly characteristic features that survive in print could equally have survived prior transcription). But whether or not we can accurately distinguish one from another, any kind of manuscript playbook that can conceivably have existed could conceivably have found its way into print.

* * *

Leah Marcus, *Unediting the Renaissance: Shakespeare, Marlowe, Milton* (London and New York: Routledge, 1996), pp. 225–6.

Milton's 1645 *Poems* is very seldom reprinted as a book—in a manner that allows us to read the subtle rhetoric of the volume as it was presented to early readers. Most frequently, editors ride roughshod over some elements of the 1645 arrangement of materials . . . out of a desire to present all of the Miltonic corpus in the precise conjectured order of composition, as a perfect reflection of the life. More recent editors, some of whom do preserve the ordering of the early editions, nevertheless characteristically omit or displace the 1645 front matter and 'speaking picture' of the author, so that their many reverberations with the rest of the collection are lost. Few readers would wish to dispense altogether with the mediating scholarship that has made Milton's work intelligible and accessible. But many in recent decades have been repelled by the gargantuan, supercanonical monolith that Milton has become, in part as a result of the vast accretion of editorial tradition behind our standard editions. To revisit the 1645 *Poems* in their original printed 'body' is to rediscover a Milton who is smaller, less ponderous, more approachable, yet paradoxically also harder to demarcate from the pressures of his time than the Milton we have inherited. In dispersing the 1645 volume's organization in favour of other principles of ordering, we have lost traces of a forgotten form of Miltonic authenticity: his strong self-depiction as an 'oral' poet who preferred speech over writing as a poetic medium and published for readers who shared the same prejudice . . . One of [the editorial tradition's] most serious elisions is the poet's own eager, conflicted participation in the transition from orality to the printed book—not only as an extension of manuscript circulation to a circumscribed audience but also as a newly fixed form that could magically embody the poet's voice, sing forth across space and time . . .

In returning to Milton's 1645 'original' . . . we are not encountering our texts in some mythically pristine, unmediated form. Nor is that chimera the unspoken object of our secret desires. What we aim to accomplish in 'Unediting the Renaissance' is to apply the same density and complexity of historical explanation to the early editions and manuscript materials as we have long applied to other elements of early modern culture. It should go without saying that anyone studying the impact of an author during any given period would do well to consult the material forms of the author's work generated during the time in question.

*   *   *

Lukas Erne, *Shakespeare as Literary Dramatist* (Cambridge: Cambridge University Press, 2003), pp. 234–44.

Giorgio Melchiori has argued that 'behind Q2 there is a play for the closet, not for the stage,' and that Shakespeare conceived the play 'as a new form of literary work that would take its place among the poetic achievements extolled by the wiser sort.'[1] I do not believe, as Melchiori does, that *Hamlet* is an isolated case, but I do agree with his insistence on the play's literariness as well as with his assessment of the relationship between the long and the short texts of *Hamlet*. Like Melchiori, I believe that 'the First Quarto reflects faithfully at least one— but a very important—aspect of the *Tragedy of Hamlet*: it reflects the new structure of the play carefully devised at an early stage in view of its presentation in the public theater.'[2]

The play's first six scenes all have their direct equivalent in Q1. Yet from what corresponds to act two, scene two in modern editions, the differences between Q1 and the long texts become more than a matter of deletions, with Q1 restructuring the action dramatized in the long texts. In Q2 and the Folio, Polonius and the King agree on the need to investigate the reasons for Hamlet's melancholy disposition and Polonius suggests to set up an encounter with the Prince and Ophelia on which they would eavesdrop. The so-called 'Fishmonger' episode with Hamlet and Polonius ensues, followed by Hamlet's encounter with Rosencrantz and Guildenstern. Next, the players are announced, they arrive, and, after the Pyrrhus speech, Hamlet asks them to prepare a play, 'The Mousetrap,' for the following day. The second act closes with Hamlet's soliloquy and his determination that 'the play's the thing / Wherein I'll catch the conscience of the king.' In the following scene which takes place the next day, the King and Polonius finally carry out the eavesdropping plan. They set up Ophelia's encounter with Hamlet and hide before he enters. After the 'To be or not to be' soliloquy follows the nunnery sequence which leaves the spying King and Polonius even more anxious than before. The next scene begins with Hamlet's advice to the players and proceeds with the performance of the Mousetrap that Hamlet had ordered the day before.[3]

Melchiori and Irace have shown that the effect of the structural rearrangement is to speed up the action.[4] While this is so, it seems equally significant that the structural changes fundamentally affect our understanding of the causal relationship between various parts of the play's action. My analysis of *Henry V* has shown how the long text—contrary to the short—contains juxtapositions (such as reminiscences of Henry's betrayal of Falstaff followed by Scroop's betrayal of Henry) that defy expectations and therefore require explanations, suggesting that the causal relationships in the play are dense and complex rather than self-explanatory. The same applies to *Hamlet*. For the order in which the long texts dramatize events seems in some ways rather odd. Polonius suggests spying on Hamlet with the help of Ophelia, but rather than putting this plan into practice, Polonius and the King wait until the next day. The succession of Hamlet's moods is perhaps even more surprising. After the arrival of the actors, he forges a plan: 'I'll have these players / Play something like the murder of my father / Before mine uncle. I'll observe his looks, / I'll tent him to the quick. If a but blench, / I know my course' (2.2.596–600). At the end of the second act, Hamlet, surely, is finally ready to take action. Yet, when he re-enters some fifty lines later, he muses on suicide and seems to have forgotten about his project.

The restructuring of Q1 makes these problems disappear by moving the 'To be or not to be' soliloquy and the 'nunnery' sequence from what we know as act three, scene one to act two, scene two. The sequence therefore follows just after the King and Corambis (as Polonius is called in Q1) have forged the eavesdropping plan. With this sequence of events, cause and effect are more easily understandable: the evesdropping plan is formed and then immediately carried out rather than postponed to the next day. Hamlet's melancholy state when he enters for the 'To be or not to be' soliloquy corresponds well to what we have last heard of him in Ophelia's report to her father. He is cheered up by the arrival of Rossencraft and Gilderstone (Q1's spelling for Rosencrantz and Guildenstern) and the players. When he has the idea to test the King by means of the Mousetrap, this is again carried out the very same day rather than postponed to the next. In the resulting sequence, the represented time is thus reduced from two days to one. The emphasis is on the swiftly moving action, on plans formed and carried out, rather than on Hamlet's delay owing to his melancholy disposition and his lack of determination.

I am not suggesting that the order of events in Q1 makes sense whereas that in the two long texts does not. Rather, the difference shows where the short version for the stage and the long version for the page fundamentally differ. If a character passes within a few lines from enthusiasm to dejection, this challenges expectations and requires explanation. The long texts thus invite us to inquire into a character who conveys a strong sense of interiority and psychological complexity. In Q1, in contrast, the Prince's character is more easily understandable and therefore can recede behind the intrigue and action which the stage play is most interested in.

In order to establish how the latter part of the play is also consciously and intelligently reworked to make it fit for the stage, it is necessary to investigate the play's structural design. The closet scene (3.4) occupies a central position within the play's architecture. Hamlet's pursuit of revenge for the murder of his father has still come to nothing. Having been given the opportunity to kill Claudius in the preceding prayer scene, he has refrained from the deed. In the closet scene, he is finally resolute and stabs the man hidden behind the arras, believing him to be Claudius. Yet, by killing Ophelia's and Laertes's father rather than the King, he becomes the object of revenge at the very moment he believes he is its subject. In a ferociously ironic reversal he not only fails to kill the murderer of his father but simultaneously becomes the murderer of another father. This pivotal moment structurally divides the play into two halves, the first showing Hamlet as the subject, the second as the object of revenge.

Carefully planned as this two-part structure is, it nevertheless threatens to result in an imbalance. The first half is filled with action and suspense from the moment the Ghost appears to the play within the play. Once Hamlet has killed Polonius, however, the play draws ineluctably toward the final confrontation between Laertes and Hamlet. Laertes is soon returned from Paris and hot for action; no delay is to be expected from him. So Shakespeare needs two devices to postpone the final confrontation: Ophelia's madness and death, and Hamlet's seavoyage to England. Ophelia's decline is highly stage effective and must have been appreciated by Elizabethan audiences that never seem to have grown tired of scenes of madness. Hamlet's seavoyage, on the other hand, is given what may well seem too much attention considering its basic lack of dramatic interest.

In the long texts, the King's plan to get rid of Hamlet by sending him to England is already announced as early as act three, scene one (3.1.167–79) and then somewhat lengthily introduced in an encounter between the King and Rosencrantz and Guildenstern (4.3). Often cut in modern productions, these passages leave no trace in Q1. The dramatization of Hamlet's return is, from the point of view of the stage, equally heavy-handed. After the lethal stabbing of Polonius has shown Hamlet's determination, Claudius is eager to get rid of the Prince and has him sail to England, accompanied by Rosencrantz and Guildenstern. At night, Hamlet finds out that the sealed message which his companions are to carry to the King of England contains an order to have him executed. Hamlet forges a new order commanding the death of Rosencrantz and Guildenstern and exchanges the two commissions. Later on pirates attack them and take Hamlet prisoner while his companions sail on to their destruction in England. The pirates treat him kindly and free him in exchange for certain services, after which Hamlet returns to Denmark.

All these intricate events take place offstage between act four, scene four, when Hamlet is leaving Denmark, and the beginning of act five when we see him back in his country. They are not directly dramatized but narrated in several installments: act four, scene six has a sailor deliver Hamlet's letter to Horatio who learns from it part of the story. The following scene opens with the King and Laertes still unaware of Hamlet's escape until another letter arrives from the Prince. At the beginning of act five, scene two, finally, another sequence has Hamlet tell Horatio those events which he did not communicate in the letter. These various passages, which are all narrative rather than dramatic, considerably slow down the pace of the action.

This fact seems to have been taken into account when the play was prepared for the stage.[5] After Ophelia's second madness scene (act four, scene five in modern editions), Q1 inserts the only scene that has no equivalent in the long texts. It has been believed that the reporter or reporters who undertook the memorial reconstruction failed to remember substantial parts of the original play and consequently had to invent a new scene.[6] It is more likely, however, that the scene is part of a conscious reworking designed to shorten and speed up the play in preparation for the stage. In order to substantiate these claims, I need to quote the scene in its entirety:

Enter Horatio and the Queene.

HOR[ATIO]. Madame, your sonne is safe arriv'de in *Denmarke*.
    This letter I euen now receiv'd of him,
    Whereas he writes how he escap't the danger,
    And subtle treason that the king had plotted,
    Being crossed by the contention of the windes,
    He found the Packet sent to the king of *England*,
    Wherein he saw himselfe betray'd to death,
    As at his next conuersion with your grace,
    He will relate the circumstance at full.
QUEENE Then I perceiue there's treason in his lookes
    That seem'd to sugar o're his villainie:
    But I will soothe and please him for a time,
    For murderous mindes are always jealous.
    But know not you *Horatio* where he is?
HOR[ATIO]. Yes Madame, and he hath appoynted me
    To meete him on the east side of the Cittie
    To morrow morning.
QUEENE O faile not, good *Horatio*, and withall, commend me
    A mothers care to him, bid him a while
    Be wary of his presence, lest that he
    Faile in that he goes about.
HOR[ATIO]. Madam, neuer make doubt of that:
    I thinke by this the news be come to court:
    He is arriv'de, obserue the king, and you shall
    Quickly finde, *Hamlet* being here,
    Things fell not to his minde.
QUEENE But what became of *Gilderstone* and *Rossencraft*?

HOR[ATIO]. He being set ashore, they went for *England*.
   And in the Packet there writ down that doome
   To be performe'd on them poynted for him:
   And by great chance he had his fathers Seale,
   So all was done without discouerie.
QUEENE Thankes be to heauen for blessing of the prince,
   Horatio, once again I take my leaue
   With thowsand mothers blessings to my sonne.
HORAT[IO]. Madam adue.

(H2^v–H3^r)

In little more than thirty lines, the scene sums up all the necessary information that the long texts spread out over different passages. All of these narrative passages, accordingly, have been omitted from the short text. This fusion of several sequences into one short scene considerably condenses the action where Q2 and F slows it down, thereby allowing for a swift, action-packed and exciting finale. The considerable difference in pace between Q1 and Q2/F *Hamlet* raises the intriguing possibility that the time-honored belief that procrastination and delay are central to the play has much to do with the text readers have studied but little with the play Elizabethan theatre-goers would have witnessed.[7]

Besides this dramatic restructuring, the new scene in Q1 also allows us to glimpse a Queen who is substantially different from her counterpart in Q2 and the Folio. In the play we know, she is a highly complex figure whose motives and allegiances are far from clear. In Q1, on the other hand, her allegiance to Horatio and Hamlet is unambiguous. She says about her second husband:

> Then I perceiue there's treason in his lookes
> That seem'd to sugar o're his villainie:
> But I will soothe and please him for a time,
> For murderous mindes are always jealous.

This is consistent with the Closet Scene in Q1 where she explicitly asserts that she ignored how her first husband died: 'as I haue a soule, I sweare by heauen, / I neuer knew of this most horride murder' (G3^r). Later on in Q1's Closet Scene, she promises Hamlet that 'I will conceale, consent, and doe my best, / What stratagem soe're thou shalt deuise' (G3^v).[8] This explicit and wholehearted allegiance to her son is again unparallelled in the long texts where her degree of complicity with Claudius is far from clear and has been the subject of critical speculation.[9]

It is a feature not just of Q1's Queen but of the short text as a whole that characterization is less multi-layered and complex than it is in the long texts. Q1's Leartes (Laertes), for instance, is a straightforward revenger out for retribution for his father's death, but he does not become a public danger by leading a rebellion. Similarly, Q1's King is more of a straightforward villain than his counterpart in the long texts.

This also applies to the play's hero as the restructuring of acts two and three discussed above has already suggested. Q1's graveyard scene, in particular, presents us with a different Hamlet from the one we are used to. The Prince who has returned from the sea-voyage is traditionally seen as a matured man, wiser and more measured, less flippant and histrionic than earlier on, calmly accepting of providence rather than madly defiant. At the funeral of Ophelia, Hamlet is accordingly on the defensive in the confrontation with Laertes: 'take thy fingers from my throat' (5.1.257) and '[a]way thy hand' (5.1.264) Hamlet begs his opponent. Yet a stage direction in Q1 is not easy to reconcile with this view of the Prince. After Ophelia's brother has jumped into her grave, Hamlet 'leapes in after Leartes' (as Laertes is called in Q1), thus attacking rather than being attacked by Ophelia's brother. Clearly, this is not the matured prince in control of his emotions which the above interpretation of his character presupposes. Hamlet's gesture has understandably disturbed critics and editors of the play. Philip Edwards, for instance, was convinced that 'Shakespeare cannot have intended Hamlet to leap into the grave and so become the attacker,' and consequently excludes the stage direction from his edition.[10] Yet a near-contemporary document that happens to survive proves Edwards wrong. An elegy of 1619 written on the death of Richard Burbage, the leading actor of Shakespeare's company, mentions that the deceased had played, among other parts, that of 'young Hamlett.'[11] Evoking what he remembers most vividly from Burbage's performance of the part, the anonymous elegist writes: 'Oft haue I seene him leap into the graue.'[12] Richard Burbage's Hamlet at the Globe of which we find a reflection in the Hamlet of Q1 seems to have been a rather different character from the one modern critics and editors imagine him to have been.[13]

The above analyses of *Hamlet* and *Henry V* have shown that the short, theatrical texts repeatedly flatten out the complex, 'life-like' characters of the long, literary texts, turning ambiguous figures, whose 'motivations' can and have been subjected to extensive analysis, into 'mere types,' the villainous king, the loyal mother Gertrude, or, in *Henry V*, the successful warrior king. This difference in characterization is best understood not in qualitative terms, equating 'life-like' with 'good' and 'types' with 'bad.' Rather, it seems useful to understand the difference in characterization between the long and short texts of Shakespeare's plays as resulting from the respective media for which they were designed. As Ong has put it:

> The modern reader has typically understood effective 'characterization' in narrative or drama as the production of the 'round' character, to use E. M. Forster's term . . . the character that 'has the incalculability of life about it.' Opposed to the 'round' character is the 'flat' character, the type of character that never surprises the reader but, rather, delights by fulfilling expectations copiously. We know now that the type 'heavy' (or 'flat') character derives originally from primary oral narrative, which can provide characters of no other kind.[14]

This account has the advantage of describing the effect ('fulfilling expectations copiously') of so-called 'flat' characterization rather than judging it solely by the standards of a modern, print-based culture. As this kind of characterization needs to be viewed in the context of the cultures of orality out of which it grows, 'round' characterization is profitably understood as part of the advent of increasing literacy:

> As discourse moves from primary orality to greater and greater chirographic and typographic control, the flat, 'heavy' or type character yields to characters that grow more and more 'round,' that is, that perform in ways at first blush unpredictable but ultimately consistent in terms of the complex character structure and complex motivation

with which the round character is endowed ... In the private worlds [writing and reading] generate, the feeling for the 'round' human character is born—deeply interiorized in motivation, powered mysteriously, but consistently, from within. First emerging in chirographically controlled ancient Greek drama, the 'round' character is further developed in Shakespeare's age after the coming of print, and comes to its peak with the novel, when, after the advent of the Age of Romanticism, print is more fully interiorized.[15]

Ong's analysis of the relationship of characterization and orality and literacy provides an enabling context for an examination of the variant texts of *Hamlet* and *Henry V*. It seems significant that the protagonists of the long texts are the complex, at first unpredictable and deeply interiorized characters Ong associates with the private world of reading while the protagonists of the short texts are considerably more typified. For audiences familiar with Kyd's *Spanish Tragedy* and his lost 'Hamlet', or with the heroic warrior king Nashe recalls having seen on stage, the title characters of the short, but not of the long, texts would have 'fulfill[ed] expectations copiously.'

The respective kinds of characters orality and literacy tend to produce can also account for differences in the speech prefixes between the long and short texts. Mountjoy in *Henry V* is simply the 'Herauld' in Q1, and Williams, who questions the King so eloquently about his responsibilites, is the '2. Souldier.' Speech prefixes in Q1 *Romeo and Juliet* similarly have characters' functions where the longer text has names: the '2. Seruingmen' of the opening stage direction of *Romeo and Juliet*, reduced to '1' and '2' in the speech prefixes, are called Sampson and Gregorie in the stage directions and the speech prefixes of the second quarto. Similarly, 'Peter' in the speech prefixes of act four, scene five is simply a 'Seruingman' in Q1. In *Hamlet*, finally, Bernardo and Francisco of the long texts are 'two Centinels' in the first quarto, and the second quarto introduces the King as 'Claudius,' a name that is absent from the first quarto. Mysteriously linked to one's identity, indicative and constitutive of personal identity and individuality, the names in the long texts suggest 'life-like' characters favored by a culture of literacy where the short texts suggest functions or types indicative of orality. [. . .]

Bradleian character analysis dominated Shakespeare criticism in the early twentieth century, but was subjected to mockery by L. C. Knights as early as 1933 in his essay 'How many children had Lady Macbeth?'[16] It fared badly both with New Critical and more recent postmodernist approaches. As Heather Dubrow has pointed out, 'character has virtually become a dirty word, quite as taboo in many circles as frank glosses on Shakespeare's sexual wordplay were to an earlier generation of editors.'[17] A better understanding of the cultural contingency of characterization might change such a state of affairs. Specifically, an assessment of Shakespeare's characters that does not teleologically take for granted the superiority of the 'round' character which a culture of literacy has brought about might profitably be included in a more extended treatment of the theatrical and literary features of Shakespeare's playtexts.

This chapter has explored some of the implications for the variant texts of *Romeo and Juliet*, *Henry V*, and *Hamlet* of the argument I developed in Part I of this study: to a degree that has not been fully recognized, Shakespeare became a dramatic author during his own lifetime, writing drama for the stage *and* the page, to be published in performance *and* in print. The two media, I have argued, have left traces in some of the variant playtexts: the literariness of the long texts contrasts in certain ways with the theatricality of the short texts, reflecting respectively an emergent culture of increasing literacy and an enduring culture of orality. I have thus tried to complicate our understanding of the 'bad' quartos, whose designation has often been lamented but perhaps not yet been properly historicized and redefined. According to the literary logic with which Shakespeare's plays were approached for most of the nineteenth and twentieth centuries, the long variant playtexts are indeed better than the short. Yet, if we restore them to the early modern culture out of which they grew, it seems less useful to consider them as bad than as simply different. This difference, as this chapter has tried to show, records crucial traces of both the plays Shakespeare and his fellows performed and of Shakespeare, literary dramatist.

....

QUESTIONS

• What material forms did the Renaissance book take?
• To what extent are there ideological meanings attached to the material form of the book?

2 | Understanding the meanings of 'authorship' in the Renaissance

Jeffrey Masten, *Textual Intercourse: Collaboration, Authorship, and Sexualities in Renaissance Drama* (Cambridge: Cambridge University Press, 1997), pp. 14–15, 19–27.

In a scholarly field dominated by the singular figure of Shakespeare, it is easily forgotten that collaboration was the Renaissance English theatre's dominant mode of textual production. In his ground-breaking study of the profession of dramatist from 1590 to 1642, Gerald Eades Bentley notes that nearly two-thirds of the plays mentioned in Henslowe's papers reflect the participation of more than one writer. Furthermore, of all the plays written by professional dramatists in the period, 'as many as half . . . incorporated the writing of more than one man.' Printed title-page statements of singular authorship 'tended . . . to simplify the actual circumstances of composition' when compared with other records.[1] There is also ample evidence of the frequent revision of play-texts, itself a diachronic form of collaboration. It was common practice for the professional writers attached to a given theatrical company to compose new prologues, epilogues, songs, characters, and scenes for revivals of plays in which they did not originally have a hand—*Doctor Faustus* and *Sir Thomas More* are famous examples. Thus 'almost any play first printed more than ten years after composition and . . . kept in active repertory by the company that owned it is most likely to contain later revisions by the author or, in many cases, by another playwright.'[2]

In a broader sense, theatrical production was itself a sustained collaboration, 'the joint accomplishment of dramatists, actors, musicians, costumers, prompters (who made alterations in the original manuscript) and . . . managers.'[3] That is, the construction of meaning by a theatrical company was polyvocal—often beginning with a collaborative manuscript, which was then revised, cut, rearranged, and augmented by book-holders, copyists, and other writers, elaborated and improvised by actors in performance, accompanied by music and songs that may or may not have originated in a completely different context.[4]

Furthermore, the larger theatrical enterprise, situated in the market-place, was the highly lucrative, capitalist collaboration of a 'company' of 'sharers,' in commerce with themselves (as their terminology suggests) and with their audience—in Jean-Christophe Agnew's useful phrase, 'a joint venture of limited liability.'[5] Plays' prologues and epilogues, the liminal speeches situated between the play and the play-house, often stage the intersections of acting company and audience in the language of a collaborative commerce; the prologue to *Romeo and Juliet* (1597) emphasizes this trans/action when it speaks of 'the two howres traffique of our Stage.'[6] Human hands—hands that applaud, but also the hands that pay to see the play, the hand-shaking that seals the bargain, the collaborating hands of exchange and commerce—make repeated appearance in this framing material: 'Do but you hold out / Your helping hands,' the prologue to *The Two Noble Kinsmen* asks, 'and we shall . . . something do to save us.'[7]

Including theatrical production in a discussion of 'collaboration' may risk an excessive broadening of the term, but it is important to suggest (as I think the play-texts themselves do) the inseparability of the textual and theatrical production of meaning in a context that did not carefully insulate the writing of scripts from the acting of plays. (Actors William Shakespeare and William Rowley can serve as figures for this convergence.) The commonplace editorial concern over a play's 'date of composition,' which assumes a relatively limited amount of time during which a text was fully composed and after which it was merely transmitted and corrupted, is obviously problematic in this broader understanding of collaboration. What does 'composition' include in such a context? (Re)writing? Copying? Staging? The addition of actors' gestures on stage? Typesetting (which, after all, is called 'composing')? When is (the writing, staging, printing of) a text complete? [. . .]

Such a reconceptualization of Renaissance dramatic collaboration has profound implications for the way we interpret these plays. As we have seen, bibliographical attention to a text is often considered to be necessarily prior to interpretation—establishing a definitive, authoritative set of words for subsequent explication—but shifting the focus from authorship to collaboration demonstrates the extent to which twentieth-century textual criticism has itself been an elaborate interpretive act framing all its efforts with Foucault's constraining author.[8] Fredson Bowers's prefatory words describing his general editorship of *The Dramatic Works in the Beaumont and Fletcher Canon* suggest, furthermore, that modern textual criticism reproduces in its own practice the privileging of author-based interpretation over collaboration:

> The texts . . . have been edited by a group of scholars according to editorial procedures set by the general editor and under his close supervision . . . We hope that the intimate connexion of one individual, in this manner, with all the different editorial processes will lend to the results some uniformity not ordinarily found when diverse editors approach texts of such complexity. At the same time, the peculiar abilities of the several editors have had sufficient free play to ensure individuality of point of view its proper role; and thus, we hope, *the deadness of compromise that may fasten on collaborative effort* has been avoided.[9]

As in Zitner's rhetoric of collaborative 'contagion,' Bowers in this remarkable statement seeks to protect from the deadly grasp of collaboration the 'peculiar abilities' of the individual working in its 'proper role.' The danger collaboration poses to this editorial paradigm is likewise figured in the notion of 'corruption' so important to twentieth-century editing of Renaissance texts, for 'corruption'—the introduction of non-authorial material into a text during the process of 'transmission'—is 'collaboration' given a negative connotation. If the making of play-texts and theatrical productions was a collaborative enterprise, how can we edit out of the 1623 folio version of *Hamlet*, for example, the 'corruption' of actors' 'interpolations'?[10] To do so is to deploy authorship as a constraint on interpretation in a way the text itself warns against:

HAM. And could'st not thou for a neede study me
  Some dozen or sixteene lines,
  Which I would set downe and insert?
PLAYERS Yes very easily my good Lord.[11]

This exchange, which I quote from the first quarto, is itself 'set downe' and 'inserted' differently in the folio and second quarto versions of the play—the latter described on its title page as 'enlarged to almost as much againe as it was,' without ascription of the augmenting agent.[12]

Though more self-consciously interpretive than bibliography, critical readings of these plays continue to rely implicitly on the assumption that texts are the products of a singular and sovereign authorial consciousness, and a reconception of collaboration thus has manifold implications here. Dwelling on collaboration in this period demonstrates at the level of material practice the claims of much recent critical theory; the production of texts is a social process. Within Hoy's paradigm of collaboration, language is fundamentally transparent of, because it is produced by, the individual author; the language one uses is (and identifies one as) one's own. But if we accept that language is a socially produced (and producing) system, then collaboration is more the condition of discourse than its exception.[13] Interpreting from a collaborative perspective acknowledges language as a process of exchange; rather than policing discourse off into agents, origins, and intentions, a collaborative focus elaborates the social mechanism of language, discourse as intercourse.[14] 'If literature were as original, as creative, as individual, as unique as literary humanists are constantly saying it is,' Morse Peckham has noted, 'we would not be able to understand a word of it, let alone make emendations.'[15] A collaborative perspective also forces a re-evaluation of (and/or complicates) a repertoire of familiar interpretive methodologies—most prominently, biographical and psychoanalytic approaches—based on the notion of the singular author. Other traditional critical categories policing the circulation of language become problematic as well—for example, 'plagiarism,' 'borrowing,' 'influence' (and its 'anxieties'), 'source,' 'originality,' 'imagination,' 'genius,' and 'complete works.'

The collaborative production of play-texts, as I have begun to suggest, was manifold, and it is important to note that collaborations between (or among) writers had differing valences. Further investigation might detail both the differences and the similarities of collaborations (between Beaumont and Fletcher, and, say, Middleton and Rowley, or Chapman, Jonson, and

Marston) that resulted from different positionings within the institutions of the theatre and outside it; crucial to such an analysis are Bentley's distinctions between 'regular attached professional' playwrights and those like Jonson situated between the theatre and a patronage network with significantly different socio-economic inflections.[16] My point here, however, is to call for a revision in the way we have read Renaissance dramatic collaboration *generally*, and the ways we have deployed it in our readings of Renaissance dramatic texts. That is, I am contending that collaborative texts produced before the emergence of authorship are of a kind different (informed by differing mechanisms of textual property and control, different conceptions of imitation, originality, and the 'individual') from collaborations produced within the regime of the author. I want to show more fully the implications of a collaboratively attuned (rather than authorially based) interpretation by examining a particular text in the Beaumont and Fletcher canon, a text of which the author-question has been often asked and (ostensibly) answered definitively: *The Knight of the Burning Pestle*.

We can take as a guide to a collaborative reading the sustained ambivalence the early printed texts of *The Knight of the Burning Pestle* demonstrate toward authorship. *The Knight*, probably initially performed between 1607 and 1610, was first printed in a 1613 quarto, the title page of which mentions no writer(s). The dedicatory epistle, however, notes:

> This vnfortunate child, who in eight daies . . . was begot and borne, soone after, was by his parents . . . exposed to the wide world, who for want of judgement, or not vnder-standing the priuy marke of *Ironie* about it (which shewed it was no of-spring of any vulgar braine) vtterly reiected it.[17]

The play, apparently unparented on its title page, is here the offspring of both a singular 'braine' and plural 'parents.' (Further, it bears publicly a 'priuy' birth-'marke' of this ambiguous lineage.) This situation is only complicated by the second and third quartos of the play (both dated 1635); these title pages announce that *The Knight* was 'Written by Francis Beaumont and Iohn Fletcher. Gent.,' but they include a different prefatory letter, 'To the Readers of this Comedy,' which cites a singular 'Author [who] had no intent to wrong any one in this *Comedy* . . . which hee hopes will please all.'[18] Finally, in these subsequent quartos there also appears 'The Prologue,' a speech transferred into this text from an earlier play, which explains, in the only sentence it alters from its 1584 pre-text, that 'the Authors intention' was not to satirize any particular subject.[19] Most modern editors emend 'the Authors intention' to 'the author's intention,' but we would want to note in this context the fertile ambiguity (or oblivion) of early modern orthographic practice, which does not distinguish genitive singular from plural or genitive plural—that is, it does not use another of authorship's more recent technologies, the apostrophe, to separate the writer's/writers' propriety from his/their plurality.

A look at the preliminary material of these quartos thus demonstrates that, though author-ship is intermittently present, it does not appear in anything approaching a definitive or mono-lithically singular form; all three quartos, like many others of this period, instead foreground in their apparatus a different network of textual ownership and production. Unlike the writer(s), the publisher Walter Burre does appear on the Q1 title-page, and he also signs the dedicatory epistle (quoted above) to Robert Keysar, the manager of the Blackfriars theatre where the play was first performed and the previous owner of the text. The epistle establishes an extended filiation for this child/text, arguing that, despite 'his' failure in the theatre, he is 'desirous to try his fortune in the world, where if yet it be welcome, father, foster-father, nurse and child, all haue their desired end.'[20] If the 'father' here is the play's writer (with Keysar as foster-father and Burre as nurse), his singularity jars with the 'parents' noted above—although the parents who first 'exposed' the text might also be read as the (boy) players. In sum, though no author (certainly no *single* author) emerges from these initial references to the play's origins, the quartos' preliminary materials do display a complex and shifting network of other authorities: the publisher Burre, the printer N.O., the acting-company manager Keysar, the inhospitable theatre audience, the players and their royal patron (Q3 advertises the text 'as it is now acted by her Majesties Servants at the Privatehouse in *Drury lane*'), the writers Beaumont and Fletcher (eventually, after both are dead), the 'gentlemen' readers, and the unnamed writer of another play whose 'intentions' are transferred over and now said to apply to the 'Authors' or 'author' of this play.

Later in the century (concurrent with the shift I earlier located in *anonymous*) the play's authorial lineage seemingly becomes more important, but it is by no means more fully stabilized. A speech that probably served as a prologue to a revival between 1665 and 1667, for example, assumes that the play is solely Fletcher's;[21] published in 1672, this prologue precedes by only seven years the ascription of the play as collaborative in *Fifty Comedies and Tragedies Written by Francis Beaumont And John Fletcher, Gentlemen* (the second folio).

I am obscuring from this textual history the fact that virtually all the recent editions of *The Knight* now place Francis Beaumont, alone, on their title pages.[22] Though the quartos situate the initially unauthored, eventually collaborated play within a collaborative network, these editions deploy an army of editorial glosses to contain the subversive ambiguities cited above, proceed to interpret the play via its relationship to Beaumont's other plays (no easy task, given the paucity of this canon) or to his class-position and family history, and separate it off from (to name some other possible contexts) other plays performed by the Children of Blackfriars, or other plays associated with the name 'Beaumont and Fletcher.'[23] The irony of reducing *The Knight of the Burning Pestle* to a single author is that it is perhaps the most wildly collaborative play of this period. By this point, it should be clear that I do not here mean 'collaborative' merely in the usual, restricted sense of two or more writers writing together; this play exposes—in a way that we lose when we read it as the creation of particular individuals acting (as Bowers might say) in their 'proper role'—the more broadly collaborative enterprise of the early modern English theatre.

From the moment the Citizen interrupts the actor speaking the prologue in his fourth line and climbs onto the stage, *The Knight of the Burning Pestle* stages the somewhat contentious collaboration of an acting company and its audience. The audience becomes, literally, a part of the play, as the boy actors reluctantly agree to improvise, at the request of the Citizen and Wife, a play called *The Knight of the Burning Pestle*—starring the Wife's serving-boy Rafe—along with their rehearsed production of *The London Merchant*. This odd juxtaposition of genres—romance-quest and city-comedy—becomes increasingly complex, as the players attempt to accommodate and fuse the divergent plots. Like the framing prologues and epilogues of other plays, *The Knight*'s opening lines (as well as its sustained amalgamation of plots) suggest the general situation of acting companies attempting to sell their representations within the proto-capitalist marketplace of early modern London: they are (in a sense that is constantly being renegotiated) bound by the desires of their audience, at the same time that they participate in the construction of those desires. The economic valence of this transaction is registered at several points in the play, as in the episode where the Citizen gives money to the actor playing the innkeeper for accommodating Rafe and thus for accommodating (literally and figuratively) the audience and its desire to see a knight-errant.

The boy who speaks for the players and negotiates with the citizens, like most prologue-emissaries between acting company and audience, invariably uses the plural and collaborative 'we' to represent the company (B1) and establishes joint ownership in 'the plot of our Plaie' (D4^v).[24] A more comprehensive view, however, would see the entirety of the play's production (that is, the intersections of the 'actors'' *The London Merchant* and 'citizens'' *The Knight of the Burning Pestle*) as the corporate effort of the players—the collaboration of actors-acting-as-actors and actors-acting-as-citizens. This negotiation in turn brings into view another, silent collaborator in the larger production, the gentlemanly audience of the private theatre where the play is presented. No representative of this audience speaks, but the Boy, and occasionally the citizens, gesture toward its ostensibly more refined tastes:

CIT. Boy, come hither, send away *Raph* and this whoresonne Giant quickely.

BOY. In good faith sir we cannot, you'le vtterly spoile our Play, and make it to be hist, and it cost money, you will not suffer vs to go on with our plot, *I pray Gentlemen rule him*. (F4^v, final emphasis added)

The play here suggests the more complex task of accommodation facing the players: negotiating between the desires of the private theatre's gentlemen-patrons and the citizens eager for 'something notably in honour of the Commons of the Citty' (B1^v), a process with economic ramifications, as these lines make clear.

These negotiations draw into play a number of divergent discourses, as I have already noted in passing; *The Knight of the Burning Pestle* is quite literally, in Barthes' famous phrase, 'a tissue of quotations drawn from the innumerable centres of culture.'[25] The range of the play's 'quotation,' its discursive diversity, is immense in a way that I can only suggestively summarize; this is nevertheless another important way in which the play figures the collaborative enterprise of theatrical writing in this period.[26] Rafe's improvised adventures in *The Knight of the Burning Pestle* appropriate and play with the discourse of romance-epic: he reads aloud an extended passage from *Palmerin de Oliva*, a romance translated into English in 1581; his subsequent adventures gesture toward episodes of *Don Quixote*, *Arcadia*, and *The Faerie Queene*; and he trains his 'squire' and 'dwarf' (two serving-boys) to speak in the antique chivalric discourse of those familiar texts.[27] Rafe's adventures also draw on a genre of plays about 'prentice worthies.'[28] The 'actors'' *The London Merchant* is a similar pastiche of genres ('prodigal' plays, romantic-comedies, city-comedies), and Jasper's appearance as the ghost of himself deploys a revenge-tragedy convention in the service of a marriage-plot. Furthermore, the play's collation of romantic comedy eventuating in marriage with Rafe's romance-quest ending in his own death may figure the emergent genre which the team of playwrights subsequently attached to this play were to make famous: tragicomedy.[29]

At a more local level, the play continually exhibits its allusive permeability. Figuring the larger theatrical practice of importing music 'originating' elsewhere to fit the current production, Master Merrythought's lines are virtually all quotation/revisions of contemporary ballads and madrigals that circulated orally and/or in print. Modern editions attempt to separate these texts out of the texture of the play by italicizing them, labeling them 'song,' and devoting appendices to their special status as music. As Zitner, with evident frustration, notes in his appendix 'The songs': 'There are perhaps forty-one passages to be sung in *The Knight*. One says "perhaps" since it is sometimes difficult to distinguish what is to be sung from what is to be spoken.'[30] (A variation on the theme with which we began: what does it matter whom one is singing?)

A similar difficulty of distinguishing parts within the collaborated texture character-izes the serving-boy/hero Rafe. As already noted, he speaks in chivalric discourse as 'the Knight of the Burning Pestle,' and his first sustained utterance in the play is a recitation from *1 Henry IV*. Likewise, his speech at the end of Act IV parodies both the septenary meter of Elizabethan verse-narratives and May Lords' May-Day speeches. The generic attentiveness of Rafe's 'tragic' death speech—about which the boy-actor complains, ' 'Twill be very vnfit he should die sir, vpon no occasion, and in a Comedy too' (K2v–K3)—signals Rafe's own construction out of allusion: the long narrative rewrites passages from *The Spanish Tragedy*, *Richard III*, and *Eastward Ho!* Furthermore (and potentially more subversive to an author-based notion of this text), Rafe's last words, 'oh, oh, oh, &c.' (K3v), are the same as Hamlet's in the Folio version of that play, where they are often presumed by modern editors to be excisable from the 'author's' text as 'actor's interpolations.'[31] Rafe's final '&c.' succinctly marks his last moments as the actor's improvisatory collaboration with, and beyond, the script.

Lee Bliss has argued that 'Rafe becomes of necessity [*The Knight*'s] self-appointed dramatist: he must create dialogue and motivation that will give life and shape to . . . rather skimpy situational clues' and 'labors manfully to impose narrative coherence.' This is, she argues, 'the young playwright's own situation.'[32] While we might agree that Rafe is the central improvisa-tory, creative figure of *The Knight of the Burning Pestle*, to construct him as a type of the 'presiding dramatist' (in Bliss's view, the young Beaumont) is to impose a constraining coher-ence on interpretation that the text militates against. For if Rafe *is* the author, he is the author as collaborator, improviser, collator of allusion—the locus of the intersection of discourses, but not their originator. More importantly, like the musical Merrythought, he does not exist out-side, or independent of, the text; he is himself a construction of those discourses, the author as staged persona, 'a tissue of quotations.' Furthermore, like the 'text' Barthes theorizes, a 'multi-dimensional space in which a variety of writings, none of them original, blend and clash' (p. 146), Rafe is without origin—as the Wife puts it in her epilogue, 'a poore fatherlesse child' (K4). And to this extent he reproduces the troubled patrilineage of the text that begets him.

According to Foucault, 'the author is the principle of thrift in the proliferation of meaning . . . a certain functional principle by which, in our culture . . . one impedes the free circulation, the free manipulation, the free composition, decomposition, and recomposition of fiction' (pp. 118–19). And though, as we have seen, a dispersal of the author in *The Knight of the Burning Pestle* may allow fiction to circulate more freely, we would be mistaken to think that the fatherless status of both the Knight (Rafe) and *The Knight* figures the freeing of fictions. 'What Is an Author?' proceeds to such a visionary close, evoking a future in which fiction seems to circulate unlimited by authorial or other constraints, but Foucault himself acknowledges earlier in the essay that a culture devoid of all such mechanisms is 'pure romanticism' (p. 119).[33]

This is a romanticism I do not want to reproduce in speaking of the early modern period. *The*

Knight of the Burning Pestle, we remember, has an extended filiation, which includes a 'foster-father' and 'nurse,' and the quarto preliminaries exhibit a network of constraining figures, including the previous owner of the text, the publisher, the actors, the theatre audience, and the readers of the printed texts—as well as the 'author(s),' whose status is by no means fixed. Rafe may be 'a poore fatherlesse child,' but he is also a servant/apprentice shown quite clearly to be constrained by a particular class-position and, in his adventures (however freely they may seem to proliferate), by the desires of his master and mistress.[34] Fiction in this play is also all too obviously limited by the discourses available to the Citizen and Wife, the generic repertoire of the actors, and their location within the competitive theatrical market.

As I've argued implicitly in the interpretation outlined above, all of these constraints are more relevant to an interpretation of this text than the author(s). Even such rigorous theorizations of the author as Wayne Booth's 'implied author' and Alexander Nehamas's 'postulated author' are problematic when applied to the interpretation of collaborative dramatic texts from this period. Nehamas, for example, writes that 'in interpreting a text . . . we want to know what *any* individual who can be its subject must be like. We want to know, that is, what sort of person, what character, is manifested in it.' The need to postulate such an author— even (only) as 'a hypothesis . . . accepted provisionally [that] guides interpretation'[35]—is specific to certain historical moments and genres. [. . .]

While these observations are obviously indebted to Foucault's conceptual shift, I would at the same time want to interrogate his imagination of a post-authorial 'constraining figure,' for it seems to register both a residue of intention left by the deceased author and a singularity that the above discussion seeks to complicate. We might speak instead of 'constraining contexts' for *The Knight* and other plays of the period; as I have argued, a more appropriate interpretation is one guided and constrained by what we know about the discourses, figures, locations, and cultural practices participating in its emergence. The ambivalence of this text and this culture toward the author is itself one of those contexts.

My terms here are plural, for, as we have seen, this text defies even the ideally liberal constraint Foucault imagines, 'fiction passing through something like *a* necessary or constraining *figure*' (p. 119, my emphasis).[36] It may be that we will not be able to emerge from the Enlightenment legacy of that necessary individual. However, our attempts to do so in our investigations of the past—to see figures (plural) rather than the singular reflections of our authorial selves, to note for example that my writing and citing in the present context collaborate with, among other things, a Chicago manual and a university press that prescribe 'my' 'style'—can be instrumental in that emergence. To revise the position from which we began, and to ask the question with which the remainder of this book will be occupied: What, or rather *how*, does it matter who are speaking?

*   *   *

Margaret W. Ferguson, 'Renaissance concepts of the "woman writer" ', in Helen Wilcox (ed.), *Women and Literature in Britain, 1500–1700* (Cambridge: Cambridge University Press, 1996), p. 145.

Despite the many changes that have occurred in historical concepts of the author and writer between the Renaissance and the twentieth century, women have consistently had an 'eccentric' relation to dominant social concepts of the writer and the author. Indeed the very phrases 'woman writer' and 'woman author' usually imply that these concepts, when unmodified, are gendered masculine. In some discursive contexts, particularly those that participate in the lively Renaissance debates about 'proper' modes of masculine and feminine behaviour . . . the idea of the 'woman writer' is a veritable paradox or oxymoron, one eliciting attitudes of outrage and/or scorn.[1] If women are prescriptively defined as 'chaste, silent and obedient', according to a well-known ideal in Renaissance conduct books, and if both writing and printing were defined, for any number of reasons, as 'masculine' activities and also in opposition to 'silence', then the phrase 'woman writer' will be seen as a contradiction in terms.[2]

*   *   *

Annabel Patterson, *Censorship and Interpretation: The Conditions of Writing and Reading in Early Modern England* (Madison: University of Wisconsin Press, 1984), pp. 10–11.

My own approach to censorship focuses only occasionally on law and the formal institutions and mechanisms whereby the press, or the pulpit, or the theatrical companies were theoretically made subject to state control. The legal history of censorship in relationship to all aspects of the printing trade has been well covered by F. S. Siebert, among others.[1] But there were certain moments in that history when the law was forced to take particular cognizance of problems of interpretation. A paradigmatic case of this kind was the trial of William Prynne for seditious libel in 1633 . . . Prynne's case . . . was both a symbolic example of the interpretive problems created by censorship, or by censorship's confrontation with the slipperiness of language, and an exceptional failure, a dramatic breakdown of the normal methods of dealing with those problems. For what we find everywhere apparent and widely understood, from the middle of the sixteenth century in England, is a system of communication in which ambiguity becomes a creative and necessary instrument, a social and cultural force of considerable consequence. On the one hand writers complain constantly that their work is subject to unauthorized or unjust interpretation; on the other hand they gradually developed codes of communication, partly to protect themselves from hostile and hence dangerous readings of their work, partly in order to be able to say what they had to publicly without directly provoking or confronting the authorities. It has been frequently pointed out that legislated control of the press by such mechanisms as prepublication licensing tends to be virtually impossible to enforce, given the various stratagems to which writers and printers could resort to evade the laws—clandestine presses, books smuggled from abroad, not to mention the costs and difficulties of administering such a system, and the inevitable fallibility or carelessness of the licensers . . . But there is a whole range of publishing in England that can be better accounted for by assuming some degree of cooperation and understanding on the part of the authorities themselves, something that goes even beyond the recognition that unenforceable laws were better than none, that the occasional imprisonment, however arbitrary, had an exemplary force. Rather, there were conventions that both sides accepted as to how far a writer could go in explicit address to the contentious issues of his day, how he could encode his opinions so that nobody would be *required* to make an example of him.

QUESTIONS

- What is a Renaissance author?
- To what extent is authorship gendered?

3 | Rethinking the notion of a single, stable text

Arthur F. Marotti, 'Malleable and fixed texts: manuscript and printed miscellanies and the transmission of lyric poetry in the English Renaissance', in W. Speed Hill (ed.), *New Ways of Looking at Old Texts* (Binghamton, New York: Medieval and Renaissance Texts and Studies, 1993), pp. 170–2.

Many individual poems, in their own time, existed in both manuscript and printed collections: in some cases publishers only reproduced one form of a text that continued to be changed and rewritten in a still vital form of manuscript tradition, no one version assuming primacy. Edward Dyer's poem 'The lowest trees have tops' is one such example. Not only did verbal changes continue to appear in the various versions, but transcribers and competitors also felt compelled to compose answers and, in at least one case, a supplement to it. Although it was published anonymously in Francis Davison's *A Poetical Rhapsody* (1602), and in John Dowland's *Third and Last Booke of Songs or Airs* (1603), in the absence of those minimal controls that would have been exercised by the contemporary publication of this author's collected verse, the poem proliferated in manuscript, accumulating variants textual scholars regard as 'corruptions' of an unavailable original text that the two printed versions are assumed to approximate. In Davison's volume, the last Elizabethan poetical anthology, the lyric appears as follows:

> The lowest Trees haue tops, the Ante her gall,
> The flie her splene, the little sparkes their heate:
> The slender haires cast shadowes, though but small,
> And Bees haue stings, although they be not great:
> Seas haue their sourse, & so haue shallow springs,
> And loue is loue, in Beggars, as in Kings.
>
> Where riuers smoothest run, deepe are the foords,
> The Diall stirres, yet none perceiues it mooue:
> The firmest faith is in the fewest wordes,
> The Turtles cannot sing, and yet they loue:
> True Hartes haue eyes, & eares, no tongs to speake,
> They heare, & see, and sigh, and then they breake.
>
> *Incerto*[1]

Since the poem, as Rollins observed, 'is made up almost entirely of proverbs and commonplaces',[2] there were unusual pressures at work in manuscript transmission to change features of the text as transcribers easily confused the lines of the lyric with their own store of familiar sayings. Add to this the possibility of changes introduced by the practice of memorial transcription and you have an extreme case of textual malleability.

Variations found in the twenty manuscript and three printed versions of this poem include the transposition of the two stanzas (BL MS. Harl. 6910), the insertion of an additional stanza in the middle (Folger MS. V.a.162; Bod. MS. Malone 19; Bod. MS. Tanner 169), and the addition of an eight-line supplement written by someone Ruth Hughey suggests 'was making use of the poem for personal reasons'.[3] Verbal variations include what look like misreadings of a transcribed source text—e.g., 'course' for 'source' and 'hollowes' for 'shallowes' in line 5—as well as misremembered words or phrases possibly occurring in the process of memorial transcription—e.g., 'smallest' for 'lowest' and 'shrubs' for 'trees' in line 1, 'riuers' for 'waters' and 'floods' for 'fordes' in line 7, and 'fairest' for 'firmest', 'loue' for 'fayth', and 'clearest' or 'sweetest' for 'fewest' in line 9.[4] While it might be an editor's nightmare, this poem should be a cultural historian's delight—in its intertextual complexity and socioliterary vicissitudes, it is a collaborative social production, as open a text as one could imagine.

*   *   *

Jonathan Goldberg, *Shakespeare's Hand* (Minneapolis and London: University of Minnesota Press, 2003), pp. 253–67, 270.

Fredson Bowers provides a good place to start. Commenting on a reading in *Romeo and Juliet* adopted by editors from Alexander Pope to George Lyman Kittredge, by John Dover Wilson in the Cambridge edition and by John E. Hankins in the Penguin, the reading that has Juliet say that 'a rose by any other name would smell as sweet' rather than 'a rose by any other word would smell as sweet,' Bowers writes: '[T]his *name* got put into the received texts in early days when no distinction was made between bad and good authority, and it has remained ever since, although it is completely wrong.'[1] [. . .]

Bowers's judgment follows upon the orthodoxy of the New Bibliography. 'Name,' the bad reading preferred by bad editors, derives from the bad quarto of *Romeo and Juliet*; 'word' is from the good quarto, and a good editor will know the difference and will know therefore that there really is no choice to be made. (The Folio text is of no importance to editors, since it is derivative, based largely on Q3, which descends from Q2; the Folio diverges from Q2 unauthoritatively.) With the clear choice between Q1 and Q2 before them, who, to paraphrase the question that Random Cloud asks in 'The Marriage of Good and Bad Quartos,' would want to be bad when they could be good?[2] Who would want to defile a good text by marrying it to a bad one? [. . .]

At this point, it might be appropriate to have before us—the texts [. . .] The 1597 quarto (Q1) of *An excellent conceited Tragedie of Romeo and Iuliet* reads:

IULIET. Tis but thy name that is mine enemie.
　　Whats *Mountague?* It is nor hand nor foote,
　　Nor arme, nor face, nor any other part.
　　Whats in a name? That which we call a Rose,
　　By any other name would smell as sweet:

So *Romeo* would, were he not *Romeo* cald,
Retaine the diuine perfection he owes:
Without that title *Romeo* part thy name,
And for that name which is no part of thee,
Take all I haue.

(D1v)[3]

In the 1599 quarto (Q2) of *The most excellent and lamentable Tragedie, of Romeo and Iuliet* the speech reads:

IULIET. Tis but thy name that is my enemie:
  Thou are thy selfe, though not a *Mountague*,
  Whats *Mountague?* it is nor hand nor foote,
  Nor arme nor face, ô be some other name
  Belonging to a man.
  Whats in a name that which we call a rose,
  By any other word would smell as sweete,
  So *Romeo* would wene he not *Romeo* cald,
  Retaine that deare perfection which he owes,
  Without that tytle, *Romeo* doffe thy name,
  And for thy name which is no part of thee,
  Take all my selfe.

(D2r–v)

And finally, to cite the lines as they appear in Brian Gibbons's New Arden edition, which shares Bowers's editorial supposition that Q2 is a good text, based on Shakespeare's foul papers, one whose readings therefore are to be preferred:

JULIET. 'Tis but thy name that is my enemy:
  Thou art thyself, though not a Montague.
  What's Montague? It is nor hand nor foot
  Nor arm nor face nor any other part
  Belonging to a man. O be some other name.
  What's in a name? That which we call a rose
  By any other word would smell as sweet;
  So Romeo would, were he not Romeo call'd,
  Retaine that dear perfection which he owes
  Without that title. Romeo, doff thy name,
  And for thy name, which is no part of thee,
  Take all myself.

(2.2.38–49)[4]

Gibbons chooses 'word' rather than 'name,' and in every other place in which the two texts offer alternatives, Q2 is the basis for his text. He, presumably, would earn Bowers's applause;

he has garnered praise, in fact, from Stanley Wells.[5] [. . .] The 1597 text is, Wells writes, 'a "bad" quarto' while Q2 'was set up mostly from Shakespeare's working papers,' although, he adds, unfortunately, they had not 'been tidied up for use in the theatre,' as the 'bad' quarto had been; thus Wells commends Gibbons's composite text, especially for making use of the theatrical evidence of Q1, as revealed in the stage directions that Gibbons derives from Q1, but Wells confirms Bowers's opinion for the choice of Q2 as the basic copytext. Not that Gibbons relies only on Q2; even Bowers admits that there are moments when an editor cannot help preferring bad readings to good ones (120); Wells notes some one hundred Q1 readings adopted by Gibbons. One of them, as should have been clear from the citations already, occurs in this passage, and Wells applauds it. It involves, in his words, 'the restitution of a phrase' ('nor any other part') at 2.2.41. For, Wells insists, the bad quarto is a much 'maligned predecessor'; the reporter sometimes remembered what the Q2 compositor left out. Such, he claims, is the case at line 41, 'nor arm nor face nor any other part,' the last part of which appears only in Q1—which Gibbons has 'restored' in his conflated text.

Gibbons at this point has not merely incorporated a Q1 reading. For to choose Q1's version of this line poses difficulties for the passage as it appears in Q2, 'nor arme nor face, ô be some other name,' with its following half-line, 'Belonging to a man.' Wells does not comment on what Gibbons has done here, which is to reverse the two phrases found only in Q2, thereby producing line 42: 'Belonging to a man. O be some other name.' Wells's silence is not surprising, however, for Gibbons's line has a long if not a New Bibliographical tradition behind it. As the apparatus in the Arden edition reveals, Gibbons reproduces an emendation that Edmond Malone made to solve this supposed textual crux, and it has to be asked whether, in giving his readers what Malone wrote, Gibbons has delivered what Shakespeare wrote. It is, to say the least, rather startling to recognize that such well-known Shakespearean lines were written by Malone. [. . .]

If one supposes that what Malone wrote is what Shakespeare wrote, one must then ask how Q2 managed not to reproduce the author's manuscript. John Jowett, who also reprints Malone's lines in the new Oxford edition of the complete works, attempts an explanation.[6] Sharing Wells's supposition that 'Q1 simply omits a verse line, as elsewhere,' Jowett argues that 'its unique "nor any other part" is especially significant as it makes sense of material in Q2 which it does not itself print.' He admits, however, that 'Q2's deficiency and mislocation have no obvious cause.' What must be assumed, he argues, is that the manuscript was particularly illegible at this point and that the phrases that found their way into Q2 were marginal additions. Perhaps, Jowett opines, 'nor any other part' at a cursory glance by the compositor seemed simply to be 'Nor arme nor face' written a second time—foul papers have such repetitions; such, at any rate, is the claim offered to explain other features of the text supposedly behind Q2—and thus the compositor, this time recognizing and eliminating a repetition, was faced with the stray half line 'Belonging to a man,' which he then misplaced. In offering this solution, however, Jowett conveniently forgets the other half-line, 'ô be some other name,' and its misplacement.

Throughout his commentary, Jowett seems haunted by the specter of Alice Walker, who rewrote and relocated the lines (in a reading adopted by Dover Wilson and G. I. Duthie in their Cambridge edition):

JULIET. 'Tis but thy name that is my enemy.
    Thou art thy self, though not a Montague.
    O be some other name! What's Montague?
    It is nor hand, nor foot, nor arm, nor face,
    Nor any part belonging to a man.
    What's in a name? That which we call a rose
    By any other name would smell as sweet.
                        (2.2.38–44)[7]

'Clearly,' Wilson comments in his notes to this line—what a relief that something should be clear at this point—'Clearly Q2 here derives from a corrected passage of Q1 in which the collator's marginal additions from the foul papers have somehow got misplaced.' Adopting Walker's reading, Wilson explains that her decision to render the line as 'Nor any part belonging to a man,' omitting 'other' before 'part,' was based on the supposition that the actor's memory anticipated 'other' in 'By any other name.' Walker's rearrangement gives us a metrical line—which Shakespeare surely wrote!—and avoids the repetitions that befoul the memories of actors and the bad texts they reconstruct. Jowett is haunted by this argument, for his own, as he admits 'is analogous to Walker's but does not depend on the hypothesis of Q1 copy for Q2.' Admit that hypothesis, and Q1 might not be so 'bad' after all (at any rate a bad quarto would have to be admitted to stand behind the good). It might allow—as it does in all the editions Bowers scorns, including Wilson's—the repetition of 'name' rather than the alternative 'word.'

For here one must face the well-known and extremely disturbing fact that Q1 does lie behind Q2 (that Q1 'contaminates' Q2, as the standard terminology of editors from Pope to Wells would have it). For a stretch of some hundred lines in act 1, scenes 2–3, Q2 reprints Q1, as is clear not merely by the virtual coincidence of words in this passage but by the replication of typographical peculiarities and other features of the accidentals.[8] Editors have wrestled with the question of the further extent of Q1's influence on Q2, and the answers have ranged from Dover Wilson's assumption that Q2 is in large part based on marked-up Q1 copy[9] to the more widely shared belief that Q1 was occasionally—and indeterminately—consulted by the Q2 compositor.

It is in terms of an assumed relation between Q1 and Q2 that Duthie explains the lines we have been examining.[10] Duthie argues that corrections in Q1 misunderstood by the compositor account for Q2's omission and mislocation of lines. In his reconstruction, Duthie supposes that the scribe marking up Q1 inserted 'Belonging to a man' directly beneath 'Nor arme, nor face' in Q1. Cramped by the interlinear space, he added the remainder of the line, 'ô be some other name,' in the righthand margin, drawing a line from those words to the place in the text where they belonged. Unfortunately, that line went through 'nor any other part,' and the compositor replaced that phrase with the marginal insertion. 'The conflation, traditional since Malone, is I believe, correct,' Duthie concludes (14)—a conclusion implicitly retracted, however, when he came to edit the play with Dover Wilson and adopted Walker's reading, one even more seductive since it preserved Q2 phrases in their proper order and also managed to eliminate memorial corruption. Duthie's initial solution to the problem seems to me ingenious, and far more elegant and cogent than Jowett's. Why, then, does Jowett not adopt it; why, indeed, does he offer his troublingly analogous reconstruction?

The answer seems to be that Duthie and Walker both assume that Q2 is bibliographically derivative, while Jowett wants, insofar as possible, to make the authority behind Q2 authorial. If something has gone wrong in the text at this point, it can only be the illegibility of the manuscript that will account for it. In the manuscript that Jowett reconstructs, two things are supposed: first, that it will allow the Q2 misreading; second, that it will not explain the Q1 reading, for in Jowett's story, a phrase that is in Q1 is missing in Q2 because the manuscript could not be read. The assumption is, therefore, that no authorial manuscript lay behind Q1. The further assumption, of course, is that there was always—in the manuscript Jowett dreams of—one possible version of these lines: the one that Malone wrote.

Duthie's reconstruction assumes a marked-up Q1, but it need not rest upon that supposition. It will also allow for a manuscript marked up in precisely the same way. To believe that, however, would produce a different manuscript from the one Jowett wants. It would be a manuscript that vested authority in the Q1 reading, making Q2 a failed attempt to understand authorial revision of lines that once authoritatively stood as they appear in Q1. Perhaps what makes Jowett nervous is not merely the fact that he too rearranges the lines as Duthie does, but also the fact that his account assumes authorial revision; for Jowett, however, the margin-alia were produced before Q1 was, in a single manuscript of the play. But to follow Duthie's argument—and to allow it its analogical force as an explanation of the state of the manuscript behind Q2—could lead one to assume that the manuscript of the play was revised and that such revision occurred after the state of the manuscript authoritatively represented by Q1.[11]

When questions about Shakespeare's text—or texts—become questions about the manu-script—or manuscripts—behind them, we pass, inevitably, into the sphere of desire, the desire for the missing object, which, in certain post-Freudian accounts, defines the nature of desire. ('To strip the veil of print,' Bowers's well-known phrase,[12] sounds uncannily like the scene Sigmund Freud described in *Beyond the Pleasure Principle*, watching his grandson play the 'Fort! Da!' game of disappearance and reappearance.) That we are dealing with a textual desire, or the desire for a text, in no way disturbs this psychoanalytic paradigm, for, as Jacques Lacan insists, the unconscious is structured as language, and the search for the absent Other is undertaken in language; the words spoken in desire come from the illusory place of the Other and are spoken toward the desire of restitution, to find the Other in one's words. It is of more than passing interest that this passage in *Romeo and Juliet*, where textual desire is enacted on the bibliographical scene, is also a moment of Juliet's desire for Romeo, enacted also as a textual desire: 'O Romeo, Romeo, wherefore art thou Romeo?' 'O be some other name'; be 'word' instead of 'name'? There is, perhaps, a complicity of desires here. But more of that in a while.

To return to strictly bibliographical questions. We seem to be faced with two possible accounts of the phantasmatic object behind the texts of *Romeo and Juliet*. In one of these—the version offered by Wells and Jowett—Q1 is a corrupt text, marked by omissions that are restored, or whose restoration is attempted, by Q2. The only full source of the play is the author's holograph, and the only text with access to it is Q2. In the other version of textual transmission, Q1 serves as the copy for Q2, and it has been marked up by consulting the author's manuscript. Implicit here, then, is the supposition that readings in Q1 might be authoritative not merely because the actors remembered what the Q2 compositor missed but also because they remembered a version of the text that did not coincide with the manuscript behind Q2. [. . .] The lines we have been examining could represent one of those moments of consultation, but, as others have shown, in the hundred or so lines where consultation is certain, we know that Q1 lies behind Q2 precisely because the texts of Q1 and Q2 are virtually identical for these lines, particularly in matters of punctuation, typography, and the abbreviations used to name the characters. At those points, Q1 was treated as authoritative, and it did not need to be marked up. However, if the lines in Juliet's speech in Q2 arose from a marked-up text, as Duthie argued, the only marked-up text in question could have been the manuscript. If he is right, that manuscript would initially have contained the lines as they appear in Q1.

From a New Bibliographical standpoint, such an argument is inadmissible. It returns us to the bad old days that Bowers attacks, when authority between good and bad had not been established and the bad quartos were considered to be early drafts of the plays. This is, for example, the opinion of P.A. Daniel in the introduction to his 1874 enface edition of Q1 and Q2. Yet his understanding of Q1 is, in fact, rather complex; for him (and, I must add, for me too), Q1 is a mixed text, sometimes authoritative, sometimes memorial reconstruction; 'in its more perfect portions,' Daniel writes, it 'affords conclusive evidence that that "copy" underwent revision, received some slight augmentation, and, in some few places, must have been entirely re-written.'[13] In the modern orthodoxy (confirmed by Harry Hoppe in *The Bad Quarto of Romeo and Juliet*),[14] where Daniel saw revision and augmentation, we are to see omission. Q1 is a memorial reconstruction of a cut Q2. There was always only one *Romeo and Juliet*.

But which one? The one supposed by Jowett, or the one I have supposed based on Duthie? Bowers, one can be sure, would find it 'completely wrong' to desire to return to the bad old days when anything was possible; the streamlined efficiency of the New Bibliography promised that would never happen again. It stands for order and economy, for logic and rationality. It knows the difference between good and bad. It has its machines, and its mechanistic view of compositors as machines, always making the same mistakes. And, as Bowers admits, it also has its proponents, like Dover Wilson, who somehow know the rules of the game and always make the wrong choices. The reason for that situation is not hard to explain, however; for all the supposed rationality of the New Bibliography, there inevitably comes the moment of unreasoned choice, the making of editorial decisions. The work of reason, moreover, is directed at a phantom, a lost text, always reconstructed on principles that will never be fully explained rationally. What, then, is a good New Bibliographer to do, producing a substitute object on the basis of a lost one?

For the passage we have been examining, Hoppe and Richard Hosley in their editions of the play make (in their terms) the only 'rational' choice; they abandon the phantom for the material fact and reprint Q2 without Malone's 'restitution.' For, as Hosley comments, 'it is not entirely clear that Q2 is corrupt.'[15] No editor before Malone conflated the texts; either the Folio (and thereby the Q2 reading) or the Q1 reading appears in the early editions.[16] What Malone wrote, Hosley argues, is not what Shakespeare wrote, and Malone can never be proved right in his emendation. Q2 is what Shakespeare wrote, and it therefore should be reprinted as it stands. This is Hosley's argument. [. . .] Q1 haunts all editions of *Romeo and Juliet;* it even haunts Q2. And there is no way of knowing when it might not be authoritative.

This fact has lead to the bibliographical commonplace that Q1 is the problem facing the editor of the play. 'The bad first quarto of 1597 may fairly be said to pose the chief editorial problem in *Romeo and Juliet*,' Hosley opens an essay on 'The Corrupting Influence of the Bad Quarto on the Received Text of *Romeo and Juliet*.'[17] 'Most, though not all, of the problems in *Romeo and Juliet* derive from the existence of the first edition,' Wells opines, hedging the case a bit. I submit that the real editorial problem is Q2, not merely because it authorizes Q1 in some always undecidable manner, although that is bad enough. If we once admit that what Malone wrote, conflating Q1 and Q2, is what Shakespeare wrote, then Bowers's touchstone disappears. If lines in this speech were revised—as both Jowett and Duthie suppose, however opposed their notion of the manuscript may be—how is one to know where the revision stopped? Now, in fact, in the account thus far given, the situation is relatively simple. Choose my version of Duthie, and one chooses a manuscript that existed in two states, temporally separate. State one lies behind the 'more perfect portions' of Q1; state two authorizes Q2. There are then two *Romeo and Juliets*, an earlier and a later one. Conflation of the two may be permissible, however, since Q2 appears to be a conflated and corrected text. One might then choose 'word' instead of 'name' on the supposition that it is the substitute that has ultimate authorial validity. So, too, one might choose Malone's lines as the best way to restore a Shakespearean revision. One would not, in this scenario, be returning to what was always there, the one and only *Romeo and Juliet* that Jowett and Wells desire; but one would at least be restoring the author's final intention.

I want to argue, however, that it is precisely the author's final intention that Q2 does not deliver. This fact about Q2 is, from a slightly different vantage point, agreed upon in deriving Q2 from foul copy that offers moments of incoherence that are especially evident in the first and second shots that Q2 reproduces at several points in the text. Editors, who want to give their readers what Shakespeare wrote, usually baulk at such moments and choose one version of what Shakespeare wrote, deciding which is best, what Shakespeare would finally have chosen had he only gotten his papers into order for the acting company. There is nothing wrong in editors so doing, so long as they do not fool themselves into thinking that in eliminating variants they are giving their readers what Shakespeare wrote or that they are privy to final intentions. Editors have good authority for what they do; their practice derives from the playhouse, however, and not from the text. No actor could possibly deliver Romeo's final soliloquy as represented in Q2, for example; it offers several versions of the same lines, and an actor will have to choose among the alternatives. So, too, do editors choose. [. . .] The authority for an editor at such a moment is not Q2, for it does not choose. The authority for editors is Q1. It represents a version of the play in which choices have been made and redundancies have been removed. I submit that we know what Q1 is, and that we can recognize it as the legitimating ancestor for edited versions of *Romeo and Juliet*. In that sense, Q2 is the real problem. An editor may not wish to make the same choices as Q1 has, but few editors will rigorously reproduce Q2. Rather, they do what Q1 has been accused of doing: They cut Q2, they emend it, they rewrite it. Q1 haunts editors of *Romeo and Juliet* because it is the dark specter of their own practice.

On its title page, Q2 announces it is '*Newly corrected, augmented, and amended.*' Although one need not take this claim literally, its multiple terms do suggest that Q2 gives evidence of a range of kinds of revision. Q2 claims authority in the sundry performances of the play as acted by the Lord Chamberlain's Men. No mention is made of the author's hand, nor is his name offered on the title page. In this, it is not unlike Q1, which also vests its authority in the playhouse. My point here is not to call into question the supposition that foul papers lie behind Q2 but to ask what their relationship might be to the playhouse. Wells, we recall, assumes that they would have been 'tidied up'—edited, in a word—for the players. I want to argue against that supposition. I submit that what stands behind Q2 is a manuscript that offers an anthology of possible performances of the play, one of which is captured by Q1. Q2's relationship to that version of the play is complex; it corrects its errors—I am not denying that, in part, Q1 may be an unreliable text—but Q2 also augments and amends the text printed in Q1, making additions and changes. Q2 is a different version—or rather, different versions—of the play. It is a selection from or an anthology of a number of productions of *Romeo and Juliet*, one of which was close to the performance represented by Q1, close enough to allow Q2 to use Q1 as its authority at some points. At some moments, such as the lines we have lingered over, Q2 offers an augmented version of Q1. But we do not know when the augmentation took place; that is, we do not know whether Q1 chose to omit lines or whether such a choice would have been impossible because the lines had not yet been written. There is no way of knowing whether new lines in Q2, including 'Thou art thy selfe, though not a *Mountague*,' as well as the problematic 'ô be some other name/Belonging to a man' were cut in the Q1 performance or added subsequent to it. Nor is there any way of knowing whether Q2 was offering substitute lines or lines meant to be added. For not only is there no way of knowing which of the two manuscripts hypothetically reconstructed lies behind Q2, but also there is no guarantee that those two possibilities are exhaustive. I am now proposing that they are not. And in this, as in much else that I have been arguing, I follow Random Cloud, who writes, '[W]e must countenance Shakespeare's writing of *Romeo and Juliet* as extending over some time and running through several different phases, and perhaps in several different manuscripts, each perhaps with its own characteristic aesthetic, offering together several finalities' (429).

The basis for this argument lies in Q2, although one must look to lines other than those about the rose for further confirmation—at Romeo's final soliloquy, for instance, or the variant sets of lines spoken by Romeo at the end of act 2, scene 2 and by Friar Laurence at the opening of act 2, scene 3.[18] For although in those cases it is clear that Q1 has made choices among possibilities left open in Q2, we have no way of knowing whether these options were there from the start—in an original, untidy manuscript—or whether they resulted from later additions. For Q2 offers different kinds of revisionary processes, some of which may represent first and second thoughts in an initial draft of the play and some of which may represent different versions in different performances of the play from season to season. It is possible that there once may have been one *Romeo and Juliet*, but insofar as Q2 is derived from foul papers, it suggests that there was always more than one *Romeo and Juliet*; these variants, I would argue, were 'tidied up' only in performance, but not in a manuscript replete with second thoughts and alternatives. If, in performance, selections necessarily were made from the authorial multiplicity, subsequent performances also occasioned further revision; there is no guarantee that such revision was authorial or that playhouse decisions necessarily were authorial either. All these versions, authorial or not, remained in the untidy and burgeoning manuscript—or manuscripts—left, once again, for the performers to choose among. The manuscript(s) became an anthology. And it is some version of that anthology that Q2 preserves.

Q2 thus represents a very complicated situation, combining both original multiplicity with temporally spaced revision. And there is no way to tell them apart; in those revisions, deletions as well as additions were made and substitutes were tried out.[19] As is clear from the remarkable coincidences between Q1 and Q2, much of the play remained unrevised. Many of the revisions are of the sort found in other instances of Shakespearean revision: a word changed here or there. Q2 is considerably longer than Q1, and it displays several moments when different versions of speeches or longer and shorter alternatives were offered, or when different characters might be allowed to speak versions of the same lines. Jowett and Wells assume that Q1 has omitted lines genuinely preserved in Q2, but there is no evidence for that except in the retrospective recasting that gives authority to a fuller version; in the case we have been examining, that fuller version is the product of editorial conflation. When Jowett hears a line in Q1 as incomplete without its Q2 addition, there is no way of knowing if he is right. 'It is nor hand nor foote, / Nor arme, nor face, nor any other part' does not necessarily cry out for 'Belonging to a man.' I submit that here, as with many of the supposed 'cut' moments in Q1, it is equally possible that Q2 has added to Q1. Furthermore, even if Q1 cuts material found in Q2, that is no argument against its authority. Q2 has to be cut in any performance (or edition) of the play. And although it prints various versions of scenes and lines, we do not know that it prints them all. Because it is often too full for the sake of performance, for all we know, it has made choices too. After all, there are lines in Q1 that are not in Q2, and Malone's conflation testifies to the desire to credit some of them as being authentically Shakespearean. On the other hand, as Hosley remarked, there is nothing obviously wrong with 'ô be some other name / Belonging to a man.' Lines that have been conflated ever since Malone may, in fact, be alternatives. Perhaps, as Walker's rewriting of the lines suggests, this speech of Juliet's was made of movable parts. And if so, that would be the case elsewhere. Editors who reproduce Malone's version operate under that supposition, but so, too, do Hosley and Hoppe when they imagine that in choosing Q2 they have not made a choice. If that is the case, I would argue that where Q1 and Q2 differ in terms of substitutions that can be explained by revisionary processes, we have no way of knowing which version is earlier or later. Nor am I convinced that such distinctions count in terms of authority.

The substitution of 'word' for 'name' is one of these moments. The fact that Q1 has 'name' does not necessarily mean that that was the earlier reading; it could mean that 'word' and 'name' were alternative possibilities in the script or scripts behind Q1 and Q2. Both might be authorial; either might not be.

What these two versions of the lines intimate is that there were as many more *Romeo and Juliet*s as we might imagine within the plausible life of the play in Shakespeare's time. An editor of the play, at least one following New Bibliographic protocols, will choose one of them, just as any actor playing Juliet chose one of the alternatives. There never was a final *Romeo and Juliet*, a single authoritative or authorial version of the play. There were only versions, from the start. As scripts to be acted, they presumed multiplicities and contingencies, the conditions of the theater. Q1 and Q2 in their very different ways both tell us that any single performance differed from other performances, just as every text of *Romeo and Juliet* differs from every other one. An edition can never give us what Shakespeare really wrote, because we have no evidence suggesting there finally was such a definitive thing. There is scarcely a Shakespeare play—even those that survive in only one text—that does not give evidence of existing in multiple versions. An editor seeking an alternative to the protocols of the New Bibliography might choose not to choose and would thus risk producing the virtually unreadable texts of *Romeo and Juliet*, opting for the 'infinitive' text. In its editorial apparatus, such an edition would give alternatives as alternatives; it would mark up the texts to allow for as many performances as the editor deemed plausible. Such a text is utopian, and, in truth, it might be no more than a composite of all the different editions of *Romeo and Juliet* that have ever been or that ever will be.[20] [. . .]

One more word: The title of this essay begins with a quotation, one more naming of the rose: 'What? in a names that which we call a Rose.' The line is yet another variant, this time from the Folio,[21] and its aberrant form has been explained,[22] once again on the basis of nonexistent marginalia; this time a marked-up copy of Q3 must be posited to explain how a question mark wandered to replace an 's' and an 's' found itself where a question mark should be. I have no desire to embrace the Folio reading as authoritative or to begin now an examination of that text of *Romeo and Juliet*. But I let the line remain at the head of this essay as a reminder of what I have been arguing: that the singular text is the phantasmatic object of a textual desire that is realized only in the deformations and multiplications of that desire in its textual manifestations. I let the line stand, since it erringly offers the plural 'names' by which we truly name the rose. If this essay has a real title, it is 'The Names of the Rose.'

* * *

Stephen Orgel, 'What is a text?', in David Scott Kastan and Peter Stallybrass (eds.), *Staging the Renaissance: Interpretations of Elizabethan and Jacobean Drama* (London and New York: Routledge, 1991), pp. 86–7.

E. A. J. Honigmann, in *The Stability of Shakespeare's Texts*, shows quite persuasively that the notion of final or complete versions assumed by virtually all modern editors of Shakespeare is inconsistent with everything we know not only about Renaissance theatrical practice, but about the way writers in fact work. Poets are always rewriting, and there is no reason to think that many of the confusions in Shakespeare's texts don't involve second thoughts, or amalgams of quite separate versions of a play. I'd want to go a great deal further than this, but the idea of the basic instability of the text seems to me an absolutely essential one . . . when we make our editions, of Shakespeare or any other dramatist, we are *not* 'getting back to the author's original text'. We know nothing about Shakespeare's original text. We might know something about it if, say, a set of Shakespeare's working notes or rough drafts ever turned up, or if we ever found the text that Shakespeare presented to the company as their working copy. But if we did find such a manuscript, that would be something different from the play—just as different as the printed text of *Sejanus* is from Jonson's play.

. . . .

QUESTIONS

- What are the advantages of reading texts in multiple versions?
- Why has the notion of a single, stable text proved historically so attractive?

4 | **The politics of editing Shakespeare**

Andrew Murphy, 'Texts and textualities: a Shakespearean history', in Andrew Murphy (ed.), *The Renaissance Text: Theory, Editing, Textuality* (Manchester and New York: Manchester University Press, 2000), pp. 197–205.

Marshall McLuhan was one of the first to recognise that '[t]he invention of typography . . . provid[ed] the first repeatable commodity, the first assembly-line, and the first mass-production'.[1] Walter Ong has built on this insight, observing that print 'embedded the word itself deeply in the manufacturing process and made it into a kind of commodity', thus creating 'a new sense of the private ownership of words'.[2] As a result, he observes, 'the old communal oral world . . . split into privately claimed freeholdings' (131). The mobile, multiplicitous, unbounded Renaissance text does not fit easily within this new dispensation which tends, as Ong puts it, 'to feel a work as "closed", set off from other works, a unit in itself' (133). The conflict prompted by the dramatic text's positioning at this juncture of a residual oral culture and an emergent print culture can clearly be seen in the publication record of texts from the Shakespeare canon from the final decade of the sixteenth century through the opening decades of the seventeenth century. Many of the texts which later generations have taken for granted as singular coherent entities appear in this period in multiple versions, some of them drastically divergent from each other. We have learned over the centuries to sort and hierarchise these versions, to discount some of them as 'bad' texts, to promote others as the genuine article as Shakespeare finally intended it.[3] In this sense, we have engaged in a similar process of privileging to that which Jack Goody sees occurring in societies where traditional oral artforms come to be encoded in written and print forms:

> One version recorded on a particular occasion (and about whose status . . . one can say very little) tends to become the model by which others are judged. In the Bagre case [in the LoDagaa society of west Africa], the production of variants has not ceased but these are often now seen against the background of my written version. Not only seen, but judged, for the written version acquires a truth value that no single oral version possesses.[4]

Rather than judging the early variant texts in this way and sorting them into categories of good and bad, true and false, authentic and derivative, we might well be better served—given the historical conditions of the constitution of Renaissance textuality—to see these individual printed versions as providing particular arrested moments of textual formation, in which the fluid text, traversed by a range of diverse inputs, has become fixed by the regime of print. Such publications are thus, to draw on a metaphor which Graham Caie deploys, like snap-shots of the moving text, holding it still in one of its shifting forms.

Print, we can thus say, arrests the mobile text, securing it in a static moment.[5] In the liminal phase where the regimes of print and orality/chirography assert competing claims, the fixity that print offers is often multiple. But as Ong has observed, 'print is comfortable only with finality' (132), and so, as print culture begins to achieve a position of ascendancy, such multiplicity is rejected in favour of a search for the singular, the definitive. As far as the Shakespeare text is concerned, this process begins as early as 1623, when we find the First Folio text staking a claim to authority by declaring that the singular texts it provides are 'absolute in their numbers, as [Shakespeare] conceived the[m]', thus centralising the author as the unique source of a unique—and definitively stabilised—meaning.[6]

There is, of course, a certain irony in the fact that the signatories to the First Folio preface should have been John Heminge and Henry Condell—Shakespeare's acting colleagues from the King's Men—close collaborators, we might say, in the shifting performative life of the text. As the Shakespeare editorial tradition got underway in the opening decades of the eighteenth century, however, Alexander Pope savaged the First Folio, attacking it specifically because it was a text assembled by actors and thus was, he believed, grossly tainted by actorly concerns.[7] Pope charges the actors with adding to and deleting from the text in order to serve their own theatrical convenience. He observes, for instance, that

> a number of beautiful passages which are extant in the first single editions, are omitted in this: as it seems, without any other reason, than their willingness to shorten some scenes: These men (as it was said of *Procrustes*) either lopping, or stretching an Author, to make him just fit for their Stage.[8]

As Gary Taylor has noted, throughout his edition, Pope 'repressed the theatricality of the plays in favor of their readerliness'[9] and this antitheatrical bias was reaffirmed in the work of Pope's successors, with Johnson, for instance, in his *Proposals* of 1756, famously complaining that, once written, the texts of the plays had been

> immediately copied for the actors, and multiplied by transcript after transcript, vitiated by the blunders of the penman, or changed by the affectation of the player; perhaps enlarged to introduce a jest, or mutilated to shorten the representation; and printed at last without the concurrence of the author, without the consent of the proprietor, from compilation made by chance or by stealth out of the separate parts written for the theatre.[10]

The hostile anti-theatricalism of the eighteenth-century editors can be seen as indicative of an increasing tendency to marginalise the multiplicitous oral and social lineages of the text, refashioning it as an isolable and wholly 'literary' object, assimilable to and intelligible within the emerging codes of an increasingly print-centred culture. Alvin Kernan has stressed the extent to which this shift in the way textuality was conceived was part of a broader reconceptualisation of the entire literary system which occurred over the course of the eighteenth century, whereby '[a]n older system of polite or courtly letters—primarily oral, aristocratic, amateur, authoritarian, court-centered—was swept away . . . and gradually replaced by a new print-based, market centered, democratic literary system'.[11]

As Mark Rose has indicated, this rise of a print-based textual culture and literary system contributed to and was facilitated by the concomitant emergence and evolution of a new understanding of copyright during the course of the eighteenth century. It is notable, in the present context, that the first piece of English copyright legislation should have been passed in 1709—the year in which the first eighteenth-century edition of Shakespeare (Nicholas Rowe's) was published by Tonson. Rowe's edition seeks to systematise the text, reducing its pluralistic codes to uniformity by, for example, standardising character names and locations and imposing consistency in act and scene divisions. As Rose has argued, the entire copyright debate and the legislation which issued from it served similarly to effect a general cohering of the text, stabilising it as the unique product of a unique author and cutting it free from the interlaced matrix of social and productive relations within which it had emerged:

> The proponents of perpetual copyright focused on the author's labor. Those who argued against it focused on the results of the labor, the work. Thus the two sides established their positions by approaching the issue from opposite directions. Yet, however approached, the question centered on the same pair of concepts, the 'author' and the 'work,' a person and a thing. The complex social process of literary production consisting of relations between writers and patrons, writers and booksellers, booksellers and readers was rendered peripheral.[12] Abstracting the author of the work from the social fabric in this way contributed to a tendency already implicit in printing technology to reify the literary composition, to treat the text as a thing.[13]

It took several decades for the implications of the 1709 legislation to be fully realised. Alvin Kernan notes that, in the period following the legislation, 'all went on, as they had before, selling and purchasing what the booksellers and authors still assumed to be perpetual rights in books old and new'.[14] In 1774, however, the *Donaldson v. Becket* case confirmed the new dispensation, effectively ending the open-ended proprietorial rights which publishers had traditionally exercised over the books they purchased and produced.

Before the century's end, then, a decisive shift had occurred within textual culture. The Renaissance playwright functioned within a broadly collaborative milieu, often drawing upon a common stock of available materials. The written playtext was released into a theatrical realm where it was subject to alteration by a variety of different agents, for a variety of different purposes. The proprietary rights in the play never rested with the author(s)—the text was sold to the theatre company, who, in turn, chose whether or not eventually to sell it on to a publisher, who would, in turn again, possess exclusive perpetual rights to it. It is indicative of the general culture of textuality prevalent in this period that of the various first quarto editions of plays from the Shakespeare canon published before 1600, only one (*Loues Labours Lost*) attributed the play to Shakespeare as author on its title page.

By the end of the eighteenth century, however, conceptions of textuality had changed. Printing served to arrest the mobile text and to privilege and centralise a single particular version.[15] The potential for seeing the author as the unique source of a unique singular meaning which printing thus indicated was confirmed by the evolution of a theory of copyright which confirmed the author in a proprietorial relationship with the text, in the process of disengaging the text from the greater social and cultural matrix out of which it had arisen. The last major eighteenth-century edition—Edmond Malone's 1790 *Plays and Poems*—very clearly located itself within the terms of the new textual dispensation. Margreta de Grazia has argued persuasively for seeing Malone's as a watershed edition which effects a break with the prior editorial tradition, but we might, perhaps, more usefully see it as reflecting the final coalescence of several strands of textual reconfiguration which had occurred over the course of the eighteenth century.[16]

Malone's approach to the text is neatly indicated by the short quotation from Wentworth Dillon, fourth Earl of Roscommon, which he offers as a kind of epigraph to his edition:

Take pains the genuine meaning to explore;
There sweat, there strain; tug the laborious oar:
Search every comment that your care can find;
Some here, some there, may hit the poet's mind:
When things appear unnatural and hard,
Consult your author, with himself compar'd.[17]

The entire stress here is on singularity—a singularity achieved by engaging with the hermetic-ally sealed world of the autonomous author. Roscommon offers Malone a textual ethic which suggests the possibility of establishing 'genuine meaning'—the singular intention of the author which the editor can discover by submitting himself to an intense scrutiny of the text on the page. The objective of the editor is to engage not with the social text, but rather with the 'poet's mind'—the editor must seek to access the traces of the unique creator of the desired ideal text. The reference point for understanding the text is not the greater social world, but rather the circumscribed sphere of the author's own canon: 'Consult your author, *with himself compar'd.*' It is the printed text itself, then, that is the final arbiter of meaning.

It seems altogether fitting that Malone should have prefaced the text of his edition with a quotation from the author of an *Essay on Translated Verse*, since what happened to the Shakespeare text by the end of the eighteenth century was that it had, in effect, become fully translated from its ambiguous and indeterminate position—set between the realms of print and orality—into a form fully harmonised with the textual conceptions of a print-centred culture. If, as Kernan has argued, Samuel Johnson was the first example of the kind of literary figure that the regime of print made possible, then we can say that, by the end of Johnson's century, Shakespeare had himself been refashioned into a similar figure, his text fixed within the terms of a cultural regime that had only begun inchoately to emerge in his own lifetime.

In 1924—the same year as Chambers's British Academy lecture—Allardyce Nicoll concluded in an article on 'The Editors of Shakespeare from First Folio to Malone' that '[w]ith Malone, the editing of Shakespeare passed from the hands of the actors and the hands of the poets to the hands of the scholars, and a new era was begun'.[18] The project of this 'new era' was consoli-dated in the work of W. G. Clark and W. A. Wright (and J. Glover), the editors of the 1863–6 Cambridge University Press edition of the complete works. As Paul Werstine has noted, the Cambridge editors 'were almost exclusively [interested] in establishing a text; few of their notes concern anything but textual questions. Thus they may be credited with opening up a space for purely textual study'.[19] As Werstine further notes, the space thus opened was occu-pied, in the opening decades of the twentieth century, by the New Bibliographers, whose intense focusing on the strictly textual served further to reinforce the disjunction between the isolated text and its oral and social contexts.

In contrast to a great number of their predecessors from Pope to Sidney Lee,[20] the New Bibliographers defended the First Folio as, in the main, a substantially reliable text, rejecting, as John Dover Wilson puts it, the 'gloomy [doctrine] of the old criticism' that 'Heminge and Condell were either knaves in league with Jaggard to hoodwink a gullible public, or else fools who did not know how to pen a preface'.[21] But the defence of Heminge and Condell mounted by the New Bibliographers did not indicate a new affirmation of the actorly or social text. In fact, the new emphasis on the fundamental soundness of F1 signalled, if anything, the onset of a more comprehensive, multifaceted attack on the oral and social dimension of the Shakespeare canon. As Hugh Grady has demonstrated, the New Bibliographic investment in F1 was all of a piece with Chambers's project in his Shakespeare lecture.[22] Like Chambers, the New Bibliographers sought to oppose the disintegrationists by reconfirming Shakespeare as the solitary author of a coherent body of unique proprietary texts assembled in the Folio in good faith by Shakespeare's colleagues.[23]

The rejection of disintegration was not, however, the only reason for the New Bibliographers' investment in F1, as we can see by examining some of the central textual analyses advanced by A. W. Pollard and W. W. Greg. Pollard's ground-breaking 1909 defence of F1 was predicated on his (in)famous division of the early quarto editions into the 'good' and the 'bad'. The 'good' quartos he described as constituting a 'family [with] no single black sheep in it . . . every member of it [being] of good average morals and utility'. Of the 'bad' quartos, he noted that 'any desirable amount of scorn and contempt' might be applied to them.[24] Pollard thus both carries forward and systematises here the traditional editorial quest for the singular, authorially sanctioned text. Within the terms of his analysis, any texts from a broader social context which cannot specifically be tied directly to the figure of the author must be rejected not just as 'inauthentic' (as Malone might have put it), but, indeed, as in some sense morally repugnant—to be repressed into a kind of textual unconscious.[25]

For W. W. Greg, Pollard's *Shakespeare Folios and Quartos* once again 'marked the opening of a new era in Shakespearian studies' and Greg himself certainly explored further the possibilities indicated by his colleague's work.[26] In the year following Pollard's book, Greg published his *Shakespeare's Merry Wives of Windsor 1602*, in which he offered the first suggestion of a possible account of how the texts characterised by Pollard as 'bad quartos' might have come into being. Greg proposed that the basis of the First Quarto *Merry Wives* was a reconstruction of the play from memory by the actor who had played the part of the Host, working in collaboration with the printer, John Busby. Greg's original suggestion here was, of course, subsequently worked up into a general theory of 'memorial reconstruction'.[27] As Laurie Maguire has stressed, subsequent reductive deployments of this term have often served to mask the complexity of Greg's original formulation. Maguire breaks down Greg's analysis of the imagined process of assemblage and transmission of Q1 *Merry Wives* into a total of thirteen distinct stages. It is worth quoting her account at some length, to indicate both the complexity of the projected process and the extent to which it indicates the variety of different influences which are imagined as shaping the text at every stage:

1) Shakespeare writes *The Merry Wives of Windsor* 'substantially as we know it', but with greater prominence accorded the plot in which the Host is cozened of his horses. 2) Minor cuts are made for performance. 3) It becomes necessary to remove the horse-stealing plot, and the task of altering the play is entrusted to another playwright in the Chamberlain's Men; Act 5 is totally recast and two alternative endings supplied (for public and Court performance) . . . 4) The actors are lazy and do not learn the new dialogue properly. 5) Furthermore, resentful of the extra work, the actors deliberately introduce allusions to excised material. 6) The Chamberlain's Men are in disgrace because of topical scandal attached to the original version of the play . . . and they exile themselves from London. 7) The 'hired man' who played the Host remains in the Capital. 8) An 'unscrupulous sta-

tioner' suborns the hired man-Host to recreate the play. 9) In the first place the Host had learned his part imperfectly and by ear. 10) The Host possibly dictates the play to someone in the stationers' office. 11) The Company further alters the original play . . . 12) Later, Shakespeare revises the phrasing of the earlier scenes . . . 13) After Shakespeare's death, in preparation for the First Folio . . . this playhouse copy was 'prepared for the press with such care as the circumstances seemed to demand'. (*Shakespearean Suspect Texts*, 75–6)

What is significant here, from the perspective of the present analysis, is that what Greg maps out is a narrative in which a complex network of factors serves to produce a range of different textual versions over the course of the early lifetime of *Merry Wives*—seven of the thirteen stages identified by Maguire can be seen as producing some sort of change to the play.[28] One of these variant versions makes its way into print in 1602—a version conceived as being heavily reliant for its genesis and dissemination both on a complex of social factors and on a set of oral procedures (reconstruction and reconfiguration based on memories of a particular enacted performance).

Greg's 'memorial reconstruction' is thus, in a way, not unlike the 'generative reconstruction' that Jack Goody has identified as occurring within the cultural transmission process in oral societies (179–80). Writing of the Bagre tradition of the LoDagaa, he observes that since there is 'no single keeper of the oral tradition, the Bagre expands, develops and contracts with each ceiling, in a "generative", "creative" way that characterizes much oral activity of a "literary" kind' (189). The difference between Greg and Goody, however, is that the whole point of anatomising this narrative of 'generative reconstruction', from Greg's perspective, is not to demonstrate the composite factors which necessarily serve to make and remake variant textualities in the Renaissance, but rather to mark such textual reconstructions as aberrant (rather as the Bagre variations which differ from Goody's own transcription have come to be seen as aberrant). Social engagement and oral lineages are, in themselves, determining markers of illegitimacy for Greg. In his view, the multiplicitous, shifting social text is an 'errant' text, wandering into complexes of variation and multiplicity, compounding error with error. Like Spenser's wandering monster, *Error*, this process produces a malignant multiplication of textuality ('Her vomit full of bookes and papers was, / With loathly frogs and toades, which eyes did lack'[29]). Like the Red Crosse Knight, the editor faces the difficult duty of cutting through this multiplicity, to pledge fidelity to a textual Una, a singular Truth.

Thus we can say of two of the pillars of the emergent New Bibliographic orthodoxy—the categorisation of the quartos into good and bad, and the theory of memorial reconstruction— that both aimed at setting the singular text on firm footing by first isolating and then discounting and invalidating the greater oral and social history of the text. In a way, this tendency within New Bibliography is none too surprising, given the movement's intense dedication to the world of print. As Greg puts it in *The Editorial Problem in Shakespeare*, the 'fresh approach to textual problems' which New Bibliography offered was distinguished by the fact that it laid 'stress upon the material processes of book-production, concerning itself primarily with the fortunes of the actual pieces of paper on which the texts were written or printed, and the vagaries of scribes and compositors'.[30]

The deep ironies of the 'materialism' espoused by the New Bibliographic movement have been much commented on over the past several years, as it has been noted that, for all their interest in the mechanics and particularities of the printed text, the New Bibliographers ultimately subordinated that material physical entity to a notional authorial ideal which they imagined as lying behind what they famously and repeatedly referred to as the 'veil of print'.[31] The ultimate end that New Bibliography held in view was the idealised realm where the author's work could float free not only from its multifaceted social context, but even from its very vehicle of transmission—the printed text. In a sense, we can view this vision as the culmination of a long tradition, whereby the culture of print, fully ascendant in the Western textual tradition, denies even its own social and material context as a productive force. The autonomous author is brought to transcend not just his or her own social moment, but even the very means of production whereby the text enters into circulation within the regime of print. *Ars est celare artem*: the end, at the last, disavows the means.

*   *   *

Gary Taylor, 'The Renaissance and the end of editing', in George Bornstein and Ralph G. Williams (eds.), *Palimpsest: Editorial Theory in the Humanities* (Ann Arbor: The University of Michigan Press, 1993), pp. 142–3.

The most important decision an editor makes is a decision which has been almost entirely ignored by editorial theory. The most important question an editor should ask is: *what shall I edit?* For Renaissance scholars in particular that means: *why edit Shakespeare?* Every edition of Shakespeare now, including the most radical, is fundamentally conservative. Even the transgressive Oxford University Press edition of *William Shakespeare: The Complete Works* committed its transgressions within the enclosed boundaries of an entrenched canonical system, and our very transgressions, and the controversy they aroused, have only served to increase Shakespeare's critical mass, thereby reinforcing his hegemony . . . we should be not editing Shakespeare, because we should be editing someone else. The Oxford University Press edition of *Thomas Middleton: The Complete Works* will radically change our perceptions of Middleton; but it will also, I believe, change our perceptions of Shakespeare more than any new edition of Shakespeare could, because it will change our perceptions of the Renaissance, of the textual space to which Shakespeare belonged, and of his place in it. Rather than editing Middleton by the light of Shakespeare, we might start editing Shakespeare by the light of Middleton. We might even start reading the Renaissance—and ourselves—in the light of Middleton, too.

The end of editing is to change literary history: to change our collective organization of the intertextual spaces of the past, and by doing so to change the kind of intertextual spaces that may be created by future readers, critics, and writers. To change our reading of the past, in order to change the future of reading.

*   *   *

Suzanne Gossett, 'Introduction' to *'Pericles': The Arden Shakespeare* (London: Thomson, 2004), pp. 46–54.

Two major cruces demonstrate the unresolvability of the *Pericles* text. As he consigns baby Marina to Dionyza, Pericles swears:

> till she be maried,
> Madame, by bright *Diana*, whom we honour,
> All vnsisterd shall this heyre of mine remayne,
> Though I shew will in't.
>
> (E4ᵛ; 3.3.28–31)

In 1793 Steevens emended to 'unscissored shall this hair of mine remain'; many editors adopt Malone's further modification, 'though I show ill in it'. The emendation is logical, considering that at Diana's altar Pericles announces the imminent marriage of his daughter and promises that

> now this ornament
> Makes me look dismal will I clip to form,
> And what this fourteen years no razor touched
> To grace thy marriage day I'll beautify.
>
> (5.3.74–7)

The confirmatory vow Pericles makes upon learning of Marina's 'death', 'He swears / Never to wash his face nor cut his hairs' (4.4.27–8), occurs only 'three months' (5.1.20) before he discovers the presumably fourteen-year-old Marina in Mytilene. In Q all that separates the two readings is a single letter: the compositor is likelier to have been confused by a manuscript 'vnsiskerd' or 'vnsiscerd' than by 'vnsisterd' and to have rationalized and vulgarized the misunderstood copy form 'k' or 'c' to 't' (RP). The emendation is supported by Twine and by Wilkins, who has Pericles vow 'solemnely by othe to himselfe, his head should grow uncisserd, his beard untrimmed, himselfe in all uncomely . . . till he had married his daughter at ripe years' (*PA*, 524). 'Ill' looks follow from 'unscissored' hair. Dyce suggested that 'will' arose from the compositor repeating the 'w' from 'shew' (Dyce², 8.95); it also could have arisen from mishearing by a reporter, or error in the expansion of shorthand notes (Davidson, 87). In the theatre the words would be indistinguishable.

Despite the neat solution there are reasons to suspect deeper corruption. If the emendation is correct the second vow reiterates the first unnecessarily; it thus seems probable that the two vows, one after the wife's death and one after the daughter's, were originally distinguished. Does Pericles at first swear, 'wilfully', that his daughter will remain his only 'heir, all unsistered' because like Leontes he will refuse to remarry, and only later swear to disregard his appearance, to remain unwashed, unshorn and in sackcloth? This is Lillo's solution in *Marina* (1738). In *Pericles* concern with dynastic continuity begins when Pericles seeks a wife 'From whence an issue I might propagate' (1.2.71) and continues to the final assignment of kingdoms.

Editors have methodically discounted the play's persistent but buried concern with sisterhood and especially with Dionyza's daughter Philoten, who 'Would euer with *Marina* bee. / Beet when they weaude the sleded silke, / With fingers long, small, white as milke, / Or when she would with sharpe needle wound, / The Cambricke' (F1ᵛ; 4.0.20–4). Since Malone, editors have emended 4.0.21 to make Marina—'she', not 'they'— the one who weaves with long white fingers, in parallel to 23. But removing the image of the two girls weaving together alters the relationship. The association of 'sisters' vows', needles and embroidery, and singing recalls *A Midsummer Night's Dream*, 3.2.204–17, where the quasi-identity of young girls is similarly destroyed by competition for men. Emilia's description of her relation to Flavina in *The*

Two Noble Kinsmen belongs to a similarly edenic past; it concludes that 'true love 'tween maid and maid may be / More than in sex dividual' (*TNK* 1.3.81–2). The surviving text of *Pericles* submerges the relation of Marina and her foster sister, who dies along with her parents but whose guilt is never demonstrated. Neither 'all unsistered' nor 'all unscissored' is thus merely or clearly an error.

Textual and interpretative difficulties intersect again in the play's most famous crux, the brothel interview between Marina and Lysimachus (4.5). Rather than Q seeming confused or non-sensical, its version of the confrontation is coherent. Lysimachus' suggestion that his sin was merely hypothetical, 'Had I brought hither a corrupted mind / Thy speech had altered it' (108–9) and his subsequent insistence that 'I came / With no ill intent' (113–14), can easily seem, in reading or in production, the awkward and embarrassed lies of a young man who expected to find the usual false 'virginities' (28) he jocularly calls for on entering. He doesn't believe the Bawd's claim that the new girl was 'never plucked yet' (47–8), casually begins conversation with Marina by asking how long she has been at her 'trade', but backtracks as he realizes what kind of a woman he has encountered. Marina's responses to him are clear and firm, and her accent and diction as much as her actual words may motivate his surprise that she can speak 'so well' (107). As she addresses Lysimachus, her speech has a 'therapeutic literalness' full of aggression and verbal wit—she will have nothing to do with euphemisms about 'trade' and 'profession' (see Ewbank, 116–17, and 4.5.71–7n.). Yet her brief lines seem scarcely adequate to bring about his conversion. Here, if anywhere, it is tempting to assume that the more extensive speeches of Marina and the different attitudes of Lysimachus in Wilkins's *Painful Adventures* may reflect a 'better' or more accurate report of the scene.

The precise history of *Painful Adventures*, the two surviving copies of which were only rediscovered in the nineteenth century, is as vexed as that of *Pericles* itself. George Wilkins, the pamphlet's author, was probably Shakespeare's collaborator on the play, responsible for the first two acts and possibly some later choruses. *Painful Adventures* proclaims itself 'the true History of the Play of *Pericles*, as it was lately presented by the worthy and ancient Poet John Gower'. Yet there are discrepancies between the play and the 'History', including not only expanded speeches but differences in motivation and event. In considerable sections Wilkins is dependent on another narrative, Laurence Twine's *The Pattern of Painful Adventures*, which had been entered in the Stationers' Register in 1576 (no copy is known of any edition of this date), published c. 1594 and republished in 1607. The differences between *Painful Adventures* and *Pericles* have been explained in many ways. Assuming that Wilkins did not participate in drafting the play, Bullough thought that his 'novel was based on an earlier version of *Pericles* than that published in 1609'. Yet Kenneth Muir pointed out that Wilkins must have completed his novel 'after Shakespeare's revision of the play had been performed, for he uses the Shakespearean names for his characters and perhaps made a few changes to bring his tale nearer to the revised version of the play'. To explain the differences in the brothel scene Muir speculated that Wilkins 'obtained the original sheets of this scene when they were superseded by Shakespeare's version' (Muir, 74).

Taylor and Jackson, on the other hand, accepted the fact of collaboration but argued that if Shakespeare took over the writing, and particularly if the King's Men were reluctant to trust Wilkins with texts because he had participated in publishing his earlier play, *The Miseries of Enforced Marriage*, and his collaboration, *The Travails of the Three English Brothers*, without the company's consent, Wilkins might not have had a copy even of his own section of the play (*TxC*, 557–8).[1] Under the circumstances Wilkins remembered what he could; when he could not, he plagiarized from Twine and occasionally invented. His text of the brothel scene, however, was fuller because it preserved a precensored version. To explain the hypothesized censorship, Taylor and Jackson claimed that the Jacobean stage authorities were 'particularly sensitive to the promiscuity of courtiers' and cited plays, including *The Second Maiden's Tragedy* (1611) and *Eastward Ho!* (1605), where the Master of the Revels edited such passages before giving his approval.

This part of Taylor and Jackson's theory is unsustainable. Other contemporary King's Men's plays, including *Measure for Measure* (1604), *Philaster* (1608–10) and *The Maid's Tragedy* (1610–11), contain equally lubricious courtiers and men in authority.[2] *Eastward Ho!* brought down royal wrath because of satire on the Scots, and *The Second Maiden's Tragedy* invited censorship through parallels to the Frances Howard scandal and the emphasis on regicide.[3] Furthermore, precisely at the time of *Pericles* there was confusion of authority in the Revels office. Edmond Tilney, seventy-two years old in 1608, was still the Master; until his death in 1610 George Buc acted as his deputy only in licensing plays for the press, not for the stage (Dutton). It is not clear whether the censorship Taylor alleges would have occurred in preparation for performance or for publication.

There are four possible bases—frequently conflated—on which one may decide to incorporate material from Wilkins into 4.5: playability; theories about the text or its transmission; the emotional logic of the scene; and attitudes towards the social content. Theatres often claim a need to expand this first, crucial encounter between Marina and Lysimachus. Theories of transmission that assume Wilkins's novella is a better report than Q and contains 'verse fossils' of the superior original permit, although they do not require, insertions. Edwards was sure Q was defective here because the reporter had misunderstood the logic of the scene. For Edwards, if Q's treatment of Lysimachus were correct the brothel-going governor would have to be a 'tester', like the Duke in *Measure for Measure* (Edwards, 24). Instead, Wilkins, who reports Lysimachus confessing 'I hither came with thoughtes intemperate, foule and deformed, the which your paines so well have laved, that they are now white' (*PA*, 536), is correct 'in reporting a humbled and ashamed Lysimachus confessing his errors . . . In preserving the apologia and omitting the confession, Q has arguably altered the balance of the play' (Edwards, 182–3). That such a judgement is essentially aesthetic was revealed when, in his edition of the play, Edwards did not incorporate material from Wilkins in 4.5 but did insert 'A straggling Theseus born we know not where' in 2.5 as 'too good to lose' (162).

The Oxford editors, believing Wilkins to be a collaborator as well as often a better reporter than the person(s) responsible for Q, import three substantial passages into 4.5. But this reconstruction contradicts Taylor's textual theories. If the boy who played Marina was the reporter, why would he misreport this key scene? It also violates their guidelines, which called for making 'much more' use of Wilkins in the share of the play they assign to him, Acts 1 and 2 or scenes 1–9 (*TxC*, 558). Furthermore, to follow Wilkins is to change the characters. By virtue of her longer speeches Marina appears more assertive, more 'feminist'. And Lysimachus is clearer about his purposes in the brothel. Rather than encountering Marina casually, Lysimachus glimpses her from his window and determines that 'since shee must fall, it were farre more fitter, into his owne armes . . . than into the hote imbracements of many' (*PA*, 533).

Attitudes towards the social content have affected the editing of the brothel scene, which some early editors preferred to think was not by Shakespeare at all. Implicit in discomfort with Q's version of 4.5 is an objection to the double standard that silently accepts Lysimachus' behaviour and the pure heroine's apparently contented betrothal to a man who frequents brothels. Yet both are consistent with early modern sexual ideology. In Marston's *Dutch Courtesan* (1605) Freevill is prepared to 'resign' the courtesan he has been maintaining because he is about to marry the pure Beatrice, who is happy to have him. That play implicitly supports Freevill's pragmatic position: 'I would have married men love the stews as Englishmen love the Low Countries: wish war should be maintained there lest it should come home to their own doors' (*Dutch Courtesan*, 1.1.65–8).[4] In *Philaster* (1608–10) the Spanish prince Pharamond's unsuitability as a husband for Princess Arathusa is demonstrated by signs that he will be unable to make the required transition from bachelor freedom to married fidelity. While on an official visit to meet his intended, the prince finds that 'the constitution of my body will never hold out till the wedding', and he is caught with the court's light lady in his chamber (Beaumont & Fletcher, 1.416). In a sinister variant, Ilford, in Wilkins's *Miseries of Enforced Marriage*, learning of his father's death, announces his intention 'shortly to goe to Church, and from thence do faithfull seruice to one woman'. His friends object, 'Its impossible, for thou hast bin a whore-mayster this seauen yeare', but Ilford replies, 'Tis no matter, I will now marry, And to som honest woman to, and so from hence her vertues shall be a countenance to my vices' (*Miseries*, 1667–79). Lysimachus is less scandalous than many of Shakespeare's heroes: Leontes and Posthumus win back wives they have seriously injured, and Bertram and Angelo not only attempt seduction but lie to their sovereigns.

A modern editor may be tempted to intervene in 4.5 to strengthen Marina's character and resistance. Taylor and Jackson, for example, give her an additional speech that versifies sections of the following passage from Wilkins:

> What reason is there in your Justice, who hath power over all, to undoe any? If you take from mee mine honour, you are like him, that makes a gappe into forbidden ground, after whome too many enter, and you are guiltie of all their evilles: my life is yet unspotted, my chastitie unstained in thought. Then if your violence deface this building, the workeman-ship of heaven, made up for good, and not to be the exercise of sinnes intemperaunce, you do kill your owne honour, abuse your owne justice, and impoverish me . . . Is there a necessitie (my yet good Lord) if there be fire before me, that I must strait then thither flie and burne my selfe. Or if suppose this house (which too too many feele such houses are) should be the Doctors patrimony, and Surgeons feeding; folowes it therefore, that I must needs infect my self to give them maintenance?
>
> (*PA*, 535–6)

Valerie Wayne applauds this part of the reconstruction because it 'presents a more articulate Marina . . . Rather than the silent or whimpering symbol of virginity's charm that an earlier generation of critics celebrated her for being, she becomes an important agent in the play's critique of those in power.' Yet Wayne objects when Oxford introduces stage directions similarly based on Wilkins: *'weeps'*, *'kneeling'*, *'He lifts her up with his hands'*, *'He wipes the wet from her eyes'*. She asks, hypothetically, 'Is it possible to adapt Marina's resistance in Wilkins without also importing her tears and abjection?' (Wayne, 'Political', *passim*; cf. 'Textual', 197).

Wayne's question indicates the quandary faced by any editor of *Pericles*. Certainly the text can be improved; rejecting the entire tradition of editorial clarification will appear perverse. However, editors' commitments, including their sexual politics, have varied radically over the centuries and need not reflect those of the authors. Since these commitments have potentially differing textual consequences and, in a postmodern age of fragmentation, any all-encompassing hegemonic explanation for the state of the text will be greeted with scepticism, more limited intervention seems appropriate.

. . . .

QUESTIONS

- What has characterized the great tradition of editing Shakespeare?
- Is editing political?
- In what respects is editing a gendered activity?
- In what ways might editing contribute to a process of canon formation?

5 | New editorial strategies

Ann Thompson, 'Teena Rochfort Smith, Frederick Furnivall, and the New Shakspere Society's Four-Text Edition of *Hamlet*', *Shakespeare Quarterly*, 49 (1998), 138.

Modern editors . . . are still grappling with the problems of how to present scholarly editions of works with complex textual histories, both in traditional book format and in CD-ROM hyper-text, and multimedia forms. We are still experimenting with parallel-text layouts, typefaces, and typographic symbols in our efforts to avoid conflation or, at least, to demonstrate how our texts have been constructed from more than one document. Teena Rochfort Smith's array of six different typefaces and multiple daggers and asterisks may have seemed over-elaborate (and probably over-expensive) in 1883, but we are now accustomed to editions that move in this direction. The latest volume in the Arden Shakespeare (third series), for example, R. A. Foakes' edition of *King Lear*, uses superscript *F*s and *Q*s to indicate Folio-only and Quarto-only passages. The editors of the New Folger Library *Hamlet*, Barbara A. Mowat and Paul Werstine, use three kinds of brackets to signal the origins of various words and passages in their text. Bernice W. Kliman also uses different kinds of brackets to distinguish Folio and Quarto read-ings in her *Enfolded 'Hamlet'*, while Jesus Tronch-Perez uses a method of linear 'super-imposition' to display variants in his 'Synoptic *Hamlet*'.[1] Many editors are experimenting with the ways in which computer technology may be able to offer us more sophisticated means of producing electronic texts.

* * *

David Scott Kastan, *Shakespeare and the Book* (Cambridge: Cambridge University Press, 2001), pp. 123–31.

There are, of course, good reasons for editions, in fact for many kinds of editions, though probably not very good reasons for as many of the same kinds of editions as indeed we have. Shakespeare should be available in editions that do attempt to restore the play he wrote before it was subjected to the demands of production in both the playhouse and the printing house; but he should also be available in editions that take the theatrical auspices of the plays seriously, recognizing that primary among Shakespeare's intentions was the desire to write something that could be successfully played. Both of these texts should be available in modernized spelling, in cheap paperbacks of individual plays and in collections of the complete works, as well as in edited old-spelling editions. And Shakespeare should be available unedited, in facsimiles of the early printings. But even a facsimile can never reveal all the material information carried by the early text—for example, the paper quality—and, what even more limits its value, facsimile makes normative a single copy of a text that almost certainly would differ in various ways from every other copy in the print run. (And therefore even an original playbook would not perfectly represent the play, though it would be very nice to have.) Each of these different texts would offer something to the reader of Shakespeare that the others do not, and each of course has fundamental limitations, denying the reader information of one sort or another that is elsewhere available and in certain circumstances would be consequential.

The Shakespeare section of the bookshop ideally might stock examples of each of these, but in truth, though we can usually find several editions of a single play (at least if the play is *Hamlet* or *King Lear*, if it is *King John* or *Pericles* we might not be able to find even one), the several editions are all too much alike, the text in modernized spelling with more or less annotation depending on whether it is intended for a scholastic market, for universities, or for the general reader. Marketing considerations rather than intellectual ones have largely determined what we can find on bookshop shelves, and marketing considerations have in large part dictated a wasteful duplication of scholarly energy and a conscious neglect of other kinds of texts that might genuinely be of value. [. . .]

But, in any case, if one wished to see the text in its full historical materiality no one of the various kinds of texts would serve. A scholar would inevitably want them all—and more: all the early printings; the restoration redactions, which were, of course, the form in which many of the plays were seen for almost 150 years; the often brilliant if quirky eighteenth-century editions beginning with Rowe's; the Globe text of the 1860s, the form in which Shakespeare first circumnavigated the world; the various important modern editions. We know that the play is not fully represented in any one edition, in spite of the overt or implicit claims it might make to being definitive. The impressive paratextual assertions of an edition's authority—the imposing introductions, the heavy annotations, the lengthy, if usually unintelligible, collation notes—all of which exist to assert the editor's control over the text, testify at least as eloquently to the text's resistant instabilities as to the editor's success in resolving them.

In truth, as this book is in part designed to show, Shakespeare's texts remain unnervingly (exhilaratingly?) fluid in spite of over 375 years of editorial efforts to stabilize them. In the absence of an authentic original, indeed in the absence of a general agreement about what an authentic original might be, each edition, like each performance, of a play becomes part of a cumulative history of what has been experienced as the play; and the more of this history that is available the more it becomes possible to measure the play's achievement and its effects.

The individual print edition, however, almost always has to think otherwise about the text; it usually must choose a single instantiation, a choice usually driven less by editorial confidence than by inescapable considerations of space, of cost, of readability, all exposing the limits of the codex as a tool of information technology.

But this brings us explicitly back to the topic with which we began, for the advent of electronic texts perhaps offers an escape from, if not a resolution of, the struggle between incompatible textual understandings and preferences. The capaciousness of the electronic environment seemingly allows an edition in this new medium to offer any number of textual versions, both the edited text of the work and any or all of the texts of the documents that previously have represented it.[1]

The fact that the electronic text does not reside on the screen on which we read it, unlike the printed text, which obviously does physically inhabit the page on which it is read, allows it a freedom from the material limits that define the book. Size is no longer a necessary consideration of textual production; the text is apparently not bound by concerns about convenience or cost. Indeed, literally the text is not bound at all.

And with that material freedom comes another. The electronic text is permeable in a way the printed text is not, not isolated from other texts in its physical integrity but existing in the same environment, so that, indeed, it is unable to 'shut out other texts' that are networked with it.[2] Any document can be linked to and thus become part of any other text. The resulting hypertext is thus the materialization of a Barthian conception of textuality itself, a textual environment in which any text can intersect and be intersected by an infinite number of others.[3] And every work within it can itself be multiply realized, available both in discrete and conflated versions, prepared according to any number of assumptions and principles; instead of an ideal(ized) text, we have the text explicitly as polymorph, its multiplicity organized as what George Landow calls 'a complex field of variants' (*Hypertext*, p. 56) rather than as a collection (or collation) of deviations from some imagined perfection.

The possibilities for editorial practice are obvious.[4] A full consideration of the possibilities for *writing itself* in hypertext (rather than what I am concerned with here: the hypertext *edition*) is well beyond the scope of this essay, indeed well beyond the scope of this writer. Nonetheless, it may be useful to observe that most of the discussions of writing in the electronic environment emphasize the reader's activity in constructing the text, exploiting the nature of the medium itself, which allows the reader endlessly and effortlessly to reshape the elements it contains. 'Electronic technology,' as David Bolter says, 'makes texts particular and individual' (*Writing Space: The Computer, Hypertext, and the History of Writing* (Hillsdale, NJ: Lawrence Erlbaum, 1991), p. 9). The electronic edition, however, offers the reader a different kind of freedom: not to restructure the elements themselves, but to engage them in ways that may well be 'particular and individual' as the reader navigates (but leaves unchanged) the materials available. But it is precisely the potential copiousness of what is there is to navigate that seems to suggest a way out of the disabling binaries of recent editorial theory.

In the past, regardless of the particular textual history of the work to be edited or the individual editor's understanding of the activity of editing itself, the nature of the codex exerts itself upon the task, helping to determine the form of the edition. Externally imposed limits of size and cost normally dictated the need to select (or construct) a single version of the work. But such contingencies no longer force an editor to choose between versions, because in hypertext there is no physical limit to the number of textual manifestations that can appear. All 'variants and variations,' as Patrick Conner has written, 'can be present and linked as nodes, and even processed into the text, so that one can reproduce any version of the text one wishes,'[5] even versions which have had no material existence, like the ideal text of the author's—or an editor's—imagination. For a Shakespeare edition, one could have an edited text (or indeed more than one), as well as digital facsimiles of all early printings; and additional resources could be included, like source texts or concordances, theater reviews, illustrations, audio clips, and even film versions, all of which can be linked to allow easy movement back and forth between them.

But this will come as no surprise. In writing this I feel something like Milton's Abdiel, who 'found / Already known what he for news had thought / to have reported' (*Paradise Lost*, VI, 19–21). Such hypertextual resources already exist and are increasingly familiar. Figure 24 [not included in this extract] is an example of a characteristic hypertext screen. This was produced with resources readily available in the Columbia library by a friend, Richard Sacks, for Columbia's version of a great books course, known familiarly as Lit./Hum. Done with more time and access to other materials it could, of course, be improved (among other things, I would not have used the 1619 *Lear* quarto—one of those texts that was intended for the aborted collection that Pavier and Jaggard had planned, but rather Butter's 1608 Q1). But the extraordinary possibilities of hypertext should be clear even from the picture. On the left there is a menu of options; on the top a clean, modernized text, familiar in its typography and textual detail; below that the related page scanned from an early text (and in principle one could have any number of early and edited texts correlated to what serves as the organizing, control text). On the right are folio and quarto texts in modern typography with variants highlighted. In the bottom right is the relevant source material from Holinshed; in the bottom left, a word search that might clarify the potentially interesting implications of one of these variants: the folio's 'Realme' and the quarto's 'kingdome,' in Albany's offer to Kent and Edgar 'you twaine / Rule in this Realme' or 'Rule in this Kingdome.'

Among the most impressive of the existing electronic editions of Shakespeare is the project developed by Peter Donaldson at MIT, called (somewhat less imaginatively than most new electronic endeavours) 'The Shakespeare Electronic Archive.' To give a sense of its extraordinary capacity, the archived *Hamlet* includes, in addition to an electronic text derived from the Oxford *Complete Works*, 'high resolution facsimiles of all pages of the First Folio in both corrected and uncorrected states, complete facsimiles of all individual copies of both *Hamlet* quartos, 1,500 works of *Hamlet* art and illustration, and several *Hamlet* films.'[6] All this material is easily accessible, and most of it is linked to the base text so a user can click on a bit of text and access a menu of the bibliographic and performative options that define that particular segment of the play.

The *Hamlet* project—and other such undertakings—either ends the need for editing or, more likely, re-establishes it. If such resources, in their ability to offer a density of relevant material that no print edition could ever manage, perhaps suggest that we are now free from the traditional obligation of textual editing to produce versions of the plays as 'their author intended them to appear,' that very density may itself reinaugurate the desire for a single text that the electronic archive has seemingly rendered both inadequate and unnecessary. No doubt such hypertextual resources could be used to confirm the truth of Wittgenstein's dictum that 'only the exhaustive is interesting,'[7] but, in their 'exhaustive' and exhausting copiousness, they may make the play (choosing my words carefully) virtually unreadable.

But the MIT project is not an edition; it is not designed to be read. It is an archive, and like any archive it yields its treasures only to diligent and capable researchers. An edition, however, is designed to present not the archive but the results of one's investigations there. If such results can be no more authoritative than the completeness of the archive and the competence of the investigator permit, they can, within those limits, present a text that can confidently and conveniently be read—not perhaps as Shakespeare's *Hamlet*, for what in truth can that mean, but as Harold Jenkins' *Hamlet*, or G. R. Hibbard's *Hamlet*, or, soon, as Ann Thompson and Neil Taylor's *Hamlet*, the editorial priority not an arrogation of creative authority but a frank admission of the edition's inevitable idiosyncrasies and limitations. [. . .]

For the scholar, however, that phrase 'just the play' is the vexing issue. What is *just* the play? The play on stage? What stage? What production? What night (or day)? The play as written? As the author first imagined it? Or after it was revised in the light of what was learned in performance? The *textus receptus*: the play as it has lived in history (for example, the editorially conflated text of *King Lear*, which at very least must be recognized as the primary form of the play that was read and acted for the last 150 years)? Which of these is 'just the play'? Which of these is not?

The familiar dichotomy of the play on the page and the play on the stage gives way to another: the play on the printed page and the play on the computer screen. On the page, the play is stabilized, by print and by editorial commitment: a commitment to the author's final intention, to the surviving best text, to the performance text of a particular production, or, as often as not, merely to the text that is out of copyright and can be reprinted without cost. The codex is always about choices and boundaries; that is both its advantage and its limitation. On the screen, the play is always potentially multiple and unstable. There is no necessity to choose between textual understandings: all available versions of the play can theoretically be included, and we can move easily between them. That is both the advantage and the limitation of the electronic text.[8] The book disciplines; it makes us take responsibility for our decisions and live with their consequences. The electronic text offers a fantasy of freedom: there is no need make choices; there are no consequences to accept.

The book's reassuring offer of closure and authority gives way to the electronic text's exhilarating promise of possibility and an immunity from all restraint. It is, however, worth pausing to disrupt this neat binary by noting that its claim is only conceptually true. The book in fact is no more complete and closed than is the electronic text open and free. The integrity of books (as opposed to that of 'the book,' which is an ideological construct) is always vulnerable to the productive, and often perverse, reading habits of individuals, who are usually happy to mark, deface, copy, misread, or otherwise appropriate the books (or parts of books) they 'read'; and, the apparent freedom of the electronic text is undermined by the not-inconsiderable costs of hardware, rights, data entry, site design and maintenance (to say nothing of the obvious difficulty of persuading anyone to pay for access, leading a number of electronic publishing ventures recently to be abandoned and others to be reconceived by their administrators as loss leaders), as well as the fact that, as electronic texts are dependent upon technologies that a reader does not own, the reader has distressingly little control over them. That is, Columbia University cannot remove a book that I own from my bookshelf, but it can easily remove the electronic version from a website that it maintains and that I have book-marked for future access. (Do check the bookmarks in your web browser's address book and see how many can no longer be found.) The issue of how long sites will be maintained, like the related issue of how compatible the always improving technologies will be with the ones they render obsolete, is an important one for thinking about the electronic environment as an alternative to so-called 'hard copy.' (How many of the essays that any of us wrote on computers in the late 1980s and early 1990s are accessible even to their authors except as printed copies on paper?)

But even with these caveats in mind, the electronic text seductively beckons, leading enthusiasts to trumpet the end of the age of print, and skeptics to murmur defensively that the book's longevity may have been underestimated. The printed book and the electronic text come to define less alternative ways of engaging the word than alternative ways of engaging the world. One might easily escape the binary these alternatives pose by saying what is no doubt true—but also no doubt uninteresting—that they both have a useful role to play, the alternatives in fact offering themselves less as an ethical choice than what might be thought an erotic one. It is not which is good, or good for us, but which we desire or can convince ourselves (or our libraries) that we need.

*   *   *

Leah Marcus, Janel Mueller and Mary Beth Rose, 'Preface' to *idem* (eds.), *Elizabeth I: Collected Works* (Chicago and London: University of Chicago Press, 2000), pp. xviii–xxii.

All of the materials in this volume are reproduced with modernized spelling and punctuation and expanded abbreviations and contractions. To accommodate the range of readers that we envisage, we offer a separate volume that presents extant texts in Elizabeth's hand in her original spelling, as well as the originals of foreign language texts not in her own hand. Unlike the clean copy versions in the present volume, *Autograph Compositions and Foreign Language Originals* (*ACFLO*) indicates Elizabeth's insertions, deletions, and other revisions in her handwritten texts. Because of limitations of space, *ACFLO* does not include original-spelling versions of English language manuscripts not in the queen's hand. As any student of early modern culture recognizes, the copying of materials was a far from standardized process. The spelling, punctuation, and even wording in any given scribal copy can vary significantly from that of every other copy; such manuscripts consequently are less reliable transmitters of Elizabeth's meaning than her own handwritten texts. The original-spelling materials collected in *ACFLO* will also allow interested readers to assess our style of modernization and translation.

In general, although we have chosen to modernize, we have wanted to keep readers in contact with the irregularities and sometimes gritty intransigence of the manuscripts: we have retained archaic and foreign words and phrases where they occur in English language texts—unless the spelling of a word is quite close to its form in modern English, in which case we have silently modernized its spelling. Thus 'sithence' and 'sith' do not become 'since' but retain their original forms. There are a number of borderline cases that we have regularized: for example, 'farder' and 'furder' become 'farther' and 'further'; Elizabeth's frequent spelling of 'hit' becomes 'it,' 'accompt' becomes 'account,' and 'burthen' becomes 'burden.' We do not correct features of the original manuscripts that may appear grammatically incorrect to modern readers, such as lack of verb-subject agreement and 'a' rather than 'an' before a vowel. We have supplied or altered punctuation and paragraphing when we have judged necessary to make many texts more readable. As we are well aware, however, to modernize is to interpret: the spelling and punctuation that enable and clarify one possible interpretation of Elizabeth's often difficult writing may well obscure other possible readings, and we invite readers to interrogate our modernizations even while making use of them.

Although we have modernized spelling and punctuation in this volume to make these materials accessible to a wide range of readers, we have simultaneously preserved some of the flavor of the early modern documents. Interspersed illustrations allow readers to consult facsimiles of the originals while reading our modernized versions. Whereas most past editors of Elizabeth's writings have freely combined readings from different versions of a text in order to create a single 'ideal' composite version, we have chosen instead to preserve the integrity of each manuscript version, recording—and where necessary, glossing—significant textual anomalies and variants in our notes. We do not silently emend apparent pen slips or repeated or dropped words; and we sometimes retain underscoring and other markings in a manuscript where those markings register emphasis. We preserve early manuscript headings as a guide to how the text was understood and classified, either by its scribe or by some other early reader. The words 'Headed' and 'Endorsed,' enclosed in square brackets, signal these early interventions upon the manuscript text. Square brackets also enclose elements supplied where a given manuscript has been damaged. However, for manuscripts also included in *ACFLO*, the companion volume to the present edition, we include the brackets signaling supplied material only in the original-spelling texts reproduced there. Because we have aimed to insure accessibility while preserving the flavor of early modern documents, our policy has been to be fairly literal in translating foreign language texts, particularly by preserving where possible the syntax and phraseology of the Elizabethan originals. Our translations of Elizabeth's poems are, however, necessarily somewhat freer because we have also aimed to retain features of their verse design.

In response to the special circumstantial nature of the historical materials that constitute this edition, we have developed principles for handling introductory material and notes that differ from some standard practices in editing literary texts. We have kept interpretation to a minimum, preferring to let readers discover for themselves the materials as they unfold during the process of reading and in our notes, rather than supplying detailed or elaborate contextualization in headnotes. Such headnotes not only would tend to direct interpretation in ways that are unnecessarily restrictive, but for the most part would reduplicate the ample scholarship that already exists. For the same reasons, we have not glossed references that we judge to be either common knowledge or common usage; we have tried to be inclusive in glossing references that are less accessible. Full references to historical persons are given only the first time they are mentioned; but a very few names go unglossed altogether, usually because we have been unable to identify them. To facilitate identification of historical persons, we have supplied an Index of Names. Obviously, however, readers will differ in their appetite for contextual details: those readers who seek additional information are invited to consult the authorities cited in the notes and in our list of frequently cited works, which will provide useful starting points for further research.

One of the key ways in which our edition departs from standard editorial practice is in our choice not to provide comprehensive lists of textual variants. Indeed, given the lack of standardization from one manuscript to another, to supply such a list for Elizabeth's writings, particularly the poems and speeches, would be impossibly unwieldy. Instead we have chosen to record selectively those variants that create what we judge to be significant differences in the meaning of a phrase or passage, which we identify in the course of a single series of notes rather than in a separate section devoted solely to textual notes. By conjoining rather than separating notes about textual variants with notes identifying persons and events, we wish to call attention to the historicity of all elements of Elizabeth's text. Similarly, in our notes we list manuscript copies and offer variants only for texts that we judge to be early or significant for some other specified reason. To list all of the extant copies of a given speech or letter would be unnecessarily cumbersome.

In order to provide a sense of the variability of manuscript and early printed evidence, we have occasionally reproduced multiple versions of selected texts, rather than a single original. In the case of Elizabeth's letters, as already noted, differences among versions are typically fairly minimal. The poems are another story. There is recurrent evidence that Elizabeth made efforts to keep most of her verses out of general circulation: some copyists of Elizabeth's verses during the period registered the faintly transgressive nature of their activity by offering their attribution to the queen quite literally '*sous rature*'—written down and then struck through, as is several times indicated in our notes to the present edition. Occasionally we offer more than one version of a poetic text in order to indicate the variety of forms in which a poem circulated among the queen's contemporaries.

The case of Elizabeth's speeches is considerably more complex. The present edition develops and applies a new paradigm for understanding their production. Past editors have assumed that Elizabeth or a surrogate delivered her speeches from a text written out in advance—a version that scholars have imagined as arising from an originary moment of composition and have privileged for its authenticity on that ground. While Elizabeth may sometimes have spoken from a prepared written text and did occasionally prepare written speeches to be read out by her principal ministers, in a larger number of instances she spoke either extemporaneously or from memory, and only wrote the speech down afterward or had it transcribed from her dictation. Sometimes, the evidence clearly suggests, if she wanted a copy of a speech she had delivered, she acquired it from one of her auditors who had written down her words later from memory. Very frequently, those attempting to record Elizabeth's speeches after the fact vent their frustration at failing to capture the original speech in its full liveliness and pungency. And yet these recorded versions can produce, along with descriptions of the queen's gestures and inflections, more vivid and vigorous texts than other later manuscript and printed versions of the same speech, even when the later versions are written entirely in, or corrected in, the queen's own hand. Texts of speeches bearing the mark of Elizabeth's hand sometimes circulated as official versions that had been reshaped after oral delivery for the purpose of dissemination to a broader public than the original audience of members of Parliament. Speeches 17 and 18—in which Elizabeth replies impromptu to parliamentary petitions urging the execution of Mary, Queen of Scots—provide particularly vivid instances of such revision for broader circulation. Sometimes, then, there are compelling reasons for preferring memorial accounts by Elizabeth's auditors over her own manuscripts as records of the speeches as delivered.

This is not to suggest that later, and sometimes less vivid, versions of a given speech are without interest. Although we part company from earlier editors by ruling out the creation of 'ideal' composite versions, we present some memorial versions of a given speech alongside printed or revised manuscript versions, so that readers can follow the interesting process by which the queen's more spontaneous rhetoric is reworked by herself and others into more considered—and often less inflammatory—language. In the case of speeches like those on Mary, Queen of Scots, already alluded to, variant versions can be understood as parts of a continuum from the queen's original utterance to the speech in process of revision by Elizabeth to the speech as it appeared later in print. However, in other instances, as in the case of the Golden Speech of 1601, the variant texts seem to preserve different memorial versions produced independently by several of Elizabeth's parliamentary auditors. By offering readers the opportunity to read and judge different versions of the speeches for themselves, we hope to leave the relations among these fascinating documents open to further study and discovery.

. . . .

QUESTIONS

- What is the future of editing?
- Are textual choices the job of the editor or the reader?

SUGGESTED FURTHER READING

Barroll, Leeds (ed.), *Shakespeare Studies*, 24 (Forum: Editing Early Modern Texts, 1996)

Hill, W. Speed (ed.), *New Ways of Looking at Old Texts*, II (Tempe, Arizona: Medieval and Renaissance Texts and Studies, 1998)

Honigmann, E. A. J., *The Texts of 'Othello' and Shakespearean Revision* (London and New York: Routledge, 1996)

Marotti, Arthur and Michael D. Bristol (eds.), *Print, Manuscript, and Performance: The Changing Relations of the Media in Early Modern England* (Columbus: Ohio State University Press, 2000)

Murphy, Andrew, *Shakespeare in Print: A History and Chronology of Shakespeare Publishing* (Cambridge: Cambridge University Press, 2003)

Rhodes, Neil and Jonathan Sawday (eds.), *The Renaissance Computer: Knowledge Technology in the First Age of Print* (London and New York: Routledge, 2000)

Taylor, Gary and Michael Warren (eds.), *The Division of the Kingdoms: Shakespeare's Two Versions of 'King Lear'* (Oxford: Clarendon, 1983)

Thompson, Ann and Gordon McMullan (eds.), *In Arden: Editing Shakespeare* (London: Thomson, 2003)

Vickers, Brian, *Shakespeare, Co-Author* (Oxford: Oxford University Press, 2002)

Werstine, Paul, 'The textual mystery of *Hamlet*', *Shakespeare Quarterly*, 39 (1988), 1–26.

NOTES

De Grazia and Stallybrass, The materiality of the Shakespeare text

1. See Ben Jonson, *Discoveries*, no. 732, in *The Complete Poems*, ed. George Parfitt (London: Penguin Books, 1975), p. 392.

2. Quoted as the epigraph to Dard Hunter's *Papermaking: The History and Technique of an Ancient Craft*, 2nd edn, rev. and enl. (New York: Knopf, 1947).

3. William Prynne, *Histrio-Mastix* (London, 1633), unpaginated preface.

4. See George Walton Williams, *The Craft of Printing and the Publication of Shakespeare's Works* (Washington, D.C.: Folger Books, 1985), p. 48.

Blayney, The publication of playbooks

1. My exclusions agree for the most part with the classifications in Harbage's *Annals*, 3rd edn. In borderline cases I have considered whether the printed book appears to be aimed at the buyers of less equivocally professional and public plays. *Cornelia* and *Summer's Last Will and Testament* are therefore included because of their authorship, *The Wit of a Woman* because of its title page, *The Second Part of The Cid* because the first part had been publicly acted, etc. I have included most university plays in English, excluding only a handful that are clearly not aimed at the 'typical' buyer of plays (such as *Sicelides: A Piscatory* and *Work for Cutlers*).

2. The figures were determined by counting items in every fifth year from 1584 and calculating the intervening years from the average number of items per line.

3. In some accounts a more tangible fallacy is found. It is therefore worth noting that the present-day concept of literary property, which includes the rights to both publication and performance, simply did not exist in early modern England. Neither 'right' existed in law, and neither the stationers nor the players imagined that they had any authority over each other's professional activities.

4. Rosalyn L. Knutson, 'The Repertory' in John D. Cox and David Scott Kastan (eds.), *A New History of Early English Drama* (New York: Columbia University Press, 1997), pp. 461–80.

5. Neither of the two early comments usually adduced as evidence is either explicit or trustworthy. The anonymous epistle prefixed to *Troilus and Cressida* in 1609 suggests merely that the unidentified 'grand possessors' of the play might have preferred to keep it unpublished. But a manuscript had been provisionally registered six years earlier by James Roberts, who had then (characteristically) declined to publish it. So neither the motive nor even the *identity* of the 'possessors' is beyond doubt—and if the play had never yet been considered worth performing in public, I cannot see why we should imagine that the players feared competition.

   In an epistle to his *English Traveler* (1633), the ever-complaining Thomas Heywood claims that some of his plays 'are still retained in the hands of some Actors, who thinke it against their peculiar profit to haue them come in Print' (Greg, *Bibliography*, 3:1222). The context, however, is an explanation of why his plays have not been collected and published as *Works* (the rest can be summarized as 'Many have been lost' and 'I have no interest in having them printed'), and Heywood is an unreliable witness. The indifference to publication that he professed in so many printed epistles is no more credible the year after he published the fourth and fifth of his *Ages* plays (the two-part *Iron Age* [1632]) than in the address he prefixed to the first of them (*The Golden Age* [1611]). He may well be right that some players in 1633 did not want *others* to sell their property to the press—but we cannot ascertain their reasons without more and better testimony.

6. Gary Taylor has suggested that the resumption of playing by the Children of Paul's, and the consequent increase in competition, might have created a perceived need to advertise.

7. That is, counting the year of publication as year 1, before the end of year 25.

8. If we express the annual number of new plays as a percentage of the annual number of items listed in the chronological index to the *Short-Title Catalogue*, the mean figures for the three periods are 1.6 percent, 1.2 percent, and 1.3 percent respectively. The first figure is distorted by the lower rate of survival of nonliterary books of the sixteenth century. Once again, therefore, the general impression is of a demand that was low but fairly constant.

9. Each of the last two reached its fifth edition in nineteen years, so they rank equal tenth.

10. In 1600 Wise trod more carefully and shared the risk of his next two plays with William Aspley,

even though one of them was the sequel to a best-seller. Once again he showed either extraordinary luck or an enviable instinct for the trade—because neither *Much Ado About Nothing* nor *Henry IV, Part 2* was reprinted for twenty-three years.

11. Approximately 74 percent in 1583–1602, 88 percent in 1603–1622, and 91 percent in 1623–1642.

12. Like other printed books, playbooks were sometimes farmed out in sections to two or more printing houses (Blayney, *Texts*, 1:31–32, 49–52), but even in a shared book it is appropriate to refer to 'the printer' of each section.

13. See in particular his 'Entrance, Licence,' 14–22; *Some Aspects*, 63–89; and *Bibliography*, 4:clxi–clxix. An *imprint* is a statement on a title page giving details of publication: the place and/or date, and often the names of one or more of the stationers responsible. A *colophon* is a similar statement placed at the end of a book.

14. In his first discussion of imprints ('First Folio,' 130–4), Greg admitted that other bookshops would 'probably' have stocked a copy or two (133). But by the time he published his first detailed analysis ('Entrance, Licence,' in response to Shaaber, 'The Meaning of the Imprint'), he no longer acknowledged that possibility.

15. The present separation of the trade in new books from the trade in used books is comparatively recent. Early modern booksellers sold books of all kinds: new, nearly new, used, and antiquarian; homegrown and imported; printed, manuscript, ruled, and blank. Many also sold other things, some related to the book trade (paper, parchment, and cardboard; pens, ink, and wax) and some not.

16. It is sometimes suggested that exchanging books acquired at cost saved money—which is economic nonsense. In a fair exchange, one batch of books worth a given sum at retail prices would be traded for a batch of different books worth exactly the same. It was immaterial how much either party had paid for his own batch: each started and finished with goods of equal value. What was increased by trading was not overall profit but the rate of turnover. While it might take several years to sell five hundred copies of a single title, ten copies each of fifty carefully chosen titles might be sold in a matter of weeks.

17. Any freeman of London had the right to retail virtually any commodity except certain controlled perishables (principally food and drink). All London booksellers were subject to the regulatory authority of the Stationers' Company, but they did not have to belong to it.

18. A few publishers even insisted on imprints claiming that their books were printed 'by' them rather than 'for' them.

19. The Dering manuscript of *Henry IV* is an abridgement of both parts, prepared before February 27, 1623. At 1½d. per sheet for thirty-two sheets, which included the equivalent of four rewritten sheets, the copy cost Dering a total of 4s. (Yeandle, 224). If London prices were comparable, a play of average length could have been copied for between 2s. and 3s.

Erne, Shakespeare as Literary Dramatist

1. Melchiori, 'The Acting Version and the Wiser Sort,' 200, 196.

2. Ibid., 207.

3. There is nothing to suggest that such restructurings were at all common. It should be noted, however, that one of the eighteen extant manuscript playbooks does give evidence of such rearrangement. As the editor of Glapthorne's *Lady Mother* has pointed out, the manuscript shows that it was 'decided to play the long serious scene between Sir Geffrey and Lady Marlove, Bonvill and Belisea (854–1056) *before* the awakening of Lovell and his scene with Grimes (735–853)' (Henry Glapthorne, *The Lady Mother*, ed. Arthur Brown [London: Oxford University Press, 1958], x). Accordingly, the person who was involved in preparing the play for the stage deleted the original warning for Sir Geffrey and Lady Marlove at lines 845–6 and added a new warning (1048–9) at the end of what is, in the manuscript, the later scene of Lovell's awakening.

4. Melchiori, 'The Acting Version and the Wiser Sott,' 207; Kathleen O. Irace (ed.), *The First Quarto of Hamlet*, The New Cambridge Shakespeare: The Early Quartos (Cambridge University Press, 1998), ii.

5. Whoever turned *Hamlet* into *Der Bestrafte Brudermord (Fratricide Punished)*—which was performed on the Continent by English comedians—appears to have been similarly dissatisfied by the longwinded, narrative handling of Hamlet's journey to England. In this version, the 'two ruffians' (Rosencrantz and Guildenstern) are ordered to kill Hamlet as soon as they reach England. Act four, scene one dramatizes their attempt to carry out this order which results in a farcical failure when Hamlet 'falls down forward between the two servants, who shoot each other.' I quote from H. Howard Furness's translation in Bullough's *Sources of Shakespeare* viii. 150.

6. See, for instance, Duthie, *'Bad' Quarto of Hamlet*, 86–93.

7. The swift pace called for by the short theatrical texts can also be inferred from 2.6 in *Romeo and Juliet*, the one scene that is made up of substantially different material from its counterpart in the second quarto. In Q1, the emphasis is on haste throughout the scene: 'Without more words I will doo all I may,' the Friar assures Romeo even before Juliet's arrival. As soon as Romeo has optimistically announced that 'come she will,' Juliet enters, and does so 'somewhat fast,' as the stage direction puts it. In the scenes closing lines, all three characters seem equally bent on speeding up the action:

    FR[IAR]: Come wantons, come, the stealing houres do passe [. . .]
    ROM[EO]: Lead holy Father, all delay seemes long.
    IUL[IET]: Make hast, make hast, this lingring doth vs wrong.

    (E4ᵛ)

    In Q2, in contrast, none of the quoted lines have an equivalent. Instead of hastening to their marriage, Romeo and Juliet express their love in lyrical conceits. Similarly, after bidding farewell to Romeo, Juliet has a speech in which she addresses Fortune in Q2, which is replaced in Q1 by the nurse entering 'hastely' to warn Juliet of her mother's arrival (G3ᵛ).

8. Matters are further complicated by the fact that the Queen's lines echo Bel-imperia in *The Spanish Tragedy* (4.1.46–8).

9. C. H. Herford, for instance, wrote of 'the veil which in Q2 is studiously made to conceal the precise measure of her complicity in the murder,' a suggestion later critics elaborated (*The First Quarto Edition of 'Hamlet,' 1603* (London, 1880)). For the Q1 Queen, see also Urkowitz, ' "Well-sayd olde Mole," ' 46–9; and Dorothea Kehler, 'The First Quarto of *Hamlet*: Reforming Widow Gertred'.

10. Philip Edwards (ed.), *Hamlet, Prince of Denmark*, New Cambridge Shakespeare (Cambridge University Press, 1985), 223.

11. The adjective with which Hamlet is here qualified is of some interest. In the long texts, the Prince's age represents a well-known problem. Early on in the play, he is referred to as 'young Hamlet' and is said to have returned from Wittenberg where he is a student. Yet, in the last act, the Gravedigger suggests that he is thirty years old. In Q1, the latter indication has disappeared and nothing contradicts the impression of Hamlet's youthful age. Yorick's skull 'hath bin here this dozen yeare' (line 1987)—not twenty-three as in the long texts—and the Prince is again referred to as 'yong' (line 1989). The elegy on Burbage thus seems to corroborate what Q1—but not Q2 and F—suggest about Hamlet's age.

12. The passage is quoted in Chambers, *Elizabethan Stage*, 11.309.

13. Even though I am less certain than Janis Lull that Q1 *Hamlet* is a memorial reconstruction, her argument that Q1 'reinterprets the play, making it affirm the very warrior values that the F version calls into question' seems to me pertinent. See Lull, 'Forgetting *Hamlet*: The First Quarto and the Folio,' in *The 'Hamlet' First Published*, ed. Clayton, 137–50, 149.

14. Ong, *Orality and Literacy*, 151.

15. Ibid., 151–3.

16. L. C. Knights, *How Many Children Had Lady Macbeth? An Essay in the Theory and Practice of Shakespeare Criticism* (Cambridge: Minority Press, 1933), often reprinted, for instance in L. C. Knights, *Explorations: Essays in Criticism Mainly on the Literature of the Seventeenth Century* (New York University Press, 1964).

17. Heather Dubrow, *Captive Victors: Shakespeare's Narrative Poems and Sonnets* (Ithaca: Cornell University Press, 1987), 17.

Masten, Textual Intercourse

1. Gerald Eades Bentley, *The Profession of Dramatist in Shakespeare's Time 1590–1642*, Princeton: Princeton University Press, 1971, p. 199.

2. Ibid., p. 263. Recent considerations of revised texts in the Shakespeare canon have worked to dissolve the notion of the single text, but continue to insist anachronistically upon the notion of a singular revising authorial consciousness; see Gary Taylor and Michael Warren (eds.), *The Division of the Kingdoms: Shakespeare's Two Versions of King Lear*, Oxford: Clarendon Press, 1983; Grace Ioppolo, *Revising Shakespeare*, Cambridge, MA: Harvard University Press, 1991. In contrast, Scott McMillin usefully explores revision as a deconstruction of authorial individuality in the *Sir Thomas More* manuscript; *The Elizabethan Theatre and The Book of Sir Thomas More*, Ithaca: Cornell University Press, 1987, pp. 153–9.

3. Bentley, *Profession of Dramatist*, p. 198. See also Stephen Orgel's important discussion of Bentley in 'What is a Text?,' *Research Opportunities in Renaissance Drama* 26 (1981), pp. 2–4.

4. This is to say nothing of the manifold collaborations that generated a play-text when/if it was eventually printed. On book-holders, see William B. Long, 'Bookkeepers and Playhouse Manuscripts: A Peek at the Evidence,' *Shakespeare Newsletter* 44 (1994), p. 3; and Long, 'Stage Directions: A Misinterpreted Factor in Determining Textual Provenance,' *TEXT* 2 (1985), pp. 121–37. Largely, of course, the participation in textual production of agents other than 'the' playwright has been viewed as intrusive and corruptive, rather than collaborative.

5. Jean-Christophe Agnew, *Worlds Apart: The Market and the Theater in Anglo-American Thought, 1550–1750*, Cambridge: Cambridge University Press, 1986, p. 111. Cf. Woolf: 'the play was a common product, written by one hand, but so moulded in transition that the author had no sense of property in it. It was in part the work of the audience' (Virginia Woolf, 'ANON.,' *Twentieth-Century Literature* 25 (1975), p. 395). It is important to notice that (in a way to which I will return below) Woolf insists upon the singlehandedness of textual production in this period, even as she stresses the collaborative role of the audience.

6. [William Shakespeare], *AN EXCELLENT conceited Tragedie OF Romeo and Iuliet*, London: by Iohn Danter, 1597.

7. Mr. John Fletcher and William Shakespeare. Gent., *THE TWO NOBLE KINSMEN*, London: Tho. Cotes for Iohn Waterson, 1634. See Agnew's discussion of the handshake's emerging contractual significance (*Worlds Apart*, pp. 86–9).

8. See Jerome J. McGann's critique of the editing/interpreting distinction in 'The Monks and the Giants: Textual and Bibliographical Studies and the Interpretation of Literary Works,' in McGann (ed.), *Textual Criticism and Literary Interpretation*, Chicago and London: University of Chicago Press, 1985, pp. 180–99. De Grazia demonstrates how the editorial apparatus itself functions to shape and constrain interpretation in editions of the Shakespeare canon; see Margreta de Grazia, *Shakespeare Verbatim: The Reproduction of Authenticity and the 1790 Apparatus*, Oxford: Clarendon Press, 1991.

9. Bowers, foreword, in *The Dramatic Works in the Beaumont and Fletcher Canon*, Cambridge: Cambridge University Press, 1966, vol. i: p. vii, my emphasis.

10. On 'verbal corruption' and actors' 'interpolations' in *Hamlet*, see Harold Jenkins's Arden edition, London: Methuen, 1982, pp. 62–3.

11. William Shake-speare, *THE Tragicall Historie of HAMLET Prince of Denmarke* (Q1), London: for N.L. and Iohn Trundell, 1603, E4^v.

12. William Shakespeare, *THE Tragicall Historie of HAMLET, Prince of Denmarke* (Q2), London: by I.R. for N.L., 1604, title page.

13. McGann argues that even the text that seems to have been materially produced by one person exists fundamentally in the realm of the social; revision in authorial manuscripts, he argues, 'reflect[s] social interactions and purposes.' See *A Critique of Modern Textual Criticism*, Chicago and London: University of Chicago Press, 1983, p. 62.

14. Stephen Greenblatt makes a related point in his discussion of 'the *collective* making of distinct cultural practices and inquiry into the relations among these practices,' though I would note that, in the next sentence, he returns to singular 'making' in labeling his subject 'plays by Shakespeare' (*Shakespearean Negotiations: The Circulation of Social Energy in Renaissance England*, Berkeley: University of California Press, 1988, p. 5, my emphasis).

15. Morse Peckham, 'Reflections on the Foundations of Modern Textual Editing,' *Proof* 1 (1971), pp. 122–55.

16. In other words, we would not want to rely too heavily on Jonson's attitude toward collaboration alone; for an alternative interpretation of dramatic collaboration in this mode, see Donald K. Hedrick, ' "Be Rough With Me": The Collaborative Arenas of *The Two Noble Kinsmen*,' in Charles H. Frey (ed.), *Shakespeare, Fletcher, and The Two Noble Kinsmen*, Columbia: University of Missouri Press, 1989, pp. 45–77.

17. *THE KNIGHT OF the Burning Pestle* (Q1), London: for Walter Burre, 1613, A2.

18. Francis Beaumont and Iohn Fletcher. Gent., *THE KNIGHT Of the BVRNING PESTLE* (Q2), London: N.O. for I.S., 1635, A3. The third quarto, often supposed to be a later reprint despite its stated date of 1635, is most easily distinguished from Q2 by its spelling of 'Beamount' on the title page: Francis Beamount and Iohn Fletcher, *THE KNIGHT Of the BVRNING PESTLE* (Q3), London: N.O. for I.S., 1635.

19. *THE KNIGHT* (Q2), A4.

20. *THE KNIGHT* (Q1), A2^v.

21. Reprinted in Zitner, (ed.), *The Knight*, pp. 163–4.

22. For example: John Doebler's edition in the Regents Renaissance Drama series, Lincoln: University of Nebraska Press, 1967; Andrew Gurr's edition for Fountainwell Drama Texts, Edinburgh: Oliver and Boyd, 1968; Michael Hattaway's New Mermaids edition, London: Ernest Benn, 1969; and Zitner's 1984 Revels Plays edition. All of these followed the 1966 publication of the play's 'standard' edition (as edited by Cyrus Hoy) in *The Dramatic Works* supervised by Bowers and cited above.

23. Eugene M. Waith's influential study of *The Pattern of Tragicomedy in Beaumont and Fletcher*, New Haven: Yale University Press, 1952, for example, discounts *The Knight* as uncharacteristic before it proceeds to an analysis of the rest of the canon (p. 5).

24. For reasons explored above, I quote not from an edition of *The Knight* governed by anachronistic notions of authorship, but rather from Q1, providing page references to that text. Joseph Loewenstein notes acting companies' use of the first-person plural in 'The Script in the Marketplace,' in Stephen Greenblatt (ed.), *Representing the English Renaissance*, Berkeley: University of California Press, 1988, p. 266; my understanding of drama's eventual emergence as textual property is greatly indebted to this article.

25. Barthes, 'The Death of the Author,' p. 146.

26. The source-tracing textual glosses and commentary in the editions mentioned above—upon which I rely heavily in the discussion of 'quotation' that follows—are themselves voluminously symptomatic and constitutive of the twentieth-century preoccupation with authorship and the transmission of textual property. For an important critique of the traditional relation of 'source' to play-text, see Jonathan Goldberg, 'Speculations: *Macbeth* and Source,' in Jean E. Howard and Marion F. O'Connor (eds.), *Shakespeare Reproduced: The Text in History and Ideology*, New York and London: Methuen, 1987, pp. 242–64.

27. The relation of *The Knight* to *Don Quixote* is a matter of some controversy, especially if one is concerned about 'Beaumont's' 'originality'; see Zitner's edition, pp. 39–42, for a summary of the issues.

28. See Zitner (ed.), *The Knight*, pp. 28–31.

29. In *The Pattern of Tragicomedy*, Waith quarantines the play from this possibility by labeling it 'Beaumont's'; see note 23 above.

30. Zitner (ed.), *The Knight*, p. 173.

31. *Hamlet*'s Arden editor, Harold Jenkins, calls these Os 'theatrical accretions to Shakespeare's dialogue' (p. 62). Terence Hawkes's perceptive essay 'That Shakespeherian Rag,' in his book of the same title (London: Methuen, 1986), first brought Hamlet's dying Os to my attention.

32. Lee Bliss, ' "Plot Mee No Plots": The Life of Drama and the Drama of Life in *The Knight of the Burning Pestle*,' *Modern Language Quarterly* 45.1 (1984), pp. 13 and 3.

33. Again, comparison with Woolf's romanticized character 'Anon.' is instructive.

34. The complexity of social class in this play is often too easily simplified by critics siding unselfconsciously with the actors and upper-class audience against the citizens' supposed lack of sophistication and their 'naive' interventions in 'art.' Bliss, for example, derides the citizens because they 'demolish the independent aesthetic status of the playwright's work and overturn the traditional ideal of drama as a clarifying mirror of men and their relation to their world' (' "Plot Mee No Plots," ' p. 4).

35. Alexander Nehamas, 'Writer, Text, Work, Author,' in Anthony J. Cascardi (ed.), *Literature and the Question of Philosophy*, Baltimore: Johns Hopkins University Press, 1987, p. 286 (first quotation); 'The Postulated Author: Critical Monism as a Regulative Ideal,' *Critical Inquiry* 8 (1981), p. 145 (second quotation).

36. Or defies, I might add, the limitations of my own dyadic rhetoric here: 'seeing *double*.' The implications of three-way collaboration and attribution are explored briefly in the last section of Chapter 4.

Ferguson, Renaissance concepts of the 'woman writer'

1. For useful discussions of the paradoxes in English Renaissance modes of authorship, see Elaine Beilin, *Redeeming Eve: Women Writers of the English Renaissance* (Princeton: Princeton University Press, 1987) and Mary Ellen Lamb, *Gender and Authorship in the Sidney Circle* (Madison: University of Wisconsin Press, 1990), both with further bibliographies.

2. See Suzanne Hull, *Chaste, Silent, and Obedient: English Books for Women, 1475–1640* (San Marino: Huntington Library, 1982).

Patterson, Censorship and Interpretation

1. F. S. Siebert, *Freedom of the Press in England, 1476–1776* (Urbana: University of Illinois Press, 1952).

Marotti, Malleable and fixed texts

1. Changing only the long *f*, I reproduce the conservative text in Hyder E. Rollins (ed), *A Poetical Rhapsody, 1602–1621*, 2 vols. (Cambridge, Mass.: Harvard University Press, 1931), I, p. 186.

2. Rollins, ed., *Poetical Rhapsody*, II, p. 168.

3. Ruth Hughey (ed.), *The Arundel-Harington Manuscript of Tudor Poetry*, 2 vols. (Columbus: Ohio State University Press, 1960), II, p. 308.

4. See the textual variants printed in Rollins (ed.), *Poetical Rhapsody*, II, pp. 164–7; Hughey (ed.), *Arundel-Harington*, II, pp. 307–8; and Edward Doughtie (ed.), *Lyrics from English Airs, 1596–1622* (Cambridge, Mass.: Harvard University Press, 1970), p. 520.

Goldberg, Shakespeare's Hand

1. Fredson Bowers, 'What Shakespeare Wrote,' in his *On Editing Shakespeare* (Charlottesville: University Press of Virginia, 1966), 120. Pope (*The Works of Mr. William Shakespear* [London: Jacob Tonson, 1723], vol. 6, 271) essentially follows Q1 at this point:

> 'Tis but thy name that is my enemy:
> What's *Mountague*? it is not hand, nor foot,

> Nor arm, nor face—nor any other part.
> What's in a name? that which we call a rose,
> By any other name would smell as sweet.

2. Random Cloud, 'The Marriage of Good and Bad Quartos,' *Shakespeare Quarterly,* 33 (1982): 421–31. This essay develops the notion of the 'infinitive text,' referred to below, which has been highly influential on the argument presented here; I also develop points first essayed in my review of the New Arden *Romeo and Juliet* in *Shakespeare Studies* 16 (1983): 343–8. My chief indebtedness in this essay is to Stephen Orgel, 'What Is a Text?' *Research Opportunities in Renaissance Drama* 26 (1981): 3–6; Orgel, 'Shakespeare Imagines a Theater,' in *Shakespeare, Man of the Theater,* ed. K. Muir, J. Halio, and D. J. Palmer (Newark: University of Delaware Press, 1983); Orgel, 'The Authentic Shakespeare,' *Representations* 21 (1988): 1–26; and his edition of *The Tempest* (Oxford: Oxford University Press, 1987).

3. Quarto texts cited from *Shakespeare's Plays in Quarto,* ed. Michael J. B. Allen and Kenneth Muir (Berkeley and Los Angeles: University of California Press, 1981).

4. *Romeo and Juliet,* New Arden edition, ed. Brian Gibbons (London and New York: Methuen, 1980).

5. Stanley Wells, 'The Bettering of Burby,' *Times Literary Supplement* 4030 (20 June 1980): 710; further citations from Wells are all from this page.

6. In Stanley Wells and Gary Taylor, with John Jowett and William Montgomery (eds.), *William Shakespeare: A Textual Companion* (Oxford: Clarendon Press, 1987): 294. Further citations from Jowett are all from this page. Wells was the secondary editor of *Romeo and Juliet* and cosigned the notes on the text.

7. *Romeo and Juliet,* ed. J. Dover Wilson and G. I. Duthie (Cambridge: Cambridge University Press, 1955, 1961).

8. The exact limits of this relationship have been the subject of much debate; for one example, see Richard Hosley, 'Quarto Copy for Q2 *Romeo and Juliet,*' *Studies in Bibliography* 9 (1957): 129–41. One feature shared by Q1 and Q2 at this point is the use of italics for the Nurse's lines. This is an especially baffling fact, and one that has not been considered sufficiently. If one supposes, as seems arguable, that the typeface here replicates the hand in which the lines were written, then the script behind the text must have been written in an italic hand. It is difficult to imagine what kind of copy would so be written; theatrical scripts were normally written in secretarial hand. Italic was reserved for presentation copies and would have been produced by a professional scribe. All accounts of Q1 assume rushed work by the actors; it seems to me very unlikely that they would have written an italic hand. Moreover, if the typography is to be trusted, italic was used only for the Nurse's part; it is doubtful that what is reproduced in Q1 is the actor's part, however, for it is hard to imagine why that part would have been written out in that hand. I have no solution to this dilemma; but it troubles the notion of memorial reconstruction.

9. See John Dover Wilson, 'The New Way with Shakespeare's Texts II. Recent Work on the Text of *Romeo and Juliet,*' *Shakespeare Survey* 8 (1955): 81–99.

10. G. I. Duthie, 'The Text of Shakespeare's *Romeo and Juliet,*' *Studies in Bibliography* 4 (1951–2): 3–29.

11. This is the theory advanced by Hardin Craig, *A New Look at Shakespeare's Quartos* (Stanford: Stanford University Press, 1961), 54–65.

12. Fredson Bowers, 'The Method for a Critical Edition,' in his *On Editing Shakespeare,* 87.

13. P. A. Daniel, *Romeo and Juliet, Parallel Texts of the First Two Quartos* (London: New Shakespere Society, 1874), v.

14. Harry R. Hoppe, *The Bad Quarto of Romeo and Juliet* (Ithaca, N.Y.: Cornell University Press, 1948). Hoppe builds upon the suppositions of E. K. Chambers in *William Shakespeare,* 2 vols (Oxford: Clarendon Press, 1930), vol. 1, 341–5, and of W. W. Greg, who endorses Hoppe's work in *The Editorial Problem in Shakespeare,* 2nd edn (Oxford: Clarendon Press, 1951), 61–4, and in *The Shakespeare First Folio* (Oxford: Clarendon Press, 1955), 225–35.

15. *The Tragedy of Romeo and Juliet*, ed. Richard Hosley (New Haven: Yale University Press, 1954), 141.

16. The F1 line that serves as the title to this essay is not repeated, for example, by Nicholas Rowe, who returns to the Q2 reading of the passage (*The Works of Mr. William Shakespear*, 7 vols. [London: Jacob Tonson, 1709], vol. 5, 2096). This line is the same in both 1709 editions.

17. Richard Hosley, 'The Corrupting Influence of the Bad Quarto on the Received Text of *Romeo and Juliet*,' *Shakespeare Quarterly* 4 (1953): 11–34.

18. A comparison between Q1 and Q2 at these points will reveal both situations that I have been suggesting. Q2 offers two versions of the 'grey eyed morn' lines, first for Romeo, then for Friar Laurence. The version of the speech in Q1 (D4r) is assigned to the friar—and it is very close to the version in Q2 that is also given to him (D4v). If Q2 represents first and second shots at the lines, Q1 has chosen the second shot; however, Q2 could also represent an alternative ending to the scene, and Romeo's version could be the second shot. The fact that it comes first in Q2 does not mean that it was written first. There is no way of knowing at what point the possibility that Romeo would speak the lines was introduced. If Hoppe is to be believed, the actor playing Romeo was one of the reporters of Q1; thus, in the performance represented by that text, the lines were not spoken by Romeo.

   Romeo's final soliloquy as represented in Q2 is clearly an anthology of possibilities; there are at least two ways of ending the soliloquy. One starts twice, 'I will beleeue, / Shall I beleeue' (L3r). Q1's 'O I beleeue' (K1v) seems closer to that first alternative, and closer to the shorter ending that is offered immediately. Still, it ends with lines that have their parallel in the longer ending provided by Q2. The situation here is manifestly complex: Either Q1 chose from the longer versions represented in Q2—chose and rearranged—or Q2 represents various additions and relocations to Q1 or a manuscript. Again, there is no way of deciding which was the case, or in what order they occurred. The supposition that this speech is faultily reported depends upon hypotheses that will not stand scrutiny: Lines said to be cut may never have existed; to claim that differences must be actors' transpositions and anticipations assumes that an author cannot make exactly the same kinds of revisions; to deny the authorial origin of lines said to be weak assumes that Shakespeare never wrote bad verse.

19. Two major instances of rewriting—act 2, scene 6 and Paris's final soliloquy in act 5, scene 3—especially embarrass Hoppe's notion of a reported text, since he believes that the actors playing Romeo and Paris were the reporters. Hoppe argues that the fatigued actors mangled the final scenes of the play and that act 2, scene 6 never was in the play as performed and thus was entirely made up from bits and pieces of the play (185). Yet it is equally possible that the end of the play was different and that Romeo's reporting in act 2, scene 6 is as 'accurate' as elsewhere (i.e., that the 'accurate' parts of Q1 are unrevised parts). The kind of melange that Hoppe finds could also be an argument in favor of Shakespeare's authorship: he too would have bits and scraps of the play in his memory. Even if, as some have supposed, this alternative scene and soliloquy are by another hand—Henry Chettle is proposed by Sidney Thomas in 'Henry Chettle and the First Quarto of *Romeo and Juliet*,' *Review of English Studies*, new series, 1 (1950): 8–16—that does not damage the possibility of recognizing the scenes as Shakespearean, once one admits that collaboration was a normal procedure in the theater (the notion that a Shakespeare play must be entirely Shakespeare's relies on a concept of authorship that is not confirmed by Elizabethan theatrical procedures, not by other plays, such as *Macbeth*, that are usually treated as 'by Shakespeare'). Furthermore, the desire to deny Shakespearean authorship for these alternatives involves the usual circular arguments about unchanging authorial style as well as the belief in the unique entity *Romeo and Juliet*.

20. One such text is Michael Warren's edition, *The Complete King Lear, 1608–1623* (Berkeley and Los Angeles: University of California Press, 1989), which offers all the substantive texts in a box; unsewn, the pages are ready for dissemination. The truly utopian text would be even more radically unstitched.

21. Reproduced with permission from the copy of the 1623 folio in the Thomas Fisher Rare Book Library, University of Toronto.

22. See S. W. Reid, 'The Editing of Folio *Romeo and Juliet*,' *Studies in Bibliography* 35 (1982): 43–66, esp. 57. Reid's explanation assumes that Q2 was marked up to tell the compositor to insert a

question mark and to delete the apostrophe in Q3 'What's.' The argument seems to be a bit strained, since it has the compositor not only reverse what was asked but remove both the apostrophe and the 's.' An alternative hypothesis, which would traffic even more spectacularly, could imagine an uncorrected state of F1 (which is not known to exist) that read, 'What in a name' and in which the two additions marked were inserted at the wrong places.

Murphy, Texts and textualities

1. Marshall McLuhan, *The Gutenberg Galaxy: The Making of Typographic Man* (London: Routledge & Kegan Paul, 1962), p. 124.

2. Walter J. Ong, *Orality and Literature: The Technologizing of the Word* (London: Methuen, 1982; reissued Routledge, 1989), p. 118. Further page references are included parenthetically in the text.

3. See Paul Werstine, 'Narratives about printed Shakespeare texts: "foul papers" and "bad" quartos', *Shakespeare Quarterly*, 41 (1990), pp. 65–86, and, most recently and comprehensively, Laurie E. Maguire, *Shakespearean Suspect Texts: The 'Bad' Quartos and their Contexts* (Cambridge: Cambridge University Press, 1996). The issue is further discussed below.

4. Jack Goody, *The Interface Between the Written and the Oral* (Cambridge: Cambridge University Press, 1987), pp. 298–9. Further references are included parenthetically in the text.

5. Even a printed edition is not, of course, *wholly* static, since, as a result of the manner in which corrected and uncorrected sheets were bound together, virtually no two copies of a Renaissance edition are identical in every detail. Thus Peter Blayney has observed in *The First Folio of Shakespeare* (Washington, DC: Folger Shakespeare Library, 1991) that 'no two copies [of the First Folio] have yet been found to contain exactly the same mixture of early and late pages' (p. 15). On the theoretical implications of such variations, see Marion Trousdale, 'A second look at critical bibliography and the acting of plays', *Shakespeare Quarterly*, 41 (1990), p. 94.

6. 'To the Great Variety of Readers', A3r.

7. By 'editorial tradition' here, I mean the tradition of having named, foregrounded editors for the text. All of the seventeenth-century folios had 'editors' also, but their presence in the text and their work of emendation went unannounced. For a useful summary of the changes made by these anonymous editors, see Paul Werstine, 'William Shakespeare', in D. C. Greetham (ed.), *Scholarly Editing: A Guide to Research* (New York: MLA, 1995), pp. 255–6.

8. 'The Preface of the Editor' in *The Works of Shakespear* (London, 1725), p. xvii. Here, as elsewhere, I have regularised long 's'.

9. Gary Taylor, *Reinventing Shakespeare: A Cultural History from the Restoration to the Present* (New York: Weidenfeld & Nicolson, 1989; reissued Oxford: Oxford University Press, 1991), p. 82.

10. *Proposals for printing, by subscription, the dramatic works of William Shakespeare, corrected and illustrated by Samuel Johnson* (London, 1756), repr. in facsimile as *Johnson's Proposals for his Edition of Shakespeare* (Oxford: Oxford University Press, 1923), p. 3 (Oxford text). Johnson was largely repeating here the narrative of theatrical dispersal and corrupt reconstruction that Theobald had proposed in his edition of 1733—see, in particular p. xxxviii of Theobald's 'Preface' to his edition. A similar anti-theatrical strain can be detected in, for example, the preface to Hammer's 1743–4 edition (pp. III–IV) and also Warburton's 1747 preface (pp. vii–viii).

11. Alvin Kernan, *Printing Technology, Letters and Samuel Johnson* (Princeton: Princeton University Press, 1987), p. 4.

12. In the case of the dramatic text we might, of course, also add the set of relations among the various other agents specified by Werstine: actors, scriveners, adapters, revisers, censors.

13. Mark Rose, 'The author as proprietor: *Donaldson v. Becket* and the genealogy of modern authorship', *Representations*, 23 (1988), pp. 62–3. See also, more generally, John Feather, 'The publishers and the pirates: British copyright law in theory and practice, 1710–1755', *Publishing History*, 22 (1987), pp. 5–32.

14. Kernan, *Printing Technology*, p. 100.

15. There are, of course, exceptions to this general trend. In *Authorizing Words*, Elsky sees Michel de Montaigne and Robert Burton as figures who exploit a certain potential for 'unfixity' within the regime of print, as they take advantage of new editions to offer changes—and sometimes contradictions—to what they have previously written. On Burton, see also Jonathan Sawday, 'Shapeless elegance: Robert Burton's anatomy of knowledge', in Neil Rhodes (ed.), *English Renaissance Prose: History, Language, and Politics* (Tempe, AZ: Medieval and Renaissance Texts and Studies, 1997), pp. 173–202.

16. See Margreta de Grazia, *Shakespeare Verbatim: The Reproduction of Authenticity and the 1790 Apparatus* (Oxford: Clarendon, 1991).

17. The quotation appears in part 2 of the first volume of Malone's edition, on the verso page facing the title page of *The Tempest*.

18. Allardyce Nicoll, 'The editors of Shakespeare from first folio to Malone', in *Studies in the First Folio* (London: Humphrey Milford/Oxford University Press, 1924), p. 178.

19. Werstine, 'William Shakespeare', p. 264.

20. A. W. Pollard's *Shakespeare's Folios and Quartos: A Study in the Bibliography of Shakespeare's Plays, 1594–1685* (London: Methuen, 1909) was prompted in part by the pessimistic assessment of the First Folio offered by Lee in his introduction to the 1902 Clarendon Press facsimile of F1.

21. Wilson, 'The task of Heminge and Condell', in *Studies in the First Folio*, p. 77.

22. See Grady, 'Disintegration and its reverberations', in Jean I. Marsden (ed.), *The Appropriation of Shakespeare: Post-Renaissance Reconstructions of the Works and the Myth* (Hemel Hempstead: Harvester, 1991), p. 120. See also Grady, *The Modernist Shakespeare: Critical Texts in a Material World* (Oxford: Clarendon, 1991), especially, pp. 57–63.

23. Ironically, it was within this same period that the first suggestions were made that the handwriting of one of the contributors to the *Booke of Sir Thomas More* fragment might be Shakespeare's. See Edward Maunde Thompson (ed.), *Shakespeare's Handwriting* (Oxford: Clarendon, 1916) and also A. W. Pollard (ed.), *Shakespeare's Hand in the Play of 'Sir Thomas More'* (Cambridge: Cambridge University Press, 1923). Pollard arranged for the pages in question to be exhibited at the British Museum.

24. Pollard, *Shakespeare's Folios*, p. 80.

25. The stress on a kind of familial morality is perhaps not so surprising here—Pollard was, after all, the (anonymous) author of *Life, Love and Light: Practical Morality for Men and Women* (London: Macmillan, 1911).

26. W. W. Greg, 'The *Hamlet* texts and recent work in Shakespearian bibliography', *Modern Language Review*, 14 (1919), p. 383.

27. Margreta de Grazia notes—in 'The essential Shakespeare and the material book', *Textual Practice*, 2 (1988), p. 76—that 'the explanation was extended by Pollard and Wilson to the rest of the "Bad Quarto" family in 1917, so that by 1939 Greg could claim that reporting was involved in the production of all the "Bad Quartos".'

28. The question of the validity of Greg's complex narrative does not concern me here (Maguire takes up this issue at pp. 76–8 of her analysis). Rather, I am concerned (a) with the various agents of intervention posited by Greg and with his determination to subordinate their roles to that of the centralised, isolated author and (b) with his desire to account for the text at hand in a way that detaches it from an imagined ideal authentic text, of which the 1602 quarto is merely a singularly poor reproduction.

29. Thomas P. Roche and C. Patrick O'Donnell (eds.), *The Faerie Queene* (New Haven: Yale University Press, 1981; first pub. London: Penguin, 1978), 1.1.20.6–7. Derrida summarises the Socratic view that writing itself is 'condemned . . . to wandering and blindness, to mourning' (Jacques Derrida, *Of Grammatology* (Baltimore: Johns Hopkins University Press, 1976), p. 39).

30. W. W. Greg, *The Editorial Problem in Shakespeare: A Survey of the Foundations of the Text* (Oxford: Clarendon, 1942; 3rd edn, 1962), p. 3.

31. See, for instance, de Grazia, 'Essential Shakespeare' and de Grazia and Peter Stallybrass, 'The materiality of the Shakespearean text', *Shakespeare Quarterly*, 44 (1993), pp. 255–83.

Gosset, Introduction to Pericles

Below is the key to the abbreviations found in this extract, given in alphabetical order:

Beaumont & Fletcher: *The Dramatic Works in the Beaumont and Fletcher Canon*, ed. Fredson Bowers, 10 vols. (Cambridge, 1966–96)

Bullough: Geoffrey Bullough, *Narrative and Dramatic Sources of Shakespeare*, Vol. 6 (1966), 349–564

Clare: Janet Clare, '*Art made tongue-tied by authority*': *Elizabethan and Jacobean Dramatic Censorhip*, 2nd edn (Manchester, 1999)

Davidson: Adele Davidson, 'Shakespeare and stenography reconsidered', *Analytical and Enumerative Bibliography*, NS, 6 (1992), 77–100

Dutch Courtesan: John Marston, *The Dutch Courtesan*, ed. David Crane (1997)

Dutton: Richard Dutton, *Mastering the Revels: The Regulation and Censorship of English Renaissance Drama* (Iowa City, 1991)

Dyce²: *Works*, ed. Alexander Dyce, 9 vols. (1864–7)

Edwards: *Pericles*, ed. Philip Edwards (1976)

Ewbank: Inga-Stina Ewbank, ' "My name is Marina": the language of recognition', in Philip Edwards, Inga-Stina Ewbank and G. K. Hunter (eds.), *Shakespeare's Styles: Essays in Honour of Kenneth Muir* (Cambridge, 1980)

Miseries: George Wilkins, *The Miseries of Enforced Marriage* (Oxford, 1963)

Honigmann: E. A. J. Honigmann, *The Stability of Shakespeare's Text* (Lincoln, Nebr., 1965)

Muir: Kenneth Muir, *Shakespeare the Collaborator* (1960)

PA: George Wilkins, *The Painful Adventures of Pericles Prince of Tyre* (1608), in Bullough, 492–546

RP: Richard Proudfoot, private communication.

Twine: Laurence Twine, *The Pattern of Painful Adventures*, in Bullough, 423–82.

TxC: Stanley Wells and Gary Taylor, with John Jowett and William Montgomery, *William Shakespeare: A Textual Companion* (Oxford, 1987)

Wayne, 'Political': Valerie Wayne, 'Political and textual corruption in *Pericles*', unpublished paper for *Pericles* seminar, Shakespeare Association of America, 1999.

Wayne, 'Textual': Valerie Wayne, 'The sexual politics of textual transmission', in Laurie E. Maguire and Thomas L. Berger (eds.), *Textual Formations and Reformations* (Newark, NJ, 1998), 179–210.

1. Honigmann—noting the presence of a Latin motto on the title-page of *The Miseries of Enforced Marriage* and the title-page notices declaring that *Miseries* and *The Travails of the Three English Brothers* were each published, most unusually, 'as . . . now played'—suggests that Wilkins may have been responsible for the publication of those plays 'against the wishes of the company' (Honigmann, 178–80).

2. Other plays 'made their way into print with very similar situations and sentiments intact', including *The Revenger's Tragedy, Women Beware Women* and Webster's tragedies, which 'revolve around the politically and sexually corrupt standards of the court' (Dutton, 197).

3. Clare calls the play 'among the most subversive of the period in its challenge to the dominant Jacobean ideology of non-resistance to the anointed ruler' (Clare, 186). Dutton and Clare disagree about the oppressiveness of the censorship—Dutton believes that the allowance of the Master of the Revels 'made for a range and complexity of expression on the social, political and even religious issues of the day that was remarkable' (Dutton, 248)—but even Clare concludes that 'There are no consistent political, moral or cultural criteria to be discerned' for censorship (Clare, 232).

4. Witgood, in Middleton's *A Trick to Catch the Old One*, similarly leaves his courtesan to marry the virginal Joyce.

Thompson, New Shakspere Society's four-text edition of Hamlet

1. Kliman's *Enfolded 'Hamlet'* appeared as a special issue of *The Shakespeare Newsletter* in 1996; Jesus Tronch-Perez, ed., *A synoptic 'Hamlet': A critical-synoptic edition of the second quarto and first folio texts of 'Hamlet'* (Valencia: Publicacions de la Universitat de Valencia, 2002).

Kastan, Shakespeare and the Book

1. The distinction is, of course, G. Thomas Tanselle's; see his *A Rationale of Textual Criticism* (Philadephia: University of Pennsylvania Press, 1989), esp. pp. 37–8, 57–8, and 68–70. See also Paul Eggert's 'Document and text: the "Life" of literary work and the capacities of edition,' *TEXT* 7 (1994): 1–24.

2. George P. Landow, *Hypertext: The Convergence of Contemporary Theory and Technology* (Baltimore: The Johns Hopkins University Press, 1992), p. 19.

3. See, for example, Roland Barthes, *S/Z* (1970), trans. Richard Miller (New York: Hill and Wang, 1975), pp. 5–6.

4. See Peter S. Donaldson, 'Digital Archive as Expanded Text: Shakespeare and Electronic Textuality,' in *Electronic Text: Investigations in Method and Theory*, ed. Kathryn Sutherland (Oxford: Oxford University Press, 1997), pp. 173–97; Peter Holland, 'Authorship and Collaboration: The Problem of Editing Shakespeare,' in *The Politics of the Electronic Text*, ed. Warren Cherniak, Caroline Davis, and Marilyn Deegan (Oxford: Office for Humanities Communication, 1993), pp. 17–23; and Philip Brockbank, 'Towards a Mobile Text,' in *The Theory and Practice of Text-Editing*, ed. Ian Small and Marcus Walsh (Cambridge: Cambridge University Press, 1992), pp. 90–106.

5. Patrick W. Connor, 'Hypertext in the Last Days of the Book,' *Bulletin of the John Rylands Library* 74 (1992): 20.

6. Donaldson, 'Digital Archive as Expanded Text: Shakespeare and Electronic Textuality,' p. 174.

7. Perhaps unsurprisingly, Richard Knowles quotes 'Wittgenstein's *mot*' in his essay on 'Variorum Commentary,' in *TEXT* 6 (1994): 41.

8. For a dark version of hypertext and digitization in general, see Gary Taylor's deliberately unmemorably titled, 'c:\wp\file.txt 05:41 10–07–98,' in *The Renaissance Text: Theory, Editing, Textuality*, ed. Andrew Murphy (Manchester: Manchester University Press, 2000), pp. 44–54. For a useful collection of essays more enthusiastically considering the effects of hypermedia technology, see *The Literary Text in the Digital Age*, ed. Richard J. Finneran (Ann Arbor: University of Michigan Press, 1996).

REFERENCES

Arber, Edward (ed.), *A Transcript of the Registers of the Company of Stationers of London: 1554–1640 AD*, 5 vols. (London, 1875–9; Birmingham, 1894)

Barthes, Roland, 'The Death of the Author', in *Image/Music/Text*, trans. Stephen Heath (New York: Hill and Wang, 1977), pp. 142–8.

Blayney, Peter W. M., *The Texts of 'King Lear' and Their Origins*. Vol. 1: *Nicholas Okes and the First Quarto* (Cambridge: Cambridge University Press, 1982)

Bullough, Geoffrey (ed.), *Narrative and Dramatic Sources of Shakespeare*, 8 vols. (London: Routledge, 1957–75)

Chambers, E. K. *The Elizabethan Stage*, 4 vols. (Oxford: Clarendon Press, 1923)

Clayton, Thomas (ed.), *The 'Hamlet' First Published (Q1, 1603): Origins, Form, Intertextulaties* (Newark: University of Delaware Press; London: Associated University Presses, 1992)

Duthie, George Ian, *The 'Bad' Quarto of Hamlet* (Cambridge: Cambridge University Press, 1941)

Elsky, Martin, *Authorizing Words: Speech, Writing, and Print in the English Renaissance* (Ithaca and London: Cornell University Press, 1989)

Foucault, Michel, 'What is an Author?', in Paul Rabinow (ed.), *The Foucault Reader* (New York: Pantheon, 1984), pp. 101–20.

Greg, W. W. *A Bibliography of the English Printed Drama to the Restoration*, 4 vols. (London: Bibliographical Society, 1939–59; reprinted 1962)

—— 'Entrance and copyright', *The Library*, 4th series, 26 (1945–6), 308–10.

—— 'Entrance, licence, and publication', *The Library*, 4th series, 25 (1944–5), 1–22.

—— 'The First Folio and its publishers', in The Shakespeare Association, *Studies in the First Folio* (London: Oxford University Press, 1924), pp. 129–56.

—— *The Shakespeare First Folio: Its Bibliographical and Textual History* (Oxford: Clarendon Press, 1956)

—— *Some Aspects and Problems of London Publishing between 1550 and 1650* (Oxford: Clarendon Press, 1956)

Kehler, Dorothea, 'The First Quarto of *Hamlet*: Reforming Widow Gertrude', *Shakespeare Quarterly*, 46 (1995), 398–413.

Melchiori, Giorgio, '*Hamlet*: The acting version and the wiser sort', in Thomas Clayton (ed.) (1992), pp. 195–210.

Ong, Walter J., *Orality and Literacy: The Technologizing of the Word* (London and New York: Methuen, 1982)

Pollard, Alfred W., *Shakespeare's Fight with the Pirates and the Problems of the Transmission of his Text* (London: Moring, 1917; 2nd edn, rev., Cambridge: Cambridge University Press, 1920)

—— *Shakespeare Folios and Quartos: A Study in the Bibliography of Shakespeare's Plays, 1594–1685* (London: Methuen, 1909)

—— and G. R. Redgrave (compilers), *A Short-Title Catalogue of Books Printed in England, Scotland and Ireland, and of English Books Printed Abroad, 1475–1640*, 2nd edn revised and enlarged by W. A. Jackson et al. 3 vols. (London: Bibliographical Society, 1976–91)

Pollard, Graham, 'The early constitution of the Stationers' Company', *The Library*, 4th series, 18 (1937–8), 235–60.

—— 'The Sandars Lectures, 1959', *Publishing History*, 4 (1978), 7–48.

Shaaber, M. A. 'The meaning of the imprint in early printed books', *The Library*, 4th series, 24 (1943–4), 120–41.

Urkowitz, Steven, ' "Well-sayd olde Mole": burying three *Hamlets* in modern editions', in *Shakespeare Study Today*, ed. Georgianna Ziegler (New York: AMS Press, 1986), pp. 37–70.

Yeandle, Laetitia, 'The Dating of Sir Edward Dering's Copy of "The History of King Henry the Fourth"', *Shakespeare Quarterly*, 37 (1986), 224–6.

Zitner, Sheldon P. (ed.), *The Knight of the Burning Pestle*, The Revels Plays (Manchester: Manchester University Press, 1984)

3

Histories

MARK THORNTON BURNETT
RAMONA WRAY

History occupies a central site in current reconceptualisations of the Renaissance. The move to situate an early modern text historically gradually gained momentum over the course of the 1980s, and was encouraged by the influential activity of critics working within the broad and fluid groupings of New Historicism and Cultural Materialism. Although revealing different political investments, these influential movements had in common an insistence upon the return of the literary work to the social, economic and cultural environment from whence it came. Such was the dominant effect of their shared venture that, although the terms for these schools of thinking have been superseded, a historicizing imperative is now regarded as an essential element in interpretive validity. In this connection, the relationship between the Renaissance literary text and its histories has come to seem crucial. How exactly does the text relate to its moment of production? Eschewing mimesis or notions of direct reflection, current critics focus on the complexity of a textual/historical interaction which is both densely constitutive and mutually interrogative. The emphasis is accordingly laid upon processes of negotiation, refraction, conversation and intervention. There can be no straightforward applications, not least because recent theorizations of history follow Hayden White in arguing for the textual or 'imaginary' status of the past. History is seen as a shifting set of discursive and material arrangements rather than a one-dimensional 'background' that lends itself to unambiguous recovery.[1] Louis Montrose describes current criticism in the extract featured here as revealing 'a reciprocal concern with the historicity of texts and the textuality of histories'.[2] The

---

[1] Hayden White, *The Content of the Form: Narrative Discourse and Historical Representation* (Baltimore and London: The Johns Hopkins University Press, 1987); *Metahistory: The Historical Imagination in Nineteenth-Century Europe* (Baltimore and London: The Johns Hopkins University Press, 1973).

[2] Louis Montrose, 'New Historicisms', in Stephen Greenblatt and Giles Gunn (eds.), *Redrawing the Boundaries: The Transformation of English and American Literary Studies* (New York: MLA, 1992), p. 410.

formulation usefully encapsulates both the historical location and material speci-ficity of texts, and the fact that all history is mediated through surviving 'textual traces', which are in turn open to interpretation and analysis.[3]

Inevitably, the claim that history is made up of 'textual traces' makes for a fundamental realignment of the ways in which the literary text intersects with, and takes energy from, other discourses. In short, the 'literary' is no longer judged to belong to a separate arena. Instead, the literary text joins all other texts as part of a level playing-field: it constitutes one site among many for the generation of social meaning. And, irrespective of their genre or category, texts displaying a variety of origins and affiliations can be subjected to literary investigation and made the subjects of familiarly formal critique. Early attempts to exemplify the interplay of culture commonly depended, probably too heavily, upon the use of a single anec-dote to connect the obscured with the privileged, the high with the low. Thus, the seminal work of Stephen Greenblatt, as the extract from *Renaissance Self-Fashioning* demonstrates, moves skillfully between the canonical Marlowe and the less instantly recognizable writings of John Sarracoll, although the latter, an Eliza-bethan merchant, is considered only briefly. Particularly in view of their emphasis upon known (and male) figures, such arbitrarily put together assemblages have come to seem inadequate. Probably because it unfolded in tandem with, as well as helped to introduce, new topics for discussion (such as censorship, patronage, power, authority and the nature of individual identity), such work has, over and above its attendant difficulties, simultaneously transfigured the field, inspiring a multiplicity of methodologically comparable arguments and propelling to the crit-ical forefront reinvigorated vocabularies (such as subversion, containment and dissidence).

If historicist work remains affected by this earlier efflorescence, it has also moved on, progressed and diversified. Hence, criticism of a historicizing tendency is now more likely to exhibit a sophisticated awareness of its own thematic investments and its specific deployments of Renaissance materials. At once this might be traced to an ongoing and unfolding dialogue between commentators of various persua-sions committed to, for instance, the post-colonial, queer and feminist historical record. (The second section below demonstrates just some of the variety of histor-ical contexts currently understood to animate Renaissance textual production, while later sections of this volume function as salutary reminders of the fact that most approaches to the Renaissance are currently informed by, and indebted to, historical paradigms.) Feminism is a case-in-point. Despite an initial uneasiness with elements of the new historicist debate—not least its generalizing undertow and seeming erasure of gender-specific questions—feminism has taken up histor-ical tools and responsibilities. And, of course, the process is two-way, with work by leading feminist scholars such as Catherine Belsey, Dympna Callaghan, Jean Howard, Ania Loomba and Kathleen McLuskie providing incisive reflections upon the possibilities and limitations of the historicist method. The result is a firmer and

---

[3] Catherine Gallagher and Stephen Greenblatt, *Practicing New Historicism* (Chicago: University of Chicago Press, 2000), p. 15.

more densely sophisticated sense of the histories of gender and the place of gender in history. Inside a more recent model, gender, rather than being addressed as an exclusive category of analysis or subordinated to an overarching discipline of power, is historically situated and integrated. It is inscribed within, and connected to, related concepts of class and race, each of which has been demonstrated as possessing an intricately-linked history of its own.

This is one way in which historical analysis has become increasingly specialized. A more general commitment to the 'local', and a drive to restore to the period a sense of conflicting particularities, have been urgently influential, as is evidenced in studies of micro-religious histories or apprehensions about the mixing of discrete castes in late sixteenth-century Ireland. In addition, Ireland's connections to Britain have been scrutinized as a part of an ongoing debate about precisely what constitutes 'Britain', its territories and peripheries. Reconceiving the Renaissance according to these principles has entailed a corresponding shift in constructions of the canon. A broader and more diffuse spectrum of early modern texts is presently investigated, from travel narratives and corporation accounts to ballads of popular invention and recollections of dreams. Not only has this exacerbated a dismantlement of canonical notions and continued the problematization of the 'literary', it has also exposed the period to more precise assessments and a deeper scrutiny. In particular, an emphasis on the variety of homes a text can inhabit has drawn attention away from ideological forms and towards structures of materialism.

The need for a more materialist apprehension of history has been voiced by several sections of the critical community. It is held in play, to single out just four examples, in Patricia Fumerton's call for a revitalized concentration on the 'ordinary', in Kim Hall's post-colonially-inspired reading of coloured objects, and in David Scott Kastan's interest in the institutional conditions of language and discourse. Even Juliet Fleming's piece on graffiti, extracted here, expresses the development, since it explores writing in a particularly unadulterated material manifestation. Dressed in these guises, history continues to be reconceived in criticism, to push at textual boundaries, and to test theoretical and generic perimeters.

1 | Theorizing the relationship between text and history

Jean Howard, 'The new historicism and Renaissance studies', *English Literary Renaissance*, 16 (1986), 24–30.

A common way of speaking about literature and history is just that way: literature *and* history, text *and* context. In these binary oppositions, if one term is stable and transparent and the other in some way mirrors it, then that other term can be stabilized and clarified, too. This is particularly crucial at a time when the notion of textuality has challenged traditional ideas about a literary work's communicative clarity and mimetic nature. By explaining literature by a ground extrinsic to itself, the ground of history, which literature supposedly reflects, the critic makes the problem of opacity disappear. But at a price. One result of seeing literature and history in this particular way is the inevitable 'flattening' of the literary work. It is emptied of its rich signifying potentiality by being used as a springboard to something else, a mere pointer back to extratextual reality, as when Duke Vincentio is read simply as a representation of James I and the whole of *Measure for Measure* reduced to a comment on this monarch's beliefs and practices. Literature thus becomes, not something to be *read*, but to be *explained*. Second, such a procedure seldom stops to question why a particular historical context has been selected to align with the literary text, as if such choices were not often arbitrary in the extreme and inimical to seeing the full intertextual network in which a literary work exists. Third, the practice reduces literature to a merely mimetic object. I don't think any serious historical criticism can dodge the fact that undertaking such criticism raises the questions of some relationship between literature and what may be considered external to itself. The key question is: what is the nature of that relationship? Does the text absorb history into itself? Does it reflect an external reality? Does it produce the real?

It increasingly seems that in confronting these issues a new historical criticism has to accept, first, that 'history' is not objective, transparent, unified, or easily knowable and consequently is extremely problematic as a concept for grounding the meaning of a literary text; second, that the very binarism we casually reinforce every time we speak of literature and history, text and context, is unproductive and misleading. Literature is *part* of history, the literary text as much a context for other aspects of cultural and material life as they are for it. Rather than erasing the problem of textuality, one must enlarge it in order to see that *both* social and literary texts are opaque, self-divided, and porous, that is, open to the mutual intertextual influences of one another. This move means according literature real power. Rather than passively reflecting an external reality, literature is an agent in constructing a culture's sense of reality. It is part of a much larger symbolic order through which the world at a particular historical moment is conceptualized and through which a culture imagines its relationship to the actual conditions of its existence. In short, instead of a hierarchical relationship in which literature figures as the parasitic reflector of historical fact, one imagines a complex textualized universe in which literature participates in historical processes and in the political management of reality.

I take as an exemplary brief example of these assumptions Don Wayne's work on the way Ben Jonson's plays help to produce an ideology for a pre-capitalist age. Wayne argues that while Jonson seemingly remained an apologist for an older feudal ideology which stressed the importance of the social collectivity over the individual, plays such as *The Alchemist and Bartholomew Fair* find him paradoxically promulgating contractual rights by which the prerogatives of the individual are secured, including the rights of individual authorship.[1] Clearly Jonson is responding to something in the social formation around him—to the emerging possibilities for printing texts as individual enterprises, to the breakdown of a national sense of community under the Stuarts, to the allure of the entrepreneurial spirit released by Puritanism and by the growth of the London merchant and professional class. Yet Wayne's chief point is that Jonson is also—through his dramatic texts—*producing* the modes of thought that encouraged and to some extent created these other changes so that it becomes nearly impossible to pinpoint an origin or single cause for social change. Many aspects of the social formation, including literary texts, work in a variety of ways and at a variety of speeds to produce the variegated entity we call history.

A major feature of a new historical criticism, therefore, must be a suspicion about an unproblematic binarism between literature and history and a willingness to explore the ways in which literature does more than reflect a context outside itself and instead constitutes one of the creative forces of history. In fact, until one truly banishes a mimetic theory of literature, several problems which have characteristically bedeviled the historical study of literature will continue to rear their heads. It is always interesting, for example, to watch what happens when people read Lawrence Stone on the Renaissance family and then try to relate what they find there to, say, Shakespeare's romantic comedies. Stone argues that marriages, at least among the middle and upper classes, were made late, were arranged by parents, were made largely for economic convenience, not love, and resulted in conjugal and parent-child relationships often lacking in warmth and intimacy.[2] What has all this to do with the picture of romantic love and rebellion against parental authority we see in Shakespeare's comedies? On the surface, not much; but what does this discrepancy mean: that Stone got things wrong? that literature is autonomous from the social realm? that Shakespeare is a universal genius who got at the enduring truths of life rather than at the anomalies of a particular historical moment? that literature is, after all, something to be read on a bus, a pure escape from the real? It is when faced with just these sorts of problems that one realizes the need for more than a simple mimetic theory of literature. A culture's discourse about love and the family need not, and probably seldom does, correspond exactly to how people live. (One could say the same about politics, economics, or personal identity.) One of the great strengths of Foucault, in my view, is his recognition that the discursive practices of an age, while producing or enabling certain behaviours, never coincide with them exactly. There is always some gap between what discourse authorizes and what people do, though 'history' may never be able to disclose that gap precisely. What is important is how and why cultures produce and naturalize particular constructions of reality: what contradictions such constructions neutralize or expose, what economic and political ends they advance, what kinds of power relations they display. Literature is one of many elements participating in a culture's representation of reality to itself, helping to form its discourse on the family, the state, the individual, helping to make the world intelligible, though not necessarily helping to represent it 'accurately.'

In any particular instance, to see how a text functions in the construal of reality means seeing it in an intertextual network of considerable historical specificity. For example, to understand how women were made intelligible in the Renaissance, one cannot look only to social 'facts,' such as how many children they had, or of what diseases and at what ages they died. One must also consider how the medical, legal, and religious spheres functioned to provide a discourse about women which may have represented them in ways quite at odds with what *we* see as the apparent 'facts' of their situation. The whole point is to grasp the terms of the discourse which made it possible to see the 'facts' in a particular way—indeed, made it possible to see certain phenomena *as* facts at all. Only then will we begin to grasp how another period shaped individuals as historical subjects; and to see literature's role in this process one must place literary representations in a much broader differential field in which *how* they correspond to or challenge other constructions of reality and *how* they take their place in a particular configuration of discursive practices and power relations can be observed.

In this rethinking of the place of literature *in* history, it seems to me that much of the historically-based literary criticism can benefit from recent developments in Marxist thought. It used to be that Marxism, while providing one of the few theoretically coherent approaches to an historical criticism, suffered from its own version of the history/literature binarism in that it saw in literature and other elements of 'the superstructure' a reflection of the dominant economic mode of production and of the class struggle it spawned. In other words, a particular privilege was given to the economic realm as the determining factor in every sort of cultural production and in the shaping of human consciousness. This assumption has been challenged, perhaps most influentially, by Louis Althusser, who argues for the *relative* autonomy of the super-structure from the material base and for the importance of the educational apparatus, the institution of literature, and other factors, in the shaping of human consciousness. In short, he acknowledges that there is not an homologous relationship between all levels of culture such that the ideologies of the superstructure can in any simple way be related to an economic base. Consequently, one finds the question of cause and effect relationship more complicated than was formerly thought, as I have already noted in regard to Wayne's work on Jonson; and one must take more seriously than before the role of literature in changing human consciousness and so, eventually, in affecting other material practices—not merely being affected by them.[3]

Furthermore, while it has always been Marxist criticism which has most insistently probed the question of literature's relationship to ideology, contemporary Marxism has developed more complex ways of approaching that question than it formerly possessed. While ideology is a vexed term with a complex history, it may be useful to distinguish two of its most common definitions: first, as the false consciousness foisted on the working classes by a dominant class; second, as any of those practices by which one imagines one's relations to the actual condi-tions of one's existence.[4] This second, Althusserian definition of ideology denies that the ideological is simply the product of a conspiratorial power group. Rather, the ideological is omnipresent; it inheres in every representation of reality and every social practice, as all of these inevitably confirm or naturalize a particular construction(s) of reality. Consequently, there is no way in which ideology can ever be absent from literature, any more than it can be absent from *any* discursive practice. Jonathan Dollimore argues, and I agree with him, that it may be useful to retain both understandings of ideology: to retain the option of seeing some literature as the conscious and direct product of one power group or class's attempts to control another group or class by the misrepresentation of their historical condition; and at the same time to recognize that in most instances power groups or classes are both less self-conscious and less monolithic than such a formulation implies and that a more complex approach to the problem of ideology requires a recognition of the pervasive, masterless (in the sense of acknowledging no one origin), and often heterogeneous nature of the ideological.

This being so, that the ideological is everywhere and traverses literature as surely as other modes of representation, the question becomes: does literature have a special way of treating the ideological? This, of course, has been an issue that has bedeviled Marxism for some time. In the 1960s Pierre Machery contended that literature, separate both from science and ideol-ogy, inevitably produced a *parody* of ideology, a treatment of it which inevitably distanced the reader from the ideological matter being treated, exposing its contradictions and laying bare the artifice surrounding its production.[5] But does literature really handle the ideological in this way? I think not, at least not in every instance. First, as Tony Bennett has recently shown, such a view rests on the premise (deriving most centrally in the twentieth century from Russian Formalism) that literature is a special and unique form of writing with its own inherent and universal properties, one of which is the way it acquires internal distance from the ideological material which traverses it.[6] But as any historian of literature can show, the literary canon is a social construct, not an empirical given. As a number of boundary cases make clear today, some texts are regularly treated as literature and as something else. For example, are Bacon's essays literature or philosophy? Are diaries literature or something else? Is travel literature really literature or history or even philosophy? While it is quite possible in practical terms to speak of a literary canon, it seems quite another matter to assume that the texts in that canon are there by virtue of some mysterious inner property which they all share. They are all there for a variety of reasons having to do with the privileging of certain artifacts by powerful groups, and their 'properties' are in large measure the result of the operations performed upon them by generations of critics.[7] Hence, while it may be useful for strategic or practical purposes to retain the category 'literature,' it seems wrong to assign to the texts gathered under that rubric a single, universal stance toward the ideological.

In fact, I would argue that a new historical criticism attempting to talk about the ideological function of literature in a specific period can most usefully do so only by seeing a specific work relationally—that is, by seeing how its representations stand in regard to those of other specific works and discourses. A work can only be said to contest, subvert, recuperate, or reproduce dominant ideologies (and it may do any of these) if one can place the work—at least provisionally and strategically—in relation to others. And, as I have argued above, the most illuminating field of reference may not be just other literary works. To return to the example of the representation of women: in order to understand the ideological function of, say, certain plays for the public theater, it may be important to see their representations of women in the light of the representations offered in masques, in conduct manuals, in medical treatises, and in Puritan polemics all written at approximately the same time.

Moreover, it seems important to entertain the possibility that neither literary texts nor other cultural productions are monologic, organically unified wholes. Only when their heterogeneity is suppressed by a criticism committed to the idea of organic unity do they seem to reveal a unitary ideological perspective or generic code. It may be more productive to see them as sites where many voices of culture and many systems of intelligibility interact. Dominick La Capra makes this point, and in doing so he draws both on the work of Jacques Derrida and on that of Mikhail Bakhtin, thus uniting deconstruction and Marxist demystification in the project of fracturing the unified surface of the text to let the multiplicity of its social voices be heard. In this project he finds two of Bakhtin's concepts, *heteroglossia* and *camivalization* (in Michael Holquist's translation), to be particularly useful in that the first suggests that novelized discourse is polyvalent, riddled with 'unofficial' voices contesting, subverting, and parodying dominant discourses, while the second suggests that the emergence in writing of these 'unofficial' voices has the revolutionary potential to expose the arbitrary nature of official constructions of the real.[8] But it is important to remember that for Bakhtin not all literature performs a carnivalizing function or is dialogic and polyvalent. There are no inherent laws governing the functioning of those texts we call literature. Consequently, one of the greatest challenges facing a new historical criticism is to find a way to talk about and discriminate among the many *different* ways in which literature is traversed by—and produces—the ideologies of its time.

*   *   *

Frances E. Dolan, *Whores of Babylon: Catholicism, Gender and Seventeenth-Century Print Culture* (Ithaca and London: Cornell University Press, 1999), pp. 2–3.

Although I continue to be interested in disparities among different registers of evidence, I am less confident that there is any kind of evidence that stands before or beyond interpretation. For instance, whereas I once resorted to court records, albeit slyly, for more reliable or more direct access to 'what really happened', I now view court records as themselves representations, shaped by occasion and convention, rather than as standards against which to check the accuracy of, say, plays. Published accounts of trials can stand as one example of how indistinguishable are 'documents' and 'representations'. Multiple narratives about the most notorious crimes and trials survive, each inflected by its author, its authorization, its intended audience, its timing. Yet we do not have 'transcripts'; that is, official, exhaustive manuscript accounts that purport to record verbatim what happened in the courtroom. Furthermore, the fullest accounts of witnesses' testimony are often those published in pamphlet form. If transcripts existed, they would not necessarily offer the historian any greater certainty. Yet their absence reminds us that we have no recourse outside of representation. I am arguing not that representations offer direct access to what really happened, but rather that even legal records, widely employed as the most reliable of documents, are 'representations' we must read with caution. In viewing legal evidence with suspicion, I am in accord with many historians who work with these records.

   Why would an enquiry into representations of Catholicism lead me to reconsider my standards of evidence and notions of history? Because early modern debates about Catholics and Catholicism were simultaneously debates about England's history and about what might constitute knowledge. If seventeenth-century English men and women had been certain of the outcome of religious and political struggles, if they had even been certain that Catholicism should or would recede into the margins and into the past, they would not have needed to write so voluminously and vituperatively against it. Since their uncertainty drove their prolixity, I make uncertainty my subject, rather than attempting to correct or compensate for it.

*   *   *

Louis Montrose, 'New historicisms', in Stephen Greenblatt and Giles Gunn, (eds.), *Redrawing the Boundaries: The Transformation of English and American Literary Studies* (New York: MLA, 1992), pp. 400–6.

In a typical new-historicist essay or book chapter, the Geertzian model of thick description is evident in the initial deployment of an exemplary anecdote as a strategy of cultural and historical estrangement. In some examples of new-historicist work, such anecdotes may be elaborated into the interpretive units from which a sustained argument emerges; in others, the method may seem merely fashionable and formulaic, a vaguely associative accumulation of historical curiosities. Thus Walter Cohen characterizes new-historicist method (or, perhaps, antimethod) as 'arbitrary connectedness': 'The strategy is governed methodologically by the assumption that any one aspect of a society is related to any other. No organizing principle determines these relationships' (34). And in order to describe this phenomenon, Dominick LaCapra offers the generous choice of 'facile associationism, juxtaposition, or pastiche . . . weak montage, or, if you prefer, cut-and-paste bricolage' (*Soundings* 193). New-historicist work has been particularly susceptible to such responses because it has frequently failed to theorize its method or its model of culture in any sustained way. Proceeding on the basis of tacit and perhaps inconsistent notions about cultural dynamics, new-historicist studies may sometimes seem to imply that the objects they analyze are connected merely by a principle of cultural contingency or by the wit of the critic ('arbitrary connectedness'); or, on the contrary, that they have a necessary connection that is grounded in a principle of cultural determinism ('containment').

Having first called his critical project a 'cultural poetics' in *Renaissance Self-Fashioning* (4–5), Greenblatt returns to and develops the term in *Shakespearean Negotiations*. This enterprise is now defined as a 'study of the collective making of distinct cultural practices and inquiry into the relations among these practices'; its relevant concerns are 'how collective beliefs and experiences were shaped, moved from one medium to another, concentrated in manageable aesthetic form, offered for consumption [and] how the boundaries were marked between cultural practices understood to be art forms and other, contiguous, forms of expression' (5). Described, in conspicuously formalist and structuralist terms, as a study of distinctions among '*contiguous* . . . forms of expression' (my emphasis), cultural poetics tends to emphasize structural relations at the expense of sequential processes; in effect, it orients the axis of intertextuality synchronically, as the text of a cultural system, rather than diachronically, as the text of an autonomous literary history.

One of the implications of Greenblatt's formulation—an implication already present in the widespread early new-historicist reliance on Geertzian notions of culture—is that 'art forms and other, contiguous, forms of expression' are expressive of some underlying causal principle or generative and restrictive cultural code, that they are thus organically related to one another, and that this genetic relationship among practices is manifested in their surface articulation as a tropological system. Thus Greenblatt writes in the essay 'Fiction and Friction':

> The relation I wish to establish between medical and theatrical practice is not one of cause and effect or source and literary realization. We are dealing rather with a shared code, a set of interlocking tropes and similitudes that function not only as objects but as the conditions of representation.
>
> (*Shakespearean Negotiations* 86)

The cultural model implicit in such new-historicist work seems to have its origins in a cross between Geertzian and Foucauldian conceptual schemes: specifically, between Geertz's integrative sense of culture, his construal of culture as a localized and collective system of symbols, and Foucault's early epistemic history, which elucidates similitudes and rejects causality 'in order to establish those diverse converging, and sometimes divergent, but never autonomous series that enable us to circumscribe the "locus" of an event, the limits to its fluidity and the conditions of its emergence' (Foucault, 'Discourse' 230). Some elements of new-historicist critical practice that have puzzled or irritated its critics may be explicable (though not, therefore, always or easily defensible) as consequences of this implicit cultural model. Certain examples of new-historicist work imply that a culture is a shared system of symbols expressive of a cohesive and closed (a 'restricted' or 'sutured') ideology. The problematic or contested consequences of such a model tend to suggest its affinities with formalist modes of analysis.

They include the methodological assumption of tropological rather than causal relations among new historicism's objects of study; the emphasis on culture as a text, on the discursivity of material life and of social and political relations; the critic's self-imposed limitation to the study of synchronic intracultural processes, exemplified in particular texts and textualized performances; and the apparent incompatibility of the cultural paradigm with the dynamics of ideological resistance, conflict, and change.

The terms in which the problematic of ideology and resistance came to be posed in new-historicist studies of the Renaissance—terms that have now become widely established in other fields of specialization—are those of a simplistic, reductive, and hypostatized opposition between 'containment' and 'subversion.' These terms—which appear to be residues of a cold war ideology that had pernicious consequences in both international and domestic policy—prove once again to be wholly inadequate instruments of analysis and debate. Nevertheless, they are significant indicators of a shift of perspective within Anglo-American literary criticism and its ambient political culture. As the problem of ideology has become an acceptable and even a central topic of critical discourse in the American academy, so the emphases in socio-cultural analysis have shifted from unity, reciprocity, and consent to difference, domination, and resistance. It is precisely this shift of emphasis from canonicity and consensus to diversity and contestation that, during the past decade, has been the focus of the national debate about the direction of the humanities—a debate that has been waged on the campuses and on the best-seller lists, in the public media and in the policy statements and funding priorities of government agencies. It is within the context of these cultural politics—and as their dis-placement—that the 'new historicism' has been constituted as an academic site of ideological struggle between containment and subversion. This struggle may be reduced to the following scenario. Critics who emphasize the possibilities for the effective agency of individual or collective subjects against forms of domination, exclusion, and assimilation have energetically contested critics who stress the capacity of the early modern state, as personified in the monarch, to *contain* apparently subversive gestures, or even to *produce* them precisely in order to contain them. According to a now-notorious argument in Greenblatt's essay 'Invisible Bullets,' the ability of the dominant order to generate subversion so as to use it to its own ends marks 'the very condition of power' (45). Thus a generalized argument for the 'containment of subversion' is itself subversive of arguments for the agency of subjects, which it reduces to the illusory and delusive effects of a dominant order. The binary logic of subversion-containment produces a closed conceptual structure of reciprocally defining and dependent terms, terms that are complementary and mutually complicit.

One can readily see that the larger assumptions and implications of a 'containment' position concerning the operations of ideology might be suspect or even alarming, not only to tradi-tionalists who cherish liberal humanist ideals of individual self-determination but also to those cultural critics who have a stake in making their own discursive practice a direct intervention in the process of ideological reproduction. At its extreme, the 'containment of subversion' pos-ition suggests a reading of Foucault that emphasizes the discontinuity of history and the inescapable subjection of subjects; it makes no theoretical space for change or for contest-ation. Such a position might be said to reinstate the Elizabethan world picture, but now transposed into the ironic mode. Recent commentators have, with increasing frequency, seized on the provocative argument of 'Invisible Bullets,' misleadingly ascribed to the essay the claims of a cultural law, and then inaccurately represented it as the central tenet of the new historicism—sometimes using it to characterize the work of those who have been explicitly engaged in contesting Greenblatt's thesis. Such assertions gain credibility and authority simply from their frequent repetition in print; nevertheless, subscription to the 'containment hypothesis' in no way characterizes the work of all those writers identified as new historicists, any more than it characterizes all of Greenblatt's work—or, for that matter, all of Foucault's.

The putatively Foucauldian new-historicist argument for the dominant's production and containment of subversion is pungently characterized by Frank Lentricchia as 'a prearranged theatre of struggle set upon the substratum of a monolithic agency which produces "opposition" as one of its delusive political effects' ('Foucault's Legacy' 234). However, such a strict containment argument oversimplifies Foucault's subtle, flexible, and dynamic conception of power by suggesting that the volatile and contingent relations of power that saturate social space are actually determined by the crystallization of power in the state apparatus. Foucault emphasizes that

> [p]ower's condition of possibility . . . must not be sought in the primary existence of a central point, in a unique source of sovereignty from which secondary and descendent forms would emanate; it is the moving substrate of force relations which, by virtue of their inequality, constantly engender states of power, but the latter are always local and unstable.
>
> (*History* 1: 93)

For Foucault, power is never monolithic; and power relations always imply multiple sites not only of power but also of resistance. He writes that such sites of resistance are of variable configuration, intensity, and effectiveness:

> The strictly relational character of power relationships . . . depends on a multiplicity of points of resistance: these play the role of adversary, target, support, or handle in power relations . . . Resistance . . . can only exist in the strategic field of power relations. But this does not mean that they are only a reaction or rebound, forming with respect to the basic domination an underside that is in the end always passive, doomed to perpetual defeat. . . . The points, knots, or focuses of resistance are spread over time and space at varying densities. Are there no great radical ruptures, massive binary divisions, then? Occasionally, yes. But more often one is dealing with mobile and transitory points of resistance, producing cleavages in a society that shift about, fracturing unities and effecting regroupings, furrowing across individuals themselves. . . . It is doubtless the strategic codification of these points of resistance that makes a revolution possible, somewhat similar to the way in which the state relies on the institutional integration of power relationships.
>
> (1: 95–96)

Foucault's flexible conception of power relations may accommodate local instances of a subversion that is produced for containment, but it also acknowledges revolutionary social transformations and other possible modalities of power and resistance. If, on the one hand, ideological dominance can never be monolithic, total, and closed, then, on the other hand, revolutionary upheavals occur relatively rarely; modes and instances of resistance—

subversions, contestations, transgressions, appropriations—tend to be local and dispersed in their occurrences, variable and limited in their consequences. Thus one need look no further than Foucault's own work for confirmation of the hopeless inadequacy of subversion-containment as an explanatory model for the dynamism and specificity of relations of power, and for the necessity to make more subtle discriminations among the modalities of resistance and among their various conditions of possibility.

Within the context of the containment-subversion debate, my own position has been that a closed and static, monolithic and homogeneous notion of ideology must be replaced by one that is heterogeneous and unstable, permeable and processual. Raymond Williams's invaluable *Marxism and Literature* theorizes ideology in just such dynamic and dialogic terms. By emphasizing 'interrelations between movements and tendencies both within and beyond a specific and effective dominance' (121), Williams clarifies the existence, at any point in time, of residual and emergent, oppositional and alternative values, meanings, and practices. The shifting conjunctures of such 'movements and tendencies' may create conceptual sites within the ideological field from which the dominant can be contested, and against which it must be continuously redefined and redefended—and so, perforce, continuously transformed. An ideological dominance is qualified by the specific conjunctures of ethnic, gender, class, profession, age, and other social positions occupied by individual cultural producers; by the heterogeneous positionality of the spectators, auditors, and readers who consume, appropriate, and resist cultural productions; and by the relative autonomy—the properties, possibilities, and limitations—of the cultural medium being worked. In other words, allowance must be made for the manifold mediations involved in the production, reproduction, and appropriation of an ideological dominance: for the collective, sectional, and individual agency of the state's subjects, and for the resources, conventions, and modes of production and distribution of the representational forms that they employ. In its emphasis on a dynamic, agonistic, and temporal model of culture and ideology—a ceaseless contest among dominant and subordinate positions, a ceaseless interplay of continuity and change, of identity and difference—such a perspective opens cultural poetics to history.

Such binary terms as *containment* and *subversion, dominance* and *contestation* are always dialectical and relative; their configuration, content, and effect are produced in specific and changing conjunctures. During the 1940s and 1950s, literary-historical scholarship was much concerned to demonstrate the ideological orthodoxy of such canonical authors as Shakespeare. In the climate of recent cultural politics, however, it has become fashionable for critics to affirm their favorite canonical literary works to be 'subversive' of their own canonicity. Frequently, such claims are based on analyses that are less historical and dialectical than formal and immanent, implying that 'subversiveness' is an essence secreted in particular texts or classes of texts. However, as Jonathan Dollimore points out in his introduction to *Political Shakespeare*:

> Nothing can be intrinsically or essentially subversive in the sense that prior to the event subversiveness can be more than potential; in other words it cannot be guaranteed a priori, independent of articulation, context and reception. Likewise the mere thinking of a radical idea is not what makes it subversive: typically it is the context of its articulation: to whom, how many and in what circumstances; one might go further and suggest that not only does the idea have to be conveyed, it has also actually to be used to refuse authority

or be seen by authority as capable and likely of being so used. It is, then, somewhat misleading to speak freely and only of 'subversive thought'; what we are concerned with . . . is a social *process*.

(13)

Crucial here is the concept of a 'context of . . . articulation,' which must include not only the social effectivity of a particular notion, formulation, or action but also the historical and social specificity of its subsequent representations; in other words, it must include the context of articulation—or, following Tony Bennett, what we might also call the reading formation—within which we retrospectively inscribe, identify, and interpret 'subversion.' Ideology can be said to exist only as it is instantiated in particular cultural forms and practices, including those traditionally categorized as literature and as criticism. All texts are ideologically marked, however multivalent or inconsistent that inscription may be. And if the ideological status of texts in the literary canon is necessarily overdetermined and unstable, it is so precisely as a condition and consequence of their canonicity. If, for example, I characterize *Hamlet* as a 'complex' text, I am not reverting to an aesthetics of immanence, unity, and closure; rather I am describing the transformation of a *text* into an open, changing, and contradictory *discourse* that is cumulatively produced and appropriated within history and within a history of other productions and appropriations. In so historically and socially sedimented a textual space—an always occupied space that signifies to a historically and ideologically sited reader—so many cultural codes converge and interact that ideological coherence and stability are scarcely possible.

* * *

Tina Krontiris, *Oppositional Voices: Women as Writers and Translators of Literature in the English Renaissance* (London and New York: Routledge, 1992), pp. 21–3.

Most women, though not all, include in the dedication or preface of their work an apology which recognizes, at least for the sake of appearance, the inferiority of the work on account of the author's sex. Dedicating a work to a man or to a respectable woman likewise provided an indirect strategy for venturing into publication. Both Margaret Tyler and Emilia Lanyer dedicate their works to respectable and aristocratic former employers. Some women present themselves as reluctant to publish what they have written and cite the persuasive influence of friends or acquaintances. This is the case with Isabella Whitney and Margaret Tyler. Others, like the young Elizabeth Cary, keep much of what they write in private circulation, until someone with greater authority prompts them to publish their work. In this respect, women usually relied on support from men sympathetic to their accomplishments, and there were a few such men around [. . .]

[These] strategies [. . .] are not peculiar to women, nor are the types of ideologies women oppose. In a period when writers depended to a large extent on patronage, when censorship on political and religious grounds was heavily imposed, and when to publish for profit was considered somewhat demeaning, male writers often developed and deployed similar strategies. But when used by female writers, such strategies acquire a different meaning because they are responses to an ideology and culture that denied women self-expression. Similarly, voicing opposition to dominant ideology is potentially more subversive in the case of a woman, because of the different position of the two sexes in Renaissance society [. . .] Thus Philip Sidney's criticism of his culture in his romance is less transgressive than Mary Wroth's in hers, not only because the *Urania* is a more oppositional work than the *Arcadia* in matters of gender, but primarily because the female author is not supposed to be writing romances in the first place. Also, a woman publishing a play about Cleopatra is not the same as a man doing it. The point is not, therefore, that women's writing is different from men's, but that it has to be *read* differently.

· ·

QUESTIONS

- How has the relationship between text and history been reconceived?
- To what extent is the relationship between text and history gendered?
- How far can any text be seen as historical evidence?

2 | Historicizing the Renaissance literary text

Stephen Greenblatt, *Renaissance Self-Fashioning: From More to Shakespeare* (Chicago and London: University of Chicago Press, 1980), pp. 193–200.

On 26 June 1586 a small fleet, financed by the Earl of Cumberland, set out from Gravesend for the South Seas. It sailed down the West African coast, sighting Sierra Leone in October, and at this point we may let one of those on board, the merchant John Sarracoll, tell his own story:

> The fourth of November we went on shore to a town of the Negroes, . . . which we found to be but lately built: it was of about two hundred houses, and walled about with mighty great trees, and stakes so thick, that a rat could hardly get in or out. But as it chanced, we came directly upon a port which was not shut up, where we entered with such fierceness, that the people fled all out of the town, which we found to be finely built after their fashion, and the streets of it so intricate that it was difficult for us to find the way out that we came in at. We found their houses and streets so finely and cleanly kept that it was an admiration to us all, for that neither in the houses nor streets was so much dust to be found as would fill an egg shell. We found little in their houses, except some mats, gourds, and some earthen pots. Our men at their departure set the town on fire, and it was burnt (for the most part of it) in a quarter of an hour, the houses being covered with reed and straw.[1]

This passage is atypical, for it lacks the blood bath that usually climaxes these incidents, but it will serve as a reminder of what until recently was called one of the glorious achievements of Renaissance civilization, and it will serve as a convenient bridge from the world of Edmund Spenser to the world of Christopher Marlowe.

What is most striking in Sarracoll's account, of course, is the casual, unexplained violence. Does the merchant feel that the firing of the town needs no explanation? If asked, would he have had one to give? Why does he take care to tell us why the town burned so quickly, but not why it was burned? Is there an aesthetic element in his admiration of the town, so finely built, so intricate, so cleanly kept? And does this admiration conflict with or somehow fuel the destructiveness? If he feels no uneasiness at all, why does he suddenly shift and write not *we* but *our men* set the town on fire? Was there an order or not? And, when he recalls the invasion, why does he think of rats? The questions are all met by the moral blankness that rests like thick snow on Sarracoll's sentences: 'The 17th. day of November we departed from Sierra Leona, directing our course for the Straits of Magellan.'

If, on returning to England in 1587, the merchant and his associates had gone to see the Lord Admiral's Men perform a new play, *Tamburlaine the Great*, they would have seen an extraordinary meditation on the roots of their own behavior. For despite all the exoticism in Marlowe—Scythian shepherds, Maltese Jews, German magicians—it is his own countrymen that he broods upon and depicts. As in Spenser, though to radically different effect, the 'other world' becomes a mirror.[2] If we want to understand the historical matrix of Marlowe's achievement, the analogue to Tamburlaine's restlessness, aesthetic sensitivity, appetite, and violence, we might look not at the playwright's literary sources, not even at the relentless power-hunger of Tudor absolutism, but at the acquisitive energies of English merchants, entrepreneurs, and adventurers, promoters alike of trading companies and theatrical companies.

But what bearing does Marlowe actually have on a passage like the one with which I opened? He is, for a start, fascinated by the idea of the stranger in a strange land. Almost all of his heroes are aliens or wanderers, from Aeneas in Carthage to Barabas in Malta, from Tamburlaine's endless campaigns to Faustus's demonic flights. From his first play to his last, Marlowe is drawn to the idea of physical movement, to the problem of its representation within the narrow confines of the theater. Tamburlaine almost ceaselessly traverses the stage, and when he is not actually on the move, he is imagining campaigns or hearing reports of grueling marches. The obvious effect is to enact the hero's vision of a nature that 'Doth teach us all to have aspiring minds' and of the soul that 'Wills us to wear ourselves and never rest' (1 *Tam* 2.6.871, 877). But as always in Marlowe, this enactment, this realization on the level of the body in time and space, complicates, qualifies, exposes, and even mocks the abstract conception. For the cumulative effect of this restlessness is not so much heroic as grotesquely comic, if we accept Bergson's classic definition of the comic as the mechanical imposed upon the living. Tamburlaine *is* a machine, a desiring machine that produces violence and death. Menaphon's admiring description begins by making him sound like Leonardo's Vitruvian Man or Michelangelo's David and ends by making him sound like an expensive mechanical device, one of those curious inventions that courtiers gave to the queen at New Year's: a huge, straight, strongly jointed creature with a costly pearl placed between his shoulders, the pearl inscribed with celestial symbols. Once set in motion, this *thing* cannot slow down or change course; it moves at the same frenzied pace until it finally stops.

One further effect of this unvarying movement is that, paradoxically, very little progress seems to be made, despite fervent declarations to the contrary. To be sure, the scenes change, so quickly at times that Marlowe seems to be battering against the boundaries of his own medium: at one moment the stage represents a vast space, then suddenly contracts to a bed, then turns in quick succession into an imperial camp, a burning town, a besieged fortress, a battlefield, a tent. But then all of those spaces seem curiously alike. The relevant contrast is *Antony and Cleopatra* where the restless movement is organized around the deep structural opposition of Rome and Egypt, or *1 Henry IV* where the tavern, the court, and the country are perceived as diversely shaped spaces, spaces that elicit and echo different tones, energies, and even realities. In *Tamburlaine* Marlowe contrives to efface all such differences, as if to insist upon the essential meaninglessness of theatrical space, the vacancy that is the dark side of its power to imitate any place. This vacancy—quite literally, this absence of scenery—is the equivalent in the medium of the theater to the secularization of space, the abolition of qualitative up and down, which for Cassirer is one of the greatest achievements of Renaissance philosophy, the equivalent then to the reduction of the universe to the coordinates of a map:[3]

> Give me a Map, then let me see how much
> Is left for me to conquer all the world,
> That these my boys may finish all my wants.
> (*2 Tam* 5.3.4516–18)

Space is transformed into an abstraction, then fed to the appetitive machine. This is the voice of conquest, but it is also the voice of wants never finished and of transcendental homelessness. And though the characters and situations change, that voice is never entirely absent in Marlowe. Barabas does not leave Malta, but he is the quintessential alien: at one point his house is seized and turned into a nunnery, at another he is thrown over the walls of the city, only to rise with the words, 'What, all alone?' Edward II should be the very opposite; he is, by his role, the embodiment of the land and its people, but without Gaveston he lives in his own country like an exile. Only in *Doctor Faustus* does there seem to be a significant difference: having signed away his soul and body, Faustus begins a course of restless wandering, but at the close of the twenty-four years, he feels a compulsion to return to Wittenberg.[4] Of course, it is ironic that when a meaningful sense of place finally emerges in Marlowe, it does so only as a place to die. But the irony runs deeper still. For nothing in the covenant or in any of the devil's speeches requires that Faustus has to pay his life where he originally contracted to sell it; the urge is apparently in Faustus, as if he felt there were a fatality in the place he had undertaken his studies, felt it appropriate and even necessary to die there and nowhere else. 'O would I had never seen Wittenberg,' he despairingly tells his friends. But the play has long before this exposed such a sense of place to radical questioning. To Faustus's insistent demands to know the 'where about' of hell, Mephistophilis replies,

> Hell hath no limits, nor is circumscrib'd
> In one self place, for where we are is hell,
> And where hell is, must we ever be.
> (567–69)

By implication, Faustus's feeling about Wittenberg is an illusion, one of a network of fictions by which he constitutes his identity and his world. Typically, he refuses to accept the account of a limitless, inner hell, countering with the extraordinary, and in the circumstances, ludicrous 'I think hell's a fable.' Mephistophilis's quiet response slides from parodic agreement to devastating irony: 'Aye, think so still, till experience change thy mind.'[5] The experience of which the devil speaks can refer not only to torment after death but to Faustus's life in the remainder of the play: the half-trivial, half-daring exploits, the alternating states of bliss and despair, the questions that are not answered and the answers that bring no real satisfaction, the wanderings that lead nowhere. The chilling line may carry a further suggestion: 'Yes, continue to think that hell's a fable, until experience *transforms* your mind.' At the heart of this mental transformation is the anguished perception of time as inexorable, space as abstract. In his final soliloquy, Faustus's frenzied invocation to time to stop or slow itself gives way to horrified clarity: 'The stars move still, time runs, the clock will strike' (1460). And his appeal to nature— earth, stars, air, ocean—at once to shield him and destroy him is met by silence: space is neutral and unresponsive.

Doctor Faustus then does not contradict but rather realizes intimations about space and time in Marlowe's other plays. That man is homeless, that all places are alike, is linked to man's inner state, to the uncircumscribed hell he carries within him. And this insight returns us to the violence with which we began, the violence of Tamburlaine and of the English merchant and his men. It is not enough to say that their actions are the expression of brute power, though they are certainly that, nor even that they bespeak a compulsive suspicion and hatred that one Elizabethan voyager saw as characteristic of the military mind.[6] For experiencing this limitlessness, this transformation of space and time into abstractions, men do violence as a means of marking boundaries, effecting transformation, signaling closure. To burn a town or to kill all of its inhabitants is to make an end and, in so doing, to give life a shape and a certainty that it would otherwise lack. The great fear, in Barabas's words, is 'That I may vanish o'er the earth in air, And leave no memory that e'er I was' (1.499–500). As the town where Zenocrate dies burns at his command, Tamburlaine proclaims his identity, fixed forever in the heavens by his acts of violence:

> Over my Zenith hang a blazing star,
> That may endure till heaven be dissolv'd,
> Fed with the fresh supply of earthly dregs,
> Theat'ning a death and famine to this land.
> (2 *Tam* 3.2.3196–99)

In this charred soil and the blazing star, Tamburlaine seeks literally to make an enduring mark in the world, to stamp his image on time and space. Similarly, Faustus, by violence not on others but on himself, seeks to give his life a clear fixed shape. To be sure, he speaks of attaining 'a world of profit and delight, / Of power, of honor, of omnipotence' (83–84), but perhaps the hidden core of what he seeks is the *limit* of twenty-four years to live, a limit he himself sets and reiterates.[7] Time so marked out should have a quality different from other time, should possess its end: 'Now will I make an end immediately,' he says, writing with his blood.

But in Marlowe's ironic world, these desperate attempts at boundary and closure produce the opposite effect, reinforcing the condition they are meant to efface. Tamburlaine's violence does not transform space from the abstract to the human, but rather further reduces the world to a map, the very emblem of abstraction:

> I will confute those blind Geographers
> That make a triple region in the world,
> Excluding Regions which I mean to trace,
> And with this pen reduce them to a Map,
> Calling the Provinces, Cities and towns
> After my name and thine *Zenocrate*.
>
> (1 *Tam* 4.4.1715–20)

At Tamburlaine's death, the map still stretches out before him, and nothing bears his name save Marlowe's play (the crucial exception to which we will return).[8] Likewise at his death, pleading for 'some end to my incessant pain,' Faustus is haunted by eternity: 'O no end is limited to damned souls' (1458).

The reasons why attempts at making a mark or an end fail are complex and vary significantly with each play, but one critical link is the feeling in almost all Marlowe's protagonists that they are *using up* experience. This feeling extends to our merchant, John Sarracoll, and his men: they not only visit Sierra Leone, they consume it. Tamburlaine exults in just this power to 'Conquer, sack, and utterly consume / Your cities' (2 *Tam* 4.2.3867–68). He even contrives to use up his defeated enemies, transforming Bajazeth into his footstool, the kings of Trebizon and Soria into horses to be discarded, when they are broken-winded, for 'fresh horse' (2 *Tam* 5.1.4242). In a bizarrely comic moment, Tamburlaine's son suggests that the kings just captured be released to resume the fight, but Tamburlaine replies, in the language of consumption, 'Cherish thy valor still with fresh supplies: / And glut it not with stale and daunted foes' (2 *Tam* 4.1.3761–62). Valor, like any appetite, always demands new food.

Faustus's relationship to knowledge is strikingly similar; in his opening soliloquy he bids farewell to each of his studies in turn as something he has used up. He needs to cherish his mind with fresh supplies, for nothing can be accumulated, nothing saved or savored. And as the remainder of the play makes clear, each of these farewells is an act of destruction: logic, medicine, law, and divinity are not so much rejected as violated. The violence arises not only from the desire to mark boundaries but from the feeling that what one leaves behind, turns away from, *must* no longer exist; that objects endure only for the moment of the act of attention and then are effaced; that the next moment cannot be fully grasped until the last is destroyed. Marlowe writes in the period in which European man embarked on his extraordinary career of consumption, his eager pursuit of knowledge, with one intellectual model after another seized, squeezed dry, and discarded, and his frenzied exhaustion of the world's resources:[9]

> Lo here my sons are all the golden Mines,
> Inestimable drugs and precious stones,
> More worth than *Asia* and the world beside,
> And from th'Antartic Pole, Eastward behold
> As much more land which never was descried,
> Wherein are rocks of Pearl that shine as bright
> As all the Lamps that beautify the Sky,
> And shall I die, and this unconquered?
>
> (2 *Tam* 5.3.4544–51)

So fully do we inhabit this construction of reality that most often we see beyond it only in accounts of cultures immensely distant from our own: 'The Nuer [writes Evans-Pritchard] have no expression equivalent to "time" in our language, and they cannot, therefore, as we can, speak of time as though it were something actual, which passes, can be wasted, can be saved, and so forth. I do not think that they ever experience the same feeling of fighting against time or of having to co-ordinate activities with an abstract passage of time because their points of reference are mainly the activities themselves, which are generally of a leisurely character. . . . Nuer are fortunate.'[10] Of course, such a conception of time and activity had vanished from Europe long before the sixteenth century, but English Renaissance works, and Marlowe's plays in particular, give voice to a radically intensified sense that time is abstract, uniform, and inhuman. The origins of this sense of time are difficult to locate with any certainty. Puritans in the late sixteenth century were already campaigning vigorously against the medieval doctrine of the unevenness of time, a doctrine that had survived largely intact in the Elizabethan church calendar. They sought, in effect, to desacramentalize time, to discredit and sweep away the dense web of saints' days, 'dismal days,' seasonal taboos, mystic observances, and folk festivals that gave time a distinct, irregular shape; in its place, they urged a simple, flat routine of six days work and a sabbath rest.[11] Moreover, there seem, in this period, to have been subtle changes in what we may call family time. At one end of the life cycle, traditional youth groups were suppressed or fell into neglect, customs that had allowed adolescents considerable autonomy were overturned, and children were brought under the stricter discipline of the immediate family. At the other end, the Protestant rejection of the doctrine of purgatory eliminated the dead as an 'age group,' cutting off the living from ritualized communion with their deceased parents and relatives.[12] Such changes might well have contributed to a sense in Marlowe and some of his contemporaries that time is alien, profoundly indifferent to human longing and anxiety. Whatever the case, we certainly find in Marlowe's plays a powerful feeling that time is something to be resisted and a related fear that fulfillment or fruition is impossible. 'Why waste you thus the time away?' an impatient Leicester asks Edward II, whose crown he has come to fetch. 'Stay a while,' Edward replies, 'let me be king till night' (2045), whereupon, like Faustus,[13] he struggles vainly to arrest time with incantation. At such moments, Marlowe's celebrated line is itself rich with irony: the rhythms intended to slow time only consume it, magnificent words are spoken and disappear into a void. But it is precisely this sense of the void that compels the characters to speak so powerfully, as if to struggle the more insistently against the enveloping silence.

* * *

Christopher Highley, *Shakespeare, Spenser, and the Crisis in Ireland* (Cambridge: Cambridge University Press, 1997), pp. 89–90.

The rebel alliance of *1 Henry IV* can be seen as reconfiguring the coalition of factions and families ranged against the English in Ireland. When Edmund Mortimer, Earl of March, marries Glendower's daughter, he completes a triangular alliance that through the marriage of Mortimer's sister to Hotspur also includes the powerful Percy family. To the king, Mortimer's marriage into a rebellious Welsh family is a provocative crossing of cultural and dynastic boundaries—and one that equips his rival and the legitimate heir to the throne with a power base; to the rebels, on the other hand, Mortimer's marriage represents an invaluable exogamic alliance that unites the north of the realm (the Percy base) with both the west and Wales in a bond of blood against the king. The rebels further strengthen their alliance by drawing in the Scots—the Percys' erstwhile rivals in the north—and a dissident group of clergy led by the Archbishop of York. United against the king by the end of Act One, then, is a heterogeneous rebel confederacy that magnifies the threat from the Celtic borderlands by compounding it with the threat of a factious nobility under Percy leadership.

Although Glendower is the member of this confederacy whose actions most insistently suggest the Earl of Tyrone's activities in Ireland, Mortimer also triggers a cluster of topical resonances about Tyrone and the politics of English–Irish conflict. In fact, in the early seventeenth century, Mortimer was invoked by Sir John Davies as an equivalent figure to Tyrone from England's own past:

> when England was full of tenants-at-will our barons were then like the mere Irish lords, and were able to raise armies against the crown; and as this man [Tyrone] was O'Neal in Ulster, so the Earl of Warwick was O'Nevill in Yorkshire, and the Bishopric and Mortimer was the like in the Marches of Wales.[1]

Mortimer, in his obscure capitulation to Glendower, embodies the oldest and most pervasive of English anxieties about contact with the Irish: like those Anglo-Norman and English settlers who had abandoned past loyalties and assimilated themselves to Gaelic culture, Mortimer 'goes native'. Moreover, in marrying Glendower's daughter and embracing her tongue, Mortimer violates the most charged and repeated of government injunctions in medieval and early modern Ireland against cultural mixing.[2]

In late sixteenth-century Ireland, Mortimer's lapse from 'civility' was most recognizable in the Old English population—that former 'store of gentlemen, and other warlike people'— which through intermarriage and promiscuous contact had 'degenerated and growen almost mere Irishe, yea and more malycious to the Englishe then the verye Irishe themselfes'. As Spenser's Irenius explains, many Old English families in order to mark their irreversible detachment from their English ancestry and to proclaim their new-found identities, had 'quite shaken off theire Englishe names and putt on Irishe, that they might be altogeather Irishe'. Significantly, among the families that had 'degendred from their antient dignities', Spenser includes 'the great Mortymer, who forgettinge how great he was once in England, or English at all, is now become the most barborous of them all, and is called *Macnemarra*'.[3] In the Glendower–Mortimer bond, then, Shakespeare gives shape to the possibility of a much-feared collusion between England's Gaelic and Old English enemies in Ireland. Appealing for support from all available quarters, Tyrone has persuaded the Old English 'gentlemen of Munster' to join the Ulster confederacy and to 'make war with us'.[4]

* * *

Dympna Callaghan, Re-reading Elizabeth Cary's *The Tragedie of Mariam, Faire Queene of Jewry'*, in Margo Hendricks and Patricia Parker (eds.), *Women, 'Race', and Writing in the Early Modern Period* (London and New York: Routledge, 1994), pp. 167–77.

The principle of difference lies at the heart of the construction of cultural others, as feminist and postcolonial theory in coincident and parallel ways have shown.[1] Therefore, it is product-ive to examine Cary's otherness as a woman writer in relation to the racialized otherness of *Mariam* rather than to allow the former completely to subsume the latter. Importantly, these modes of cultural otherness (gender and 'race') are structurally connected aspects of the colonialist dialectic between self and other that emerged in the Renaissance:

> These encounters with the 'other' . . . necessitated a concomitant confrontation with the self, provoking a re-evaluation of the known in relation to the newly discovered unknown. Significantly, and ironically . . . England's preoccupation with strangers and strange lands intensified the culture's re-examination of its own estranged others.[2]

There is no reason to suppose that Cary as a woman writer (herself an embodiment of otherness) was peculiarly exempt from the preoccupation with alterity that characterized the burgeoning imperialism of her milieu.[3] We know, for instance, that Cary had read Pliny, and would therefore be familiar with classical anthropology.[4] When Cary's former tutor, John Davies, begins his 'The Muse's Sacrifice, Or Divine Meditations' (1612) with a dedicatory encomium to Cary and two of her female contemporaries, he depicts a writer singularly preoccupied with the intellectual exploration of linguistic and geographical otherness characteristic of the generic male humanist scholar, but uncharacteristic of women:

> With feete of State, *dost make thy* Muse to *mete*
> *the* scenes of Syracuse *and* Palestine.
> Art, Language; *yea; abstruse and holy* Tongues
> *thy* Wit *and* Grace acquir'd *thy* Fame *to raise.*[5]

There is good reason, then, not to dismiss the Palestine of Cary's *Mariam* as a mere back-drop, as a matter of incidental 'local color.' Rather, Palestine is the locus of complex racial and religious coordinates, at once the displaced center of Christianity and the home of the infidel. This setting is part of the way in which *Mariam* participates both in an aesthetic convention of otherness and in an intellectual fascination with Judaism which swept England from the reign of Henry VIII. The connection between the ancient Israelites and contemporary Jewry came under close scrutiny as the result of complex intellectual and political developments, which included the glorification of Hebrew, the interest in a universal language, the search for the lost ten tribes of Israel, and the belief that the conversion of the Jews was a necessary aspect of Christian eschatology. This occurred despite the fact that the Jews had been exiled from England in 1290 and were not readmitted (and then only on an unofficial basis) until the philo-semitic momentum reached its climax in the 1655 meeting with Rabbi Menasseh ben Israel at the Whitehall Conference.[6] Further, a connection had been firmly established between the Jews and the peoples of the New World. Explorers hoped to come upon the lost tribes, and Peter Martyr's English translation of an account of the Spanish voyages of exploration, *The Decades of the New World* (1555), describes the Americas as a 'spirituall Israel.' Indeed, the Native Americans actually encountered were deemed to bear considerable resemblance to Jews since they practiced circumcision and spoke a language which, to the explorers' ears was reminiscent of Hebrew.[7] Both Cary's proficiency in Hebrew, undoubtedly one of the 'abstruse and holy tongues' referred to by Davies, as well as her reading Lodge's

1602 translation of Josephus's *Antiquities of the Jews* (written in Greek), which is thought to be her source for *Mariam*, are ways in which she participated in the intellectual ethos of her time.[8]

Yet, the negotiation of otherness, in English Renaissance culture as in Cary's text, is conflicted because it entails simultaneously the impetus to constitute and affirm self-identity via a relation with the other that can manifest itself as either irresistible fascination, a disquieting sense of affinity, or outright repulsion and denigration.[9] There are, for example, anti-racist sentiments (sometimes alongside overtly racist ones in the discourses of Coryate, Purchas, and Sir Thomas Browne, who occasionally attempt to establish the Jews as a 'nation,' rather than a 'race.'[10] However, there coexisted with such notions, as with philo-semitism more generally, a strong current of diabolization of the Jews.[11] As David Katz points out in his book-length study of the subject: 'These English philo-semites wanted Hebrew without tears, philo-semitism without Jews.'[12] This renders the distinction between 'theological' and 'racial' anti-semitism quite unfeasible.[13] The former is so virulent that it far exceeds the bounds of the simply 'religious' and is distinct from other forms of religious intolerance such as that directed against Catholics:

> . . . it is the demonological, supernatural element in the early modern attitude to the Jews which renders it quite different from other forms of opposition to religious minorities and outcasts. 'Ye are of *your* father the devil,' John admonished the Jews, 'and the lusts of your father ye will do.' . . . The Jews were thought to have some cosmic connection with the Antichrist. They were believed to carry a particular smell (*Foetor Judicus*), to poison Christians, desecrate hosts, murder children and use their blood for ritual purposes.[14]

It is within this cultural frame, one where there was both reverence and repulsion for Jews, that Cary's setting must be seen to signify. Palestine provided an unusually suitable site for the depiction of male tyranny and female resistance, and for a protagonist who embodies an unstable mixture of antithetical elements—female virtue and rebellion. Both fantasized and actual, Palestine is a place where Cary can unbalance the polarized binarisms which constituted the category 'woman.'

The play's production of femininity, alternatively vilified as wanton and valorized as virtuous, is crucially dependent upon 'race.' That is, the cultural polarization of the category 'woman' is constructed via racial marking. Paradoxically, the stark coloration of virtuous femininity as white and licentious femininity as black is destabilized by the fact that these polarities are set in relation to one another amid Jews, peoples of an allegedly already compromised ethnicity. 'Race' enables Cary to stage some of the contradictions that constitute the Renaissance condition of femininity, and by exploring femininity through it *The Tragedie of Mariam* gains a double focus on the otherness of woman. Racialized difference and geographical otherness, in fact, become preconditions of the representation of resisting femininity.

Yet 'race' also works to make female resistance simultaneously possible and ethically insupportable. Mariam's ambivalent position in the play as stoic and virtuous, especially in death, but also as disobedient and vituperative is in part a function of her anomalous racial position. Within the conventions of Renaissance culture, Jewish women seem to be portrayed in a far more positive light—as literally less racialized—than the invariably patriarchal Jewish males. For example, Jessica, daughter of Shylock, who converts to Christianity in Shakespeare's

Merchant of Venice, and Abigail, the daughter of Barabas, who flees to a convent in Marlowe's *The Jew of Malta*, are identified with Christianity rather than Judaism,[15] their fathers do not have the same propensity toward conversion and assimilation. The archetypal Jewish patriarch is Abraham, of course, to whom Gentiles bear an inescapably filial relationship. He is, as St Paul writes, 'the father of us all.[16] Yet Abraham is hardly benevolent. He figures in Christian mythology as the murderous patriarch who circumcises Isaac and later ties him to the altar fully prepared to wield his knife, his hand stayed only by the timely intervention of the angel of the Lord.[17]

The significant parallels between Herod and the conventional, racialized representation of the Jew as the tyrannical patriarch (though he is not, of course, Mariam's father) make her insubordination quite legitimate (this is especially true when we recall that this same Herod is the notorious figure who massacred the innocents):

> Yet I rather much a milke-maide bee,
> Than be the Monarke of *Judeas* Queene.
> It was for nought but love, he wisht his end
> Might to my death, but the vaunt-currier prove:
> But I had rather still be foe than friend,
> To him that saves for hate, and kills for love.
>
> (I.i.59–64)[18]

Mariam here is very much constructed as the victim-subject of the jealous husband-monarch who 'kills for love.' [. . .] But Mariam is not only a victim: in some sense, she is the rebellious figure who heralds the coming of Christ. As Elaine Beilin has noted, Lodge's translation of Josephus marks the events of Herod and Mariam's tumultuous marriage with a countdown to the birth of Christ in the margin.[19] For Mariam is also an amalgam figure of the apostate Jewish woman, based on the Virgin Mary, the eternal 'daughter mother,' 'purged at once of the evil embodied in her ancestry.'[20] Like Mary, Mariam represents the mercy of Christianity which again tempers the patriarchal rigor of the Old Testament.[21]

While earlier literary models had the Virgin Mary represent the advent of the New Law and the demise of the Old, Leslie Fiedler argues that the thematic fusion of the identity between the Virgin and the Jewish woman was a relatively new, Renaissance development. In the popular medieval ballad of *Hugh of Lincoln* a Gentile boy is slain for his devotion to the Virgin, but a beautiful Jewish girl helps her father ensnare the child. In contrast, in the Renaissance, Fiedler writes:

> By the time Shakespeare was dreaming Shylock and Jessica, there had begun to grow both in him and in his audience a longing unsatisfied by either The Prioresses Tale or 'Sir Hugh, or the Jew's Daughter,'—for a representation of the female principle in Jewish form more human than the Blessed Virgin, yet, unlike the Jew's daughter of the ballad, benign and on the other side.[22]

This seems to indicate that an ever-increasing weight of the indictment for the killing of Christ is borne by the Jewish male, who is positioned as more racially debased than his female counterpart. Consider Thomas Adams's 'defense' of women published in 1629:

Though Christ honoured our sex, in that he was a man, not a woman: yet hee was borne of a woman, and was not begot of a man. And howsoever wicked women prove the most wicked sinners: yet the worst and greatest crime that ever was done, was committed by a man, not by woman; the crucifying of our Lord Jesus; not a woman had a hand in it.[23]

Here, men (irrespective of race) are marked by the crucifixion, while women are exonerated by virtue of the fact that they are seen as non-participants in the course of human history. Mariam is thus placed differently in relation to the racialization of Jews than Herod. This suggests a complex interrelation between gender and 'race,' and simultaneously endorses and interrogates Mariam's resistance to Herod.

For what is problematic about Mariam's rebellion against Herod, which is not so of Jessica's deception of Shylock or Abigail's disobedience to Barabas, is that, while daughters can refuse to obey Jewish fathers, wives are not permitted to disobey husbands, let alone forswear the marriage bed.[24] Cary deals with this by accentuating the production of racialized difference between Herod and Mariam and positing it as the circumstance of Mariam's wifely rebellion. Paradoxically, then, Herod becomes both more Jewish than Mariam and racially debased—an Edomite—while Mariam becomes both less Jewish than Herod and 'pure' Jew. Mariam's mother, the ever-railing Alexandra, attacks her son-in-law in a fashion that constitutes Herod and Mariam's marriage as virtual miscegenation:

> Base *Edomite* the damned *Esaus* heire:
> Must he ere *Jacobs* child the crown inherit?
> Must he, vile wretch, be set in *Davids* chair?
> No, *Davids* soule within the bosome plac'te
> Of our forefather *Abram*, was asham'd
> To see his feat with such a toade disgrac'te,
> That seat that hath by *Judas* race been fain'd
> Thou fatall enemy to royall blood. . . .
> Was he not *Esaus* Issue, heyre of hell?
> Then what succession can he have but shame?
> Did not his Ancestor his birth-right sell?
> O yes, he doth from *Edoms* name derive,
> His cruell nature which with blood is fed:
> That made him me of Sire and sonne deprive,
> He ever thirsts for blood, and blood is red.
>   (I.ii.89–111)

The differences of power and morality between Herod and Mariam presented here are over-determined not only by gender, but also by 'race,' and class. The phrase 'Judah's race' (which the printing produces as the racial epithet, 'Judas race') is telling also because it extends beyond the parameters of our twentieth-century understanding of 'race' into the realm of class and social hierarchy, which in the Renaissance is so thoroughly naturalized that it attaches to blood. In literal terms, 'Judah's race' suggests the general sense of lineage as in 'a race of kings' and refers to the long dynastic conflict between the descendants of Esau (Isaac's son who was tricked out of his inheritance by his twin, Jacob) and those of his brother. These Edomites were enemies to Israel until subdued by those of Mariam's blood, a history that would have been familiar to Renaissance readers.[25] Proper sovereignty, according to the voluble Alexandra, is deformed by the loathsome, reptilian Herod.

Although the question of lineage in terms of the contest for power dealt with in Lodge's Josephus, it is not nearly so racialized as in *Mariam* where Mariam's encounters with Salome leave us in no doubt about the fact that a specifically racialized difference is thought to exist between the Edomites and those of Jacob's line. [. . .] Crucially, Salome and Mariam, who are the central as well as the most sexualized female characters of the play (as opposed to Doris and Alexandra, who are so preoccupied with the advancement of their children that they become de-sexualized mothers), have their moral coloring reflected in the pigment of their skin. Mariam's diatribe, however, implies not merely that her antagonist's darkness is an accurate reflection of her 'blacke acts,' and base blood: 'base woman . . . *Mariam's* servants were as good as you / Before she came to be *Judeas* Queen' (II.iii.233–4). It also implies that her transgressions have their origins in her inferior heritage.

The racialization of Salome, then, permits the irresistible logic of her proto-feminist pronouncements about female desire and the injustice of divorce law: 'Ile be the custom-breaker: and beginne/To show my Sexe the way to freedomes doore' (I.iv.319–20). As the stage villain, whose literary antecedents include the medieval Vice and the Renaissance Machiavel, Salome has a certain verbal license. However, these traditional and invariably male figures typically rail at women and indict them for concupiscence.[26] Salome constitutes a singular formal innovation. She is endowed with the license of the Vice-Machiavel but to reverse ends: she critiques male prerogative, articulates her outrageous sexual desires and asserts her will with impunity. In contrast, Mariam is ensnared in the Renaissance patriarchal trap, and her juxtaposition with Salome foregrounds and problematizes the cultural construction of female virtue and agency as mutually incompatible elements. Salome represents an unorthodox means of escaping Mariam's dilemma, namely the complete refusal of all the strictures men impose on female behavior; even while in typical Machiavellian form, she endangers the tragic protagonist.[. . .]

As Mariam progresses toward death and exoneration, she becomes whiter—more dazzlingly white than 'fair'—and less sexualized (that is, within the dominant ideology of 'race' she is de-racialized), while an increment of associations with voracious blackness accrue to Salome. Yet in a symptomatic erasure of 'race,' one feminist critic argues that Salome is imagistically based on the reference in Matthew's gospel to 'a painted sepulcher,/That is both faire, and viley foule at once' and that 'Mariam . . . is exempt from this portrayal. Part of her tragedy is the lack of whitewash: the beauty of Mariam is an indication of spiritual purity and innocence.'[27] It is certainly true that Salome exhibits the glamor of evil, but the notion that she is 'whitewashed,' even though intended as a figurative rather than a literal description, betrays singular inattention to the specifically racialized construction of feminine evil that Salome's character embodies. Far from being 'whitewashed,' she is conspicuously dark and morally tarnished, while Mariam is insistently blanched and purified.[28] [. . .]

Only when Herod repents her execution does Mariam's whiteness become unproblematic. The reiteration of de-racialized female beauty and morality is such that it signals that Herod has become unhinged by his malevolent uxoriousness:

> she was faire.
> Oh what a hand she had, it was so white,
> It did the whiteness of the snowe impaire
> I never more shall see so sweet a sight
>
> (IV. viii.2091–4)

He marvels that the sun can still shine when such a one is lost rather than 'some *Egiptian* blows/Or *Æthiopian* doudy' (IV.viii.2136–7). 'If she had been like an *Egiptian* blacke,/And not so fair, she had bene longer lived' (IV.viii.2181–2). Of course, Herod has had plenty of opportunity to revoke the execution order before Mariam's death. He momentarily repents his rashness by displacing the racialized/demonized difference between his sister, 'my blacke tormenter,' and the luminous virtue of his wife onto the primal distinction between dark and light:

> What meant I to deprive the world of light:
> To muffle *Jury* in the foulest blacke,
> That ever was an opposite to white.
>
> (IV.iv.1502–4)

These pervasive cultural elisions between darkness, black skin, evil, and the 'racialization' of femininity—especially the repeated vilification of wanton femininity as black—were founded in the belief that Africans and women were demonic and that the devil was black.[29] Such associations constitute not just the 'imagery' of this text, but the conceptual content of 'race' in the Renaissance.

That Mariam's virtue is presented very traditionally in terms of whiteness should not cause us to dismiss the way in which beauty itself becomes markedly de-racialized. Indeed, it is precisely the fact that the equation of beauty with whiteness is 'conventional' that requires explanation. What is significant and remarkable is the way the racialization of demonized femininity and the de-racialization of sanctified femininity, as well as the preoccupation with moral difference as analogous to racial difference, saturate this play. Cary manipulates the terms of the convention by making the culturally pervasive equation of inner purity with whiteness work simultaneously to construct and problematize the conventional ideology of femininity. In a culture where femininity is polarized as literally black or white, women are still unstable signifiers. Cary's use of the conventions for constructing gender virtues reveals them to be dangerously dependent on a deracinated essentialism: virtue is white, but white is really black. The text discloses female virtue as grounded not in femaleness but in convention.

Nonetheless, Herod's misogynous ravings are lent a certain plausibility by the fact that it is with a treachery of emotion, thought, and speech rather than with actual infidelity that Mariam suffers both self-recrimination and indictment by the play's Chorus. For Mariam, while physically virtuous, has erred in her voluble upbraidings of Herod for the murder of her grandfather and brother, and in her inability to set her mind to perfect obedience once she discovers that he intended to have her murdered had he failed to return from Rome. Herod charges: 'Foul pith contain'd in fairest rinde . . . thine eye/Is pure as heaven, but impure thy minde' (IV.iv.1453–5). Similarly, Doris impugns Mariam's physical purity for the years of adulterous 'marriage' she has spent with Herod: 'In heav'n, your beautie cannot bring you,/Your soule is blacke and spotted, full of sinne' (IV.viii.1849–50). Doris's case against Mariam as the 'other woman' is actually quite strong, and for a Renaissance audience, the outrageous cultural otherness of such marriage practices might well have sullied Mariam's protestations about her spotless virtue.

There is, in fact, no female subject position available in the play that is both viable and virtuous, except perhaps for the unsullied femininity of the dramatically insipid Graphina, servant lover of Pheroras. She is more virtuous than Mariam, whose racial characteristics she parallels by practicing that 'fair virgin art' despite her inferior class position:

> For though the Diadem on *Mariams* head
> Corrupt the vulgar judgements, I will boast
> *Graphinas* brow's as white, her cheekes as red.
>
> (II.i.583–5)

Graphina represents the play's ostensible ideal of femininity (which significantly enough, does not wholly comport with the cultural equation of female silence with chastity).[30] Like the humble milkmaid of Mariam's fantasy, Graphina is not presented with the obstacles to virtue that Mariam must endure. Once again lower-class femininity becomes a fantasized location, somewhere beyond the absolute and brutal power of Herod, which has impeded Mariam's path to perfect virtue.

In its complex imbrication with gender and class, we can begin to see how 'race' shapes notions of female purity and beauty as well as the issues feminist criticism has shown to be the focal and contradictory concerns of *The Tragedie of Mariam*, namely wifely obedience versus female agency and autonomy.[31] For 'race' is never a discrete entity; it constituted by an inherent interrelatedness with other categories. Even the specular economy of the black—white dichotomy, the metaphysics of race on which much of the play's production of femininity relies, functions throughout as a fundamental binarism whose analogical extensibility encompasses gender, hierarchy, and morality as much as color. None of these categories, therefore, can be properly disarticulated from 'race' understood in its non-positivist sense.

*　*　*

Mark Thornton Burnett, *Constructing 'Monsters' in Shakespearean Drama and Early Modern Culture* (Basingstoke: Macmillan, 2002), pp. 11–12.

If the record of 'monstrous' human exhibits is substantial, that of 'monstrous' animals is generally more sketchy, suggesting that different exhibitions stimulated different reactions. Possibly, the human 'monster' was to prove more enduring because the exhibition touched more closely upon the viewer's experiential sense of self. Certainly, the contexts invoked in Jonson's *The Alchemist* (1610) posit the crowd-pulling potential of a non-normative animal display. Amazed at the crowd about his house, Lovewit wonders: 'What should my knave advance, / To draw this company? He hung out no banners / Of a strange calf with five legs to be seen, / Or a huge lobster with six claws?'[1] His comment bears out the ways in which some animals with non-typical physical features—such as the pig with claws, the ram with four horns and the sow with six legs—received mention not only in dramas but also in ballads and legal pronouncements.[2] Also displayed in increasing numbers in the period were baboons, birds from Peru, beavers, camels, dromedaries, tropical fish, elks, lions and possums.[3] Invariably publicity material labelled such animals as 'outlandish' or 'straunge', reinforcing the notion that it was their unfamiliarity that authorized the 'monstrous' designation.[4] One might also suggest that spectacles involving strange species worked to secure a sense of national superiority: to capture a foreign 'monster', and to reduce it to the level of a fairground curiosity, was to push back the boundaries of the 'known' and to domesticate an otherwise alien environment. On occasions, it seems that the alien environment was purposefully produced and that specious animals were created to satisfy the demand for exoticism. When a clerk in Thomas Nabbes' play, *Covent-Garden* (1632–3), jokes about having a 'Baboone . . . kill'd . . . stuff't' and shown 'at countrey Faires . . . for a *Ginney Pigmie*' (a Guinea pygmy), he opens up the possibility that at least some 'monstrous' animals on display were elaborate deceptions.[5] It is tempting to speculate that, in such cases, two species were surgically fused into one, as in the case of Barnum's 'Fejee Mermaid', or that a stuffed assemblage of fur and feathers might have sufficed for more gullible spectators. Other sources lend support to the hypothesis, suggesting that, at times, dissimulation fed the early modern appetite.[6] In this connection, the real/unreal binary often seen as separating fair and theatre quickly dissolves.

. . . .

QUESTIONS

- What is involved in historicizing the Renaissance text?
- How useful is the anecdote in mapping a historical field, and what are the alternatives?
- How far does this section demonstrate the variety of historical contexts animating Renaissance textual production?

3 | Historicizing beyond 'literary' boundaries

Catherine Gallagher and Stephen Greenblatt, *Practicing New Historicism* (Chicago and London: University of Chicago Press, 2000), pp. 14–16.

- Out of the vast array of textual traces in a culture, the identification of units suitable for analysis is problematized. If every trace of a culture is part of a massive text, how can one identify the boundaries of these units? What is the appropriate scale? There are, we conclude, no abstract, purely theoretical answers to these questions. To a considerable extent the units are given by the archive itself—that is, we almost always receive works whose boundaries have already been defined by the technology and generic assumptions of the original makers and readers. But new historicism undertakes to call these assumptions into question and treat them as part of the history that needs to be interpreted.

- Similarly, we ask ourselves how we can identify, out of the vast array of textual traces in a culture, which are the significant ones, either for us or for them, the ones most worth pursuing. Again it proves impossible to provide a theoretical answer, an answer that would work reliably in advance of plunging ahead to see what resulted. We have embarked on what Ezra Pound in an early essay calls 'the method of Luminous Detail' whereby we attempt to isolate significant or 'interpreting detail' from the mass of traces that have survived in the archive, but we can only be certain that the detail is indeed luminous, that it possesses what William Carlos Williams terms 'the strange phosphorus of the life',[1] in the actual practice of teaching and writing.

- If an entire culture is regarded as a text, then everything is at least potentially in play both at the level of representation and at the level of event. Indeed, it becomes increasingly difficult to maintain a clear, unambiguous boundary between what is representation and what is event. At the very least, the drawing or maintaining of that boundary is itself an event.

- In the larger perspective of the cultural text, representations similarly cease to have a settled relationship of symbolic distance from matter and particularly from human bodies. The way bodies are understood to function, the difference between men and women, the nature of the passions, the experience of illness, the border line between life and death are all closely bound up with particular cultural representations, but they cannot simply be reduced to those representations. The body functions as a kind of 'spoiler', always baffling or exceeding the ways in which it is represented.

- The unsettling of the relation between imitation and action, between background and foreground, and between representation and bodily reality gives rise to a sense of archival and interpretive inexhaustibility. There is always something further to pursue, always some extra trace, always some leftover, even in the most satisfyingly tight and coherent argument. Moreover, works that are at first adduced only in order to illuminate a particular cultural object develop an odd tendency to insist upon themselves as fascinating interpretive enigmas.

- If a whole culture is regarded as a text—if all the textual traces of an era 'count' as both representation and event—then it is increasingly difficult to invoke 'history' as censor. That is, for new historicism, history cannot easily exercise that stabilizing and silencing function it possessed in analyses that sought to declare the limits of the sayable and thinkable. Of course, certain things are easier—and certainly safer—to say and think, at a given time and place, than other things, and it is important to know and keep in mind the relative ease. But in any culture that has left a complex record of itself—and certainly in any culture that we study—there turn out to be virtually no boundaries that are not transgressed by someone or other (or imagined by those in power to be transgressed in some dark corner). Against the determinism that attempts to insist that certain things in a given period were beyond conception or articulation, new historicism invokes the vastness of the textual archive, and with that vastness an aesthetic appreciation of the individual instance.

* * *

Mary Fuller, *Voyages in Print: English Travel to America, 1576–1624* (Cambridge: Cambridge University Press, 1995), pp. 58–65.

With the 1596 publication of *The Discoverie of Guiana*, Ralegh promised Elizabeth a gold-rich empire more lucrative than Peru—whose inhabitants, moreover, would be eager to swear allegiance to her. In 1616, Ralegh staked his life and his wife's estate on his ability to find, claim, and work the Guianan gold mines which he had located twenty years earlier, and lost. After his unsuccessful return in 1618, Ralegh spent the weeks before his execution producing narratives which he hoped would satisfy James, and asked on the scaffold that no writing be promulgated after his death to discredit him.[1] In contravention of this request, the *Declaration of the Demeanor and Cariage of Sir Walter Raleigh* appeared shortly thereafter to justify James' proceedings against him and to specify and give evidence of the charges which led to the revival of the 1603 sentencing.[2]

Bacon's *Declaration* stresses over and over the clear evidentiary grounding of James' proceedings, making their very clarity a reason for their publication:

> for Actions not well founded, it is aduantage to let them passe in vncertaine Reports; but for Actions, that are built vpon sure and solide grounds, (such as his Maiesties are) it belongeth to them, to be published by open manifeste. (p. 1)

> His Maiesties iust and honorable proceedings . . . thus made manifest to all his good Subjects . . . [were] not founded vpon coniectures or likelyhoods; but either vpon confession of the partie himselfe, or vpon the examination of diuers vnsuspected witnesses. (p. 62)[3]

In fact, these claims are not borne out by the *Declaration*'s argument, which is often confused (accusing Ralegh simultaneously of conflicting projects) and everywhere partial. The rhetorical strategy, however, is to contrast a discourse grounded in *evidence*—testimonies and confessions—and firm inferential procedures, with one of imaginations, equivocations, and fictions, a discourse of dissimulation. (The opposition Bacon sets up recalls Gilbert's and Sidney's defenses of their own discourse in a similar, if less intense, polemic context.)

The first part of the text concerns the Guiana project. To begin with, Ralegh is accused of using the pretext of Guianan mines to gain his liberty and commit acts of piracy and invasion. There is some difficulty here, since no acts of piracy were committed. As for the occupation of San Thomé, Ralegh himself was not present, detained at the coast by illness and the need to hold open the means of departure for the company. While he could be held responsible for the acts of his subordinates, that Ralegh encouraged them to attack San Thomé seems doubtful; when Keymis returned with news of the proscribed Anglo-Spanish engagement in which Ralegh's son had died, adding that it had seemed best to him not to lead his men to the mine, his reception was sufficiently chastening that he commited suicide.

In the absence of acts, the *Declaration* falls back on words spoken by both Ralegh and others as an index of his true intentions, shifting the focus—as Karen Cunningham has argued for the 1603 trial—to guilty knowledge and intention, whether or not accompanied by guilty acts.[4] Perhaps the climax of invective (and irony) is reached with the attribution of these words to Ralegh's son as he led the ill-omened attack on San Thomé: 'Come on my hearts, here is the Mine that ye must expect, they that looke for any other Mine, are fooles' (*Declaration*, 35). (Ralegh said at his hearing, 'The voyage had no success but what was fatal to me, the loss of my son and wasting of my estate.'[5] Bacon cites young Walter Ralegh's words as further evidence that 'this Mine was not only imaginary, but moueable, for that which was directed to bee 3.miles short of Saint Thomé, was after sought 30.miles beyond S. Thomé': an instance of having his argument (imaginary *and* movable) both ways.[6]

Ralegh's own conversation, Bacon continues, indicates that the mine which he had represented as 'reall, and of certainty, for that [he] had seene of the Oare . . . with his eyes' (3) was in fact a more speculative goal, so that the voyage's aim was not (as announced) to open and work a known mine but to find a possible one. Ralegh had claimed personal, bodily witness of the thing, when his actual experience was only of a possibility, a mine existing at the other end of a chain of inference; he offered, again, not things but proofs of things.

> When he was once at Sea, hee did not much labor to nourish and maintaine the beliefe, that he meant to make his voyage vpon the profite of the Mine, but fell a degree, as if it were sufficient to bring home certainty and visible proofe, that such a Mine there was, though hee brought not home the riches of it. For soone after his setting foorth from *Ireland*, hee professed, that if hee brought home but a handfull or basket full of Oare, to shew the King, hee cared for no more, for it was enough to saue his credit. (29)

Ralegh is charged with having an interest not in profit but in proof—intending to 'save his credit' with one basket of ore rather than to fill the King's treasury with the mine's riches. 'Being charged therewith, hee confessed the speech, with this argument and inference, that if there had beene a handfull of the Mine, it followed there was a Mine to be confessed; as if so many Ships, so many lives of men, such charge of provisions, and such an honourable Commission, had beene but for an experiment' (29–30). Here, Bacon accuses Ralegh not of lying about a mine in order to pursue other, less licit projects, but of 'falling a degree,' a culpable shrinking of intention from working the mine to merely bringing back 'certainty and visible proofe, that such a Mine there was.' Ralegh confessed this intention, conceiving his project, it seems, not as one of justifying the expenditure of ships, men, and provisions by a commensurate profit, but of enabling him to substantiate his own language with material proof, a token of reliability to generate further credit and further, more lavishly equipped expeditions. Ralegh's conviction that a 'handfull of the mine' would, in providing evidence of his claims, justify the voyage speaks to a preoccupation with his own credit as a truthful speaker, a preoccupation unlikely to serve his interests with the hostile James.

To Ralegh, however, just such an absence of prudent calculation as is evidenced here in the shift from profit to proof guaranteed the purity of his intentions and absolved him of any apparent culpability. As an argument of his innocence, he wrote to James that 'when I had gotten my liberty . . . I voluntarily lost it; . . . when I was master of my life I rendered it again; . . . though I might elsewhere have sold my ships and goods, and put five or six thousand pounds in my purse, I have brought her into England.'[7] Truth told at one's own cost had another kind of authority than external evidence, one which had been turned to account by Chief Justice Popham in Ralegh's 1603 trial to enhance the weight of Cobham's accusation of Ralegh as a co-conspirator: 'of all other proofs, the accusation of one, who by his confession accuseth first himself, is the strongest, for that hath the force of a verdict of twelve men.'[8] When Ralegh points to the 'voluntary loss' of his return to England, he argues for a privilege which transcends evidence, like the transcendent privilege he claims for his speech from the scaffold:

But this I say, for a Man to call God to Witness to a Falsehood at any time is a grievous sin, and what shall he hope for at the Tribunal Day of Judgment? But to call God to Witness to a falshood at the time of Death, is far more grievous and impious, and there is no hope for such a one. And what should I expect that am now going to render an Account of my Faith? I do therefore call the Lord to Witness, as I hope to be saved, and as I hope to see Him in his Kingdom, which I hope will be within this quarter of this Hour; I never had any Commission from the King of France, nor any Treaty with the French Agent, nor with any from the French King; neither knew I that there was an Agent, nor what he was, till I met him in my Gallery at my Lodging unlooked for. If I speak not true, O Lord, let me never come into thy Kingdom. (Harlow, 307)

Ralegh begins his speech with a repeated expression of gratitude that he has not died in the darkness of the Tower, but has been 'brought into the Light to Die' (307). This gratitude, while it may express a simple preference, suggests as well a sense that this bringing into the light will also be a discovery of his manifest truth, that the display, the *evidence* of his person on the scaffold 'in the sight of so Honourable an Assembly' will support the argument for the defense which he was not allowed to articulate in front of the King's Bench.[9]

Bacon does a good bit of work to discredit the truth-claims of Ralegh as suffering and dying subject. Locally, he simply denies the relevance of Ralegh's scaffold speech. 'Soueraigne Princes cannot make a true iudgement vpon the bare speeches or asseuerations of a delinquent at the time of his death, but their iudgement must be founded vpon . . . reall proofes, as all this former discourse is made vp and built vpon' (*Declaration*, 63). Ralegh's argument, or the argument of his body, was a powerful one, however, necessitating the *Declaration* itself. After hearing Ralegh perform in court during the 1603 trial, one witness had said that 'whereas, when he saw Sir Walter Raleigh first, he was so led with the common hatred that he would have gone a hundred miles to have seen him hanged, he would, ere they parted have gone a hundred to save his life.'[10] Bacon's anxiety about the power of these bare speeches is attested to by another kind of response, aimed to discredit the body as a liar, and suffering as a performance.

The *Declaration*'s second response to Ralegh's personal appeal was contained in another part of the text. While the first forty pages sort through claims and counter-claims about the Guiana expedition, roughly the last third of the text narrates Ralegh's attempts to escape custody once in England, particularly through his subornation of the French physician Manourie. To the heroic, truthful, and self-denying Ralegh presented on the scaffold, this part of the narrative opposes a body both grotesque and deceptive. Ralegh asked Manourie to provide him with the means to pretend sickness, in order to buy time for an escape. The *Declaration* describes in detail the successive administrations and their physical effects: for instance, a skin ointment leaves 'his face full of blisters of diuers colours, hauing in the middest a little touch of yellow, and round about it like a purple colour' (51). Manourie's drugs are solicited for what appear to be increasingly violent symptoms, as Ralegh requests progressively stronger emetics and more blisters. As the prisoner's apparent illness and mental disturbance worsened, his keeper Sir Lewis Stukely feared for Ralegh's life, calling in physicians who, unable to 'discouer this disease,' recommended that the patient not be exposed to the air. The medical examination becomes a place where the grotesque body can be shamelessly displayed, both by Ralegh and, with other intentions, Bacon, and the testimony of the physician makes available an unusual, even uncomfortable degree of intimacy and sensory detail.

> *Sir Walter Raleigh*, seeing that all these things fell out according to his intention, was exceedingly contented thereat, especially that in the presence of the saide Physicians, the vomit began to worke both vpwards and downewards. And because hee doubted that the Physicians would aske to see his water, hee played *Mannowry* to doe something to make it seeme troubled and badde, which to content him, (giving him the Vrinall into his bed) *Mannowry* rubbed the inside of the glasse with a certain Drugge, which assoone as hee had made water therein, the Vryne euen in the hands of the Physicians, turned all into an earthy humour, of a blackish colour, and made the water also to haue an ill sauour. (53)

Bacon displays a Ralegh disfigured by pimples, gleefully vomiting, defecating, and passing a foul-smelling black urine in front of an audience convinced of his body's truth and anxious for his life. Pretending for three days to eat nothing, the prisoner was 'jocund and merry' as he asked the physician to smuggle in food for him—a leg of mutton and three loaves consumed in secret.

It is hard not to read Ralegh's evacuative symptoms as a figure for faked confession, especially since Bacon notes that Ralegh composed his *Apology* during the interval gained by pretended illness.[11] Repeated evacuations of the self's whole contents make available not a true interiority but a false appearance; apparent starvation or self-denial merely covers secret, gleeful indulgence. Inasmuch as Ralegh's staged illness serves as a figure in this text for his trial and execution (a figure he was to use himself),[12] Bacon's account argues that neither the validating danger nor the self-wounding giving up of inner contents are anything other than a charade at the expense of the credulous.

The problematizing of Ralegh's words, actions and finally of his body by the *Declaration* had the effect of discrediting any explanatory claims. Not only Ralegh is compromised; even Bacon's exposition had to abandon Ralegh's conscience and his final speech as undecipherable by human agency, as if notions of discovery itself, of revealing the truth buried beneath appearances, had become unintelligible. The skepticism aroused by Ralegh's last voyage was a far cry from the hopes expressed in Hakluyt's dedication to him of Peter Martyr's *Decades* in 1587:

> Reveal to us the courts of China and the unknown straits which still lie hid: throw back the portals which have been closed since the world's beginning at the dawn of time. There yet remain for you new lands, ample realms, unknown peoples; they wait yet, I say, to be discovered and subdued, quickly and easily, under the happy auspices of your arms and enterprise, and the sceptre of our most serene Elizabeth.[13]

The optimism of this passage concerns not only Ralegh himself but the epistemological possibility of discovery as well. Hakluyt's dedication works on a visionary model of discovery as apocalypse, literally the drawing aside of a concealing medium to reveal 'new lands, ample realms, unknown peoples.' Edmundo O'Gorman has criticized this notion of America as existing behind the veil, waiting to be found. ' "Discover" implies that the nature of the thing found was previously known to the finder'; it assumes 'that things are something in themselves, *per se* . . . that all things are endowed for all time, for anyone and anywhere, with a set being, predetermined and unalterable.'[14] In fact, 'the historical appearance of America' was 'the result of an inspired invention of Western thought and not . . . the result of a purely physical discovery' (4). O'Gorman's general argument speaks to the particular difficulties faced by Ralegh in his personal project, that of 'discovering' Guiana. Even taking Ralegh at his word, the notion of proving a discovery and an intention by presenting James with 'a handfull of the mine' was not only politically naive, but in its failed trajectory pressures the notion that a discourse tied to 'things as things were' disposed of resources any more stable than the poet's lie, even when those 'things' were inert objects, pieces of a continent. Ralegh began seeking permission to return to Guiana in 1607, on the strength of a refiner's report (but the refiner was 'a poor fellow,' and had been promised a reward) about a stone taken on the 1596 expedition (one which Ralegh had been ready to throw away).[15] The second voyage to Guiana was underwritten by a previous voyage, but that voyage itself had failed to substantiate Ralegh's claims, indeed gave rise to the same kinds of accusations—of fabrication, misrepresentation—which met the second. Here, too, Ralegh's response to such accusations was to generate a text.

Ralegh's *Discoverie of the Large, Rich, and Bewtifvl Empyre of Gviana* identifies itself as a defensive gesture against the potential ambiguity of the material in its broadest reference: the content of narrative, marks of experience on the body, objects.

> Because there haue been diuers opinions conceiued of the golde oare brought from *Guiana* and for that an Alderman of London and an officer of her maiesties minte, hath giuen out that the same is of no price, I haue thought good by the addition of these lines to giue aunswere as well to the said malicious slaunder, as to other objections . . . Others haue deuised that the same oare was had from *Barbery* and that we caried it with vs into *Guiana* surely the singularitie of that deuice, I do not well comprehend, for mine owne parte, I am not so much in loue with these long voiages, as to deuise, thereby to cozen my selfe, to lie hard, to fare worse, to be subiected to perils, to diseases, to ill fauours, to be parched and withered, and withall to sustaine the care and labour of such an enterprize, excepte the same had more consort, than the fetching of *Marcasite* in Guiana or the bying of gold oare in *Barbery*.[16]

Ralegh's text responds to three allegations, two of which appear above: that the gold ore brought back from Guiana contains no gold; that Ralegh acquired the ore not in Guiana but in East Africa; that Ralegh never left England at all, but concealed himself in Cornwall for the duration of the supposed voyage. The narrative was called into service to verify both the object and the 'parched and withered' body of the travelers; but those things were themselves supposed to testify, to prop up or substantiate Ralegh's claims. The imaginary and movable mine emblematizes Ralegh's personal experience as a discoverer: one characterized by arrivals or consummations continually deferred—over hours, years, decades, centuries. By these deferrals, movements, slippages, the objects of Ralegh's discovery remained continually elusive.

* * *

Bruce R. Smith, *Homosexual Desire in Shakespeare's England: A Cultural Poetics* (Chicago and London: University of Chicago Press, 1991), pp. 6–7.

Forman's own dream about Queen Elizabeth . . . illustrates graphically how sixteenth-century structures of power and sixteenth-century structures of knowledge shaped sixteenth-century images of sexual desire. In January 1597 Forman

> dreamt that I was with the Queen, and that she was a little elderly woman in a coarse white petticoat all unready. She and I walked up and down through lanes and closes, talking and reasoning. At last we came over a great close where were many people, and there were two men at hard words. One of them was a weaver, a tall man with a reddish beard, distract of his wits. She talked to him and he spoke very merrily unto her, and at last did take her and kiss her. So I took her by the arm and did put her away; and told her the fellow was frantic. So we went from him and I led her by the arm still, and then we went through a dirty lane. She had a long white smock very clean and fair, and it trailed in the dirt and her coat behind. I took her coat and did carry it up a good way, and then it hung too low before. I told her she should do me a favour to let me wait on her, and she said I should. Then said I, 'I mean to wait *upon* you, and not under you, that I might make this belly a little bigger to carry up this smock and coat out of the dirt'. And so we talked merrily; then she began to lean upon me, when we were past the dirt and to be very familiar with me, and methought she began to love me. When we were alone, out of sight, methought she would have kissed me.[1]

The attack by a man—specifically a tall man—with bristling red hair, the white gown that becomes dirtied, the mounting familiarity that proceeds from talking to touching to leaning to kissing: all of these things in the 'manifest content' of the dream point to a 'latent' sexual meaning (if 'patent' isn't the better word in this case) that was as clear to Forman as it is to post-Freudians like ourselves. Witness his erotic pun on 'waiting *upon* you'. But what about the detail that the attacker was, of all things, a weaver? That, surely, is an aspect of the dream's eroticism that is understandable mainly in terms of Elizabethan structures of power, which replicated Elizabethan structures of knowledge in setting the Virgin Queen at a tantalizing distance above the animality of a rude mechanical. For the original watchers/dreamers Bottom the weaver must have had a *machismo* that eludes twentieth-century analysts of *A Midsummer Night's Dream*. The 'reddish beard' of the queen's attacker is another detail that seems partly universal, partly peculiar to the sixteenth century. Samson was neither the first nor the last hero whose virility has been predicated on his hair. But why red? The structure of Elizabethan knowledge established parallels among body fluids, organs of the body, psychological traits, and planetary influences—categories logically separate to us but to the Renaissance mind causatively interlinked as aspects of one grand hierarchical order. Red was the colour of the heart's blood, productive of a 'sanguinary' humour and controlled by the planets Mars and Venus by association with their namesakes' prowess in love. A red beard was erotic because Elizabethan thinking made it so. The very fact that Forman should have an erotic dream about the queen shows us, in just the terms Michel Foucault proposes, how structures of power in society help define sexuality in that society: Forman's dream suggests how much of the political success of 'Gloriana' consisted in arousing the sexual energies of her male subjects and deflecting those energies toward politically useful goals.

* * *

Adam Fox, *Oral and Literate Culture in England 1500–1700* (Oxford: Oxford University Press, 2000), pp. 325–34.

In their deployment by people of humble origin, railing rhymes and lampooning songs could be very much the products of the 'alternative' society of the alehouse. Almost all were said to have been composed over a pot of ale and handed out or repeated in taverns and inns. 'If anie man aske who made this rime | Yt was Steven Corkrum in a drinkinge time', concluded one squib composed at a tippling-house in Pyworthy, Devon, in May 1612 and sung on 'ale-benches and other places in most scoffing, lewd and obscene manner'.[1] Denied the right openly to question those in authority, it was only away from their watchful eyes that people were able to vent grievances freely. The alehouse offered a sanctuary for relative freedom of speech, for cathartic release in story and song, jest and mockery; it provided the chance to ridicule in private those whom it was an offence to challenge in public. These ballads of popular invention were, like so much oral culture, inherently subversive and irreverent, implicitly running counter to the norms and values of society's elite and sometimes challenging them explicitly.

Indeed, many of the libels brought before the Jacobean Star Chamber which were composed by those of lowly social status, and therefore tended to be directed at persons of higher rank, had subversive overtones of some kind. It was this perceived threat to the social order which caused the Star Chamber to take an ever more dim view of the crime. Counsel for the plaintiff in a case of 1608 made it clear that persons of 'good credit'

> should not be defamed, scandalized or slaundered by men of base and lewde condicion which are evill affected, by publishinge of scornfull and reprochfull lybells and pamphletts. And wheras lybelles, lybellers and lybellinge and the publishinge, devulginge and castinge the same abrode are thinges very odyous and hatefull in anie well governed comonwelth, movinge muche contencion, malice and sedicion amongst the people and are often tymes the causes of breache of the peace of the lande and of insurrections and rebellyons, and are alsoe directly againste the lawes and government of this . . . realme of Englande . . . and hath ever byne accompted noe small offence.[2]

Such rhetoric was reinforced by sentences involving large fines, whipping and branding, and even the cutting-off of an offender's ears in cases with seditious implications.[3] But whatever the consequences, a great many people 'of base and lewde condicion' were clearly undeterred by them. John Pearse, a husbandman from Dorset, threatened with the Star Chamber for making a libellous song in 1618, boasted 'that hee did not care a straw for it, for he had aunsweared there far worse matters than these'. 'Wee care not for the Star Chamber!', shouted the ridiculers of the Lancashire bailiff, John Wood. 'Wee will have a trick that Wood . . . shall not be able to looke towards the Star Chamber'.[4]

Equal contempt for the law and its agents was evident among the group of artisans and tradespeople from Thaxted in Essex who, in March 1622, concocted a shaming ballad against a councillor and notable citizen of the town, Richard Turner, whom they accused of harshly beating his daughter, Anne. They laughed in the face of authority and when the mayor of Thaxted

> by way of reprofe, [told] them that makeinge of libells would indanger the losse of theire

eares, [they] did make a scoffe of [him] and at his admonitions, and did thereuppon publishe that a sow of one in the town had lost her eares for makinge libells and . . . [they] made a representation of the mayor and bayliffes of [Thaxted] in innes and alehouses as sittinge in their sessions, to the great scandall of the government of the said corporacion.

Their composition, entitled 'Whip Her Arse Dick', had been 'reported and sunge, published and divulged . . . in divers innes, alehouses and other places in the said towne of Thaxted and county of Essex'. They had made copies and 'taught and instructed . . . young children to singe the same to wrong and provoke [Turner]'. It began:

> Hye thee home Anne,
> Hye thee home Anne,
> Whippe Her Arse Dicke,
> Will have thee anon.
> All those that love puddinge,
> Come unto Parke Street,
> And learne the songe,
> Of Whippe Her Arse Dicke.

Through this combination of oral and visual dissemination, the song, it was said, soon 'became publique, common and notorious in the eyes, eares and tongues' of all Richard Turner's neighbours.[5]

The effect of this kind of ridicule could be devastating on its victims. As local people, known by everyone, they were exposed to a public shaming from which there was no escape and little redress. To some, taking the matter up to Westminster may have represented the best form of satisfaction, but 'the blott of infamie' did not easily fade. Of course, the complaints of libel victims were likely to maximize or even exaggerate the extent to which they had been damaged by the offence, but it is likely that such claims were not without substance. Richard Turner was apparently ruined both privately and professionally by his detractors who succeeded in their plan to 'robb and take from [him] his good name, credit and reputation and to make and cause [him] to be contemptuous and ridiculous to the said town of Thaxted'. Thereafter he was 'often forced to neglect his busines abroad, [while] hopeing in time the said scandalous libell, rime or songe may cease and end'. The same fate awaited others similarly abused. That substantial inhabitant of Tiverton, Robert Reede, the victim of a rhyme and a pair of cuckold's horns fastened upon his door in February 1610, became a laughing-stock among his neighbours. Long after the incident, it was said that when people passed him in the street they 'still doe most disgracefullie poynt att [him], and with their hands and fingers make the signe or token of hornes and poynt att [him] therewith', with such resulting shame to him and his wife that it 'were likely not only to cause a seperacion between them but alsoe were lyke to have bereaved them both of their lyves through the grief, sorrowe and discontentment which they conceyved att the said scandalous imputations'.[6] [. . .]

Very similar circumstances surrounded the 'sundrie reproachefull, scandalous and infamous libells . . . in words as in writings' directed against Henry Collins of Winscombe in Somerset. Collins was another wealthy clothier who employed 'many poore and distressed people', and was also a village constable who regularly presented miscreants to the authorities. In doing so he incurred the wrath of one John Hawker who, as a weaver and 'a common haunter of alehouses, a night walker, and a notorious offender in many other disorders and greevous misdemeanors', had both professional and personal reasons to resent Collins. On 16 May 1624, Hawker, together with fellow weavers William Staple and George Bullford, invented 'balletts, rymes, songs and other infamous speeches' claiming that Collins, a married man, had been seen in the trees of Maudlines Grove with Hawker's niece Ann. They alleged that he had also lived incontinently with many women, that he was a bad debtor, and thus a person of no credit. They deliberately sang these ballads in front of Collins's circle of friends, 'the better sorte' of the neighbours, and among his 'kinsfolkes'. The result, he claimed, was that he was shunned by all and became afraid even to leave his house. Professionally he was 'utterlie forbarred and frustrated from the following of his trade and thereby utterly undonne and overthrowne'. When the ill fame reached Collins's wife she believed the 'rumors and rimes to be true' and 'did theruppon become frantick'.[7]

The 'better sort', so often the victims of these scurrilous songs, could frequently be heard denouncing libellers and their alehouse culture. Such was the reaction to the ballad composed in 1612 by James Ball of Wellingborough, 'out of his evill and malitious mind', and directed against a local widow, Ellinor Grobye. One gentleman of the town, Hugh Chervock, deposed that while Ellinor was 'reported to be an honest and civil poore woman amongst her neighboures', Ball was 'held to be, amongst the more and better sorte of his neighboures, a man of a troublesome disposition'. Another of these respectable neighbours, John Hackney, claimed to be greatly shocked by the ballad which was 'such a thinge as he never heard of in his life and that he thought that yt was a libell' which Ball performed 'in a laughing and very scoffing manner and made a Maye game thereof'.[8]

As these examples suggest, it is sometimes possible to gauge the audience's response to such ballads and libels in a way that is rarely allowed by cheap printed texts. Of course, reactions often depended upon the quality of the performance and the content of the material involved, and they might vary according to the attitudes of readers or hearers both to the authors and their subjects. Ridiculing material of this kind was very likely to evoke strong opinions on all sides. Hilarity was clearly the intended result and it usually seems to have been achieved. 'There was good laughing at the . . . readinge' recalled Christopher Horder, a West Country husbandman, of a 'filthie libell' which he had heard in 1603. But other people, either from genuine indignation or a sense of feigned propriety, expressed distaste and disgust at the obscene or the irreverent. Christopher Auncell, an apprentice from Wimborne Minster in Dorset, who claimed to have found a copy of a very saucy rhyme on the ground in his master's back yard, protested that 'it was a fowle piece of worke and that he would not have been the contriver of it for forty pounds'. Most compositions were greeted with a mixture of reactions, no doubt. When in May 1609, for example, Simon Girdler of Tenterden in Kent flagrantly performed a drunken jig outside the house of John Tylden, a godly magistrate of the town, 'being a man of sober and very religious behaviour', it occasioned the hysterical merriment of some and the abhorrence of others: 'his said behaviour being so publique [it] was not only laughed at by divers then seeing him and by others who after heard thereof . . . but also some others then seeing him so behave him selfe were much greeved and ashamed thereof and for shame went from him and left him alone in such manner'.[9]

Libels were obviously an effective way in which people might jeer at, and wound, their betters. The effects might be just as damaging to victims as any physical assault, indeed perhaps much more so, for, whatever the widening horizons and affiliations of the 'better sort' in this period, the loss of reputation among their immediate neighbours still mattered greatly to most. Slanderous rhymes might be sung among the victim's friends and family and, if they could be written out, posted up in public or left on their doorsteps. Often they were inspired by malicious or spiteful motives and had no justification other than petty personal jealousies. But they might also be a powerful articulation of popular opinions and sensibilities, the communal expression of a sense of justice. Brought to bear upon those who offended against perceived norms, they could be an informal censor and regulator of the most potent kind. Thus, enclosing or battening landlords, forestalling or hoarding tradespeople, officials thought to be overbearing in the pursuit of their duties, all risked the ignomiy of being 'balladed'.

Such was the fate of Andrew Abington, lord of the manor of Over Compton on the Dorset–Somerset border. During a protracted dispute with his tenants over enclosure of the commons, he found himself the object of a number of libellous protests. Notwithstanding that they were said to be 'simple unlearned people', the local husbandmen and their families managed to find someone to draw up a bond, to which twenty-six of them subscribed, claiming release from their obligations to Abington. They sent him, in addition, a pseudonymous letter of derision which was also read out at public meetings; and finally, in August 1616, they fastened this 'infamous libell' to the church gate at Trent in Somerset, about a mile from the manor house.

> *Heere be Andrew Abington's Commandementes*
>
> Thou shalt do no right nor thou shalt take no wronge
> Thou shalt catche what thou canst
> Thou shalt paie no man
> Thou shalt comitt adulterye
> Thou shalt beare false wittnes against thy neyghbor
> Thou shalt covett thy neighbors wiefe
> Thou shalt sell a hundred of sheepe to Henrye Hopkines after
> Thou shalt drawe the best of them
> Thou shalt sell thy oxen twice
> Thou shalt denye thye owne hand

With this parody of the Ten Commandments, which emphasized their view of Abington's behaviour as a mockery of Christian charity, the tenants 'did not only singe, repeat, publishe and divulge the said slanderous and vicious libell in innes, taverns and other places in [the] countyes of Dorset and Somerset and elsewhere, [but also] sold abroad coppyes thereof'. Here, apparently, was another example of a particularly striking libel that had a commercial value in written form. All this was said to have had the desired effect of bringing the squire and 'his wiefe and children into publicke disgrace and infamye'.[10]

Millers were another group which might also feel the force of such communal censure. Their position of power within the local economy and community meant that they were traditionally figures of popular suspicion and even contempt, usually portrayed as lechers or misers. It was the former image upon which the Rotten brothers had drawn in their ballads of Anne Bellamie from Moseley. The latter image provided one theme for 'A pleasante newe songe of a faithfull drunkard dwellinge in Essex who was a myller', which cropped up in the summer of 1608.[11] Similarly caricatured and riduculed was the Puritan, depicted as a zealous hypocrite no less often in these local libels than in the plays and pamphlets of professional humorists.

The 'godly' were especially vulnerable to lampooning if, when they held positions of office, they were perceived as being too 'busy' or 'precise' in regulating the behaviour of their neighbours. For there were in general many examples of mocking verses composed against authority figures such as churchwardens and constables, bailiffs and justices, or the mayor and aldermen of corporations. Commonly would some allegation of corruption or abuse be so dispersed, as Isaac Cotton noted in 1622, 'cast forth [in] certain rhymes or libells conteyninge as it were a dialogue full of scurrility and rude terms, scoffing and inveighing against [the] authority of officers and civil government, with menances for subversion of the same and other base matter unfit to be spoken of'.[12] [. . .]

As we have seen, the libels composed against Thomas Shillito, the high constable of Barkston, West Riding, were widely popular partly because of their professional performances, but also because the tenor of their contents must have struck a chord with many.

> Would God I weare a head constable,
>   And had a Justice of my name,
> Then would I whipp and stock the poore,
>   And think it neither sinne nor shame.[13]

The 'Justice' referred to here was Shillito's brother, George, and men of this stamp were by no means immune from such treatment. 'You thinke to oppresse men with your riches and autho-rytie!', bawled a Nottinghamshire man at a squire and Justice of the Peace whom he was alleged to have libelled in 1608. 'Gaping and framinge a deformed mouthe in most scornefull manner', he 'putt out his tounge at [him]', uttering these 'and divers other such sawcye and malepart words to the great scorne and dyrision of justice'. At another level, the scandalous sexual behaviour of Thomas Smith, a Justice of the Peace for Berkshire, so offended a group of yeoman farmers from Buscot and Lechlade that they tried to shame him into repentance with various mocking nicknames like 'Justice balle, bald pated knave and whoremaster knave', and more forcibly with a ballad which they sang among the neighbours, including at a wedding.[14]

The wider threat to the social and political order which this kind of derogation of authority was seen to pose is well illustrated by some libels contrived in Northampton during the summer of 1607. A large and diverse group of the local inhabitants was responsible for what were clearly a very successful pair of ballads. One was 'made against the knightes and justices of the county', and was 'bought and sold for money' as far north as Leicester and as far south as Dunstable in Bedfordshire, where an innkeeper, Thomas Holland, paid 12*d.* for a copy. The other was composed in scandal of the ecclesiastical officials within the diocese of Peterborough and published on 22 September, the day of Archbishop Bancroft's visit to the town. It was found in the church of Allhallows and at 'inns and alehouses, in sadlers and smiths, and other tradesmen's shops'; a gentleman, Thomas Burton, 'said he would give an angell for a coppie of it, and shewe it to his lord', while Edward Thorowgood, a woolen-draper, promised to 'sende it into Cambridgeshire to his friendes'. This ballad, which took the form of a dialogue between a man and a woman, included a typical jibe at one dignatory:

> He turnes his hat up in the brim,
> > And lookes as though his eyes wold burne,
> He snappes poore people by the nose,
> > And scornfully from them doth turne.

The libellers were said to have claimed that it was legitimate to publish such material, provided that it did not touch the person of the king nor his privy councillors. In so doing, their indict-ment protested, they 'bredd a most dangerous opinion in the harts of the comon people as though it were lawfull to libel and traduce their governors both ecclesiasticall and temporall (so [long as] they be no Lords of the Counsaile)' and also helped to 'continue and maintaine the hatred and dispight bred in many of the baser sort of people against the gentlemen of the country' at the time of the uprisings in the Midlands.[15]

It may have been the case that in prosecuting their assailants at Westminster, some libel victims were seeking to exploit such official anxieties over subversion and disorder. In general, the very fact that those from the most humble levels of society were presented before the Star Chamber at all and, moreover, that they themselves might sometimes present others, is indica-tive of the fact that the law, even in the form of its most grandiose court, was coming to loom increasingly large in the lives of people all the way down the social order. This was an unprecedentedly litigious age and even Star Chamber business, dominated as it was by the gentry, involved people from the middling and lower ranks of provincial society as either plaintiff or defendant in almost half the defamation cases during James I's reign.[16] The paradox of the libels examined here is that they were usually a supremely parochial phenomenon but one disputed and settled at the most elevated of levels. As such they were the reflection of a society which was at once intensely disparate and localized, yet ever centralizing and moving in the directions of incorporation and nationality.

William Shakespeare was lucky. If Sir Thomas Lucy had prosecuted him for libel in the Star Chamber he would probably have incurred a very large fine at the least. Even his crude first effort at poetry, if such it was, rates rather well when compared with the muse of many of his more humble contemporaries. But whereas it is not surprising to find someone of Shake-speare's stamp composing and disseminating 'bitter ballads', it is altogether more remarkable to discover the practice among the obscure tradesmen and artisans, yeomen, and husband-men of England's small towns and villages. To be able to observe the way in which such ordinary provincial people concocted rhymes and songs, had them committed to paper and then circulated, both by performance and public posting, provides us with one of the most graphic, immediate, and illuminating insights into the relationship between oral and literate culture that we are likely to find. In this context, as in other spheres of contemporary life, writing provided not a substitute but a valuable supplement to dissemination by word of mouth; it added a visual and a physical dimension to the ethereal quality of sound. Text was only ever an auxiliary and a stimulus to the primary media of reciting and singing. And yet the fact that it was utilized at all for something as ephemeral as the doggerel verses of alehouse scurrility, speaks volumes about the perceived value and the widespread use of the written word in Shakespeare's England.

* * *

QUESTIONS

• What is involved in historicizing non-literary texts?
• Read in context, what do these texts have to offer to today's reader?
• What other kinds of non-literary texts might profitably offer a way into the Renaissance?

4 | Broadening the material perspective

Patricia Fumerton, 'Introduction: A New New Historicism', in Patricia Fumerton and Simon Hunt (eds.), *Renaissance Culture and the Everyday* (Philadelphia: University of Pennsylvania Press, 1999), pp. 3–4.

This newly emergent historicism focuses primarily on the common, but the common in both a class and cultural sense: the low (common people), the ordinary (common speech, common wares, common sense), the familiar (commonly known), the customary or typical or taken-for-granted (common law, commonplace, communal), etc. A new new historicism sites particular clusters of such myriad commonality within the context of the manifold details of cultural practice and representation [. . .] To the extent that this new historicism of the everyday looks beyond (and below) the politics of the court or the state apparatus and its cultural instruments, it is not so much 'political' as 'social' historicism (although clearly there is some overlap between these terms and movements).

* * *

David Scott Kastan, *Shakespeare after Theory* (New York and London: Routledge, 1999), pp. 17–18.

The most powerful and productive recent critical models of a historical engagement with Shakespeare—those critical practices that either wear by choice or have had attached to them the labels of New Historicism and Cultural Materialism—have been regularly charged with exactly the narcissism that history should counter. Their historical readings seem to some too overtly self-interested to be compelling as historical accounts, significant more as records of our present needs and anxieties than as reconstructions of those of Shakespeare's time.

This paradox emerges, I would say, not from their historical naïveté but from their theoretical sophistication, which forces them to acknowledge the situatedness of the critic as it determines the questions that are asked of the past. Thus, their 'presentist' commitments are not only visible from the first but also part of their very understanding of how the past is logically conceivable [. . .] But the past is never just there to be interrogated; indeed, its absence is precisely what makes it past and what insists that our knowledge of it be inescapably partial, in both senses of the word, products both of the traces that have survived them and of the shaping concerns of those who study them [. . .]

In its often dazzling demonstrations of the circulation of discourses through culture, New

Historicism has rarely paid much attention to the specific material and institutional conditions of the discursive exchanges it has explored. Its idea of representation is a dynamic and cultural semiosis, but one too often lacking in both a convincing account of how a text actually enters and exists in the world and any sustained attention to what Roger Chartier calls 'the effect, in terms of meaning, that its material forms produced'.[1] In the very process of relocating literature from a hermetic literary history into the dense cultural system in which it is seen to function, New Historicism too often re-mystifies it as an effect of discourse, alienating the works it studies from the enabling forms in which they were encountered.

It is this abstract tendency that I think has given rise to a familiar critique of its practices: the charge of abstraction and idealization of power. A sharper focus on the material relations of discourse to the world in which it circulates would give its cultural analysis more historical purchase, fixing it more firmly in relation to the actual producers and consumers of those discourses, locating it, that is, in the world of lived history. Only then is discourse truly enlivened, recognized as a product of human desire and design.

*   *   *

Kim Hall, *Things of Darkness: Economies of Race and Gender in Early Modern England* (Ithaca and London: Cornell University Press, 1995), pp. 215–26.

The circulation of jewels, as much as poems, was an integral part of court culture (Fumerton 69). More jewelry was worn in the sixteenth century than before or since, much of it inspired by European involvement in travel and trade (Cocks 16).[1] Pendants and brooches were made in the shapes of ships, elephants, and the various sea monsters that were the stuff of travel lore. According to Patricia Fumerton, both jewels and poems were seen as 'ornamental' and both worked to establish subjectivity in much the same way. The incessant exchange of ornaments among aristocrats marked the boundaries of aristocratic identity, continually asserting a 'private' self in an atmosphere of public display and exchange (68–70). This somewhat paradoxical mode of marking aristocratic identity with the display and exchange of objects becomes in fact the creation of a 'white mask' of English identity when the objects kept for display are adorned with representations of black Africans.

The wearing of black cameos became a fad in European courts; these cameos were mass-produced in Italian workshops during the last quarter of the sixteenth century (*Princely Magnificence* 70).[2] Joan Evans quotes part of a 1576 inventory list from the goldsmith John Mabbe that includes 'a brouche of gold like a Mores-head, the ground being Mother of pearl . . . a broache with a very fair Agott like a Blackamore enamelled all white about the said agott . . . a jewell with an Agott having a woman cut on it like a More' (98). The increased circulation of these gems was also part of the Renaissance's renewed interest in and emulation of classical antiquity (Cocks 15). Many pieces were restorations of antique classical gems, as in the antique pendant [not illustrated in extract] which has been re-made and surrounded with modern additions—black figurines and scarabs. These additions make the pendant a peculiarly Renaissance piece with its combination of classical past and increased interest in the newly discovered variety in foreign cultures. Still other jewels were simply given a classical 'air' with the inclusion of classical garb, as in the double 'Moor and emperor' cameo and the single cameo of a black male. Later in England the association of Africans with classical antiquity is realized in the practice of giving servants classical-sounding names such as Pompey or Scipio (Fryer 24; Tuan 146), which, with its supposedly comic juxtaposition of high and low culture, mimics a larger pattern of African degeneration and Greco-Roman ascendancy.[3] It also suggests another way in which England linked its classical past with its current pursuit of empire. The humanist project of restoring the glories of classical antiquity also helped England find an imperial model to imitate in the expansion of its own borders. This blend of Africa and Rome is especially intriguing in the Diana cameos. The quiver of arrows and the crescent moon headpiece, which mark this as a Diana figure, are also the symbols used to connect Elizabeth to Diana (Strong, *Miniature* 85). There is no tradition of a black Diana in European art; however, Diana was traditionally the protector of slaves. Furthermore, her temple at Ephesus was said to have been built by Amazons and [. . .] Amazons quickly become linked with African and Asian women in early colonialist discourses.

More specific examples of jewel exchanges confirm the relationship between developing white English subjectivity and self-representation and the use of blacks as decorative signifiers. The well-known Gresley jewel features a black woman surrounded by Cupids. The jewel covers the miniature portraits of Catherine Walsingham and Sir Thomas Gresley and commemorates the couple's marriage. Fumerton suggests that such covers serve to protect and hide the private self even as they structurally reveal the private inside of the pendants (74). Additionally, the cover may actually create the 'outer' self in that the black outside cover must be opened to reveal the white skins within [. . .] the image of a white embedded in darkness, of discovering and merchandising a precious whiteness from 'dark' continents, is a typical colonialist gesture in Elizabethan England that works to define and preserve the value of whiteness. More significant, the black cameo is on the obverse side of Catherine Walsingham's miniature, which implies a special connection between white femininity and blackness which I shall return to later in this chapter.

Elaborating on the paradox of public/private within Elizabethan gift culture, Fumerton further asserts: 'On the one hand, the public self faced outward upon gift culture: it "gave" of itself selflessly for the increase of the commonality (or put less idealistically, for a particular regime of commonality). On the other hand, the private self faced inward toward secrecy: it *withheld* itself from the cultural whole' (69). This jewel embodies both gestures: the enclosing of the portrait within the case of blackness hides the self just as the opening of the case reveals the aristocratic bodies within. However, this particular jewel also celebrates a public event— the marriage of Walsingham and Gresley—and thus represents another type of 'increase' as well. If it 'tells little of the couple's love,' as Fumerton notes (74), it speaks volumes about the social function of marriage: the duplication/replication of the self through procreation and the continuation of aristocratic bloodlines. Such a commemorative jewel speaks to this 'increase of the commonality' and lends added resonance to the declaration that opens Shakespeare's sonnets: 'From *fairest* creatures we desire increase' (1.1; emphasis added). Both the jewel and Shakespeare's sonnet rely on the association of aristocratic identity with the Elizabethan cult of fairness.

Perhaps the best known of these black cameos is the Drake pendant, given to Sir Francis Drake by Queen Elizabeth during the winter of 1586–87. According to Roy Strong, this jewel is notable because 'it pinpoints exactly the moment when this act became an acknowledged sign of regal favour' (*Miniature* 85). From the moment of this gift, the queen's miniature portrait became a popular and coveted personal adornment, and the mass production of her legendary 'fairness' began in earnest. Not much is known about the occasion for Drake's receipt of the portrait.[4] In 1586 Drake, authorized to raid the Spanish West Indies, returned from this first voyage as a naval commander. Although the voyage was not a financial success, his capture of Santo Domingo and Cartegna (and the destruction of a Spanish fort in Florida) did substantially raise English morale (Hampden 248). The jewel itself has a black African profile superimposed on a white European profile; it may be yet another version of a 'Moor and emperor' cameo. It is, however, tempting to speculate that this is a reference of sorts to Drake's success over the Spanish. Anti-Spanish rhetoric in England often made note of Spain's ill-defined—and therefore dubious—racial origins: these twin heads may be a sign of that mixture.[5] More concretely, enclosing this representation of the queen's fairness within a black jewel again makes material the creation of 'fairness' as a particular quality of Englishness.

Significantly, this jewel is featured in a Gheeraerts portrait of Drake done in 1594. One hand rests on a globe that is turned to display the continent of Africa. This gesture may be a reminder of his famous circumnavigation, which would also involve [. . .] a conquering of Africa. It might also visually represent English desires for 'possession' of Africa, made possible by breaking Spanish control over that trade. The pendant itself is visually linked to the globe. The objects are parallel to each other, and both contain the only bright color in the portrait: the rubies of the pendant are linked to the red lines indicating the Tropics of Cancer and Capricorn above and below the continent. As a closed locket, the jewel covers the portrait of Elizabeth inside, hinting at a private relationship with the queen while publicly advertising Drake's status as adventurer-gentleman. The positioning of the pendant near his genitals links Drake's imperial and navigational prowess with his masculinity. Louis Montrose's persuasive readings of the psychology of the male subject and female queen in court culture provides for a reading of Drake's representation of imperial/masculine prowess against the overwhelming fact of Elizabeth's power: 'Within legal and fiscal limits, she held the power of life and death over every Englishman, the power to advance or frustrate the worldly desires of all her subjects. Her personality and personal symbolism helped to mold English culture and the consciousness of Englishmen for several generations' (Montrose, 'Shaping Fantasies' 77). If Montrose is correct, then the placement of this gift, hinting at a certain intimacy between ruler and subject, might in this portrait paradoxically reflect Drake's imperial and masculine pride as well as a certain unease in relation to a powerful female ruler.

*   *   *

Juliet Fleming, *Graffiti and the Writing Arts of Early Modern England* (Philadelphia: University of Pennsylvania Press, 2001), pp. 60–7.

The simple visibility of graffiti as such vanishes when it is considered within a culture which practised a wide variety of wall-writing.[1] The Elizabethan interior as it has survived under the auspices of the National Trust presents us with a potent instance of domestic peace. Chastely whitewashed, or wrapped in the decorous and domestic pleats of the famous 'linen-fold' panelling, it seems to preserve for us the graceful silence of the pre-commodity home. In fact, brightly painted walls and ceilings formed the decorative focus of most rooms in Tudor and Stuart England; surviving rooms display an exuberance of colour and design that, together with the inclusion of *trompe l'oeil* and figurative effects, and a tendency to continue patterns over studs, panels and beams, proves uncongenial to modern taste.[2] Tapestry and wainscotting apart, Tudor and Stuart methods of interior decoration included ballad sheets and tables pasted directly onto the wall, or attached to cloth hangings; 'wall papers' produced specifically for the purpose by printers who recycled spoiled pages by printing decorative patterns (sometimes incorporating mottoes) on their backs; and painted cloths.[3] These last so regularly contained writing that they became known for their sententiousness: Shakespeare's Tarquin reminds himself, 'Who fears a sentence or a old man's saw/Shall by a painted cloth be kept in awe' (*The Rape of Lucrece*, 244–5); while an exchange between Jacques and Orlando (*As You Like It*, 3, 2, 266–70) equates painted cloths and posy rings as the sites for the moral truism:

JACQUES: You are full of pretty answers. Have you not been acquainted with goldsmiths' wives, and conn'd them out of rings?

ORLANDO: Not so; but I answer you right painted cloth, from whence you have studied your questions.[4]

From the middle of the sixteenth century until the beginning of the seventeenth, wall-painting was perhaps the most common form of interior decoration. Painted walls (and, for that matter cloths) are not best understood as 'poor man's tapestry': each constitutes a medium and a practice with its own technical opportunities and sophisticated generic conventions, and each found a place in wealthy as well as more modest interiors. Documenting more than 300 surviving wall-paintings in the 1930s, Reader classified them as 'arabesque' work in black and white, 'naturalistic' floral ornament painted in rich colours, panels divided by strapwork and filled with cartouche, representations of tapestries and other hangings, and figure subjects taken from contemporary pastimes and from biblical and classical sources.[5]

Any of these decorative schemes could contain writing: as a whole they comprise a field of art that deserves more serious critical attention than it has hitherto received. Produced in a period that spans the English Reformation, Elizabethan wall-painting necessarily addresses itself to the vexed (and state-legislated) imbrication of word and image: its ideal analysis would proceed under the aegis of a calligraphic term (perhaps *calligramme*, or *graf*, if *graffiti* will not do) that encompassed word and image, and did not presume to know the difference between writing and painting.[6] Archaeological evidence gathered by Reader and others shows that the writing on the interior walls of the Elizabethan house included classical *sententiae*, biblical verse and commentary, prayers, heraldic mottoes, injunctions to fear God and obey the Prince, exhortations to charity and righteous living, and reminders of mortality.[7] Typical of the last, with its tropes of flowers and clay, and its theme of the insubstantiality of earthly life, is the inscription recorded by Reader from a farmhouse in Chiddingly, East Sussex:

> In lyfe theare ys no suer staye
> For fleashe as flower doth vade awaye
> This carcas made of slyme and claye
> Must taste of deathe theare is no waye.
> While we have tyme then lett us praye
> To god for grace bothe night and daye.[8]

Stoke Poges Manor House, built by the Earl of Huntingdon in 1553, has a series of painted sayings in one room, of which Reader found the following still legible: 'Feare the Lord, Obey the Prince', 'Love thi neighbour', 'Beware of Pride', 'Speak the truth' and 'Bear no malice'; while on the wall of a four-room cottage in Chalfont St Peter Reader found the black-letter inscription: 'When any thing thou takest in hand to do or Enterpryse/fyrst markewell the fynall end there of that maye Aryse. Fear God.[9]

That wall-painting could be associated with an adherence to outlawed religious practices is suggested by a passage from John Barclay's *Argenis* (1625), where Timoclea hides Poliarchus in a secret vault left by 'the first Builders' of the house, whose access was hidden beneath the floorboards of her chamber:

> In the entrance, a little way was playstered, that it might be adorned with Letters and Pictures. But the dampe ayre, not quickened by the Stars influence, had somewhat blemished the Imagery: yet there was to bee seene the Portraiture of an Altar, and a man putting his counterfeit Frankincense into this fire: over which these Verses were to bee, though hardly, read:

> > You Gods, that here below, your worship have;
> > Be this *Joves* Palace, or grim *Pluto's* Cave,
> > Or hee that doth in his blue armes enfold
> > Earths Globe, doe here his three-forkt Scepter hold:
> > This Vault still faithful to the Lords maintaine:
> > No treachery, no theft this darknesse staine . . .
> > Let rest and peaceful silence still appeare,
> > Whilest this chaste Family burne Incense here.
> > All guilty soules let hellish horror fright,
> > But good men here enjoy a quiet night.[10]

Secret chapels are very likely to have been decorated with the kinds of wall-painting newly prohibited in parish churches; and it is easy to imagine the discreet painting of forbidden images, on a more modest scale, on the interior walls of recusant households. But the images and political statements that survive from the period are more commonly uncontroversial; they range from the ubiquitous 'Obey the Prince' to the inscription of Elizabeth's motto, 'Semper Eadem', at an inn in County Dublin. While the dominance of such exhortations may suggest the extensiveness of Tudor state supervision, or the possibility that public and private spheres were not yet distinct from each other, slogans such as 'God save the Quene' (like the coronation mugs that are the very type of British domesticity) may serve instead to remind us that dynastic or nationalist sentiment is a reassuring thing.[11] The Elizabethan domestic interior may have been comfortable to its occupants not because it offered refuge from state interference, but because it provided a personal field within which the subject who had learned to desire her own political subordination was permitted—indeed instructed—to write.

Such, after all, is the burden of the two nearly identical passages from Deuteronomy (6: 4–9 and 11: 18–21) that underpin the practice of wall-writing in post-Reformation England, and that were themselves often written on domestic walls.[12] Tyndale rendered the first as follows:

Hear Israel, the Lorde thy God is Lorde only and thou shalt love the Lorde thy God with all thyne hearte . . . And these wordes which I commaunde the this day, shalbe in thine herte and thou shalt whett them on thy childer, and shalt talke of them when thou art home in thyne housse and as thou walkest by the waye, and when thou lyest doune and when thou rysest upp: and thou shalt bynde them for a sygne uppon thyne hande. And they shalbe papers of rembraunce betwene thyne eyes, and shalt write them uppon the postes of thy house and uppon thy gates.

Against this passage, which is crucial to the Reformation project of a vernacular bible, Tyndale inserts the barbed marginal note, 'It is heresy with us for a laye man to loke of gods worde or to read it.' He goes on to explain his choice of the term 'whett' (from the Hebrew root ShNN, to sharpen or repeat), as meaning 'exercyse': exercise your children in God's commandments, and put them into use or practice with them. A marginal gloss to the Geneva Bible elaborates on the meaning of Tyndale's term: 'some read, ye shall whet them upon thy children: to whit, that they may print them more depely into memorie'. The Christian has God's truth imprinted in her mind and heart through education as well as through Grace: the pedagogic trajectory whereby repetition is transformed into memory can be explained, here as nowhere else, as the action of Grace itself.[13]

The Reformed Christian is thus advised, following Deuteronomy, to rehearse God's truth in conversation, bind it on hand and brow, and copy it on to walls. Luther pleased himself with imagining 'the whole Bible to be painted on houses, on the outside and the inside, so that all can see it'; while Calvin, equally sensitive to the fact that the distracted householder may need to be continually reminded of his duty, advised, 'Let us have Gods lawe written, let us have the sayings of it painted on our walles as in tables, and let us have things to put us in minde of it early and late.[14] Indeed, Calvin argues that God holds memory aids to be so necessary that He *repeats* the injunction to write them (in Deuteronomy 6: 4–9 and again in Deuteronomy 11: 18–21). The Bible text thus enacts what Calvin understands to be the burden of its own passages: 'This repetition therefore is not superfluous, where God telleth us again, th[at] it is good for us to have his lawe written everywhere.'[15]

Some Reformers showed themselves more chary of the prosthetic nature, and the material dimension, of such mnemonic devices. The Bishop's Bible (1578) glosses Deuteronomy 6: 9 by explaining that the injunction to write 'upon the postes of thy house, and upon thy gates' means nothing 'but continual meditation of the lawe'; while Joseph Hall, arguing that it is not the outward show but 'the heart and reins [that] are those that God looks after', used the same passage to illustrate the difference between Christians and Pharisees:

God charged them to binde the Law to their hand, and before their eyes, *Deut.* 6 wherein, as *Jerome* and *Theophylact* well interpret it, he meant the meditation and practice of his Law: they, like unto the foolish Patient, which when a Physitian bids him take that pre-script, if they could but get a list of parchment upon their left arme next their heart, and another scroll to be upon their forehead . . . thought they might say with *Saul, Blessed be thou of the Lord, I have done the commandment of the Lord.*[16]

But surviving wall-writings such as the Chiddingly inscription suggest that the pious Eliza-bethan did indeed go to bed at night and wake in the morning in the written shadow of the

Law: 'Therefore at night call unto minde / how thou the daye hast spent: / Praise God, if naught amisse thou finde: / if ought, betimes repent.'[17]

Such admonitions, concerned as they are with testing, counting and timeliness, are over-determined in their early English context, posing both in their content and in themselves the crucial question of whether there *is* ever time or place for repentance. *Pace* Calvin, the repetition of God's law within a predestined world is precisely superfluous; the wall-written prayer (and by extension any prayer) is reduced to the statement of an intention to pray—or to remember to pray.[18] What, after all, following Deuteronomy, should one write on posts, gates, and frontlets for the eyes?—nothing more nor less than the injunction to do so. But what has one done in doing this? The answer, even for Calvin, is nothing at all, for the only 'true decking', the one that makes us acceptable to God, is already to 'beare his Lawe *in minde*'.

Calvin attempts to displace the carnal potential of the writing practices he endorses by displacing it first on to women (who he finds would do better to beautify their bodies, clothes, and houses with 'remembrance of Gods lawe' than with 'bracelets and other fine toyes'); and then on to the Jews, who in their use of mezzuzot and tefillin took an 'excellent lesson' and 'turned it into a charme and sorcerie . . . lyke to the *Agnus Dei* in popery, and such other geugawes as the papists hang about their necks'.[19] For Calvin, to believe in the efficacy of words in their material dimension is to commit precisely the idolatry that the passage warns against. So, even as he writes on his walls, the Reformed Christian must 'marke that God will not bee served by the wrytynge of some sentence of his lawe upon a post or a doore, or at the entry of a house', and undertake instead the impossible achievement of ensuring that that law is 'so engraven in our heartes, as it may never be wiped out again'. Impossibly, and therefore fruitfully, Reformed Christianity structures itself across the problem of the signifier, the problem that is the material dimension of language.

. . . .

QUESTIONS

- What is the status of the material in current reconceptions of history?
- How far are these critics extending the notion of what constitutes a readable text?
- What sorts of texts might materially-oriented critics select for analysis in the future?

SUGGESTED FURTHER READING

Brant, Clare, and Diane Purkiss (eds.), *Women, Texts and Histories 1575–1760* (London and New York: Routledge, 1992)

Bruster, Douglas, *Drama and the Market in the Age of Shakespeare* (Cambridge: Cambridge University Press, 1992)

Dollimore, Jonathan, *Radical Tragedy: Religion, Ideology and Power in the Drama of Shakespeare and his Contemporaries* (Brighton: Harvester, 1984)

—— and Alan Sinfield (eds.), *Political Shakespeare: New Essays in Cultural Materialism* (Manchester: Manchester University Press; Ithaca: Cornell University Press, 1985)

Halpern, Richard, *The Poetics of Primitive Accumulation: English Renaissance Culture and the Genealogy of Capital* (Ithaca and London: Cornell University Press, 1991)

Klein, Bernhard, *Maps and the Writing of Space in Early Modern England and Ireland* (Basingstoke: Palgrave, 2001)

Macdonald, Joyce Green, *Women and Race in Early Modern Texts* (Cambridge: Cambridge University Press, 2002)

Norbrook, David, *Writing the English Republic: Poetry, Rhetoric and Politics, 1627–1660* (Cambridge: Cambridge University Press, 1999)

Orlin, Lena Cowen, *Private Matters and Public Culture in Post-Reformation England* (Ithaca and London: Cornell University Press, 1994)

Sinfield, Alan, *Faultlines: Cultural Materialism and the Politics of Dissident Reading* (Oxford: Clarendon, 1992)

NOTES

Howard, The new historicism

1. Don E. Wayne, 'Drama and Society in the Age of Jonson: An Alternative View', *Renaissance Drama*, 13 (1982), pp. 103–29.

2. Lawrence Stone, *The Family, Sex and Marriage in England 1500–1800* (New York, 1977).

3. See, in particular, Althusser's key essay, 'Ideology and Ideological State Apparatuses' in *Lenin and Philosophy and Other Essays* (New York, 1971), pp. 127–86.

4. For the first understanding of ideology see Karl Marx, *The German Ideology* (London, 1965); for the second understanding see Althusser, 'Ideology and Ideological State Apparatuses.'

5. Pierre Macherey, *A Theory of Literary Production*, trans. Geoffrey Wall (London, 1978), esp. pp. 51–65.

6. Tony Bennett, *Formalism and Marxism* (London, 1979), esp. ch. 2, 'Formalism and Marxism,' pp. 18–43.

7. Bennett, p. 9 and Terry Eagleton, *An Introduction of Literary Theory*, esp. 'Introduction: What is Literature?', pp. 1–16.

8. For LaCapra's view of the multiplicity and self-divisions of texts see 'Rethinking Intellectual History and Reading Texts,' esp. pp. 52–5 and 58–61. M. Bakhtin's work on *heteroglossia* and *carnivalization* can be found in *The Dialogic Imagination Four Essays*, ed. Michael Holquist, trans. Caryl Emerson and Michael Holquist (Austin, 1981), pp. 259–422.

Greenblatt, Renaissance Self-Fashioning

1. 'The voyage set out by the right honourable the Earle of Cumberland, in the yere 1586. . . . Written by M. John Sarracoll marchant in the same voyage,' in Richard Hakluyt (ed.), *The Principal Navigations, Voyages, Traffiques & Discoveries of the English Nation*, 12 vols. (Glasgow: James MacLehose & Sons, 1903–5), 11:206–7. On the English in Sierra Leone prior to this voyage, see P. E. H. Hair, 'Protestants as Pirates, Slavers, and Proto-missionaries: Sierra Leone 1568 and 1582,' *Journal of Ecclesiastical History* 21 (1970), pp. 203–24. On the region in this period, see Walter Rodney, *A History of the Upper Guinea Coast, 1545–1800* (Oxford: At the Clarendon Press, 1970).

2. At the opening of *Tamburlaine* there is a wry reminder of how exotic Europe would appear to a Persian: 'Europe, where the Sun dares scarce appear, / For freezing meteors and congealed cold' (1 *Tam* 1.1.18–19). Quotations of Marlowe's plays with the exception of *Doctor Faustus*, are modernized from *The Works of Christopher Marlowe*, ed. C. F. Tucker Brooke (Oxford: Clarendon Press, 1910). Quotations of *Doctor Faustus* are modernized from the A text of W. W. Greg's *Marlowe's 'Doctor Faustus' 1604–1616: Parallel Texts* (Oxford: At the Clarendon Press, 1950). My own reading of the play supports recent arguments for the superiority of the A text; see Fredson Bowers, 'Marlowe's *Doctor Faustus:* The 1602 Additions' (*Studies in Bibliography* 26 [1973], 1–18) and Constance Brown Kuriyama (*English Literary Renaissance* 5 [1975], 171–97).

On the relationship of Spenser and Marlowe, see Douglas Bush, 'Marlowe and Spenser,' *Times Literary Supplement*, 28 May 1938, p. 370; T. W. Baldwin, 'The Genesis of Some Passages which Spenser Borrowed from Marlowe,' *English Literary History* 9 (1942), pp. 157–87, and reply by W. B. C. Watkins in *ELH* 11 (1944), 249–65; John D. Jump, 'Spenser and Marlowe,' *Notes and Queries* 209, new ser. 11 (1964), pp. 261–2. See also Georg Schoeneich, 'Der literarische Einfluss Spensers auf Marlowe' (Diss., Halle, 1907).

3. See Ernst Cassirer, *The Individual and the Cosmos in Renaissance Philosophy*, trans. Mario Domandi (New York: Barnes & Noble, 1963), esp. chap. 1, 'Nicholas Cusanus.' In *Doctor Faustus* Marlowe plays upon the residual religious symbolism of the Elizabethan stage (though this is more true of the B text than the A text), but he does so only to subvert it, locating hell psychologically rather than spatially.

On maps in Marlowe, see Ethel Seaton, 'Marlowe's Map,' *Essays and Studies by Members of the English Association* 10 (1924), pp. 13–35; Donald K. Anderson, Jr., 'Tamburlaine's "Perpendicular" and the T-in-O Maps,' *Notes and Queries* 21 (1974), pp. 284–6.

4. Here, as elsewhere in my discussion of *Doctor Faustus*, I am indebted to conversations with Edward Snow and to his essay, 'Marlowe's *Doctor Faustus* and the Ends of Desire,' in *Two Renaissance Mythmakers: Christopher Marlowe and Ben Jonson*, ed. Alvin B. Kernan (Baltimore: Johns Hopkins University Press, 1977), pp. 70–110.

5. The agreement depends, in part, on the pun on Aye/I (the latter is the reading of the A and B texts). 'Experience' may also have the sense of 'experiment,' as if Faustus's whole future were a test of the proposition that hell is a fable.

6. See Richard Madox's Diary for 14 December 1582: 'Although the soldiers are strong and sufficiently courageous, they are utterly inept at trading and the exploring of unknown lands. Because, indeed, being always among enemies and in a hostile place, they believe they are [here] exposed to the usual dangers; for this reason they can never enter into dealings with others without suspicion. Suspicion, however, breeds hatred and hatred open war, and thus those they ought to attract and attach to themselves by human kindness and clemency, they frighten off by impudence and malice, and in this way all love perishes. Especially because of ignorance of languages, each is a barbarian to the other' (*An Elizabethan in 1582*, ed. Donno, p. 186). In the light of this passage, perhaps the odd conjunction of admiration and destructiveness in Sarracoll's account may be traced to the difference between the merchant's view of the town and the view (and consequent actions) of the soldiers who were with him.

7. Snow, 'Marlowe's *Doctor Faustus* and the Ends of Desire,' p. 101.

8. The futility of naming cities after oneself was a commonplace in the period; see, for example, Ralegh's *History of the World* (1614):

This was that *Seleucia*, whereto *Antigonus the great* who founded it, gave the name of *Antigonia*: but *Seleucus* getting it shortly after, called it *Seleucia*; and *Ptolemie Evergetes* having lately won it, might, if it had so pleased him, have changed the name into *Ptolemais*. Such is the vanity of men, that hope to purchase an endless memorial unto their names, by works proceeding rather from their greatness, than from their virtue; which therefore no longer are their own, than the same greatness hath continuance. (V, v, 2, p. 646)

9. The cutting edge of this career was the conquest of the New World where fertile lands, rich mines, and whole peoples were consumed in a few generations. It is estimated that the Indian population of New Spain (Mexico) fell from approximately 11 million in 1519 to approximately 1.5 million in 1650, and there are similarly horrifying figures for Brazil. In 1583 a Jesuit, José de Anchieta, observed of the latter that 'the number of people used up in this place from twenty years ago until now seems a thing not to be believed' (quoted in Immanuel Wallerstein, *The Modern World-System* [New York: Academic Press, 1974], 80, n. 75); appropriately, it is on this great enterprise (among others) that the dying Tamburlaine, with infinite pathos, reflects.

10. E. E. Evans-Pritchard, *The Nuer* (Oxford: At the Clarendon Press, 1940), p. 103; quoted in E. P. Thompson, 'Time, Work-Discipline, and Industrial Capitalism,' *Past and Present* 38 (1967), p. 96.

11. See Keith Thomas, *Religion and the Decline of Magic* (London: Weidenfeld & Nicolson, 1971), p. 621; likewise, Christopher Hill, *Society and Puritanism in Pre-Revolutionary England*, 2nd edn (New York: Schocken, 1967), chap. 5.

12. See Natalie Zemon Davis, 'Some Tasks and Themes in the Study of Popular Religion,' in *The Pursuit of Holiness in Late Medieval and Renaissance Religion*, ed. Charles Trinkaus and Heiko A. Oberman (Leiden: E. J. Brill, 1974), pp. 307–36. I am also indebted to Professor Davis's essay, 'Ghosts, Kin and Progeny: Some Features of Family Life in Early Modern France,' *Daedalus* 106 (1977), pp. 87–114.

13. On time in *Doctor Faustus*, see Max Bluestone, 'Adaptive Time in *Doctor Faustus*,' in *From Story to Siege: The Dramatic Adaptation of Prose Fiction in the Period of Shakespeare and his Contemporaries* [*Studies in English Literature*, n. 70] (The Hague: Mouton, 1974), pp. 244–52; David Kaula, 'Time and the Timeless in *Everyman* and *Dr. Faustus*,' *College English* 22 (1960), pp. 9–14.

Highley, Shakespeare, Spenser, and the Crisis in Ireland

1. Quoted in Nicholas Canny, 'The Ideology of English Colonization: From Ireland to America', *William and Mary Quarterly*, 30 (1973), p. 591.

2. *1 Henry IV*, ed. David Bevington (Oxford: Clarendon, 1987), III.i.201–2.

3. Sir Edmund Spenser, *A View of the Present State of Ireland*, ed. W. L. Renwick (London: Scholartis Press, 1934), pp. 62, 84, 86.

4. Quoted in G. A. Hayes-McCoy, 'The Completion of the Tudor Conquest and the Advance of the Counter-Reformation, 1571–1603', in T. W. Moody, F. X. Martin and F. J. Byrne (eds.), *A New History of Ireland*, 9 vols. (Oxford: Clarendon, 1976–84), III, p. 123.

Callaghan, Re-reading Cary's The Tragedie of Mariam

1. Bill Ashcroft, Gareth Griffiths and Helen Tiffin, *The Empire Writes Back: Theory and Practice in Post-Colonial Literatures* (New York: Routledge, 1989), p. 175.

2. Emily C. Bartels, 'Malta, the Jew, and the Fictions of Difference: Colonialist Discourse in Marlowe's *The Jew of Malta*,' *ELR* 20: 1 (1990), p. 2.

3. See Margaret T. Hodgen, *Early Anthropology in the Sixteenth and Seventeenth Centuries* (Philadelphia: University of Pennsylvania Press, 1964).

4. See Lady Georgiana Fullerton, *The Life of Elisabeth Lady Falkland, 1585–1639* (London: Burns & Oates, 1883), p. 266. See also *The Lady Falkland: Her Life*, ed. Richard Simpson (London: Catholic Publishing & Bookselling Co., 1861), p. 113. For further biographical information, see Kenneth B. Murdoch, *The Sun at Noon: Three Biographical Sketches* (New York: Macmillan, 1939).

5. Alexander B. Grosart (ed.), *The Complete Works of John Davies of Hereford*, 2 vols. (n.d.; repr. New York: AMS Press, 1967), vol. 2, p. 5.

6. Jews were expelled from Spain in 1492 and from Portugal in 1497. See Jonathan I. Israel, *European Jewry in the Age of Mercantilism, 1550–1750* (Oxford: Clarendon Press, 1985); John Edwards, *The Jews in Christian Europe 1400–1700* (New York: Routledge, 1988); David S. Katz, *Philo-semitism and the Readmission of the Jews to England 1603–1655* (Oxford: Clarendon Press, 1982).

7. See Katz, *Philo-semitism*, p. 134.

8. The Beinecke Library at Yale University has the 1602 edition of Lodge, but I have consulted the Newberry Library's 1620 edition. Flavius Josephus, *The Famous and Memorable Works*, trans. Thomas Lodge (London: Simon Waterson, 1620). Dunstan makes the case for Cary's use of Lodge. Elizabeth Cary, Viscountess Falkland, *The Tragedy of Mariam* (1613), ed. A. C. Dunstan, The Malone Society Reprints (Oxford: Horace Hart for Oxford University Press, 1914), pp. xiii–xix.

There is an earlier version of the Herod–Mariam story translated into English, which indicates something of the extent of contemporary interest in this aspect of Jewish history.

Joseph Ben Gorion, *A Compendium and Most Marvellous History of the Latter Times of the Jews Common Weale*, trans. Peter Morwyn (1575; London: Colophon, John Wallie, 1579).

Fullerton claims that Cary 'perfectly understood' Hebrew in her youth (Fullerton, *The Life*, p. 7; Simpson, *Lady Falkland*, p. 4). There has been far less interest in Cary's intellectual endeavors than in recovering her emotional traumas. The biography of Cary written by her daughter is largely about her conversion to Catholicism, which critics tend to read primarily as a matter of 'personal experience,' the limits of which have been well established in feminist critiques of essentialism. At a time when intellectual and political thought was virtually synonymous with theological doctrine, conversion to Catholicism was an intellectual position on contemporary texts and arguments arrived at only after intense study, not just a matter of private soul-searching. See Kenneth L. Campbell, *The Intellectual Struggle of the English Papists in the Seventeenth Century: The Catholic Dilemma*, Texts and Studies in Religion, vol. 30 (New York: Edwin Mellen Press, 1986); Peter Milward, *Religious Controversies in the Jacobean Age* (London: University of Nebraska Press, 1986); George H. Tavard, *The Seventeenth-Century Tradition: A Study in Recusant Thought* (Leiden: E. J. Brill, 1978). Cary's interest in the Jews is clearly part of an intellectual and theological interest, one she shared with English Protestants, who were after all responsible for convening the Whitehall Conference.

9. The trope of foreignness applied to other nations, 'another country, a country of others,' where it was possible to explore what was forbidden in the domestic environment (Ann Rosalind Jones, 'Italians and Others,' in David Scott Kastan and Peter Stallybrass (eds.), *Staging the Renaissance: Reinterpretations of Elizabethan and Jacobean Drama* [New York: Routledge, 1991], p. 251).

10. See James Finn, *Sephardim: Or the History of the Jews in Spain and Portugal* (London: Gilbert & Rivington, 1841), p. vi; Katz, *Philo-semitism*, pp. 170–1. Sir Thomas Browne inquires into the 'vulgar and common error' 'That Jews stink.' This turns out to be a meditation on whether Jews constitute a nation or whether they have distinct, physiologically based, racial characteristics. He concludes that a 'metaphorical expression' has been transformed into a 'literal construction' and that it is dangerous to 'annex a constant property unto any nation' (Thomas Browne, *The Works of the Learned Sir Thomas Browne* [London: Thomas Basset, Richard Chiswell, Thomas Sawbridge, Charles Mearn, & Charles Brome, 1686], p. 169). Coryate describes Jews of different nationalities in Venice:

I observed some few of these Jewes especially some of the Levantines to bee such goodly and proper men, that then I said to my selfe our English proverbe: To look like a Iewe (whereby is meant sometimes a weather beaten warp-faced fellow, sometimes a phrenticke and lunaticke person, sometimes one discontented) is not true.
(Thomas Coryate, *Coryats Crudities* [London: W. S[tanby], 1611], p. 232)

Spelling of the authors' names in these entries conforms to the title-pages of the works consulted.

11. Katz, *Philo-semitism*, pp. 2–3.

12. Ibid., p. 244.

13. G. K. Hunter has argued that in Elizabethan England Jews were regarded as theologically and morally wanting rather than as racially other. He bases his argument on the possibility of conversion. Yet historical evidence shows that conversion did not secure a Jew's freedom from anti-semitism. Since they were regarded as innately treacherous, it was felt that one could never be sure about the authenticity of Jews' conversion. G. K. Hunter, 'The Theology of Marlowe's *The Jew of Malta*,' *Journal of the Warburg and Courtauld Institutes* 27 (1964), pp. 211–40. See also Michael Ferber, 'The Ideology of *The Merchant of Venice*,' *ELR* 20:3 (1990) p. 441. *The Merchant of Venice* and *The Jew of Malta* are examples of this stereotyped representation from the drama. We also know that Stephen Gosson wrote a play called *The Jew* which was performed at the Bull in 1579, recorded as 'representing the greediness of wordly chusers, and bloody mindes of Usurers' (N. W. Bawcutt (ed.), *The Jew of Malta* by Christopher Marlowe [Baltimore: Johns Hopkins University Press,

1978], p. 4). On the distinction between anti-Catholicism and anti-semitism, see Katz, *Philo-semitism*, p. 162.

14. Katz, *Philo-semitism*, pp. 3–4. Purchas notes that Papists are 'the common adversarie' of both Jews and Protestants. He writes of the 'Partition-wall which separateth Jew and Catholike' on grounds of the Jewish intolerance for idolatry, and fulminates against Catholics who seem rather further from conversion to true Christianity than Jews. Samuel Purchas, *Purchas His Pilgrimage, Or Relations Of The World And The Religions Observed In All Ages and Places Discovered, from the Creation unto this Present*, vol. I (London: William Stansby for Henrie Fetherstone, 1613), p. 184.

15. Even this view must be tempered by Sir Thomas Browne's proposition that the Jews were an impure race because of the strong sexual desire Jewish women had for Christian men. See Katz, *Philo-semitism*, p. 170.

16. Leslie A. Fiedler, *The Stranger in Shakespeare* (1973; London: Paladin, 1974), p. 99.

17. There are also medieval legends about Jewish fathers who kill their children when they become converts to Christianity (Bawcutt, *Jew of Malta*, p. 9).

18. All play quotations are taken from Dunstan's *Mariam*. In the interests of readability, I have emended 'v' to 'u' and 'ſ' to 's' throughout.

19. See, Elaine V. Beilin, *Redeeming Eve: Women Writers of the English Renaissance* (Princeton: Princeton University Press, 1987), p. 165. Ferguson notes that Mariam's beheading conjures up the ghosts of Mary Queen of Scots and of Christ's harbinger, 'John the Baptist, beheaded by Herod's servants at Salome's request,' 'Spectre of Resistance,' p. 245. This is, of course, a different Herod (Antipas) and a different Salome (the daughter of Heroditas), but Valency has observed that all the Herods were so evil that they became a sort of historical amalgam, so that the wickedness of one Herod invariably summons up the deeds of the others (Maurice J. Valency, *The Tragedies of Herod and Mariamne* [Morningside Heights: Columbia University Press, 1940], pp. 19–67).

20. Fiedler, *Stranger in Shakespeare*, p. 99.

21. This phenomenon has its literary antecedents in the Virgin's intervention in Chaucer's *The Prioress's Tale* and in the ballad of *Hugh of Lincoln* where a Gentile child is slain for his devotion to the Virgin. See Fiedler, *Stranger in Shakespeare*, p. 98.

22. Fiedler, *Stranger in Shakespeare*, p. 101.

23. Quoted Charles H. and Katherine George, *The Protestant Mind of the English Reformation 1570–1640* (Princeton: Princeton University Press, 1961), p. 282.

24. See Fiedler, *Stranger in Shakespeare*, p. 106. Obviously, in terms of the plot, actual conversion is not a choice available to Mariam, even though, as we have seen, she is symbolically marked by Christianity.

25. Ferguson suggests that the marriage of Herod and Mariam is an 'interfaith union' ('Running on,' p. 43). It is not clear that English Renaissance Christians were particularly aware of any religious difference between Edomites and Jews. Purchas writes:

Idumaea lyeth Southward from Judea: It had the name of *Edom*, the surname of *Esau*, sonne of *Isaak*. . . . It was subdued by David, according to the Prophecie, *The elder shall serve the younger*. They rebelled under *Ioram* the sonne of *Jehsophat*; as *Isaak* had also prophecied. From that they continued bitter enemies to the people of God, till Hircanus, the sonne of Simon compelled them to accept both the Jewish Dominion and Religion: after which they were reckoned among the Jews.

He also remarks, in a chapter entitled 'Of the divers Sects among the Jewes,'

The *Herodians* were Jewes, otherwise agreeing with the rest; but they thought *Herod* to be the Messias, moved by *Jacobs* prophecie falsely interpreted, *That the Scepter should not depart from Juda till Shilo came*. When as therefore they saw *Herod* a stranger to possesse the kingdome, they interpreted as aforesaid.

(Purchas, *Pilgrimage*, pp. 83, 128)

Similarly, the issue of 'colonization' tends to strike modern readers of the play as a relevant theme given the relation between Palestine and Rome. However, Renaissance culture's interest in the Jews does not take this form.

26. See my *Woman and Gender in Renaissance Tragedy: A Study of Othello, King Lear, The Duchess of Malfi and The White Devil* (Atlantic Highlands: Humanities Press, 1989), pp. 123–39.

27. Fischer, 'Elizabeth Cary,' p. 235.

28. On the question of Mariam's execution see Frances Dolan, ' "Gentlemen, I have one thing more to say"; Women on Scaffolds in England, 1563–1680,' *Modern Philology* 92.2 (1994), 157–78.

29. See Harry Levin, *The Power of Blackness* (New York: Alfred Knopf, 1958) and Winthrop Jordan, *White over Black* (Chapel Hill: University of North Carolina Press, 1968).

30. For a splendid analysis of Graphina as an instance of appropriate but restrained female utterance see Ferguson, who reminds us that *graphesis* means Writing ('Running on,' p. 47).

31. Feminist critics have noted that this is what is unusual about Cary's treatment of her theme, in comparison with both her source and with other Renaissance dramatic treatments of the Herod–Mariam story. For example, Beilin comments 'Cary structures the play to make Mariam's conflict between obedience to and rebellion against Herod's authority the central concern' (*Redeeming Eve*, p. 166).

Burnett, Constructing 'Monsters'

1. Ben Jonson, *Three Comedies*, ed. Michael Jamieson (Harmondsworth: Penguin, 1966), V.i.6–9.

2. N. W. Bawcutt (ed.), *The Control and Censorship of Caroline Drama: The Records of Sir Henry Herbert, Master of the Revels, 1623–73* (Oxford: Clarendon, 1996), p. 142; R. W. Ingram (ed.), *Coventry*, Records of Early English Drama (Toronto: University of Toronto Press, 1981), p. 443; I. P., *A meruaylous straunge deformed swyne* (London, 1570?; S.T.C. 19071).

3. Bawcutt (ed.), *Control and Censorship*, pp. 83, 152, 175, 189, 204; George Chapman, *Sir Gyles Goosecappe* (1601–3), in *The Tragedies*, ed. Allan Holaday (Cambridge: Brewer, 1987), I.i.11–12; Thomas Crosfield, *The Diary*, ed. Frederick S. Boas (London: Milford, 1935), p. 79; David Galloway (ed.), *Norwich, 1540–1642*, Records of Early English Drama (Toronto: University of Toronto Press, 1984), pp. 115, 126, 142, 150, 215; Jasper Mayne, *The City-Match*, in W. C. Hazlitt (ed.), *A Select Collection of Old English Plays*, 4th edn, 15 vols. (London: Reeves and Turner, 1874–6), XIII, p. 248; Thomas Randolph, *Hey for Honesty* (1626–28?/1648–49?), in *The Poetical and Dramatic Works*, ed. W. Carew Hazlitt, 2 vols. (London: Reeves and Turner, 1875), II, I.i. p. 393.

4. Bawcutt (ed.), *Control and Censorship*, p. 204; Galloway (ed.), *Norwich*, p. 115.

5. Thomas Nabbes, *The Works*, ed. A. H. Bullen, 2 vols. (London: Wyman, 1887), I, II.ii. p. 27.

6. Zakiya Hanafi, *The Monster in the Machine: Magic, Medicine, and the Marvellous in the Time of the Scientific Revolution* (Durham and London: Duke University Press, 2000), pp. 36, 47; Stephen Pender, 'In the Bodyshop: Human Exhibition in Early Modern England', in Helen Deutsch and Felicity Nussbaum (eds.), *'Defects': Engendering the Modern Body* (Ann Arbor: University of Michigan Press, 2000), p. 108; *The terrible, horrible, monster of the West* (London, 1649; Wing T765), sig. A1ʳ.

Gallagher and Greenblatt, Practicing New Historicism

1. Ezra Pound, 'I Gather the Limbs of Osiris', *New Age* (1911–12); William Carlos Williams, *In the American Grain* (New York: New Directions, 1956), p. v.

Fuller, Voyages in Print

1. Lewis Theobald, *Memoirs of Sir Walter Raleigh; His Life, his Military and Naval Exploits, his Preferments and Death: In which are Inserted, The Private Intrigues between the Count of Gondamore, the Spanish Ambassador, and the Lord Salisbury then Secretary of State*, 2nd edn, (London: W. Mears, 1719), p. 39.

2. Francis Bacon, the *Declaration of the Demeanour and Cariage of Sir Walter Raleigh* (London, 1618, repr. New York: Da Capo, 1970).

3. The pagination of the copy used for the Da Capo facsimile is incorrect here; though the page quoted from is numbered 62, it should be 66. The incorrect pagination begins at 65, numbered 61, and continues to the end of the text.

4. Karen Cunningham, ' "A Spanish Heart in an English Body": the Ralegh Treason Trial and the Poetics of Proof,' *Journal of Medieval and Renaissance Studies* 22, no. 3 (fall 1992), 327–51.

5. V. T. Harlow, *Ralegh's Last Voyage* (London: Argonaut, 1932), 303. Further citations in text as 'Harlow.'

6. *Declaration*, 35. Harlow offers a detailed explanation for Keymis' maneuverings, arguing that two mines were known to him and Ralegh, one near San Thomé and the other at some distance.

7. Letter to James, September 24, 1618, in Edward Edwards, *The Life of Sir Walter Ralegh*, 2 vols. (London: Macmillan, 1868), II, 369.

8. David Jardine (ed.), *Criminal Trials*, 2 vols. (London: Charles Knight, 1832), I, 420; cited in Cunningham, ' "A Spanish Heart," ' 337.

9. This argument about the privileged position of the prisoner on the scaffold will be familiar to readers from Michel Foucault's chapter, 'The Spectacle of the Scaffold' (in *Discipline and Punish*, trans. Alan Sheridan [New York: Vintage, 1979], 32–72) and from Stephen Greenblatt's chapter on Thomas More, 'At the Table of the Great,' in his *Renaissance Self-Fashioning* (University of Chicago Press, 1980). I want to stress here Ralegh's sense of his position 'on stage' as also in the light.

10. Letter to Sir John Chamberlain from Sir Dudley Carleton, cited in Edwards, *Ralegh* I, 410.

11. 'Sir Walter Raghleys Large Appologie for the ill successe of his enterprise to Guiana' is printed by Harlow, 316–34.

12. Most famously, in the quip on the ax: 'This is a sharp Medicine, but it is a physician for all diseases.' Ralegh also greets the witnesses to his execution with words which powerfully suggest a figurative reading: 'I desire to be born withal, because this is the Third day of my Feaver: And if I shew any weakness, I beseech you to attribute it to my Malady, for this is the Hour I look for it' (Harlow, 306).

13. E. G. R. Taylor (ed.), *Original Writings and Correspondence of the Two Richard Hakluyts*, 2 vols. (London: Hakluyt Society, 1935), II, p. 367.

14. Edmundo O'Gorman, *The Invention of America* (Bloomington, Indiana University Press, 1961), 9, 40.

15. See Ralegh's 1607 letter to Robert Cecil, in Edwards, *Ralegh* II, 389–91.

16. Walter Ralegh, *Discoverie of the Large, Rich, and Beautiful Empire of Guiana*, ed. Sir Robert H. Schomburgk (London: Hakluyt Society, 1848), xi, xiii.

Smith, Homosexual Desire

1. Quoted in A. L. Rowse, *Simon Forman: Sex and Society in Shakespeare's Age* (London: Weidenfeld & Nicolson, 1974), p. 20.

Fox, Oral and Literate Culture

1. PRO, STAC8/236/29, m. 2.

2. PRO, STAC8/159/6, m. 2.

3. BL, Lansdowne MS, 639, fo. 103; BL, Lansdowne MS, 620, fo. 50ᵛ; Hudson, 'A Treatise of the Court of Star Chamber', in *Collectanea Juridica*, ed. Hargrave, ii. 224.

4. PRO, STAC8/77/4, m. 4; PRO, STAC8/307/9, m. 2.

5. PRO, STAC8/282/12, m. 3.

6. PRO, STAC8/253/18, m. 4.

7. PRO, STAC8/88/7, m. 2.

8. PRO, STAC8/153/5, mm. 4, 8.

9. PRO, STAC8/190/7, m. 13; PRO, STAC8/153/29, m. 1; PRO, STAC8/51/2, m. 2.

10. PRO, STAC8/42/14.

11. PRO, STAC8/185/23, m. 2.

12. BL, Lansdowne MS, 639, fo. 88.

13. PRO, STAC8/167/27, m. 2; PRO, STAC8/275/22, m. 2.

14. PRO, STAC8/208/31, m. 3; PRO, STAC8/256/9.

15. PRO, STAC8/205/19; PRO, STAC8/205/20; Huntington Library, Ellesmere MS, 5956.

16. 265 out of the 577 defamation causes (46 per cent) involved men and women from these middling and lower levels of society as either plaintiff or defendant.

Kastan, Shakespeare after Theory

1. Roger Chartier, *Forms and Meanings: Texts, Performances, and Audiences from Codex to Computer* (Philadelphia: University of Pennsylvania Press, 1995), p. 2.

Hall, Things of Darkness

1. This was also the first era in which princes 'made a formal association between certain specific jewels and their own dynasty, declaring them to be inalienable heirlooms' (*Princely Magnificence* 3).

2. Patricia Fumerton and Roy Strong ascribe this to an increased supply of black onyx in the period, but there are such cameos made of white sardonyx as well as artifacts made of other materials. It may be that more black onyx is used and that these cameos are in part sparked by the importance of blackness in the sonnet as well.

3. I owe this point to John Michael Archer's paper ' "False Soul of Egypt": Antiquity and Degeneration in *Antony and Cleopatra*,' circulated at the Shakespeare Association of America panel, 'Race, Ethnicity and Power in Shakespeare and His Contemporaries' (April, 1993).

4. The correct date was only comparatively recently changed from 1574 to 1586.

5. This would be a highly ironic gesture as well, given Camden's recording of the earlier controversy over Drake's 'most inhumanely exposed in an island that negro or blackamore maid who had been gotten with child in his ship' (reprinted in Hampden, *Francis Drake, Privateer* 244). As I noted in the Introduction, Drake was involved in England's entrance into the slave trade on other levels as well.

Fleming, Graffiti and the Writing Arts

1. The following account is dependent on the work of Francis Reader, who recorded surviving English domestic wall-paintings in the 1930s ('Wall-paintings of the 16th and early 17th centuries recently discovered in Bosworth House, Wendover, Bucks.', *Archaeological Journal*, LXXXVII (1930), pp. 71–97; *idem*, 'Tudor Mural Paintings in the Lesser Houses of Bucks.', *Archaeological Journal*, LXXXIX (1932), pp. 116–73; *idem*, 'Tudor Domestic Wall-Paintings I', *Archaeological Journal*, XCII (1935), pp. 243–86; *idem*, 'Tudor Domestic Wall-Paintings II', *Archaeological Journal*, XCIII (1936), pp. 220–62. Watt usefully digests and elaborates Reader's work in Tessa Watt, *Cheap Print and Popular Piety 1550–1640* (Cambridge: Cambridge University Press, 1991), pp. 179–253.

2. Following Reader, Watt puts the height of the vogue for English wall-painting at 1530–80 and suggests that its decline may be attributable to 'the growing ownership of paintings and prints as we now know them [which] changed ideas about what "art" should be, and made the use of every odd surface for painting seem old-fashioned and inferior' (*Cheap Print*, p. 199).

3. In 1568, Herman Schinkel, a Delft printer, answered charges that he had printed prohibited

ballads by claiming 'that they were printed in his absence by his servant, and on his return he refused to deliver them and threw them in a corner intending to print roses and stripes on the other side, to paper attics with' (James Knowles, 'Papering Rooms', *Notes and Queries*, second ser., II (July 1856), pp. 7–8); see also Reader, 'Tudor Mural Paintings', p. 163. H. Jenkinson, 'English Wall-Paper of the Sixteenth and Seventeenth Centuries', *Antiquaries Journal*, XV (1925), pp. 237–53, argues that although very few have survived, decorative printed papers were 'both plentiful and popular in their day' and were used not only to decorate walls but also to cover books and line boxes.

4. Reader, 'Tudor Domestic Wall-paintings I', p. 246; Watt, *Cheap Print*, p. 219.

5. Reader, 'Tudor Mural Wall-paintings', pp. 119–20.

6. The term *calligramme* was used by G. Apollinaire to describe his experimental poem-pictures (*Calligrammes* [Paris, 1918]). An imagistic arrangement of text ('non rebus sed verbis', as it were), the *calligramme* has its own ancient, modern and post-modern history. Like the rebus, of which it is the inverse, the *calligramme* stages a confrontation between word and image. According to Adam Gopnik and Kirk Varnedoe (*High and Low: Modern Art/Popular Culture* (New York: Harry N. Abrams, 1991), p. 70), it was Garrucci (1856) who extended the meaning of graffiti to include drawings as well as inscriptions. Contemporary graffiti writers sometimes use the term *graf* to describe their own conflation of word and image. For discussion of the Protestant tradition of 'visual stories', see Watt, *Cheap Print*, pp. 185f., 224, where she notes that the term *table* describes a broadside or painting 'caught somewhere between decorative "imagerye" and the schematic arrangement of printed words'.

7. Tessa Watt cites William Bullein's description of an inn whose parlour is decorated with painted cloths 'with pleasaunte borders aboute the same, with many wise sayinges painted upon them' and with emblems and Latin inscriptions painted on the walls and chimneys. She concludes, as I would not, that this is a 'literary' rather than a 'realistic' description (Bullein, *A dialogue . . . wherein is a goodly regimente against the fever pestilence*, 3rd edn (1573), sig. Kᵛ; Watt, *Cheap Print*, p. 193).

8. Reader, 'Tudor Mural Paintings', p. 121. For a fuller description of this inscription and the decorative scheme that contained it, see Mainwaring Johnstone, 'Mural Paintings in Houses', p. 75. A broadside ballad expressing identical sentiments, in slightly different order, was printed in 1555 by John Tysdale, and again in 1566 by William Powell; it begins 'Remember man both night and daye/Thou must nedes die, there is no nay/Thy mortall body formed of clay/Will sone resolve and passe a waye.'

9. Reader, 'Tudor Mural Paintings', p. 120.

10. John Barclay, *Barclay his Argenis*, trans. K. Long (London, 1625), pp. 12–14.

11. Watt suggests that as texts such as 'Feare God' may have held talismanic power for the people who wrote them on their walls; alternatively, once it had become familiar it might 'simply have faded into the background like "Home Sweet Home" on a nineteenth-century American sampler' (*Cheap Print*, p. 220).

12. The text of the first passage survives on a wall in Feering, Essex (see Carrick, 'Wall Painting', p. 6; Watt, *Cheap Print*, p. 217), and in Kelvedon, Essex (see Fred Roe, 'Tudor Wall Painting at Kelvedon', *Connoisseur*, LXXXV [January 1930], p. 24).

13. Regina M. Schwartz, *Remembering and Repeating: Biblical Creation in 'Paradise Lost'* (Cambridge: Cambridge University Press, 1988), p. 5, cites this passage in the context of a discussion of repetition and memory. On the importance of the classical *sententia* as a form that is not only memorable in itself but that has the power to bring the reader to consciousness of what she knows, and so appears to 'speak the language of oracles', see E. McCutcheon, *Sir Nicholas Bacon's Great House Sententiae*, English Literary Renaissance Supplements (Amherst: University of Massachusetts Press, 1977), p. 45.

14. See Ernest B. Gilman, *Iconoclasm and Poetry in the English Reformation: Down went Dagon* (Chicago and London: University of Chicago Press, 1986), p. 35; Watt, *Cheap Print*, p. 185.

15. John Calvin, *Sermons on Deuteronomy*, trans. Arthur Golding (London, 1583), p. 473.

16. Joseph Hall, *Works* (London, 1634), vol. 1, p. 379.

17. W. Phiston, trans., *The Welspring of Wittie Conceites* (London: Richard Jones, 1584) sig. N3ᵛ.

18. Watt notes that Elizabethan edifying ballads, even those that are 'thoroughly Protestant', display 'little sense of a predestined elect': characteristically, they continue to represent grace as a gift that is offered by Christ to all and is available up to the last minute of life (*Cheap Print*, pp. 105–6).

19. Calvin, *Deuteronomy*, p. 276. Samuel Purchas, by contrast, describes Jewish observance as the type of prophylaxis acceptable to Calvin: '*The sentence* Hear Israel etc. *and another sentence is to be written on the postes of the House.* He which hath his *Phylacteries* on his head and arms, and his knots on his garment, and his Schedule on his doore, is so fenced he cannot easily sinne' (*Purchas his Pilgrimage* [London, 1613], p. 154).

REFERENCES

Carrick, M., 'Wall Paintings in Feering and Kelvedon', in *Historic Buildings in Essex* (Colchester: Essex Historic Buildings Group, 1985), pp. 328–39.

Cocks, Anna Summers, *An Introduction to Court Jewellery* (Owings Mills, Md: Stemmer House, 1982)

Cohen, Walter 'Political criticism of Shakespeare', in Howard and O'Connor (eds.) (1987), pp. 18–46.

Donno, Elizabeth Story (ed.), *An Elizabethan in 1582: The Diary of Richard Madox, Fellow of All Souls*, Hakluyt Society, Second Series, no. 147 (London: Hakluyt Society, 1977)

Eagleton, Terry, *Literary Theory: An Introduction* (Oxford: Blackwell, 1983)

Evans, Joan, *English Jewellery from the Fifth Century AD to 1800* (London: Methuen, 1921)

Ferguson, Margaret W., 'Running on with Almost Public Voice: The Case of E. C.', in Florence Howe (ed.), *Tradition and the Talents of Women* (Urbana: University of Illinois Press, 1991), pp. 37–67.

—— 'The Spectre of Resistance: *The Tragedy of Mariam*', in David Scott Kastan and Peter Stallybrass (eds.), *Staging the Renaissance: Reinterpretations of Elizabethan and Jacobean Drama* (London and New York: Routledge, 1991), pp. 235–50.

Fischer, Sandra K., 'Elizabeth Cary and Tyranny, Domestic and Religious', in Margaret Patterson Hannay (ed.), *Silent but for the Word: Tudor Women as Patrons, Translators, and Writers of Religious Works* (Kent, Ohio: Kent State University Press, 1985), pp. 225–37.

Foucault, Michel, 'The Discourse on Language', in *The Archeology of Knowledge*, trans. Alan Sheridan (New York: Pantheon, 1972), pp. 215–37.

—— *The History of Sexuality: An Introduction*, trans. Robert Hurley (New York: Pantheon, 1978)

Fryer, Peter, *Staying Power: The History of Black People in Britain* (London: Pluto Press, 1984)

Fumerton, Patricia, *Cultural Aesthetics: Renaissance Literature and the Practice of Social Ornament* (Chicago: University of Chicago Press, 1991)

Garruci, R., *Graffiti de Pompéi*, 2nd edn (Paris, 1856)

Greenblatt, Stephen, *Renaissance Self-Fashioning: From More to Shakespeare* (Chicago: University of Chicago Press, 1980)

—— 'Invisible Bullets: Renaissance authority and its subversion, *Henry IV* and *Henry V*', in Jonathan Dollimore and Alan Sinfield (eds.), *Political Shakespeare: New Essays in Cultural Materialism* (Manchester: Manchester University Press, 1985), pp. 18–47.

—— *Shakespearean Negotiations: The Circulation of Social Energy in Renaissance England* (Berkeley, CA: University of California Press, 1988)

Hampden, John, *Francis Drake, Privateer: Contemporary Narratives and Documents* (Alabama: University of Alabama Press, 1972)

Howard, Jean E. and O'Connor, Marion F. (eds.), *Shakespeare Reproduced: The Text in History and Ideology* (London and New York: Methuen, 1987)

Hudson, William, 'A Treatise of the Court of Star Chamber', in F. Hargrave (ed.), *Collectanea Juridica: Consisting of Tracts Relative to the Law and Constitution*, 2 vols. (London, 1791–2), II, pp. 1–240.

LaCapra, Dominick, *Soundings in Critical Theory* (Ithaca: Cornell University Press, 1989)

Lentricchia, Frank, 'Foucault's legacy', in Veeser, H. Aram (ed.), *The New Historicism* (New York: Routledge, 1989), pp. 231–42.

Montrose, Louis A., '*A Midsummer Night's Dream* and shaping fantasies of Elizabethan culture: gender, power, form', in Margaret W. Feguson et al. (eds.), *Rewriting the Renaissance: The Discourses of Sexual Difference in Early Modern Europe* (Chicago: University of Chicago Press, 1986), pp. 65–87.

Princely Magnificnce: Court Jewels of the Renaissance, 1500–1630 (London: Debrett's Peerage, 1980)

Strong, Roy *The English Renaissance Miniature* (London: Thames & Hudson, 1983)

Tuan, Yi-Fu, *Dominance and Affection: The Making of Pets* (New Haven: Yale University Press, 1984)

Williams, Raymond, *Marxism and Literature* (Oxford: Oxford University Press, 1977)

4

Appropriation

MARK THORNTON BURNETT

The first section of this anthology suggested that every edition produces a fresh work out of an existing arrangement; in the same way, it can be argued that every reading, performance or citation creates a wholly new text from a familiar Renaissance utterance. Peter Hulme and William H. Sherman's collection, *'The Tempest' and Its Travels*, is one of a number of recent studies which demonstrate the mobility of a single Shakespearean play from its inception through the Restoration and eighteenth and nineteenth centuries to postmodernity.[1] As the varied and various *Tempests* described prove, with the reiteration of the text comes an inevitable shift in its meaning, emphasis and orientation, one which entails an acknowledgement not only of the determining power of history but also of the irrecoverability of the earlier juncture. Nor is it only drama that is appropriated; other literary genres continue to be of interest to later periods, while particular authorial figures and even the Renaissance itself have also proved to possess irresistible recasting potential.

Critics invested in appropriation concern themselves with the expanding status of the literary, with the extent to which appropriation bears the signature of its moment of production, and with the relations between textual meanings and ideological change. Moreover, the key questions posed by such critics—'What becomes of the "original" text when it is removed to contexts far from its first location?' and 'What does this particular repetition tell us both about the culture that is drawn to reproduction and the text that is appropriated?'—become more urgent as artists and filmmakers take greater inventive liberties with Renaissance materials, and Renaissance materials are seen to interact with the contemporary instruments of mass media. The shaping of a new work out of an 'original', particularly in relation to Shakespeare, has been the concern of performance critics throughout the

---

[1] Peter Hulme and William H. Sherman (eds.), *'The Tempest' and Its Travels* (London: Reaktion, 2000).

twentieth century. More recently, theoretical work on appropriation has opened up the field to embrace not only performance but also translation in other representational mediums, such as film, television, video, DVD, creative writing, music, the visual arts and the internet. Turning their attention to these types of interaction, scholars of the early modern have learned to deploy the theoretical vocabularies of film and television, merging current understandings of Renaissance studies with the latest developments in visual technologies to produce sophisticated analyses of a range of artistic productions.

Such transmigratory criticism is sensitive to the standing of reproduction at the present moment and, conscious of the power of early modern nomenclature, is especially alive to issues of value and status. These preoccupations have been simultaneously taken up by critics of a materialist persuasion. Through an examination of a broader range of originary contexts, materialist critics argue that names and texts from the early modern period carry in their train powerful capital. Those who examine Shakespeare's influence upon, and place in, common English cultural practices—in marketing and advertising, for example, or in the education system and the Stratford-upon-Avon tourist industry—have played crucial roles in establishing that the invocation of Shakespeare operates largely to reinforce his reputation as an economic and symbolic commodity.

Emerging from these types of critical exploration is the suggestion that Shakespeare has historically served conservative purposes; indeed, as important arguments have made clear, the dramatist is often at his most powerful when he is put to work for a national agenda. However, over the past twenty years, work on appropriation of Renaissance texts in a broader geographical field has encouraged a parallel sense of mobility. As an exportable body of association, Shakespeare has long gravitated to a variety of international homes, not least China and Japan. Consequently, many critical approaches now single out cross-cultural practices as important, highlighting novels, dramas, films and poetry that openly move between existing categories, attachments, identifications and languages. In a particularly illuminating manifestation, this mode of interpretation has framed itself within post-colonial paradigms, as Ania Loomba's essay on the Kathakali *Othello*, a hybrid production which assumes an ambiguous stance towards the protagonist's racial alterity, reveals. The work of Loomba, and other post-colonial critics, eschews any easy assumption about the ways in which Shakespeare continues to be repeated 'abroad', since it concentrates upon detailing the particular contextual nuances of local realization and reception.

If appropriation is one space for playing out national and international politics, it is also one in which sexual politics, and class discussion, find a ready home. In particular, reflections upon gender and sexuality, and upon marginality and otherness, have been significantly nuanced across new versions of old texts, often being traced in opposition to totalizing cultural narratives. Sarah Werner's discussion of a female-directed theatrical production is typical of this trend: her study works to reveal the conflict that rises to the surface when commercially-entrenched attitudes to Shakespeare are at odds with self-consciously gendered attempts to rewrite his potential. Similarly, prevailing conceptions of the past can be interrogated if plays such as Marlowe's *Edward II* (1592?) are staged or filmed through the lens of contemporary gay history: Lawrence Normand's piece below on Derek Jarman's film of Marlowe's drama abundantly illustrates this shift in thinking, approach and awareness. The example of Marlowe reminds us that it is not only Shakespeare who is subject to reinvention. Yet it remains the case that, with films such as Shekhar Kapur's *Elizabeth* (1998) and the 2003 celebrations testifying to a particular hold on the popular collective psyche, only Elizabeth I comes anywhere close to Shakespeare in terms of being written and written over.

Processes of reinvention sometimes have unexpected results. The most recent appropriation theory has linked Shakespeare's widespread deployment in modernity to a more general blurring of signification and nomenclature. Such work focuses upon a loosening of application and an absorption into the dramatist's name of stereotypical 'Renaissance' associations (which have themselves evolved from the ways in which the period has been reimagined as fantasy in theatre festivals, advertisements, films, romances and exhibitions). Like Elizabeth, who, beyond her associations with female power and political agency, has been appropriated so as to reinforce popular notions about what constitutes the 'Renaissance', Shakespeare has become inseparable from the 'Renaissance', with one fading into, and being incorporated within, the other. In practice, this means that the conventional eulogization of Shakespeare as a literary genius has been complicated, and a stereotypical connection between Renaissance and European artistic achievement broken. From a traditionalist point of view, it is even possible to talk about the 'end of the "Shakespearean" '. Certainly, in recent films such as Tim Blake Nelson's *'O'* (2002) or Gil Junger's *Ten Things I Hate About You* (1999), there is only a passing regard for the playtext, with Shakespeare having been transformed into no more than a vaguely symbolic 'essence'. Future appropriations will almost certainly dissolve these expansions and displacements even as they continue to interpret the new in the guise of the old.

1 | The relationship between an 'original' and appropriation

Daniel Fischlin and Mark Fortier, 'General Introduction', to Daniel Fischlin and Mark Fortier (eds.), *Adaptations of Shakespeare: A Critical Anthology of Plays from the Seventeenth Century to the Present* (London and New York: Routledge, 2000), p. 1.

For almost four hundred years, playwrights have been taking Shakespeare's works and remaking them, in an overwhelming variety of ways, for the stage. In fact, Shakespeare himself was an adapter, taking existing materials from various sources and crafting them into 'new' artistic creations. However, much of the long history of appreciating and thinking about Shakespeare has stressed his unsurpassed originality, the sanctity of his texts, and the cultural taboo on presuming to alter them. This view is, nevertheless, beginning to change. As critical theory has taken hold in academic institutions, students and scholars have become increasingly interested in such issues as text and source, text and context, authorship, originality, interpretation, and the production of meaning. These interests have allowed what has always been true to come into sharper focus: that Shakespeare's works have, from their inception, been both the product and the source of an ongoing explosion of re-creation.

* * *

Samuel Schoenbaum, *Shakespeare's Lives* (Oxford: Clarendon Press, 1991), pp. 550–9.

The great tide of popular biography has surged on undiminished, and unruffled by Freudian perturbations. Ivor Brown, who with George Fearon wrote *Amazing Monument: A Short History of the Shakespeare Industry* (1939), has himself helped sustain that industry with *Shakespeare* (1949), *Shakespeare in his Time* (1960), *How Shakespeare Spent the Day* (1963), *The Women in Shakespeare's Life* (1968), and *Shakespeare and the Actors* (1970)—not to mention a one-act play, *William's Other Anne* (1937), dramatizing some of his pet notions. Other titles of the past quarter-century include Hazelton Spencer, *The Art and Life of William Shakespeare* (1947); Charles Norman, *So Worthy a Friend: William Shakespeare* (1947); Leonard Dobbs, *Shakespeare Revealed* (1948); Marchette Chute, *Shakespeare of London* (1949); Frank Ernest Hill, *To Meet Will Shakespeare* (1949); Hesketh Pearson, *A Life of Shakespeare* (1949); M. M. Reese, *Shakespeare: His World and His Work* (1953, rev. 1980); F. E. Halliday, *Shakespeare: A Pictorial Biography* (1956), *Shakespeare in His Age* (1960), and *The Life of Shakespeare* (1961); Hugh R. Williamson, *The Day Shakespeare Died* (1962); Peter Quennell, *Shakespeare: The Poet and His Background* (1963); and Roland Mushat Frye, *Shakespeare's Life and Times: A Pictorial Record* (1968). To this list, select rather than exhaustive, may be added two handy repositories of information, including the biographical: Halliday's *A Shakespeare Companion* (1952, rev. 1964, 1969) and *The Reader's Encyclopedia of Shakespeare* (1966), edited by Oscar James Campbell and Edward G. Quinn.

As a group these are books that the professional journals for the most part feel no compulsion to review. Most of the authors mine the same secondary sources—Chambers, Fripp, and (later) Eccles—in order to acquaint a heterogeneous audience of non-scholars with the facts and problems of Shakespeare's life. All document lightly when they document at all; none prints the records *in extenso*. Biography of this order requires no sojourns in the record office and no immersion in the Warwickshire ambience; Chute composed her entire Life without straying from the New York Public Library. Under the circumstances a certain amount of duplication is inevitable. One wonders, for example, why Frye should have troubled to compile his 'Pictorial Record' when Halliday's equally attractive (and cheaper) 'Pictorial Biography' was already available. But what astonishes us about these biographies is not how much they overlap but their variety of approach to their subject. In them are exhibited the techniques of journalism, fiction, and austerely factual narrative, of subjective and impersonal Life-writing; one encounters an historian's braggadocio, the encyclopaedist's urge to encompass Shakespeare's whole world, an eccentric's unhinged vision. How unlike (to illustrate the point) are the biographies published in the same year by Marchette Chute and Ivor Brown!

'I, for one,' Brown declares,

absolutely refuse to believe that he kept himself out of his writing, that his Sonnets are a formal exercise, and that his plays are examples of abstract and remote dramaturgy, from whose themes and persons and language he carefully withdrew all personal feeling and opinion. Only the dullest of study-bound professors could pretend that authorship so vibrant as Shakespeare's is possible on those lines. My own opinion (and certainly not mine alone) is that he portrayed and betrayed himself continually.[1]

Behind this manifesto lurks the ghost of Frank Harris. As a youth Brown read the puff for *The Man Shakespeare* by 'Jacob Tonson' (i.e., Arnold Bennett) in *The New Age*, and was thus introduced to the poet's 'tragic life story'. In his autobiography, *The Way of My World*, Brown long afterwards recalled the impact of Harris on his formative mind: 'this was a typically lush piece of writing, but it was a strong stimulant to one who had been bored almost into Bard-hatred by the academic mandarins. In persuading me that Shakespeare was a human being and therefore to be read with affection instead of studied with distaste, Tonson's service won, and has retained, my deep gratitude.[2]

Despite his professional writer's disdain for dry academics, Brown brings to his task some of the academic virtues: a grounding in the best authorities (Gray, Smart, Alexander) and a sturdy common sense with respect to legendary accretions and the tantalizing blank spaces in Shakespeare's career. Moreover, as a drama critic with practical awareness of the machinery of stage production, he can venture upon his subject through the theatre door, a means of access usually denied university-tied scholars. But literary amateurism carries its penalties. Brown expresses some odd views. Unwilling to reduce Anne Whateley of Temple Grafton to the 'sad status of a shadow born of a misprint', he suggests that dashing Will simultaneously courted two Annes, that he took out a licence to marry the younger and prettier Whateley lass, but that Miss Hathaway, having the stronger claim by virtue of her belly's testimony, sent her champions posting, money in hand, to Worcester for the bond. Thus was poor Anne Whateley left at the church door. Brown regards the anti-Stratfordians seriously enough to entertain the notion that Shakespeare took over hints and ideas from his noble acquaintances, and sometimes even touched up their manuscripts, for they were busy writers who preferred to remain aloof from the degrading theatre; if *Love's Labour's Lost* was not inspired by Bacon, then maybe a member of the Southampton clique was the original begetter.

To these vagaries of speculation must be added excesses of style; too often animation deteriorates into purple journalese. Brown thus describes Shakespeare's transition from his Fourth Age of High-Fantastical to the Fifth Age of Bitter Comedy:

> The ugliness of things leaped up at Shakespeare: like assassins surrounding a man from all quarters the deadly sins of envy, lust, jealousy and tyrannical ambition sprang out from behind the arras of his happy high-fantastical imaginings; they stabbed at his ecstasy in living. . . . the sun sank sharply in his sky. The pettiness of man and the frailty of woman began to obsess his meditation and obscure his laughing outlook on the glittering, turbulent panorama of the town. Nor was there the old comfort in the country. The earth which had been so fair a frame for meadows painted with delight became a pestilent congregation of vapours.[3]

Such a style is symptomatic of a simplistic critical vision. This Shakespeare turns out joyous plays when he is happy, tragedies when life oppresses him. By the time he wrote *Antony and*

Cleopatra the Dark Lady was dead, and the dramatist could forgive her by making her an Egyptian lass unparalleled—'The ecstasy and the agony were over,' Brown observes, the expected cliché at his fingertips. In the hands of such a critic a concordance becomes an instrument of medical diagnosis. From Shakespeare's references to ulcers, abscesses, boils, and plague sores, Brown surmises that 'in the early years of the century Shakespeare himself suffered from a severe attack of staphylococcic infection and was plagued with recurrent boils and even worse distresses of the blood and skin. . . .'[4]

Happily, Chute does not burden Shakespeare with boils. She refrains altogether from making biographical inferences from the works. The Sonnets, that irresistible quarry for subjective biographers, she relegates to an appendix (they receive barely a mention in the text). 'Many attempts have been made to interpret the sonnets as autobiographical', she concludes, 'and no doubt the desire to discover something about Shakespeare's private life is legitimate enough. But each reader finds a different story in the sonnets and reaches a different conclusion, and perhaps it is just as well. No single theory can safely be formed about them, and in the meantime William Shakespeare remains securely in possession of his privacy.'[5] The traditions and legends furnish matter for another appendix; here, rather than in the Life proper, one finds Fuller, Ward, Aubrey, Davies, and Rowe, the wit-combats with Jonson, the schoolteaching stint in the country, the fornication with Mistress Davenant, Southampton's largesse, the deer-poaching, and the merry meeting with Drayton and Jonson at which Shakespeare had one cup too many. Chute trusts to contemporary documents exclusively, the latest belonging to 1635, and this she accepts only because it includes the testimony of Cuthbert Burbage, Shakespeare's last surviving fellow. Nor does she attempt to round out her narrative with interpretative analysis of the canon—'The book is not a literary biography,' she insists. A wise prohibition, for her occasional critical remarks have a dispiriting *naïveté*. She lacks the equipment to evoke the genius and intellectual power of her subject; the climate of thought in which he breathed does not interest her. That with so many exclusions Chute should have been able to produce any biography at all is something of a triumph. That it should be as good as it is borders on the miraculous.

This legerdemain she accomplishes by dwelling upon Stratford and London, grammar school and Court, theatres and companies. A danger of the method is that background may become foreground, but somehow she overcomes this. Chute has a way of placing Shakespeare at the centre of Elizabethan circumstance; the poet (as one reviewer remarked) comes 'to dominate, and, enigma as he is, almost to take life at second-hand from the life around him'. Such an achievement—the creation of a biographical illusion—requires art. Yet, despite her exaltation of the fact, Chute does not entirely escape the temptation of conjecture: she postulates a break that 'evidently' took place between Anne and William Shakespeare within three years of their marriage, although no evidence of estrangement has come down.

Chute's total rejection of the Shakespeare-Mythos must have transient appeal to the historian confronted with incompatible and unverifiable traditions. But Malone long ago recognized that such data may harbour golden kernels of truth. 'What then are we to think of tradition as an element in the making of a biography?' Sir Edmund Chambers has asked more recently, and he goes on to supply a reasoned answer:

It is obviously far less reliable than record, which may be misinterpreted, but at least gives a germ of fact, which has to be worked in at its appropriate place. Tradition is attractive. It may deal with more picturesque and intimate matter than record. On the other hand, it may be due to invention. . . . In any case there is room for errors of transmission, either through inexact memories, or through the natural human instinct to leave a story better than you found it. Nevertheless, tradition cannot be altogether disregarded. A country neighbourhood is self-contained and tenacious of outstanding local personalities. . . . Our attitude towards tradition must therefore be one, neither of credulity nor of complete scepticism, but of critical balance. There are criteria to be borne in mind. Does the tradition arise early or late? Does it come from more than one independent source? Does it help to explain record, or contradict it?[6]

By failing to ask these questions, Chute betrays her inadequacy as a serious biographer. But perhaps this is (as Pope said in another connection) to try the citizen of one country by the laws of another. *Shakespeare of London* makes no pretences to being a critical Life, as the absence of any documentation mutely testifies. Chute is a responsible popularizer who has in one respect taken the easy way out. Within her self-imposed limits, she has produced an admirably sane book. That is no contemptible achievement.

Leonard Dobbs sorts oddly with Brown, Chute, and the rest, but then it is the eccentric's prerogative not quite to fit in with any company. His life was a succession of misfortunes. Dobbs sat for a research scholarship in science at Cambridge but was ill throughout the examination week and failed. When he finally took thirds in mathematics and science he concluded, not unreasonably, that he was not cut out for a life of research in pure science. Next Dobbs tried schoolteaching but was unable to enforce discipline; a severe motorcycle accident, which, his memorialist remarks, 'may not have been altogether unwelcome to him', terminated his pedagogical career. He took up sculpture but lacked the strength to work in stone. In Majorca, Dobbs made and sold marmalade but used too much sugar. A turning-point was his meeting with Hesketh Pearson just after (Pearson recalls) Leonard had 'cracked his head open by doing physical jerks in a room, the ceiling of which made it unsuitable for high jumping'. Pearson's *Life of Shakespeare* stimulated Dobbs, between moods of hilarity and dismal brooding, to expound upon the poet at a pub in Whatlington. The biographer encouraged him to put his views down on paper. 'New ideas poured from him in such abundance', Pearson recalls, 'that I began to get alarmed, begging him to steady himself and commence at once on the first volume of what promised to be a library if he went on like that.' After Dobbs's death in 1945, at the age of forty-two, *Shakespeare Revealed* was published through the good offices of Hugh Kingsmill. The latter sensibly withheld endorsement of the ideas developed in what was the last of Dobbs's calamities.

In these strange pages he works out his theory that Shakespeare used his fellow dramatists as models for the leading characters in his plays, which therefore become autobiographical allegories. Shakespeare represented Jonson as Falstaff, the rejection of the latter by Henry V corresponding to the separation of the two playwrights when Jonson left to join a rival company. In *Hamlet* Shakespeare expiated his guilty conscience over dethroning Marlowe with *Titus Andronicus*. 'This allegorical interpretation', Dobbs goes on, 'can, I think, be completed, if we regard the Queen, whom Claudius marries after killing her husband, as symbolizing the art which Marlowe was the first to possess, and which Shakespeare won from him as the seal of the kingship of the drama which he had usurped. Note the subtlety of this idea. . . .'[7] Alas, *Shakespeare Revealed* contains many such subtleties.

None of the remaining members of this heterogeneous crew aspires to match Dobbs for idiosyncratic originality, but their books contribute to the variety of biographical strategy already noted. These writers offer workaday Lives (Quennell), contentious Lives (Rowse), lightly fictionalized Lives (Hill); odd theories and old prejudices. According to Norman (*So Worthy a Friend*) Shakespeare addressed his Sonnets to both Southampton and Pembroke, in Cleopatra the Dark Lady and Mistress Davenant (in life separate) merge, Anne harboured bitter thoughts about the marital bed, and 'A scholarly thesis that the *Contention* and *True Tragedie* are merely surreptitious theater copies of Part Two and Part Three [of *Henry VI*] falls to pieces on examination', which is not forthcoming. In *The Day Shakespeare Died* Williamson presents 'a Catholic actor–playwright who was of no particular account to his contemporaries'. The same author reminds us, as we have not been reminded for half a century, that 'had Sidney Lee not abandoned his real name, Solomon Lazarus, he might have been less uncritically accepted in the first place as an authority on Anglicanism'.[8] The mean-spiritedness of this pointless remark (as though anybody did not know Lee was a Jew, whatever that has to do with his knowledge of Elizabethan Anglicanism) is alien to the temper of M. M. Reese, who accepts the serious obligation of the popularizer in an age when the advance of specialization has made information that should be available to all the province of the few. 'Scholarship', he writes, 'that will not mediate its conclusions in terms acceptable to ordinary men ends by strangling both itself and the object of its attentions.'[9] In *Shakespeare: His World and His Work* Reese mediates the findings of the specialists. To be sure his own scholarship is at second hand, he sometimes makes mistakes and sometimes displays greater confidence than the facts warrant, as when he assumes that Shakespeare sold his theatrical shares for a substantial capital sum. But one can hardly imagine a better ordered or more lucidly presented introduction to the dramatist's age, life, and work than this one, which fairly glows with reasonableness. Of the remaining popular biographies, Rowse's, having stirred the most controversy, most deserves comment here.

Fellow of All Souls, authority on the England of Elizabeth, versifier, and writer of best-selling autobiographical memoirs (*A Cornish Childhood, A Cornishman at Oxford*), Dr Rowse has produced a solid middle-brow biography in a hearty middle-brow style, all roast beef and Yorkshire pudding, to which his fondness for such archaisms as 'pshaw' lends a not unattractive period quaintness. In keeping with his style the author manifests a pre-Freudian innocence which puts him at a disadvantage in dealing with such matters as the sexuality of the Sonnets. No aroma of the record office scents this effort; as any good popularizer must, Rowse takes his facts from Chambers, Fripp, and Eccles. But although he offers not a single new document, Rowse does not disclaim originality. In the marriage (her second) of the Countess of Southampton to Sir Thomas Heneage on 2 May 1594, he discovers the occasion of *A Midsummer Night's Dream*. This suggestion had been put forward, but not pressed, by Stopes almost half a century previous in her life of Southampton.

Rowse maintains that the Sonnets were written between 1592 and 1595, when, for part of the time, plague closed the theatres; that Southampton is the Lovely Boy; that Marlowe furnished the pattern for the Rival Poet; and that Mr W.H.—Sir William Hervey (or Harvey, as Rowse prefers), the Countess of Southampton's third husband—handed over the Sonnets to the printers in 1609 and was in this sense alone the 'onlie begetter'. In presenting his case

Rowse brings his formidable historical expertise to bear on the contemporary events alluded to in the poems. He argues forcefully, with little regard for the sensibilities of those who differ from him (Hotson's ideas are dismissed as, of all suggestions, 'the craziest'). But the language of verse, being imaginative and ambiguous, admits of more than one possible interpretation. Moreover, Marlowe, first suggested as the Rival as early as 1859, had no known connection with the Southampton set. It is in the nature of a fact that it puts an end to responsible speculation, but controversy about the Sonnets has gone on merrily since Rowse's biography, and few if any have had to change their allegiance. For the rest in this substantial book (484 pages), Rowse displays his customary magic with political and social history, Warwickshire and the Court; he has his finger on the pulse of the age, although on the theatres and companies he is negligible.

One can scarcely imagine better timed publication: October 1963, on the eve of the quater-centenary year. The appearance of the book was heralded by a series of four leader-page articles by Rowse in *The Times* for September 17–20, carried under the general title, 'Historian Answers Questions about Shakespeare'. An added headline in larger type proclaimed, over the first instalment, 'Only the Dark Lady Still a Mystery'. Early on in this piece Rowse declares. 'I am prepared to stake my reputation as an Elizabethan scholar on the claim that all the problems of the Sonnets save one—the identity of Shakespeare's mistress, the Dark Lady—are susceptible of solution, and that I have solved them.' These words forecast the tone of the book, in which Rowse emerges as the Sir Positive At-all of Shakespearian biography. '. . . I am overwhelmed by what historical investigation, by proper historical method, has brought to light. It has enabled me to solve, for the first time, and definitively, the problem of the Sonnets, which has teased so many generations and led so many people into a morass of conjecture.' Everything is 'now cleared up'. 'Now, for the first time, certainty as to dating has been achieved and the consequences are immeasurable.' '. . . the picture builds up gradually, inescapably, to certainty and conviction'. 'The game [of dating the Sonnets] has now come to an end, for good and all.' And so on; Rowse likes such words as 'fixes', 'confirms', and 'certainty'. Counterpointing the claims are sneers at the literary scholars, a miserable lot of dodos struggling along without Rowse's mastery of historical method. How this method differs from that of historically oriented literary students he nowhere explains, but I gather from my own conversations with him that the historian occupies himself with certainties, firmly stated, and not with specula-tions, in which the literary folk pointlessly indulge—a distinction made by Rowse in another *Times* article (17 January 1964). Apparently he speaks for himself rather than for his guild as a whole; other historians with whom I have discussed this question do not make positiveness an article of their creed. However this may be, Rowse's arresting pronouncements quickly gave his book notoriety.

A row inevitably followed; first in the correspondence columns of *The Times*, later in reviews and rejoinders to reviews. With the exquisite good taste for which it is celebrated, *Private Eye* on 18 October 1963 edified its readers with an anonymous broadside entitled, 'Swan of All Souls'. The piece quoted authentic samples of the Swan's verse ('The phallic crocuses are up and out | Standing on tiptoe as if to shout . . .'), as well as an extract from that 'new monu-ment to egotistical niggling', *I Am Shakespeare*: 'Once the solution is stated categorically, it seems so obvious that one can only have contempt for those pseudo-experts, lamentably lacking my own historical insight, impeccable taste and implacable self-admiration, who have for so long perversely ignored all the clues which stare them in the face. What other English poet is there who combines in his verse the same admiration for the upper classes, the same interest in sex and the same feeling for nature?' Later the same year there appeared, in poignant contrast to both Rowse and *Private Eye*, Dover Wilson's urbane polemic, *An Introduction to the Sonnets of Shakespeare for the Use of Historians and Others*. A destructive notice of Rowse in the *TLS* ('Shadow and Substance in Shakespeare', 26 December 1963) drew an angry defence from the victim, finally giving the anonymous reviewer (John Crow) another chance to denounce 'Dr. Rowse's fat bad book'.

Since then thunderbolts hurled from All Souls have periodically resparked controversy; on 26 April 1969 a leader-page article, this one on Mr W.H., belatedly marked Shakespeare's birthday in *The Times* and elicited the usual spate of letters, all of them (except one from Rowse himself) unfavourable. Throughout this ordeal of public exposure he did not once relapse into diffidence. 'Really!' he exclaimed in *The Times* on 17 January 1964. 'What is the point of affecting a lack of confidence one does not feel? I should not have *dared* to put out such a book if I were not sure of my ground. No historian would dream of it, let alone a leading Elizabethan historian with much more to lose than a lot of reviewers, for the most part knowing little of the subject.'

Upon bringing out his Life, Rowse, like his great metaphysical poet predecessor (but without the word-play), found that when he had done he had not done: Rowse had claimed to have solved all the problems of the Sonnets save one; everything 'except for the identity of Shakespeare's mistress, which we are never likely to know'. Subsequently, at the Bodleian Library, while working his way through the case-books of Simon Forman, a contemporary of Shakespeare—Forman was born in 1552 and died in 1611—who enjoyed considerable success as physician, astrologer, and lecher, Rowse found his Dark Lady. She was Emilia Lanier, née Bassano, the daughter of Baptista Bassano and Margaret Johnson, who, although unmarried, lived together as man and wife. The Bassanos were a family of Court musicians who had come to England from Venice to serve Henry VIII. Their descendants stayed on at Court in the same capacity; Baptista's will describes him as 'the Queen's musician'. By the time she was seventeen in 1587, Emilia was an orphan with a dowry of £100, not a negligible sum in those days, but she was scarcely an heiress. She mended her fortune, however, by becoming the mistress of Henry Carey, 1st Lord Hunsdon, then well advanced in years. As Lord Chamberlain he supported the players in their sporadic skirmishes with the municipal authorities, and he was himself the patron of an acting company; for a while, just before his death, in 1596, he sponsored Shakespeare's company, the Chamberlain's Men. In 1593 Emilia consulted Dr Forman, who cast her horoscope, and said of her in his diary that 'She is now very needy, in debt, and it seems for lucre's sake will be a good fellow, for necessity doth compel.' So she was promiscuous. On one occasion Forman, sent for by Emilia's maid, stayed all night with Emilia. In January 1600 she sent for Forman, who wondered 'whether she intendeth any more villainy'. By then he was finished with her.

His case established to his own satisfaction, Rowse recast his biography, mainly (one suspects) to give Emilia a showcase, and in 1973 published it as *Shakespeare the Man*. In the Preface to his emended second printing he claims that the resurfacing of Emilia 'has triumphantly vindicated the answers I have put forward all along, and the method by which they were found . . . The discovery of the Dark Lady completely corroborates, and puts the coping-stone on, my previous findings'—i.e., the chronology of the Sonnets and the identity of Fair Youth, Rival Poet, and Mr W.H. On 29 January 1973 *The Times* carried a feature article, headed 'Revealed at Last, Shakespeare's Dark Lady', by A. L. Rowse. Once published, *The Times* article was summarized in newspapers and magazines the world over, and for weeks afterward the correspondence columns reverberated with responses: heated, facetious, or merely informative. In the same year Rowse brought out a revised edition of the Sonnets, titled *Shakespeare's Sonnets: The Problems Solved*, complete with paraphrases for those who prefer to read their poetry as prose, and with sufficient reference to Emilia in the annotations.

But is she the Dark Lady? She was promiscuous, and her dates do accord with Rowse's dating of the Sonnets. Coming as she did from a musical family, she may well have been accomplished at the virginals. All this is in accord with what the poems suggest. Rowse observes that the husband's Christian name, William, makes an admirable basis for puns, lending another dimension to the word-play of the Will sonnets ('Whoever hath her wish, thou hast thy Will, | And Will to boot, and Will in over-plus.'). Rowse, however, is wrong about the name of the lady's husband: she married Alfonso—not such a good name for puns—not William, Lanier. And was Emilia dark? Stanley Wells was the first to look more closely at the passage in Forman's case-book, which Rowse conveniently reproduced in facsimile in his *Shakespeare the Man*. The key word is not 'brown' at all, but 'brave': she was very brave in youth, here meaning 'splendid', 'fine', 'showy'. We are left with a promiscuous lady, of whom there were others in Elizabethan London. *The Times*, which had announced in a front-page headline 'A. L. Rowse discovers Shakespeare's Dark Lady', quickly beat a prudent retreat, and the correspondence which followed used the non-committal heading, 'Another Dark Lady'. The next year, in 1974, Rowse had a chance to retrace his steps in *Simon Forman: Sex and Society in Shakespeare's Age*. Again he tells Emilia's story. She is now brave, not brown, and her husband's name is correctly given, in passing, as Alfonso. Nowhere does Rowse allude to past errors, and about his thesis he remains impenitent, all the more convinced 'that here in this Italianate woman we have the Dark Lady'. Others are less persuaded.

. . . .

QUESTIONS

• What sorts of relationship does the appropriation have to the 'original'?
• What are the key questions for a critic investigating this relationship?

2 | Shakespeare, the 'Renaissance' and cultural value

Barbara Hodgdon, *The Shakespeare Trade: Performances and Appropriations* (Philadelphia: University of Pennsylvania Press, 1998), pp. 232–4.

Today, the Birthplace Trust Gift Shop entices [. . .] willing [. . .] consumers to buy into Shakespeare, to celebrate tourism itself as a commodity with a souvenir that promises a magical return to the scene of its origin, authenticating their connection to the sites and sights of Stratford. Just as the Birthplace asserts ideological control over the Shakespeare narrative, the Shop (which visitors must pass through as they exit from the property) is the discursive field where that ideology becomes most fully materialized, and where, through the agency of the souvenir, that narrative moves into the visitor's private time and space.

Representing an even more complex assemblage of material objects than any one of Stratford's museum spaces, the Shop is a micro-universe of Bardic consumer culture. Here, the categories through which we know and think Shakespeare are expressed in commodities arranged in a jumbled array reminiscent of a neighbourhood grocery store. And like such stores, what doesn't go out doesn't come back: not only do things have to be worth having around, they must be also be worthy of Shakespeare—a worth determined by the watchful eye of the Trust, which has the authority to define and monitor its own marketplace. Those seeking an alternative account of Stratford's universal hero or searching for contradictions or tensions that disrupt his cultural memory must look elsewhere, for the same strategies of legitimation that govern the properties operate here. With a few exceptions that either edge toward parody or kitsch or cater to mass-mediated fads, the choice of objects is shaped by expectations not only that consumer culture desire aligns with and conforms to those stand-ards of taste and authenticity revered by the Trust but that what visitors wish to take away is nothing less than a means for re-membering Shakespeare within the contextual landscape of England's national heritage.

* * *

Michael Anderegg, *Orson Welles, Shakespeare, and Popular Culture* (New York: Columbia University Press, 1999), pp. 61–73.

In one of the first important studies of Shakespeare and film, Jack Jorgens described some of the traditional ways Shakespeare adaptations have been categorized in terms of stylistic modes and approaches: the 'theatrical,' the 'realistic,' and the 'filmic.' The theatrical mode 'uses film as a transparent medium' to 'capture the essence of a theatrical performance'; the realistic mode ' "takes advantage of the camera's unique ability to show us *things*—great, sweeping landscapes or the corner of a friar's cell, a teeming market-place or the intimacy of a boudoir, all in the flash of a moment" ',[1] and the filmic mode demonstrates what he calls the work of the 'film poet, whose works bear the same relation to the surfaces of reality that poems do to ordinary conversation.'[2] Immediate objections can be raised to this scheme, of course: no medium is transparent; realism cannot be so easily defined; all films are, by defin-ition, filmic. Jorgens, who presents these categories without embracing them, is the first to admit that 'good Shakespeare films often move fluidly between modes and styles, merge several simultaneously, so that it is not possible to make simple judgments.'[3] These categories, nonetheless, can help point to distinct elements in each of [Orson] Welles's films: *Macbeth* as 'theatrical,' *Chimes at Midnight* as 'realistic,' and *Othello* as 'filmic.'

These primarily formal strategies are closely related to the distinct production histories of each of Welles's Shakespeare films. With *Macbeth*, the unlikely sponsor (Republic Pictures, known primarily for its cliffhanger serials and B westerns), the modest budget, and the brief (three-week) production schedule, all encouraged Welles to adopt an enclosed, claustrophobic, highly set-oriented, long-take method of filming. The look and mood of this film—the paper-mâché sets, the tackily inconsistent costumes, the wide-angle and deep-focus photography, the wildly variable quality of style and performance—can be seen to have had their origin in the means of production even while they serve to express Welles's vision of Shakespeare's play. In adapting *Macbeth*, Welles, in the words of Lorne Buchman, 'shortened the play by two-thirds, cut entire scenes, excised characters, added others, [and] rearranged what remained of the play.'[4] Welles constructed a deliberately deglamorized world for Macbeth; the whole production has a lean and hungry look. The film's style, rightly described as 'expressionistic,'[5] has analogues to films like Edgar G. Ulmer's *Detour* (1945) and William Cameron Menzies' *Invaders from Mars* (1953), both of which employ expressionist techniques in part as a defense against minimal budgets. Although *Macbeth* was not, like *Detour*, a bottom-drawer production, Welles employed a B picture approach in order to keep what would have been a potentially expensive film within reasonable bounds.

The very different style evident in *Othello* in part derives from a very different production context. Rather than working within a preset, clearly defined budget, and within the institutional constraints of a specific studio or production organization, Welles had at his disposal varying amounts of money over several years. Reflecting Welles's peripatetic existence as a Hollywood outsider and exile from America, *Othello* exhibits evidence of having been filmed in different locations at different times, even within a single scene. In contrast to the claustrophobic unity of *Macbeth*, *Othello* appears open and fundamentally fragmented in terms of both time and space. Welles, once again, drastically cuts and rearranges Shakespeare's text, eliminating, for example, virtually all of Iago's self-justifying soliloquies. He creates a sound design that has the effect of making what dialogue remains difficult to follow. His methods result in an 'opening up' of one of Shakespeare's most tightly constructed plays. If the visual style of *Macbeth* has affinities with the Hollywood B movie, the visual style of *Othello* finds its affinities in the European art cinema tradition.

With *Chimes at Midnight*, we have a production history that can be conceived of as a kind of composite of those of the other two films. As with *Macbeth*, Welles was working within a reasonably firm, limited budget and a precisely delineated, albeit more generous, time frame. The filming itself was restricted in terms of space as well: a few Spanish locations and an equally restricted number of studio sets. And, as he had with *Macbeth*, Welles had at his disposal, and drew on, a recent theatrical production of the same material. As with *Othello*, on the other hand, Welles was working outside the dominant Anglo-American traditions of Shakespearean production. The entire film was produced in Spain, and the casting included Spanish, French, and other European performers, along with the established Shakespeareans like John Gielgud (Henry IV) and Ralph Richardson (narrator). As with *Othello*, Welles therefore relied heavily on dubbing non-English-speaking actors with, frequently, his own voice. Even more drastically than with *Othello*, Welles also chose to de-emphasize the linguistic dimension of Shakespeare and to rely more on visual equivalents to the written text.

In both *Othello* and *Chimes at Midnight*, Welles's effectual destabilization of narrative form, thematic consistency, and unity of character is carried out to an extent that it can resemble incoherence. On the one hand, Welles restructures Shakespeare's plays so as to present us with the ending at the beginning—particularly in *Othello*, which opens with the funerals of Othello and Desdemona, but also with the opening of *Chimes*, where we can see and hear the aged Shallow and Falstaff speaking lines from the fourth act of *Henry IV, Part II*; he then proceeds, on the other hand, to construct in each film a narrative which precisely fails to explain what the initial scene has shown us. The need for explication is much stronger in *Othello*, and in both films an implicit, intricate act of closure is gradually revealed by the end of the narrative not to be closure at all. Welles in these late Shakespearean films (perhaps in all his films) resists the sense of inevitability, of the already done, that critics of mass culture like Adorno have sometimes identified as the essence of cinema.[6]

Another way of understanding the differences between Welles's three films would be to suggest that each reproduces in formal terms the central thematics of the Shakespeare text upon which it is founded. In *Macbeth* the mise-en-scène and photography combine to re-create the self-enclosed and self-referential world of its protagonists. *Othello*, filmed with off-kilter camera angles, discontinuous editing, elliptical sound bridges, and vertiginous compositions, plays out the growing disorientation that becomes the focus of Othello's experience in Cyprus. *Chimes at Midnight* articulates the essential dynamics of the Hal/Falstaff relationship through a style that emphasizes the physicality of the body and at the same time separates out distinctly opposed spaces through a mise-en-scène that contrasts the court and tavern worlds. Eschewing both the artificially 'theatrical' space of *Macbeth* and the essentially naturalistic and geographically identifiable world of *Othello, Chimes* opts for a style less dependent on either the manipulation of obvious artifice or on the foregrounding of formal cinematic techniques than its predecessors.

As an alternative to Jorgens's primarily stylistic distinctions, Shakespeare films in general could be categorized by pointing to the material circumstances of their production. To simplify matters somewhat, we could identify two basic types: those made from the center and those made at the margins. The former merge the cultural authority of Shakespeare with institutional support, whether commercial (major studio), governmental (Kosintsev's *Hamlet* and *King Lear*, for instance), or both (Olivier's *Henry V*). In these works, the cultural authority is both assumed and reinforced: the performance of Shakespeare's text is simultaneously an affirmation of the value and status of that text. The marginal films, among which Welles's figure prominently, challenge, or at least qualify, the cultural supremacy of Shakespeare by, to one extent or another, pushing the source text toward its own margins or by revealing, through the film's low-budget strategies and absence of gloss and finish, the fragmentary and tentative authority of the original. As we have been relearning in the past few decades, Shakespeare's plays themselves, as they have come down to us, can be defined as extremely unstable texts, never entirely 'finished,' works in progress, playhouse documents, even sketchy blueprints for an edifice that we can never satisfactorily reconstruct. But this, needless to say, is not the image of Shakespeare as he is understood in the larger culture. When Kenneth Branagh's *Hamlet* (1996) is publicized as including the full, original text, what is ignored is that we have no way of knowing precisely what the original text is. Branagh's film, for all its virtues, presents a Shakespeare in full high-Victorian garb—a Shakespeare that Sir Henry Irving and Sir Herbert Beerbohm-Tree would have been proud to produce. Welles, on the other hand, presents a Shakespeare from hunger, what we might term, paraphrasing Jerzy Grotowski, a 'poor' Shakespeare.

No film in commercial release, one must concede, could ever be as 'poor' as a theater presentation can be: Welles's Shakespeare films were not precisely cheap (though they were cheaper than most): I am referring, rather, to certain stylistic considerations and production circumstances that give us a 'poverty effect' (just as, in Roland Barthes' terms, specific narrative devices and techniques can give us a 'reality effect').[7] Although a long take, as with the ten-minute-plus of the murder of Duncan in Welles's *Macbeth*, may serve a variety of useful purposes, it registers as an effect of minimal resources: Welles filmed the scene that way, some viewers will assume, in order to save money. Actually, long-take filming can be just as time-consuming, and hence expensive, as breaking the scene down into numerous setups, but the impression of cheapness and speed is what I am getting at here. The obvious absence of synchronous sound in so much of *Othello* and *Chimes at Midnight* provides the viewer with a similar projection of 'poverty effect.' And Welles, as the record clearly shows, did cut corners in his Shakespeare films, employing, for example, stand-ins for reverse shots simply because he could only afford to hold on to his actors for brief periods of time. My point is simply that Welles's Shakespeare films, as marginal products, are not surrounded by the same aura of class and respectability that surrounds most Shakespeare adaptations.

Welles's Shakespearean trilogy is comparable in ambition if not in effect to the trilogies of Laurence Olivier, Franco Zeffirelli, and Kenneth Branagh. In contrast to Welles, however, Olivier and Branagh project, in different ways, issues of national purpose and national identity: 'Britishness' of one sort or another. Olivier's films—especially *Henry V*—are intimately linked to Shakespeare's unmatched place in English history and culture as well as his high value as a cultural export. Branagh, although—as a Belfast boy—ostensibly reacting against the very English, respectful, traditional attitude Olivier supposedly brings to Shakespeare, nevertheless falls rather easily into what Harold Bloom would term the 'Anxiety of Influence.' He surrounds himself with paternal and maternal figures drawn from the great tradition of British Shakespeare—John Gielgud, Paul Scofield, Derek Jacobi, Judi Dench—while he makes a gesture toward a more international Shakespeare by casting, usually in minor roles, such Americans as Denzel Washington, Keanu Reeves (in *Much Ado About Nothing*, 1993), Jack Lemmon, Billy Crystal, and Robin Williams (in *Hamlet*). Both Olivier and Branagh provide, albeit in somewhat different ways, an official Shakespeare. As John Collick notes, 'Most people have been brought up to equate Shakespeare with great British actresses and actors dressed in period costumes and speaking in mellifluous accents.'[8] The films of Olivier and Branagh, though they reveal specific and distinctive cultural and formal strategies and styles of their own (Olivier draws from art-historical design in *Henry V*, Freudian theory in *Hamlet*, televisual staging in *Richard III*; Branagh associates King Henry V with Tim Burton's *Batman*), are also intimately associated with the establishment British Shakespeare of the Old Vic (Olivier) and the Royal Shakespeare Company (Branagh) insofar as the genesis of their films comes from previous stage productions and from the iconography of the classical British acting fraternity.

Zeffirelli's Shakespeare films would seem to offer a specifically European approach in that the Italian director's style inherits simultaneously from a neorealist film aesthetic and from opera, so that in, especially, *Taming of the Shrew* (1966) and *Romeo and Juliet* (1968), we are presented with a carefully observed, highly detailed material world in conjunction with a sweeping romantic tone underlined by a strong emphasis on music and spectacle. Zeffirelli, however, exhibits almost as much of the traditions of British Shakespeare as he does a more specifically Italian one; he has, after all, spent a good part of his working life in England, directing Shakespeare and opera on the London stage, and he has expressed his admiration for Olivier's Shakespeare films.[9] As a result, Zeffirelli's Shakespearean productions have some-thing of the air of 'Euro-pudding' about them: the variety of influences and the emphasis on spectacle do not add up to anything like a stylistic unity. By the time of *Hamlet* (1990), most traces of neorealism and opera have disappeared, and in spite of his location filming, he produces a Shakespeare film that has more in common (in its mise-en-scène, at least, espe-cially costumes and setting) with Victorian and Edwardian stage productions than with his two earlier films, at the same time that the casting of Mel Gibson and Glenn Close, together with an orthodox group of British Shakespeareans, has obvious appeal for a primarily Anglo-American market.

To place Welles's Shakespeare films in their specific cinema-historical contexts, we can compare the circumstances of their production with the near simultaneous Shakespeare films of Laurence Olivier, Akira Kurosawa, and Sergei Yutkevitch. Olivier's *Henry V* (1944), *Hamlet* (1948), and *Richard III* (1955) were all financed by the two major British producers J. Arthur Rank and Alexander Korda, with significant governmental encouragement and institutional support. Each film was conceived of as a prestige production, expected to bring honor and, hopefully, some American dollars, to Great Britain. Each film (especially *Hamlet*) was provided by its distributor with a carefully orchestrated publicity campaign. *Hamlet* was released in the United States under the auspices of the prestigious Theatre Guild, a highly unusual step by that organization. Handsome illustrated booklets were prepared as press kits, and *Hamlet* gener-ated not one but two hardcover, lavishly illustrated volumes, one of which included both Shakespeare's play and Olivier's script.[10] *Richard III* had its U.S. premiere on NBC television in 1956, an event publicized as a significant cultural moment for both Shakespeare and for television, and one that returned a quick half million dollars to Olivier's backers.

Kurosawa's *Throne of Blood* (1957), an adaptation of *Macbeth*, and a film that is often pointed to as an ideal Shakespeare adaptation in spite of the fact (because?) it does not include on its sound track a single word written by Shakespeare, was produced, distributed, and exhibited under, once again, highly favorable conditions. As an 'art cinema' artifact, *Throne of Blood* received extensive cultural support; it was embraced by Shakespeareans in part because its translation to another medium was so complete that comparisons to the original could be made in general rather than specific terms. Yutkevitch's *Othello* (1955) was produced at a government-run studio and was the product of a cultural moment when the Soviets, partially freed from the shadow of Stalin, were in the process of redefining their relationship to culture in general and to the West in particular.[11] Significantly, none of these 'successful' Shakespearean films reached a large enough popular audience so as to make a lot of money (an accomplishment perhaps more tricky than Bernstein [Everett Sloane], in *Citizen Kane*, quite realized). The undoubted critical success of a number of these films has served to obscure the fact that they were either barely profitable or not profitable at all, their seeming popularity artificially inflated by careful handling and publicity. Though Olivier's *Hamlet* ran in New York for over a year, it played at one theater only and hence could never generate large grosses. And even though an estimated 62.5 million people saw *Richard III* on television, Olivier's film still lost money.[12]

Welles's approach to filming Shakespeare may be more closely related to the circumstances of early modern theatrical practice than are the more orthodox projects of his contemporaries. In a very real sense, as a number of critics have recently emphasized, Shakespeare's plays themselves flourished first in the actual margins of Tudor and Stuart cultures, at the edges of the city of London proper. 'The popular theatre in particular . . . was a threateningly liminal space, whose "mingling of kings and clowns" . . . blurred a whole range of distinctions, evoking the specter of adulterating, crossbreeding, and hybridity.'[13] Welles's Shakespeare films, regarded in this light, are part of a countertradition of Shakespeare, what might be thought of as 'Shakespeare from the Provinces,' a tradition that includes amateur and school productions, abbreviated texts, 'foreign' (i.e., non-Anglo-Saxon) stagings—almost any Shakespeare taking place outside the theater capitals of London (including London, Ontario) and New York. These forms of 'derivative creativity,' to employ Michael Bristol's term,[14] have, in fact, always been around: Shakespeare's own company engaged in provincial performance, employed severely cut texts, performed in makeshift acting spaces, and so forth.

Welles's Shakespeare films could be further marginalized as provincial in the sense that they are products of an American sensibility. Actually, there is very little that can be characterized as specifically American about Welles's approaches to Shakespeare's text; the films combine traces of Hollywood genre elements (this is particularly true of *Macbeth*) with European, art-cinema practices. The marginal status of these films lies precisely in a simultaneous awareness and incorporation of the 'great tradition' of British Shakespeare (Gielgud and Richardson in *Chimes*, for example) and a decisive movement away from the center. This is precisely what is meant by marginal: not outside the circle but at the edges of it, reaching simultaneously toward the center and outside the line. Even *Othello*, which might seem most divorced from theater practice, is not innocent of theatrical traditions. Having Roderigo and Iago witness the elopement of Othello and Desdemona is an interpolation that goes back at least to Oscar Ashe's London production in 1907; Welles makes much of having based his visual design on the work of the Renaissance painter Carpaccio, but Beerbohm-Tree did the same in 1912; in the nineteenth century the French actor Charles Fechter, playing in London, made use of a mirror to emphasize Othello's growing consciousness of racial difference, and a mirror figures prominently in Welles's film.[15]

Perhaps because Welles appears to have one foot in each camp, to be both at the center and at the periphery, practitioners of cultural studies and various other modes of poststructuralism have been hesitant to embrace his Shakespeare films. The discourse surrounding *Othello* is particularly telling: in at least four recent studies (Vaughan, Donaldson, Collick, and Hodgdon), Welles's *Othello* has been taken to task for being insufficiently sensitive to issues of race and gender. I will consider the race question [later]; the gender argument, it seems to me, is founded on little more than dubious assumptions concerning Welles's personal life and the difficulties surrounding the production of the film that have scant force as evidence. Vaughan, for example, writes: 'Constructed by a male auteur who was known to have difficulty in his own relationships with women, Welles's *Othello* fetishizes the female body and demonstrates the tyranny of the male gaze'; Collick claims that 'the protracted search for an actress to play Desdemona hints at an indecisiveness on Welles's part and an inability to come to terms with the sexual implications of the Othello–Desdemona relationship in the film'; Donaldson supports a psychoanalytic point in this fashion: 'The emphasis on the failure of the beloved's eyes to return an anxious gaze in a reassuring way may draw on Welles's memory of his dying mother's eyes'; and Barbara Hodgdon, apropos of *Filming Othello*, Welles's 1978 documentary, finds that 'not only is [the film] organized as a series of male conversations or monologues, with Welles . . . at its center; but none of the three Desdemonas who worked on the film [i.e., *Othello*] appears to tell her story.'[16] These comments perhaps reveal, as much as anything else, the limits of contextual criticism.

In spite as well as because of the marginal nature of Welles's Shakespeare films, they undeniably provide a more challenging reading of the plays and, not incidentally, a more useful pedagogic tool than, for example, the vast majority of the BBC/Time-Life Shakespeare plays. Whereas the latter are far more 'faithful' to the texts of Shakespeare than are any of Welles's films, with a few notable exceptions they are also, in their bland refusal to explore interpretive possibilities and to challenge theatrical (or even televisual) orthodoxies, dead on arrival. But because the BBC versions have the aura of 'official' Shakespeare and because the videos have been aggressively marketed to schools and colleges worldwide, they have filled a significant pedagogic niche. If, however, the goal is to challenge viewers to think about Shakespeare rather than simply absorb the plays passively, Welles's films provide a far more useful model.[17] The gaps, omissions, and quirks of Welles's texts call for some kind of answering intelligence, a challenge to either Welles or Shakespeare. Although John Collick can claim that a film like Welles's *Othello* (or Derek Jarman's *The Tempest*, 1979) is 'as institutionalized within the economy of commercial cinema as any other movie,' thereby ironing out rather significant differences in production, distribution, and exhibition, he nevertheless recognizes that 'it is in these fragmented and contradictory movies that the coherence and apparent consensus over what constitutes culture, Shakespeare, and film, breaks down to reveal an uncertain and grotesque vision of society and social relationships.'[18] Welles's films, to put the matter somewhat differently, are unlikely to be perceived as definitive versions of the Shakespearean texts from which they derive.[19]

Welles's Shakespeare films, as we will see, have been more celebrated in Europe than in England and North America, in part because they place less emphasis on language and in part because the theatrical understanding of Shakespeare in Europe—and here I am thinking of such venues as the Deutsches Theater (Berlin), the Piccolo Teatro (Milan), and the Théâtre de Soleil (Vincennes)—is far bolder and experimental, more playful and elastic, than the equivalent venues in Great Britain and North America. As Dennis Kennedy has observed,

> the authoritative and thorough-going rethinkings of the plays we associate with Leopold Jessner or Giorgio Strehler or Ariane Mnouchkine have not occurred to the same degree in the home countries. Even Peter Brook, reinventing the plays in English since 1945, has done his most radical work on Shakespeare in French.[20]

At the same time, of course, it needs to be acknowledged that Shakespeare has a rather different cultural status in Europe, that his plays are often presented in modern translations, and that French cineastes, in particular, are less likely to be familiar with Shakespeare's original text than most English-speaking reviewers and critics. No European critic, in short, is likely to be bothered by the fact that Welles, like many of the producers of Shakespeare in non-English-speaking countries, has virtually translated Shakespeare into another idiom.

Welles's Shakespeare films, in short, circulate more clearly within a range of European postwar appropriations of Shakespeare than they do within an Anglo-American tradition of Shakespeare performance. Or, perhaps more accurately, they exhibit, as do many contemporary Shakespeare productions, 'a tension between a decentering aesthetic and the desire to retain the plays as touchstones of traditional Western culture.'[21] Bringing the witches back at the very end of his film of *Macbeth*, which echoes the similar employment of voodoo drums in the Harlem *Macbeth* in 1936, may not have been an interpretive invention on Welles's part, but it is a strategy that has been latterly associated[22] with the theatrical influence of Samuel Beckett and the critical influence of Polish critic Jan Kott; the ending of Polish-born director Roman Polanski's 1971 film of *Macbeth*, which shows us Malcolm's younger brother, Donalbain, drawn to an encounter with the witches just as his older brother is being crowned king of Scotland, makes the point explicit, but it was already implicit in Welles.

European cinephiles, furthermore, who were quick to enshrine Welles in a pantheon of auteurs, easily incorporated the Shakespeare films into the Wellesian cinema, recognizing in them themes and dramatic emphases present as well in *Citizen Kane, The Magnificent Ambersons, The Stranger, Lady from Shanghai, Touch of Evil,* and *Mr. Arkadin*: the destructive consequence of power, even when employed in a just cause; the inevitability of betrayal; the loss of paradise—all of these films are, in their own way, Shakespearean texts, if in no other sense than in the way they impose a large, poetic intensity on questions of family and domesticity and thus wed the social with the personal. So Henri Lemaitre, for example, could write: 'Perhaps the most Shakespearean film in the history of the cinema is not one of those drawn from his works, but rather a creation of the most Shakespearean of the masters of the camera, Orson Welles—the film, *The Lady from Shanghai*.'[23] In the specific context of a discussion of *Touch of Evil*, Robin Wood has captured the general affinities between Welles and Shakespeare by pointing to 'the efforts to create a visual-poetic world equivalent to the "world" of a Shakespearean tragedy; in the constant reaching out for a tragic weight and grandeur; in the attempts to find a cinematic style that will fulfill a creative function analogous to that of Shakespeare's verse.' (Wood, however, suggests that *Touch of Evil* may be closer in spirit to Shakespeare's near-contemporary John Webster, 'in whose plays the Elizabethan creative energies degenerate into morbidity and decadence.')[24] What Welles's films and Shakespeare's plays perhaps share most directly, apart from their interest in power relations, is a compelling evocation of evil as something at once attractive and horrifying, both in terms of its appeal to characters within the fiction and to audiences outside of it.

Whether produced at the center or from the margins, however, one thing is certain: Shakespeare films, as Welles was no doubt aware, have seldom been big box office. Only such a presumption explains the methods he employed to produce *Macbeth* at Republic: a low budget was all that could justify making a Shakespearean film at all. That Welles returned to Shakespeare twice again, and planned other projects along the way, shows a tenacity quite divorced from sound business acumen. If Warner Brothers and MGM were not able to succeed with Shakespeare, who could? Certainly, the conjunction of Shakespeare and Welles's modernist, avant-garde, and even postmodern cinematic practice was almost guaranteed to produce films of narrow commercial appeal. Welles made few concessions, in these films, to the requirements of popularity. After *Macbeth*, he was working completely outside mainstream Hollywood and had gone over, willingly or not, into the European personal cinema, a cinema that was poised to make an extraordinary cultural, though never truly popular, international impact. This picture is complicated, however, by Welles having positioned himself, or been positioned, as an international maverick during much of the period in question. His limited access to more or less standard modes of production, distribution, and exhibition severely compromised his European films, which were often financed by dubious speculators, processed in not always reliable labs, and released in piecemeal fashion by organizations and people ill-suited to the task.

Welles's Shakespeare films, in other words, were not rationalized productions, even when compared not to Hollywood but, more appropriately, to the international art cinema of the 1950s. It is worth noting, in this context, that the important European and international auteurs who came to prominence in the 1950s—Ingmar Bergman, Federico Fellini, and Akira Kurosawa, notably—made films that were produced, distributed, and exhibited under comparatively ideal conditions, either because of government subsidy (Bergman), major studio backing (Kurosawa), or, with Fellini, a film industry enjoying, by the end of the 1950s, a renaissance both in terms of prestige and commercial popularity which allowed it to support offbeat projects. These highly individualistic filmmakers did not, for the most part, have to struggle to find minimum financing, essential facilities, or sympathetic distributors. Welles, on the other hand, in each of the three instances where he adapted Shakespeare to film, did so within formal constraints that virtually demanded as well as allowed an expressionist, highly fragmented solution to the questions posed by the Shakespeare text.

Hollywood's earlier experiences with Shakespeare, in other words, would have suggested both to Welles and to Republic Studios that, given the size of the potential market for Shakespeare on film, containing costs was the crucial issue. Welles knew that filming Shakespeare successfully in Hollywood would involve creative production techniques. The desire to see Welles's *Macbeth* as originating from a conflict between the commercial imperatives of Hollywood, on the one hand, and the aesthetic aspirations of the artist-genius, on the other, thus needs to be resisted. Welles was just as sensitive as studio head Herbert J. Yates and producer Charles K. Feldman to commercial values, even if he was often unable or unwilling to turn that knowledge into practice. Welles's purpose in filming *Macbeth* at a studio known primarily for its low-budget movies was precisely to demonstrate that a financially successful adaptation of Shakespeare could be made in Hollywood. The conflict, in other words, was not over whether Shakespeare could be transformed into popular art, but over how best to accomplish that goal. Welles and Republic were both, in their own way, attempting to reach a large, popular audience for Shakespeare films.

By the time of *Othello* and *Chimes at Midnight*, the project I ascribed to Welles at the outset of this study—reconciling Shakespeare (high culture) with popular culture—was no longer viable. Neither film is 'accessible' in the way the earlier *Macbeth*—at some point in time—was meant to be. Indeed, the motives behind the 1992 'restoration' of *Othello* (and the plans to 'restore' *Chimes at Midnight*), I will argue, testify to the irreconcilable differences between these Shakespeare films and the popular audience one might hope to discover for them. An ironic reversal here takes place. Shakespeare, essentially a popular artist, is rescued by Welles from the late nineteenth-century high classicism which had threatened to imprison and limit him, had threatened to turn him, in Gary Taylor's words, into 'the badge of cultural elitism and the instrument of pedagogical oppression,'[25] but in the process the sixteenth-century playwright now becomes a distinctly modernist figure. As we will see, the deconstruction Welles performs on Shakespeare's *Othello* and 'Henriad' plays (and, to a lesser extent, on *Macbeth*) produces a series of irresolutions and complexities that elucidate and sharpen the tensions already present in Shakespeare while at the same time undermining the narrative and structural foundations of Shakespeare's dramaturgy.

* * *

Michael Bristol, *Big-Time Shakespeare* (London: Routledge, 1996), pp. 5, 91.

Although he is probably not as bankable as, say, Clint Eastwood, there is nevertheless a considerable market for a range of cultural goods that carry the Shakespeare trademark. Film versions of the plays such as Kenneth Branagh's *Henry V* and *Much Ado About Nothing* or Zeffirelli's *Hamlet* and his earlier *Romeo and Juliet* have shown that Shakespeare can be profitable in the context of commercial film production. Even more remarkable perhaps is the success of such *avant-gardiste* productions as William Reilly's *Men of Respect*, Peter Greenaway's *Prospero's Books*, and Gus Vant Sant's *My Own Private Idaho*, all of which rely on their audience's prior knowledge of a Shakespeare text. In general the overall level of economic activity in publishing, movies, video production, and commercial theatre that exploits the general public's knowledge of Shakespeare's currency is an apt usage, since his image actually appears on VISA cards issued by certain banks in the UK, and a scene from *Romeo and Juliet* is depicted on the back of £20 notes [. . .] As cultural capital, Shakespeare is fully negotiable in all financial markets. It is simply untrue that 'you can't make money doing Shakespeare'. For an actor like Tommy Lee Jones, who has in fact done some Shakespeare, action films and other standard Hollywood formats do provide much more lucrative opportunities than an ascetic commitment to artistic quality can offer. In these terms, serious Shakespearean performance is just small time. Venues such as university theatres or off-off-Broadway generally offer low-budget productions to small audiences. Still, the same logic that makes it possible to turn a small amount of money into Shakespeare can also be used to turn a small amount of Shakespeare into money. To convert a limited stock of cultural capital into a generous cash flow requires complicated forms of leverage. Shakespeare must be carefully positioned within a complex network of cultural assets and investments.

* * *

Courtney Lehmann, *Shakespeare Remains: Theatre to Film, Early Modern to Postmodern* (Ithaca and London: Cornell University Press, 2002), pp. 165–6, 168–9, 170, 175–6, 176–7, 180–8.

Kenneth Branagh is a figure who stretches the limits of our thinking about postmodern authorship. In many ways, his work corresponds to Corrigan's formula for the commercially conditioned auteur, for Branagh envisions authorship as a practice that takes place within the sphere of reception as much as production, and his films consistently generate paratexts that focus on the 'commercial performance of the business of being an auteur' (Corrigan 104). But Branagh challenges Corrigan's 'giddy' definition of authorship, for as a postcolonial subject, he is simultaneously threatened by postmodernism's privileging of 'the leveling, equalizing indifferent operations of the commodity form' which, as Terry Eagleton observes, 'respects no unique identity [and] transgresses all frontiers' (36). Branagh's quest to achieve a unique identity is a quest that he articulates, ironically, in the name of Shakespeare. [. . .] More than any other contemporary figure working with Shakespeare, Branagh *embodies* the dramatic tensions that constitute the Shakespearean corpus, exposing the tenacity of the Shakespearean remainder—the irreducible surplus that reveals a history of conflict beneath the 'worked over,' 'smoothed out' surface of his shimmering adaptations. What makes Branagh's work even more valuable for analyses of Shakespearean authorship in the age of adaptation is the fact that this remainder assumes both personal and geopolitical dimensions [. . .] Branagh employs strategies of surrogation in order to reinvent not only his Shakespearean source material but also the sources of his own identity. In basing his authorial mission on the omission of his own site of origin, however, Branagh's work returns us to the empty search for Shakespeare with which we began, revealing the extent to which any authorial mission assumed in the name of 'Shakespeare' is, like the cinematic specter of Sycamore Grove, a structure with a hole in the middle. But this void is also the space of possibility and, therefore, the landmark of the postmodern auteur's intervention in the cultural pathology of authorship. What most distinguishes Branagh from other directors working on Shakespeare, then, is how he uses this space to generate a singular confrontation between the postmodern and the postcolonial, the 'national' and the 'popular.' [. . .]

As a product of the infantilized Protestant population of Northern Ireland, Branagh, like his compatriots, suffers from an identity in a state of arrested development. At once subject to the disapproving gaze of big brother England and the menacing disdain of the Republic, the Belfast or Ulster Protestants are caught in a condition of 'double isolation.' As Tom Nairn explains in *The Break-up of Britain*, the Ulster Protestant's are not ' "Irish," in the sense that Catholic based agrarian nationalism ha[s] established. . . . But they [are] not really "British" either: they were always, and they still remain, profoundly and embarrassingly different from the society they imagine they are a frontier of' (233–4). As documented in the work of many writers and artists of the Irish Renaissance, this Anglo-Irish predicament of 'double isolation' can lead to a debilitating state of identity confusion; offering a glib synopsis of this predicament, Oscar Wilde once observed that ' "I am Irish by race, . . . but the English have condemned me to speak the language of Shakespeare" ' (quoted in Kiberd 35). But what exactly does it mean to be *condemned* to speak the language of Shakespeare? For James Joyce, the answer goes something like Caliban's rant in *The Tempest*: 'you taught me Shakespeare, and my profit on't, is that I have learned how to curse.' Shakespearean drama, according to Joyce, strikes a chord of empathy with the Irish experience, for 'the note of banishment, banishment from the heart, banishment from home, sounds uninterruptedly from *The Two Gentlemen of Verona* onward till Prospero breaks his staff, buries it certain fathoms in the earth and drowns his book' (Joyce, quoted in Kiberd 271). Shakespeare, in other words, has an uncanny capacity to convey the problem historically faced by the Irish as strangers in their own land, sounding the anomalous depths of the ' "mixed" experience of the Irish people, as both exponents and victims of British imperialism' (Kiberd 15). [. . .]

'Hidden in the classic writings of England,' Kiberd relates, 'lay many subversive potentials, awaiting their moment like unexploded bombs. So the young Irish man and woman could use Shakespeare to explore, and explain, and even perhaps to justify themselves' (268). Seeking to escape the memory of real bombs, Branagh's appropriation of the Bard is, at first glance, subversive only to the extent that Shakespeare enables him to subvert his own Irish heritage.

Caught in the debilitating adolescent role of being 'English at school and Irish at home,' Branagh's life and art have assumed a schizophrenic pattern of Yeatsian self-conquest, dominated by two conflicting principles, both of which may be coined from Shakespeare's name. The first half of this equation may be described as the 'Will principle,' or, Branagh's will to overcompensate for his Anglo-Irish lack of belonging by out-Englishing the English with the help of Shakespeare, the quintessential signifier of this 'happy breed of men.' The second half of this Shakespearean negotiation is the 'Billy principle' which, by contrast, represents the return of Branagh's repressed Irish identity. A household name throughout Ulster, 'Billy' signifies the name of Branagh's father, brother, countless friends, and ultimately, 'King Billy,' also known as King William of Orange, the folkloric hero of Northern Ireland's Protestant Community. [. . .]

Branagh's crisis of authorization is articulated in the tensions his films generate between reception and production—tensions which, in turn, stem from a conflict between the directorial body and the acting body. [. . .] In the context of the performative logic of late auteurism, the directorial body, generally speaking, is less easily colonized than the acting body, for the postmodern auteur preemptively divides and conquers the self by continually dispersing and reinventing it along an 'extratextual path.' This radical relocation of authorial agency from the sphere of production to reception leads to the *reductio ad absurdum* that 'auteur movies' are, paradoxically, 'made before they get made' (Corrigan 105). Conversely, the actor's body— while capable of having a similar affect on film reception in 'star' discourse—is a distinctly more vulnerable body. As W. B. Worthen argues, despite the attempt of actor training to render this body pre-cultural and preideological, 'the text of the social—behavior, language— is registered as bodily nature' and, therefore, inescapably inscribed on the actor's body (*Shakespeare and the Authority* 111). What happens, then, when the director's body and the actor's body belong to the same person? It is not uncommon for directors—most notably, Hitchcock—to 'pop up' in their films in ways that intentionally disrupt the diegesis and bemuse or baffle audiences; others, like Orson Welles, exploit the merger of directorial vision and performing vessel in ways that magnify the significance of both auteur and actor, often to such a powerful degree that we cannot tell where the diegesis ends and reality begins. By contrast, Branagh's 'two bodies'—not unlike the medieval king's—are dramatically discontinuous, for they belong to the postmodern and the postcolonial, respectively. Indeed, if Branagh's 'divine' directorial body supports a vision of Shakespearean community as the seamless product of ideological quilting, then his 'natural' actor's body bears the scars of this process, emerging in his often extraordinary attempts to present his own body as a healthy alternative to the recurring specter of the body-in-pain.

Branagh's acting body generates a narrative quite different from the directorial body's proleptic, even apotropaic rhetoric of inclusion, for in the course of production, this body emerges rigidly poised against the very differences Branagh courts at the level of reception. In *Henry V*, for example, Branagh's body is armor-laden and literally steeled against attack. [. . .]

In *Peter's Friends* and *Much Ado About Nothing*, the process of 'healthy' identity-formation is inscribed not on the *tabula rasa* of the mind, but rather, directly on the body. Though one might expect Branagh to play the titular character in *Peter's Friends*, Branagh casts himself as a relatively minor character—one of 'Peter's friends'—all of whom gather at Peter's house for a holiday reunion. But as friendships devolve into fights and holiday spirits give way to depression, the difference between Branagh and Peter acquires major significance. Representing the spread of social dis-ease that threatens to disband the reunion, Peter ushers in the New Year by announcing his status as a diseased body par excellence: the AIDS victim. Consequently, *Much Ado About Nothing* works hard to distinguish this pale, enfeebled, deficient body from the impeccably healthy bodies of its cast members, who appear robust and tan from a shooting schedule that literally takes place under the Tuscan sun. What is particularly interesting about this film is the way in which Branagh's directorial promise of making *Much Ado* a Shakespeare film for 'the world' (*Much Ado Screenplay* x) is belied by the caste system that the film unconsciously endorses in positioning the one naturally dark-skinned actor, Denzel Washington, at the margins of its Utopian community. Serving as a convenient synecdoche for all the non-white others that the film's putatively international scope fails to encompass, Washington functions more powerfully as a reminder of how 'the Irish'—and, by extension, Branagh—'became white,' that is, by subscribing to the same system of discrimination in America that the English subjected the Irish to in Britain. [. . .]

The bookend film to *Mary Shelley's Frankenstein, Hamlet* marks the apotheosis of Branagh's family romance. If, in his *Hamlet* prequel, *A Midwinter's Tale*, Branagh's actorly body is conspicuously absent, then in *Hamlet*, Branagh's emphasis on size and scale returns with a vengeance as he sets out—like Hamlet himself—to prove himself a 'good' son to his Shakespearean father once and for all.[1] But what stands out in this film even more than Branagh's chiseled physique is *Shakespeare's* body. Shot in eighty millimeter film and hyped as the only 'full-text' film version of *Hamlet* ever made, this four-hour epic self-consciously subscribes to the view that size matters, as Branagh's comments on the film suggest: ' "We want this *Hamlet* to be a big, big treat. We're trying for more epic sweep than is usually contemplated . . . there will be thousands of extras for some sequences. The Ghost is going to be a lot scarier than some faintly benign old sort walking on stage in a white shirt. It ain't gonna be three-and-a-half hours of talking heads" ' (quoted in Arnold 36–7): Branagh's somewhat strained appropriation of American slang, replete with the bravura promise of a 'big and bad' *Hamlet*, smacks of overcompensation, suggesting his deep-seated insecurities about taking on this quintessentially English role. More provocatively, his remarks betray a certain degree of anxiety about the fortitude of the Shakespearean 'corpus' in an all-action, no-talking-heads culture. Like Hamlet's own struggle with the exposure of his father's weaknesses, Branagh's rhetoric encodes his own fears about the vulnerabilities of his Shakespearean source which, as we have seen throughout this analysis, suggests the ultimate body-in-pain. But Branagh deftly deflects this anxiety onto surrogate fathers, claiming that the main challenge he faces in adapting *Hamlet* is contending with 'the ghosts of other performances' (quoted in Crowl 6). Serving as a sequel to the matricidal fantasy staged in *Mary Shelley's Frankenstein, Hamlet* invites Branagh both to worship and to kill the paternalistic 'ghosts' of other *Hamlet* performances in a film that is, ultimately, less about a pouting prince's aspirations to the Danish throne than it is about this displaced Irishman's aspirations to the mantle of English theatrical royalty.[2]

Much has been made of the fact that it was Derek Jacobi's impersonation of Hamlet that jump-started Branagh's love-affair with Shakespeare back when he was merely a wide-eyed fifteen-year-old from Belfast. At a time when Branagh claimed to be interested only in soccer and girls, he was surprised to find his attention riveted on a television serialization of Robert Graves's *I, Claudius*. As he recalls: 'I was particularly impressed by the actor playing the title role. His name was Derek Jacobi' (Introduction, *Hamlet* xi–xii). Inspired by Jacobi's acting, Branagh purchased his first ticket to a Shakespeare play—*Hamlet*—in which the fabled actor was playing the lead. And the rest is history. After seeing Jacobi's performance, Branagh 'resolved to become an actor,' exclaiming: 'I believe that much of what has followed in my life was affected by that experience' (xii). Indeed, just over a decade later, in 1988, Jacobi directed Branagh as Hamlet in Renaissance's theatrical production of the play. Yet Branagh's memories of this dream-come-true were not fond: 'I felt much more crushingly the weight of the ghosts of other performances,' he claims, recalling his intimidation by 'the weight of expectation that comes with any young actor playing the role. . . . It was not a relaxed experience' (Crowl 6). But in 1996, Branagh was able to get his revenge by playing Hamlet to Jacobi's Claudius, as well as by directing the film himself, consolidating his creative energies in an effort to replace the memory of his theatrical father in the popular imagination. The problem is, however, that while Shakespeare's Hamlet ultimately proves himself a good son by following the Ghost and killing Claudius, Branagh's celluloid prince appears more intent on following in Claudius's, that is, *Jacobi's* immortal footsteps.

Here again a conflict between Branagh's 'two bodies' emerges, for while Branagh the actor hopes to exorcise the ghost of Jacobi's Hamlet, Branagh the director clearly emulates Jacobi. This extra-diegetic fascination is apparent in the uncanny family resemblance the film establishes between stepfather and son. In contrast to the other members of the court, Hamlet and Claudius are the only two figures who have bleach-blonde hair cut in a military flat-top style, which accentuates their difference from the distinctly non-cropped, darker hair of the rest of the cast. Likewise, their costumes distinguish them from the crowd: Claudius and Hamlet both wear black, plain, and form-fitting outfits which they occupy with the stiff posture of bowling pins, quite unlike the relaxed poses, softer hues, and more lavish designs bedecking the other members of the vaguely nineteenth-century court. These pale, svelte, and decidedly phallic images of Claudius and Hamlet could not be further removed from the image of Old Hamlet, whose peppery hair, incandescent eyes, gargantuan physique, and sulfurous breath make a grotesque spectacle of Shakespeare's more sympathetic Ghost. Consciously or unconsciously, then, the film posits a mirroring relationship between Jacobi's Claudius and Branagh's Hamlet that clearly articulates Branagh's desire to be like Jacobi—to be, in effect, his natural son.

At one level, this extraordinary physical resemblance suggests that Branagh identifies with Jacobi in imaginary terms as his 'ideal ego.' Imaginary identification, as Žižek explains, involves imitating the other 'at the level of resemblance—we identify ourselves in the image of the other inasmuch as we are "like him" ' (Žižek, *Sublime* 109). But why, then, doesn't Branagh simply cast Jacobi as Old Hamlet, making it easy for this would-be son to be like his otherwise inimitable Shakespearean precursor? The answer, I would argue, is because Branagh must come to identify with Jacobi in *symbolic*, rather than imaginary, terms; he must succeed from the realm of the 'ideal ego' to that of the 'ego ideal' by identifying himself with precisely the point at which Jacobi is 'inimitable, at the point which [he] eludes resemblance' (Žižek 109). This transition from imaginary to symbolic identification entails a pivotal change of perspective in which the subject learns to align himself *not* with the position from which he appears likeable to himself but with the position from which he appears likeable to *others*. In casting Jacobi as Claudius, Branagh cleverly streamlines both of these identificatory gazes by evoking the primal scene of his adolescent, imaginary desire to be like Jacobi in *I, Claudius* and by placing his

Hamlet in a symbolic position to 'kill' this father-figure according to the dictates of the play. Consequently, as Branagh's Hamlet thrusts the poison down the throat of Jacobi's Claudius, he is quite literally giving Jacobi a taste of his own medicine. Supplanting his lifelong experience of transferential desire for Jacobi, Branagh reconciles auteur and actor as he stage-directs and succeeds Jacobi as Hamlet. But it is not until Jacobi's final day on the set that Branagh's succession is complete, when Jacobi 'springs a surprise' on him:

> He holds up a small red-bound copy of the play, that successive actors have passed on to each other with the condition that the recipient should give it in turn to the finest Hamlet of the next generation. It has come from Forbes Robertson, a great Hamlet at the turn of the century, to Derek, via Henry Ainley, Michael Redgrave, Peter O'Toole and others— now he gives it to Ken. (Jackson 211)

Like father, like son. No longer the Belfast-born step-son of the English theater, Branagh is hereby offered a new patrilineage by none other than Derek Jacobi, who christens him both natural son of and heir apparent to English theatrical royalty.

It seems particularly significant as well as strange that Branagh selected Belfast for *Hamlet's* United Kingdom debut, staging a return to the primal scene of his birth—and rebirth—with the Renaissance Theatre and Film Company. But for an audience eager to claim this prodigal son as their own, disappointment followed. Rather than acknowledging his familial and political debt to Belfast, Branagh opted to absent himself from a potentially infelicitous encounter with his own site of origin, preferring to remain, like Hamlet, at 'school'—in Hollywood. [. . .] In keeping with the haunting spirit of *Hamlet*, however, Branagh was present at the premiere as a ghost, that is, in the form of a videotaped message voicing his support for 'First Run Belfast,' the local charity sponsoring the study or staging of drama *outside* of Northern Ireland (Burnett 82). Thus Branagh completes his family romance by setting a ghostly precedent for subsequent generations, offering them tacit encouragement to follow his lead in 'adapting' to greener, quintessentially English pastures—perhaps even to become, like Branagh himself, ghost sons of a willfully forgotten Ireland in favor of Shakespeare's sceptered isle.

After several intervening non-Shakespearean films, Branagh adds a coda to his repertoire of cinematic and personal adaptation with a musical version of *Love's Labour's Lost*. A far cry from Shakespeare's prominence and preeminence in *Hamlet*, in *Love's Labour's Lost*, the Bard plays second fiddle to twentieth-century troubadors like Irving Berlin, Cole Porter, and George Gershwin. In his reflections on this film in relation to his career as an actor, Branagh claims that as far as he is concerned, it 'is dangerous to have a single hero' ('Salerno Transcript,' http://www.branaghcompendium.com/artic-sal99.htm)—an admission that contextualizes his otherwise abrupt turn away from all things English in favor of distinctly American genres and icons. Anxious, perhaps, to avoid the kind of hero worship that threatened to sabotage his *Hamlet*, in *Love's Labour's Lost* Branagh trades Derek Jacobi for Fred Astaire, as his actorly body attempts to take on the ultimate illusion of transcendence: Americanization.

Our first indication that Branagh has crossed the Atlantic in hopes of reinventing himself on American shores is the film's carefully selected location in place and time. Skillfully avoiding the aura of repression that plagues Shakespeare's unconventional comedy, Branagh situates *Love's Labour's Lost* in the thick of the wildly expressive musical culture of the nineteen thirties, setting the film before America's involvement in World War Two but conspicuously after the repeal of prohibition. While this setting offers Branagh a wide range of musicals to emulate, it is clear from the film's opening scene that his point of reference for the mood of *Love's Labour's Lost* is the sauntering grace of Fred Astaire and, more specifically, *Top Hat* (Mark Sandrich 1935)—the Astaire/Rogers classic that Branagh screened for the cast and crew on the first day of rehearsal. Despite the fact that Branagh modestly assures the media that 'I'm not Fred Astaire . . . I can tell you' ('The Guardian Interview,' http://branaghcompendium-.com/articntfguard99.htm), his bodily transformation from a hardbody to a considerably more delicate slimbody clearly generates an illusion of height and grace befitting comparison with Astaire. But Branagh's emaciated look in this film seems to work too hard for this analogy, for he much more clearly resembles another dance hero of the 1930s: James Cagney.

James Cagney might be called the working-class Fred Astaire. Known for his unusual combination of gangster and dancer roles and his bulldog energy, this Irish-American actor played parts in the thirties that correspond in stunning ways to Branagh's own postmodern penchant for merging high and low culture in the name of 'life-enhancing populism.' Preceding Astaire's *Top Hat* by two years was Cagney's role as the tap-dancing entrepreneur who puts the show on at all costs in *Footlight Parade* (Lloyd Bacon 1933)—a Busby Berkeley classic famous precisely for the goofy mix of 'singing, dancing, and synchronized swimming' that *Love's Labour's Lost* sets out to emulate (Thompson 31). Before this film, however, was Cagney's even more memorable performance as the gangster in *Public Enemy* (William Wellman 1931). This film left an indelible mark on Branagh's career, for his professional transition from the Royal Shakespeare Company to Renaissance hinged on the success of the Company's debut play, *Public Enemy*—the semi-autobiographical story of a working-class Belfast teenager who, in Branagh's own words, has 'a Jimmy Cagney fixation' (*Beginning* 169). But it is Cagney's role as the aspiring actor-manager Bottom in Max Reinhardt and William Dierterle's 1935 version of *A Midsummer Night's Dream* that seals these unmistakably proto-Branagh identities with a Shakespearean imprimatur. Like 'bully Bottom,' Branagh has always wanted to 'play all the parts' in an effort to overcome his suspicious Shakespearean credentials as the Belfast-born grandson of 'rude mechanical' dockworkers. Unlike Bottom and, for that matter, Cagney, Branagh has succeeded in this enterprise only by repressing his working-class Irish origins.

Perhaps this explains Branagh's conspicuous erasure of Cagney from his musical tribute to the 1930s, as well as the reason that, when asked about Cagney's influence on the film, Branagh's associates rigorously deny any association with this screen legend of the 1930s who, like Branagh, is patently 'no Fred Astaire.' But if Branagh really believes that it is 'dangerous to have a single hero,' then why not embrace both Astaire *and* Cagney—the ideal coordinates of his personal and professional enterprise of bringing together high and low, national and popular in the name of Shakespeare? Quite simply, Cagney represents the wrong national-popular culture, for he threatens the film's glamorous, *Top Hat*-like diegetic reality with *the* reality of class and social antagonisms stemming from his irrepressible identity as a working-class Irish-American—an identity immortalized in his musical tribute to the 1930s: *Yankee Doodle Dandy* (Michael Curtiz 1942). There is little doubt that *Love's Labour's Lost* owes as much to Cagney and *Yankee Doodle Dandy* as it does to Astaire and *Top Hat*. However, in order for Branagh's audience to believe in the escapist fiction of the 'high life' his film works so hard to construct, any hint of the 'low life'—the labor, sweat, alienation, and bodily expenditure associated with both dance and industrialization so prominent in Cagney's films—must be repressed. Ultimately, then, Branagh's actorly pursuit of Americanization in *Love's Labour's Lost* reveals what his directorial body constantly attempts to hide: that a melting pot, in which post-colonial identities are subject to often violent erasure, is preferable to the hard labor of ideological quilting.

. . . .

QUESTIONS

- Is it the capital or the content of Shakespeare and/or the Renaissance text that has guaranteed marketability?
- Can you think of your own examples of how the commodification process might work?

3 | The politics of appropriation

Heidi Hutner, *Colonial Women: Race and Culture in Stuart Drama* (Oxford: Oxford University Press, 2001), pp. 45–6.

The adaptations of *The Tempest* that follow John Fletcher's *The Sea Voyage* were written and performed after the Interregnum. In these plays, the echoes of the socio-politics of *The Tempest* and the political events of the seventeenth century are obvious—usurped kingdoms, rebellious lower classes, and restored thrones.[1] As George Guffey notes, 'Shakespeare's play was itself a "restoration" comedy'. That is, it centred upon the restoration of the rightful Duke of Milan to the throne that had earlier been wrested illegally from him.[2] The adaptations of *The Tempest* after 1660 explore the cultural anxiety concerning the overthrow of Charles I in the 1640s and the uncertainties of Restoration politics. With the exception of Thomas Durfey's *A Common-Wealth of Women*, patriarchal authority is never fully restored in any of these adaptations. Katherine Eisaman Maus suggests that although the idea of the family and patriarchy as the origin of the state was a significant political weapon for the Stuarts and their allies in the earlier seventeenth century, 'as the century wore on, patriarchalism seemed increasingly nostalgic—an attempt to recover the lost monarchical privilege enjoyed by the early Stuarts'. Hence, in Restoration adaptations of *The Tempest*, the figure of the 'father-king' becomes 'anachronistic'[3] [. . .] Father-kings and their societies in the drama of the Restoration are morally corrupt, and the line between rebel and legitimate king is thus obscured [. . .] The king's (and father's) power becomes weakened because of his own corruption, and he is unable or unwilling to discipline his daughters and prevent them from going native, that is, living out the desires that had been channelled into 'proper' behaviour in the plays of the early seventeenth century. In the *Tempests* of the Restoration, Shakespeare's and Fletcher's distinctions between the power of fathers and daughters, and between Europeans and natives, blur.

* * *

Michael Dobson and Nicola J. Watson, *England's Elizabeth: An Afterlife in Fame and Fantasy* (Oxford: Oxford University Press, 2002), pp. 217–18, 255–6, 257–9, 262–7.

Two mutually cancelling versions of Gloriana's private self—one associated with genres predominantly coded masculine, one with women's genres—were entwined together like a double helix throughout the bulk of the century, making up the genetic resources for modernist, post-modernist, and popular versions of Britain's inner self. By the 1970s, however, in the context of feminism, permissiveness, the now widely available Pill, and a steeply rising divorce-rate, the issue of Elizabeth's failure to marry and reproduce all but vanishes. In a cultural environment in which sexuality was now severed from marriage and reproduction, and in which women increasingly were expecting to wield equal power in the public sphere, the Virgin Queen was magically transformed into a role model for career women, eventually coming to double the career-politician-cum-dominatrix, Mrs Thatcher, who in the 1980s reunited femininity and the realities of state power. This coincidence opened the way to new satiric portrayals of the Queen as outside the proper reproductive cycle. Finally, the figure of this flirtatious but non-reproductive Queen became peculiarly charged for the 1990s, the decade of spin—all promise and no delivery. At the end of the century we find ourselves looking at a post-modern Elizabeth whose status far outweighs any real power, an Elizabeth for a culture which has successively come to disbelieve in the power of the established Church, the viability of a dynastic monarchy, the coherence of the island-nation, the nobility of a long-dead imperial project, the necessity of heterosexual reproduction (let alone within the nuclear family), and perhaps even in the power or appropriateness of the cultural transmission of a national heritage. [. . .]

The years since this revisited, post-Thatcher end of the Essex affair have brought still further pressures to bear on the national identity which Gloriana once underwrote—the constitutional break-up of Britain, the increasing encroachment of the European Union on domestic policy and America on foreign, the further collapse of Anglican worship, the problematic imperatives of multiculturalism—and with them has come a definite sense of the vanishing of England's Elizabeth into Past Times.[1] Elizabeth, however, seems as gamely willing to dramatize even this troubled state of the national psyche as ever, as three very successful recent reworkings of her figure will show. The dream of identifying a real subjectivity within the icon understood through the tropes of the Queen undressed and unmasked is as strong as ever: as Alison Weir conventionally remarked in 1998, 'Today, . . . with our passion for uncovering the most private secrets of our national figures, we are determined to discover the reality that lay behind Elizabeth's carefully contrived public image.'[2] However, the undressing and re-dressing of Elizabeth, one of the longest-serving tropes in the repertoire of her representations, has acquired a new valence over the *fin de siècle*, as is unconsciously demonstrated by the relevant programme in Simon Schama's television series *The History of Britain* (2000). The metaphor that governs his peroration is that with the accession of James, Mary, Queen of Scots and Elizabeth I became the *de facto* lesbian parents of a united Britain. The traditionally upbeat flavour of such a happy moment in 'our island story', however, is (unsurprisingly) absent in an era of devolution; the viewer is uncomfortably conscious of looking at a long, long series of shots of the tomb of Elizabeth. This moribund effect is underscored unintentionally by the disintegration of the very trope used in the eighteenth century to naturalize and locate the vitality of the nation, the undressed body of the Queen. Although the programme begins with a shot of the

Queen's underclothes, they are mounted on a headless dummy. This rather unsettling effect is only amplified if you know that these are *not* actually the Queen's underclothes, but a 'body' or bodice purchased after her death to serve as the basis for the funeral effigy carried on top of her coffin. They point not towards the living body, but the uninhabited posthumous icon. [. . .]

This self-propagandizing queen for the decade of spin, less Protestant Blessed Virgin than mere Madonna, appears again in the same year at the climax of Shekhar Kapur's award-winning film *Elizabeth*, which caps its cocktail of inherited commonplaces with a belatedly cogent last ten minutes. The film culminates with a vision of the young and sexually active Elizabeth (Cate Blanchett) turning herself into Elizabeth I as a career decision, alluding to her predecessor in the role, Mr Crisp, as she does so. (' "Look", she says to Kat Ashley. "I have become a virgin." ')[3] Sexual renunciation is here conceived as women's magazine makeover; and the dressing-room scene is reprised not so much so that we can see the Queen without her clothes on, but so that we can see her put them on. Yet this is none the less a death scene, accompanied by the mournful strains of the requiem mass's 'requiem aeternam', dramatizing the heroine's willed transformation of herself into 'stone', at once a simulacrum of a statue of the Virgin and a prophecy of the marble effigy on her own tomb. Renouncing her unfaithful and treacherous favourite Leicester (with whom she has earlier engaged in as passionate an affair as any 1950s novelist could have devised, unfortunately without checking whether he was already married), she shears her hair and replaces it with a wig, covers her face and hands with white lead in a parody of the ceremony of anointing, and constricts herself within the whalebone of the Ditchley portrait white dress, which here becomes a wedding-dress, signifying that she is, as she says, 'married to England'. With this makeover she ceases to be normal and modern and becomes 'Elizabeth', setting herself up as a citation within the dictionary of visual quotations that make up popular history. The film rewinds feminine subjectivity back into history; as Elizabeth moves from her dressing-table mirror out into the throne-room, she definitively exits from the private. Indeed, the novelization marketed at the time of the film's release, closing with an account of what happens there when she meets Leicester again for the first time, understands this transformation as essentially that of becoming the Madame Tussaud's waxwork of Elizabeth in advance:

> Then she stopped beside the man standing apart from the rest of her courtiers. 'Lord Robert.'
> Robert had been rigid with shock from the moment Elizabeth had entered the room. Now, obeying the command, implicit in her voice, he bent to kiss her hand. He was shaking all over, but Elizabeth's hand was quite still. And deathly cold.
> As was the frozen mask when he steeled himself to look up at her. There was nothing there. And nor was there anything in the hidden depths of Elizabeth's soul. For she had been true to her resolution. She had cut out her heart.[4]

In the film the effect is more ambiguously optimistic, of self-making, even self-citation, but what is striking is the way that the film requires the woman to occupy the historical fantasy body, 'the hyper-sign' (to borrow Barbara Hodgdon's term) that is the Queen by the end of the action.[5] In keeping with this transformation, *Elizabeth* ends with a rolling summary of subsequent history, reminiscent of Britten's Queen vanishing into legend: 'Elizabeth reigned for another forty years . . . | By the time of her death England was the richest and most powerful country in Europe | Her reign has been called the Golden Age | Elizabeth | The Virgin Queen.'

Although Kapur is a good deal more sentimental about the 'sacrifice' of the young woman's sexuality than Patricia Finney, neither seems very invested in either heterosexual normalization or in homoerotic perversity, despite bedroom scenes ranging from the torridly heterosexual (Kapur) to the routinely lesbian (Finney). Distinctively, the 1990s Queen is depicted as sensibly non-reproductive and narcissistic by rational choice, and what is typically underscored by the fates of the supporting cast of proxies is the unwisdom of choosing love when you inhabit a sexual and reproductive body—Kapur's lady-in-waiting dies in Leicester's arms through wearing a poisoned dress sent to the Queen so as to satisfy his sexual fantasy, Finney's lady-in-waiting dies of a botched abortion. Hence Elizabeth's counterparts and proxies in Finney's novel—the dwarf Thomasina and the child Pentecost—embody a femininity that is only ambiguously or hypothetically involved in the reproductive cycle. Self-pleasuring, self-narrating, self-iconizing, a one-woman limited liability company, this newly virginized Elizabeth decisively exits the heterosexual romance to become a triumphant icon, and nothing but a triumphant icon.[6]

But triumphant icon of what? An Elizabeth as utterly self-fashioned as this is barely the emblem or trace of a self, never mind a nation, and, as far as Kapur and Finney are concerned, the national and especially imperial history for which Elizabeth once stood appears in any case all but over. The ultimate successes of Elizabeth's realm recorded by *Elizabeth*'s closing titles are in the past tense: Kapur's shorthand for English nationalism is the use of Edward Elgar's 'Nimrod' variation on the soundtrack, music which associates that nationalism with the long-dead Edwardian era of empire. His film thus gives the impression, rather like Shakespeare and Fletcher's *Henry VIII* nearly four centuries earlier, of being nostalgic, if nostalgic it is, not just for Elizabeth but for what at the close of this story was still her country's future, though it is now definitively the past. [. . .]

The continuing vitality of Queen Elizabeth I as *the* English celebrity, rivalled as such only by the national poet himself, is of course most signally demonstrated by the famous success of *Shakespeare in Love* (1998), in which our continuing collective desire for the Queen is beautifully foregrounded, aroused, and registered by the script's Mr Puff-like insistence on keeping us waiting for her throughout most of the film. If history is only what you can remember, it is still what can be re-enacted as fantasy in front of an audience who have come together in part to identify themselves as its legatees. Judi Dench's commanding eight-minute impersonation of Shakespeare's most judicious critic has been perhaps the most conspicuously successful of all screen Elizabeths, and it manages to combine and reinflect so many of the possible roles and positions by which the last four centuries of English culture have made meaning for Elizabeth that even the most cursory attention to her part in the film might sum up a good deal of our study.

In *Shakespeare in Love* as elsewhere—as David Scott's 1840 painting of Elizabeth watching *The Merry Wives of Windsor* at the Globe suggests—the Queen is herself a site of the national drama, and she steps dramatically forward at the close of the première of *Romeo and Juliet* which provides this film's climax to take the stage as the film's dea ex machina. She is once more construed, Bernhardt-like, as herself a star theatrical performer (with all the potential for camp, for pathos, and for glory that this implies), with her court and her nation as captivated audience to her celebrity. *Shakespeare in Love* furthermore manages cannily to underline and reuse other earlier understandings of Elizabeth's roles, as multiply gendered personification of state power, and as focus and sponsor of the national culture. At one level Dench's queen is the official enforcer of sexual normality: she is the only character who immediately sees through Shakespeare's impersonation of his beloved Lady Viola's aunt when he accompanies Viola to the palace at Greenwich, for example, and the only spectator to recognize that the role of Juliet is being created not by a boy but by an actress. With the authority of the state, Elizabeth insists at the film's close that Viola must return to her proper role as Lord Wessex's new wife and that Shakespeare should refrain from wearing drag next time he visits her court. But the Queen is also the sponsor of cross-dressing: the play she commissions at the end of the film is for once not *The Merry Wives of Windsor* but *Twelfth Night*, the most sexually ambivalent of all Shakespeare's comedies, and even in the act of recognizing Lady Viola's disguise she ruefully perceives this boy-Juliet as her double and proxy: 'I know something of a woman in a man's profession, yes, by God, I do know about that' (148).[7]

While Dame Judi Dench is only the latest of a long series of major actresses to lend the role of Elizabeth glamour and to borrow more from it, her particular casting, however, brings far more to the role than a mere mutually reinforcing celebrity. As a formidably intelligent actress with a very distinguished career, Dench's presence in the role affirms Elizabeth's continuing identification as a model of female achievement, familiar since contemporaries first praised her as 'learned and wise above her sex': but by allusion to this actress's earlier signature successes *Shakespeare in Love* underscores Elizabeth's multiply gendered state power and national body. For viewers of the film familiar with Dench's career on the stages of London and Stratford, her casting as Lady Viola's severe but ultimately benign honorary parent—Fairy Queen as Fairy Godmother—is redoubled by memories of earlier Dench performances, as Juliet and as Viola, and as a series of legitimately and illegitimately powerful older women: Titania, Volumnia, Cleopatra, and another queen who trespasses upon what is construed as a man's profession, Lady Macbeth. For the wider audience of popular film, though, Dench is more closely associated with two other powerful women. Dench had narrowly missed an Oscar a year earlier for her equally definitive performance in John Madden's previous film *Mrs Brown* (a piece of work which had none the less stamped her as the screen's preferred Victoria for our time), so in Dench's person in *Shakespeare in Love*, the old Elizabeth and the old Victoria are reconciled at last. And then, of course, she had also played that other lady M, 007's superior in Her Majesty's secret service: she made her debut in the role (in *Goldeneye*, 1997) by assuring Bond, with a line that might ideally have rehearsed her for one long-running take on Elizabeth, that she isn't the sort of sentimental feminine type who would vacillate over signing death warrants: 'If you think I don't have the balls to send a man out to die, you're mistaken.' But Dench's M is an enabler as well as a prohibiting governess—she may complain about some of his conduct, but she goes on sending Mr Bond off on his romantic adventures—and so is her Elizabeth, saving the players from the officious Master of the Revels, guaranteeing Shakespeare's subsequent career, and choosing not to betray the soi-disant boy-player 'Thomas Kent' 's secret identity as Viola. Despite personifying the nanny state, Dench's Elizabeth hereby manages to be the soul of a Merrie England licensed sexually to thrill, and the Queen's national jollity is affirmed, too, during her first sequence in the film, when she laughs uproariously at Lance the clown in *The Two Gentlemen of Verona* and, more English still, throws a sweet to his dog Crab.

Crucially, though, Dench's Elizabeth exceeds even her own Englishness. Norman and Stoppard's script not only celebrates the London theatre business of the 1590s as a founding instrument of English national self-definition, but depicts it as Hollywood *avant la lettre*, supplementing its *No Bed for Bacon* or *1066 And All That* jokes about English school-boy history with gags about scriptwriters' analysts and venal backers. Although the film is in its own cheerful way just as post-imperial as are the desolating meditations of Nola Rae—in that the colonial enterprise, exemplified here by Lord Wessex's project for establishing a tobacco plantation in North America, is represented as morally dubious, associated not with gallant sea-dogs but with sordid commerce—*Shakespeare in Love* keeps open the possibility of a transatlantic escape, since this queen's protegée and double Lady Viola will eventually be shipwrecked off America and reborn there, alone, 'a new life beginning on a stranger shore' (154). While Dench's old queen, like the Elizabeth played by Bette Davis in *The Private Lives of Elizabeth and Essex* (1939) and *The Virgin Queen* (1955), might be construed as the repressive Old World incarnate (as we will see in our afterword), she also enjoys in Viola a vicarious rejuvenated rebirth in the New World. In this film Merrie England and Virginia coexist.

As the Public Orator put it in 2000, capping Dench's Oscar with an honorary degree from Oxford, he felt that he was presenting 'two Queens at once. We have seen Dame Judi Dench as Queen Elizabeth and as Queen Victoria, both of whom she portrayed with such skill that we thought we were seeing those monarchs themselves, familiar as they are to us all from our earliest childhood.'[8] We thought we were seeing those monarchs themselves, familiar as they are to us all from our earliest childhood: however knowingly *Shakespeare in Love* sets out to pander to a transatlantic collective fantasy of celebrity, however remote its playful, mass-media version of English history may be from the schoolbook solemnities of Froude and Neale, this, surely, is precisely the praise to which costume drama, historical fiction, and historical biography alike still aspire. Elizabeth is familiar because she was long ago adopted as part of a constitutive myth, and one which is more than ever the founding story of the origin of modern Englishness now that the National Curriculum mandates the study of no history before the Tudors. Yet she is also very strange to us, and so we go on wanting a closer look. Like the audiences for Thomas Heywood's chronicle plays soon after Elizabeth's death, we want another chance to gaze at the royal icon, miraculously restored by drama to the present tense of performance; like the readers of *The Secret History* or *Young Bess*, we want to look into history and find it peopled with recognizable selves acting out the nation as a story. Nations constitute themselves by stories: so long as we can find ourselves in the national past and that past in ourselves, it belongs to us. Hence the woman who embodied the English nation at such a crucial point in its development—and whose posthumous profile has consequently been under special pressure at moments like the eighteenth century, when that nation was being remade as part of Britain, or the end of the twentieth, when that British identity was being partially unmade once again—has been placed time and time again in works which provide us with imaginary roles in or around her story, vantage points from which to feel and to bear witness. The success with which a line of different genres of imaginative writing has brought the past variously alive through the affective mechanisms of romance—making Elizabeth a princess to be rescued, a lover to be wooed by proxy, a parent to forbid and to authorize—has made those sentiments available in modified forms even outside her own nation, as Dench's pan-global triumph itself demonstrates. But it is within her erstwhile realm that her mythos is most various, most rich, and most needed: as a readership or as an audience, we still identify ourselves around this enigmatic and ever-alluring figure. In Heywood we are bystanders at the opening of the Royal Exchange and fellow soldiers ready to resist the invading Armada; in sentimental fiction, eavesdroppers on the privacy of the real woman partly concealed by her robes or the voyeuristic readers of love-letters and confessions, privy to the heartbreakings that underlie official history; in Victorian and modern biography, we are detectives pursuing the Queen's real motives; in boys' adventure fiction, youth to be inspired to serve the national destiny by our chivalric devotion to her virgin image; in *Shakespeare in Love*, voyeurs of a romance plot and spectators of historical drama alike. From historical icon, Elizabeth is made into narrative in the great age of historical fiction, and in recent film (and mime) she has been returning towards iconic celebrity once more.

   The desire to revivify the past that continues to animate the successive representations of Elizabeth is nicely dramatized by our Frontispiece, John Hassall's *The State Entry of Queen Elizabeth into Bristol* (c.1910). If charmingly old-fashioned in its collective optimism, this paint-ing none the less exemplifies and explicates an affective investment in the living spectacle of Gloriana that has outlived the many political formations it has underwritten over the last four centuries. Here is the icon in movement, set within a busy, animated street scene: the Virgin Queen is just coming into view. She is in white, the bride of her country: she is flanked by soldiers and preceded by a marshal's drawn and upright sword, a symbol of the state's power. Immediately to our right, two small children are entranced, as we are meant to be, and our excitement is mirrored in the faces in the theatre-like gallery on the far side of the street. We have pressed ourselves into the front rank of the crowd, only just clear of the path of the oncoming soldiers (one is looking sternly at us to check we won't be in the way) and of the smooth-skinned flower-strewing pages. Radiant in the centre of the composition, crowned and gauzily beruffed, the Queen looks like her official portraits—kept a distance from us by her attendants, but not entirely remote, now that she has drawn so close. Except that in one respect she doesn't look like those portraits at all. Her eyes do not look unseeingly straight out at us: they are glancing downwards. The key impression the picture strives to give us is that the icon is inhabited, England's Elizabeth is a living woman yet once more: the pageant of history is alive, this perpetual secret at its centre, and as the procession draws level with us we are part of it. We go on hoping that the Virgin Queen will look up and meet our gaze. We are of her own country, and we adore her by the name of Eliza.

*   *   *

Lawrence Normand, '*Edward II*, Derek Jarman, and the state of England', in J. A. Downie and J. T. Parnell (eds.), *Constructing Christopher Marlowe* (Cambridge: Cambridge University Press, 2000), pp. 177, 180–3, 189–93.

The title of Derek Jarman's book *Queer 'Edward II'* indicates his intention in his film *Edward II*: to represent being queer, that is to have a certain sexuality and consequent political stance in Britain in the 1980s and 1990s. On the other hand, Jarman seemed to ignore politics when he declared that he 'chose this play solely for its subject' 'a gay love affair',[1] a characterisation of

Marlowe's play that foregrounds a twentieth-century notion of a same-sex relationship. It looks as though Marlowe's play was just a pretext for Jarman to make a film that is really about being queer in 1991. The name 'Marlowe' carried enough cultural authority to help him find money to make the film: 'can you imagine an original script on "Edward II" finding funds?', Jarman asked; and went on, '[h]ow to make a film of a gay love affair and get it commissioned. Find a dusty old play and violate it' (Jarman, p. 110, Preface). In some ways that is what he does: he cuts and changes the text of Marlowe's *Edward II*, and gives it a modern setting. But Jarman's remarks are misleading if they suggest that he was indifferent to the qualities of this Renaissance play. He turned to the English Renaissance in *The Tempest* (1979) and *The Angelic Conversation* (1985) for material that advanced his project of producing images of England's history that speak to the present. Jarman's response to *Edward II* was to produce a film that is as scrupulous in its sexual politics as Marlowe's play, though their relations to historical circumstances are necessarily different. Jarman's statement, 'Marlowe outs the past—why don't we out the present?',[2] is accurate if it means that Marlowe's dramatisation of homoerotic love is honest and critical: and it is the starting point of this essay which shows that configurations of same-sex desire are historically relative, and implicated in a field of complex social and political forces. [. . .]

Jarman's film is fully sexualised. It demonstrates the Foucauldian dictum that in the modern world the truth of the subject's sexuality is an effect of power. Gaveston reads Edward's letter while two sailors are having sex, and when he first meets Edward on his return from exile their kiss on the lips is sexual. Power and sex are more obviously entwined than in Marlowe: the Bishop of Winchester is humiliated by being stripped and forced by Gaveston into mock fellatio. Edward's neglect of Isabella appears as his not responding to her kiss. Mortimer, the epitome of a violent masculinity, is seen having masochistic sex with two Wild Girls. Gaveston wins momentary power over Isabella by teasingly trying to kiss, then mocking her. Edward's ferocious stabbing of the policeman who killed Gaveston comes after he tenderly combs his hair. Isabella's cruelty is signalled by her vampirish killing of Kent. In these incidents and imagery sex is entwined with power, and power is realised through sex. And there is no ground which defines the natural or the authentic: power is realised as the satisfaction of sexual desire, sexual desire as the effect of the play of power, and sex as the means to power. Isabella and Mortimer come to desire each other as the advantage of their political co-operation becomes clear; and the fulfilment of their political desires appears as their both sitting on the throne bubbling with sexual intimacy—repeating the image of Gaveston and Edward sharing the throne at the start.

Marlowe's play also dramatises the power–sex interplay, and reading it through the film highlights that. But Jarman is specifically modern in producing a film that centres on sexual politics. Kate Chedgzoy identifies the complexity of Jarman's ideology in which a 'post-modern aesthetic combines with a passionate commitment to radical sexual politics and an equally deeply-felt love of the English cultural past'.[3] I would like to pursue some of the implications of this. The film's postmodernity is evident in the eighty or so short scenes using minimal Marlovian dialogue; the formal, painterly composition in the film frame; and the mixing of contemporary and historical references.[4] The film's historical framings slip easily from modern to Renaissance to medieval, and this fluidity provokes the viewer into seeing aspects of these historical moments in each other. Unlike researchers of sexuality who generally insist on its historical relativity, Jarman's 'commitment to radical gay politics', which is founded on a sense of 'a shared sexual identity',[5] combines with his ambition of 'reclaiming . . . the Queer Past'[6] to produce a film that insists on the historical continuity of gay oppression and the transhistoricity of gay sexuality. The screenplay reshapes the play, but improvised fragments of dialogue, and the highlighting of other lines, make the contemporary and fictional historical scenes interpenetrate. Transforming the Poor Men into sailors having sex on a bed in the same room as Gaveston and Spenser makes explicit the gay subculture shared by these young men. Gaveston's line, 'there are hospitals for such as you' (1.1.35), which in the play sneers at the men's poverty, is translated into a sexual sneer associating homosexuality with AIDS. Jarman, like Marlowe, characterises Gaveston as contemptuous of others, and Jarman is unconstrained in showing Gaveston's, as well as Isabella's behaviour, as cruel or repellent in ways that might seem anti-gay or mysogynist. Jarman's 1990s' sexual context transforms non-sexual or ambiguous lines from the play into sexual ones in the film, such as Lancaster's, 'arm in arm, the king and he doth march' (1.2.20). The purpose of this radical transforming of the play into the contemporary is, as Chedgzoy suggests, political. The homophobia of the Conservative government found legal expression in 1988 in the passing of Section 28 of the Local Government Act which threatened local authorities with prosecution for actions that 'promoted' homosexuality. For many younger lesbians and gay men it was the first time they had faced a threat from the state against their ways of life, and for many older men like Jarman it was the return of the state oppression that prevailed before the 1967 Sexual Offences Act partially decriminalised male homosexuality. The Conservative government's intention to restrict and stigmatise homosexuality by legal action was Jarman's evidence that English state power had depended since at least the time of Edward II on the repression of homosexuality. This political thesis underpins the film's aesthetic that combines a Renaissance play with the contemporary sexual political scene. As Colin MacCabe writes, '[f]rom the moment that Mortimer appears with the dress and bearing of an SAS officer in Northern Ireland, the equations between past and present, between state and sexuality, are clearly visible on the screen'.[7]

Jarman's sexual politics can be clearly differentiated from Marlowe's. First, Jarman produces a history based on gay identity. The film shows contemporary history in rollups and Walkmans, OutRage! and protests against state-sponsored homophobia; but it also connects with Marlowe and the 1590s; and beyond that to the 1310s and 20s when Edward was King. So a gay history is produced, or rather a gay myth, of English ruling-class power being founded on the repression of homosexuality. From the point of view of the dominant class, to allow homosexuality to become fused with power is to risk undoing the ideological structure that is used to capture and hold power. As Gregory Bredbeck has shown, that discursive structure, defined in the early modern period as sodomy, represents same-sex desire as the very epitome of disorder, subversion, and rebellion, and therefore the very thing that has to be repressed for order to emerge. If homosexuality did not exist it would be necessary for the ruling class to invent it in order to have something sufficiently threatening to justify its political repression. By giving the play a modern context Jarman turns Marlowe's aristocracy into the bourgeoisie as the dominant class. Marlowe's barons disappear and only Mortimer remains as the military leader of a bourgeois nexus: he is an SAS officer, and following him are churchmen, police, and civilians who look like a Conservative constituency association. The banishment which Edward

is forced to sign is written on House of Commons notepaper dated 1991. The sexual relationship between Edward and Gaveston appears contemporary too: they are about the same age,
and have a relationship of equality. The word 'minion' almost disappears from Jarman's script
and along with it the quite different ways of seeing a homoerotic relationship between men
that Marlowe offers us, including Marlowe's construction of a powerful king and his dependent sexual partner. For Jarman sexuality is the basis for personal identity and a radical politics
that contests established power structures. The riot scene is between straights and queers,
with Edward shouting, 'March with me my friends', to a crowd of lesbians and gay men from
OutRage! in a scene which, Jarman wrote, should resemble 'the Poll Tax riot'. Spenser joins
Edward on Gaveston's recommendation as 'one of us' (a Thatcher phrase ironically reversed),
and Lightborn spares the King when he falls in love with him. The power struggle is between
groups defined by their sexuality. Figures not defined by this binary are either torn between
both sides like Kent, or, like the young Prince Edward, forced to construct an identity within it.
[. . .]

   These opposed interpretations of Edward have come to centre on the meaning of Edward's
death, and in both Marlowe and Jarman the endings are subject to authorial reshaping of their
sources (which for Jarman is Marlowe's play, of course). Ever since William Empson suggested
that Marlowe's dramatisation of Edward's death, by thrusting a red-hot poker into the anus,
invoked the anal sex that Edward and Gaveston were supposed to have practised, editors,
critics, and directors have responded to this idea. Homophobic critics have been happy to see
this death as a punishment for presumed sexual acts of which they disapproved. Such a
punitive, moralising reading of the protagonist dispels the ironies that are characteristic of
Marlowe's other tragedies, and aligns itself with, say, Ferneze's view of Barabas, or the
Chorus' of Faustus. In these plays (including the B-text of *Doctor Faustus*) the protagonists'
deaths are brought about by acute physical suffering, and that suffering itself offers a problem
of interpretation. But other critics sympathetic to King Edward's homoeroticism have also
emphasised the sexual meanings of the killing of the King.[8] In these cases it has been interpreted as being so terrible in its extreme, homophobic cruelty that the audience sympathises
with the victim, as it does with Barabas. This attempt by Edward's enemies to destroy his body
and his royalty, according to this reading, reveals Mortimer and Isabella to be the true destroy-
ers of the social order, and therefore the true sodomites in trying to dissolve the created order
of monarch and state. The sodomy that most critics have identified in Marlowe, and that
Jarman isn't interested in because he has no concept of sodomy, is faced by Edward alone, and
concerns the dissolution of his identity as king. Jarman cuts and disperses the speeches that
Marlowe assigns to Edward in the last scenes throughout the film. This avoids what a modern
audience is unlikely to find of much concern—the dissolution of the sacred category of king,
and the revelation that kingship is not intrinsic to the person, nor affirmed by God, but
dependent on power. In Marlowe's play Edward suffers this attempted dissolution not as a
homosexual, as in Jarman's film, but as a king. Jarman includes and displaces what editors and
critics have assumed to be Edward's staged death with a spit (the authority for which comes
from Holinshed), representing it as a nightmare from which Edward awakes to find Lightborn
transformed from murderer to lover. Jarman places scenes between Edward and Lightborn
throughout the film, making the audience expect Marlowe's violently rendered death, but
then overturns that by confirming instead the film's focus on the truth and power of sex. It is

Lightborn's emergent love for Edward that makes him switch loyalties from Isabella and Mortimer; he abandons his promise to Isabella to kill Edward and becomes the king's lover and political supporter, signalled by a tender kiss. Jarman's reversing the action of the play invites an active response from viewers, which might include identifying with a sexual desire that is so powerful as to subvert state power and establish its own loyalties: '[w]ith this kiss a whole history of homophobia and violence is annulled, a whole new history becomes possible'.[9] This is one of many moments which engage viewers' wishes, anxieties or desires, and open up various possibilities of interpretation and response.

Jarman's rewriting of Marlowe's ending is anticipated in Marlowe's rewriting of Holinshed's account of Edward's death; and in both cases the changes work to diminish homophobia. But the critical assumption that Marlowe stages Edward's death in the manner detailed in Holinshed is probably wrong. Orgel notes that the insistence on the red-hot spit shows a wish to make the murder 'precisely what Marlowe refuses to make it, a condign punishment, the mirror of Edward's unspeakable vice'; and he argues that Marlowe may have designed the play so that its scrutiny of power can be screened by Edward's sexuality, 'a way of protecting the play, a way of keeping what it says about power intact'.[10] Readings of the play that insistently focus on sexuality, in Orgel's view, obscure its dramatisation of power. This insistence on sexuality is evident in the added stage directions in Act Five, Scene Five of the 1995 'World's Classics' edition of David Bevington and Eric Rasmussen. The editors state that they only add stage directions 'where they seem clearly intended to be performed' (p. xxv), but the added stage direction '[*Matrevis and Gurney bring in a table and a red-hot spit*]' (p. 398) is unwarranted in indicating what was intended for stage performance.[11] Although Lightborn tells Matrevis and Gurney to 'get me a spit, and let it be red-hot' (5.5.32), no further mention is made of the spit. Then Lightborn asks Gurney and Matrevis for 'A table and a feather-bed', and the dialogue continues:

GURNEY: That's all?
LIGHTBORN: Ay, ay: so, when I call you, bring it in. (5.5.35–7)

When the murder starts Lightborn calls only for the table (5.5.112)—which, as Orgel notes, is something that requires two people to carry—and then orders Matrevis and Gurney to 'lay the table down, and stamp on it,/ But not too hard, lest that you bruise his body' (5.5.114–15). The red-hot spit is redundant to Lightborn's Machiavellian intention of murdering the King without marking his body, which is done by crushing with a table without bruising (perhaps also with the mattress of 'this bed' [5 .5. 74] that Lightborn invites Edward to lie on). Stamping on a table along with Edward's 'cry' (5.5.116) would be enough to suggest the grotesque violence of the death. If this reading of Marlowe's staging of Edward's death is correct then Marlowe anticipated Jarman in redirecting attention away from the chronicles' homophobic accounts to a dramatisation that emphasises political meanings: Edward's responses as king in the face of a designedly low and treacherous death.

Jarman's *Edward II*, like other of his films, uses the history and literature of the English Renaissance to explore what he saw as the grim English present under a Conservative government. 'English' is the right word, for Jarman was a cultural conservative who loved that country's landscapes and literature, while also detesting what he saw as its hypocritical, repressive political values.[12] His homosexuality was the source of his political radicalism, which increased in the late 1980s as the government supported homophobic legislation, including Section 28, at the same time as gay men were suffering most from HIV disease. Jarman's HIV positive status had been diagnosed in 1986, and by the time he made *Edward II* he was involved in the gay activist group OutRage!, and had become the most prominent public figure to talk openly about being HIV positive. The making of *Edward II* was an integral part of the personal and political strands of his life. The presence of members of OutRage! in *Edward II* indicates the precise logic of Jarman's sexual politics. Queer love in the film is not confined to the private realm but is political; OurRage!'s demonstrations, often theatrical or parodic and always high profile, are designed to make the same point. Both represent a kind of protest through performance that is 'self-consciously imitative of actual events, providing a polemical antithesis to spectatorship and passivity'.[13]

I have been discussing the film and play as if the film worked with fixed sexual identities and the play worked without sexual identities, but rather with sex dispersed through other discourses. I want to end by complicating that impression. In the film we see not the fixity of sexual identities but their terrifying contingency. In the scene after Isabella has been accused by Edward of fawning on Mortimer and causing Gaveston's exile we see her changing. Tilda Swinton plays the speech beginning 'Would, when I left sweet France, and was embarked,/ That charming Circe, walking on the waves,/ Had chang'd my shape' slumped on her knees in the bottom of the frame, facing the camera, her body symmetrically composed and motionless. As she speaks, we witness the birth of a new consciousness as the power exerted on her by Edward produces the knowledge that she must act differently to create power for herself: 'I must entreat him, I must speak him fair' (1.4.172–3, 184). Circe, then, is the apt reference, for Isabella's new-found power leads to sexual pleasure with Mortimer. Edward too changes to become, for example, a butcher-like killer of Gaveston's killer, though he is constant in his love for Gaveston. But the pre-eminent figure in whom identity is unfixed and in the process of being formed as the film goes on is Prince Edward. As he wanders around the set directing a torch's beam at sights that amaze him—a naked rugby scrum, his father's violence directed at his mother, a huge opened carcass—the audience shares his point of view and his bewilderment at this fearful semiotic excess. Neither play nor film ends with Edward's death, but rather with the return of Prince Edward as the new king. Marlowe and Jarman diverge markedly in their treatment of young Edward, with Marlowe's Prince voicing patriarchal continuity, and Jarman's constructing an improvised subjectivity from various signs of power he has previously encountered. In Marlowe's astonishingly swift final scene the Prince is transformed from being 'yet a child' to a sovereign uttering words of judgement and condemnation, the power of which comes from his occupying authoritatively the patriarchal place vacated by his father: 'in me my loving father speaks,/ And plainly saith, 'twas thou that murder'dst him' (5.6.17, 41–2). The new king's subjectivity, as Marlowe dramatises it, is split in a way that intensifies rather than undermines his power, between the voicing of royal authority and the weeping of a loving son. The final tableau, ordered by Edward, of Edward II's hearse with Mortimer's head on it effects a reordering of events that reestablishes royal legitimacy and sovereignty. Jarman's prince improvises a new subjectivity through partial identifications that we have seen him make through the film: from Mortimer's world he wears a soldier's uniform and fires a toy machine gun; from Edward, whose letters he delivered and read, he picks up family loyalties;

from Isabella he acquires ruthlessness and a cold heart, and some remarkable earrings. The little boy dancing to 'The Sugar Plum Fairy' on top of the cage containing Isabella and Mortimer is uncanny, scary—you might say, queer. He has no certain place in ideology; he is a self-assembled figure constructed of signs of power from others (who all fail), a bricolage of partial identifications that do not construct anything like a simple sexual identity, but will enable him to capture and exercise enough power to survive in what lies ahead (which includes being queer as well as being king). This is a long way from Marlowe's new king's orthodoxy but perhaps no less radical in its analysis of sex and power.

*   *   *

Sarah Werner, *Shakespeare and Feminist Performance: Ideology on Stage* (London and New York: Routledge, 2001), pp. 77–87.

In 1995, Gale Edwards directed *The Taming of the Shrew* for the Royal Shakespeare Company on their main stage in Stratford-upon-Avon. While this production marked the company's fifth *Shrew* in thirteen years and the second by a woman, it also marked only the third time a woman had directed in the Royal Shakespeare Theatre.[1] The low frequency of women directing on the main stage and relativity high frequency of women directing *Shrew* creates some interesting contexts for Edwards' production. The absence of female directors at the RSC follows the pattern of male Shakespeare that I have traced in the previous chapters. But what does it mean that this play seems to be marked at the RSC as more female than others? The 'Shrew option,' as director Susan Lily Todd calls the practise of hiring women to direct this play, acknowledges and circumvents the play's notorious misogyny. The playscript centers on silencing a woman and climaxes with making her the mouthpiece for a nostalgic and regressive notion of women's duty to prostrate themselves before their husbands.[2] By inviting a female director to be the voice behind the mouthpiece, a predominantly male company can distance itself from the suggestion that women need to be made to obey their male lords. But if this move places female directors in the position of Shakespeare (the authorial director substituting for the authorial playwright), it also places them in the position of Katherine, authorized to proclaim the inferiority of women. Having a woman direct *The Taming of the Shrew*, in other words, sets up oppositional ideologies: the female director's presence legitimizes women's interpretations of Shakespeare, while the playscript's patriarchal thrust silences women.

Staging the production in the main theatre of the company creates additional tensions. The audience for the RSC's base in Stratford is largely made up of tourists, particularly overseas tourists who come to see Shakespeare performed in the town of his birth. Another portion of the audience is school parties taken to see Shakespeare as part of their studies. Both of these groups expect to see productions of the plays that are in some sense traditional, that is that put forward readings illustrating Shakespeare's universal genius and that help audiences to understand and appreciate it. It is not unusual, during intervals and after shows, to hear audience members complain that the actors were not in Elizabethan dress or to hear those well-versed in the play grumble about changes made to the script. The architecture of the Royal Shakespeare Theatre reinforces these expectations with its proscenium-arch stage that has resisted all attempts at modification and has been criticized by generations of directors and reviewers for its inflexibility. Robert Shaughnessy argues that the theatre's 'predominantly pictorial mode of

Shakespearean production,' where viewers sit in a darkened auditorium separated from a remote spectacle they can only passively observe, sets up a consumerist relationship between spectators and stage (Shaughnessy 1994: 19). As he points out, the seat prices replicate this dynamic as well, with spectators paying increasingly higher prices for the closer and more central seats (Shaughnessy 1994: 20). By presenting Shakespeare in a space that remains inaccessible to viewers, RSC productions on the main stage work against political engagement with the play. Shakespeare becomes a product that viewers can buy, a commodity whose presence is confirmed not just by the ticket prices but by the souvenir shops and the larger-than-life photos from past productions hanging in the lobbies and corridors. For those visitors to Stratford who have spent the day doing the Shakespeare sights—his birthplace, his house, his daughter's house, his grave—going to the RSC is one last step on the Shakespeare tour.[3]

In such a context, the tension between patriarchal script and feminist intervention can also be seen as a tension between Shakespeare as commercial package and as object of inquiry. While a feminist director may see him as a playwright whose politics should be interrogated, his or her Stratford audience is more likely to see him as a playwright to be consumed. Michael Bogdanov's 1978 RSC production of *The Taming of the Shrew* famously exploited this tension by welcoming his audience with an Italianate set that fitted smoothly into proscenium-arch, pictorial expectations. This set—and its accompanying traditional projection of Shakespeare—was then demolished during what appeared to be a fight between a drunken male audience member and a female usher. This couple turned out to be an updated Sly and Hostess, who then became Petruchio and Katherine. By literally destroying the timeless Bard and replacing him with a twentieth-century version, Bogdanov strove to jolt the audience into seeing the piece through new eyes, eyes that would be willing to see it as an indictment of male violence against women rather than as a comedy. Some in the audience were shocked into a re-evaluation of Shakespeare's play. Michael Billington, reviewer for the *Guardian*, wondered 'whether there is any reason to revive a play that seems totally offensive to our age and our society'; his conclusion was that 'it should be put back firmly and squarely on the shelf' (Billington 1993: 124). Others, however, responded to this production as evidence of the play's farcical possibilities, continuing to value it as comedy.[4]

The tensions between traditional comedy, feminist inquiry and audience expectations were even more strongly present for Gale Edwards. In an interview with Elizabeth Schafer after the production had closed, she is caustic about the challenges the play presents a female director:

> A woman directing *The Taming of the Shrew*, whoever she is, might as well get a loaded shotgun and put it against her temple, because half the critics will be disappointed and will criticise it if the view of the play is not radical and feminist because they expect that from a woman; then the other half will shoot you down in flames because you're doing a feminist, 'limited' view of a play which is meant to be about the surrender of love. So you *cannot* possibly win. You're absolutely fucked.
>
> (Schafer 1998: 57; emphasis in original)

Unlike Bogdanov, who was convinced that his interpretation was true to Shakespeare's intentions, Edwards could not pretend that she was going to be faithful to the play: 'My theory about *The Taming of the Shrew* is that it is about the surrender of love and it *is* about her giving up everything and saying, "I love you and you can tread on my hand." That is the right way to do it and I couldn't do that production. That was a *huge* artistic and moral dilemma for me' (Schafer 1998: 71; emphasis in original). Edwards only agreed to direct *Shrew* because the temptation to work at the RSC was so strong (see Alderson 1995, Cornwell 1995, Schafer 1998: 71). However, having taken on the play, she found herself confronted not only by her own hesitations but by the demands of others:

> There is a tremendous pressure when a woman takes on a text like this, that somehow this woman is going to solve the play, a play we've been wrestling with for years, or enlighten us or turn it on its head. . . . People don't think, gee, a man is going to direct *King Lear*, this'll be really good because a man is directing. If I directed *Hamlet*, as I have directed *King Lear*, *The Winter's Tale* and *The Tempest*, I would not be subject to this amount of scrutiny or interest. And therein lies the rub. It's what part of the play is about isn't it? . . . How strange it is to be a strong woman.
>
> (Alderson 1995)

Acutely aware of the contradictions inherent in being a woman directing a play about taming women and of the vulnerability involved with doing so at a prominent national theatre, Edwards could have been frozen by the responsibilities placed on her. Instead, the similarities she saw between her situation and Katherine's became a way of revealing those demands and throwing them back to her audience.

Caught between viewers' contradictory desires for a traditional comedy and a feminist indictment, Edwards chose to offer both: the scripted narrative of a happy love story between a shrew and the man who tames her was played out on stage alongside a critique of that narrative. By alternating between these two stories, Edwards made visible the gaps and silences of Shakespeare's script and put the burden of 'solving' the play onto her audience. Instead of creating a story for Katherine that provided a rationale for her behavior and thoughts, this production emphasized its absence. Katherine's silence was neither self-explanatory nor readily subsumed into a happy ending, but rather it was something that audiences were forced to confront.

Edwards' production of *Shrew* made it clear that the frame and the taming story were centered on and driven by their male heroes. The performance opened with Sly tossed out into a storm by his wife (Edwards' substitution for the Hostess) and falling asleep into a compensatory dream starring himself as Petruchio and his wife as Katherine. By setting up the taming as a male fantasy, Edwards allowed the script to play out its patriarchal storyline and made questions about what Katherine is feeling irrelevant: she behaves as she does because that is what Sly/Petruchio wishes. But by casting Josie Lawrence as Katherine, Edwards disrupted Petruchio's control. Lawrence is a well-known comic with her own television series (*Josie*) and a regular on the popular improvisational sketch show *Whose Line is it Anyway?* and her fame generated power on stage. While Shakespeare's script suggests that Petruchio controls the story—his words dominate the play—Edwards' production prioritized verbal and physical comedy. The affections of the audience gravitated towards the person who made them laugh, creating a rapport that shaped how they reacted to events on stage. Lawrence's comic persona established Katherine as an appealing character from her first entrance, snarling at her sister's suitors. She walked on stage as if she owned it, setting the tone in the early scenes by taking control of Katherine's image. Her belittlement of the suitors ridiculed their depiction of her as a shrew. They appeared weak and foolish, while she seemed strong and smart, not so much shrewish as impatient with their ineptitude. Her first scene with Petruchio began with him quaking before her, nervously calling her 'Kate' as his desire to establish his mastery floundered in the face of her presence. But Edwards refused to allow the production to settle into a story of Katherine's strength. While Lawrence/Katherine began the wooing scene in a position of power, Siberry/Petruchio was soon as successful in controlling the laughter— a pattern of competition for control over each other and the audience that continued throughout the production. Using Lawrence's appeal to counter that of Petruchio, Edwards allowed the audience to fluctuate between finding the taming plot compelling and revolting.

The most graphic examples of these alternating stories came with the contrast between the scenes set in Petruchio's house and the later reconciliation as the couples were on their way to Bianca's wedding. These two depictions of their relationship stood in stark contrast and neither one could erase the presence of the other. During their stay at his house, Katherine and Petruchio's marriage was represented as consisting of his violent domination of her. Although the initial banquet scene was played for laughs, with the servants and Petruchio juggling the food across the room, it was also implicitly violent: Petruchio pretended to beat his servants and Katherine hid under the table from the flying meats. By the time the stage had cleared and Petruchio re-emerged to deliver his soliloquy, 'Thus have I politicly begun my reign' (4.1.169– 92), the tone was deadly serious. During the soliloquy, which Siberry delivered to the audience, Katherine emerged upstage accompanied by solemn music. She looked just as Petruchio described her, starved and exhausted, and her onstage presence graphically illustrated the physical actions behind his falconry metaphors. She literally upstaged Siberry/Petruchio, a material presence that his voice could not erase and an extratextual reminder of the violence of Shakespeare's script. Katherine remained on stage during the next scene, the walls of the set moving to box her in on three sides; her trapped misery counteracted the wooing games Bianca was playing with Tranio, Lucentio and Hortensio, and reminded us precisely of what is taught at the taming school Hortensio said he would attend. After their exit, Lawrence addressed the audience with her opening lines of the next scene: 'The more my wrong, the more his spite appears. / What, did he marry me to famish me?' (4.3.2–14). By making Katherine's first thirteen lines a soliloquy instead of a speech to Grumio, Edwards gave Lawrence/ Katherine equal dramatic time with Siberry/Petruchio, counteracting his description of the taming with her experience of it. What the audience saw and heard invited them to judge Petruchio's treatment of Katherine as cruel, and to sympathize with her confusion and despair.

But when Petruchio and Katherine were on their way to Bianca's wedding and he asked her to agree with him that the sun is the moon, their relationship was presented as one of mutual appreciation and loving flirtation. Katherine, although a bit slow to pick up her cues at first, soon responded to Petruchio's name games, assuring him flirtatiously that 'sun it is not, when you say it is not, / And the moon changes even as your mind' (4.6.20–1). Twisting her finger at the side of his head to indicate that he is crazy, she was about to kiss him when they were interrupted by the appearance of Vincentio. Katherine's encounter with Vincentio provided an opportunity to continue her sexual flirting with Petruchio. Taking his suggestion to embrace the 'fair lovely maid' (4.5.34) one step further, she looked at Petruchio so that he could acknowledge and appreciate her challenge in wondering aloud at the lucky maid's future bedfellow. When Petruchio corrected her by pointing out that Vincentio is an old man, Katherine graciously acknowledged her mistake. There was no trace of the earlier cruelty and power imbalance in their marriage. Instead, they were presented as willing participants in a comic love story.

The deferred kiss returned as a climax in the next scene. Having just witnessed the discovery of Lucentio's real identity and his marriage to Bianca, Katherine suggested to her husband that they follow the group home. He refused to do so until she gave him a kiss, which, she made clear, she was reluctant to do 'in the midst of the street' (5.1.125). Petruchio insisted, and she complied; the couple then shared what Siberry has described as 'a big, long "screen" kiss' (Siberry 1998: 56). Edwards' production set up this moment as a willing reconciliation between the two, who then walked off arm in arm, accompanied by a glowing sunset and swelling music. The kiss in the street came as a seemingly natural conclusion to Katherine and Petruchio's growing flirtation in the earlier sun/moon scene, and the audience on the first night I saw the play applauded the moment loudly. Although the movie stereotypes of pink sunsets and passionate clinches also send up the moment, the embrace in the street fulfilled the earlier promise of a kiss, and the audience responded with relief.[5]

Despite their wildly differing natures, no effort was made to provide a coherent transition from the depiction of Petruchio's cruelty and Katherine's despair to that of the loving couple we saw a few scenes later. No explanation was given for Katherine's acquiescing to Petruchio's sun/moon games, let alone why she seemed to be charmed by him. Nor does the happy kiss erase the violent taming: Katherine entered the street scene eating what appeared to be a chicken leg, a visual and unmistakable reminder of her earlier starving self. Despite that reminder, and the obvious implication that she was only allowed to eat as a reward for her good behavior in the sun/moon scene, the audience I first saw the play with chose at this moment to endorse the love story over the taming critique. By forcing the audience to recognize the violence of the taming, and then encouraging them to approve the love story, Edwards moved the audience back and forth between the two positions of critiquing and endorsing the patriarchal politics of the playscript without appearing to privilege either. Although the audience's initial attraction to Katherine upset the traditional stereotype of a shrew, their subsequent laughter in the 'wooing' scene with Petruchio returned to a masculinist understanding of the plot. The pair of taming soliloquies in the middle of the play undercut the patriarchal plot, but the flirtatious sun/moon debate made that plot seem a pleasant one. The triumphant kiss in the street clinched the love story, only to have that story seem increasingly unlikely as the production moved towards its final moments. It is in these last scenes that Edwards' strategy paid off.

Katherine's final speech, notorious for its extreme submission, carries so much extratextual weight as to be almost unreadable, particularly for those who wish to believe in a universal Shakespeare. The literal text is, perhaps, all too readable—a rhythmically even and generally straightforward lesson on the duties a wife owes her husband. But, if anything, its blatant servility increases the desire to make the speech say something else. For many modern readers and viewers of *The Taming of the Shrew*, this is where the playscript collapses in on itself, the moment where Petruchio's patriarchal domination of Katherine becomes so bitter that the comedy can no longer be sustained. In an oft-cited criticism, George Bernard Shaw wrote in 1897 that

> No man with any decency of feeling can sit it out in the company of a woman without being extremely ashamed of the lord-of-creation moral implied in the wager and the speech put into the woman's own mouth.
>
> (Wilson 1961: 188)

The fact that scholars and reviewers nearly a century later continue to quote Shaw without referring to the context of his article (a dismissal of Garrick's *Catherine and Petruchio* in which he praises Shakespeare's realism) reveals the degree to which the play's ending has become the focal-point of any production or interpretation.[6] As we have seen, directors have frequently adapted the speech to make it more palatable, and feminist scholars repeatedly turn to it as the focus of their inquiries. With all this attention on her words circulating through the cultural energy of the play, Katherine's submission speech bears the burden not only of resolving the playscript and its performance, but of answering the larger issues of gender relationships that reverberate in early twentieth-first-century western culture.

This extratextual burden carried by Katherine's speech became part of the dynamic of Edwards' *Shrew*, which relied on audience expectations to fill in the script's character gaps. When Petruchio and Katherine first entered the scene, she was dressed in a modified version of the dress she and Petruchio had argued about with the tailor. They appeared to be a happily married couple on equal footing with each other. But when Katherine re-entered at Petruchio's bidding, and discovered that he had been betting on her obedience, the entire context and tone of the scene changed. No longer part of a power-sharing couple, Katherine performed her speech of submission but abandoned her husband immediately after. After her disappearance into the toy theatre that appeared upstage (following the exit of the rest of the characters), the play returned to the Sly frame. The broken-hearted Petruchio became newly repentant Sly, who begged his wife's forgiveness when she came to bring him out of the storm. What appeared to be a patriarchal revenge fantasy turned out to be something so horrible that even the plot's creator shunned it. As the summary in the program describes it, 'Petruchio slowly realizes what he has been attempting to do to Katherine in the name of love. By the end of the speech his dream has become his nightmare . . .' (Royal Shakespeare Company 1995).

Because the production had vacillated so wildly between contesting and upholding the playscript's patriarchal comedy, viewers found themselves entering Katherine's speech without a solid basis from which to interpret it—would it continue in the vein of a love story or return to a critique of that plot? Rather than appearing clearly as a sincere endorsement or an ironic rejection of the text's message of submission, Lawrence/Katherine's performance of the speech was a blank space waiting to be filled with meaning. Our awareness as viewers of the performative aspects of the moment—our sense that Lawrence/Katherine was reciting a speech rather than releasing thoughts and emotions into words—did not answer the question of what Katherine meant her words to be. Instead of being able to read the moment as a revelation of her character, we were put in the position of reading it as a revelation of our own desires. If this speech was a performance, what was it a performance of? What did we want Katherine to be saying? Typically, actor training and audience experience set up a psychologically coherent character that develops through the actor's physical embodiment of the textual role. But Edwards and Lawrence radically destabilized that coherency by altering the audience's relationship to the performance. By moving the audience back and forth between incompatible endorsements and critiques of the taming plot, the production replicates in its viewers Katherine's own position within the script, moving from one set-piece to the next with little sense of continuity or development on which to build a unified character. It was impossible for viewers to read the ending as telling Katherine's story, since there was never a clear sense of what 'her' story is. All the audience had to go on was its own sense of what was an appropriate ending for the play.

Edwards' production refused to allow its viewers the false luxury of sitting back and having Shakespeare solved for them. This *Shrew* created gaps in the logic of the story that had to be filled by its viewers. In the final moments of the play, the two storylines—taming romance and feminist critique—collided and the audience realized that they could not have it both ways. When Petruchio/Sly (who wanted a happy ending as much as any viewer) realized the mistake of his revenge fantasy, Edwards created a space for the audience to share his remorse. We realized that our desire for a happy ending implicated us in a regressive and harmful ideology, and thus we recognized the danger of consuming Shakespeare blindly. In this way, Edwards' *Shrew* offered a feminist production that could be presented on the RSC main stage without succumbing to a passive acceptance of its politics.

. . . .

QUESTIONS

- Why does reinvention seem to serve so many opposing political interests?
- What differences are there between queer and feminist modes of appropriation?
- To what extent does the appropriation of the Renaissance text reinforce its universal status?

4 | International appropriation

Dennis Kennedy, 'Afterword: Shakespearean Orientalism', in Dennis Kennedy (ed.), *Foreign Shakespeare: Contemporary Performance* (Cambridge: Cambridge University Press, 1993), p. 301.

If we are to make the study and performance of Shakespeare fully contemporary and fully international we must worry less about his textual meaning and more about his prodigious appropriation (or misappropriation) in a global context. Shakespeare is not everywhere, but he is certainly more places than any other dramatist and perhaps more than any other artist [. . .] His work has become the closest thing we have to a common cultural inheritance, but it is an inheritance that is thoroughly redefined by each culture that receives it.

*   *   *

Ania Loomba, 'Local manufacture made-in-India Othello fellows', in Ania Loomba and Martin Orkin (eds.), *Post-Colonial Shakespeares* (London: Routledge, 1998), pp. 151–63.

The Kathakali *Othello* is over two hours long. Produced by the International Centre for Kathakali in New Delhi, it includes only five scenes: Roderigo and Iago's initial meeting, the Senate scene, Othello and Desdemona's meeting in Cyprus, a long scene that amalgamates Cassio's meeting with Desdemona, her pleading with Othello on Cassio's behalf, Iago snatching the handkerchief from Emilia and planting seeds of suspicion in Othello's mind, and finally, the bedchamber scene. If the original play were played in full, the production would go on for twelve hours or more, as in fact Kathakali performances often do.

Like Noh and Kabuki, Kathakali is a highly formal style of theatre which evolved at about the same time as Shakespearean drama. This 'story-play' is a hybrid form that drew upon various earlier arts. Its dramatic principles are based upon Bharata's *Natyashastra*, the encyclopaedia of Indian dramaturgy and theatrical techniques which dates between 200 BC and AD 200. Its elaborate and heavy costumes, mask-like make-up and a complex gestural code or *mudras*, in which over 500 facial, eye or hand gestures are used to 'speak' to the audience, are drawn from an earlier form of theatre, *Kutiyattam*. From the religious theatre *Taiyyam*, Kathakali takes its repeated theme of battles between good and demonic figures. In the *Othello* production, Iago and Othello become such archetypes. The famous martial art form of Kerala, *Kalarippayat*, contributes to Kathakali's choreography and rigorous methods of training. Under colonial rule, Kathakali's patronage by the landed aristocracy or rich households began to crumble and collapsed further with the breakdown of princely estates. Today's 'patrons' are either just those audiences who have grown up with the form, or else state-sponsored schools or institutions such as the International Centre for Kathakali (see Zarrilli 1984).

During the time we were studying this production, I also began reading Salman Rushdie's latest novel, *The Moor's Last Sigh* (1995), which traces its central character's origins to the same Malabar coast to which Kathakali belongs. However, these two rewritings of Shakespeare's Moor are born of two very different kinds of 'post-colonial' dynamics. *The Moor's Last Sigh* is the product of a sophisticated English-speaking intellectual hankering for a remembered home. The Kathakali *Othello* is crafted within a centuries-old form that has only recently begun to become internationally visible. Rushdie, the high priest of diasporic post-coloniality, and master of the hybrid tongue, is at pains to delineate the long and intricate history of cultural and racial intermingling in this region: today's population is almost evenly divided between Christians (mainly Roman Catholics and Syrian Orthodox), Muslims and Hindus. But at the same time, Rushdie's 'hybrid' Kerala is described in terms that are remarkably similar to his 'hybrid' Bombay, with whom he seems more comfortable (both the Bombay of this novel and the one described in *Midnight's Children*). Rushdie's vocabulary and images remain fairly similar for these two fairly dissimilar terrains and cultures because the crucial point for him is that each is 'impure'. The Kathakali production, on the other hand, skirts all questions and histories of difference in its powerful appropriation of this story about difference. It is anxious to craft a vocabulary that will allow it to experiment with plays like *Othello* without violating its own specific codes of signification.

For at least two hundred years, Othello's origins and Moorishness have been the focus of critical debate: what shade of black was he? Where did he come from? What exactly does his blackness mean? Rushdie expands these questions to embrace both the history of racial conflict in early modern Europe and communal and religious strife in contemporary India. His Moor's mother, Aurora, belongs to the Catholic da Gama family of Cochin, pepper traders by profession. She marries the Jewish Abraham Zogoiby, whose mother attempts to forbid this match 'because it was unheard of for a Cochin Jew to marry outside the community' (Rushdie 1995: 70). For Abraham's mother, Moors are the real threat, and she accuses Aurora's family of not being pure 'Christy's' but having Moorish blood in them. Her anger against Aurora erupts as 'A curse on all Moors. . . . Who destroyed the Cranganore synagogue? Moors, who else. Local-manufacture made-in-India Othello fellows. A plague on their houses and spouses' (ibid.:72). Abraham then reveals that he knows of the Moorish blood in his own lineage. As a young boy he had discovered, in a trunk in the synagogue, the crown of the last Moorish Sultan of Granada. In one dramatic sentence, Rushdie brings together the European drive to overseas expansion with the will to cleanse its interior of non-white peoples:

> Thus Abraham learned that, in January 1492, while Christopher Columbus watched in wonderment and contempt, the Sultan Boabdil of Granada had surrendered the keys to the fortress-palace of the Alhambra, last and greatest of all the Moors' fortifications, to the all-conquering Catholic Kings Fernando and Isabella. . . . He departed into exile with his mother and retainers, bringing to a close centuries of Moorish Spain.
>
> (Ibid.: 79–80)

Both Jews and Moors fled South, and Boabdil took on a Jewish lover who stole his crown and moved to India. Abraham asks, 'Mother, who is worse? My Aurora who does not hide the Vasco connection, but takes delight; or myself, born of the fat old Moor of Granada's last sighs in the arms of his thieving mistress—Boabdil's bastard Jew?' (ibid.: 82–3).

Rushdie plays on the images of both *Othello* and *The Merchant of Venice* as he weaves the histories of Jews and Muslims. Aurora and Abraham's fourth child is the Moor, whose hybrid genes and abnormal rate of growth become a metaphor for the fecundity of metropolitan India. Against this chaotic history, the novel charts the growth of fundamentalist communal identities in Bombay, evoking the rise of the right-wing militant organization the Shiv Sena, and the violence that followed the destruction of the Babri mosque in Ayodhya in December 1992. His Moor flees back to Spain where he dies, looking at the 'Alhambra, Europe's red fort, sister to Delhi's and Agra's' and hoping to awake in better times (ibid.: 433). His hero's expulsion from Bombay also mirrors Rushdie's own distance from India. But where Othello's last sigh testifies to the agonizing split between Moorish past and Christian present, black skin and white mask, the recurring motif of the Moor's last sigh in Rushdie's novel indicates not psychic but historical and geographic schisms: the hybridity of the post-colonial polity rather than of the individual subject.

The Kathakali *Othello* inflects the Moor's agonies in a different direction and erases the schisms central both to Shakespeare's play and Rushdie's novel. It flamboyantly reshapes Othello's tragedy in the language of a four hundred year-old form first devised to perform stories from the Hindu epic *Ramayana*. Its Othello is neither a black man nor a Moor, but takes the form of a Hindu warrior. Historical arrivals on the Malabar coast do not inflect his story; nor do the contemporary ideologies of belonging and exclusion in India colour his identity. Thus, while one post-colonial revision restlessly searches the globe for histories and motifs which foreground the question of difference, the other uses centuries of stagecraft to reach out and mould difference in its own image. As part of a post-colonial appropriation of Shakespeare, these silences disappoint us. But they speak eloquently about the dynamics of the post-colonial evolution of Kathakali.

The International Centre of Kathakali was founded in 1960, with the aim of addressing the specific problems 'involved in adapting Kathakali to the modern stage' (Zarrilli 1984: 305). It has produced several plays outside of the traditional Kathakali corpus such as *Mary Magdalene*, *David and Goliath*, and *Salome*. The Kathakali Centre thus marks the attempt to forge traditional, regional traditions into a national (and perhaps nationalist) conception of the Indian Arts. It is one of many similar institutions conceived within the Nehruvian ideal of a multicultural yet united India, evoked lyrically and nostagically in *The Moor's Last Sigh* as the

> dawning of a new world . . . a free country, above religion because secular, above class because socialist, above caste because enlightened, above hatred because loving, above vengeance because forgiving, above tribe because unifying, above language because many-tongued, above colour because multi-coloured, above poverty because victorious over it, above ignorance because literate, above stupidity because brilliant.
>
> (Rushdie 1995: 51)

In the face of an aggressive and escalating communalism, the need to affirm a secular nationalism seems enormous. And yet so many of the ethnic, linguistic and class tensions of contemporary India are precisely the product of the exclusions engendered by the post-colonial nationalist state, as Bengali writer Mahasweta Devi's short story 'Shishu' (Children) so gut-wrenchingly illustrates. In this, a well-meaning government officer, Mr Singh, learns that the relief supplies he has come to distribute to a drought-ridden region are regularly stolen by mysterious children. Many years earlier, tribals called the Agarias had opposed government attempts to mine the region for iron and coal. Their myths forbade the attempt to carve the belly of the earth. But national 'development' has little space for such local 'fairy stories' and the rebellious Agarias were driven into the forests and into starvation. Singh's own attitudes towards the tribals replicates colonialist views of non-Western peoples—they are mysterious, superstitious, uncivilized, backward. At the chilling climax of the tale, Singh is brought face to face with these 'children' who thrust their starved bodies towards him:

> They cackled with savage and revengeful glee. Cackling, they ran around him. They rubbed their organs against him and told him they were adult citizens of India. . . .
> Singh's shadow covered their bodies. And the shadow brought the realization home to him.
> They hated his height of five feet and nine inches.
> They hated the normal growth of his body.
> His normalcy was a crime they could not forgive.
> Singh's cerebral cells tried to register the logical explanation but he failed to utter a single word. Why, why this revenge? He was just an ordinary Indian. He didn't have the stature of a healthy Russian, Canadian or American. He did not eat food that supplied enough calories for a human body. The World Health Organization said that it was a crime to deny the human body of the right number of calories.
>
> (Devi 1993: 248–50)

Even as it is careful to demarcate what is available to citizens of different nations, 'Shishu' reminds us that anti-colonial nationalism has rarely represented the interests of all the peoples of a colonized country. I place this story against Rushdie's evocation of the nationalist ideal to indicate some of the tensions between the local, the national and the international, and between tradition and modernity, all of which are part of Kathakali's contemporary contexts.

What can Kathakali negotiate, and what must it still be silent about? The introduction of women actors may be the most radical change in Kathakali, which until recently was, like Shakespeare's plays in their original context, enacted solely by men. In the *Othello* production, a woman actor only occasionally played Desdemona. Female roles require special training, and according to Sadanam Srinathan, the man whom I saw play Desdemona, real women do not have the 'energy' to enact true femininity. Some of my students, who saw both Srinathan and a woman actor as Desdemona, preferred him for exactly these reasons. The elaborate non-realistic, exaggerated style of Kathakali privileges obvious impersonation rather than any form of naturalistic identification—its mask-like make-up, intensive massages administered to dancers through their training, heavy costumes and formalized gestural codes literally remould the stage body, privilege cross-dressing and establish a theatrical code where impersonation is flaunted.

The appropriate context for the Kathakali adaptation of Shakespeare is thus within indigenous performative and intellectual histories rather than in simply the colonial heritage of English literary texts in India. Of course, the centrality of Shakespeare to colonial and post-colonial Indian education cannot be entirely irrelevant to this production of *Othello*, since Kerala's education system is no exception to the rest of the country, and entirely canonical ideas about Shakespeare's greatness permeate the larger culture. But although some of Kathakali's high-born patrons, learned about its forms and traditions, might also have been schooled in, or familiar with, Shakespeare, Kathakali itself features patterns of training and teaching and the aesthetic philosophies that remained relatively isolated from English education. Within an indigenous high cultural sphere, certain theatrical or musical practices were protected by the elite as embodying an essential spiritual Indianness. Here the Fanonian model of agonistic hybridity is modified by a dualism in which one aesthetic code does not necessarily displace the other.[1]

For Sadanam Balakrishnan, the writer, director and chief actor of *Othello*, the production is an ongoing experiment, which will take at least another year to reach maturity. Scenes have been added each time the play has been performed, and over the next year he hopes a satisfying and creative meeting of the English play and the Indian form will take place. For him, the challenge lies in working within the rigid conventions of Kathakali, and flexing them to tell an alien story. For example, he told me that it would be virtually impossible to play *King Lear* as Kathakali forbids a king to appear without his headgear, and how else could one show a disordered Lear? For him, the daring and innovation lay in playing upon the rules of Kathakali, rather than in producing a new version of *Othello*. Balakrishnan was referring to a 1989 production of *Lear* in Kathakali, jointly mounted by The Kerala State Arts Academy and Keli, a Paris-based theatre group formed by Australian director David McRuvie and French actress Annette Leday, in which Lear did appear without his crown and aroused much criticism in Kerala (see Zarrilli 1992). Balakrishnan's response, like the earlier critiques, can be read both as a conservatism about Kathakali's class-based conventions and a genuine scepticism about a superficial grafting of forms.

For me and my class, the most disturbing element about this production was its almost total erasure of Othello's difference, whether we understand that as a difference of colour or religion. In the context in which it was being performed, what does it mean to recall that Othello was not just a black man but a Moor? Although in early modern England 'Moor' became almost an umbrella term for non-Europeanness, it originally simply meant 'Muslim'. For Kathakali to adopt a Muslim protagonist would be as radical as it was for Shakespeare to stage a black hero. Although Kathakali is necessarily shaped by cultural borrowings (the female headdress is supposed to have derived from the headcoverings of Egyptian women, for example), and although its own social context would have provided it with a rich and complex basis for adapting the racial conflict that lies at the heart of Shakespeare's play, the Kathakali *Othello* repeats its own brand of insularity and virtually erases any notion of Othello's difference. Othello's hands are painted black, it is true, and the narration which accompanies the dancing identifies him as 'malechh', a term that means outcaste, polluted or dirty. His soldier's epaulets add a nice touch of modernity, or Westernization. But on the whole there is little attempt to place Othello socially. Othello's green make-up identifies him as a *pacca* figure, which in Kathakali includes divine figures, kings and heroic characters who are upright and moral and possess 'calm inner poise' (Zarrilli 1984: 170). His blue dress extends such connotations as blue signifies the colour of Lord Krishna's dark skin, and hence empties darkness of social prejudice. Iago, on the other hand, is resplendent in black clothes and is placed within the group of 'black beard' characters who are vile schemers. Thus the binaries of good and evil that Kathakali inherits from religious theatre are mapped on to Shakespeare's play in a fashion that ironically reinforces those readings of the play according to which Iago represents 'motiveless malignity' and Othello is actually a white man!

How could the question of race be inflected for us in India? Should Iago be a Brahmin, outraged by a lower-caste Othello? I was in fact disturbed by the opulence of Iago's costume—class differences, at least to my untrained eye, were totally erased by this production. Should Othello be a tribal? Or a Muslim? Would not these readings simply reinforce existing prejudices about violent Muslims and tribals? My students and I pondered further over this production's erasure of all social difference except that of gender. Was this simply a conceptual lack on the part of Sadanand Balakrishnan, or did it derive from Kathakali's aesthetic codes and modes of representation? Kathakali make-up is not only highly codified but also takes 2–4 hours to put on. As with many stylized forms of theatre, the outside and inside of each character are thus rendered inseparable. This also means that characters cannot fundamentally change in the course of theatrical action (although Kathakali's facial makeup is not quite a mask and permits, indeed facilitates, changes in expression and extremely nuanced muscle movements). In the case of *Othello* this poses a major problem, for Shakespeare's play charts a movement whereby Othello the noble and calm general becomes agonized and disordered; the loving husband becomes the murderer of his wife: the victim of racial prejudice mouths misogynist platitudes as he smothers the white woman he loves.

The murder poses a problem for feminist critics who point out that any reading of Othello as victim must also take note of his power over Desdemona. But within the Kathakali tradition, Desdemona's murder poses an altogether different problem: good women are never killed on stage and 'nari-hathya' or female murder is not allowed. The *Othello* production flouts tradition in this regard, but its transgression works only to reinforce a misogynist interpretation of the play. If Othello is uncritically depicted as the prototype of a good man, his jealousy cannot be understood as something that is generated in and through his racial position. It becomes a 'universal' (and therefore 'understandable') male response to real or imagined female transgressions. To erase the racial politics of *Othello* is therefore to flatten it into a disturbingly misogynist text. Of course it is true that the audience knows that Desdemona is chaste. As one of my students pointed out, Desdemona's make-up and costume place her as a *Minukku* character which in Kathakali signifies benign femininity bordering on divinity. Thus if Othello as a *Pacca* can do no evil, Desdemona as *Minukku* in no way merits her death. This student pointed out too that in a traditional Kathakali battle between good and evil, the two circle each other, but the killing takes place centre stage or right. But in this case, Othello is forced to leave the 'clean' right half and move over to Desdemona's space and the performance closes with Othello, grief stricken, in a faint on her side: 'The convention's "double-coding" system thus allows one register to subvert another'.[2]

My class kept returning to the question of whether or not the strict gestural code of Kathakali could profitably interact with Shakespearean drama, and indeed with its modern Western stage conventions. Gender stereotyping is also compromised by the miming central to Kathakali stagecraft. Othello resolves that Desdemona 'must die, else she'll betray more men' (V. ii. 6). In the Kathakali production, Othello 'speaks' these lines by miming Desdemona the seductress who will charm other men. On the eve of the murder, he thus becomes the wife as well as the husband, the victim and the murderer. Even though Othello's split as Christian and Infidel, Turk and Venetian, European and Outsider is erased, we briefly glimpse another sort of doubleness that resonates with Kathakali's flamboyant enactment of gender difference. But of course, as on Shakespeare's stage, this is a male tradition of enacting women. Even though it flourished in a matrilineal society, Kathakali is notoriously masculine, not just by virtue of employing only male actors but in its aesthetic codes and its themes. Still, we noted that its Desdemona was not particularly passive: she answers back and is vigorous in her own defence. Sadanam Balakrishnan attributes this to the need for constant movement in Kathakali. Unlike on a conventional stage, Desdemona cannot be still. Thus Kathakali's various conventions and histories interact with, subvert or simply bypass those of Shakespeare's play.

The Kathakali *Othello* does not, then, offer a significant new interpretation of the play. It is not anti-colonial. It does not play upon or transgress colonial histories of the play, or of colonial Shakespeare in India, except at the very level of its existence. It does not even engage overtly with contemporary discourses about community and identity, although in its very silences we can read contemporary fissures of gender, caste, religion and ethnicity. Why then does the International Centre for Kathakali play with Shakespeare? I have tried to suggest that it is actually not interested in Shakespeare at all, except as a suitably weighty means through which it can negotiate its own future, shake off its own cramps, revise its own traditions, and expand its own performative styles. Only the Shakespeareans in the audience are concerned with its transgressions, or cognizant of those moments in which it either improves upon the original or fails to do justice to it. And even as 'Shakespeare' remains central for my own analysis of this production, the Kathakali *Othello* obliges me to mark the ways in which it 'provincializes' Shakespeare.[3]

*   *   *

Lawrence W. Levine, *Highbrow/Lowbrow: The Emergence of Cultural Hierarchy in America* (Cambridge, Mass.: Harvard University Press, 1988), pp. 20–1, 23.

At the dedication of Shakespeare's statue in Central Park in 1872, his familiarity to Americans was taken for granted. 'Old World, he is not only thine', the inscription on the temporary pedestal proclaimed[1] [. . .] Shakespeare's popularity can be determined not only by the frequency of Shakespearean productions and the size of the audiences for them but also by the nature of the productions and the manner in which they were presented. Shakespeare was performed not merely alongside popular entertainment as an elite supplement to it; Shakespeare was performed as an integral part of it. Shakespeare *was* popular entertainment in nineteenth-century America. The theatre in the first half of the nineteenth century played the role that movies played in the first half of the twentieth: it was a kaleidoscopic, democratic institution presenting a widely varying bill of fare to all classes and socioeconomic groups [. . .] Shakespeare was presented as part of the same milieu inhabited by magicians, dancers, singers, acrobats, minstrels and comics. He appeared on the same playbills and was advertised in the same spirit. This does not mean that theatergoers were unable to make distinctions between Shakespearean productions and the accompanying entertainment. Of course they were. Shakespeare was, after all, what most of them came to see. But it was a Shakespeare presented as part of the culture they enjoyed, a Shakespeare rendered familiar and intimate by virtue of his context.

*   *   *

Francesca T. Royster, *Becoming Cleopatra: The Shifting Image of an Icon* (New York: Palgrave, 2003), pp. 9–17.

This book is concerned less with what race Cleopatra was than what she *is*—her afterlife beyond her own life and beyond Shakespeare's depiction as a means of performing and often deconstructing racial and gender subjectivity. A racial performance depends on its moment. But it also depends on the past, the memory banks of past images and fantasies of self and other. Perhaps this is one reason why Cleopatra has had such an important place in African American arts. Through parody, ventriloquism and other forms of revision, African American performers have commandeered the Cleopatra image, using it to stage, among other things, the precarious conditions of performing blackness.

There are striking parallels between Cleopatra's images as 'courtesan queen,' 'betrayer,' 'dark exotic' and 'supermommy' and the negative representations of African American women. But most evocative of all to me have been the ways that the Cleopatra icon evokes the availability of black women's bodies and the figuration of their bodies as commodities. As feminist critic Patricia Hill Collins has pointed out, 'From the mammies, jezebels, and breeder women of slavery to the smiling Aunt Jemimas on pancake mix boxes, ubiquitous Black prostitutes, and everpresent welfare mothers of contemporary popular culture, negative stereotypes applied to African-American women have been fundamental to Black women's oppression.'[1]

For example, over the years, African American performer Josephine Baker has been compared to a bicycle, a machine gun, a kangaroo, a perpetual motion machine, a leopard, a savage, a clown and a man as well as 'that contrary character about whom Shakespeare

wrote, "Age cannot wither her, nor custom stale her infinite variety"—the "Jazz Cleopatra," '
as biographer Phyllis Rose describes Baker in *Jazz Cleopatra: Josephine Baker in her Time*.[2]
Baker repeatedly used the image of Cleopatra in her autobiographical writing and in her self-
designed costumes. Baker's literary and stage careers were built on dramatizing the process of
becoming the desired object. And like Cleopatra's lovers, Baker's audience figured her body
and her allure as infinitely sustainable. The first Parisians to see her perform in *La Revue Negre*
'gobbl[ed] her up as cultural food to prepare for a coming age of creativity,'[3] according to
Rose. Rose herself confesses that when approaching the project of writing about Baker, she
found herself complicit in this fantasy of Baker's always sustainable desirability: 'When I
started this book, I wanted something from Josephine Baker: a certain spontaneity, fearless-
ness, energy, joy. At the same time, I was soon writing about the way in which European
audiences of the 1920s, seeking a renewal that was decidedly racial, focused their fantasies of
finding joy, freedom, and energy all the more easily on Baker because she was black.'[4]

Baker shares with Shakespeare's Cleopatra not just her talent at variation but also her
promise to keep coming back—to be resurrected—to create a new condition of need: 'Other
women cloy the appetites they feed/but she makes hungry where most she satisfies' (*Antony
and Cleopatra* 2.2.238–239). To sustain this energy, Baker took the basic model of the grass-
skirted savage and animated her through repetition. Her savage appeared again and again,
each time modified but with elements of the same. The grass skirt became a skirt of whimsical
bananas; the bananas became metallic spikes. Next she dressed up her savage image in
sequins and went for a stroll down the fashionable streets of Paris—accompanied by a chee-
tah, to remind her audience of her mythic jungle roots. In one of her production numbers for
the film *Zou Zou* (1934), directed by Marc Allegret, Baker appears in a cage, albeit a gilded
one. Like bebop, Josephine Baker takes on the already known quantity of the exotic; she riffs,
she improvises, but there is the gesture always of engagement with the already known.
(Compare, for example, Miles Davis's twisting and bending of the song 'Some Day My Prince
Will Come.' It is a gesture that incorporates the familiar while stretching out the longing of the
tune through its bent notes, estranging and occupying the familiar through repetition.)

As an exotic, the Cleopatra icon has been coded in Western eyes in a way necessarily
controlled by a discourse of power that served to strengthen the European self by distinguishing itself from the Orient. While sometimes presenting a fantasy of freedom, that freedom is
most accessible to the group doing the defining. As cultural critic Edward Said has contended
in *Orientalism*, 'because of Orientalism the Orient was not (and is not) a free subject of
thought or action. This is not to say that Orientalism unilaterally determines what can be said
about the Orient, but that it is the whole network of interests inevitably brought to bear on
(and therefore always involved in) any occasion when that peculiar entity "the Orient" is in
question. . . . [In the process] European culture gained in strength and identity by setting itself
off against the Orient as a sort of surrogate and even underground self.'[5]

While promising reinvention, Cleopatra as a sign is also a coded event. Every time the
Cleopatra icon is cited, there is enacted the tension between her promise of renewal and
the heavily determined nature of Cleopatra's function as an icon of orientalism. However, the
shape of Cleopatra's encoded associations with orientalism become even more complex as we
consider her applicability to an African American context, and the ways that blackness and
orientalism are sometimes fused and other times opposed in the configuration of difference. In

her critique of Said's *Orientalism*, Melani McAlister has pointed out that the creation of a homogenous 'us' versus 'them' subjectivity in Said's formulation becomes complicated when the lens shifts from Europe to the United States, especially as 'African Americans, both civil rights activists and black nationalists, have claimed certain histories as their own, and these claims have challenged, complicated and conspired with dominant discourses that have represented the region as a resource for American nationalism and a site for the expansion of U.S. power. Thus in the post-war period, the us–them dichotomies of orientalism have been fractured by the reality of a multiracial nation, even if that reality was recognized only in its disavowal.'[6] While the older history of a European orientalism shapes Cleopatra, so too does the ongoing relationship among the United States, African Americans and international policy.

In the essay 'Signature, Event, Context,' Jacques Derrida asks: 'Could a performative utterance succeed if its formulation did not repeat a "coded" or iterable utterance, or in other words, if the formula I pronounce in order to open a meeting, launch a ship or a marriage were not identifiable as conforming with an iterable model, if it were not then identifiable in some way as a "citation"?'[7] Derrida here speaks of the inescapability of normative forces and, with it, of 'history' to determine the faces, bodies and acts of the cultural icon. Cultural icons bring into bold relief the constructedness of fundamental aspects of identity, especially gender and race.

The available palette of cultural icons from which we can choose has everything to do with cultural favorites of the past as well as with our own *habitus*—our modes of distinction, the ways that we exercise our social power in a public space and the ways that our identities are interpolated by others. The tactics by which we choose to use cultural icons are influenced by these outside forces; and the ways that symbols like Cleopatra become assigned to certain people are also determined by social relations. As icons like Cleopatra have become embedded in stereotype, the tracing of social relations that spawn them become all the more difficult because one of the functions of stereotypes is to disguise or mystify the social relations that they serve.[8]

For example, the relationship between Antony and Cleopatra in Shakespeare's play might be viewed as a central paradigm for the ways that the multiple energy of black women's bodies can be appropriated and sold back to us. Antony seeks change and revitalization from Cleopatra's energy—an energy that is formulated by others in the play as anti-Roman, anti-western and uncivilized. Repeatedly Antony describes the process of loving Cleopatra as a process of dissolution of his public and eventually his private self. At first this dissolution is described as a pleasure: 'Let Rome in Tiber melt and the wide arch / Of the ranged empire fall! Here is my space' (1.1.35–36). Quickly, though, his relationship with Cleopatra becomes one of entrapment, his passion a source of shame: 'O whither hast though led me, Egypt? See / How I convey my shame out of thine eyes, / By looking back what I have left behind / 'Stroyed in dishonour' (3.11.50–54).

Antony describes his doting on Cleopatra as a kind of onanism, a wasteful spilling of seed. In one of his moments of greatest humiliation, he describes his political failure as a failure to perpetuate the 'lawful race' of Rome: 'Have I my pillow left unpress'd in Rome, / Forborne the getting of a lawful race, / And by a gem of women, to be abus'd / By one that looks on feeders?' (3.13.106–109)

I discuss this paradigm as a Renaissance commonplace [later], but for now I want to point out that such an easy movement from the pleasure of being consumed by love to shame is reflected in several of Shakespeare's works, including Sonnet 129: 'Th' expense of spirit in a waste of shame is lust in action.' In *Troilus and Cressida*, Troilus warns Cressida even before their lovemaking begins that 'This is the monstrosity in love, lady, that the will is infinite / And the execution confined; that desire is boundless / And the act a slave to limit' (3.2.75–78).

As Shakespeare critic Coppélia Kahn has pointed out, such anxieties do important cultural work in *Antony and Cleopatra*. The rumors and innuendo about Cleopatra and especially her reputed sexual control over Antony are the shared topics of conversation that bond the men of the play and help to further define the standards of the good warrior.[9] In Act 2, scene 2, Antony, Enobarbus and Pompey trade stories about Cleopatra while jockeying for positions of power and loyalty. But Cleopatra herself becomes a cipher, not quite ever clearly conveyed in our sight:

LEPIDUS: What manner o' thing is your crocodile?
ANTONY: It is shaped, sir, like itself, and it is as broad as it hath breath; it is just so high as it is, and moves with its own organs. It lives by that which nourisheth it, and the elements once out of it, it transmigrates.

In her influential book *The Common Liar*, Janet Adelman argues that the slipperiness of descriptions of Cleopatra in this passage, where 'the only accurate description is a reproduction of the thing itself,'[10] reveals less the nature of Cleopatra than of the person doing the describing. Even Cleopatra's enemies desire to be moved by her, desire to have her but also to be changed through 'knowledge' of her. Cleopatra's body is thus constructed as other, the dark terrain that the Romans want to invade, experience and control.

bell hooks brilliantly describes this colonizing paradigm as 'eating the other.' Getting 'a bit of the Other,' in modern British slang, means having sex. But 'eating the other' also can describe a less specific dynamic of cross-cultural desire that can express itself in language, political policy, social interactions and images.[11] From Sally Hemmings and Thomas Jefferson, to the interracial romance in Marc Forster's film *Monster's Ball* (2001), representations of interracial sexual adventure often mystify and suppress the underlying dynamics of racial inequality, economic and other forms of power at play, by presenting sex itself as a form of freedom.

Racialized sexual encounter for the Antonys of the world is a form of initiation, a way of leaving the safe world of the familiar to experience an adventure eventually instructive in how to master difference. Cleopatra is to be consumed, her own motives a mystery. When Harold Bloom writes that 'Antony is Shakespeare's desire to be different, his wish to be elsewhere: he is the *otherness* of Shakespeare's art carried to its farthest limit,'[12] he is participating in the long-standing tradition of writing Antony and Cleopatra into the adventure of eating the other. And one of the rules of this tradition is that it requires that our desires become Antony's desires; by force of rhetoric, he becomes 'us' while Cleopatra becomes the cipher beyond our reach—certainly *not* us. In this view, Antony becomes a kind of director figure, choreographing desire, while Cleopatra remains the entertainer, the 'diva' whose experiences of being the object of desire (and her own desires) are never explored but instead are kept from us. My study of Cleopatra swims against the tide of mostly male and white Shakespearean critics who are primarily interested in Antony rather than Cleopatra, embracing him as the emblem of a fallen self.[13]

What could we see if we took the point of view of Cleopatra instead of Antony? In what ways can the tactical appropriation of Cleopatra create insight, freedom and power for real women? According to bell hooks, 'Popular culture provides countless examples of black female appropriation and exploitation of "negative stereotypes" to either assert control of their representation or at least reap the benefits of it.'[14] What might be some of the reasons that women become Cleopatra and what are the costs?

In her constant wrestling with the *being* of the racial strictures in her life and the demands of *becoming* or reinventing herself, Josephine Baker harnesses the Cleopatra legend to signify what I call her 'divahood.' In my use of the word 'diva,' I am calling on its connotations in the African American, especially queer African American, cadence: the strategic use of an outsize theatrical self to protect oneself from persecution. Through her pointed appropriation of and then contesting with the Cleopatra icon, Baker demonstrates that the pleasure of performing the 'other' does not travel in one direction only. Hers is a tactical appropriation.

In the following instance, Baker gains pleasure by subverting her audience's expectations by being the consummate not-Cleopatra. In her autobiography, *Josephine* (1977), written with Jo Bouillon, Baker describes a 1929 South American cruise she took with her lover, Pepito. At that time, she was enjoying great fame as the strange black actor who came to Europe as a minstrel performer and who emerged a glamour queen. Pepito is notorious mostly as her lover, suspect for his dark Italian coloring and his financial dependence on Baker. Baker and Pepito find themselves the objects of fascination on the cruise—a situation further exacerbated by the fact that they are a public couple but are not married. As entertainment, the cruise ship plans a costume contest. Baker reports overhearing two American tourists gossiping about her: 'Naturally Josephine Baker will win first prize with her bananas!' One of the tourists is dressed as Cleopatra, the other as a marquise. But rather than dress in their public guises, already occupied by the tourists (one as the glamour queen, the other as a personage of noble connections), Baker and Pepito decide to dress as their darkest projections. Pepito dresses as that looter and marginal dweller in European history: the pirate; Baker dresses as the mammy, a figure very different from the youthful, topless, grass-skirted, sleek and nubile exotic captured in Paul Colin's 1927 *Bal Negre* poster or from the more queenly, authoritative glamour of Cleopatra:

> I stuffed my cheeks with cotton, blackened my face with a candle, attached pillows fore and aft, slipped on the petticoat of the Gypsy costume I had bought in Spain, stuffed balloons I had wheedled from a child into my blouse, draped myself in shawls and stuck black paper on my front teeth. Barefoot, knock-kneed, fat and gap-toothed, I waddled into the first-class salon. Everyone burst out laughing. The two Americans, one decked out as Cleopatra, the other as a marquise, looked daggers. I knew what they were thinking: She'll do anything for attention. And the purser announced: 'First prize for the ugliest costume goes to . . . Miss Josephine Baker.'[15]

Via the Cleopatra image, the American tourists tried to beat Josephine Baker at her own game—to out exoticize the sure-to-be-outrageously exotic. But Baker steals the show—not by being a better Cleopatra but by subverting these expectations created by her iconography by

being outrageously *banal*. Baker subverts the glamour of the Cleopatra-queen icon by performing the version of blackness that the travelers thought they left behind—a version of
blackness much closer to the American minstrel shows in which Baker herself once participated. What is shocking about Baker's slide from Cleopatra to mammy is her apparent ease at
moving between these two fantasies. Her description exposes the constructedness of these
fantasies and subverts the necessary distance between them.

In 'Cultural Identity and Cinematic Representation,' cultural critic Stuart Hall suggests that
we can think of identity as 'real' in the sense that it has a material and historical entity, but
that this realness is under a state of constant change: 'identities come from somewhere,
have histories. But like everything that is historical, they undergo constant transformation.'[16]
Cleopatra's 'infinite variety'—her flexibility both within Shakespeare's play (in her own view
and in the view of her onlookers) and in the variety of shapes she takes in the history of her
appropriation—speaks of the ebb and flow of identity. But as we track Cleopatra's capacity to
perform the 'becoming' of identity, and as we track the becoming of Cleopatra's identity (two
different but related moves), we also must note the undeniable force of Eurocentrism in
shaping past transformations and most likely future ones. The central crux for me in writing
this book is the tension between being and becoming, between history and reinvention. As
Hall writes, identity 'is a matter of "becoming" as well as "being." It belongs to the future as
much as to the past.'[17]

QUESTIONS

- In what ways is a cross-cultural engagement with Shakespeare distinguished from a
national appropriation?
- In what ways does the introduction of race complicate Shakespearean reinvention?
- Would you agree that film and theatre allow for contrasting possibilities for
reinvention?

5 | The impact of new media and the end of the 'Shakespearean'

Richard Burt, '*Shakespeare in Love* and the end of the Shakespearean: academic and mass
culture constructions of literary authorship', in Mark Thornton Burnett and Ramona Wray
(eds.), *Shakespeare, Film, Fin de Siècle* (Basingstoke: Macmillan, 2000), pp. 226–7.

Many mass culture spin-offs have a post-hermeneutic relation to Shakespeare's plays: that is,
they are so far from the original as not to be interpretable as Shakespearean at all. By speaking
of the end of the Shakespearean, I mean to suggest that this distinction between the hermeneutic and the post-hermeneutic is now in the process of breaking down, that the reception of
Shakespeare as a biographical author or an author-function, which serves to establish what is
and what is not canonically written by Shakespeare, involves distancing Shakespeare as a
character and author from anything that might be said to be characteristically 'Shakespearean'
about his writings. The very proliferation of Shakespeare editions and Shakespeare in mass

culture might then be read as a symptom of this psychotic breakdown of authority rather than as an expansion of it (to be used, in the dominant critical fantasy, for ennobling, civilizing ends, whether those ends are conceived as the carrying on of a tradition or the dismantling of it, the policing of the boundary between high and mass culture or the transgression of it). This is what I take to be, in effect, the breakdown not so much of Shakespeare's cultural authority as an author but of the specifically Shakespearean—that is, those characteristics that can be said to define his writings as *his* writings. The character of Shakespeare produced inside of mass culture in which realism rules, to put the point another way, is displaced by the character of Shakespeare understood as the letters, the authorial signature *in* the works themselves. Mass culture screenwriters, directors and costume designers cannot dispense with academics just as academics cannot dispense with mass culture productions of Shakespeare in order to legit-imate their (some might say 'merely') academic authority. As the distinction between the Shakespeare canon and the Shakespeare apocrypha dissolves before us, it may soon be time to speak of the Shakespeare apocalypse.

*   *   *

John Russell Brown, *New Sites for Shakespeare: Theatre, the Audience and Asia* (London and Routledge, 1999), pp. 191–2, 193, 197.

What might happen in the future to our staging and understanding of Shakespeare's plays: how will we change our ways, if at all? The obvious answer is that we are bound to change because every generation has done so. But now the changes are likely to be faster and more basic. As soon as we look at theatre in general, beyond the well-established companies that stage Shakespeare, innovation is to be found everywhere. Theatre is being forced to alter because of new methods of finance, organization, and public relations, and because it finds itself in a very new society with new expectations. Some theatres are searching for ways to change because they realise that the alternative is death, by sudden financial failure or a slow attrition of the audiences they have previously relied on. In certain respects, change is inevit-able [. . .] new technology has radically altered the production resources of theatre so that it can offer many new sensations and control them with new speed and sensitivity. Moreover, all these changes are occurring at a time when theatre must redefine itself against the more easily accessible and reproducible forms of film, video, and television; it is being forced to learn how to make the very most of its unique ability to present live performers and share with an audience the moment of fresh invention and creation [. . .] Perhaps the most certain indication that theatre is about to undergo a great change—and Shakespearean productions with it—is that more and more influences can be identified that do not come out of current theatre practice.

. . . .

QUESTIONS

• In what senses might future forms of appropriation be inevitably cross-cultural?

• What new terminology will be required to describe future forms of appropriation?

SUGGESTED FURTHER READING

Aebischer, Pascale, Edward J. Esche and Nigel Wheale (eds.), *Remaking Shakespeare: Performance Across Media, Genres and Cultures* (Basingstoke: Palgrave, 2003)

Burt, Richard, *Unspeakable ShaXXXspeares: Queer Theory and American Kiddie Culture* (Basingstoke: Macmillan, 1998)

—— , and Lynda E. Boose (eds.), *Shakespeare, the Movie, II: Popularizing the Plays on Film, TV, Video, and DVD* (London and New York: Routledge, 2003)

Cartelli, Thomas, *Repositioning Shakespeare: National Formations, Postcolonial Appropriations* (London and New York: Routledge, 1999)

Chedgzoy, Kate, *Shakespeare's Queer Children: Sexual Politics and Contemporary Culture* (Manchester: Manchester University Press, 1995)

Hattaway, Michael, Boika Sokolova and Derek Roper (eds.), *Shakespeare in the New Europe* (Sheffield: Sheffield Academic Press, 1994)

Johnson, David, *Shakespeare and South Africa* (Oxford: Clarendon Press, 1996)

Marsden, Jean I. (ed.), *The Appropriation of Shakespeare: Post-Renaissance Reconstructions of the Works and the Myth* (Hemel Hempstead: Harvester Wheatsheaf, 1991)

Taylor, Gary, *Reinventing Shakespeare: A Cultural History from the Restoration to the Present* (London: Hogarth, 1989)

Williams, Gweno, ' "Why may not a lady write a good play?": Plays by early modern women reassessed as performance texts', in S. P. Cerasano and Marion Wynne-Davies (eds.), *Readings in Renaissance Women's Drama: Criticism, History, and Performance, 1594–1998* (London and New York: Routledge, 1998), pp. 95–108.

NOTES

Schoenbaum, Shakespeare's Lives

1. Ivor Brown, *Shakespeare* (London, 1949), 155.
2. Ivor Brown, *The Way of My World* (London, 1954), 138–9.
3. Brown, *Shakespeare*, 164, 165.
4. Ibid. 218.
5. Marchette Chute, *Shakespeare of London* (London, 1951), 300–1.
6. E. K. Chambers, *Sources for a Biography of Shakespeare* (London, 1946), 66, 67.
7. Leonard Dobbs, *Shakespeare Revealed* (London, n.d.), 119.
8. Hugh Ross Williamson, *The Day Shakespeare Died* (London, 1962), 12.
9. M. M. Reese, *Shakespeare: His World and His Work* (London, 1953), pp. viii–ix.

Anderegg, Orson Welles, Shakespeare, and Popular Culture

1. Jorgens is here quoting from Arthur Knight, 'Three Problems in Film Adaptation,' *Saturday Review*, 18 December 1954, 26.
2. Jack J. Jorgens, *Shakespeare on Film*, 7–10.
3. Jorgens, *Shakespeare on Film*, 15.
4. Lorne M. Buchman, *Still in Movement: Shakespeare on Screen*, 6.
5. See James Naremore, 'The Walking Shadow: Welles's Expressionist *Macbeth*,' *Literature/Film Quarterly* 1, no. 4 (fall 1973): 360–6.
6. 'Certainly every finished work of art is already predetermined in some way but art strives to overcome its own oppressive weight as an artefact through the force of its very construction. Mass culture on the other hand simply identifies with the curse of predetermination and joyfully fulfils it.' Theodor W. Adorno, 'The Schema of Mass Culture,' in Bernstein, (ed.), *The*

Culture Industry, 53–84 (quotation from 62). Welles's entire career could be read as a refusal to accept that predetermination.

7. See Roland Barthes, 'The Reality Effect,' in *The Rustle of Language*, trans. Richard Howard, 141–8.

8. Collick, *Shakespeare, Cinema, and Society*, 60.

9. See Ace G. Pilkington, 'Zeffirelli's Shakespeare,' in Davies and Wells (eds.), *Shakespeare and the Moving Image*, 165–6.

10. This tendency has been carried on by Kenneth Branagh, especially in the lavishly illustrated screenplay book *Hamlet by William Shakespeare* (New York: Norton, 1996).

11. See Laurie E. Osborne, 'Filming Shakespeare in a Cultural Thaw: Soviet Appropriations of Shakespearean Treacheries in 1955–6,' *Textual Practice* 9, no. 2 (1995): 325–47.

12. Bruce Eder, liner notes, *Richard III*, dir. Laurence Olivier, 1955 (videodisk, Voyager, 1994). Kenneth Branagh's *Henry V* and *Much Ado About Nothing*, in part because of preselling to secondary markets like cable television and video, are exceptions to the rule that Shakespeare films can't make money; Branagh's *Hamlet*, on the other hand, cost $24 million and only grossed $11.3.

13. Patricia Parker, *Shakespeare from the Margins: Language, Culture, Context*, 15.

14. Michael Bristol, *Big-Time Shakespeare*, 61.

15. These examples are drawn from Julie Hankey (ed.), *Othello: Plays in Performance*, 138, 91, and 237.

16. Virginia Mason Vaughan, *Othello: A Contextual History*, 200; Collick, *Shakespeare, Cinema, and Society*, 96; Peter S. Donaldson, *Shakesperean Films/Shakespearean Directors*, 124 *n*18; Barbara Hodgdon, 'Kiss Me Deadly; or, The Des/Demonized Spectacle' in Vaughan and Cartwright (eds.), *Othello: New Perspectives*, 222.

17. Like the far more obviously 'experimental' and 'underground' Shakespeare films discussed by Graham Holderness ('Shakespeare Rewound,' *Shakespeare Survey* 45 [1993]: 63–74), Welles's Shakespeare films, too, 'can be used to challenge traditional notions and to provoke debate about some central issues of both text and performance' (70).

18. Collick, *Shakespeare, Cinema, and Society*, 63, 73.

19. And thus they are relatively safe from the danger articulated by James C. Bulman: 'Because film and video allow us repeated viewings of a single performance, they encourage us to assimilate that performance to the condition of a literary text—a stable artifact rather than a contingent, ephemeral experience.' Bulman, 'Introduction: Shakespeare and Performance Theory,' in Bulman (ed.), *Shakespeare, Theory, and Performance*, 2.

20. Dennis Kennedy (ed.), *Foreign Shakespeare: Contemporary Performance*, 6.

21. Dennis Kennedy, *Looking at Shakespeare: A Visual History of Twentieth-Century Performance*, 302.

22. Kennedy (ed.), *Foreign Shakespeare*, 10.

23. Henri Lemaitre, 'Shakespeare, the Imaginary Cinema and the Pre-cinema,' in Charles W. Eckert (ed.), *Focus on Shakespearean Films*, 36.

24. Robin Wood, 'Welles, Shakespeare, and Webster,' *Personal Views*, 136–52 (quotations from 136–37 and 152).

25. Gary Taylor, *Reinventing Shakespeare*, 384.

Lehmann, Shakespeare Remains

1. Branagh describes *A Midwinter's Tale* as a 'little *Hamlet* film' (quoted in Arnold 41).

2. For an elaborate discussion of Branagh's extra-cinematic intentions and identifications, see Courtney Lehmann and Lisa S. Starks, 'Making mother matter: repression, revision, and the stakes of "reading psychoanalysis into" Kenneth Branagh's *Hamlet*.'

Hutner, Colonial Women

1. See George Guffey, 'Politics, weather, and the contemporary reception of the Dryden–Davenant *Tempest*', *Restoration*, 8 (1984), pp. 1–9, for a fascinating account of the way Dryden's and Davenant's revisions include political relations between Spain, France and England.

2. Guffey, ibid., p. 2.

3. Katherine Eisaman Maus, 'Arcadia lost: politics and revision in the Restoration *Tempest*', in Mary Beth Rose (ed.), *Renaissance Drama as Cultural History: Essays from Renaissance Drama 1977–1987* (Evanston: Northwestern University Press, 1990), p. 202.

Dobson and Watson, England's Elizabeth

1. It is no coincidence that the 1980s had already seen two plays invested in the triumph of Mary, Queen of Scots (Liz Lochhead's *Mary, Queen of Scots Got Her Head Chopped Off*, and Dario Fo's *Elizabeth: Almost By Chance a Woman*, though the first is interested in Mary, Queen of Scots as an embodiment of Scotland, and the second in her as the embodiment of Catholic Europe), not to mention a revival of Friedrich Schiller's play, *Maria Stuart*, at the National Theatre in 1997 and of Gaetano Donizetti's *Maria Stuarda* at the London Coliseum in 1998.

2. Alison Weir, 'The queen who still rules us', *Spectator*, 17 Oct. 1998, 12.

3. Tom McGregor, *Elizabeth: Based on the Screenplay by Michael Hirst* (New York, 1998), 244.

4. Ibid., 246.

5. Hodgdon, *The Shakespeare Trade*, 143.

6. Lest all this seems far-fetched, it is pertinent to mention Mavis Cheek's *Aunt Margaret's Lover* (1994), written for a *Cosmopolitan*-oriented readership, in which the central character, a childless woman in her late thirties, takes a lover, no strings attached, explicitly on the model of Elizabeth. (Hence the use of the Darnley portrait on the paperback's cover.)

7. Marc Norman and Tom Stoppard, *Shakespeare in Love* (screenplay, London, 1999), 148.

8. This being Oxford, the Orator in fact spoke in Latin: both the oration and the English translation quoted here are published in *Encaenia 28 June 2000* (Oxford, 2000).

Normand, Edward II, Derek Jarman . . .

1. Derek Jarman, *Queer 'Edward II'* (London: BFI Publishing, 1991), p. 26, Preface.

2. Ibid.

3. Kate Chedgzoy, *Shakespeare's Queer Children: Sexual Politics and Contemporary Culture* (Manchester and New York: Manchester University Press, 1995), p. 195.

4. *Queer 'Edward II'* has 82 sequences but they don't correspond exactly with the film. For example, the first sequence shows the death of Edward I which is absent from the film; and the last sequence has Edward in the throne room speaking: 'But what are Kings, when regiment is gone'—also not in the film. Instead the last shot is of lesbians and gay men from OutRage! standing silent and still as the camera slowly pans across them.

5. Chedgzoy, *Shakespeare's Queer Children*, p. 184.

6. Derek Jarman, *Dancing Ledge*, S. Allen (ed.) (London: Quartet, 1991), p. 7.

7. Colin MacCabe, 'A post-national European cinema: a consideration of Derek Jarman's *The Tempest* and *Edward II*', in Duncan Petrie (ed.), *Screening Europe: Image and Identity in Contemporary European Cinema* (London: BFI Publishing, 1992), p. 14.

8. See Gregory Bredbeck, *Sodomy and Interpretation: Marlowe to Miltan* (Ithaca and London: Cornell University Press, 1991), p. 76; Bruce R. Smith, *Homosexual Desire in Shakespeare's England: A Cultural Poetics* (Chicago and London: University of Chicago Press, 1991), p. 220; Lawrence Normand, ' "What passions call you these?": *Edward II* and James VI', in D. Grantley and P. Roberts (eds.), *Christopher Marlowe and English Renaissance Culture* (Aldershot: Scolar Press, 1996), p. 191.

9. MacCabe, 'Post-national European cinema', in Petrie (ed.), *Screening Europe*, p. 16.

10. Stephen Orgel, *Impersonations: The Performing of Gender in Shakespeare's England* (Cambridge: Cambridge University, Press, 1996), p. 48.

11. The editors are more cautious in their note to 5.5.112–13: 'Whether such a horrible method of murder was simulated by the Elizabethan acting company is not certain' (Marlowe, *'Doctor Faustus' and other Plays*, ed. D. Bevington and E. Rasmussen (Oxford and New York: Oxford University Press, 1995), p. 491).

12. See Michael O'Pray, *Derek Jarman: Dreams of England* (London: BFI Publishing, 1996), pp. 8, 98. 104.

13. Ian Lucas, *Impertinent Decorum: Gay Theatrical Manoeuvres* (London: Cassell, 1994), p. 161.

Werner, Shakespeare and Feminist Performance

1. Edwards' production of *Shrew* followed Buzz Goodbody's 1973 *As You Like It* and Di Trevis' 1988 *Much Ado About Nothing* at the Royal Shakespeare Theatre, Stratford-upon-Avon; Trevis directed in a touring production of *Shrew* in 1985. The five productions of *Shrew* in the thirteen-year interval were Barry Kyle's in 1985, Jonathan Miller's in 1987, Bill Alexander's in 1990 for the national tour and revived in 1992 for the main stage, and Edwards' in 1995; this does not include Adrian Noble's *Kiss Me Kate* in 1987, which made for the unusual back-to-back *Shrew*s in Stratford that year.

2. See Lynda Boose for the relationship between Katherine's speech and early sixteenth-century marriage sermons and the speech's nostalgic reordering of societal structure ('Scolding brides and bridling scolds: taming the woman's unruly member', *Shakespeare Quarterly*, 42 (1991), pp. 182–3, and 'The Taming of the Shrew: good husbandry and enclosure', in Russ McDonald (ed.), *Shakespeare Reread: The Texts in New Contexts* (Ithaca and London: Cornell University Press, 1994), pp. 195–6).

3. Graham Holderness writes about the way in which the tourism of Stratford-upon-Avon participates in the 'Shakespeare myth' ('Bardolatry: or, The cultural materialist's Guide to Stratford-upon-Avon', in Graham Holderness (ed.), *The Shakespeare Myth* (Manchester: Manchester University Press, 1988), pp. 2–15). See also Barbara Hodgdon, *The Shakespeare Trade: Performances and Appropriations* (Philadelphia: University of Pennsylvania Press, 1998), pp. 191–240.

4. Bogdanov's was perhaps the most influential production of *Shrew* in the late twentieth century. For more on his production from the participants' point of view, see Bogdanov's interview with Christopher McCullough ('Interview with Michael Bogdanov', in Holderness (ed.), *The Shakespeare Myth*, pp. 89–95) and Paola Dionisotti's account of playing Katherine in that production (Carol Rutter, *Clamorous Voices: Shakespeare's Women Today* (London and New York: Routledge, 1989), pp. 1–4, 22–3). Graham Holderness discusses the production in his stage history of *Shrew* ('The Taming of the Shrew': Shakespeare in Performance* (Manchester: Manchester University Press, 1989), pp. 73–94). Penny Gay also includes it in her feminist stage history of the comedies (*As She Likes It: Shakespeare's Unruly Women* (London and New York: Routledge, 1994), pp. 104–11). Gay's discussion is particularly useful for the distinction she makes between those reviewers who were sensitive to the production's gender critique and those who responded solely to the farcical elements and Jonathan Pryce's star power as Petruchio.

5. Not every audience reacted the same way: the second time I saw the play, at a matinee a month later, the audience did not applaud their kiss. Regardless of the frequency of such applause, it suggests audiences came to the play expecting to see a romantic comedy and wanting that expectation to be fulfilled.

6. Ann Thompson, for instance, quotes Shaw in her Cambridge edition of the play (*The Taming of the Shrew* (Cambridge: Cambridge University Press, 1984), p. 21), as does Brian Morris in his Arden edition (*The Taming of the Shrew* (London and New York: Methuen, 1981), p. 144), Barbara Hodgdon quotes this passage in her examination of *Shrew* (*The Shakespeare Trade*, p. 28), and Michael Billington refers to Shaw in his review of Edwards' *Shrew* (*The Guardian*, 24 April 1995). Shaw's 6 November 1897 *Saturday Review* article, however, is far from a straightforward condemnation of the gender politics of the play. While he is uncomfortable

with Katherine's final speech, he enjoys the taming itself: 'The process is quite bearable, because the selfishness of the man is healthily good-humoured and untainted by wanton cruelty, and it is good for the shrew to encounter a force like that and to be brought to her senses' (Edwin Wilson (ed.), *Shaw on Shakespeare: An Anthology of Bernard Shaw's Writings on the Plays and Productions of Shakespeare* (New York: E. P. Dutton, 1961), p. 188). Shaw is often quoted as evidence of his dislike of the play's gender politics, but it is also possible to read his reaction as stemming from the discomfort of watching Katherine's submission 'in the company of a woman'—perhaps his enjoyment of the moment is stifled by not being in the safety of a men's club.

Loomba, Local manufacture made-in-India . . .

1. I should qualify that I am not suggesting that this dually schooled audience is not caught in the colonial trauma in other ways.

2. I would like to thank Bhavana Krishnamoorthy for these insights.

3. Dipesh Chakrabarty (1992) asks historians of India to try and 'provincialize Europe' by shedding Eurocentric historical categories and methods.

Levine, Highbrow/Lowbrow

1. The dedication of Shakespeare's memorial was covered in the *New York Times*, 24 May (1872).

Royster, Becoming Cleopatra

1. Patricia Hill Collins, *Black Feminist Thought*, 2nd edn. (New York: Routledge, 2000), 5.

2. Phyllis Rose, *Jazz Cleopatra: Josephine Baker in Her Time* (New York: Vintage Books, 1991), 262.

3. Rose, 30.

4. Rose, x–xi.

5. Edward Said, *Orientalism* (New York: Vintage Books, 1979), 3.

6. Melani McAlister, *Epic Encounters: Culture, Media, and U.S. Interests in the Middle East, 1945–2000* (Berkeley: University of California Press, 2001), 11.

7. Jacques Derrida, 'Signature, event, context,' in *Limited, Inc.*, ed. Gerald Graff (Evanston, IL: Northwestern University Press, 1988), 18.

8. Collins, 69.

9. Coppélia Kahn, *Roman Shakespeare: Warriors, Wounds and Women* (New York: Routledge, 1997), 112–21.

10. Janet Adelman, *The Common Liar: An Essay on 'Antony and Cleopatra'* (New Haven, CT: Yale University Press, 1973), 1.

11. bell hooks, 'Eating the other' in *Black Looks: Race and Representation* (Boston: South End Press, 1992), 21–40.

12. Harold Bloom, *Shakespeare and the Invention of the Human* (New York: Riverhead Books, 1998), 559.

13. In T. S. Eliot's conception of the play, for example, Cleopatra is 'but a gorgeous prostitute, playing for her own advantage,' while Antony is 'a poor creature who allows his politics to spoil his pleasure and his pleasure to spoil his politics.' Quoted in Barbara Hodgdon, *The Shakespeare Trade: Performances and Appropriations* (Philadelphia: University of Pennsylvania Press, 1998), 83.

14. hooks, 65.

15. Josephine Baker and Jo Bouillon, *Josephine* (Paris: Laffont, 1976), 79.

16. Stuart Hall, 'Cultural Identity and Cinematic Representation,' *Framework*, no. 36 (1989), 70.

17. Hall, 70.

REFERENCES

Alderson, Kate, 'Whose show is it anyway?' *The Times*, 21 April 1995

Arnold, Gary, 'Branagh breathes new life into classics', *Insight on the News*, 15 January 1996, pp. 37–8.

Barthes, Roland, 'The Reality effect', in *The Rustle of Language*, trans. Richard Howard (New York: Hill & Wang, 1986), pp. 141–8.

Bernstein, J. M. (ed.) *The Culture Industry: Selected Essays on Mass Culture* (London: Routledge, 1991)

Billington, Michael, *One Night Stands: A Critic's View of British Theatre from 1971–1991* (London: Nick Hern Books, 1993)

Branagh, Kenneth, *Beginning* (New York: St Martin's Press, 1989)

—— Introduction to *'Hamlet' by William Shakespeare: Screenplay, Introduction and Film Diary* (New York, W. W. Norton, 1996), pp. xi–xv.

—— *'Much Ado About Nothing' by William Shakespeare: Screenplay, Introduction, and Notes on the Making of the Movie* (New York: W. W. Norton, 1993)

Bristol, Michael, *Big-Time Shakespeare* (London: Routledge, 1996)

Buchman, Lorne M., *Still in Movement: Shakespeare on Screen* (New York: Oxford University Press, 1991)

Bulman, James C. (ed.), *Shakespeare, Theory, and Performance* (London and New York: Routledge, 1996)

Burnett, Mark Thornton, 'The "very cunning of the scene": Kenneth Branagh's *Hamlet*', *Literature/Film Quarterly*, 25/2 (1997), 78–82.

Chakrabarty, Dipesh, 'Post-coloniality and the artifice of history: who speaks for "Indian" pasts?', *Representations*, 37 (Winter), 1–24.

Collick, John, *Shakespeare, Cinema, and Society* (Manchester and New York: Manchester University Press, 1989)

Cornwell, Jane, 'An Australian in Stratford', *Southern Cross*, 19 April 1995.

Corrigan, Timothy, *A Cinema without Walls: Movies and Culture after Vietnam* (New Brunswick: Rutgers University Press, 1991)

Crowl, Samuel, 'Hamlet "most royal": an interview with Kenneth Branagh', *Shakespeare Bulletin*, 12/4 (1994), 5–8.

Davies, Anthony and Wells, Stanley (eds.), *Shakespeare and the Moving Image: The Plays on Film and Television* (Cambridge: Cambridge University Press, 1994)

Devi, Mahasweta, 'Shishu', in S. Tharu and K. Lalita (eds.), *Women Writing in India*, Vol. 2 (New York: The Feminist Press, 1993), pp. 236–50.

Donaldson, Peter S., *Shakespearean Films/Shakespearean Directors* (Boston: Unwin Hyman, 1990)

Eagleton, Terry, 'Nationalism: irony and commitment', in T. Eagleton, F. Jameson and E. W. Said, *Nationalism, Colonialism, and Literature* (Minneapolis: University of Minnesota Press, 1990), pp. 23–39.

Eckert, Charles W. (ed.), *Focus on Shakespearean Films* (Englewood Cliffs, NJ: Prentice-Hall, 1972)

Hankey, Julie (ed.), *Othello: Plays in Performance* (Bristol: Bristol Classics Press, 1987)

Hodgdon, Barbara, *Shakespeare in Performance: Henry IV, Part II* (Manchester and New York: Manchester University Press, 1993)

—— *The Shakespeare Trade: Performances and Appropriations* (Philadelphia: University of Pennsylvania Press, 1998)

Jackson, Russell, 'The Film Diary', in *'Hamlet' by William Shakespeare: Screenplay, Introduction and Film Diary* (New York: W. W. Norton, 1996), pp. 179–213.

Jorgens, Jack. T., *Shakespeare on Film* (Bloomington: Indiana University Press, 1977)

Kennedy, Dennis, *Looking at Shakespeare: A Visual History of Twentiety-Century Performance* (Cambridge: Cambridge University Press, 1993)

—— (ed.), *Foreign Shakespeare: Contemporary Performance* (Cambridge: Cambridge University Press, 1993)

Kiberd, Declan, *Inventing Ireland: The Literature of the Modern Nation* (Cambridge, MA: Harvard University Press, 1995)

Lehmann, Courtney and Starks, Lisa S., 'Making mother matter: repression, revision and the stakes of "reading psychoanalysis into" Kenneth Branagh's *Hamlet*', *Early Modern Literary Studies*, 6/1 (2000), 1–18.

Nairn, Tom, *The Break-up of Britain: Crisis and Neo-Nationalism* (London: New Left Books, 1977)

Parker, Patricia, *Shakespeare from the Margins: Language, Culture, Context* (Chicago: University of Chicago Press, 1996)

Rushdie, Salman, *Shame* (London: Picador, 1984)

—— *The Moor's Last Sigh* (London: Jonathan Cape, 1995)

Schafer, Elizabeth, *MsDirecting Shakespeare: Women Direct Shakespeare* (London: The Women's Press, 1998)

Shaughnessy, Robert, *Representing Shakespeare: England, History and the RSC* (Hemel Hempstead: Harvester Wheatsheaf, 1994)

Siberry, Michael, 'Petruccio', in R. Smallwood (ed.), *Players of Shakespeare, 4: Further Essays in Shakespearean Performance by Players with the Royal Shakespeare Company* (Cambridge: Cambridge University Press, 1998), pp. 45–59.

Thompson, Bob, 'Sing along with Shakespeare', *Toronto Sun*, 4 August 1999, p. 31.

Vaughan, Virginia Mason, *Othello: A Contextual History* (Cambridge: Cambridge University Press, 1994)

—— and Cartwright, Kent (eds.), *Othello: New Perspectives* (Rutherford, NJ: Fairleigh Dickinson University Press, 1991)

Wood, Robin, *Personal Views* (London: Gordon Fraser, 1976)

Worthen, W. B. 'Drama, performance, performativity', *PMLA*, October 1998, 1093–107.

—— *Shakespeare and the Authority of Performance* (Cambridge: Cambridge University Press, 1997)

Wilson, Edwin (ed.), *Shaw on Shakespeare* (New York: E. P. Dutton, 1961)

Zarrilli, Philip B., 'For Whom Is the King a King? Issues of Intercultural Production, Perception and Reception in a *Kathakali King Lear*', in Janelle G. Reinelt and Joseph R. Roach (eds.), *Critical Theory and Performance* (Ann Arbor: University of Michigan Press, 1992), pp. 16–40.

—— *The Kathakali Complex* (New Delhi: Abhinav, 1984)

Žižek, Slavoj, *Enjoy Your Symptom! Jacques Lacan In Hollywood and Out* (New York: Routledge, 1992)

—— *The Sublime Object of Ideology* (London: Verso, 1989)

5

Identities

CLARE McMANUS

The early modern period, as the General Introduction has shown, is often figured as the crucible of the modern subject. In the wake of the rejection of the universal, stable self, however, that subject has changed. Yet ideas of the self (the 'I', the 'me', as opposed to the 'other'), identity (the defining content of the self) and subjectivity (the experience and articulation of selfhood and identity) remain among the most important concerns animating current critical interventions into the Renaissance. Much current work explores the nature of identity after its theoretical deconstruction. It points to a constructed subject, the self forged under the pressure of historical, social and discursive circumstance. Among the forces working on this subject are class, gender, nationhood, race and sexuality, categories which are themselves the focus of many current readings of the Renaissance. The identities created by these forces can be read in an individual's self-creation or self-description, in the use of categories of identity to define others, and in the identities fashioned in literary and cultural texts.

The factors which shape subjectivity are rarely found or read in isolation. Rather, categories such as gender, class, race and sexuality are seen as a converging web of influences, operating in complex ways and each affecting the other. For instance, early modern women's identities are not read as simply 'feminine' but, as Joyce Green MacDonald makes clear in her analysis of *Oronooko* (1688), as a gendered identity which is also inflected by the discourses of ethnicity and class. To extend the example, the identity of *Oronooko*'s narrator could be further explored by considering her status as an *English*woman, a heterosexual woman, and a Christian woman. This recognition of the complexity of identity formation goes hand in hand with the exploration of the ways in which the categories through which the subject is defined are themselves historically contingent, created, as 'Histories' explores, by the pressures of a particular historical moment. Diane Purkiss's revelation of the strange familiarity of the early modern warns against taking past identities for present ones and Katharine Eisaman Maus's intense awareness of the historical contingencies of present day explanations of inwardness and subjectivity also warns of the limits of theoretical objectivity.

Stephen Greenblatt, in his seminal work on early modern identities, writes that 'Self-fashioning is always, though not exclusively, in language'.[1] Identity is, among other things, a textual creation. In the wake of Jacques Derrida's recognition of the shifting, inconstant nature of language, in which the play of meaning brings with it deferred or rejected significances which undermine every attempt to make language simple and transparent, it would seem that an identity built through language has its foundations based on sand.[2] The linguistic system through which we think ourselves into being and articulate our experience of that existence is radically indeterminate and the identities language creates are equally contingent. This has especially forceful implications when it comes to considering the nature and status of literature. Literature, as 'Textuality' shows, is no longer the expression of a stable authorial identity, instead both it and the idea of the author are far beyond the control of any individual. Furthermore, just as the identity category of the author has become unreliable, so too, within the literary text, the idea of character has changed. In the extracts below, Alan Sinfield explicitly sees Shakespeare's tragic female characters as constructs, formed by the forces of language and of gender, while Lorna Hutson's reading of Shakespeare's sonnets opens up the sheer textuality of what at first seems to be an emotional relationship between the speaker and beloved. Formed in and by language, author, character and reader are all vulnerable to the shifting nature of the linguistic text.

With the recognition of the 'play' of language comes the realization that meaning cannot always (or ever) be fully controlled and this understanding has influenced many readings of the formation of the Renaissance subject. Following the work of Michel Foucault, identity is seen as contingent, as precariously dependent upon the simultaneous negotiation of power and meaning by an individual and the working out of power upon the individual.[3] As Greenblatt's overarching concept of *self*-fashioning implies, subjectivity and identity is partly about self-definition (often, importantly, a self-definition made against the identity of the other) but it is also implicated in the perception and definition of the self by others, or put another way, the imposition of an identity onto an other. This has a particular impact when that identity is ethnic or racial and its effects can be felt in the commonplace Renaissance categorisation of Africans, Indians, Turks and the Irish as 'savages' or 'barbarians'. The creation of identity, then, is bound up with the circulation of power through society and its negotiation by those who have it (e.g. men,

---

[1] Stephen Greenblatt, *Renaissance Self-Fashioning: From More to Shakespeare* (Chicago and London: University of Chicago Press, 1980), p. 9.

[2] See, for instance, Jacques Derrida, 'Of Grammatology' in *A Derrida Reader: Between the Blinds*, ed. Peggy Kamuf (Hemel Hempstead: Harvester Wheatsheaf, 1991), pp. 31–58, and 'Différance' in *Literary Theory: An Anthology*, ed. Julie Rivkin and Michael Ryan (Oxford: Blackwell, 2000), pp. 385–407.

[3] See, for example, Foucault's *The History of Sexuality* trans. Robert Hurley (Harmondsworth: Penguin, 1990–2), 3 vols. *Discipline and Punish: The Birth of the Prison*, trans. Alan Sheridan (London: Penguin, 1991).

monarchs, colonists, military leaders) and by those upon whom it is imposed (e.g. the poor, women, the colonised). Indeed, the issue of agency—the possibility of self-expression or self-creation between the gaps of discourse and history—is one of the most important in current critiques of subjectivity. The chances of such self-expression are perhaps better than they may at first appear. In his discussion of 'everyday practices, [and] "ways of operating" ', Michel de Certeau writes of 'the clandestine forms taken by the dispersed, tactical, and make-shift creativity of groups or individuals already caught in the nets of "discipline" '. Later, he concludes: 'People have to make do with what they have.'[4] One result of this is that we may find agency in the multiple but seemingly marginal ways in which those who do not appear to wield cultural power 'make do' with what their culture offers them. So, for instance, the explosion of interest in Renaissance women's writing has shown that we might think of early modern women as authors, not necessarily of canonical literature (although that was also the case), but of manuscript commonplace books, tomb inscriptions and religious meditations. Likewise, elite women's patronage of theatre, architecture and court masques shows how they worked within gendered restrictions and found ways to figure as cultural authorities, if not always as literary authors.

As the stress on the possibilities of agency and indeed the very title of this chapter suggests, current Renaissance criticism emphasises plurality, inclusivity and a refiguring of the relationships between selves. This involves a focus on identities which have not traditionally been at the centre of critical attention. Indeed, many of the identities currently under consideration are elusive and marginal—those of women, those documented in popular culture or travel writing, the more ephemeral records of sexual or gendered identities, and the voicelessness of those whose experiences are not recorded at all. Attention has also recently turned to those whose identities are fashioned through their own use of a discourse which oppresses them but who can use that very discourse to 'write back' against their oppressors. This group is described by Ania Loomba—following Gayatri Spivak who in turn follows Antonio Gramsci—as 'the subaltern'. This term, which is most often used to refer to the colonized subject, draws attention to the hegemonic differences of class, gender, race and faith that distinguish individuals from each other and recalls the negotiations involved in every act of historical documentation and interpretation. However, the voice of the subaltern is hard to hear, and much critical work has focused instead on travel writing describing the European experience of America, India or Ireland. Using this model, readers return to canonical texts such as Shakespeare's *Tempest* (1611) to discover English perceptions of the other (whether the play is read as Mediterranean or American). So Caliban's enchanted dream, his curse and Prospero's begrudging recognition of his recalcitrant slave with the words 'This thing of darkness I / Acknowledge mine' (5.1.278–79) are well-trod territory for those wishing to explore a mediated representation of otherness through the lens of early modern English culture. Indeed, just as

---

[4] Michel de Certeau, *The Practice of Everyday Life*, trans. Steven F. Rendall (Berkeley: University of California Press, 1988), pp. xi, xiv–xv, 18.

'Histories' has already shown the impossibility of a direct access to the past, some sort of compromise and mediation seems integral to every effort to find the other. That said, the focus of critical attention on this diverse other has vitally reconfigured the Renaissance.

The creation of identity, then, is bound up with power, with the perception of an imposed identity which positions the other as, for example, Irish, as black, as female, as poor or as voiceless. From this, many left-wing critics have argued, the responsibilities of a newly inclusive criticism of the Renaissance and the academy which teaches it are clear. Yet the limits of these responsibilities and the debates over where the imposition of identity begins and ends are ongoing. Indeed, the boundaries of identity are constantly being pushed back; for instance, recent criticism has engaged with the influence of death upon subjectivity and has challenged the hierarchies of identity to the extent that it questions the primacy of humanity over other creatures. The extracts by Erica Fudge and Jonathan Dollimore show that even the seemingly stable demarcations between the living and the dead, between the human and the non-human shift with time and with political and social necessity. Such work contributes to an ongoing discussion over the nature and interpretation of the self. The debate around identity has changed the face of the Renaissance and it promises to continue doing so.

1 | Language, the self and identity

Alan Sinfield, *Faultlines: Cultural Materialism and the Politics of Dissident Reading* (Oxford: Clarendon Press, 1992), pp. 52–4.

When is a character not a character? Desdemona, Olivia, Lady Macbeth, and subjectivity

Desdemona is not usually regarded as a problem . . . Traditionally, she has been celebrated as one of Shakespeare's great women characters—celebrated mainly, of course, by men, since they have dominated the discourses of criticism. But surely there is a great mystery. On her first appearance, Desdemona is spectacularly confident, bold and unconventional. Summoned to the Senate to explain her elopement with Othello, she justifies herself coolly and coherently, confessing without a blush that she was 'half the wooer' (1.3.176). . . . Further, she speaks up uninvited, and on the outrageous theme of women's sexual desire, demanding to go with her husband to Cyprus so that they may consummate the marriage:

> if I be left behind,
> A moth of peace, and he go to the war,
> The rites of love for which I love him are bereft me.
> (1.3.255–7)

Despite such extraordinarily spirited behaviour, Desdemona becomes the most conventional spouse. Mainly we see her wheedling for the restoration of Cassio, in the sad posture of the wife trying to manage her husband:

> my lord shall never rest,
> I'll watch him tame, and talk him out of patience;
> His bed shall seem a school, his board a shrift.
>
> (3.3.22–4)

Even this she does ineptly: despite her earlier intuition on how to address the Senate, she is now stupidly blind to the effect she is having. When Othello starts to abuse her, she is abjectly fearful and consequently dishonest, making matters worse. In her denials, even, she is strangely acquiescent:

> those that do teach young babes
> Do it with gentle means, and easy tasks;
> He might ha' chid me so, for, in good faith,
> I am a child at chiding.
>
> (4.2.113–60)

She allows herself to be killed with slight protest (5.2.23–85).

Now, I don't think it implausible, in principle, that Desdemona could be so disheartened by Othello's attitude that she might eventually lose all her original spirit and intelligence. How this happens might be elaborated through action, dialogue, and soliloquy. It may not be easy, but Shakespeare is reckoned to be good at this sort of thing—in Othello's case, we may observe his changing attitudes in considerable detail. Desdemona is a disjointed sequence of positions that women are conventionally supposed to occupy. The bold Desdemona of the opening romantic initiative is one possible position—we see it also in Rosalind in *As You Like It*, Jessica in *The Merchant of Venice*, Perdita in *The Winter's Tale*. The nagging spouse is another. Linda Woodbridge wants to believe that early modern authors created full, lively characters, rather than following their own stultifying theories of womanhood, but in this respect she is uneasy nonetheless: 'Although Desdemona is no domineering shrew, her behaviour at one point comes dangerously close to stereotype.'[1] The final Desdemona, who submits to Othello's abuse and violence, takes the posture of other abused women in texts of the period—sitting like Patience on a monument, as Viola puts it in *Twelfth Night*. . . . It is almost as if the Wife of Bath were reincarnated as Griselda. If most critics have not noticed this discontinuity in Desdemona, it is because each of her appearances is plausible in itself, insofar as it corresponds to one of the models for 'woman' that prevail in our cultures; and because, as Catherine Belsey observes, 'discontinuity of being' can be read as the 'inconstancy' that is supposed to be typically 'feminine'.[2]

Desdemona has no character of her own; she is a convenience in the story of Othello, Iago, and Venice. Othello asks, 'Was this fair paper, this most goodly book, / Made to write 'whore' upon?' (4.2.73–74). The writing is done by Othello, Iago, Roderigo, Brabantio, the Duke, and Lodovico—they take Desdemona as a blank page for the versions of her that they want. She is written into a script that is organized through the perceptions and needs of male dominance in heterosexuality and patriarchal relations. . . .

Janet Adelman has identified a similar pattern in the presentation of Cressida. Despite her argument elsewhere that we should 'respond to Shakespeare's characters as whole psycho-logical entities,' Adelman finds that 'characters may not always permit us to respond to them in this way.'[3] The early scenes of *Troilus and Cressida*, she shows, 'establish not only some sense of Cressida but also the expectation that we will be allowed to know her as a full character, that she will maintain her relationship with us' (p. 122). But from the time when she arrives in the Greek camp, she appears as 'a mere character type, a person with no conflict or inwardness at all.' There are several ways, Adelman says, in which we might imagine motiv-ations for Cressida, but the text affords 'no enlightenment.' Thus the play seems to enact the fantasy that Cressida becomes radically unknowable, irreducibly other, at the moment of her separation from Troilus (pp. 127–8). Adelman's argument as to why this should be is complex and psychoanalytic; ultimately, she says, 'the necessities of Troilus' character, rather than of Cressida's require her betrayal of him . . . she becomes a whore to keep him pure' (pp. 137–38). And this suits not only Troilus, of course: Adelman could easily have shown how Cressida's behavior has seemed, to many critics, no more than we expect. Like Desdemona, Cressida is organized to suit her role in the story of the men. A character is not a character when she or he is needed to shore up a patriarchal representation.

*   *   *

Lorna Hutson, 'Why the lady's eyes are nothing like the sun', in Clare Brant and Diane Purkiss (eds.), *Women, Texts and Histories 1575–1760* (London and New York: Routledge, 1992), pp. 17–18.

I suggest that the naturalness of Shakespeare's *Sonnets* (the comprehensibility of their moral symbolism) depended on the fact that by rejecting as 'false' and 'superficial' the analogical techniques normally used in sonnets, they managed to persuade us of the possibility of a love and a poetry that might remain true to its subject. The possibility is so congenial to our way of thinking that we scarcely feel the need to gloss it, but how is it constructed? . . . [I]n sonnet 82, the subject is described as being 'as faire in knowledge as in hew', so that his inward beauty is identified as a kind of connoisseurship, a capacity to value and to validate the text as a cultural artefact. And this is typical of the beauty ascribed to him. For though we tend to read the *Sonnets* as if they were explorative of an emotional relation between the poet and his mascu-line subject, an equally prominent feature is the text's exploration of an *interpretative* and *mutually authenticating* relation between the *text* and its *subject*. Indeed, the *Sonnets* enable us to experience the inward beauty of intellectual discrimination which enables the friend—'as faire in knowledge as in hew'—to judge the text, as itself an effect of the text. In the play of antitheses, we glimpse this authenticating, discriminating subject, the 'friend', in the process of being made up out of a comparative rhetoric which ambiguously privileges the contingen-cies of gender, of noble birth and a peculiarly 'economic' attitude to the text which is foreign to our assumptions about the purpose of reading. . . . For, of course, it was only for men that Renaissance humanism identified the interpretative practices of reading with the prudence, or practical reason, which enables deliberation about action in political life. Only for men could the activity of reading be expected to increase the power to act and speak in emergency, to discover in the emergent moment an argument, a 'colour' for one's own uses. . . . So, since only a man can effectively reproduce from a discourse which celebrates beauty, this power of discursive reproduction becomes his intrinsic beauty, and only a man can therefore be 'truly' beautiful. The sonnets put this in a cleverly 'moronic' or oxymoronic fashion: only a man can have 'a Womans face with natures owne hand painted' [(20.1)].

*   *   *

Douglas Trevor, 'George Herbert and the scene of writing', in Carla Mazzio and Douglas Trevor (eds.), *Historicism, Psychoanalysis and Early Modern Culture* (London and New York: Routledge, 2000), pp. 228, 229–35, 251–2.

> *A Lord I had,*
> *And have, of whom some grounds, which may improve,*
> *I hold for two lives, and both lives in me.*
> George Herbert, 'Love Unknown'

> *You see that there are reasons why I advise you to read religious authors*
> *from time to time; I mean good ones, of course.*
> Jacques Lacan, Seminar VII

[. . .] Herbert's descriptions of writing demonstrate the complicated sense of agency that permeates his verse, agency that is at once acted upon and self-acting. As numerous studies have demonstrated, the Reformation theology that shaped Herbert's religious beliefs also influenced his poetic praxis.[1] And yet, as the diverse interpretations spawned by these doctrines—in both Herbert's day and our own—make clear, the verses that comprise *The Temple* resist uniform explication through the lenses provided by theological and doctrinal texts. Building on the work of scores of Herbert scholars themselves invested in exploring the intersection of historical contexts with poetic stylistics,[2] Michael Schoenfeldt has recently utilized theoretical paradigms and methodological practices associated with the new historicism in order to explore 'the historically embedded language of Herbert's poetry.'[3] Reacting to these literary strategies, Richard Strier points out that '[s]ince the Reformation posits the centrality of an internal, nonritual experience, it becomes a special difficulty for New Historicism.[4] While the sociocultural orientation of the new historicism can prove invaluable—as I hope to show—in establishing the terms by which human agency was explicated by Herbert, understanding Herbert's notion of selfhood means stepping beyond, or back from, the emphasis often placed by new historicists on social exchanges and public self-fashionings.

In this essay I pursue a reading of Herbert's verse that emphasizes his attention to the material processes of writing and his rendering of the self as it is shaped and enriched through Christian belief. Through Herbert's work, I argue that early modern confessional lyricists offer a way of historicizing and explicating fundamental concepts and concerns of Lacanian psychoanalysis. I also consider the ways in which Jacques Lacan's own theorization of psychoanalysis is explicitly and implicitly indebted to Judeo-Christian motifs and significantly influenced, as Lacan himself insists, by early modern religious discourses. Questions of devotion, so integral to Herbert's project as a poet, also play a part in Lacan's self-presentation as the most truly

Freudian of Sigmund Freud's followers. While mindful of the enormous differences between a Renaissance English parson and a twentieth-century French psychoanalyst, I suggest nonetheless that Herbert's laboriously and self-consciously fashioned scene of writing anticipates the scene of analysis as it is imagined by Lacan, that the latter constructs his own rhetoric of devotion keenly aware of his Renaissance precursors, and that the Jewish science of Freud's psychoanalysis is—in the hands of his foremost French disciple—rendered as peculiarly reformed through allusions and analogies that secularize religious topoi while at the same time spiritualizing psychoanalytic terminology.

Through his frequent descriptions of collaborative scenes of composition, Herbert demonstrates a distinctly Protestant understanding of human agency whereby the self is irrevocably split by sin, capable of being saved only by the grace of God. And yet to posit that the devotional subjects of Herbert's confessional lyrics yearn for salvation is not to argue that such subjects desire unified, holistic selves, or even think in such terms. In Protestant theology the movement is often simultaneously toward a self enriched by God and away from a self that is fallen. Donne, for instance, thanks his Lord in *Devotions Upon Emergent Occasions* for having 'clothd me with thy selfe, by stripping me of my selfe,' while, in Paul Harland's wonderful reading of *Devotion XVII*, the 'island of which Donne speaks is a pun, for if no man is an I-land, a domain of self alone, every man is potentially a Christ.'[5] Such alterity is grounded, according to Protestant theologians, in scripture itself. Martin Luther, for instance, glosses Galatians 3:28 ('There is neither Jew nor Greek, there is neither bond nor free, there is neither male nor female: for ye are all one in Christ Jesus') by insisting that 'in Christ, where there is no law, there is no difference of persons, there is neither Jew nor Grecian, but all are one.'[6]

Luther's indifference to individual identity mirrors his insistence that it is through the grace of God alone that the human soul can be saved, a position itself developed principally through readings of the Pauline Epistles and Augustine's later works. Again according to Luther, Christ enriches the life of the believer, while to exist without Christ in oneself is to be damned, 'for "I" as a person separate from Christ belongeth to death and hell . . . Christ therefore, saith he [Paul], thus joined and united unto me and abiding in me, liveth this life in me which now I live; yea Christ himself is this life which now I live. Therefore Christ and I in this behalf are both one.'[7]

Intriguingly, Lacan comes to resemble Herbert and other early modern Protestant lyricists and theologians when he emphasizes the reliance of the self on an external gaze in which—paradoxically—the language of self-scrutiny resides.[8] Reading Lacanian psychoanalysis through Protestantism—and, in this essay, Herbert in particular—reveals the debts that Lacan owes to Renaissance religious thinkers. While contemporary Lacanian theorists are for the most part hesitant to acknowledge these debts, Lacan certainly was not [. . .] At one point in *Seminar VII*, for example, he insists that if you want to 'understand Freud's position relative to the Father, you have to go and look up the form it is given in Luther's thought.' And even more pointedly, in the same seminar, Lacan traces some of the images Freud has invested 'with the quality of scientific authentication' back to Luther: 'His [Luther's] choice of words is in the end far more analytic than all that modern phenomenology has been able to articulate in the relatively gentle terms of the abandonment of the mother's breast.'[9] Precisely because he predates psychoanalysis, because he is ungently polemical and rebellious, and vehement in his doctrinal convictions, Luther is useful to Lacan. He articulates nothing less than 'the essential turning point of a crisis from which emerged our whole modern immersion in the world.'[10] He invents, in other words, the subject on which the tenets of Lacanian psychoanalysis are based.

According to Philip Rieff, psychoanalysis represents a return to early modern modes of self-introspection: 'To the therapeutic of the mid-twentieth century, as to the ascetic of the Reformation movements, all destinies had become intensely personal and not at all communal. The way to this self-knowledge, which may be in itself saving, is to trace back a person's conduct from symptom to the inner conditions responsible for that symptom.'[11] That these symptoms might themselves be diagnosed in vastly different ways, depending upon the historical surround of the subject, Debora Shuger has made clear.[12] More fundamentally, however, for both Herbert and Lacan, self-knowledge is in many ways an impossibility, as human agency is understood as not only fractured but *constituted* by its collaboration with another: God, in Herbert's nomenclature, the Other in Lacan's. [. . .] Jonathan Dollimore is right, I think, to point out that 'post-structuralism rediscovered what the Renaissance already knew: identity is powerfully—one might say essentially—informed by what it is not.'[13] For the poet acutely aware of the material context of his work, perhaps no person better embodies displaced identity than the secretary who writes on behalf of another.

In Jonathan Goldberg's account of early modern secretaries, the (male) writer is acknowledged as 'a living pen' of his master, but also as a pen enriched rather than demeaned by its subservience to another. Reading Angel Day's *The English Secretary* (1586, 1592), Goldberg concludes that 'the self that the secretary acquires is founded in an institutionalized selflessness (the privacy and privation that define the structure of the secret shared, that neither is without the other, and that the secretary must be that necessary absence in which the lord has presence).'[14] Prior to turning his back on a career at court, Herbert might well have imagined himself becoming a secretary to a prominent member of the English aristocracy; when he comes to imagine more lasting rewards, it should perhaps not surprise us that he employs a vocabulary resonating with worldly implications. [. . .] In any event, if not in his thoughts, such professional skills were at least in his hand; according to Amy Charles, '[t]he persistence of the secretary *e* in Herbert's handwriting supports the conclusion that secretary was the hand he learned first and turned to, probably without realizing it, under stress or in haste.'[15]

Herbert's celebration of his God translates into devotional terms the secretary's dutiful obedience to his master, an obedience made material in writing. Not unlike courtiers who must place all of their faith in their patrons if they hope to advance, Herbert's speakers occasionally comment upon their devotional obligations in terms that suggest the problems that inner autonomy can pose for both courtly and divine supplicants. As the speaker of 'The Holdfast' explains,

> I threatned to observe the strict decree
> > Of my deare God with all my power & might.
> > But I was told by one, it could not be;
> > Yet I might trust in God to be my light.
> Then will I trust, said I, in him alone.
> > Nay, ev'n to trust in him, was also his:

> We must confesse that nothing is our own.
> Then I confesse that he my succour is:
> But to have nought is ours, not to confesse
> That we have nought. (1–10)

Each expression of self-authored action here prompts qualification: The speaker can neither obey his God with 'power & might' nor 'trust in him,' nor even confess his own nothingness. Human agency is always deferred to the same actor, Christ. In 'Aaron' this transference is rendered corporeally as the speaker takes up residence in the Son of God's body, gaining a better costume in the process: 'Onely another head / I have, another heart and breast, / Another musick, making live not dead, / Without whom I could have no rest: / In him I am well drest' (11–15). The suggestion that Christ's body is the holiest of residences, that in it one becomes well attired in the dress of one's master, draws on the cultural context out of which *The Temple* emerged, a context in which household service could lead to social advancement. It also echoes somewhat Luther's gloss of Galatians 2:20: 'Therefore he [Paul] saith: "Now not I, but Christ liveth in me,' Christ is my form . . . adorning and beautifying my faith, as the colour or the clear light do garnish and beautify the wall.'[16]

A similar merging of selves—these more explicitly authorial—occurs in 'Providence,' where the speaker is not clothed by God but rather finds his verse enriched through collaboration. In 'Assurance' the anguish of an independent existence in which the speaker rightly fears confrontation with 'cold despairs' and 'gnawing pensivenesse' is put off by the prompt intervention of his savior: 'Thou didst at once thy self indite, / And hold my hand, while I did write' (16, 29–30). Just as devotion is, in the terms of the Protestant Reformation, largely textually based and rooted in reading (especially the Bible), a common characteristic of Herbert's descriptions of religious life is their attention to writing. The two practices, reading and writing, collapse into each other in the companion poems 'The Holy Scriptures' (I and II), which fetishize the Bible at its graphic level: 'Oh Book! infinite sweetnesse! let my heart / Suck ev'ry letter' (I: 1–2). [. . .] Imbibing the language of God means appropriating it as one's vocabulary for self-understanding: '[F]or in ev'ry thing / Thy words do finde me out, & parallels bring, / And in another make me understood' (II: 10–12). And to the extent that such vocabulary permits replication in the poet's own writings, we should expect to find it there as well, the very letters that make up scripture reconstituting—being regurgitated as—Herbert's verse. [. . .]

Herbert represents his dependence on the language of God here by suggesting that it is through appropriated words that self-understanding occurs. Lacan reformulates this sentiment in a number of ways, first by insisting that analysis depends on the speech of the analysand and the presence of the analyst, which by itself creates a dialogue: '[T]here is no speech without a reply, even if it is met only with silence, provided that it has an auditor.'[17] But the discourse of the Other, symbolized by the analyst's silence and the analysand's ensuing verbal free association, attests to a self-division that looms behind all utterance: The ego is never, according to Lacan, 'identical with the presence that is speaking to you.' Rather, there is always distance 'between the subject's ego *(moi)* and the 'I' *(je)* of his discourse.'[18] In 'Holy Scriptures' (II), the Other is figured by 'Thy words,' the words of God that 'finde' the speaker 'out' (11). As a religious poet, one who reads the Bible and through this reading comes to write verse, Herbert often emphasizes the materiality of devotional language, which in turn materializes alterity: Scriptural verses are evoked with their 'leaves' in mind (6), and the Bible is, finally, valued over the natural world: 'Starres are poore books, & oftentimes do misse: / This book of starres lights to eternall blisse' (13–14).

Herbert's high regard for the writing life, the kind of existence centered around transcribing and attesting to the effects of doctrinal inspiration, is glimpsed in the first stanza of 'The Windows' when he puns on the title of his book, transferring the authorship of *The Temple* to God and suggesting that it is within such a *material* realm that the poet/speaker is empowered to attest to God's glory:

> Lord, how can man preach thy eternall word?
>   He is a brittle crazie glasse:
> Yet in thy temple thou dost him afford
>   This glorious and transcendent place,
>   To be a window, through thy grace. (1–5)

Such acknowledgment of God's contribution to, even ownership of, his own written praise is not far removed from 'Providence' or any of the other poems in which the realm of *scripted* devotion (both scribally and performatively) witnesses the exercise of divine grace on the poet/speaker. Herbert's desire to remove his own agency from the temple he has built is a desire to authenticate his love for God by insisting that it originates with God himself. It also attests to another desire, left unspoken, to grant himself solace. In the analytic setting, a similar search for 'truth,' which Lacan reveals as lying 'at the very heart of analytic practice' ('inscrit au coeur même de la pratique analytique'), refers to the successful identification of an unconscious tendency, which results in the analyst's experiencing tranquility ('cette paix qui s'établit à reconnaître la tendance inconsciente').[19] If the God-figure is dead for Lacan, as is maintained in *Seminar VII*, he is perhaps resurrected as the unconscious: all-knowing, all-powerful, and maddeningly elusive.[20] [. . .]

When Jacques Derrida turns to Freud's own scene of writing he comes to see in the analytical techniques espoused a seemingly endless accretion of interpretative gestures: '[T]he substitution of signifiers seems to be the essential activity of psychoanalytic interpretation,' he writes.[21] Derrida uncovers in psychoanalytic practice, through the scribal metaphors that litter Freud's accounts of the unconscious, the way in which written performance reifies the deferral of desire. It is, according to Derrida, within the account of writing that the unconscious is summoned as necessarily absent by the textual trace it leaves behind as a copy. The real scene of such transcription is never, in effect, captured; rather, '[e]verything begins with reproduction. Always already.'[22] Neither is the original scene of writing one of whole or self-contained agency. Instead, the traces that remain attest to a 'two-handed machine, a multiplicity of agencies or origins.'[23]

It is toward this deferred scene of writing, a scene repeatedly pushed away by its own textual traces, that Herbert's poetry so often directs itself, in the process articulating Christian faith as one of perpetually deferred and hence inexhaustible longing. Lacan describes the practice of psychoanalysis as similarly enamored, not of God but rather of the unconscious, which is always 'on another stage, in another scene . . . repeated.'[24] Returning to Herbert's poetry with renewed recognition of how faith is a desire for that which is always already elsewhere reminds us that belief in any set of doctrines and praxes is never reducible to the contents of these doctrines and praxes themselves. Herbert's language of devotion character- izes itself by an acute awareness of the psychology of longing, by its recognition that the scene of writing can only insufficiently record any encounter with the divine, but that the partiality of these transcriptions itself attests to the wonder and completeness offered through com- munion with the Other.

*   *   *

Ania Loomba, 'Shakespeare and cultural difference', in Terence Hawkes (ed.), *Alternative Shakespeares, Vol. 2* (London and New York: Routledge, 1996), pp. 172–3.

The 'speech' or the 'voice' of the subaltern subject has become a shorthand for her conscious- ness, her ability to express herself, her cultural tools, her capacity for opposition, as well as the state of the colonial archives through which these can be recovered, all of which are in danger of being read as interchangeable. The question of orality, for example, is minimized by an emphasis on writing and records. Caliban's poetry has long been read as evidence of an oral culture, sensibility and intelligence that undermines and challenges Prospero's view of him as a brute. And if *The Tempest* became a parable it was also because, for a variety of anti-colonial activists, it encoded, or could be altered to indicate, the possibility of subaltern resistance. Caliban's curse became an evocative symbol of native articulation, but it was a symbol that suggested a specific model of that articulation as, to borrow Partha Chatterji's term for nationalist ideologies in India, a 'derivative discourse' (1986). It is Prospero's gift of language that initiates the resistance of his slave. This model has been extremely influential within current theories of colonial discourse. Thus, while it is customary for any criticism dealing with 'colonialism', 'cultural difference' and 'race' to gesture towards the native presence, to the threat she poses to dominant culture, and to the violence she evokes from the latter, we often find that her rebelliousness turns out to be a matter of the 'slipperiness', the 'ambivalence', the 'ambiguity', the 'contradictions' of colonial discourse itself. Theorizing subaltern agency remains a genuine problem, for early modern and post-colonial critics, largely because indigenous cultures are understood as unrecoverable after the colonial holocaust.

*   *   *

Katharine Eisaman Maus, *Inwardness and Theater in the English Renaissance* (Chicago and London: University of Chicago Press, 1995), pp. 26–30.

[S]ome new-historicist and cultural-materialist critics of early modern English literature have tended to deny or downplay the significance of a rhetoric of inwardness in early modern England, even though evidence abounds for its importance in the period. I believe that this denial arises from, or is symptomatic of, a false sense of what is necessitated by the premises of cultural-materialist and new-historicist criticism. Despite differences in the details of their approaches, such critics characteristically work from philosophical positions that reject as illu- sory the possibility of a subjectivity prior to or exempt from social determination. That is, they are making a claim not only about English Renaissance subjectivity, but about subjectivity *tout court*: a claim 'that the self,' in Annabel Patterson's words, 'is always necessarily a product of its relations.'[1] At the same time, they want to resist speciously imputing modern assumptions about 'the self' to a historically distant culture: they are especially suspicious of the kind of triumphantly individualist rhetoric that used to characterize a good deal of Renaissance history and literary criticism. Admitting the significance of conceptions of personal inwardness for the English Renaissance, they imagine, would be tantamount to embracing a naive essentialism about human nature.

This consequence simply does not follow, however. Perhaps the historicist argument makes the philosophical argument seem more plausible; for if our intuitions about subjectivity are demonstrably absent in other cultures or periods, then those intuitions are unlikely to represent transhistorical constants, or to reflect stubborn facts about human nature. But the philosophical argument does not need to be made in historicist terms—and in fact, in some of its most influential formulations is not so made—nor does the historicist project require this particular philosophical agenda.[2] The difference is worth keeping in mind, because philosophical claims about the necessarily social constitution of *any* subjectivity, Renaissance or modern, sometimes seem to get confused with historicist claims about an early modern form of subjectivity supposedly less inward-looking than our own.

Since [. . .] the idea of 'inward truth' in early modern England is intimately linked to transcendental religious claims, antagonism to those claims perhaps contributes to the recent tendency to underestimate the conceptual importance of personal inwardness in this period. I share the religious incredulity of many new-historicist and cultural-materialist critics. I suspect, however, that if the religious categories in which the English Renaissance tried to comprehend itself often seem to us to involve glaring mystifications of social and political dynamics, so too our secularist interpretive axioms may blind us to their own explanatory limitations. Perhaps our suspicion of privacy, inwardness, subjectivity, soul, and so forth—our conviction that such terms beg to be debunked—has less to do with their inherently unsatisfactory features than with our sense of what counts as a satisfactory explanation. Perhaps it is not the people of early modern England but we, the postmodern academic heirs of Wittgenstein, Lacan, Marx, Austin, and Foucault, who experience difficulty thinking of individuals apart from external matrices, who imagine 'the supposedly "private" sphere . . . only through its similarities and dissimilarities to the public world,' and who are attracted to the notion that selves are void. If so, it is disingenuous to pretend that by discovering the externally constituted nature of Renaissance selves we have identified one feature of a great gulf set between 'them' and 'us.'

So distinguishing between what I would call a 'philosophical' argument and a 'historical' one seems important. And this distinction is related to another: the difference between the origins of an idea and its effects once it becomes culturally available. The new-historicist critique insists, correctly in my view, that the 'self' is not independent of or prior to its social context. Yet that critique often seems to assume that once this dependence is pointed out, inwardness simply vaporizes, like the Wicked Witch of the West under Dorothy's bucket of water. It may well be true that Renaissance notions of interior truth turn out to be philosophically defective: they are rarely elaborately or rigorously argued for. But lack of rigor neither limits the extent of, nor determines the nature of, the power such ideas can exert. Murkiness and illogicality may, in fact, enhance rather than limit their potency.

Instead of dismantling Renaissance distinctions between inward and outward, public and private, then, or evaluating their theoretical acceptability, I [suggest] a more pragmatic enterprise, analyzing some of the ways the distinction matters, and some of the ways in which it is used. What is at issue—ethically, politically, epistemologically, theologically—when someone in early modern England appeals to a difference between external show and form internal, or between outer and inner man? How are the boundaries drawn that separate what counts as 'inside' from what counts as 'outside'? How does the existence of such categories help shape thought and behavior? These investigations need not comprise a rejection, but rather an attempt to refine and advance a historically self-conscious discussion of the early modern period.

[. . .] English Renaissance culture [valued] two fantasies: one, that selves are obscure, hidden, ineffable; the other, that they are fully manifest or capable of being made fully manifest. These seem to be contradictory notions, but again and again they are voiced together, so that they seem less self-canceling than symbiotically related or mutually constitutive. Thomas Wright insists that 'we cannot enter into a man's heart' in *The Passions of the Mind*, a treatise devoted to the techniques of mind-reading. Ralegh argues for the incommensurability of animal with human perception, and then guesses at what cats and goats might see as they look out of their peculiar eyes. Hamlet claims that theatrical externals conceal an inaccessible inwardness, but stages a play to discover his uncle's secrets. James I writes that a king 'can never without secrecy do great things' only a couple of pages before describing him 'as one set on a scaffold, whose smallest actions and gestures all the people gazingly do behold.'[3] Thus the public domain seems to derive its significance from the possibility of privacy—from what is withheld or excluded from it—and vice versa. 'Counsels if they be wrapped up in silence,' writes the essayist Robert Johnson, 'are very fortunately powerful in civil actions, but divulgated lose their force.'[4] Just so, the revelatory power of theater is predicated upon disguising; just so, divine omniscience indicates, even as it repairs, the limitations of mortal vision.

The elaboration in early modern England of this dialectic of vision and concealment is surely an important chapter in the history of self-conceptions, whether we are inclined to see that history in terms of rupture or of continuities. At the same time I would emphasize that it is merely a chapter, not the whole story. For the 'idea of the subject' is, in fact, not *an* idea, nor is it simply commensurate with [. . .] 'inwardness' [. . .]. 'Subjectivity' is often treated casually as a unified or coherent concept when, in fact, it is a loose and varied collection of assumptions, intuitions, and practices that do not all logically entail one another and need not appear together at the same cultural moment. A well-developed rhetoric of inward truth, for instance, may exist in a society that never imagines that such inwardness might provide a basis for political rights. The intuition that sexual and family relations are 'private' may, but need not, coincide with strong feelings about the 'unity of the subject,' or with convictions about the freedom, self-determination, or uniqueness of individuals, or with the sense that the self constitutes a form of property. It seems to me a mistake to assume that all these matters can be discussed at once, that they are necessarily part of the same cluster of ideas.

. . . .

QUESTIONS

- Each of these critics focus on the workings of particular discourses (race, gender, sexuality, or inwardness) in the textual or linguistic formation of the subject. What is the impact of these different emphases?
- How effective are the metaphors of the voice, the text and writing, and what are their implications for Renaissance identities? How does Loomba's analysis interrogate the voice as a metaphor for subaltern identities?
- Where does the idea of the constructed subject leave the analysis of 'character' (i.e. the textual representation of the self or the other) and what does this suggest about the relationship between the text, the author and the reader?

2 | Theorizing the other

Diane Purkiss, 'Material girls: the seventeenth-century woman debate', in Clare Brant and Diane Purkiss (eds.), *Women, Texts and Histories 1575–1760* (London and New York: Routledge, 1992), pp. 69–70.

The kind of attention paid collectively to the texts of the late Elizabethan and Jacobean 'woman debate' signed with female names [including *Jane Anger her Protection for Women* (1589), *A Mouzell for Melastomus*, by Rachel Speght (1617), *Ester hath Hang'd Haman,* by Ester Sowernam (1617), *The Worming of A Mad Dogge,* by Constantia Munda (1617), and *The Women's Sharp Revenge,* by Mary Tattle-well and Joan Hit-Him-Home (1640)] suggests that many critics understand feminism to be a relatively recognizable political and literary category which, though historically variable, is also visible across historical boundaries. [. . .] [T]he identification of oppositional resistance as expressed by a single author may be a difficult matter historically; texts we recognize as feminist in our present circumstances might in their historical context represent not feminist univocality, but an awkward combination of contra-dictory speaking-positions such as the assumption of a negotiating stance on the terrain of politics, a subversive play with the question of gender in terms unfamiliar to modern feminism, and the production of femininity as a saleable commodity in the literary market. What we recognize in these texts may be the processing of woman as a theatrical role or masquerade which can never be equated with an essential woman or audible authorial voice but which, rather, troubles the very existence of such a self-identical figure. [. . .] Because they purport to be by women, they seem to offer a visible female self-consciousness about gender, a site upon which female agency is fully and openly displayed in a manner recognizable or nameable as feminism. In other words, they excite the desire to recognize the present in the past, to name what we can term as our *own* history. But because what is at stake in these texts seems at first glance so familiar and understandable, it is possible that their estranging or culturally autono-mous aspects may not be fully noticed; moreover, because they can so readily be situated in the context of gender politics, they are never fully situated in the political and discursive specificities of the early modern period.

*   *   *

Joyce Green MacDonald, 'The disappearing African woman: Imoinda in *Oronooko* after Behn', *English Literary History*, 66 (1999), 77–8.

In [Behn's] Oronooko and Imoinda we can thus trace an example of what Homi Bhabha has called 'mimicry' in the colonialist text: their black skins and the signs of cultural alterity which literally mark their bodies (the narrator somewhat fancifully compares their facial scarification to the body painting of the Picts) come to signify primarily as touches of exoticism within the determinedly patriarchal story of gender identity being written for them.[1] And yet even within this absorption of black Africans by a white European narrative of slavery and the sexual and racial relations it dictates, Behn's Imoinda somehow confounds the construction of a seamless account. Her [. . .] 'extraordinary prettiness' [is] augmented rather than lessened by 'her being carved in fine flowers and birds all over her body' (*Oronooko*, 44). Behn's pregnant Imoinda initially resembles, but ultimately diverges from, the ideal of the English mother whose employment in discourses of eighteenth-century colonialism has been so brilliantly traced by Felicity Nussbaum.[2] Her sexual history and her status as a sexually desiring subject, the active role she takes in fighting for her freedom by her husband's side, and the alien origin traced in her very skin, all mark Behn's production of her as finally—and only—Other than the white woman who tells her story.

    Imoinda's status as breeding stock in the minds of the planters is a literal exhibition of how, for women in this period, reproduction has become the only means of production. What is missing from Behn's portrait of an African woman, however, is an acknowledgement of the material bases of difference between women which slavery threw into such sharp relief. Behn recognizes gender difference within her representation of Africans, and also acknowledges the operations of gender within whiteness. As a white *woman*, Behn's narrator responds to the beauty and honorable qualities of Oronooko and [. . .] Imoinda, and is curiously powerless to intervene in the public crisis of Oronooko's capture and [. . .] public mutilation. As a *white* woman, she sails upriver and delights in displaying her undergarments to the uncomprehending Indians who inhabit Surinam's interior. But, in flattening all Imoinda's labor into sexual labor, the white narrator declines to recognise how work—sexual and otherwise—distinguished black women from white ones, resulting in her reproduction of an African woman in terms of the emerging social definitions of women of her own race.

*   *   *

Margo Hendricks, 'Civility, barbarism, and Aphra Behn's *The Widow Ranter*', in Margo Hendricks and Patricia Parker (eds.), *Women, 'Race,' and Writing in the Early Modern Period* (London and New York: Routledge, 1994), pp. 225–6, 227–9, 234–9.

We have been unable to address questions of race to any adequate degree in this book, and we are not exonerated in this deficiency by the most visible complexion of European Renaissance society. Rather, it is its very whiteness that we need to learn to see.[1]

As one of the small but growing number of scholars of color engaged in the study of Renaissance English culture and colonialism, I am heartened by the current attention being paid to early modern European racialism and racism. Yet implicit in Wayne's comment cited above is an uncomplicated assumption about what 'race' means in the early modern period. Intrinsic to this type of reasoning is a perception that early modern English people equated 'race' with color in the same way that citizens of the United States currently do. In this presumption, 'race' is used as if it were a universal paradigm rather than a mediated social practice.

In his introduction to *The Bounds of Race*, Dominick LaCapra obliquely refers to this particular linguistic inflection, arguing that 'race' has come to be a 'valorized and often unmarked center of reference'; and consequently,

> [it becomes] decidedly difficult to overcome the tendency to privilege whiteness as the master-text . . . and to identify the nonwhite as 'other' or 'different.' It is equally difficult to avoid the growing tendency to substitute a commercialized exoticism or an anodyne, commodified discourse on race for problems of racial stereotyping and oppression.[2]

Recognition of critical complicity in the transmission or reification of such ideological tendencies has generated an incipient awareness of the complex history of the idea that we call 'race.' To resist concomitantly the 'commercialized exoticism' attendant upon 'race' *and* 'make the categories of race [as well as those of class and gender] . . . historically contingent and relational rather than foundational concepts,'[3] feminist and cultural scholars cannot limit their readings to seeing the 'whiteness' of Renaissance studies. Such a move will only make more precise the ideological binarism produced by racial categories, not undo it. Rather than marking 'whiteness,' the imperative that faces cultural and feminist scholarship is theoretically and historically to map the discursive and social practices that prompted seventeenth-century Englishmen and women to define themselves not only in terms of nationalism but also, increasingly, in terms of color.

This imperative, then, is the context of my reading of Aphra Behn's *The Window Ranter*. One of the earliest professional women writers, Behn actively participated in the literary construction of late seventeenth-century English ideologies of cultural and social identity. Her relationship to the court of Charles II, as well as her own lived experiences, resulted in Behn's complex and often contradictory assumptions about race, class, and gender. Though she was politically conservative (Tory), Behn's writings reveal a social consciousness deeply affected by the colonial infrastructure of early modern capitalism. As a colonial subject and a writer complicitous in the production of English hegemonic discourses, Behn (and her writings) represents a particular resonance in early modern English culture. At a moment when 'questions of race' were complicated by English overseas expansion, Behn dramatizes the politics of a particular notion of race and its effect on English colonialism. [. . .]

The idea of civility

From its earliest engagement with the 'New World,' England strategically invoked the binarism of civility to carry out its imperial mission. In his study *Savagism and Civility*, Bernard Sheehan argues that, conceptually, this binarism construed a civilized society as definable by its sense of discipline, its religious morality, a legal system, and political authority.[4] Thus, as a value judgment, the discourse of civility always articulates a paradigm where native cultures exist as a 'primal state' in which 'savages might be either noble or ignoble, either the guardians of pristine virtue or the agents of violent disorder' but always different, always alien.[5]

In its articulation in English cultural discourses, the trope of civility draws upon very specific yet ambivalent ethnographic images of what English colonizers might expect to find in the

New World.[6] On the one hand, these narratives represented the native peoples as treacherous, lazy, religious idolaters, ignorant of civil government, and sexually licentious. On the other hand, Arthur Barlow could write in 1584, 'We found the people most gentle, loving, and faithful, void of all guile and treason and such as lived after the manner of the Golden Age.'[7] It is Thomas Harriot's view, however, which seems to reflect the habit of mind of the English who traveled to the New World:

> In respect of us they [the natives] are a people poor, and for want of skill and judgement in the knowledge and use of our things do esteem our trifles before things of greater value. . . . And . . . so much the more is it probable that they should desire our friendships and love and have the greater respect for pleasing and obeying us. Whereby may be hoped, if means of good government be used, that they may in short time be brought to civility and the embracing of true religion.[8]

The imposition of this value system, intricately intertwined with English imperial expansion, onto the native peoples of the English colonies was not without its contradictions. As Karen Kupperman writes,

> Discussion of the Indian character is complicated by the assumption that there was a native hereditary class system. The praise of Indian courtesy, dignity, and trustworthiness was often restricted to the Indian nobility. . . . What all this means is that status, not race, was the category which counted for English people of the early years of colonization. Put in its most direct form this means that it was not the case that the 'savage' was forever set apart from civilized mankind by qualities which were peculiar to him. The 'meaner sort,' the low-born, whether Indians or English, were set apart by qualities peculiar to them.[9]

English attitudes toward the American Indians in the first few decades of the colonizing project (1580s to 1620s), according to Kupperman, were shaped by the class affiliation of the narrator; thus, the ability to 'bring' the native to 'civilization' was largely dependent upon the native's social position. Kupperman goes on to argue that this view linked 'in roughly the same terms . . . English people of low status' and 'the rank and file Indians.'[10]

Though I am in general agreement with Kupperman's overall analysis, it seems to me that she ignores the centrality of 'race' to discussions of status in England's colonial discourses. In his pioneering study *The Idea of Race*, Michael Banton observes that within Western history we can map the multiple ways in which 'race' has been employed to describe personal identity—lineage, nation, typology, biology, and status. According to Banton, as a particular culture's social relations and practices changed or as nation-states from Europe extended their territorial claims across oceans, 'race' proved an effective polyseme in the process of constituting and authenticating an official explanation for social, cultural, and phenotypical differences. What becomes obvious, if the scholar steps outside her own particular historical consciousness, is the fact that a genealogy of 'race' reveals that the concept has never had a fixed meaning, but has been variable.

In its conceptual shifts, 'race' often leaves residues of previous significations to inflect current usage.[11] Kupperman's insistence that 'status' was 'the category which counted for English people,' however, seems to elide the presence of these residues. Conceptually and politically, 'race' permitted the English to explain hierarchies of lineage, status, or typology without changing the language. In other words, a writer could describe the inferiority of the Irish 'race' and the superiority of the aristocratic 'race' in the same text with little concern for conflicting meanings, since the text's audience would be expected to supply the requisite definition of the word 'race.' In this manner, the literary circulation of 'race,' unlike that of 'status,' infuses a more concrete and definitive resonance to the discourse of civility.

In a trenchant essay on 'the other question,' Homi K. Bhabha argues that it 'is the force of ambivalence that gives the colonial stereotype its currency: ensures its repeatability in changing historical discursive conjunctures; informs its strategies of individuation and marginalization.'[12] It is in the margins of such 'ambivalence' that Behn locates her dramatic depiction of [Nathaniel] Bacon's [1676] rebellion. Though Behn ends with an image of a self-consciously unified English settlement, she begins with the drama of a class-based division among the English. And this 'drama' is displayed along a familiar early modern racial grid—an anxiety about lineage. [. . .]

Before concluding my reading of *The Widow Ranter*, I want to look at the interlinking of miscegenation and the idea of civility in Behn's play. [. . .] Early in the play the audience learns that Bacon's 'Thirst of Glory cherish'd by sullen Melancholy . . . was the first motive that made him in love with the young Indian Queen, fancying no Hero ought to be without his Princess' (I.i). On the one hand, literary convention can help us understand why Behn consciously elects not to represent Bacon's actual wife in the play: romantic love in Restoration comedy rarely takes place in marriage since the phenomenon is about courtship. On the other hand, however, literary convention cannot explain why Behn chooses to construct a miscegenous relationship. Behn's construction of the fantasy of Semernia, I believe, serves to deflect a very real anxiety in the racial ideology of English colonialism—unrestrained English female sexuality.

In an instance of form(al) mediation, Semernia, as an American Indian, displaces the unmarried upper-class English woman as the object of upper-class masculine erotic desire. In much of colonial English ethnography, American Indian women were stereotyped as sexually active and aggressive. In *A Map of Virginia*, one of the narrators reports that the women of Powhatan's nation 'solemnly invited [John] Smith to their lodging; but no sooner was he within the house but all these nymphs more tormented him than ever with crowding and pressing and hanging upon him, most tediously crying, "Love you not me?" '[13] William Strachey reported that American Indian men permitted their wives full sexual freedom, arguing 'uncredible yt is, with what heat both Sexes of them are given over to those Intemperances, and the men to preposterous Venus, for which they are full of their owne country-disease (the Pox) very young.'[14]

It is this 'baggage' which Behn cannot displace in her representation of Semernia, though the Englishwoman tries. As Behn draws her, Semernia's 'Indianness' is concealed by the rhetoric of a conventionalized version of English femininity. Semernia is virtuous, attractive, loyal, honorable, and she is in love with the heroic Bacon. Confiding in her servant Anaria, the Queen gives expression to the struggle between her passions and her reason: 'Twelve tedious Moons I pass'd in silent Languishment; Honour endeavouring to destroy my Love, but all in vain' (V.iii). Though married to Cavernio, Semernia is not unaffected by the presence of Bacon. When the Englishman describes, with a 'faltring' tongue, the effects of love—'It makes us tremble when we touch the fair one; . . . the Heart's surrounded with a feeble Languishment, the eyes are dying, and the Cheeks are pale' (II.i)—Semernia's reaction mirrors Bacon's words:

'I'll talk no more, our Words exchange our Souls, and every Look fades all my blooming Honour' (II.i).

As a married woman, Semernia recognizes the 'symptoms' as something to fear, and she quickly seeks the protective standard of virtuous distance. In fact, to guard her 'honour,' Semernia exhorts Bacon to take 'all our Kingdoms—make our People slaves, and let me fall beneath your conquering Sword: but never let me hear you talk again, or gaze upon your Eyes' (II.i). By the play's conclusion, Bacon's desire to possess Semernia does exact the enormous toll her prophetic words bespeak. In the end, her husband-king dead, her people dispossessed and slaughtered, Semernia's dilemma is resolved when Bacon mistakenly kills the Queen. The American Indian woman's body has channeled male interest until the Englishwomen can be safely engaged or wedded.

With Semernia's death, Behn effectively brings to closure her narrative of the romance. Bacon's death is somewhat anti-climactic: he commits suicide after successfully routing the Jamestown forces allied against him. Nonetheless, the play ends with two significant articulations. The first is the imposition of a class hierarchy among the English settlers. The army which pursued Bacon was composed of both gentry and lower-class men, and their class differences become resolved in pursuit of a common enemy. Even so, the play concludes with the Acting Governor dislodging Justices Whiff and Whimsey—'your Places in the Council shall be supplied by these Gentlemen of Sense and Honour' (V.v).

The second articulation of Behn's narration occurs just after Bacon slays Semernia. The General claims, 'There ends my Race of Glory and of Life' (V.iii). Behn's ambiguous use of the word 'Race' produces two parallel readings. In the first instance, 'Race' straightforwardly signals the end of Bacon's ambitious endeavor. On a second and more ideological level, Bacon's words are much more revealing of a cultural anxiety about miscegenation if we read 'Race' as a reference to lineage. In what follows I want to make a case for the second reading in light of the discourse of civility.

Bacon's rhetoric dramatizes the anxiety concerning the acquisition and transmission of property that circulates within the discourse of 'race.' In an earlier statement, Bacon declared that Semernia was 'the dear Prize, for which alone he toil'd!' (V.iii). If we link his use of the word 'toil'd' with his earlier declaration to 'defend every inch of Land,' Bacon's pursuit of Semernia takes on the rhetoric of property. Symbolically, Bacon's pursuit is about the English efforts to acquire American Indian lands. In a letter, John Winthrop argued, 'That which lies common, and hath never beene replenished or subdued is free to any that possesse and improve it.'[15] If we read Bacon's pursuit of Semernia as parallel to his efforts to possess American Indian lands, then it is not inappropriate to extrapolate a reading that sees both the woman and the lands as the 'property' of another person, in this case Cavernio.

The acquisition of Semernia not only would signify Bacon's mastery of the American Indians (including their enslavement) and what they control but also the English man's right to lay claim to the American Indian female body. In Bacon's colonialist endeavors, Cavernio stands between the Englishman's accumulation of property—whether lands or the object of his erotic desire, Semernia. Given that Semernia is the wife of Cavernio and, in the context of early modern English ideologies regarding marriage, 'belongs' to him, Bacon's actions represent an encroachment upon the property of the American Indian. The 'warrior prince,' far from being civilized, symbolizes social disorder and immorality. Yet from the English perspective, Bacon's position is typical of a general colonialist attitude.

It is this ambivalent racial inscription which makes Behn's *The Widow Ranter* a deeply troubling text. By framing the discourse of civility in a miscegenous romance, Behn doubly insures the eradication of the American Indians, but at the expense of obscuring the problematic paradox of Bacon's undertaking. Should Semernia become the 'property' of Bacon (whether as his wife or his mistress), any offspring are of Bacon's 'Race.' What better way to shift the balance of power in the New World than by increasing dramatically the number of sympathetic natives who identify with a patrilineal authority and culture? More importantly, what better way to achieve this goal than through sexual and marital relations with American Indian women?

In her able study, Mary Dearborn argues that one of the 'single most important received metaphor[s] of female ethnic identity' is 'the story of Pocahontas.'[16] This myth lies at the very center of Behn's depiction of Semernia, altered, however, to meet the objectives of the late seventeenth-century colonizing project. What this 'metaphor of female ethnic identity' tells us is that, from the standpoint of the civilizing mission propounded by the English, miscegenation is both desirable *and* dangerous. And, given the overall objective of early modern English colonialism, the danger far outweighed the pleasures.

Miscegenation threatens the idea of assimilation that lies at the heart of civility. Unlike genocide, miscegenation can (and often does) result in the proliferation of 'natives' who reject 'civility.'[17] What is more frightening, from the standpoint of the colonizers, is the possibility that the 'savage' would come to dominate both in numbers and in culture.[18] If miscegenation could 'civilize,' could it not also create 'savages' who preferred polygamy or a communal existence based on the absence of competition and greed?[19] Furthermore, if miscegenation erases the boundaries between the English and the American Indians, what then becomes of the ineradicable measure of 'difference' required to justify the colonizing project?

Ultimately, it was the loss of 'Englishness' within an erotic, miscegenous space of 'civilized conquest' that most alarmed the colonizers. As Bacon pursues Semernia, is he civilized man or 'savage' native? Do we excuse Bacon's blatant disregard of the Christian prohibitions against adultery, lust, and murder because the individuals who provoked this behavior were considered 'savages'? Or, do we condemn him for his failure to remain a 'true' Englishman? Finally, when Bacon takes his own life for love of an American Indian woman—'Come, my good Poison, like that of Hannibal; long I have born a noble Remedy for all the Ills of Life. I have too long surviv'd my Queen and Glory' (V.iv)—has he succumbed to 'Indian savagism'? Or is his death the return of his 'English civility'?

As Behn writes it, what seemed most important to the colonial project was unity among the English, as Bacon's last words indicate: 'Now while you are Victors, make a Peace—with the English Council, and never let Ambition,—Love,—or Interest, make you forget, as I have done, your Duty and Allegiance' (V.v). [. . .]

The discourse of civility allowed Behn to invent an 'American Indian' who is both assimilable and unequivocally alien. Behn drew upon existing racialist ideologies and, in incorporating them into the discourse of civility, produced a new discourse that spoke to unalterable differences that were not easily exoticized. In creating *The Widow Ranter*, she unconsciously exposes the principal contradiction of her class-based discourse of civility: aristocratic civility is incompatible with colonialism and imperialism. However, when the discourse of civility is constructed upon a racialized binarism, as is the case with *The Widow Ranter*, then the justifications for genocide, cultural hegemony, and slavery become more easily enunciated and defensible.

Homi Bhabha argues, 'the objective of colonial discourse is to construe the colonized as a population of degenerate types on the basis of racial origin, in order to justify conquest and to establish systems of administration and instruction.'[20] As 'race' becomes imbricated in the geopolitics of early modern England, then the moral impetus of ideologies such as civility becomes a sailor's knot, tightening its hold not on the American Indians but on the English immigrants. The 'most visible complexion' of 'race' in the early modern English discourse, to return to Valerie Wayne's observation, is indelibly etched not in color but in the paradox of civility. Only when the concept of civility proves to be an ideological contradiction in the colonial project does the idea of 'race' shift its meaning.

In the end, while the African woman's body became the primary locus for the economic enactment of English imperialism in the Americas from the eighteenth century onward, the American Indian woman functioned as the initial register for a discourse of 'race' where color fixed difference. Thus, while the phenotypical differences between the American Indians and the English, in the English racial consciousness, were not as stark as the differences between Africans and English, they were important to the construction of a newer racial ideology. Essentially, and this is where I diverge from scholars such as Kupperman, the differences were enough to produce a binarism of inferiority/superiority.

Ultimately, the task that faces Renaissance scholars is not just to make visible the 'whiteness' that is presumed to be the center of the concept, as Wayne has argued. Rather, we must begin to question the implicit racial assumptions being reread as a homogeneous society attempts to extend its hegemony beyond its own geographic boundaries. How does that society mark itself as different from the peoples it wishes to conquer? What effect does this marking have on the conquerors' own sense of identity? Only when we address these issues shall we begin to see the real property of the idea of 'race.' And perhaps, there will no longer be a need to 'exonerate.'

* * *

David Scott Kastan, 'Is there a class in this (Shakespearean) text?', *Renaissance Drama* 25 (1993), 101–7, 114.

We be men and nat aungels, wherefore we know nothinge but by outward significations.

Thomas Elyot

Money changes everything

Cyndi Lauper

At least two considerations may prevent a quick and confident 'yes' to my titular question. The first is perhaps the more easily confronted. Historians have usefully reminded us that the language of class relations applied to the social formation of early modern England is an anachronism.[1] Indeed 'class' is a nineteenth-century analytic category and as such was obviously conceptually unavailable to the people of Tudor and Stuart England.[2] But their own social vocabularies of 'estate' or 'degree,' while insisting on social differentiation on the basis of status rather than on the basis of income and occupation, no less powerfully testify to a system of social inequality that the concept of class would help articulate and analyze. Classes, in the most precise economic definition, perhaps can be said to come into being only within the social conditions of bourgeois production, but classes, in their abstract social sense, can be seen to have existed as long as social organization has permitted an unequal distribution of property, privilege, and power. [. . .]

It may well be, then, that any anxiety about the deployment of the language of class in the discussion of Shakespeare's plays is an unnecessary scruple. Even if the culture did not experience its social relations overtly as class relations, certainly social stratification and the tensions resulting from the forms of inequality are evident in the plays and can be usefully examined. Hymen, at the end of *As You Like It*, announces the delight of the gods 'when earthly things [are] made even' (5.4.109), but the plays again and again reveal that to be a delusive hope or a utopian dream, belied by social differentiation and conflict, that is, belied precisely by an *unevenness* that is reproduced both on stage and in the playhouse itself. Like the Chorus in *Henry V* who imagines the socially diverse Elizabethan audience as 'gentles all' (1 Cho. 8), the king addresses his troops as 'a band of brothers' (4.3.63), all 'gentled' in their shared enterprise, but the resistant reality of social difference is made clear in the body count at Agincourt:

> Where is the number of our English dead?
> Edward the Duke of York, the Earl of Suffolk,
> Sir Richard Keighley, Davy Gam esquire:
> None else of name, and of all other men
> But five and twenty.
>
> (4.7.100–04)

Even in the leveling of death, twenty-five of Henry's 'brothers' retain their subaltern anonymity. In *Coriolanus*, Menenius's fable of the Belly idealizes the body politic as a harmoniously ordered whole, but Menenius immediately undermines his own corporate image: 'Rome and her rats are at the point of battle' (1.1.161). The familiar fable here offers not a full articulation of the Roman polity but a tactical advantage for a privileged segment of it. Menenius buys time for Marcius's arrival to quell the uprising, and the tendentiousness of the elaborated analogy is revealed in the slide from imagining Rome as a unified, if differentiated, social body of patricians *and* plebs to seeing Rome only as its patricians and needing to defend itself from the 'rats' that would feed upon it.

Yet even if 'class' can be more or less happily accepted as an effective heuristic if not a properly historical category to describe and analyze the stratification of social relations in these plays (as well as in early modern England itself), a more problematic issue still remains to be addressed. The question 'is there a class in this text?' cannot be answered merely by assessing the propriety of the analytic vocabulary. If the question were (to quote Mary Jacobus) 'is there a woman in this text?'[3] the continuing difficulty emerges clearly. Certainly women's roles are written into Shakespeare's plays, but boy actors were, of course, required to play the female parts; so the answer must be both 'yes' and 'no.' Women are prescribed but were themselves not present on stage; they were *represented* in the transvestite acting tradition of the popular Elizabethan theater. To speak of the women in Shakespeare's plays is, then, to speak not of women as historical subjects but only of the heavily mediated representation of women that the commercial theater offered: male actors, speaking words written by a male writer, enacting female roles. Increasingly, therefore, we have come to see the need to analyze not simply 'the women in Shakespeare' but their representation. In a significant sense, there are no women, only males playing 'the woman's part.' If these 'parts' have something significant to say about women in early modern England, it is, then, not least because of the mediations that make them present.

But if a transvestite acting tradition determines the presentation of women on the stage, a similar fissure between the represented object and the representing agent affects the presentation of class. Plays may well present a variety of class locations (and locutions), but they are, of course, all themselves mediated by the modes of representation in the theater.[4] Though kings and clowns notoriously mingled on the English Renaissance stage, kings and clowns were not themselves present, only the actors that played them. In 1602, Richard Vennar of Lincoln's Inn attempted to resolve, or at least reduce, the problematic of class representation by offering an aristocratic historical pageant, *England's Joy*, to be enacted at the Swan, as the playbill announced, 'only by certain gentlemen and gentlewomen of account' (Chambers 3: 500). Vennar's promise of gentle instead of common players would not, of course, have fully closed the gap between those who are represented and those who represent, but it would at least have avoided any severe social dislocation between the two. But Vennar never produced his play, attempting to run off with the considerable receipts without ever performing it (and leaving the theater to be sacked by the outraged audience). In the commercial theater, however, aristocratic roles were not performed by 'gentlemen and gentlewomen,' nor were the actions of royalty represented, as the Chorus in *Henry V* desires, with 'Princes to act.' Actors of lower social rank, of course, mimed their social betters. Stephen Gosson, in his *Playes Confuted in Fiue Actions*, says that the players were 'either men of occupations . . . or common minstrals, or trained up from their childhood to this abominable exercise' (sig. G6v), though some of these 'glorious vagabonds,' as the academic authors of the *Parnassus* plays noted contemptuously, achieved an underserved social eminence: 'With mouthing words that better wits have framed, / They purchase lands, and now Esquiers are made' (*2 Return from Parnassus*, lines 1927–28). Class positions, then, appear on Shakespeare's stage exactly as women do, only in the mediations of a transvestite acting tradition. The oft-noted crossdressing of the Renaissance stage unnervingly crossed class as well as gender lines; not only did boy actors play women but commoners played kings.

In recent years, feminist scholarship has powerfully, if variously, considered the implications of crossdressing both in and outside of the theater for understanding the Renaissance sex-gender system,[5] but little attention has been paid to the implications of crossdressing for understanding the socioeconomic ordering of Elizabethan and Stuart England. 'How many people crossdressed in early modern England?' (95), Jean Howard has recently asked; and while she admits that the number must have been 'limited,' her estimate must be considerably revised upward if we include transgressions of class identity as well as of gender.

If sexual crossdressing, like that of the notorious Mary Frith, was seen as scandalously bizarre, social crossdressing was seen as dangerously common. Regularly protest was heard against the 'mingle mangle,' as Philip Stubbes called it, produced by this social transvestism, 'so that it is verie hard to knowe, who is noble, who is worshipful, who is a gentleman, who is not' (sig. C2v). In addition to five 'Acts of Apparel,' at least nineteen proclamations to regulate dress were issued in Tudor England in order to preclude 'the confusion . . . of degrees' that results 'where the meanest are as richly appareled as their betters' (Hughes and Larkin 3: 175).[6] Though these sumptuary laws clearly were written for economic as well as political motives, being in part designed to cut down on imported luxuries and to protect the English wool trade by restricting the market for imported fabrics, the deep anxiety they voice about the 'unmeasurable disorder' that crossdressing might bring about is unmistakable. The proclamation of 1559 laments 'the wearing of such excessive and inordinate apparel as in no age hath been seen the like' (Hughes and Larkin 2: 136). People did crossdress and in considerable numbers, and the state strove to prohibit it, acutely aware that such crossdressing threatened the carefully constructed hierarchical social order of early modern England. Regulation of dress was necessary to mark and secure social difference, in order to prevent, as William Perkins writes, 'a confusion of such degrees and callings as God hath ordained, when as men of inferiour degree and calling, cannot be by their attire discerned from men of higher estate' (sig. GG2v). Or, as Gosson wrote in 1582, 'if priuat men be suffered to forsake theire calling because they desire to walke gentlemanlike in sattine & velvet, with a buckler at theire heeles, proportion is so broken, unitie dissolued, harmony confounded & the whole body must be dismembered and the prince or the heade cannot chuse but sicken' (sig. G7v). 'Many good Lawes haue been made against this Babylonian confusion,' remarked Fynes Moryson, 'but either the Merchants buying out the penaltie, or the Magistrates not inflicting punishments, have made the multitude of Lawes hitherto unprofitable' (*Itinerary* 4: 233–4).

But social crossdressing, legally prohibited on the streets of London, was of course the very essence of the London stage. Actors crossdressed with every performance, and although the early Tudor iterations of the sumptuary laws specifically exempted 'players in enterludes' from its edict, none of the Elizabethan proclamations restating them mentions this exemption.[7] On stage, men of 'inferior degree' unnervingly counterfeited their social betters, imitating not merely their language and gestures but their distinctive apparel. If there was no effort to produce historically accurate representations (recall Henry Peacham's drawing of the scene from *Titus Andronicus*), the stage did attempt to provide convincing representations of social rank. Philip Henslowe's wardrobe contained such gorgeous items as 'a scarlett cloke with ii brode gould Laces: w^t gould byttens of the same downe the sids,' another in 'scarlett w^t buttens of gould fact w^t blew velvett,' and 'a crimosin Robe strypt w^t gould fact w^t ermin' (*Diary* 291–2). Edward Alleyn apparently paid more than twenty pounds for a 'black velvet cloak with sleeves embroidered all with silver and gold.' But if such dress obviously permitted a lavish aristocratic display, its wearing was arguably criminal. The 1597 proclamation on apparel prohibited the wearing of 'cloth of gold or silver . . . or cloth mixed or embroidered with pearl, gold, or silver' to any 'under the degree of a baron, except Knights of the Garter [and] Privy Councilors to the Queen's majesty' and denied the wearing of velvet 'in gowns, cloaks, coats, or other uppermost garments' to all 'under the degree of a knight, except gentlemen in ordinary office attending upon her majesty in her house or chamber, such as have been employed in embassage to foreign princes, the son and heir apparent of a knight, captains in her majesty's pay, and such as may dispend £200 by the year for term of life in possession above all charges' (Hughes and Larkin 3: 176).

Understandably, then, the theater, with its constitutive transgressions, was a politically charged arena in an age when social identities and relations seemed distressingly unstable, an instability in part constituted by the contradictory definition of status, as in the proclamation, both in terms of rank (a knight or baron) and in terms of wealth ('such as may dispend £200 by the year'). This contradiction reveals the vulnerability of the traditional culture based on hierarchy and deference to the transformative entrepreneurial energies of a nascent capitalism; and in the antitheatrical tracts that proliferated after the building of the Theatre in 1576 and the Curtain in 1577 the cultural anxiety about the fluidity of social role and identity found shrill voice. The oft-cited Deuteronomic prohibition (22.5) against males wearing female dress was regularly linked to a fear of social inferiors aping their betters. Gosson finds it equally objectionable that in the theater a boy would 'put one the attyre, the gesture, the passions' of a woman and that 'a meane person' would 'take vpon him the title of a Prince with counterfeit port, and traine' (*Playes Confuted*, sig. E5r). William Rankins, in his hysterical account of the monstrous contaminations of playing, insists that 'Players ought not amidst their folly present the persons of Princes' (sig. C3r). But anxiety was directed not merely at dressing 'up,' at the potential derogation of authority that its miming might effect; it was equally directed at dressing 'down' (Rankins is as worried about the counterfeiting of rustics as he is of royalty). What was worrisome was that class positions could be mimed at all.

Though Stephen Greenblatt, following Tom Laqueur's work on Renaissance anatomical knowledge, provocatively sees the transvestite acting tradition of the pre-Restoration stage as the inevitable result of a culture whose idea of gender was 'teleologically male' (88), viewed from the perspective of class rather than gender, a theater dependent upon cross dressing seems notably less inevitable or natural and perhaps more profoundly unsettling to the fundamental social categories of the culture. If the theater is not, as Jonas Barish enthusiastically claims, guilty of an 'ontological subversiveness' (331), at least in the context of the social anxieties of late sixteenth-century England the theater, with its shape-shifting of professional actors, was indeed a threat to the culture of degree. Acting threatened to reveal the artificial and arbitrary nature of social being. The constitutive role-playing of the theater demystifies the idealization of the social order that the ideology of degree would produce. The successful counterfeiting of social rank raises the unnerving possibility that social rank is a counterfeit, existing 'but as the change of garments' in a play, in Walter Ralegh's telling phrase. In the theaters of London, if not in the *theatrum mundi*, class positions are exposed as something other than essential facts of human existence, revealed, rather, as changeable and constructed. When 'every man wears but his own skin, the Players,' as Ralegh writes, 'are all alike' (147).

But if role-*playing* intellectually challenged the would-be stable and stabilizing social hierarchy, the role-*players* were themselves perhaps a greater social threat.[8] If the actors' ability to represent a full range of social roles disturbingly identified these *as* roles, the actors' conspicuous existence in society exposed the instability of the social categories themselves. Their success was perhaps the most visible of the contradictions that daily belied the fantasy of a stable social hierarchy. The actors' extravagant presence on the streets of London, no less than the substantial amphitheaters that they were able to erect, was an unmistakable sign of the vulnerability of the traditional culture of status to the transformative energies of capitalistic practice. [. . .]

If it isn't quite accurate to say that the theater, with its imitative disruption of the traditional culture of status, brought that culture to an end, certainly the theater's conspicuous presence signaled its vulnerability to dissolution in the transformative energies of the nascent capitalism of early modern England; and if it isn't quite accurate to say that the entrepreneurial successes of the acting companies actually brought 'class' into being, certainly in the visible signs of their abundant energies and aspirations they brought class into view.

* * *

Thomas Healy, 'Selves, states, and sectarianism in early modern England', *English*, 44 (1995), 195, 198–99.

[W]hat predominantly fashions the imagined communities of the integrated self or state—the supposed wide horizontal comradeship of this age—is a sectarian identity, usually founded on religious difference. Further, it is precisely this sectarianism which promotes the doubleness and alienation [Richard] Helgerson notes in the writings emerging from these communities.[1] [. . .] The more claims to wholeness are made in the language of self-definition, the more forces are recognised, within and without the imagined national community, which disrupt a sectarian rhetoric's claim to accurate, hegemonic, self-representation. [. . .]

[. . .] In its portrayal of Roman Catholicism in foreign, and, so it was believed, irreligious environments, the commercial drama of the late sixteenth and seventeenth centuries presents an otherness to Protestant identities, providing spectacles by which the integrity of the self and state can be interrogated within locations imagined as different from England, yet in terms defined by Protestant assumptions: locations where the alien quality of the reprobate 'other' can be carefully managed. [. . .] [A] supernatural organisation of the world which saw constant attempts by the forces of the Antichrist to challenge the godly, and which believed the majority of humanity necessarily damned, found cultural expression in plays which exploit the implications of these conditions. [. . .] It is [. . .] important to recognise how the pervading cultural mentality of Protestantism influenced plays, ones designed for popular entertainment, which enact the anxieties engendered by Roman Catholic reprobate alterity. Although this was a religion some of the audience still professed—others might recall from familial acquaintance, and still others, probably the majority, would feel unclear about in terms of doctrinal tenets—this drama reflects a social and emotional consensus about Catholic alterity derived from the dominant Protestant ideology's perspective on what it perceived as a reprobate religion [. . .] . In doing so, this drama promoted sectarian identification with an English perspective and helped consolidate the imagined border by which the national community distinguishes itself from that which lies outside. At the same time, it enticed involvement with what was being enacted, drawing attention to an alterity which remained resonate for the spectators because its otherness was not incomprehensibly alien. Its characters, after all, spoke the language, looked like, and frequently directly addressed the audience.

* * *

Alan Bray, 'Homosexuality and the signs of male friendship in Elizabethan England', *History Workshop*, 29 (1990), 2–3.

Elizabethan society was one which lacked the idea of a distinct homosexual minority, although homosexuality was none the less regarded with a readily expressed horror. In principle it was a crime which anyone was capable of, like murder or blasphemy. . . . It was, according to John Rainolds, not only a 'monstrous sin against nature' but also one to which 'men's natural corruption and viciousness is prone'. It is why it was sometimes attributed to drunkenness and why a sixteenth century minister accused of sodomy said when first confronted that what he had done he had done in his sleep. . . . It was not part of the individual's nature: it was part of all human nature and could surface when the mind was dulled or sleeping, much as someone might commit murder in a drunken fit or in a dream.

*   *   *

Valerie Traub, *Desire and Anxiety: Circulations of Sexuality in Shakespearean Drama* (London and New York: Routledge, 1992), pp. 94–116.

[W]hat is at stake when gender difference is signified through the sign of heterosexual inter-course, as in the work of feminist Lacanian Jacqueline Rose;[1] or when critics use synonymously such terms as sexual difference and sexual identity, androgyny and bisexuality, femininity/masculinity and heterosexuality? The difficulty most readers will have in even *identifying* a problem is precisely the problem. I hasten to point out that the first term in each of the above pairings (i.e., sexual difference, androgyny, femininity/masculinity) denotes a *gender* relation and the second term (sexual identity, bisexuality, heterosexuality) an *erotic* one. In other words, gender and sexuality pose as synonymous in our critical discourse in a way that not only despecifies our analyses but denies and delegitimates erotic difference. Whose interests are served by this denial of difference?

In 'Thinking Sex: Notes for a Radical Theory of the Politics of Sexuality,' Gayle Rubin challenges

> the assumption that feminism is or should be the privileged site of a theory of sexuality. Feminism is the theory of gender oppression. To automatically assume that this makes it the theory of sexual oppression is to fail to distinguish between gender, on the one hand, and erotic desire, on the other.[2]

The preceding examples make it clear, I hope, that feminists need to theorize more accurately the specific relations between gender and sexuality, beginning by questioning the assump-tions that this relationship is isomorphic and historically constant. For the purposes of dissect-ing this relationship, we must be willing to place sexuality at the center, rather than on the implied periphery, of our analyses, and only after that (1) detail the way *specific* erotic dis-courses and practices are informed by or associated with gender discourses and practices, and (2) analyze how race, ethnicity, and class differences inform the relationship between sexuality and gender at specific moments in time. To assume that gender *predicates* eroticism is to ignore the contradictions that have historically existed between these two inextricably related yet independent systems. While they are always connected, there is no simple fit between them. Gender # sexuality.[3]

Feminists, materialist feminists, cultural materialists, and new historicists implicitly draw on a psychoanalytic construct whenever they pose the question of 'desire.' 'Desire,' like 'power,' has taken on a certain currency in contemporary critical discourse, in part because the popularization of Lacanian psychoanalysis has offered so much to two broadly defined readerships: to gender critics, Lacanians offer a reading of the simultaneous construction of gender and sexuality that problematizes even as it upholds patriarchal prerogatives; to historical critics, Lacanians offer a theory of the radical contingency of a speaking subject always constructed through social practices. The psychoanalytic construct 'desire' combines these concerns into a tripartite structure of a radically discontinuous subjectivity, gender, and sexuality, in which the unruliness of the unconscious undercuts the subject's pretensions to self-identity.

According to the psychoanalytic narrative, subjectivity, gender, and sexuality are constituted contemporaneously. I want to argue that it is precisely the capacity of 'desire' to connote this mutual complicity and constitutiveness that has rendered it such a powerful, provocative, and perversely hegemonic construct. Perversely hegemonic because, despite its disruptive Lacanian valences, 'desire' often works as a totalization that conceals the dynamic divisions inherent in its construction: rather than holding the specificity of gender and sexuality in mutual tension, it conflates and then collapses them into the supposedly larger matrix of subjectivity.

For instance, discussions regarding the meaning of female presence and the possibility of female power in early modern texts often hinge on assumptions about 'feminine desire.' By relying on a Lacanian revision of the Freudian dictate that there is only one 'libido' (a masculine one), in which the structural exigencies of phallocentrism not only delimit but deny the possibility of 'feminine desire,' some critics come perilously close to writing out of representation and history all female agency.[4] By focusing their analyses on 'woman' only as she is positioned within a supposedly monolithic symbolic order, critics lose sight of the degree of agency constructed from the contradictions and fissures within the symbolic. For it is in the schism between 'woman-as-representation' and the plurality of women that a negotiation for power within and against the phallocentric order takes place.[5]

However, merely to reassert the presence of female agency in the form of 'feminine desire' is not an adequate response to the problem of women's subjectivity. First, any assertion of agency must address those constraints placed on women's lives by the conceptual and material demarcations of a phallocentric system. But secondly (and this is my main concern), reinserting 'feminine desire' into discourse reinscribes women's eroticism as always already defined and reified by the gender category 'feminine.' The adjectival link between 'feminine' and 'desire' neutralizes the difference between an ascribed gendered subject-position and the erotic experiences and expressions of a female subject. In a move that obscures the constructedness of subjectivity, gender, and sexuality, the female subject is defined in terms of a desire that is implicitly passive, heterosexually positioned in relation to man. Generated as an appeal, 'feminine desire' in fact operates as a trick, a double bind for women always already confined by their previous definition. *How* a woman's sexuality is positioned in accordance to gender ascriptions, and the possibility of *resistance* to that positionality are questions foreclosed by the appeal to 'feminine desire.'

This mutually referential circularity of gender and sexuality in our critical discourse not surprisingly can be traced to Freud. In his attempt to advance over late nineteenth-century sexologists by dividing sexuality into three independent variables—physical characteristics, mental characteristics, and object choice—Freud implicitly recognized the possibility of conflict between biological inheritance, gender role behaviour, and erotic identification.[6]

And yet, in spite of this theoretical move toward greater specification, in practice Freud continued to conflate gender and sexuality, and to link both to biological inheritance. Despite his well-known disclaimer that passivity is not the exclusive province of women, nor aggressiveness the sole prerogative of men, Freud reproduced precisely these gender determinisms to connote erotic positioning and style. This becomes most evident when, in his case histories, the signifiers for male homosexuality become 'effeminacy' and 'passivity,' and for lesbianism, 'masculinity' and 'activity.'[7] Consider the following statement:

> [I]t is just those girls who in the years before puberty showed a *boyish character and inclinations* who tend to become hysterical at puberty. In a whole series of cases the hysterical neurosis is nothing but an excessive over-accentuation of the typical wave of repression through which *the masculine type of sexuality is removed and the woman emerges*.[8]

In this remark we can see two characteristic moves. First, through a rhetorical sleight-of-hand, the phrase 'masculine type of sexuality' collapses into one construct precisely those components Freud had taken such pains to distinguish. In its relationship to 'boyish character and inclinations,' the phrase 'masculine type of sexuality' refers to what Freud called sexual attitude or character (gender role conformity); in its relationship to sexuality, the phrase refers to homoerotic object choice. In the second rhetorical conflation, 'woman' in the final clause becomes the sign, not only of proper gender role behavior, but heterosexual object choice. Both gender role conformity and heterosexuality correspond to the essential woman. Likewise, the young boy who expresses a 'feminine attitude' takes on a 'passive role' toward a male object,[9] the desire to be touched on his genitals rather than be the agent of phallic penetration is a 'passive aim.' '[P]assive homosexuals,' according to Freud, 'play the part of the woman in sexual relations.'[10]

The vocabulary employed by Freud demonstrates that, theoretical protestations to the contrary, his work is caught within a nineteenth-century paradigm of 'inversion' which assumes that 'normal' heterosexuality follows unproblematically from ascribed gender role, and that disruptions in gender role result in deviant object choice. Despite the gender of the persons involved, Freud's concept of homoeroticism (like his concept of heterosexuality) is based on a gender model of 'masculine' activity and 'feminine' passivity.

Whenever critics use 'desire' to refer simultaneously to gender and eroticism, we implicitly reassert this dualistic, patriarchal, normalizing history inherent in 'desire's' formulation. Even when no explicit reference to 'desire' is made, critics often unwittingly follow Freud in referring *gender* conflict (whether between men and women, or within a woman) to *bisexuality*. Consider, for example, the following statement by Karen Newman, in her otherwise brilliant analysis of ambivalence toward female power in *The Taming of the Shrew*: 'We might even say that this conflict [between female speech and silence] shares the *bi-sexuality* Freud claims for the hysterical symptom, that the text itself is *sexually ambivalent*.'[11] Newman is arguing that *The Taming of the Shrew* empowers Kate, even as it subordinates her, by putting the power of speech (even if it is an encomium to subordination) in her own mouth. Such an argument is largely persuasive—except when it is led, via Freud, to conflate gender and sexuality. Whatever *gender* ambivalence the text expresses, it is distinct from the text's consistently *non-ambiguous* definition of female erotic desire as the projection and fulfillment of male heterosexual fantasy. In *The Taming of the Shrew*, female desire is encoded as the desire-of-the-man.

While many gender and historical critics remain caught within the circularity of this conflation of gender and eroticism, gay and lesbian cultural analysts are asserting a counter-discourse of 'desire.' In this discourse, gender and eroticism not only are explicitly differentiated, but each is given greater specificity, and both are referred back to their cultural origins. As in psychoanalytic literature, gender is conceived as a matter of core gender identity (the persistent experience of oneself as male, female, or ambivalent: I am a man, I am a woman, I am both/neither), but the 'core' here does not pre-exist representation; rather, it is constructed through representation, specifically through the acquisition of language and clothing which are gender encoded. In addition, gender is a matter of gender *role* (the degree to which one complies with the societal expectations of 'appropriate' behavior) and gender *style* (the personal choices one makes daily to assert agency within the confines of gender). Generally believed to be in place by the age of three, core gender identity is the least flexible of these constructs. Although it is usually 'consistent' with anatomical sex,[12] transsexuals demonstrate not only the occasional fallibility of this process but also the highly inflexible nature of core gender identity once it is constituted. Gender role, while also ascribed by culture, is open to greater improvisation as each child positions him/herself in relationship to activities culturally coded (and historically variable) as 'masculine' or 'feminine.' Gender style is an even more personal matter, and can be complicit with or in contradiction to one's gender role behaviour. The difference between gender role behaviour and individual gender style can be understood by recognizing that a woman who identifies as 'feminine' might choose to wear jeans, work boots, and a leather jacket without disrupting her own sense of gender role (whatever it might do to others' expectations). Most feminists, it could be argued, are feminists precisely because their core gender identity (woman) does not correspond to many conventional social expectations of the 'feminine'; even so, there is a great deal of variety in our gender styles.

Eroticism, like gender, is also given greater differentiation in this counter-discourse. Most importantly, eroticism is defined as independent of gender identity, behavior, and style. As a recent article in *Outlook* put it: 'Wearing high heels during the day does not mean you're a femme at night, passive in bed, or closeted on the job.'[13] Of course, there are periods in history when wearing high heels is an erotic signifier—indeed, in the 1940s and 1950s North American 'butch-femme' lesbian culture, high heels were erotic signifiers of the first degree (as they were, for that matter, in North American culture generally). But what they signified within that context—passivity, availability, self-confidence, sexual courage—is still a matter of debate.[14] The point is that there is no necessary connection between eroticism and gender role conformity—any connection is a matter of culturally contingent signifying practices.

Eroticism itself is increasingly being defined less as a fixed identity dependent on the gender of one's partner, and more as a dynamic mode based on the sum of one's erotic *practice*. The gender of object choice is only one variable among many, including erotic identification, fantasy, and preference for specific activities, all of which intermingle and conflict in various ways.[15] Erotic identification refers to one's sense of self as an erotic object or subject—the position one takes up at any given moment in any given erotic encounter (initiating, receiving, playful, passionate, bored, etc.). In contrast to psychoanalysis' designation of activity and passivity as rigid states of being, in this counter-discourse one's erotic identification can switch from one moment to the next, one partner to the next, one year to the next; most people do, however, have a general erotic script that provides the degree of safety mixed with excitement necessary for erotic arousal and orgasm.[16] Fantasy, obviously, has two levels, both conscious and unconscious, with conscious fantasy further distinguished by those one enacts and those one merely dreams. As Cindy Patton argues, 'fantasy and actual practice are separate and different. . . . Fantasy can retain qualities of ambiguity, impossibility, and a connection with atemporal desire that no experience at any given moment can have.'[17] Preferences for specific activities (scenes and situations, combinations of oral, genital, and anal stimulation) and types of partners (male, female, gender-identified 'masculine' or 'feminine,' vulnerable, nurturing, aggressive, nonemotional, etc.) further differentiate and individuate each person's erotic mode.

From the perspective of this counter-discourse, psychoanalysis reduces sexuality to one variable—object choice (whether 'latent' or manifest)—which is presumed to flow directly from gender identity. The contradiction at the heart of this problem, as well as the alternatives posed by this counter-discourse, can be better understood by imagining oneself in the following voyeuristic scenario: When viewing a love scene on a movie screen, you experience pleasure by watching an interplay of power and erotic desire. Your eye is drawn to particular body zones, and you are aroused not only by body type and position, but also by the 'scene,' the pace of interaction, the affective content. But whether you are aroused by watching a woman's body or a man's, two women together or two men, a woman with a man, or any other combination imaginable, the mere fact of your excitement does not explain what is happening on the dual levels of identification and erotic desire. That is, is your arousal dependent upon a process of identification with or desire for an eroticized object? To state it simplistically, do you *want* or do you *want to be* one of the images on the screen? Which one? Can you tell? Does your identification and/or desire shift during the interaction? And are your desire and identification dependent upon the *gender* or any one of many other constituents of the image: power, class, status, age, relative aggressiveness, vulnerability, energic level, clothing, skin color/texture, hair type/length, genital size/shape . . .? Do specific acts (sucking, penetration, kissing) seem more relevant to your identification and/or desire than the gender of persons involved?

Rather than explain the manifold possibilities inherent in this phenomenon—desiring and identifying with the same gender; identifying with one gender and desiring the other; desiring both genders; desiring or identifying on some basis other than gender—psychoanalysis asserts that desire will follow gender identification. Men desire women because their gender role positions them as active; women desire men because their own 'lack' must be filled. Men who desire men do so because they have taken up a 'feminized' passive position in relation to other males; lesbians desire women in imitation of active male desire. All sexuality engages in a structurally heterosexual mode of operation based on the duality of passivity and activity: whatever your biological sex, if you identify as/with a man, then you will desire a woman, and vice versa. That this theory fails to address the presence of 'masculine' gay men and 'feminine' lesbians is only made more evident by post-Freudian efforts to differentiate between the 'true invert' and the seduced, corrupted 'pervert.'[18]

For those who actually live the contradictions inadequately addressed by psychoanalysis, the conflation of gender and sexuality is specious at best. Contemporary lesbians and gay men at various moments have constructed their own erotic significations through the use of a deviant vocabulary: 'butch, rough-fluff, and femme,' 'top/bottom,' and sign systems of hanky codes and key signals. It may seem as though the gender polarities that structure these signifying systems remain within the psychoanalytic frame of reference. Not completely, however: while butch/rough-fluff/femme designations continue to conflate gender and eroticism, they recognize an implicit continuum rather than a dichotomy of identifications, and there are no rigid assumptions structuring who can be involved with whom (i.e., a butch can be with another butch, a rough-fluff, or a femme). And, the S/M rhetoric of top/bottom asserts each individual's erotic position as a matter of play, varying with each erotic 'scene.' Similarly, the position of hankies on the hip and keys on the belt can be altered at any time.

And yet, the difficulty of extracting a new erotic vocabulary out of the polarities of gender testifies both to the enduring consequences of a highly gender-inflected language, and to the imaginative limitations of us all; we can barely conceive of an eroticism even partially free of gender constraints. At most we seem to be able to enact a politics of what Jonathan Dollimore calls transgressive reinscription, wherein dominant categories and structures are appropriated, inverted, and perverted.[19] The virtue of such a politics is that it does not defer pleasure and social change to an indefinite and impossibly pure future. But whatever the political limitations of contemporary erotic practice, the tactics employed indicate the need to push erotic theory toward the recognition that, both within an intra-psychic framework and on a systematic, structural level, the 'sex/gender system' is related to but incommensurate with sexuality. Gender, sexuality, and subjectivity are separate but intersecting discourses.

To attempt to historicize 'desire,' to tease out the mutually implicated but distinct relation between gender and eroticism, is the obvious task. Such a project involves specifying erotic discourses and practices; describing institutional delimitations on erotic practice; detailing the resistance of subjects to the ideological and material constraints upon their erotic lives; and tracing the play of erotic discourses and practices within history. Both the congruences and the contradictions between dominant ideology and material practice must undergo thorough analysis. More problematically, insofar as the material and subjective experience of the erotic can also contradict—desire, after all, is experienced not only in the contact between bodies, and between bodies and institutions, but through the experience of subjective need, want, anxiety, and fulfillment—the subjective quality of desire's historical formulation must also be approached.

The contradictions with which I am most concerned—between gender and eroticism; between dominant discourses and subversive practices; between subjective, internal need, and material, institutional pressures—all are foregrounded in the early modern British experience of homoeroticism. By 'experience' I mean to suggest the whole matrix of discourses and practices, the negotiations, interchanges, assertions, withholdings, and refusals that occurred in reference to erotic desire between members of the same gender.

Before I proceed, it is perhaps important to acknowledge that by positing the presence of homoerotic desire and anxiety in early modern society and texts, I move against the social constructivist stance that locates the advent of 'homosexuality' in either the eighteenth or the nineteenth century. [. . .] I do not mean to dispute the evidence that homosexuality in the modern sense (as a distinct mode of identity) came into being under the auspices of sexo-logical discourse. Nor do I mean to imply, as some 'essentialists' do, that the 'experience of homoeroticism' is unproblematically available to the historically inquiring eye—that it exists in some pure form, unmediated by language, political discourse, and the process of historical narrativization. I *do* mean to contest two assumptions that currently hinder historical analysis: that because of our inevitably skewed apprehension of it, early modern homoerotic experience can be treated as if it never existed; and that because neither homosexuality nor heterosexual-ity existed in the precise forms they do today, we cannot posit some form of historical connec-tion between their postmodern and early modern forms.

I thus put into play the following hypothesis: like all forms of desire, homoerotic desire is implicit within all psyches; whether and how it is given cultural expression, whether and how it is manifested as anxiety, is a matter of culturally contingent signifying practices. What is culturally specific is not the fact or presence of desire toward persons of the same gender, but the meanings that are attached to its expression, and the attendant anxieties generated by its repression. In this, I reject the dominant constructivist trend that sees specific desires as being *produced* independently by discursive practices, and return to Freud's assertion of the poly-morphous perversity and nondifferentiated nature of the infant's earliest desire. However, whereas Freud myopically focuses on the family as site of erotic development, I, like the social constructivists, emphasize the ideological character of the process of subjectification, by which the various modalities of desire are manipulated and disciplined: some are, in Foucault's terms, incited by discursive practices and institutions; some are, in the terms of psychoanalysis, dis-placed or repressed. That cultural forms that could be considered homoerotic have existed in virtually all societies argues for this erotic modality's inherent position as potentiality; that what differs from society to society is whether homoeroticism is ritualized or privatized, gender-encoded or free of gender associations, vilified, tolerated, or celebrated implies the constitu-tive import of complex and often contradictory discursive practices and social investments.[20]

The critical approaches that have been employed to address the textual representation of early modern homoeroticism have functioned in fairly conventional ways. For many years, the dominant critical discourse on homoeroticism in Shakespearean drama has been that of nar-cissism: Shakespeare's most basic identity configuration, the mirror image, has provided a fertile field for the psychoanalytic rehearsal of Freud's linkage of narcissism, paranoia, and homosexuality.[21] Whereas I agree that questions of self and other are usefully posed through the self-reflexivity of the mirror, and that narcissism, like jealousy and madness, plays an important role in the structure of dramatic conflict, I disagree that such 'identity themes' are necessarily linked to one erotic mode. I therefore question not only this model's normalizing pretensions, but also its presupposition of the object of inquiry. That is, it takes as a given what remains more properly a question: *is* there a connection between narcissism and homoerotic desire beyond the rather obvious banality of gender similitude? The commonsense proposition that heterosexual arousal depends on gender difference, whereas homoerotic excitement depends on gender sameness obscures both the implication of gender in larger systems of power and the role of difference in erotic arousal. Erotic arousal is always imbricated with power differences—it functions by means of exchanges, withholdings, struggles, negoti-ations. Arousal can be generated through the play of all kinds of differentiations: clothes, looks, gestures, ornaments, body size and type. Because of the institutionalized character of heterosexuality, gender has appeared as the sole determinant of arousal, but I suspect that gender is only one among many power differentials involved: arousal may be as motivated by the differences *within* each gender as by gender difference itself. [. . .]

Currently, the critical trend is to move away from psychoanalytic paradigms in one of two directions. First, in the model of male homosociality developed by Eve Sedgwick, male homo-erotic desire is situated in relation to male homosocial bonds and the patriarchal traffic in women.[22] This paradigm provides important access to the complex and historically varying relation between erotic and gender systems, as the structural congruity and differences between homo*social* and homo*sexual* desire engenders a thematics at once homophobic and misogynist. Although homosociality and homosexuality appear to exist on a continuum, the former is constituted by a disavowal, indeed, a violent repudiation, of the latter. Homosociality in fact underscores patriarchal heterosexuality. Precisely because of the focus on homosocial-ity, however, in Sedgwick's work the specific *sexuality* of homoerotic *practice* is elided. Draw-ing the social back into the erotic illuminates the desire which sustains patriarchal configur-ations, but it does little to articulate the meanings of homoerotic sexuality. Structural congruity is not isomorphism. For the purpose of Sedgwick's analysis, the overshadowing of the erotic by the social seems to serve as a necessary means to foreground the intersection of *women's* oppression and homosociality; but, as a methodological problem it becomes more acute in the work of other feminist critics enamored of the homosocial paradigm who are less consistently careful than is Sedgwick to assert allegiance to an antihomophobic politics. The uncritical use of this model thus risks reproducing a homophobic discourse in the interest of advancing a particular feminist agenda. That the model also tends to deny the availability of female agency is a related, though separate problem.

Invigorated by Sedgwick's contribution, a pre-existing 'gay and lesbian studies' criticism of early modern texts has increased in rigor and sophistication.[23] Whereas I view this evolving body of work as refreshingly progressive, and am especially pleased to see critics of various erotic identifications engaged in its formulation, this criticism unfortunately re-enacts some of the problems of progressivism in general: that is, it uncritically accepts the polarizing structure of its problematic. Within Shakespearean criticism, this method seems to align itself along one of only two axes: either Shakespeare, as victim of dominant ideology, participated in the homophobia that is seen as defining early modern discourse, or he defied such homo-phobia in celebrating homoerotic love. (Or, correlatively, Shakespeare was or was not homo-sexual.) The oppositional structure of this paradigm not only reproduces a false binarism of desire/attraction versus anxiety/phobia, but also employs a reductive account of cultural power—namely, that cultures (and authors) either unequivocally deny or affirm *any* erotic mode.[24]

That neither denial nor affirmation provides an adequate theoretical model to account for the complexity of Shakespearean representations of homoeroticism is suggested, firstly, by the lack of unitary discourse on homoeroticism in early modern England. Not only did legal, moral, religious, and literary discourses understand and evaluate homoeroticism differently, but within each discourse there existed contradictory positions. Officially condemned yet routinely ignored, a sinful potential within all subjects yet also a specific illegal physical act, homoeroti-cism (or more accurately, sodomy and buggery) was a matter of contradictory social invest-ments. Prosecutions were relatively rare (those that did occur often involved child molestation, rape, or some explicit political motivation), and punishments, despite the fact that sodomy was a capital crime after Henry VIII's statute of 1533, were usually moderate.[25]

In addition, Alan Bray argues persuasively that those institutions which condemned sodomy did so in such absolute, apocalyptic, and heretical terms, and within such a broad display of 'unnatural' sins, that men who engaged in homoerotic activities routinely distanced such condemnations from the meanings they attached to their own behaviors.[26] As Jonathan Goldberg notes, sodomy 'always was embedded in other discourses, those delineating antisocial behavior—sedition, demonism, atheism.'[27] Thus, when James I wrote his treatise on kingship, *Basilikon Doron*, for example, he

> listed crimes that were treasonous and warranted death. Among them was sodomy. James, of course, was notorious for his overtly homosexual behaviour. Yet, his treatise does not simply dissimulate; rather, it shows that sodomy was so fully politicized that no king could possibly apply the term to himself.[28]

Although Goldberg seems to assume that James was, in modern terms, a homosexual, the fact remains that the king's publicly expressed affection for Buckingham (among other things, he fondled him and called him his wife) held no necessary implication of sodomy. A distance inserts itself between the discourse on sodomy and the subject of that discourse, *even as that subject discourses*. It is not only that through a kind of selective blindness the cognitive dissonance of those early moderns participating in homoerotic practices was kept at a minimum, but that sodomy itself was an unstable, internally contradictory category.

The contradiction posed here between discourse and practice cannot be neatly described as oppositional: homoerotic activity was not only condemned, but was afforded a social logic, a psychic space, within which it could be pursued. The implication of this ideological configuration is far-reaching; in Goldberg's words, sodomy 'was disseminated throughout society, invisible so long as homosexual acts failed to connect with the much more visible signs of social disruption represented by unorthodox religious or social positions.'[29] Sodomy was not, as in modern terms, sexually immoral in and of itself; whatever immorality accrued to it was by virtue of its power of *social* disruption.

If male homoeroticism was officially invisible unless associated with other social transgressions, female homoeroticism was even more so. Indeed, how *women* understood their own homoerotic desires is still very much under-investigated and under-theorized. Two strategies suggest themselves as ways of exploring the female homoerotics of Shakespearean drama: a 'revisioning' of close female friendship in the sense proposed by Adrienne Rich, and enacted by such scholars as Carroll Smith-Rosenberg and Lillian Faderman;[30] and a detailed examination of the erotic predicaments of the cross-dressed heroines of the comedies. We might want to look, for instance, at the relationships between Rosalind and Celia in *As You Like It*, Helena and Hermia in *A Midsummer Night's Dream*, and Marina and Philoten in *Pericles*, and ask why we assume that the images of 'a double cherry' and of 'Juno's swans . . . coupled and inseparable' are qualitatively different, somehow less erotic, than the 'twin'd lambs' of Polixenes and Leontes in *The Winter's Tale*.[31] To pose the question in this way is to highlight the fact that, whatever the actual erotic practice of women historically, in terms of critical discourse female homoeroticism must be thought into existence.

For now, however, I must limit myself to the second strategy. Most critics would agree that the device of cross-dressing involves the suggestion of homoeroticism. A problem arises, how-ever, in delineating precisely what kind of homoeroticism is represented. The materialist critic often turns to the theatrical practice of using boy actors to play female parts; from that material practice, it can be argued [. . .] that the homoeroticism embodied by the cross-dressed heroine is implicitly male: If Olivia is attracted to Viola/Cesario, or Phebe to Rosalind/Ganymede, the presence of boy actors suggests that the homoerotic exchange occurs between the transvestized boy actor playing Olivia or Phebe and the boy actor who (once dramatically transvestized as Viola or Rosalind) is now back in masculine dress.

But before we too quickly ratify the maleness inherent in this action, is it not also possible that these exchanges express female desire? If we focus on the text rather than theatrical practice, the desires circulating through the Phebe/Rosalind/Ganymede relation, or the Olivia/Viola/Cesario interaction, represent woman's desire for woman. Indeed, this is the reading Jean Howard implicitly proposes, with Olivia bearing the brunt of an anti-homoerotic humor. I will argue that the female (and male) homoeroticism of *As You Like It* and *Twelfth Night* is a mutual exchange (though not without anxieties and complications) which the contemporary practice of employing *female* actors for these parts can heighten.

But objections immediately present themselves to this 'feminist formalism.' If Phebe is attracted to the 'feminine' in Rosalind/ Ganymede, could this be merely an indication of her preferred erotic style (that is, having a small, lithe lover), and having no reference to object choice (a female)? In other words, is it possible to separate early modern erotic *style* from gender inflections? Is such a separation merely the imposition of late twentieth-century pre-occupations upon an earlier era? Or, does the foregoing analysis of Freud suggest that the conflation of gender and sexuality is a distinctly *modern* formulation?

In the absence of historical analysis of female homoeroticism, such questions are impossible to answer. Indeed, women's general illiteracy, which impeded first-hand recording of their experience, combined with the relative absence of legal and ecclesiastical documents pertain-ing to women's erotic investments in one another confounds the very possibility of historical analysis. If the materialist feminist's method is to return to the site of inscription, how does one read the difficulty of such a return?[32] The dearth of historical materials supports a number of possibly conflicting interpretations: assuming that women *did* engage in homoerotic behaviors, as cross-cultural anthropological evidence would suggest they did, it is possible that the nature of their erotic contacts did not invite sexual interpretations (by themselves? by others?); that such behavior was unremarkable insofar as it did not threaten the basis of the social contract—the open lineage family; that women's relative confinement in the household not only privatized their sexual contact but prevented the formation of those wider social networks which provided the embryonic basis of male homoerotic subcultures; and that the internal distancing evident in male homoeroticism was even more pronounced in that of female.

What evidence we do have suggests that in early modern England women were not sum-moned before courts on accusations of 'sodomy'; according to Louis Crompton, England's 'buggery' statute 'was not interpreted as criminalizing relations between women.'[33] Randolph Trumbach observes that the pre-eminent judicial scholar, Sir Edward Coke 'took for granted that a woman's action came under the sodomy statute primarily "if she commit buggery with a beast." '[34] Crompton provides evidence, however, that in other Western European countries

(France, Spain, Italy, Germany, and Switzerland) sexual acts between women 'were regarded as legally equivalent to acts of male sodomy and were, like them, punishable by the death penalty.'[35] The French sodomy statute, for instance, specifically criminalized female penetration of other women. According to James Saslow, however, across Western Europe punishment was rarely inflicted for female–female sexual acts: 'The total number of known prosecutions ranges from four in sixteenth-century France to two in Germany and one each in Spain, Italy, Geneva, and the Netherlands.'[36] Whatever the significance of this widespread reluctance to prosecute, it seems clear that in terms of criminal *law*, England was uniquely unconcerned with female homoeroticism. It may be that the ideology of Catholic countries was less tolerant, more apt to link homoeroticism with heresy, than that of Protestant ones. Saslow speculates that, in general,

> male authorities viewed lesbianism [*sic*] itself as more grave the more it laid claim to active male prerogatives: In Spain, two women were merely whipped and sent to the galleys for sex 'without an instrument,' but the penalty for penetration with a dildo was burning, suffered by two fifteenth-century nuns.[37]

The minimal concern about female homoeroticism displayed by the English did not derive from an assumption that women were asexual. As the plethora of cases involving pre-marital sexuality, adultery, and bastardy make clear, the reticence surrounding homoerotic activity contrasts sharply with the *lack* of impunity in cases of heterosexual transgression. Here the drama's concerns with the regulation of female heterosexual activity seem to parallel that of the culture for, as Katharine Eisaman Maus demonstrates, 'anxiety about female sexual fidelity ran high in English Renaissance culture'; she reports that the majority of defamation suits were prompted by the opprobrious terms whore, whoremaster, and cuckold.[38]

Curiously, the term 'sodomitess' was used synonymously with 'whore' as a generic insult, and yet, unlike 'whore,' it was not employed as accusation in the courts. The question of why the 'sodomitess' lacked legal culpability when so many other insults (scold, shrew, adulteress, whore) carried the onus of defamation leads only to more questions. Were specific erotic behaviors associated with the legally and socially execrated 'whore,' while others were reserved for the socially denigrated but legally unculpable 'sodomitess'? Or was female sodomy defined as a matter of erotic *excess*, of quantity rather than kind? Whereas we have come to believe that early modern ideology regarding women's sexuality was informed by the patriarchal need to control women's reproductive capacities, we do not yet know the extent to which erotic behavior between women either challenged or existed coextensively with that political mandate.

Not only were the regulatory mechanisms toward heterosexual and homoerotic transgressions asymmetrical, so too was the erotic system inconsistent with the gender system—as evidenced by the fact that when women cross-dressed, they did *not* experience impunity. Although there was no English law against cross-dressing (as there was in France), from at least 1580 on, women wearing 'masculine' attire were regularly castigated from pulpits and by pamphlets, and by 1620 were perceived to be such a threat that James I spoke out against the practice.[39] The gender and class infraction of female cross-dressing *was* linked to prostitution through labeling cross-dressers as 'whores' and 'trulls,' but it does not seem to have occasioned accusations of homoerotic deviancy automatically—not, at least, for women.[40]

That the anti-theatricalists regularly, even obsessively, returned to the allegedly sodomitical transgressions of the *male* cross-dresser, including those of the boy actor, underscores the asymmetry most palpably expressed later on in the eighteenth century: women who not only cross-dressed but *passed* as men were prosecuted for *fraud*, while their male counterparts were called to court for sodomy (a rather telling instance of woman's metaphysical positioning —to uphold, indeed embody, the truth).[41] And, notoriously, in the nineteenth century Queen Victoria refused to sign an anti-sodomy bill until all references to women were deleted—she professed complete disbelief in the possibility of women engaging in such acts.[42]

The official invisibility of early modern female homoeroticism, however, tells us little about its *popular* cultural significations. What does seem clear is that in England, women's sexuality did not derive wholly from gender identity or role ascriptions. That is, deviations in gender role did not automatically implicate women as 'unnatural' in their sexual tastes; deviations in erotic behavior were not necessarily coded as gender transgressions. The conflation of gender and eroticism that we so often bring to our critical activity does not adequately address early modern women's homoeroticism.

Whatever its significations, they were not identical to those of male homoeroticism, which had both a greater social and discursive presence and, one would suspect, a greater range of practice. In contrast to the silence surrounding female homoeroticism, many early modern English words denote male homoerotic activity: ganymede, catamite, ingle, androgyne. As terms of disparagement, they conflated youthful androgyny, 'effeminacy,' and transvestism in one package of gender and erotic transgression.[43] Yet there is also some evidence to suggest that the discourse of sodomy did not always map easily onto the discourse of, for instance, the ganymede—that the categories in certain contexts might have been distinguished and dis-articulated (to us) to an extraordinary degree.

In short, the meanings of homoerotic desire during the early modern period seem to have been remarkably unfixed, with contradictory meanings existing across a complex and fractured field of signification. The discourses of homoeroticism were neither monological nor mono-vocal. Most importantly, homoerotic activity—for men or women—was not a primary means of identification of the self. Homoeroticism had little to do with any of the social roles, statuses, and hierarchies in which an early modern subject might be located and thereby define him or herself. Early moderns simply did not essentialize homoeroticism in quite the way we do. [. . .]

My use of two seemingly opposed yet not directly antonymic terms—homo/eroticism and hetero/sexuality—is a response to the early modern social configuration. In the early modern period, neither heterosexuality nor homosexuality (or sexuality itself for that matter) existed in our modern senses of the terms. Yet, despite the absence of both concepts from the early modern consciousness, it is still possible to speak of crucial differences in the social organiza-tion of those activities which we now term 'homo' or 'hetero.' Although neither an originating cause nor an organizing principle, heterosexual object choice was involved in the social forma-tion both subjectively and institutionally in the following ways: as a subjective state of desire, if not for an object proper, then for the results that union with that object would hopefully ensure (family, name, property, rank, lineage—all that is connoted by the early modern term 'house'); as a well-defined and well-investigated erotic act (fornication) organized around the presence or absence of female chastity; and as a dominant ideology which found its teleology in the material institution of marriage. Insofar as elite marriages were primarily dedicated to breeding, the perpetuation of lineage, and the consolidation and dispersal of property, and to the extent that these social mandates were threatened by the expression of unregulated female sexuality, it could be said that in certain contexts, heterosexual *desire* was in excess of marriage, even at odds with it. If this were true, hetero*sexuality* would be that which the upper classes displaced onto the laboring classes, as landed gentry and aristocrats indulged in a patriarchal fantasy of marriage that secured lineage and property without sexual intercourse.[44] Despite this possible difference in the erotics of class, however, my use of the linguistic root 'sexuality' is meant to imply heterosexuality's institutional and political mandate, in which identity was situated in relation to one's sexual congress as a socially ascribed subject-position—as husband, mistress, wife, widow or widower, for instance. To that extent, hetero-sexuality performed a crucial function of subjectification *vis-à-vis* the dominant social order.

In contrast, homosexuality—as subject position, ideology, or institution—did not exist. What did exist discursively, in the form of sodomy and buggery, were a number of dispersed acts, organized around penetration: anal intercourse between males or between males and females, intercourse with children, fellatio, and bestiality—none of which in England referred to specific acts between women.

Following the implicit lead of the documentary discourses of law, religion, and morality, many critics thus focus on early modern homoeroticism as an *act*, defining it in terms of sodomitical practice. To do so, however, is to conflate homoeroticism with other forms of so called 'sexual confusion,' to ignore the gender asymmetry of sodomy's definition, and to obviate the subjective motivation for and experience of homoerotic activity. Legal, ecclesi-astical, and moral discourses positioned homoeroticism as other, and within that logic, refused the power of speech to those who would speak from the position of their own intentionality. I want to argue that to the extent that material practice did not exhaust homoeroticism's mean-ing—either for those who experienced it or those who represented it in literature—what is in excess remains in the amorphous register of erotic *desire*.[45] More accurately, homoeroticism was a position taken in *relation* to desire—a position, however, that was neither socially mandated nor capable of conferring identity or role.

And yet, even as I formulate homoeroticism as a position taken in relation to desire, I am in danger of reifying what is really a relational process—desire or eroticism—and granting it a certain structural autonomy. Such a method risks attributing agency to desire by raising it to the status of ontology or attributing to it a teleology. It represents, at best, an interim strategy, a way to keep the exigencies of materiality and subjectivity poised in mutual tension, while at the same time insisting on the material and subjective asymmetry between hetero/sexuality and homo/eroticism. [. . .]

Several implications evolve from the problems and methodology I have outlined here. First, by arguing that eroticism *is* cultural practice—material, ideological, and subjective—I encourage literary and cultural critics to recognize and distinguish the workings of eroticism in the texts and cultures they analyze. If even the most sophisticated feminist materialist analyses misrec-ognize gender as a signifier in such a way that eroticism is conveniently forgotten, clearly both gender and historical critics need to rethink their assumptions about the meaning and signifi-cance of erotic practice.

Secondly, [. . .] is the belief that the problems posed by erotic desire demand feminist analysis from two angles simultaneously: historical materialist analysis of ideological and material practices, and psychoanalysis of subjective states of desire. Indeed, the case of early modern homoeroticism(s) demonstrates the extent to which the opposition between the material (institutions and practices) and the psychic (desires and fantasies) is a false one. Despite psychoanalysis' belatedness, its construction within the specific problematics of modernity, and its unfortunate history as a normalizing institution, its recognition that eroticism involves several modes of desire is crucial to the possibility of a non-normalizing analytic. To investigate homoeroticism only from the standpoint of ascertainable material practice, our understanding of which is limited, for the early modern period, to the dominant discourses of legal and religious records, is to ignore the subjective erotic dramas of countless early modern people. We cannot know the content of those subjective dramas, but we can reconstruct partial (that is, both incomplete and necessarily biased) approximations of their meaning from the contemporary rhetorical strategies employed to describe them. To my mind, this is where a historical, discourse-based model faces its greatest challenge: to delineate not only those statements that circulate throughout the social fabric, but also to 're-vision' and put into play those historical meanings that have been repressed, lost, or unspoken.

The viability of the kind of critical *rapprochement* I advocate—feminist-historical-materialist-psycho-analysis—depends on the continuing deconstruction of psychoanalysis' will to mastery. The first move in such a project is the internal displacement of those totalizations that obscure historical and social processes. One such totalization, I hope to have demonstrated, is 'desire' itself.

The work I've begun here is only a small first step in the much larger project of deconstructing 'sex-desire' in the words of Foucault, in the interests of 'bodies and pleasures.'[46] Insofar as gay men and lesbians are still subject to institutionalized oppression (including the recent revision of the archaic 'sodomy' law to specifically criminalize homosexual acts in the state in which I live, and the revoking of the right to freedom of speech in matters homoerotic in Great Britain), asserting the specificity of homoeroticism is politically progressive.

It is not, however, radically deconstructive, if only because it continues to pay implicit obeisance to the prestige of object choice as the primary criterion of sexuality. A more radical project would not only move beyond the regime of object choice, but also beyond the representational strategy that supports it: the hegemony of the phallus. Both the phallus and object choice depend on a binary system that reifies eroticism by privileging one erotic position over all others. Even in Lacanian psychoanalysis, in which the phallus represents a 'lack-in-being,' the recourse to phallus-as-signifier-of-desire defines the problematic of presence/absence as ontologically originating in the male body. Rather than demystifying male sexuality as it exposes subjectivity as a (w)hole, it reproduces male genitalia as transcendental signifier (not of presence but of absence), in an inversion that leaves the privilege of the term undisturbed. Male sexuality remains both the referent and repetition of the problem of subjectivity 'itself.'[47] And the static relations between power and desire remain uncontested, with power always the 'substitute of choice' for what we always already, and always will, essentially lack.

The deconstruction of erotic binarism would involve putting into play more heterogeneous and heteronomous representations, by recognizing what Jonathan Dollimore has called the 'creative perversity of desire itself.'[48] People of all erotic persuasions—and I stress that this is not solely the task of erotic minorities—can renegotiate the terms by which desire is lived and understood, setting into critical motion the various contingencies that structure arousal and foster erotic satisfaction. Beginning to conceptualize desire as the sum of discontinuous and incongruent discourses, practices, identifications, fantasies, preferences for specific activities, as well as object choice(s), we could do worse than adopt as a critical strategy the kind of rhetorical displacement evident on the following political T-shirt:

> so-do-my
> neighbors
> parents
> friends

  Deconstructing 'desire' opens up a field of inquiry, a way of thinking about bodies, pleasures, and history that allows us to ask previously unapproachable questions. Indeed, questions that hitherto seemed ahistorical may be viewed with a new historicity. For instance, what precise intersections of discourses, both early modern and postmodern, on power, gender, bodies, and pleasures produce the possibility of reading *Twelfth Night*'s Antonio as akin to the macho 'Castro clone' encased in leather in San Francisco? Or, why is it possible to interpret Sebastian as the 'bisexual' who can go either way? And why does Viola and Rosalind's adoption of 'doublet and hose' seem to speak to our own taste for androgynous and practical fashions?
  But where is Olivia?
  Perhaps sitting at her computer, wearing high heels.

. . . .

QUESTIONS

- How do the categories of race, gender, class and sexuality overlap in this work and how is each category affected by the workings of history?
- The identities examined above are alike in their marginality, but what other features do these 'others' share and what distinguishes them from each other? Is there an implicit 'self' in contrast to these 'others'?
- What are the problems or difficulties involved in accessing the experiences, the subjects of this criticism?

3 | Centres and margins

Ania Loomba and Martin Orkin (eds.), 'Introduction: Shakespeare and the post-colonial question', in *Post-Colonial Shakespeares* (London and New York: Routledge, 1998), p. 4.

Current scholarship has offered sophisticated readings of the webbed relations between state power, the emergence of new classes and ideologies, the reshaping of patriarchal authority, the development of the idea of an English nation, sexual practices and discourses, and the real and imaginary experiences of English people in the Americas, Africa and Asia. These experiences built upon and transformed ideologies about 'others' which filtered down from earlier times, particularly the experience of the Crusades, or which emerged in interactions with other Europeans such as the Spanish, the Italians and the Dutch, or, most importantly, those that were developed in relation to those living on the margins of English society—Jews, gypsies, the Irish, the Welsh and the Scots. Political criticism of Shakespeare as well as of early modern England has begun to show, with increasing detail and sophistication, that it is virtually impossible to seal off any meaningful analysis of English culture and literature from considerations of racial and cultural difference, and from the dynamics of emergent colonialisms.

* * *

Paul Brown, ' "This thing of darkness I acknowledge mine": *The Tempest* and the discourse of colonialism', in Jonathan Dollimore and Alan Sinfield (eds.), *Political Shakespeare: Essays in Cultural Materialism* (Manchester: Manchester University Press, 1985), pp. 49–51.

In 1614 John Rolfe, a Virginia planter, wrote a letter seeking the Governor's blessing for his proposed marriage with Pocahontas, abducted daughter of Powhatan, chief-of-chiefs. This remarkable document [. . .] confirm[s] Rolfe in the position of coloniser and Pocahontas in the position of a savage other [. . .] [and] is [. . .] a production of [Rolfe's] civilised 'self' as a text to be read by his superiors, that is, his Governor and his God. What lurks in Rolfe's 'secret bosome' is a desire for a savage female. [. . .] The letter, then, rehearses the power of the civil subject to maintain self-control and to bring the other into his service, even as it refers to a desire which might undermine that mastery.

 After his initial calls for Rolfe to be denounced as a traitor, James I allowed the 'princess', newly christened 'Lady Rebecca', into court as visible evidence of the power of civility to transform the other. Pocahontas was to die in England a nine day's wonder. [. . .] The Pocahontas myth was only beginning, however. [. . .]

 Even this partial analysis [. . .] serves to demonstrate the characteristic operations of the discourse of colonialism. This complex discourse can be seen to have operated in two main areas: they may be called 'masterlessness' and 'savagism'. Masterlessness analyses wandering or unfixed and unsupervised elements located in the internal margins of civil society (. . . Rolfe's subjective desire [. . .]). Savagism probes and categorises alien cultures on the external margins of expanding civil power ([. . .] the Amerindian cultures of Virginia). At the same time as they serve to define the other, such discursive practices refer back to those conditions which constitute civility itself. Masterlessness reveals the mastered (submissive, observed, supervised, deferential) and masterful (powerful, observing, supervising, teleological) nature of civil society. Savagism (a-sociality and untrammelled libidinality) reveals the necessity of psychic and institutional order and direction in the civil regime. In practice these two concepts are intertwined and mutually reinforcing. Together they constitute a powerful discourse in which the non-civil is represented to the civil subject to produce for Rolfe a 'laborinth' out of which, like Theseus escaping from the Minotaur's lair, he is to 'unwinde' his 'selfe.'

* * *

Stephen Greenblatt, *Renaissance Self-Fashioning: From More to Shakespeare* (London and Chicago: University of Chicago Press, 1980), pp. 179–92.

It is not possible [. . .] to outline the dense network of analogies, repetitions, correspondences, and homologies within which even this one episode of Spenser's immense poem is embedded. But I can point briefly to three reiterations by the culture of important elements of the destruction of the Bower of Bliss: the European response to the native cultures of the New World, the English colonial struggle in Ireland, and the Reformation attack on images. The examples suggest the diversity of such reiterations—from the general culture of Europe, to the national policy of England, to the ideology of a small segment of the nation's population—while their shared elements seem to bear out Freud's master analogy: 'Civilization behaves towards sexuality as a people or a stratum of its population does which has subjected another one to its exploitation.'

In the texts written by early explorers of the New World, a long arduous voyage, fraught with fabulous dangers and trials, brings the band of soldiers, sailors, and religious fathers—knight, boatman, and palmer—to a world of riches and menace. The adventurer's morality is the morality of the ship, where order, discipline, and constant labor are essential for survival, and they are further united by their explicit religious faith and by an unspoken but powerful male bond. The lands they encounter are often achingly beautiful: 'I am completely persuaded in my own mind,' writes Columbus in 1498, 'that the Terrestrial Paradise is in the place I have described.'[1] So Spenser likens the Bower of Bliss to Eden itself, 'if ought with Eden mote compayre,' and lingers over its landscape of wish fulfillment, a landscape at once lavish and moderate, rich in abundant vegetation and yet 'steadfast,' 'attempred,' and well 'disposed.' If these descriptive terms are shared in the Renaissance by literary romance and travelers' accounts, it is because the two modes of vision are mutually reinforcing: Spenser, like Tasso before him, makes frequent allusion to the New World—to 'all that now America men call (2.10.72)—while when Cortes and his men looked down upon the valley of Mexico, they thought, says a participant, of Amadis of Gaule.[2] The American landscape has to European eyes the mysterious intimations of a hidden art, as Ralegh's description of the Orinoco suggests: 'On both sides of this river, we passed the most beautiful country that ever mine eyes beheld: and whereas all that we had seen before was nothing but woods, prickles, bushes, and thorns, here we beheld plains of twenty miles in length, the grass short and green, and in diverse parts groves of trees by themselves, as if they had been by all the art and labor in the world so made of purpose: and still as we rowed, the Deer came down feeding by the water's side, as if they had been used to a keeper's call.'[3]

Spenser, to be sure, has no need of the 'as if'—he credits art as well as nature with the making of the paradisal landscape—but this difference should not suggest too sharp a contrast between an 'artless' world described by the early voyagers and the poet's 'artificial' Bower. The Europeans again and again record their astonishment at the Indians' artistic brilliance: 'Surely I marvel not at the gold and precious stones, but wonder with astonishment with what industry and laborious art the curious workmanship exceedeth the matter and substance. I beheld a thousand shapes, and a thousand forms, which I cannot express in writing; so that in my judgment I never saw anything which might more allure the eyes of men with the beauty thereof.'[4]

But all of this seductive beauty harbors danger, danger not only in the works of art which are obviously idolatrous but in the Edenic landscape itself. The voyagers to the New World are treated, like Guyon and the Palmer, to mild air that 'breathed forth sweet spirit and holesom smell' (2.12.51), and they react with mingled wonder and resistance: 'Smooth and pleasing words might be spoken of the sweet odors, and perfumes of these countries,' writes Peter Martyr, 'which we purposely omit, because they make rather for the effeminating of men's minds, than for the maintenance of good behavior.'[5] Similarly, if the New World could be portrayed as a place 'In which all pleasures plenteously abownd, / And none does others happiness envye' (2.10.58), a Golden World, it could also serve—often in the same text and by virtue of the same set of perceptions—as a screen onto which Europeans projected their darkest and yet most compelling fantasies: 'These folk live like beasts without any reasonable-ness, and the women be also as common. And the men hath conversation with the women who that they been or who they first meet, is she his sister, his mother, his daughter, or any other kindred. And the women be very hot and disposed to lecherdness. And they eat also one another. The man eateth his wife, his children. . . . And that land is right full of folk, for they live commonly 300 year and more as with sickness they die not.'[6] In 1582 Richard Madox, in Sierra Leone with Edward Fenton's expedition, heard from a Portuguese trader comparable stories of African customs: 'He reported that near the mountains of the moon there is a queen, an empress of all these Amazons, a witch and a cannibal who daily feeds on the flesh of boys. She ever remains unmarried, but she has intercourse with a great number of men by whom she begets offspring. The kingdom, however, remains hereditary to the daughters, not to the sons.'[7]

Virtually all the essential elements of the travel narratives recur in Spenser's episode: the sea voyage, the strange, menacing creatures, the paradisal landscape with its invisible art, the gold and silver carved with 'curious imagery,' the threat of effeminacy checked by the male bond, the generosity and wantonness of the inhabitants, the arousal of a longing at once to enter and to destory. Even cannibalism and incest which are the extreme manifestations of the disordered and licentious life attributed to the Indians are both subtly suggested in the picture of Acrasia hanging over her adolescent lover:

> And oft inclining downe with kisses light,
> For fear of waking him, his lips bedewd,
> And through his humid eyes did sucke his spright,
> Quite molten into lust and pleasure lewd.
>
> (2.12.73)

In book 6 of *The Faerie Queene* Spenser offers a more explicit version of these dark imagin-ings;[8] here in book 2 the violation of the taboos is carefully displaced, so that the major threat is not pollution but the very attractiveness of the vision. Sexual excess has caused in Verdant a melting of the soul,[9] and this internal pathology is matched by an external disgrace:

> His warlike armes, the idle instruments
> Of sleeping praise, were hong vpon a tree,
> And his braue shield, full of old moniments,
> Was fowly ra'st, that none the signes might see.
>
> (2.12.80)

The entire fulfillment of desire leads to the effacement of signs and hence to the loss both of memory, depicted in canto 10 and of the capacity for heroic effort, depicted in the figure of the boatman who ferries Guyon and the Palmer to the Bower:

> Forward they passe, and strongly he them rowes,
> Vntill they nigh vnto that gulfe arryve,
> Where streame more violent and greedy growes:
> Then he with all his puisaunce doth stryve
> To strike his oares, and mightily doth dryve
> The hollow vessell through the threatfull wave,
> Which, gaping wide, to swallow them alyve
> In th'huge abysse of his engulfing grave,
> Doth rore at them in vaine, and with great terrour rave.
>
> (2.12.5)

The threat of being engulfed that is successfully resisted here is encountered again at the heart of the Bower in the form not of cannibalistic violence but of erotic absorption. Verdant, his head in Acrasia's lap, has sunk into a narcotic slumber: all 'manly' energy, all purposeful direction, all sense of difference upon which 'civil' order is founded have been erased. This slumber corresponds to what the Europeans perceived as the *pointlessness* of native cultures. It was as if millions of souls had become unmoored, just as their ancestors had, it was thought, somehow lost their way and wandered out of sight of the civilized world. Absorbed into a vast wilderness, they lost all memory of the true history of their race and of the one God and sank into a spiritual and physical lethargy. It is difficult to recover the immense force which this charge of idleness carried; some sense may be gauged perhaps from the extraordinary harshness with which vagabonds were treated.[10]

That the Indians were idle, that they lacked all work discipline, was proved, to the satisfaction of the Europeans, by the demonstrable fact that they made wretched slaves, dying after a few weeks or even days of hard labor. And if they were freed from servitude, they merely slid back into their old customs: 'For being idle and slothful, they wander up and down, and return to their old rites and ceremonies and foul and mischievous acts.'[11] That the European voyagers of the sixteenth century, surely among the world's most restless and uprooted generations, should accuse the Indians of 'wandering up and down' is bitterly ironic, but the accusation served as a kind of rudder, an assurance of stability and direction. And this assurance is confirmed by the vast projects undertaken to fix and enclose the native populations in the mines, in encomiendas, in fortified hamlets, and ultimately, in mass graves. A whole civilization was caught in a net and, like Acrasia, bound in chains of adamant; their gods were melted down, their palaces and temples razed, their groves felled. 'And of the fairest late, now made the fowlest place.'[12]

Guyon, it will be recalled, makes no attempt to destroy the Cave of Mammon; he simply declines its evil invitations which leave him exhausted but otherwise unmoved. But the Bower of Bliss he destroys with a rigor rendered the more pitiless by the fact that his stubborn breast, we are told, embraced 'secret pleasance.' In just this way, Europeans destroyed Indian culture not despite those aspects of it that attracted them but in part at least because of them. The violence of the destruction was regenerative; they found in it a sense of identity, discipline, and holy faith.[13] In tearing down what both appealed to them and sickened them, they strengthened their power to resist their dangerous longings, to repress antisocial impulses, to conquer the powerful desire for release. And the conquest of desire had the more power because it contained within itself a version of that which it destroyed: the power of Acrasia's sensuality to erase signs and upset temperate order is simultaneously attacked and imitated in Guyon's destruction of the exquisite Bower, while European 'civility' and Christianity were never more ferociously assaulted than in the colonial destruction of a culture that was accused of mounting just such an assault.

One measure of European complicity in what they destroyed is the occurrence of apostacy or at least fantasies of apostacy. Bernal Diaz del Castillo tells one such story about a common seaman named Gonzalo Guerrero who had survived a shipwreck in the Yucatan and refused to rejoin his compatriots when, eight years later, Cortes managed to send word to him: 'I am married and have three children, and they look on me as a *Cacique* here, and a captain in time of war. Go, and God's blessing be with you. But my face is tattooed and my ears are pierced. What would the Spaniards say if they saw me like this? And look how handsome these children of mine are!'[14] The emissary reminded him that he was a Christian and 'should not destroy his soul for the sake of an Indian woman,' but Guerrero clearly regarded his situation as an improvement in his lot. Indeed Cortes learned that it was at Guerrero's instigation that the Indians had, three years before, attacked an earlier Spanish expedition to the Yucatan.

We have, in the tattooed Spanish seaman, encountered an analogue to those disfigured beasts who try to defend the Bower against Guyon and, in particular, to Gryll, who, having been metamorphosed by Acrasia into a hog, 'repyned greatly' at his restoration. Such creatures give a local habitation and a name to those vague feelings of longing and complicity that permeate accounts of a sensuous life that must be rejected and destroyed. And if the Yucatan seems too remote from Spenser's world, we need only turn to our second frame of reference, Elizabethan rule in Ireland, to encounter similar stories. In Spenser's own *View of the Present State of Ireland*, probably written in 1596, Eudoxius asks, 'is it possible that an Englishman brought up naturally in such sweet civility as England affords could find such liking in that barbarous rudeness that he should forget his own nature and forgo his own nation? . . . Is it possible that any should so far grow out of frame that they should in so short space quite forget their country and their own names? . . . Could they ever conceive any such devilish dislike of their own natural country as that they would be ashamed of her name, and bite off her dug from which they sucked life?'[15] In reply, Spenser's spokesman, Irenius, speaks bitterly of those Englishmen who are 'degenerate and grown almost mere Irish, yea and more malicious to the English than the very Irish themselves' (48); these metamorphosed wretches even prefer to speak Irish, although, as Eudoxius observes, 'they should (methinks) rather take scorn to acquaint their tongues thereto, for it hath been ever the use of the conqueror to despise the language of the conquered, and to force him by all means to learn his.[16] Irenius locates the source of this unnatural linguistic betrayal, this effacement of signs, in the subversive power of Irish women. The rebel Englishmen will 'bite off her dug from which they sucked life' because another breast has intervened: 'the child that sucketh the milk of the nurse must of necessity learn his first speech of her, the which being the first that is enured to his tongue is ever after most pleasing unto him,' and 'the speech being

Irish, the heart must needs be Irish.'[17] The evil metamorphosis caused by Irish wetnurses is completed by miscegenation: 'the child taketh most of his nature of the mother . . . for by them they are first framed and fashioned' (68). As the fashioning of a gentleman is threatened in book 2 of *The Faerie Queene* by Acrasia, so it is threatened in Ireland by the native women.

It is often remarked that the *View*, which Spenser wrote after his completion of *The Faerie Queene*, expresses a hardening of attitude, a harsh and bitter note brought on by years of tension and frustration. It may well reflect such a change in tone, but its colonial policies are consistent with those with which Spenser had been associated from his arrival in Ireland as Lord Grey's secretary in 1580, that is, from the time in which *The Faerie Queene* was in the early stages of its composition. When Spenser 'wrote of Ireland,' Yeats comments, 'he wrote as an official, and out of thoughts and emotions that had been organized by the State.'[18] It was not only in his capacity as an official that Spenser did so: in art and in life, his conception of identity, as we have seen, is wedded to his conception of power, and after 1580, of colonial power. For all Spenser's claims of relation to the noble Spencers of Wormleighton and Althorp, he remains a 'poor boy,' as he is designated in the Merchant Taylor's School and at Cambridge, until Ireland. It is there that he is fashioned a gentleman, there that he is transformed from the former denizen of East Smithfield to the 'undertaker'—the grim pun unintended but profoundly appropriate—of 3,028 acres of Munster land. From his first acquisition in 1582, this land is at once the assurance of his status—the 'Gent.' next to his name—and of his insecurity: ruined abbeys, friaries expropriated by the crown, plow lands rendered vacant by famine and execution, property forfeited by those whom Spenser's superiors declared traitors.

For what services, we ask, was Spenser being rewarded? And we answer, blandly, for being a colonial administrator. But the answer, which implies pushing papers in a Dublin office through endless days of tedium, is an evasion. Spenser's own account presses in upon us the fact that he was involved intimately, on an almost daily basis, throughout the island, in the destruction of Hiberno-Norman civilization, the exercise of a brutal force that had few if any of the romantic trappings with which Elizabeth contrived to soften it at home.[19] Here, on the periphery, Spenser was an agent of and an apologist for massacre, the burning of mean hovels and of crops with the deliberate intention of starving the inhabitants, forced relocation of peoples, the manipulation of treason charges so as to facilitate the seizure of lands, the endless repetition of acts of military 'justice' calculated to intimidate and break the spirit. We may wish to tell ourselves that a man of Spenser's sensitivity and gifts may have mitigated the extreme policies of ruthless men, but it appears that he did not recoil in the slightest from this horror, did not even feel himself, like his colleague Geoffrey Fenton, in mild opposition to it.[20] Ireland is not only in book 5 of *The Faerie Queene*; it pervades the poem. Civility is won through the exercise of violence over what is deemed barbarous and evil, and the passages of love and leisure are not moments set apart from this process but its rewards.

'Every detail of the huge resettlement project' in Munster, writes Spenser's biographer Judson, 'was known to him as it unfolded, including its intricate legal aspects, and hence his final acquisition of thousands of acres of forfeited lands was entirely natural.'[21] Natural perhaps, but equally natural that his imagination is haunted by the nightmares of savage attack—the 'outrageous dreadfull yelling cry' of Maleger, 'His body leane and meagre as a rake' and yet seemingly impossible to kill[22]—and of absorption. The latter fear may strike us as less compelling than the former—there is much talk, after all, of the 'savage brutishness and loathly filthiness' of native customs—but the Elizabethans were well aware, as we have already seen, that many of their most dangerous enemies were Englishmen who had been metamorphosed into 'mere Irish.' Spenser's own career is marked by conflicting desires to turn his back on Ireland forever and to plant himself ever more firmly in Munster;[23] if the latter course scarcely represented an abandonment of English civility, it may nonetheless have felt like the beginning of the threatened transformation. I do not propose that Spenser feared such a metamorphosis on his own behalf—he may, for all we know, have been obscurely attracted to some of the very things he worked to destroy, though of this attraction our only record is his poetry's fascination with the excess against which it struggles—only that he was haunted by the fact that it had occurred over generations to so many of his countrymen. The enemy for Spenser then is as much a tenacious and surprisingly seductive way of life as it is a military force, and thus alongside a ruthless policy of mass starvation and massacre, he advocates the destruction of native Irish identity.

Spenser is one of the first English writers to have what we may call a field theory of culture, that is, the conception of a nation not simply as an institutional structure or a common race, but as a complex network of beliefs, folk customs, forms of dress, kinship relations, religious mythology, aesthetic norms, and specialized modes of production. Therefore, to *reform* a people one must not simply conquer it—though conquest is an absolute necessity—but eradicate the native culture: in the case of Ireland, eliminate (by force, wherever needed) the carrows, horseboys, jesters, and other 'idlers'; transform the mass of the rural population from cowherds with their dangerous freedom of movement to husbandmen; break up the clans or sects; prohibit public meetings, councils, and assemblies; transform Irish art, prohibiting the subversive epics of the bards; make schoolchildren ashamed of their parents' backwardness; discourage English settlers from speaking Irish; prohibit traditional Irish dress; eliminate elections of chiefs, divisible inheritance, and the payment of fines to avoid capital punishment. And always in this immense undertaking, there is the need for constant vigilance and unrelenting pressure, exercised not only upon the wild Irish but upon the civilizing English themselves. 'So much,' writes Spenser, 'can liberty and ill example do' (63) that the threat of seduction is always present, and the first inroad of this seduction is misguided compassion: 'Therefore, by all means it must be foreseen and assured that after once entering into this course of reformation, there be afterwards no remorse or drawing back' (110). Pitiless destruction is here not a stain but a virtue; after all, the English themselves had to be brought from barbarism to civility by a similar conquest centuries before, a conquest that must be ever renewed lest the craving for 'liberty and natural freedom' (12) erupt again. The colonial violence inflicted upon the Irish is at the same time the force that fashions the identity of the English.

We have returned then to the principle of regenerative violence and thus to the destruction of the Bower of Bliss. The act of tearing down is the act of fashioning; the promise of the opening stanza of canto 12—'Now gins this goodly frame of Temperance / Fairely to rise'—is fulfilled at the close in the inventory of violence:

> But all those pleasant bowres and Pallace braue,
> *Guyon* broke downe, with rigour pittilesse;
> Ne ought their goodly workmanship might saue

> Them from the tempest of his wrathfulnesse,
> But that their blisse he turn'd to balefulness;
> Their groues he feld, their gardins did deface,
> Their arbers spoyle, their Cabinets suppresse,
> Their banket houses burne, their buildings race,
> And of the fairest late, now made the fowlest place.
>
> (2.12.83)

If the totality of the destruction, the calculated absence of 'remorse or drawing back,' links this episode to the colonial policy of Lord Grey which Spenser undertook to defend, the language of the stanza recalls yet another government policy, our third 'restoration' of the narrative: the destruction of Catholic Church furnishings. In the *Inventarium monumentorum superstitionis* of 1566, for example, we may hear repeated echoes of Guyon's acts:

Imprimis one rood with Mary and John and the rest of the painted pictures—burnt. . . .

Item our rood loft—pulled down, sold and defaced. . . .

Item our mass books with the rest of such feigned fables and peltering popish books—burnt. . . .

Item 3 altar stones—broken in pieces. . . .[24]

In 1572 Spenser, a student at Pembroke, could have witnessed a similar scene at nearby Gonville and Caius where the authorities licensed the destruction of 'much popish trumpery.' Books and vestments, holy water stoops and images were 'mangled, torn to pieces, and mutilated'—*discerpta dissecta et lacerata*—before being consigned to the bonfire.[25]

There is about the Bower of Bliss the taint of a graven image designed to appeal to the sensual as opposed to the spiritual nature, to turn the wonder and admiration of men away from the mystery of divine love. In the Bower the love survives only in the uncanny parody of the Pietà suggested by Verdant cradled in Acrasia's arms. It is not surprising then to find a close parallel between the evils of the Bower and the evils attributed to the misuse of religious images. Devotion to the representations of the Madonna and saints deflected men from the vigorous pursuit of the good, enticed them into idleness and effeminacy. With their destruction, as Hugh Latimer writes, men could turn 'from ladyness to Godliness.'[26] Statues of the virgin were dismembered by unruly crowds, frescoes were whitewashed over and carvings in 'Lady Chapels' were smashed, in order to free men from thralldom to what an Elizabethan lawyer calls, in describing the pope, 'the witch of the world.'[27]

But the art destroyed by Guyon does not pretend to image holy things; it is designed to grace its surroundings, to delight its viewers with its exquisite workmanship. Against such art there could be no charge of idolatry, no invocation of the Deuteronomic injunctions against graven images, unless art itself were idolatrous. And it is precisely this possibility that is suggested by Guyon's iconoclasm, for Acrasia's realm is lavishly described in just those terms which the defenders of poetry in the Renaissance reserved for imagination's noblest achievements. The Bower's art imitates nature, but is privileged to choose only those aspects of nature that correspond to man's ideal visions; its music is so perfectly melodious and 'attempred' that it blends with all of nature in one harmony, so that the whole world seems transformed into a musical 'consort'; above all, the calculation and effort that lie behind the manifestation of such perfect beauty are entirely concealed:

> And that which all faire workes doth most aggrace,
> The art, which all that wrought, appeared in no place.

'Aggrace' has virtually a technical significance here; Castiglione had suggested in *The Courtier* that the elusive quality of 'grace' could be acquired through the practice of *sprezzatura*, 'so as to conceal all art and make whatever is done or said appear to be without effort and almost without any thought about it.'[28]

Spenser deeply distrusts this aesthetic, even as he seems to pay homage to its central tenets; indeed the concealment of art, its imposition upon an unsuspecting observer, is one of the great recurring evils in *The Faerie Queene*. Acrasia as demonic artist and whore combines the attributes of those other masters of disguise, Archimago and Duessa.[29] Their evil depends upon the ability to mask and forge, to conceal their satanic artistry; their defeat depends upon the power to unmask, the strength to turn from magic to strenuous virtue. Keith Thomas notes that in the sixteenth and seventeenth centuries the Protestant 'emphasis upon the virtues of hard work and application . . . both reflected and helped to create a frame of mind which spurned the cheap solutions offered by magic, not just because they were wicked, but because they were too easy.'[30] *Sprezzatura*, which sets out to efface all signs of 'hard work and application,' is a cult of the 'too easy,' a kind of aesthetic magic.

But what can Spenser offer in place of this discredited aesthetic? The answer lies in an art that constantly calls attention to its own processes, that includes within itself framing devices and signs of its own createdness. Far from hiding its traces, *The Faerie Queene* announces its status as art object at every turn, in the archaic diction, the use of set pieces, the elaborate sound effects, the very characters and plots of romance. For the allegorical romance is a mode that virtually by definition abjures all concealment; the artist who wishes to hide the fact that he is making a fiction would be ill-advised to write about the Faerie Queene.

If you fear that images may make a blasphemous claim to reality, that they may become idols that you will be compelled to worship, you may smash all images or you may create images that announce themselves at every moment as things made. Thus did the sixteenth-century kabbalists of Safed circumvent the Hebraic injunction against images of the Godhead;[31] their visions are punctuated by reminders that these are merely metaphors, not to be confused with divine reality itself. So too did the more moderate Protestant Reformers retain a version of the Communion, reminding the participants that the ceremony was a symbol and not a celebration of the real presence of God's body. And so does Spenser, in the face of deep anxiety about the impure claims of art, save art for himself and his readers by making its createdness explicit. Images, to be sure, retain their power, as the sensuous description of the Bower of Bliss attests, and Spenser can respond to the charge that his 'famous antique history' is merely 'th'aboundance of an idle braine . . . and painted forgery' by reminding his readers of the recent discoveries, of 'The Indian *Peru*,' 'The *Amazons* huge riuer,' and 'fruitfullest *Virginia*':

> Yet all these were, when no man did them know;
> Yet haue from wisest ages hidden beene:
> And later times things more vnknowne shall show.
> When then should witlesse man so much misweene
> That nothing is, but that which he hath seene?
> What if within the Moones faire shining spheare?
> What if in euery other starre vnseene
> Of other worldes he happily should heare?
> He wonder would much more: yet such to some appeare.
>
> (2 Proem 3)

For a moment the work hovers on the brink of asserting its status as a newfound land, but Spenser immediately shatters such an assertion by invoking the gaze of royal power:

> And thou, O fairest Princesse vnder sky,
> In this faire mirrhour maist behold thy face,
> And thine owne realmes in lond of Faery,
> And in this antique Image thy great auncestry.
>
> (2 Proem 4)

In an instant the 'other world' has been transformed into a mirror; the queen turns her gaze upon a shining sphere hitherto hidden from view and sees her own face, her own realms, her own ancestry. That which threatens to exist independent of religious and secular ideology, that is, of what we believe—'Yet all these were, when no man did them know'—is revealed to be the ideal image of that ideology. And hence it need not be feared or destroyed: iconoclasm gives way to appropriation, violence to colonization. J. H. Elliott remarks that the most significant aspect of the impact of the new world upon the old is its insignificance: men looked at things unseen before, things alien to their own culture, and saw only themselves.[32] Spenser asserts that Faerie Land is a new world, another Peru or Virginia, only so that he may colonize it in the very moment of its discovery. The 'other world' becomes mirror becomes aesthetic image, and this transformation of the poem from a thing discovered to a thing made, from existence to the representation of existence is completed with the poet's turn from 'vaunt' to apology:

> The which O pardon me thus to enfold
> In couert vele, and wrap in shadowes light,
> That feeble eyes your glory may behold,
> Which else could not endure those beames bright,
> But would be dazled with exceeding light.
>
> (2 Proem 5)

The queen is deified precisely in the act of denying art's claim to ontological dignity, to the possession or embodiment of reality.

Such embodiment is the characteristic achievement of great drama, of Marlowe and supremely of Shakespeare, whose constant allusions to the fictionality of his creations only serve paradoxically to question the status of everything outside themselves. By contrast, Spenser's profoundly *undramatic* art, in the same movement by which it wards off idolatry, wards off this radical questioning of everything that exists. That is, if art like Shakespeare's realizes the power we glimpsed in Wyatt, the power in Althusser's words, to 'make us "perceive" . . . from *the inside*, by an *internal distance*, the very ideology' in which it is held, Spenserean allegory may be understood as a countermeasure: it opens up an internal distance within art itself by continually referring the reader out to a fixed authority beyond the poem. Spenser's art does not lead us to perceive ideology critically, but rather affirms the existence and inescapable moral power of ideology as that principle of truth toward which art forever yearns. It is art whose status is questioned in Spenser, not ideology; indeed, art is questioned precisely to spare ideology that internal distantiation it undergoes in the work of Shakespeare or Marlowe. In *The Faerie Queene* reality as given by ideology always lies safely outside the bounds of art, in a different realm, distant, infinitely powerful, perfectly good. 'The hallmark of Spenserean narration,' Paul Alpers acutely observes, 'is confidence in locutions which are at the same time understood to be provisional.'[33] Both the confidence and the provisionality stem from the externality of true value, order, meaning. For Spenser this is the final colonialism, the colonialism of language, yoked to the service of a reality forever outside itself, dedicated to 'the Most High, Mightie, and Magnificent Empresse . . . Elizabeth by the Grace of God Queene of England Fraunce and Ireland and of Virginia, Defendour of the Faith.'

. . . .

QUESTIONS

- How useful are the spatial metaphors of centres and margins to these readings of Renaissance identities and what interconnections are suggested by this ordering motif?

- What is the impact of the critical focus on the marginal on the study of the Renaissance? Can access to marginal texts, voices and experiences ever truly be gained through the mediation of canonical texts or representations?

- How do the above selections embody metaphorical centres and margins? In what ways do Greenblatt and Brown complicate the straightforward idea of English culture as 'central' and what impact might this have on the cultural canon?

4 | The limits of the human

Jonathan Dollimore, *Death, Desire and Loss in Western Culture* (London: Allen Lane, Penguin Press, 1998), pp. 84–5, 90–3.

Death and identity

Our nature consists in movement. Absolute stillness is death.

(Pascal, *Pensées*, p. 126)

The preoccupation with death probably always involved problems of identity, but in the early modern period they became more acute. In the context of secure faith and a belief in an underlying order in Creation, the meditation on death might well arrive at a view of human identity as being essentially or ultimately coherent and unified, though not of course immediately so—not, that is, in the existential experience of self. Thomas Browne speaks of the importance of knowing oneself but also of the difficulty of doing so. Modern psychoanalysis might concur with his contention that 'the greatest imperfection is in our inward sight . . . and while we are so sharp sighted as to look through others, to be invisible unto ourselves; for the inward eyes are more fallacious than the outward' (*Christian Morals*, p. 249).[1] There is also something proto-psychoanalytic about Browne's belief that our dreams may 'intimately tell us ourselves' in ways which conscious introspection cannot (*On Dreams*, p. 176; cf. *Letter to a Friend*, pp. 190–92). The revealing difference is, of course, that for Browne dreams tell us about our selves, rather than our unconscious. Freud's sense of the unconscious as being the place of our repressions, of our other selves (plural) and of forbidden desires which can wreck the socially organized ego, is not Browne's: 'Persons of radical integrity will not easily be perverted in their dreams' (*On Dreams*, p. 176). And, although he concedes that man is a conflicted being, living in 'divided and distinguished worlds', Browne nevertheless has faith in the possibilities of integrating the conflicting demands of, for example, faith and reason with those of passion and desire (*Religio Medici*, pp. 53, 34). He also believes that, in spite of bad dreams, inner division and the corruption of the world, one really can become who one truly is:

> Though the world be histrionical, and most men live ironically, yet be thou what thou singly art, and personate only thyself. Swim smoothly in the stream of thy nature, and live but one man. To single hearts doubling is discruciating . . . He who counterfeiteth, acts a part; and is, as it were, out of himself . . . (*Christian Morals*, pp. 252–3)

Browne contains mutability within an ethical-religious perspective. Even so, he retains an acute sense of death in life, and of the potential instabilities in identity which this entails. Those who experienced these things in ways which could not be contained or resolved in Browne's terms were much more troubled. It is in Elizabethan and Jacobean drama that we find an exploration of identity in terms of what Browne calls its histrionical/ironic mode—that is, identity as necessitating the duplicitous opposite of an authentic, honest subjectivity. Time and again in such drama Browne's belief in the ultimate accessibility of true identity is repudiated.[2]
[. . .]

The death of man?

Modern theories of identity have been preoccupied with the alleged recent disintegration of Western humanism. The argument usually goes like this. Western culture was once underpinned by a confident ideology of subjectivity. The individual experienced himself as unified and (spiritually if not socially) self-determining by virtue of his imagined possession of a presocial or asocial essence from which spiritual (if not social) value and freedom derive. It was this concept of subjectivity which fed the predominantly masculinist Western ideologies of individualism, and its universal counterpart, 'man'. But these ideologies were relatively short-lived. Often the fully unified subject was said to have emerged in the Renaissance, become ideologically consolidated in the Enlightenment, and experienced its high point in the nineteenth century, before collapsing in our own time (and in a way corresponding to the crisis of the West, of capitalism or empire). This collapse is not usually regarded with regret; in some post-modern versions of this narrative, the modern 'decentred' and mobile subject is also fantasized as the subversion of, or at least the radical alternative to, the ideologies which the individual and man once served.

It is ironic that, far from being the critical act of demystification which it so often aspires to be, the explanatory model at work here—from unity, fullness and freedom to disunity, crisis and fragmentation—echoes, often unawares and in secular form, one of the founding myths of western-European culture, and of Western subjectivity, namely the Fall. We repeat this Fall narrative imagining it as a narrative of the ending of something, whereas in fact it is the narrative of its continuation.

[. . .] [T]he crisis of subjectivity was present at the inception of individualism in early Christianity, and it has been as enabling as it has been disturbing (enabling because disturbing). The Fall narrative dramatizes this very crisis, indicating as it does that what simultaneously subverted and energized the subject of Western culture was not desire *per se*, but transgressive desire haunted by the death which it brought into being. This of course is what happened in Eden: Adam and Eve, by transgressing God's law, brought death into the world.

Most significant in this tradition has been death's manifestation as a pernicious mutability which always undermines identity. William Drummond writes of how death not only destroys, but in the process (and long before death proper) cruelly transforms everything into its own opposite: 'all Strength by it is enfeebled, Beauty turned in deformity and rottenness, Honour in contempt, Glory into baseness' (pp. 148–9). Working thus through mutability, death inverts, perverts, contradicts and finally destroys. As a result, man is permanently unstable and conflicted: 'His Body is but a Mass of discording humours . . . which though agreeing for a trace of time, yet can never be made uniform.' This very discord is at once natural and the agency of death—it is the '*inward cause of a necessary dissolution*'. Man is an entity so inherently and radically unstable, so contradictory, both psychically and physically, that 'we should rather wonder how so fragile a matter should so long endure, than how so soon dissolve, and decay'. This is hardly the fractured, dispersed post-modern subject, but the latter's antecedents are surely here. (And one significant difference between Drummond and some post-modernists is that, intellectually speaking, he at least knew where he was coming from.) Mutability is also experienced as a condition of radical psychic insecurity; Drummond succinctly remarks our perpetual vulnerability even, or especially, at the height of our power, when 'the glance of an Eye is sufficient to undo [us]' (pp. 148, 155, 151–2; my emphasis).

What we might now call the neurosis, anxiety and alienation of the subject in crisis is not so much the consequence of its recent breakdown, but the very stuff of the subject's creation, and of the culture—western-European culture—which it sustains, especially in its most expansionist phases (of which Drummond's own period—what we now call 'the Renaissance'—was undoubtedly one). If man is inhabited by mutability, and in a way which leads him inevitably deathward, it is this same mutability which imparts to him a restless, agonized energy. The crisis of the self is not so much the subjective counterpart of the demise, disintegration or undermining of western-European culture as what energizes both the self and that culture. That is why, for Drummond, the terrible disharmony which is the dynamic of life as death, and which makes for the futility of desire, by the same token generates a kind of negative, forward-directed energy:

> [Man] hath no sooner acquired what he did desire, but he beginneth to enter into new Cares, and desire what he shall never be able to acquire . . . He is pressed with Care for what is present, with Grief, for what is past, with Fear of what is to come, nay, for what will never come. (p. 153)[3]

Again, it is in Augustine's *Confessions* (c. 397–401) that we find one of the most influential precedents for the way in which 'modern' subjectivity is founded in that same sense of crisis which imparts the restless expansionist energy which is the making of civilization itself. Augustine suggests how individualism was from the beginning energized by an inner dynamic of loss, conflict, doubt, absence and lack, and how this feeds into our culture's obsession with control and expansion—the sense that the identity of everything, from self to nation, is under centrifugal and potentially disintegrative pressures which have to be rigorously controlled. This is a kind of control that is always exceeding and breaking down the very order it restlessly quests for, and is forever re-establishing its own rationale even as it undermines it. The experience of instability is inherited by Augustine and deployed in a religious praxis; the subject in crisis becomes a crucial element in the triumph of Western individualism and all that this has meant. It is this which we have inherited; what we are living through now is not some (post-)-modern collapse of Western subjectivity but another development of its enduring dynamic.

*　*　*

Erica Fudge, *Perceiving Animals: Humans and Beasts in Early Modern English Culture* (Basingstoke: Macmillan, 2000), pp. 1–8.

There was a Bear Garden in early modern London. In it the spectators watched a pack of mastiffs attack an ape on horseback and assault bears whose teeth and claws had been removed. We know this from the numerous reports of the baitings which have survived. What we don't understand is the nature of their enjoyment. This book began as an attempt to comprehend the pleasure through an examination of the ways in which the spectators related to animals, those silent and, until recently, forgotten creatures of history.[1] What emerged from my reading surprised me. An anxiety could be traced in the ways in which animals were represented: an anxiety which was not about the animals. My attempt to read the Bear Garden revealed a struggle more significant than the one played out by the dogs and the bears, it revealed a struggle over the nature of being human itself. [. . .] [I]f anthropocentrism—placing the human and human vision at the centre—leads [. . .] to anthropomorphism—seeing the world in our own image—and anthropomorphism allows for the animalisation of humans then anthropocentrism paradoxically destroys *anthropos* as a category. By centralising the human, making the human vision the only vision, the separation of the species is impossible. At the heart of the debate about animals lies a debate about humanity which has social and political ramifications. If an animal can beg, then is a (human) beggar also an animal? The implications of this question are played out in the sense that in order to assert human status writers have to make exclusions. Some humans are aligned with animals: in fact, some humans are not human at all.

. . . .

QUESTIONS

- How do these critics define 'humanity', 'identity', 'subjectivity' and the 'self'? In what ways might the dead, or the animal be categorized as 'other', as 'marginal', or as in a state of historical flux?

- Are the particular political and social responses and responsibilities which these criticisms advocate the legitimate purpose of criticism and/or the legitimate function of reading?

- What, if any, are the limits of theorizations of identity?

SUGGESTED FURTHER READING

Andreadis, Harriette, *Sappho in Early Modern England: Female Same-Sex Literary Erotics, 1550–1714* (Chicago: University of Chicago Press, 2001)

Baker, David and Maley, Willy (eds.), *British Identities and English Renaissance Literature* (Cambridge: Cambridge University Press, 2002)

Berry, Philippa, *Shakespeare's Feminine Endings: Disfiguring Death in the Tragedies* (London and New York: Routledge, 1999)

Bhabha, Homi, *The Location of Culture* (London and New York: Routledge, 1994)

Chedgzoy, Kate (ed.), *Shakespeare, Feminism and Gender* (Basingstoke: Palgrave, New Casebook, 2001)

Foucault, Michel, *The History of Sexuality*, trans. by Robert Hurley (Harmondsworth: Penguin, 1981–8), Vols. 1–3

Hulme, Peter and Sherman, William H. (eds.), *'The Tempest' and its Travels* (London: Reaktion Books, 2000)

Kamps, Ivo and Singh, Jyotsna G. (eds.), *Travel Knowledge: European 'Discoveries' in the Early Modern Period* (Basingstoke: Palgrave, 2001)

Kelly-Gadol, Joan, 'Did women have a renaissance?' in Renate Bridenthal and Claudia Koonz (eds.), *Becoming Visible: Women in European History* (Boston: Houghton Mifflin, 1977), pp. 137–64.

Neill, Michael, *Issues of Death: Mortality and Identity in English Renaissance Tragedy* (Oxford: Clarendon Press, 1997)

Smith, Bruce R., *Homosexual Desire in Shakespeare's England: A Cultural Poetics* (Chicago and London: University of Chicago Press, 1991)

Spivak, Gayatri Chakravorty, *In Other Worlds: Essays in Cultural Politics* (London and New York: Methuen, 1987)

NOTES

Sinfield, Faultlines

1. Linda Woodbridge, *Women and the English Renaissance* (Brighton: Harvester, 1984), p. 195.

2. Catherine Belsey, *The Subject of Tragedy* (London: Methuen, 1985), p. 149.

3. Janet Adelman, ' "This is and is not Cressid": the characterisation of Cressida', in Shirley Nelson Garner, Claire Kahane, and Madelon Sprengnether (eds.), *The(M)other Tongue: Essays in Feminist Psychoanalytic Interpretation* (Ithaca, NY: Cornell University Press, 1985), p. 140. However, Adelman believes that Desdemona 'remains a vigorous and independent character, larger than Othello's fantasies of her' (p. 140).

Trevor, George Herbert and the scene of writing

1. See, for example, Barbara Kiefer Lewalski, *Protestant Poetics and the Seventeenth-Century Religious Lyric* (Princeton: Princeton University Press, 1979), esp. chapter 9.

268

2. See in particular Diana Benet, 'Herbert's experience of politics and patronage in 1624,' *George Herbert Journal*, 10, 1–2 (1986–7), 33–45; Sidney Gottlieb, 'The social and political backgrounds of George Herbert's poetry,' *'The Muses Common-Weale': Poetry and Politics in the Seventeenth Century*, ed. Claude J. Summers and Ted-Larry Pebworth (Columbia: University of Missouri Press, 1988), 107–18.

3. Michael C. Schoenfeldt, *Prayer and Power: George Herbert and Renaissance Courtship* (Chicago: University of Chicago Press, 1991), 12. For Schoenfeldt's acknowledged, although qualified, indebtedness to the new historicism, see 13.

4. Richard Strier, *Resistant Structures: Particularity, Radicalism, and Renaissance Texts* (Berkeley: University of California Press, 1995), 73.

5. John Donne, *Devotions upon Emergent Occasions*, ed. Anthony Raspa (Oxford: Oxford University Press, 1987), 'Prayer II,' 13; Paul W. Harland, ' "A true transubstantiation": Donne, self-love, and the passion,' in *John Donne's Religious Imagination: Essays in Honor of John T. Shawcross*, ed. Raymond-Jean Frontain and Frances M. Malpezzi (Conway: University of Central Arkansas Press, 1995), 162–80, 172.

6. Martin Luther, *A Commentary on St Paul's Epistle to the Galatians*, ed. Philip S. Watson, based on the Middleton edition of the 1575 English version (London: James Clarke, 1953), 343.

7. Ibid., 168.

8. Schoenfeldt *Prayer and Power*, 53. See also Jonathan Goldberg, *Voice Terminal Echo: Postmodernism and English Renaissance Texts* (New York: Methuen, 1986), esp. 115–16.

9. Jacques Lacan, *Seminar VII: The Ethics of Psychoanalysis, 1959–1960*, ed. Jacques-Alain Miller, trans. with notes by Dennis Porter (New York: W. W. Norton, 1992, first pub. Editions du Seuil, 1986), 97, 93.

10. Jacques Lacan, *Seminar VII*, 93.

11. Philip Rieff, *The Feeling Intellect: Selected Writings* (Chicago: University of Chicago Press, 1990), 12–13. For a sustained critique of the ways in which psychoanalysis redeploys Judeo-Christian motifs and theories of the self see Suzanne R. Kirschner, *The Religious and Romantic Origins of Psychoanalysis: Individuation and Integration in Post-Freudian Theory* (Cambridge: Cambridge University Press, 1996).

12. Debora Kuller Shuger, *The Renaissance Bible: Scholarship, Sacrifice, and Subjectivity* (Berkeley: University of California Press, 1994), 195.

13. Jonathan Dollimore, *Radical Tragedy: Religion, Ideology, and Power in the Drama of Shakespeare and His Contemporaries* (Durham: Duke University Press, 1993, first pub. Harvester Wheatsheaf in 1984), 'Introduction to the second edition,' xi–lxviii, xxxi.

14. Goldberg, *Writing Matter: From the Hands of the English Renaissance* (Stanford: Stanford University Press, 1990), 265, 269.

15. Amy M. Charles, *A Life of George Herbert* (Ithaca: Cornell University Press, 1977), 213.

16. Luther, *Commentary on Galatians*, 168.

17. Jacques Lacan, 'The function and field of speech and language in psychoanalysis,' in *Ecrits: A Selection*, trans. Alan Sheridan (New York: W. W. Norton, 1977), 30–113, 40. All passages in the original French are from *Ecrits I* and *II* (Paris: Editions du Seuil, 1966).

18. Ibid., 90.

19. Ibid., 118; *Ecrits I*, 214.

20. See Lacan, *Seminar VII*, 179–82.

21. Jacques Derrida, 'Freud and the scene of writing,' in *Writing and Difference*, trans. with additional notes by Alan Bass (Chicago: University of Chicago Press, 1978), 196–231, 210.

22. Derrida, 'Freud and writing,' 211.

23. Ibid., 226.

24. Lacan, 'The subversion of the subject and the dialectic of desire in the Freudian unconscious,' *Ecrits*, 292–325, 297.

Maus, Inwardness and Theater

1. Annabel Patterson, *Censorship and Interpretation: The Conditions of Writing and Reading in Early Modern England* (Madison: University of Wisconsin Press, 1984), p. 139.

2. Various forms of the philosophical argument are made in general terms by such writers as Freud, Marx, Foucault, Lacan, Derrida, Dewey, and Wittgenstein; except in the case of Foucault, perhaps, their arguments do not stand or fall upon a particular reading of Renaissance culture.

3. James I and VI, *Basilikon Doron* (Edinburgh, 1595), pp. 119, 121.

4. Robert Johnson, *Essays* (London, 1601), F8ᵛ–G1ʳ.

MacDonald, The disappearing African woman

1. See, for example, Homi Bhabha, 'Of mimicry and man: the ambivalence of colonial discourse', *October* 28 (1984): 125–33. [. . .] [See also] 'The other question', (*Screen* 24:6 [1983]: 18, n.1). Gwen Bergner's 'Who is that masked woman? or, The role of gender in Fanon's *Black Skin, White Masks*' (*PMLA* 110 [1995]: 75–88). [. . .] Ann DuCille's 'The occult of true womanhood: critical demeanour and black feminist studies' (*Signs* 19 [1994]: 591–629). [. . .]

2. See especially Nussbaum's discussion of polygamy and Richardson's *Pamela*, in her *Torrid Zones: Maternity, Sexuality, and Empire in Eighteenth-Century English Narratives* (Baltimore: The Johns Hopkins University Press, 1995), 73–94.

Hendricks, Civility, barbarism, and . . . The Widow Ranter

1. Valerie Wayne (ed.), *The Matter of Difference: Materialist Feminist Criticism of Shakespeare* (London: Harvester Wheatsheaf, 1991), 11.

2. Dominick LaCapra (ed.), *The Bounds of Race: Perspectives on Hegemony and Resistance* (Ithaca: Cornell University Press, 1991), 2.

3. Margaret Ferguson, 'Juggling the categories of race, class, and gender: Aphra Behn's *Oroonoko*,' in Hendricks and Parker, ch. 12.

4. Bernard W. Sheehan, *Savagism and Civility: Indians and Englishmen in Colonial Virgina* (Cambridge: Cambridge University Press, 1980), 2.

5. Sheehan, *Savagism and Civility*, 2.

6. See Ann Rosalind Jones and Peter Stallybrass, 'Dismantling Irena: the sexualizing of Ireland in early modern England,' in *Nationalisms and Sexualities*, ed. Andrew Parker, Mary Russo, Doris Sommer, and Patricia Yaeger (London: Routledge, 1992), 157–71.

7. Louis B. Wright (ed.), *The Elizabethans' America: A Collection of Early Reports by Englishmen on the New World* (Cambridge, Mass.: Harvard University Press, 1965), 109.

8. Thomas Harriot, *A Brief and True Report of the New-Found Land of Virginia*, in *The Elizabethans' America*, ed. Louis B. Wright (Cambridge, Mass.: Harvard University Press, 1965), 129–30.

9. Karen Ordahl Kupperman, *Settling with the Indians: The Meeting of English and Indian Cultures in America, 1580–1640* (New Jersey: Rowman & Littlefield, 1980), 121–2.

10. Kupperman, *Settling with the Indians*, 122.

11. See Michael Banton's *The Idea of Race* (London: Tavistock, 1977) and *Racial Theories* (Cambridge: Cambridge University Press, 1987) for an incisive analysis of the history of 'race.' See also *Anatomy of Racism*, ed. David Theo Goldberg (Minneapolis: University of Minnesota, 1991).

12. Homi K. Bhabha, 'The other question: difference, discrimination and the discourse of colonialism,' in *Out There: Marginalization and Contemporary Cultures*, ed. Russell Ferguson, Martha Gever, Trinh T. Minh-ha, and Cornel West (New York: MIT Press, 1990), 71.

13. Wright, *The Elizabethans' America*, 185.

14. Quoted in Kupperman, *Settling with the Indians*, 59.

15. John Winthrop, cited in *The Invasion Within: The Contest of Cultures in Colonial North America* (Oxford: Oxford University Press, 1985), 137. What is not clear in this declaration is the English attitude toward cultivated 'Indian' lands.

16. Mary Dearborn, *Pocahontas' Daughters: Gender and Ethnicity in American Culture* (New York: Oxford University Press, 1986), 97.

17. Here I am thinking of the literary and film trope of the 'half-breed' who self-consciously rejects 'white' culture for American Indian culture.

18. For example, the Maryland colony enacted one of the earliest prohibitions against English-African miscegenation: 'any White man that shall beget any Negroe Woman with Child whether Free Woman or Servant, shall undergo the same Penalties as White Women.' These penalties included indentured servitude for seven years for the man or woman and thirty-one years for the child(ren) of such unions. Occurrences of English-African miscegenation in the Virginia colony in the first half of the seventeenth century were also generally punished. There is, however, no record of legal opposition to marital relations between Englishmen and American Indian women in the early stages of English colonialism in the Virginia colony. See William Browne *et al.* (eds.), *Archives of Maryland* (Baltimore, 1883–1912), vol. 1.

19. See Felicity Nussbaum, 'The other woman: polygamy, *Pamela*, and the prerogative of empire,' Hendricks and Parker, ch. 8.

20. Bhabha, 'The other question,' 75.

Kastan, Is there a class?

1. See, for example, valuable discussions on the language of social ordering by Burke, Cressy, and Wrightson.

2. Among the many influential considerations of class consciousness, see Lukàcs, Mészáros (ed.) (esp. E. J. Hobsbawm's 'Class Consciousness in History'), and Thompson.

3. See Mary Jacobus's fine article by that name. Jacobus's essay, like my own, obviously finds its title in a play upon Stanley Fish's *Is There a Text in This Class?*

4. [S]ee Annabel Patterson's *Shakespeare and the Popular Voice.*

5. [S]ee especially [. . .] Belsey, Howard 93–128, Levine, and Rackin.

6. On sumptuary legislation in early modern England, see Harte and two useful earlier studies by Hooper and Baldwin.

7. For example, in 1 Henry VIII c. 14: 'Players in enterludes,' along with 'ambassatures Hencemen,' 'Harroldes of armes,' 'Mynstrelles,' and men 'weryng any apparrell of the Kyngs lyverey geven hym by the King, for the tyme beyng of his Attendance aboute the Kyngs Grace' are specifically exempted from the act's provisions. In Elizabethan England, however, dispensations again are made to 'henchmen, heralds, pursuivants at arms, runners at jousts, tourneys, or such martial feats, or such as wear apparel given by the Queen's majesty' (Hughes and Larkin 3: 180), but the specific dispensation for players has disappeared.

8. Among the many useful studies of the status of players in Elizabethan England, see Agnew 101–48, Bradbrook 17–66, and Edwards 17–39.

Healey, Selves, states and sectarianism

1. Richard Helgerson, *Forms of Nationhood: The Elizabethan Writing of England* (Chicago and London: University of Chicago Press, 1992), p. 22.

Traub, Desire and Anxiety

1. See Jacqueline Rose's analysis of Leonardo da Vinci in *Sexuality in the Field of Vision* (London: Verso, 1986), p. 226.

2. Gayle Rubin, 'Thinking Sex: Notes for a Radical Theory of the Politics of Sexuality,' *Pleasure and Danger: Exploring Female Sexuality*, ed. Carole Vance (London: Routledge and Kegan Paul, 1984), p. 307.

3. Jonathan Dollimore, 'Shakespeare, cultural materialism, feminism, and Marxist humanism,' *New Literary History* 21:3 (Spring 1990), pp. 471–93.

4. Sigmund Freud, 'Femininity,' *New Introductory Lectures on Psychoanalysis*, ed. James Strachey (New York: W. W. Norton, 1965), p. 116.

5. See Teresa de Lauretis, *Technologies of Gender: Essays on Theory, Film, and Fiction* (Bloomington: Indiana University Press, 1987), and 'Feminist Studies/Critical Studies: Issues, Terms, and Contexts,' in *Feminist Studies/Critical Studies* ed. de Lauretis (Bloomington: Indiana University Press, 1986), pp. 1–19.

6. Sigmund Freud, 'The psychogenesis of a case of homosexuality in a woman' (1920), *The Standard Edition of the Complete Psychological Works of Sigmund Freud*, ed. J. Strachey, Vol. 18, p. 170.

7. Freud, 'Psychogenesis,' p. 154, and 'Leonardo da Vinci and a memory of his childhood' (1910), *Standard Edition*, Vol. 11, pp. 59–137.

8. Freud, 'General remarks on hysterical attacks' (1909), *Dora: An Analysis of a Case of Hysteria*, ed. Philip Rieff (New York: Macmillan, 1963), p. 157, my emphasis.

9. Freud, 'From the history of an infantile neurosis' (1918), *Three Case Histories*, ed. Philip Rieff (New York: Macmillan, 1963), p. 305.

10. Freud, 'Leonardo da Vinci,' p. 86.

11. Karen Newman, 'Renaissance family politics and Shakespeare's *The Taming of the Shrew*', *ELR* 16:1 (1986), p. 99, my emphasis.

12. Nancy Chodorow, *The Reproduction of Mothering: Psychoanalysis and the Sociology of Gender* (Berkeley: University of California Press, 1978), p. 150. See also Julia Epstein, 'Either/Or—Neither/Both: sexual ambiguity and the ideology of gender,' *Genders* (Spring 1990), pp. 99–142 for an excellent analysis of the ideological character of 'biological' gender categories.

13. Arlene Stein, 'All dressed up, but no place to go? Style wars and the new lesbianism,' *Outlook: National Lesbian and Gay Quarterly* 1:4 (1989), p. 38.

14. See Joan Nestle, 'Butch-Fem relationships: sexual courage in the 1950s,' *Heresies: A Feminist Publication on Art and Politics* 3:4 (1981), pp. 21–4.

15. [S]ee Esther Newton and Shirley Walton, 'The misunderstanding: toward a more precise sexual vocabulary,' *Pleasure and Danger: Exploring Female Sexuality*, ed. Carol Vance (London: Routledge and Kegan Paul, 1984), pp. 242–50.

16. Robert Stoller, *Observing the Erotic Imagination* (New Haven: Yale University Press, 1985).

17. Cindy Patton, *Sex and Germs: The Politics of AIDS* (Boston: South End Press, 1985), p. 105.

18. See Henry L. Minton, 'Femininity in men and masculinity in women: American psychiatry and psychology portray homosexuality in the 1930s,' *Journal of Homosexuality* 13:1 (Fall 1986), pp. 1–21, and Kenneth Lewes, *The Psychoanalytic Theory of Male Homosexuality* (New York: Simon and Schuster, 1988).

19. See Jonathan Dollimore, 'Subjectivity, sexuality, and transgression: the Jacobean connection,' *Renaissance Drama* 17 (1986), pp. 53–81.

20. [S]ee *Hidden From History*; also *The Gay Past: A Collection of Historical Essays*, ed. Salvatore J. Licata and Robert P. Petersen (New York: Harrington Park Press, 1985).

21. See, in particular, the way that appeals to narcissism work in W. Thomas MacCary, *Friends and Lovers: The Phenomenology of Desire in Shakespearean Comedy* (New York: Columbia University Press, 1985); Leonard Tennenhouse, 'The Counterfeit Order of *The Merchant of Venice*' and Joel Fineman, 'Fratricide and Cuckoldry: Shakespeare's Doubles' in *Representing Shakespeare: New Psychoanalytic Essays*, ed. Murray M. Schwartz and Coppélia Kahn (Baltimore: Johns Hopkins University Press, 1980), pp. 54–109.

22. Eve Kosofsky Sedgwick, *Between Men: English Literature and Male Homosocial Desire* (New York: Columbia University Press, 1985). Sedgwick has recently come under attack, most notably by David van Leer in 'The beast in the closet: homosociality and the pathology of manhood,' *Critical Inquiry* 15:3 (1989), pp. 587–605.

23. See, for instance, Joseph A. Porter, 'Marlowe, Shakespeare, and the canonization of heterosexuality,' *South Atlantic Quarterly* 88:1 (1989), pp. 127–47 and *Shakespeare's Mercutio: his History and Drama* (Chapel Hill: University of North Carolina Press, 1988). At the 1989 Shakespeare Association of America Conference, at least fifteen seminar papers dealt with homoeroticism.

24. Joseph Pequigney, for instance, sees his task as securing the 'identity' of both Shakespeare and his characters as 'homosexual.' His impulse to produce 'evidence' of 'classic male homosexual relationships' works against my thesis in multiple ways. See *Such is My Love: A Study of Shakespeare's Sonnets* (Chicago: University of Chicago Press, 1985), and 'The Two Antonios and Same-Sex Love in *Twelfth Night* and *The Merchant of Venice*,' unpublished manuscript presented to the Shakespeare Association of America, 1989.

25. The most critically sophisticated analyses of early modern legal discourse on homosexuality are Ed Cohen, 'Legislating the Norm: From Sodomy to Gross Indecency,' *South Atlantic Quarterly* 88:1 (1989), pp. 181–217, and Bruce Smith, *Homosexual Desire in Shakespeare's England* (Chicago: University of Chicago Press, 1991). Helpful as more general analyses of early modern homoeroticism are Stephen Orgel, 'Nobody's Perfect: Or Why Did the English Stage Take Boys for Women,' *South Atlantic Quarterly* 88:1 (1989), pp. 7–29, and Jonathan Goldberg, 'Sodomy and Society: The Case of Christopher Marlowe,' *Southwest Review* 69:4 (Autumn 1984), pp. 371–8. Each is influenced by Foucault as well as by Alan Bray.

26. Alan Bray, *Homosexuality in Renaissance England* (London: Gay Men's Press, 1982), p. 92.

27. Goldberg, 'Sodomy and Society,' p. 371.

28. Ibid., p. 376.

29. Ibid., p. 372.

30. Adrienne Rich, 'When we dead awaken: writing as re-vision', *College English* 34:1 (Oct. 1972), pp. 18–25; Carroll Smith-Rosenberg, 'The female world of love and ritual: relations between women in nineteenth-century America,' *Signs* 1 (Autumn 1975), pp. 1–29. See also Rich's important, if problematic, essay 'Compulsory heterosexuality and lesbian existence,' *Signs* 5:4 (Summer 1980), pp. 631–60.

31. *A Midsummer Night's Dream* III.ii.198–216; *As You Like It* I.iii. 73–4; *Pericles* IV. Prologue 15–40; *The Winter's Tale* I.ii.62–75.

32. James Holstun [. . .], ' "Will You Rent Our Ancient Love Asunder?": Lesbian elegy in Donne, Marvell, and Milton,' *ELH* 54:4 (Winter 1987), pp. 835–67. [. . .] For a further exploration of this question, see my 'The (in)significance of "lesbian" desire in early modern England,' *Erotic Politics: The Dynamics of Desire on the English Renaissance Stage*, ed. Susan Zimmerman (London: Routledge, 1992).

33. Louis Crompton, 'The myth of lesbian impunity: capital laws from 1270 to 1791,' *The Gay Past*, ed. Licata and Petersen, p. 11. See also Brigitte Eriksson (trans.), 'A lesbian execution in Germany, 1721: the trial records,' ibid., pp. 27–40; Judith C. Brown, *Immodest Acts: The Life of a Lesbian Nun in Renaissance Italy* (Oxford: Oxford University Press, 1986).

34. Randolph Trumbach, 'London's sodomites: homosexual behavior and western culture in the eighteenth century,' *Journal of Social History* 11:1 (Fall 1977), pp. 1–33 (p. 13).

35. Crompton, 'The myth of lesbian impunity,' p. 11.

36. James M. Saslow, 'Homosexuality in the Renaissance: behavior, identity, and artistic expression,' *Hidden from History: Reclaiming the Gay and Lesbian Past*, ed. Martin Duberman, Martha Vicinus, and George Chauncey Jr. (New York: New American Library, 1989), pp. 90–105 (p. 95).

37. Ibid., p. 96.

38. Katharine Eisaman Maus, 'Horns of dilemma: jealousy, gender, and spectatorship in English Renaissance drama,' *ELH* 54:3 (1987), p. 562.

39. In addition to Howard's far-reaching analysis of cross-dressing and anti-theatricalist rhetoric in 'Crossdressing, the theater, and gender struggle in early modern England,' see Mary Beth Rose, 'Women in men's clothing: apparel and social stability in *The Roaring Girl*,' *ELR* 14:3

(1984), pp. 367–91; and Laura Levine, 'Men in women's clothing: anti-theatricality and effeminization from 1579 to 1642,' *Criticism* 28:2 (Spring 1986), pp. 121–43.

40. Saslow disagrees, stating ambiguously that 'the perception of female sexual deviance [what kind of deviance?] was conflated with other forms of unorthodoxy, gender and doctrinal,' 'Homosexuality and the Renaissance,' p. 95. Howard suggests that 'In the polemical literature women who crossdressed were less often accused of sexual perversion than of sexual incontinence, of being whores . . . in part because the discursive construction of woman in the Renaissance involved seeing her as a creature of strong sexual appetites needing strict regulation' 'Crossdressing,' p. 424.

41. Lynn Friedli, ' "Passing Women": a study of gender boundaries in the eighteenth century,' *Sexual Underworlds of the Enlightenment*, ed. G. S. Rousseau and Roy Porter (Chapel Hill: University of North Carolina Press, 1988), pp. 234–60.

42. Vera Brittain, *Radclyffe Hall: A Case of Obscenity?* (London: A Femina Book, 1968), p. 21.

43. Saslow, 'Homosexuality in the Renaissance,' p. 99.

44. I am indebted to Peter Stallybrass for helping me to clarify my understanding of early modern heterosexuality.

45. In his nuanced discussion of the transformations of legal discourse over the course of the sixteenth and seventeenth centuries, Bruce Smith also distinguishes between the discourses of acts and desires. See *Homosexual Desire in Shakespeare's England*.

46. Michel Foucault, *The History of Sexuality*, Vol. 1 (New York: Random House, 1978), p. 157.

47. See, in this regard, Luce Irigaray, *This Sex Which Is Not One*, trans. Catherine Porter (Ithaca: Cornell University Press, 1985): 'We might suspect the *phallus* (Phallus) of being the *contemporary figure of a god jealous* of his prerogatives; we might suspect it of claiming, on this basis, to be the ultimate meaning of all discourse, the standard of truth and propriety, in particular as regards sex, the signifier and/or the ultimate signified of all desire, in addition to continuing, as emblem and agent of the patriarchal system, to shore up the name of the father (Father),' p. 67.

48. Jonathan Dollimore, 'Shakespeare, cultural materialism, feminism, and Marxist humanism,' p. 484.

Greenblatt, To fashion a gentleman

1. Christopher Columbus, *Journals and Other Documents*, p. 287.

2. Tasso, *Gerusalemme Liberata* (book 15, stanzas 28ff.), relates the quest for the realm of Armida to Columbus's voyages. Spenser's Maleger carries arrows 'Such as the *Indians* in their quiuers hide' (2.11.21). Bernal Diaz del Castillo recalls the first reaction to the sight of the Aztec capital in *The Conquest of New Spain*, trans. J. M. Cohen (Baltimore: Penguin, 1963), p. 214. On Spenser and the New World, see Roy Harvey Pearce, 'Primitivistic Ideas in the *Faerie Queene*,' *Journal of English and Germanic Philology* 45 (1945), pp. 139–51; A. Bartlett Giamatti, 'Primitivism and the process of civility in Spenser's *Faerie Queene*,' in *First Images of America: The Impact of the New World on the Old*, ed. Fredi Chiappelli, 2 vols. (Berkeley: University of California Press, 1976), 1:71–82.

3. Ralegh, *The Discovery of Guiana*, ed. V. T. Harlow (London: Argonaut Press, 1928), p. 42.

4. Peter Martyr, *The Decades of the New World*, trans. Michael Lok, in *A Selection of Curious, Rare, and Early Voyages and Histories of Interesting Discoveries chiefly published by Hakluyt . . .* (London: R. H. Evans and R. Priestly, 1812), p. 539.

5. Ibid., p. 530.

6. *Of the newe landes*, in *The First Three English Books on America*, ed. Edward Arber (Birmingham: Turnbull and Spears, 1885), p. xxvii; cf. Wilberforce Eames, 'Description of a wood engraving illustrating the South American Indians (1505),' *Bulletin of the New York Public Library* 26 (1922), pp. 755–60.

7. Elizabeth Story Donno (ed.), *An Elizabethan in 1582: The Diary of Richard Madox, Fellow of All Souls*, Hakluyt Society, Second Series, No. 147 (London: Hakluyt Society, 1977), p. 183. The

editor notes that 'in the older maps the mountains of the moon figure as a range extending across the continent from Abyssinia to the Gulf of Guinea.'

8. At 6.8.43, the cannibals who capture Serena consider raping her, but they are stopped by their priests.

9. Compare Redcrosse who, when he dallies with Duessa, is described as 'Pourd out in loosnesse on the grassy grownd,/Both carelesse of his health, and of his fame' (1.7.7).

10. On vagabonds, see Frank Aydelotte, *Elizabethan Rogues and Vagabonds* (London: Frank Cass & Co., 1913).

11. Martyr, *Decades*, p. 628. On charges of idleness, see Edmund S. Morgan, *American Slavery, American Freedom: The Ordeal of Colonial Virginia* (New York: Norton, 1975).

12. Cortes 'had ordered that all houses should be pulled down and burnt and the bridged channels filled up; and what he gained each day was thus consolidated. He sent an order to Pedro de Alvarado to be sure that we never crossed a bridge or gap in the causeway without first blocking it up, and to pull down and burn every house' (Bernal Diaz, *Conquest*, p. 369).

13. I am indebted here to Richard Slotkin, *Regeneration through Violence: The Mythology of the American Frontier, 1600–1860* (Middletown, Conn.: Wesleyan University Press, 1973).

14. Bernal Diaz, *Conquest*, p. 60.

15. *A View of the Present State of Ireland*, ed. W. L. Renwick (Oxford: Clarendon, 1970), pp. 48, 64, 65. Our primary purpose is to explore aspects of Elizabethan policy in Ireland as a reiteration of a characteristic cultural pattern rather than to detail the direct influence of Ireland upon *The Faerie Queene*; for the latter, see M. M. Gray, 'The influence of Spenser's Irish experiences on *The Faerie Queene*,' *Review of English Studies* 6 (1930), pp. 413–28; Pauline Henley, *Spenser in Ireland* (Folcroft, Pa.: Folcroft Press, 1920).

16. Ibid., p. 67. Cf. Louis-Jean Calvet, *Linguistique et colonialisme: Petit traité de glottophagie* (Paris: Payot, 1974) and Stephen J. Greenblatt, 'Learning to curse: aspects of linguistic colonialism in the sixteenth century,' in *First Images of America* 2:561–80.

17. *View*, pp. 67–68. Children 'draweth into themselves together with their suck, even the nature and disposition of their nurses, for the mind followeth much the temperature of the body; and also the words are the image of the mind, so as they proceeding from the mind, the mind must be needs effected with the words' (p. 68).

18. Yeats, *Essays and Introductions*, p. 372.

19. R. Dudley Edwards, *Ireland in the Age of the Tudors: The Destruction of Hiberno-Norman Civilization* (London: Croom Helm, 1977); Nicholas P. Canny, *The Elizabethan Conquest of Ireland: A Pattern Established, 1565–76* (Hassocks, Sussex: Harvester Press, 1976); David Beers Quinn, *The Elizabethans and the Irish* (Ithaca: Cornell University Press, 1966). For an apologetic account of Spenser's involvement, see Pauline Henley, *Spenser in Ireland*; for an enigmatic indication of Spenser's personal profit from the Smerwick massacre, see Anna Maria Crinò, 'La relazione Barducci-Ubaldini sull'impresa d'Irlanda (1579–1581),' *English Miscellany* 19 (1968), pp. 339–67.

20. Alexander C. Judson, *The Life of Edmund Spenser* (Baltimore: Johns Hopkins University Press, 1945), pp. 107–8.

21. Ibid., p. 116. The reference to the 'fennes of Allan' in 2.9.16 indicates that it was written after Spenser acquired New Abbey, a ruined Franciscan friary in County Kildare, in 1582 (see Josephine Waters Bennett, *The Evolution of 'The Faerie Queene'* [Chicago: University of Chicago Press, 1942], p. 131n.).

22. It has been frequently noted that Maleger and his band resemble accounts in Spenser's *View* and in other reports on Ireland of Irish kerns.

23. We should perhaps note in this connection that Guyon leaves the Bower immediately after its destruction: 'But let vs hence depart,' says the Palmer, 'whilest wether serues and wind' (2.12.87).

24. Quoted in Philip Hughes, *The Reformation in England*, 3 vols. (New York: Macmillan, 1954), 3:408.

25. John Venn, *John Caius* (Cambridge: Cambridge University Press, 1910), p. 37. In a letter of the vice-chancellor, Dr. Byng, to the chancellor, Lord Burghley, dated 14 December 1572, the 'trumpery' is catalogued: 'vestments, albes, tunicles, stoles, manicles, corporas clothes, with the pix and sindon, and canopie, besides holy water stoppes, with sprinkles, pax, sensars, superaltaries, tables of idolles, masse bookes, portuises, and grailles, with other such stuffe as might have furnished divers massers at one instant.' The Latin account is from John Caius, *The Annals of Gonville and Caius College*, ed. John Venn, Cambridge Antiquarian Society Octavo Series no. 40 (Cambridge, 1904), p. 185. Caius adds that iconoclasts used hammers to smash certain objects.

26. Quoted in John Phillips, *The Reformation of Images: Destruction of Art in England, 1535–1660* (Berkeley: University of California Press, 1973), p. 80.

27. Keith Thomas, *Religion and the Decline of Magic* (London: Weidenfeld and Nicolson, 1971), p. 69.

28. *The Book of the Courtier*, trans. Singleton, p. 43. On *sprezzatura*, see Wayne A. Rebhom, *Courtly Performances: Masking and Festivity in Castiglione's 'Book of the Courtier'* (Detroit: Wayne State University Press, 1978), pp. 33–40.

29. On demonic artists, see A. Bartlett Giamatti, *Play of Double Senses: Spenser's Faerie Queene* (Englewood Cliffs, N.J.: Prentice-Hall, 1975), pp. 106–33. We may observe that Spenser seems on occasion to invoke positive versions of self-concealing art:

> Then came the Bride, the louely *Medua* came,
> Clad in a vesture of vnknowen geare,
> And vncouth fashion, yet her well became;
> That seem'd like siluer, sprinckled here and theare
> With glittering spangs, that did like starres appeare,
> And wau'd vpon, like water Chamelot,
> To hide the metall, which yet euery where
> Bewrayd it selfe, to let men plainely wot,
> It was no mortall worke, that seem'd and yet was not.
>
> (4.11.45)

   Spenser's suspicions of aesthetic concealment can be allayed by its use in a virtuous context, but we might also note that in this instance the device both hides and does not hide its own artifice. The art is designed to seem natural and yet at the same time to let men plainly know, through a kind of 'self-betrayal,' that it is not natural. For conflicting arguments on the status of artifice in Spenser, see C. S. Lewis, *The Allegory of Love*, pp. 326–33, and Hans P. Guth, 'Allegorical Implications of Artifice in Spenser's *Faerie Queene*,' *Publication of the Modern Language Association* 76 (1961), pp. 474–9.

30. Keith Thomas, *Religion and the Decline of Magic*, p. 275.

31. See Gershom Scholem, *Sabbatai Sevi* (Princeton: Princeton University Press, 1973).

32. J. H. Elliott, *The Old World and the New, 1492–1650* (Cambridge: Cambridge University Press, 1970).

33. Paul Alpers, 'Narration in *The Faerie Queene*,' *English Literary History* 44 (1977), p. 27.

Dollimore, Death, Desire and Loss

1. All references to Browne are to the edition edited by Symonds, unless otherwise stated.

2. I've explored this at length in *Radical Tragedy*; see esp. Part III, 'Man Decentred'.

3. Compare Machiavelli (1469–1527): 'nature has created men so that they desire everything, but are unable to attain it; desire being thus always greater than the faculty of acquiring, discontent with what they have[,] *and* dissatisfaction with themselves[,] results from it' (cited in Greenblatt, *Sir Walter Ralegh*, p. 40).

Fudge, Perceiving Animals

1. [See] Keith Thomas, *Man and the Natural World: Changing Attitudes in England 1500–1800* (London: Penguin, 1984). [. . .] Joyce E. Salisbury, *The Beast Within: Animals in the Middle Ages* (London: Routledge, 1994); Harriet Ritvo, *The Animal Estate: The English and Other Creatures in the Victorian Age* (London: Penguin, 1990); and Kathleen Kete, *The Beast in the Boudoir: Petkeeping in Nineteenth-Century Paris* (London: University of California Press, 1994).

REFERENCES

Agnew, Jean-Christophe, *Worlds Apart: The Market and the Theater in Anglo-American Thought, 1550–1750* (Cambridge: Cambridge University Press, 1986)

Baldwin, Frances Elizabeth, *Sumptuary Legislation and Personal Regulation in England* (Baltimore: Johns Hopkins University Press, 1926)

Belsey, Catherine, 'Disrupting sexual difference: meaning and gender in the comedies', *Alternative Shakespeares*, ed. John Drakakis (London: Methuen, 1985), pp. 166–90.

Bradbrooke, M. C., *The Rise of the Common Player: A Study of Actor and Society in Shakespeare's England* (Cambridge, MA: Harvard University Press, 1964)

Burke, Peter, 'The language of orders in early modern Europe', in M. L. Bush (ed.), *Social Orders and Social Classes in Europe since 1500: Studies in Social Stratification* (London: Longman, 1992), pp. 1–12.

Chambers, E. K. *The Elizabethan Stage*, 4 vols. (Oxford: Clarendon Press, 1923)

Cressy, David 'Describing the social order of Elizabethan and Stuart England', *Literature and History*, 3 (1976), pp. 29–44.

Drummond, William, *Poems and Prose*, ed. R. H. MacDonald (Edinburgh: Scottish Academic Press, 1976)

Edwards, Philip, *Threshold of a Nation: A Study in English and Irish Drama* (Cambridge: Cambridge University Press, 1979)

Gosson, Stephen, *Playes Confuted in Fiue Actions* (London, 1582)

Greenblatt, Stephen, *Shakespearean Negotiations: The Circulation of Social Energy in Renaissance England* (Berkeley: University of California Press, 1988)

—— *Sir Walter Ralegh: the Renaissance Man and his Roles* (New Haven: Yale University Press, 1973)

Harte, N. B. 'State control of dress and social change in pre-industrial England', in D. C. Coleman and A. H. John (eds.), *Trade, Government and Economy in Pre-Industrial England* (London: Weidenfeld & Nicolson, 1976), pp. 132–65.

Henslowe, Philip, *Diary*, ed. R. A. Foakes and R. T. Rickert (Cambridge: Cambridge University Press, 1961)

Hooper, Wilfred, 'The Tudor sumptuary laws', *English Historical Review*, 30 (1915), pp. 433–49.

Howard, Jean E., *The Stage and Social Struggle in Early Modern England* (London: Routledge, 1994)

Hughes, Paul L. and Larkin, James F., *Tudor Royal Proclamations*, 3 vols. (New Haven: Yale University Press, 1964–9)

Jacobus, Mary, 'Is there a woman in this text?' *New Literary History*, 14 (1982), pp. 117–41.

Levine, Laura, 'Men in women's clothing: anti-theatricality and effeminization from 1579 to 1632', *Criticism*, 28 (1986), pp. 121–43.

Lukàcs, Georg, *History and Class Consciousness*, trans. R. Livingstone (London: Merlin, 1971)

Mészàros, Istvân (ed.), *Aspects of History and Class Consciousness* (New York: Herder & Herder, 1972)

Moryson, Fynes, *An Itinerary* (1617), 4 vols. (Glasgow: MacLehose, 1907)

Patterson, Annabel, *Shakespeare and the Popular Voice* (Oxford: Blackwell, 1989)

Rackin, Phyllis, 'Androgyny, mimesis, and the marriage of the boy heroine on the English Renaissance stage', *PMLA*, 102 (1987), pp. 29–41.

Symonds, J. A. (ed.), *Sir Thomas Browne's Religio Medici, Urn Burial, Christian Morals and other essays* (1643) (London: W. Scott, 1886)

Thompson, E. P., 'Eighteenth-century English society: class struggle without class?' *Social History*, 3 (1978), pp. 133–65.

Wrightson, Keith, 'Estates, degrees and sorts: changing perceptions of society in Tudor and Stuart England', in Penelope J. Corfield (ed.), *Language, History and Class* (Oxford: Blackwell, 1991), pp. 30–52.

6

Materiality

EWAN FERNIE
CLARE McMANUS

As this anthology makes clear, recent criticism tends to reject abstractions and general ideas such as 'the human condition' or 'the Great Chain of Being'. Instead, perhaps influenced by new scientific and medical understandings of the human body and the physical world in the twentieth and twenty-first centuries, critics have turned towards materiality and the detailed and changing world of concrete bodies, commodities and things. The most obvious example of this approach in current Renaissance studies is the increased awareness of the physicality of the book. As we saw in 'Textuality', to think about typefaces, title pages, bindings, and paper simultaneously brings criticism down to earth and explodes the authority of the author and the organic status of the text into the wider material and economic world of which they are a part. For instance, Erica Fudge's recognition that early modern texts about animals were in fact stuck together with glue made from the bodies of animals radically alters the status of the creatures that those books described.[1] The material conditions of a text can profoundly change the ways in which that text might be read.

Given the recent preoccupation with Renaissance identities explored in the last section, considerations of materiality have understandably homed in on the human body. And it is striking that something of the current critical obsession with human materiality can be discerned throughout early modern literature itself. Driven by a newly secular curiosity about human nature, the Renaissance cultivated, in Jonathan Sawday's phrase, a 'culture of dissection' in anatomy theatres across Europe. This is discernible, to cite only a few literary instances, in the hideous moments of mutilation in Thomas Nashe's *The Unfortunate Traveller* (1594), in Philip Sidney's presentation of a 'blazoned', dismembered Stella (*Astrophil and*

---

[1] Erica Fudge, *Perceiving Animals: Humans and Beasts in Early Modern Culture* (Basingstoke: Macmillan, 2000), p. 2.

Stella (1591), sonnet 106), in the opening sonnet of Mary Wroth's *Pamphilia to Amphilanthus* (1621), in the *memento mori* of Gloriana's skull in *The Revenger's Tragedy* (1607), and in the murder of Christopher Marlowe's Edward II by anal penetration with a red-hot poker (1592?). Bruce R. Smith has argued that the Renaissance self was thoroughly embodied, indicating that the '*True Knowledge of a Man's Own Self* (1602), as inscribed by Philippe de Mornay and translated by Anthony Munday, turns out to be *physiological* knowledge'.[2] Gail Kern Paster has demonstrated that the early modern subject's passions and desires were conceived largely physiologically, as material rather than psychological events.[3] We tend still to separate mind from body, psychology from physical health, but these and other critics stress the organic unity of mind, body and soul during the Renaissance.

In current criticism, the body is widely regarded as, in Foucault's words, 'totally imprinted by history'. Foucault argued that the elision of human materiality in traditional criticism evades recognising the influence of historical power over subjectivity. He, therefore, set out to expose and explore the body as saturated by such power, and much recent Renaissance criticism has followed his lead, reading the body as an ideological text, 'a volume in perpetual disintegration', endlessly rewritten according to changing cultural discourses of, among other things, gender, race, sexuality and class.[4] Renaissance critics, like, for instance, Nancy Vickers and Louis Montrose below, have demonstrated how the rhetoric and literature of the period is influenced, at the levels of both content and form, by the culturally con-figured Renaissance body which it simultaneously helped to create. The phrase 'writing the body' was so well used in the criticism of the early 1990s as to become almost threadbare, but it usefully points to the intersections between the body and language that can be seen in, for instance, the connections between literary dilatoriness and conventional Renaissance notions of the female body drawn by Patricia Parker in what follows.

The question of exactly how far the body is discursively constructed has been hotly debated. In the extract below, Jonathan Dollimore is sceptical about the extent to which it is a product of discourse and, as we saw in the General Introduction, Stephen Greenblatt and Catherine Gallagher regard the body as the 'spoiler' of theory—that is, as an ultimately unreconstructable given. Equally importantly, Lacanian theory distinguishes between social and cultural ideas of the body (which are thoroughly internalised by individual subjects) and the chaotic and fundamentally inconceivable materiality from which those perceptions are formed. Recent critical shifts are perhaps best exemplified in the developing work of Judith Butler. In *Gender Trouble* (1990), Butler argued for the thoroughly discursive nature of the body, but the later *Bodies that Matter* (1993) offers a more nuanced position:

[2] Bruce R. Smith, *Shakespeare and Masculinity* (Oxford: Oxford University Press, 2000), p. 7.
[3] Gail Kern Paster, 'The body and its passions', 'Forum: body work', *Shakespeare Studies* 29 (2001), 44–50.
[4] Michel Foucault, 'Nietzsche, genealogy, history', in *Language, Counter-Memory, Practice: Selected Essays and Interviews*, ed. D. F. Bouchard, trans. D. F. Bouchard and Sherry Simon (Oxford: Blackwell, 1977), p. 148.

Language and materiality are fully embedded in each other, chiasmic in their interdependency, but never fully collapsed into one another. [. . .] Always already implicated in each other, always already exceeding one another, language and materiality are never fully identical nor fully different.[5]

This kind of compromise formulation—which maintains the specificity of the body and language while hailing their common ground and mutual influence—stakes out a shared territory for many Renaissance critics.

The re-examination of Renaissance bodies has opened up new perspectives on the issues dealt with in 'Identities' above. With reference to supposed bodily differences of gender, race, sexuality and class, explanations based in biology and culture have been brought together, and tested against each other. 'The body' as the focus of critical attention has multiplied into 'bodies', but conclusions about bodily difference in the period vary widely. For example, in *Making Sex* (1990), Thomas Laqueur draws on the history of medicine to argue for a one-sex model of Renaissance gender, in which women are less perfect, less developed versions of men, while Paster shows below that women were discursively constructed as leaky vessels but that, owing to unhelpful obstetrical techniques and reproductive practices, this discursive construction had some basis in material fact.[6] As this focus on the body's sexual construction would suggest, sexuality and desire intro- duce a range of complications into studies of the Renaissance body. Bodies that desire, bodies that are desired and physical relations between them, as well as desires that are induced in the bodies of readers and audiences by the textual and theatrical performance of desire, have all been analysed by critics. It might seem that desire and the body are mutually conditioning but Valerie Traub below ends her investigation of the Renaissance's physiological understanding of desire between women by arguing that sexual identity should be liberated from biological determination. But almost all this recent work shows the influence of Foucault in treating the body not as something only 'natural' or easily explicable but as the site of identity formation and the locus of expression, through which power is dis- played and performed.

The focus on the body in recent scholarship has attracted some criticism. A number of left-leaning critics, for instance, have suspected that it sustains a covert individualism which does not readily lend itself to a collective political perspective. Others have answered this charge by turning their attention from personal to institutional, symbolic bodies. The theory of the 'king's two bodies', in which the monarch's mortal body stood apart from her or his immortal body politic that symbolised the nation, is a common critical starting point for the interpretation of Elizabeth I's intricate negotiation of her gendered position. Likewise, investigators of early modern religious discourses have attended to the Christian churches'

---

[5] Judith Butler, *Bodies that Matter: On the Discursive Limits of 'Sex'* (London and New York: Routledge, 1993), p. 69.

[6] Thomas Laqueur, *Making Sex: Body and Gender from the Greeks to Freud* (Cambridge, MA, and London: Harvard University Press, 1990). See the extract from Paster below.

belief that they fed on the body and blood of Christ and so reconstituted his body, and critics of colonialism have unravelled the misogynistic representation of America as a female body, ripe for the taking. Critical attention to these imagined corporate bodies, and the discourses which upheld them, clearly has large-scale political pertinence.

If contemporary criticism has moved from minds or souls towards bodies, it has taken another step away from the immaterial in its related engagement with the category of the object. The sheer appeal and interest of the fragmentary physical traces of the early modern past partly derives from the sharpened sense explored in 'Histories' that this past is unreachable. Jonathan Gil Harris testifies below to the powerful experience of coming into contact with what is supposed to be a stray strand of Shakespeare's hair. He then proceeds to analyse this precious follicle as 'a commodity whose reliquary synecdochial value has been and continues to be produced by means of its passage through multiple modes and sites of exchange, whether as an auctionable item, gentlemanly gift, or scholarly curio'. As with the body, objects in contemporary Renaissance criticism tend to be theorized in such terms of human labour and culture. The cultural circulation of objects reveals much about what individuals and societies value and how they relate to each other.

The new orientation towards materiality has enabled current critics to replace the early modern subject in its wider physical context as an object among others, which, once again, decentres the human. The vision that critics working on materiality have elaborated of human bodies in a material world resonates with the environmental impulse in contemporary culture and politics. And yet, that there are dangers of seeing human beings as things is clearly revealed by the early modern but still continuing practice of slavery. This particular bodily condition of being owned, denied agency and used as an object touches on ethical and political concerns raised already in 'Histories' and 'Identities' and suggests the need of a revised criterion of human distinctiveness. Dympna Callaghan raises the question below of how a sceptical materialist view of human life as essentially physical can be related to Marxist materialism, which famously critiques the process of 'reification' by which human beings are turned into things. There is also an urge in recent critical writing to rehabilitate the spiritual through the material. Spirituality is filtered through materiality and vice versa in, for instance, the intensely embodied Christ of Aemilia Lanyer's passion poem *Salve Deus rex Judaeorum* (1611) and John Donne's plea for his God to 'ravish' him in Holy Sonnet X (published 1633). Recent theoretical debates (based on the work of, for instance, Emmanuel Levinas, the later Jacques Derrida and Slavoj Žižek) have stimulated a new interest in spirituality as such. But these theories of what is irreducible to materiality are only part of the intense and wide-ranging debate that the turn towards materiality has stimulated. What is at stake is nothing less than our understanding of the constitution of human identity and of differences of gender, sexuality and race, as well as of the intellectual and ethical question of the relationship between the human and the wider physical environment. In this context, discussion of the material Renaissance is likely to continue vigorously.

1 | Rematerializing the subject: the body in history

Francis Barker, *The Tremulous Private Body: Essays on Subjection* (London and New York: Methuen, 1984), pp. 1–25.

> February 9th (Lord's day). Up, and at my chamber all the morning and the office doing business, and also reading a little of *L'escholle des filles*, which is a mighty lewd book, but yet not amiss for a sober man once to read over to inform himself in the villainy of the world. At noon home to dinner, where by appointment Mr. Pelling come and with him three friends, Wallington, that sings the good base, and one Rogers, and a gentleman, a young man, his name Tempest, who sings very well indeed, and understands anything in the world at first sight. After dinner we went into our dining-room, and there to singing all the afternoon. (By the way, I must remember that Pegg Pen was brought to bed yesterday of a girl; and among other things, if I have not already set it down, that hardly ever was remembered such a season for the smallpox as these last two months have been, people being seen all up and down the streets, newly come out after the smallpox.) But though they sang fine things, yet I must confess that I did take no pleasure in it, or very little, because I understood not the words, and with the rests that the words are set, there is no sense nor understanding in them though they be English, which makes me weary of singing in that manner, it being but a worse sort of instrumental musick. We sang until almost night, and drank a mighty good store of wine, and then they parted, and I to my chamber, where I did read through *L'escholle des filles*, a lewd book, but what do no wrong once to read for information sake. And after I had done it I burned it, that it might not be among my books to my shame, and so at night to supper and to bed.
> (*The Diary of Samuel Pepys*, entry for 9 February 1668)

The scene of writing and of reading is, like the grave, a private place. We must explore the contents of this privacy, in relation to what is publicly speakable, and draw the diagram of the structure of confessions and denials of desire that gives this passage its peculiar numinosity, and, in principle, as a representative, a special place in history of the bourgeois soul.

In Pepys' chamber, unlike the quiet tomb in which the dismembered but visible body of Marvell's beloved was recently interred, if not echoing songs, at least ghostly mutterings can indeed be heard, rustling among the feints and side-steps of the text's involuted speech. Where in Marvell's poem ['To His Coy Mistress'] sex was the objective, publicly invoked and celebrated, and death the price of its refusal, here we have entered a different, secluded domain to which sex has been banished; a silent bedroom, traversed by whispers which intimate—of necessity, obliquely—a sexuality which cannot any longer be frankly avowed.

The discourse of the Navy Office clerk is, no doubt, attenuated. That is part of its charm and is certainly the stylistic register which has characterized its reproduction and transmission in the history of writing. Not too verbose, barely literary; after all that rhetoric that preceded it, a breath of fresh air. With the verbal excess of the Renaissance behind us, not to say *sotto voce* those other excesses of the recent revolution, we emerge at last into a clear, known world of facts and events, of business and leisure, and into a discourse appropriate to that world. A discourse shorn of its ornaments; a plain style for our bourgeois times. At least, this is how we have been taught to read Pepys' text by those commentators who have identified its signifi-cances for us in a way characterized by nothing so much as a plainness, an obviousness given in the image of a mind writing down mundane events according to the clear order of their unfolding, providing a text whose regularities, it is said, are determined only by the pattern of the empirical, whose transcription it is. 'Up, and at my chamber all the morning and at the office doing business.' This is the discourse we have learned to read, which in its unalterable presence leaves us strictly nothing to say. Nothing further can be said. Everything is here and now, perceived and written down. What is beyond perception is never paused over. The text is not a fiction and cannot thus be criticized. We have been trained to read in silence, fixed by its light, taut factuality—by a small technique of sensibility rather than a grand gesture of power—into the inexorable domain of the quotidian real.

And we have acceded in this discourse to a social reality which is, whatever dangers it may hold, essentially simple. It is here, there, given, waiting to be written down. Clarified already in its common-sense existence, life needs only the perceiving mind and the writing hand, tracing and recording its contours, to become text. The apparency of the bourgeois world and its texts is born. [. . .]

Yet, for all that, the plain style works as a mask, or at best a detour, for both Pepys, the 'I' that writes and is written, and for the commentators who have reconstructed what turns out to be so little of him. The material history of the text ought to provide a converse image of this mystificatory clarity. A text ciphered and partly coded, hidden in a difficult early seventeenth-century shorthand, written in secret and kept locked away during Pepys' lifetime (and him driven blind by it), bequeathed, lost for so long a period to the *public* domain. Against what odds of obscurity has all this imputed transparency been achieved. And at what risk, or perhaps promise, of truncation of the bourgeois soul it has come to represent.

It is most signally in the practice of writing advanced by the text itself that this fore-shortening is achieved. The passage deploys two recensions of the same alibi on either side of an interpolation which is, in part, parenthesized. Perhaps this is the typical structure of all bourgeois discourse? At any rate, the a-libi-dinous justification of reading 'for information sake' belongs properly to what has been called hitherto the discourse of the clerk, and no doubt also provides, in general if not actually by the local authority of these particular lines, the basis for the informational mode of reading that has characterized the reception of Pepys' text.

But what is remarkable here is not the relative lack of opacity of the self-deception (to and for whom is Pepys writing this secret text?) but the indirect, if none the less urgent, manner of its self-exposure in another discourse within and around that of the clerk. Unspeakable in their 'proper' place, the pleasures of the lewd text, *L'escholle des filles*, surface, and are in turn denied, elsewhere; in confessions and disavowals apparently disconnected from their real source, the guilty reading; yet forever connected back to it by the sign of their very excess over the textual motivations which only apparently justify their actual disposition in the passage.

So, the proposition that Pepys reads the lewd text over 'to inform himself in the villainy of the world' (the grammatical third person is significant, as if, which is the case, he is trying to speak of someone else, another self, although 'in' speaks eloquently if ambiguously of where Pepys already thinks he is in relation to the sin of the world) barely succeeds in even containing another discourse, one concerning desire, disease, the mess of the body and its passions, that disrupts and intrudes upon the calm order of plain speech. In spite of the steps the discourse of the clerk takes to forestall these others, and of the fact that, arguably, this is its principal *raison d'être*, it nevertheless ruses with itself, and becomes self-treacherous.

In this way we can begin to understand the precision of verbal usage which otherwise looks erroneous. The item 'yet *I must confess* that I did take no pleasure in it', which purports to refer to a certain kind of singing that Pepys despises, provides an efficient instance. The whole passage is dominated by its initial 'Lord's day', which functions doubly: from an informational point of view it is a temporal mark—all the *Diary*'s Sundays are identified in this way—but discursively it is an admonition whose minatory value must be contained within the punctuational *cordon sanitaire* of the bracket within which it has been confined. But the insulation that separates the 'Lord's day' from the rest of the passage is not impervious to every kind of charge. While it serves effectively to permit the efficient pursuit of 'business' which is mentioned, unproblematically, in passing, it otherwise merely redoubles the anxiety associated with the lewd reading. So that when we come to Pepys' comment on his lack of enjoyment of the singing, a religious idiom is incited. Singing is perhaps bodily enough a practice to have given the right clues without such an overt confession of the need to confess. In any case, only truly Pepysian efforts of common sense, or informational reading, could avert the recognition that what is at stake here is the simultaneous admission and denial of the furtive pleasures of the French text, displaced onto an apparently innocuous, and, significantly, public and social pastime. By the same token, perhaps, the tongue loosened by alcohol has its part to play here. The 'sober man' of informational reading, the bourgeois citizen grave in the dignity of his public demeanour, is, we can now see, almost inevitably not just one who has drunk 'a mighty good store of wine', but one who must blurtingly confess himself to have done so.

The text employs massive means—not of repression, for everything is said, eventually, even if it is not acknowledged as having been said—but of diversion: we are asked to look 'by the way' at 'other things'. But just as no amount of raucous singing by Pepys and his friends will ever drown out the loquaciousness of the half-silence in which the forbidden book is enjoyed, so, the more the text denies interest, diverts attention, only the more clearly does it identify its unacknowledged drives. No doubt, as the empiricist would have it, the parenthesis of smallpox and childbirth at the centre of the passage is simply part of the 'day's residue', faithfully noted by the honest recorder. But why these sentences, just here, deployed in quite this relation to the others? Can it be with total fortuitousness that Pepys speaks 'by the way' of a young woman 'brought to bed' in an idiom not only of childbirth but of sexuality (as if the connotative, and indeed material, connection were not explicit enough)? And to speak in the same breath of disease, dis-ease, an affliction punishing the body so loathed by Pepys, as by any sober man on the Lord's day, and moreover, a privatized affliction after which people are 'newly come out' to be 'seen all up and down the streets'. The connotative relations established here are clear: from the bedroom to the public scene; from sickness to health; from private, sick sexuality to sexless public health.

It is the same 'fortuitousness', which is uncanny but far from arbitrary, that governs what we are told of the quasimythical Mr Tempest. Envied for his class, his youth and his sexuality (we now know what the metaphor 'sings very well indeed' means), he is also feared for his perspicacity. Truly a tempest come to disturb the calm order of the bourgeois *domus*, a man who 'understands everything in the world at first sight', as if, a good sight-reader of music, his ability will flow over to penetrate the concealments and immediately see through to the hidden text with which Pepys pleasured himself that morning and which he will surely take to bed with him that night. It is because of the threat represented by Tempest that Pepys finally burns *L'escholle des filles*, to make finally sure. In the presence of such a seer it is not enough to hide the text, like the *Diary* itself, in layers of cipher and, at the moments the language of prurience calls most 'frank', in a garble of foreign languages (see how Pepys *tells* his desire that the truth of his own text should not be read—'I understood not the words . . . there is no sense nor understanding in them though they be English'), but all that guilt must be absolutely consumed by a cleansing, purifying fire. The smallpox of sexuality is to be cauterized by a sacred flame, just as London itself, visited for its sins by plague a few years earlier, is then purified by fire.

So. An image of a man. A typical man. A bourgeois man. Riven by guilt, silence and textuality. Forbidden to speak and yet incited to discourse, and therefore speaking obliquely in another place. Who says sing when he means fuck, who fears sex and calls it smallpox, who enjoys sex and calls it reading, who is fascinated and terrified by texts and so reads them once, but only for information's sake, who is sober and drunk. Who would rather burn his body, who would rather go blind, but who, as in the storm of rage with which he tears, elsewhere in the *Diary*, his wife's pathetic love-letters, obliterates the texts instead.

A representation of a representation, moreover. Behind it all, not even an adulterous act, but an act of reading. A lewd book.

The enclosure of the Pepysian moment is its decisive quality. The text itself rehearses the situation it discloses as it inlays seclusion within seclusion. The very writing, which as its epistemological principle grasps the outer world as an accessible transparency, recedes from that world towards an inner location where the soul—or, as the modern terminology has it, positionality in discourse—apparently comes to fill the space of meaning and desire. The boundaries of the outer context, designated as much by discourse as by a physical separation of space, are clearly defined, and the real energies and interests of the text then locate themselves within these frontiers. The diagram of the text is as a series of concentric circles at the furtive heart of which is the secret declivity of the soul itself. The I surrounded first by discourse, then by the *domus*, the chamber, and finally by the public world, is placed at the heart of its own empire, in silence and very largely in terror. The *Diary* for all the fullness of its days, despite being so richly populated with others and with the furniture of gossip and events, is thus the record of a terrible isolation. At the moment when the soul reaches out to appropriate the outer world, the very gesture reinforces the division by which it is other than what it seeks to apprehend. The obverse face of the reception of the *Diary* as a documentary record of the life and times of the Restoration is its status as an inner history, one of the first of the autobiographies in that tradition of subject-centred discourse which [. . .] Descartes began.

But despite its intimacy, Pepys' tormented situation is not peculiar to him but marks out a social condition which was novel at the time. In it, a complex of overdetermined relations coalesce, governing bourgeois subjectivity at its founding moment. By no means the tortured predicament of a single, aberrant individual—even its individuation is historically produced—this situation is the result of the revolutionary process that preceded it. The political upheaval of the mid-century established, as all revolutions must if they are to be thoroughgoing, a new set of connections between subject and discourse, subject and polity, and in doing so altered fundamentally the terms between which these mutually constitutive relations held. In the space of a relatively few years a new set of relations between state and citizen, body and soul, language and meaning, was fashioned. The older sovereignty of the Elizabethan period was disassembled, and in its place was established a conjunction of novel social spaces and activities, bound together by transformed lines of ideological and physical force, among which new images of the body and its passions were a crucial, if increasingly occluded, element. It is a history of this new emergence which is the concern of the present, intransitive, essay.

Having issued on to this situation, the historical process then appeared to drain itself away, effacing its own marks as it hands the subject over to the depoliticized privacy newly marked out for it. But the outcome is none the less historical for the fact that a property of its historical form is an apparent dehistoricization of its own achievement. That Pepys is now located as a private citizen in a domestic space, over against a public world is not, thus, a natural fact, but merely one of the more grossly structural features of a historical settlement (however provisional, as are all historical situations) which the century acceded to by means of an extreme and often bloody effort. None of the main features of this settlement can be read as the sign of an eternal condition. The apparent directness of its profoundly evasive discourse; the apparent ease of access of its discourse, launched from an inner place, to an outer, clarified world; the guilty secrecy not only of its writing but of its sexuality; the privatization of its bodies and their passions; all are instances of a new ensemble of what can only be described as power relations, in so far as they designate a type and a locatedness for subjectivity and fix it *in place* among a new set of divisions, dominations, of the social formation constructed from and among the debris of the older regime. That they are recognizable in all their aspects today indicates the viability of the construction and need not tempt us to underestimate its novelty (nor, for that matter, to assume its permanence).

The context of the inauguration of Pepys' situation has already been extensively defined. The broad process of transition from the feudal to the capitalist mode of production (which, unlike the political transformation, cannot be dated with chronometric precision) and the rise of the modern state provide the general co-ordinates within which the reformulation of the subjectivity appropriate to them can be mapped. But what has been less frequently treated is the manner in which the grand historical process interpenetrates the detail of what until recently has been regarded as barely historical features of social life. The gross restructuring of a political system or a mode of economic production may even supply the explanatory basis for an understanding of the more intimate textures, but will remain in any case abstract and incomplete unless that supplementary work of definition and evocation is carried out. In the long run the tragicomedy of the body and the soul may even prove decisive.

The Pepysian settlement, then, must be taken as a moment of definite importance not only for the ideological, economic and political history of the seventeenth century and its foundation of the modern situation, but also within the corporeal history of that establishment. We shall attempt to grasp the precise status of the body in that settlement below, but for the moment it is necessary to note the mere fact, for the body has certainly been among those objects which have been effectively hidden from history. Not least because one of the principal components of that establishment of the modern which the Pepysian situation signals is the very de-realization of the body which subsequent historiography has been heir to. When

Hamlet—himself, as we shall see, on the threshold of modernity—called for this 'too too sullied flesh' to 'melt, / Thaw and resolve itself into a dew' (I.ii.129–30), the seventeenth century would soon take him at his word. The consequence is there to be read in Pepys. The passions and the anxiety of the discourse-text swirl around an apparent absence which is none the less always there, if never 'in person'.

If the new ensemble of terms and relations is established conjuncturally around a particular corporeal status, this is not because the body is the essential foundation of the structure. Not only would it be wrong to assign such ontological pre-eminence to any one moment in the ensemble, but it is a related and relational body which is at stake. However necessary it may be to isolate the body for analytic purposes, the body in question is not a hypostatized object, still less a simple biological mechanism of given desires and needs acted on externally by controls and enticements, but a relation in a system of liaisons which are material, discursive, psychic, sexual, but without stop or centre. It would be better to speak of a certain 'bodiliness' than of 'the body'. It is the instance of a suturing of discourse and desire to the organism (itself, of course, a historical entity although subject to a longer, evolutionary, timespan in which today disease, diet and working conditions are the key determinants), and thus fully social in its being and in its ideological valency. Rather than an extra-historical residue, invariant and mute, this body is as ready for coding and decoding, as intelligible both in its presence and its absence, as any of the more frequently recognized historical objects. The site of an operation of power, of an exercise of meaning.

The work of description which has played the central part in opening up the possibility of a political history of the body is that carried out by Michel Foucault who traces the lineaments of the bourgeois order in studies of two of its essential components—the history of its madness and of its penality—and identifies there a transition, effected over a long period of time, from a socially visible object to one which can no longer be seen. It has its roots in the 'Great Confinement' of the seventeenth century which gathers into the new institutions of confinement that promulgated themselves throughout the whole of Europe during that century, the dispossessed elements of the population who were to become, for the new order, no more than a detritus. The sick, the poor, the orphaned, the homeless, the unemployed, the criminal and the mad, who had once been integrally present, were now, by an act of separation, first excluded from the scene, and then made useful. Within the houses of confinement they could be made to labour, and their labour regulated. The example was socially instructive, and their organized incarceration encoded symbolically and contributed in actuality to a complete restructuring of the social whole along new productive lines. The process matures in *l'âge classique* and is consummated in the nineteenth century with the global triumph of the bourgeois class.

Crucial to this transition was the relocation of the body. The scope of penality changes: the body involved in punishment, in spectacular, public, corporal pain, is removed into 'complete and austere institutions', where, within these closed and silent prisons, asylums and hospitals, it becomes the object—and at its most efficient, the subject—of discipline. The central penal task is no longer to exact a recompense of pain, but to cure, by exemplary labour and other techniques, the prisoner's delinquent soul. She or he becomes the object of secret and overt surveillance rather than spectacular visibility. Technical measurement replaces the older art of judicial torture, and becomes the ground for the elaboration of the modern knowledges—

penology, forensic psychiatry, *diagnosis* in all its medical and juridical forms—which are, for Foucault, instances of power in its contemporary form. From a precise violence of the body, to a precise knowledge of the modern soul; which is born, in Foucault's narrative, precisely in the moment of the disappearance of the body from public view; or, as the example of Pepys shows, at the moment when the very division between the public and the private is constructed in its modern form. It is thus that the pre-eminence of the soul in Pepys' text is predicated on, and a part of the history of, the body, newly banished from the sphere in which his troubled subjectivity now appears to be sovereign.

In pursuit of the decisive reshaping of the body politic and its subjectivity that was effected in the seventeenth century and which results in the Pepysian situation, it will be necessary to trace a path back across the years of the revolution, and to read [. . .] in the pervasive publicity of the Jacobean stage, the crisis of the older polity, and the main determinants of the outcome registered in Pepys and which in essential outline we have still to endure today. The historical settlement which preceded the bourgeois order of whose inner structure Pepys' predicament is an early instance, was profoundly different from that modernity of subjection which the revolution inaugurated. Only efforts of de-historicization similar to those practised by the Pepysian commentators, whose impressive but insidious simplicity we have already noticed, could hope to achieve even a partial assimilation of the pre-revolutionary to the present.

In particular the sign of the literary greatness of Shakespeare has played a major part in remaking the late feudal world in the image of the bourgeois settlement that grew up inside it, and eventually brought it down. If not the invariability of a quotidian discourse like that of the clerk, at least its more elevated version, the timelessness of great art, has had to be mobilized in order to secure the necessary abolition of historical difference: Shakespeare's texts, their universality, their 'broad humanism'—even their beauty—have served, in the hands of left and right, to secure in an alien history a value and a point of reference by which the other can be identified as the same, and thus tamed, explained, and even appreciated.

This is not the place for an extensive critique of Shakespearian criticism or of the role of 'Shakespeare' in British culture, but the mere citation of the commanding position of the Shakespearian text within the reception of the pre-revolutionary discursivity will suffice to identify the order of difficulty to be encountered in trying to insist on the necessity of redrawing the map of that other world. In one sense, of course, all history is contemporary history, so what is at issue is not that Shakespeare's corpus has been reproduced in order to be reshaped to present needs: this is the general task of all historiography, and to believe otherwise would be to advance a hubristic objectivism. Nor is it necessary to deny that there are features in the Shakespearian text which lend themselves particularly well to the uses that have been found for them: this probably accounts for their 'greatness' in so far as the literary tradition has been able to celebrate what is, unknown to itself, a narcissistic self-confirmation, 'recognizing' in Shakespeare's transitional and contradictory *oeuvre* those elements which are truly its own. It is simply that another history must be written if our account of that corporal past is not to be merely a case of recapitulating in the pre-revolutionary texts the themes and structures which it was precisely the task of the revolution to establish, by *destroying* the polity whose complex index the Shakespearian discourse was.

The effort of historiographical denial of the situation for discourse and the body *abolished* by the Pepysian settlement is stamped on the other side of the coin of Shakespeare's present greatness: the minority of the other Jacobeans. Above all it is evident in the indictment for sensationalism which has so frequently secured the Jacobeans' inferior status in the calm and hygienic moral order that obtains in literary criticism, if nowhere else. In part, the charge of sensationalism goes to the substantive and recklessly bodily contents of the scenes and images that are said to elicit the sensation, and we shall return to them; but also, connected inextricably with this, it more covertly denigrates the Jacobean *mode* of representation itself, which is also alien to the history which succeeded it and the historiography which has refused its significance. The reception of the Jacobean text has proceeded in a fashion entirely subjugated to the partitive sign of the *literary* greatness of Shakespeare's verse: the word has found a place of privilege over the image. It is against this measure that a crux like that in which the Duchess of Malfi is shown the wax figures of the corpses—the bodies—of Antonio and his children by her tormentors, which is in essence spectacular although words are also spoken, has been judged in principle inferior to the kind so frequent in Shakespeare which is effected, allegedly, in language although accompanied by stage business. But what is at stake in opposing this organizing principle of the traditional reproduction of the Jacobean representational situation is not the banal plea for the 'living theatre' against the academicism of the play-*text*; still less is it designed to reinforce an existentially untenable opposition between word and image, and thus to enforce a spurious choice between them, but rather an assessment of the cost of this organization of the reception, recognizing the subsequent decisions that have been made regarding the relative weighting of language and spectacle within the historical retroaction of developments familiar to Pepys and his epoch, but not yet fulfilled in the theatre-world of the early seventeenth century.

Those who have attacked sensationalism would doubtless deny that they are carrying out the belated cultural work of the bourgeois revolution: but it is hard not to see in the attack on sensation the hand of a Protestant asceticism, and in the demotion of the spectacle a continuity with the seventeenth century's own iconoclasm in favour of the Word. [. . .]

At the level of representation what has been elided—or acknowledged only in the condemnatory form of the charge of sensationalism—is the theatricality of this theatre, the innocent foregrounding of its device.

When a play like *The Revenger's Tragedy* cannot be regarded as particularly extraordinary for the fact that, almost without content and verging constantly on self-parody, it moves from one quoted stage device to another, we are clearly far from that occlusion of writing itself which is effected in the post-Pepysian world by the attribution to discourse of an instrumental transparency. Tourneur's text is constructed by tireless reference to its own signifying; each sequence is a matrix of citation, imitation and reworking of the range of theatrical tropes and mechanisms at work on the Jacobean stage, and in this sense is only a usefully typical example of the early seventeenth-century theatre as a whole. The masques and the masks, the quaint devices and the stereotyping of character and situation, the relentless artifice and even the all-pervasive metaphor of the theatre itself are not the exceptions to the rule of this theatre, but the rule itself. Even Shakespeare's writing culminates in *The Tempest*, that spectacle which has been criticized so frequently for its improbability, its lack of narrative, its absence of dramatic tension, criticized, in short, for being what the formalists would have called 'unmotivated'.

But if the Jacobean texts continually remark beneath their breath or in loud clear voices, 'Regard me: I am a play', or if it was sometimes necessary for them, in order to achieve a sufficient extraordinariness, to double the stakes and let the play within the play raise the density of representation to the second power, they are not thus unacceptable to naturalizing criticism on aesthetic grounds alone, but because they share an unbroken continuity—across the proscenium *which is not there*—with the world in which they were performed, and which they perform. It is difficult, perhaps impossible, now to imagine a settlement in which the means of representation are so clearly visible as such: an artisanal world in which the device is naked not out of polemical technique but as its normal condition; a discursive situation before production has quite 'disappeared' into, in one of its modalities, the closed factory, or at the level of representation, into the conventions of that bourgeois naturalism which has nothing to do with nature, and everything to do with naturalizing the suppression of the signs of the artefact's production. A world of other visibilities than our own, which is founded on *their* elision, and whose suppression the reception of the texts rehearses.

Brecht understood this when he turned back to this early stage for material for his own alienated political theatre. But if Brecht's project was, by the elaboration of that series of theatrical interventions now known by the portmanteau 'alienation effect', to distance and break the mystificatory illusion near the end of its reign, the Jacobean theatre was, so to speak, anti-naturalist before the event. [. . .]

But the reception of the Jacobean text-world we have been discussing does not reject solely these formal properties of that discursivity. It is their inextricable conjunction with the corporeality of the early seventeenth-century world that fully explains their denial by criticism anxious to disavow a materiality on whose de-realization its tradition is founded. Almost without exception, the depravity of the tragic dramatist who resorts to sensation is most clearly in evidence, it is said, in the presentation on stage of the body and the violence done to it. But is it utterly accidental, or even simply Webster's doubtful opportunism, that in the waxworks scene in *The Duchess of Malfi* it is the *corpses* of Antonio and the children that are displayed; or that in the same series of torments, at the far limits of theatrical pathos, the masque of the lunatics, doubling the spectacle within the spectacle, is in such close proximity to the episode of the severed hand? Is there not, perhaps, a more internally robust connection between the dramatic scene and the seen body than one merely of perversity of taste when Macbeth's head is brought in, or Annabella's bleeding heart on the point of a dagger? Or when the body of Sejanus, like that of Cinna the poet before him, is torn in pieces at a moment of politics in a mass form? It is, of course, possible that merely a certain delicacy of touch in respect of corporeal pain, an artistry which we have lost, smears the poison of Vindice's revenge on the lipless skull of his raped and murdered mistress, from where, transmitted by a half-dead kiss, it eats away first the mouth and then the brain of the old Duke, while Hippolito holds down the man's dying tongue with the point of his knife. Or perhaps just a reflection of the available technology? But it would be better, more historically sensitive, to ask what inner cast of sociality governs the putting out of Gloucester's eyes and the corporeal extravagance of the now significantly seldom performed *Titus Andronicus*. For despite the fact that our own world has its share of torturers, a mark of difference from ourselves can be read in these and the other versions of the spectacular body with which the Jacobean stage is redolent.

Especially when beyond that missing proscenium, in 'reality' itself, lies the mutilation that Prynne suffered for his discursive offences, or the public death which was exacted on another stage (Marvell does not fail to grasp the essential connection in his 'An Horatian ode') of the king himself. These images of the body are not instances of the arbitrary perversity of single dramatists, nor even the casual brutalities hidden away in underground cells or distant camps by violent but irredeemably furtive governments, but the insistence in the spectacle of a corporeality which is quite other than our own. The visibility of this body in pain—the pre-disciplinary body extant before that incarceration which is disclosed, in their different ways, both by Foucault's work and by the Pepysian text—is systemic rather than personal; not the issue of an aberrant exhibitionism, but formed across the whole surface of the social as the locus of the desire, the revenge, the power and the misery of this world.

The spectacular body in whose language Lady Macbeth must define her conditions and demands, and against whose measure Hamlet's anachronistic inwardness will have to be assessed, is everywhere present as the object and site of the confrontations which articulate the drama of this settlement. Continually evoked and displayed, close to language itself, the impersonal body is almost promiscuous in the repeated urgency with which it installs itself in the metaphors and concepts of this world, as well as in its practical situations. But properly it can only be regarded in this way because a certain emphasis is polemically necessary against the decentration it later suffers in history and in historiography alike. 'That a king may go a progress through the guts of a beggar' (*Hamlet*, IV. iii. 29–30) is extraordinary (if it is so at all) for its insistence on the democracy of mortality in contrast with the hierarchized body politic of the living world, not for the corporeal expression in which the idea emerges. The proliferation in the dramatic, philosophical and political texts of the period of corporeal images which have become dead metaphors for us—by a structured forgetting rather than by innocent historical wastage—are the indices of a social order in which the body has a central and irreducible place. Whether judicially tortured as the visible sign of the vengeance of the king on the transgressor, or disassembled lovingly on stage in the cause of poetry, it is the crucial fulcrum and crossing point of the lines of force, discursive and physical, which form this world as the place of danger and aspiration to which the Jacobean texts repeatedly attest. The glorious cruelties of the Jacobean theatre thus articulate a mode of corporeality which is structural to its world. Although the involvement of the body in punishment is only an essential and typical section across the way in which discourse invests it with a fundamental (and therefore, in this world, *superficial*) meaning, it none the less represents a generalized condition under which the body, living or dead, is not that effaced residue which it is to become, beneath or behind the proper realm of discourse, but a materiality that is fully and unashamedly involved in the processes of domination and resistance which are the inner substance of social life. The stage of representation and that other scaffold of corporal punishment are, as Marvell saw, effectively continuous with each other. On both, the spectacularly visible body is fully in place within signification, coterminous with the plane of representation itself.

Unlike the secret half-life to which the Pepysian corporeality has been assigned, but from which it continues nevertheless to agitate the newly sovereign speech of a disembodied and Cartesian subjectivity, this early body lies athwart that divide between subject and object, discourse and world, that characterizes the later dispensation. The body of the world and that of the text are frequently identified with each other in the ideology of the Renaissance, but the metaphor should be understood with a nominalism appropriate to a period that antedates the deleterious separations on which modernity is founded. At the signifying centre of the culture they are at one with each other in the figure of the Passion, where the word and the body are inextricably identified in an act of punishment and signification from which all other meanings flow: the spirit who is the one real Subject of this world is wholly immanent, incarnate, in the flesh. The Jacobean body is at once sacred and profane, tortured and cele-brated in the same gesture, because it traverses even the polarities of the culture's invest-ments: or rather, it is the medium and the substance in which, ultimately, those meanings are inscribed. It has this polyvalent but unambiguous status because drawn on its surface are the means by which the culture, even at its most metaphysical, can determine not only its consonances but its inner discords as well. The underpinnings of the more quotidian disputes which texture the life of this society return in their grounding to that unseparated word made flesh which is the principle of its representational practices (practices which cannot, thus, be regarded as *representational* in the strictest sense). A mode of discourse operates here which, basing itself in incarnation, exercises a unitary *presence* of meaning of which the spectacular body is both the symbol and the instance.

That the body we see is so frequently presented in fragments, or in the process of its effective dismemberment, no doubt indicates that contradiction is already growing up within this system of presence, and that the deadly subjectivity of the modern is already beginning to emerge and to round vindictively on the most prevalent emblem of the discursive order it supersedes. But despite the violence unleashed against the body, it has not yet been quenched. However much it has been subsequently ignored, it remains in the texts themselves as a vital, full materiality. The Jacobean body—the object, certainly, of terrible pressures— is distributed irreducibly throughout a theatre whose political and cultural centrality can only be measured against the marginality of the theatre today; and beyond the theatre it exists in a world whose most subtle inner organization is so different from that of our own not least because of the part played by this body in it. In the fullest sense which it is now possible to conceive, from the other side of our own carnal guilt, it is a *corporeal* body, which, if it is already touched by the metaphysic of its later erasure, still contains a charge which, set off by the violent hands laid on it, will illuminate the scene, incite difference, and ignite poetry. This spectacular visible body is the proper gauge of what the bourgeoisie has had to forget.

* * *

Jonathan Sawday, *The Body Emblazoned: Dissection and the Human Body in Renaissance Culture* (London and New York: Routledge, 1995), pp. 4–5.

[T]he foundations of a western 'science' of the body were laid in the period which is our concern, and many of the academic institutions which fostered the study of the body may be thought of, themselves, as being 'Renaissance' foundations. Take, for example, the Royal College of Surgeons in London. The Royal College of Surgeons is derived from the unified Barber-Surgeons Company. This company had been founded in 1540 and, together with the College of Physicians, had operated as one of the regulating bodies for health-care in early-modern London. The College's collections of human material originated with the Hunterian collection formed in the mid-eighteenth century. [. . .] These collections [. . .] form part of the taxonomic process of categorization and classification which began in the sixteenth century, but only reached its full extent in the years after the founding of the Royal Society in 1660. [. . .] [A]mongst the collections [. . .] can be found the enormous skeleton of 'The Irish Giant', Charles Byrne, who died in June 1783, in terror lest his body would be turned over to the anatomists. In order to thwart their desires, he requested that he be buried at sea. The request was in vain. [. . .] 'Byrne's skeleton today still forms the centrepiece of the Hunterian museum in the Royal College of the Surgeons of England.' [. . .]

What unites this sad story of a frightened Irishman and a Renaissance foundation is this: the 'culture of dissection' was devoted to the gathering of information and the dissemination of knowledge of the 'mystery' of the human body. As such, its ends were proclaimed as being both 'useful' and 'noble'. But the 'culture of dissection' also promoted the beginnings of what Michel Foucault has analysed as the 'surveillance' of the body within regimes of judgement and punishment. [. . .] Within the ornate architecture of the Renaissance and Baroque anatomy theatres, the body was produced (in a theatrical sense) as the flimsy vehicle for a complex ideological structure which stretched into every area of artistic and scientific endeavour in the early modern period. The positive role of this new structure of knowledge was, undoubtedly, the establishment of a regime which was to spread incalculable benefit throughout the populations of early modern Europe. [. . .] But in telling that story we should not neglect the darker side—which features a dying man, a will whose provisions were ignored, and a surgeon bribing an undertaker.

*   *   *

Terry Eagleton, *The Ideology of the Aesthetic* (Oxford: Blackwell, 1990), p. 7.

[F]ew literary texts are likely to make it nowadays into the new historicist canon unless they contain at least one mutilated body. [. . .] At the same time, it is difficult to read the later Roland Barthes, or even the later Michel Foucault, without feeling that a certain style of meditation on the body, on pleasures and surfaces, zones and techniques, has acted among other things as a convenient displacement of a less immediately corporeal politics, and acted also as an *ersatz* kind of ethics. There is a privileged, privatised hedonism about such discourse, emerging as it does at just the historical point where certain less exotic forms of politics found themselves suffering a setback.

. . . .

QUESTIONS

- What different historical narratives of the body are offered by Barker and Sawday?
- What are the implications of these narratives for subjectivity?
- How does Barker's view of the political implications for rematerialising the subject compare with Eagleton's?

2 | Theorizing the body: text and ideology

Nancy Vickers, 'Diana described: scattered woman and scattered rhyme', *Critical Inquiry* 8 (1981), 265–6.

[Petrarch's] role in the history of the interpretation and the internalization of woman's 'image' by both men and women can scarcely be overemphasized. [. . .] [T]he 'scattered rhymes' undeniably enjoyed a privileged status: they informed the Renaissance norm of a beautiful woman.[1]

   We never see in the *Rime sparse* a complete picture of Laura. This would not be exceptional if we were considering a single 'song' or even a restricted lyric corpus: gothic top-to-toe enumeration is, after all, more appropriate to narrative, more adapted to the 'objective' observations of a third person narrator than to those of a speaker who ostensibly loves, and perhaps even addresses, the image he describes. But given an entire volume devoted to a single lady, the absence of a coherent, comprehensive portrait is significant.[2] Laura is always presented as a part or parts of a woman. When more than one part figures in a single poem, a sequential, inclusive ordering is never stressed. Her textures are those of metals and stones: her image is that of a collection of exquisitely beautiful disassociated objects.[3] Singled out among them are hair, hand, foot and eyes: golden hair trapped and bound the speaker; an ivory hand took his heart away; a marble foot imprinted the grass and flowers; starry eyes directed him in his wandering.[4] In terms of qualitative attributes (blondness, whiteness, sparkle), little here is innovative. More specifically Petrarchan, however, is the obsessive insistence on the particular, an insistence that would in turn generate multiple texts on individual fragments of the body or on the beauties of woman.

*   *   *

Patricia Parker, *Literary Fat Ladies: Rhetoric, Gender, Property* (London and New York: Methuen, 1987), pp. 8–17.

> To play with mimesis is thus, for a woman, to try to recover the place of her exploitation by discourse, without allowing herself to be simply reduced to it. It means to resubmit herself—inasmuch as she is on the side of the 'perceptible,' of 'matter'—to 'ideas,' in particular to ideas about herself that are elaborated in/by a masculine logic, but so as to make 'visible,' by an effect of playful repetition, what was supposed to remain invisible: the cover-up of a possible operation of the feminine in language. . . . One must assume the feminine role deliberately, which means already to convert a form of subordination into an affirmation, and thus to begin to thwart it.
>
> Luce Irigaray

Much of this essay will have to do with walls or partitions; so we begin with a rhetorical partition, a division of the subject into parts. The first, which might be called 'The Body in Question,' comes in several sections and is perhaps appropriately by far the largest. [. . .]

   First, the question of 'fat ladies.' We will begin with a woman called Rahab, the redeemed harlot of Jericho from the biblical Old Testament. No record of the conquest of Jericho by Joshua (whom, in Milton's words, the Gentiles Jesus call) indicates that she was physically fat. She was simply the harlot associated with the walls at the entrance to the Promised Land. Her name in Hebrew, however, means 'wide' or 'broad.'[1] Her conversion from the heathen to the Israelite cause involves a turning from letting in men to letting in men—a prelude to the final act of the story in which, as the song goes, the walls come tumbling down. As a figure thus associated both with walls and with discrimination, with taking in the *right* men, she becomes in the biblical tradition of which she is a part a principal Old Testament figure for the Church. The Church figured as female is that other redeemed harlot who in the space between the First and Second Coming of another Joshua, Christ—that is, between the disappearance and final triumphant return of the Master of Creation, Time and History—expands or dilates in order, so to speak, to take in more members, before that ultimate apocalyptic end. One of the iconographic embodiments of this female figure—ambiguously recalling both Mary the Mother and the harlot Mary Magdalene—is the figure most often called *Mater Misericordiae* and pictured as opening her cloak wide enough to encompass the gathered members of the Church or the Body of Christ.

The name of Rahab in Hebrew ('broad, wide') was translated into Latin by the Church Fathers as *dilatio* or dilation, and her opening and expansion in that crucial meantime or threshold period before Apocalypse became known technically as the 'dilation of Christendome,' a phrase used repeatedly by St Thomas More and others in the Renaissance for the period of spreading or widening through the 'dilation of the Word,' the crucial activity of that interim of deferred Judgment or Second Coming in which a promised end is yet postponed. 'Dilate' comes to us from the same Latin root as Derrida's 'différance' and involves—commonly throughout Renaissance usage in several languages—that term's curious combination of difference and deferral, dilation, expansion, or dispersal in space but also postponement in time. The dilation of Rahab or of the Church, then, involves symbolically two orifices: expansion to take in a multiplicity of members (as in Donne's sexual pun in the Sonnet on the Church as she who is—he is addressing Christ her Master—'most trew, and pleasing to thee, then/When she's embrac'd and open to most men'); and the propagation, through the mouth, of the Word, again an activity not unexpectedly linked with a Church figured as symbolically female, since one of the oldest topoi of misogyny is the fabled inability of women to keep that particular orifice shut. There is, as Lee Patterson has recently reminded us, at least one recorded instance of the view that Christ revealed himself to women immediately after his Resurrection because he knew that women would spread the word.[2]

This particular figure—of Rahab, understood as dilation, expansion, and deferral, and used as a figure for the space and time of language, discourse, and history before a Master's apocalyptic return—is the figurative fat lady who first interested me when I started to think about romance and about its characteristic association with such dilation or potential vagrancy (or often simply its dilatory refusal to come to a 'point').[3] But it was only much later that I began to discover how pervasive and multivalent this entire complex of 'dilation' in the Renaissance actually was and how frequently associated with figures of the feminine. This is a link which arises out of romance itself. Spenser used the term 'dilate' both for the dilation of history before its deferred apocalyptic (or 'sabbath') ending and for the activity of narrating or telling tales, including by implication the dilatory expansion of his own poem; but he also associates this expansion with a dangerous female temptress or enchantress in a canto which is perhaps not by accident the fattest, most dilated canto in the entire poem—a dilation specifically linked with the 'gate' of a 'Dame' called 'Excesse' ('No gate, but like one, being goodly dight / With boughes and braunches, which did broad dilate / Their clasping armes, in wanton wreathings intricate,' *The Faerie Queene*, II.xii.53–5). Overcoming this temptress and the dilated body of the text in question becomes the quest of the knight of Temperance, in a version of what Marvell calls the contest between Resolved Soul—here, the male knight—and the potentially distracting ensnarements of Created Pleasure, the bower of Acrasia. His project, we might say, is to bring this dilated 'matter' (with the possibility of a pun on both *materia* and *mater* as in Hamlet's 'Now, mother, what's the matter?') to a 'point.' Though this knight does not use his sword, the word 'point' (which designates in so many Renaissance English puns at once 'end,' sword, and their phallic counterpart) is Spenser's own in the very canto opening which projects the knight's victory over this 'matter' in advance even of his setting out ('And this brave knight . . . / Now comes to *point* of that same perilous sted, / Where Pleasure dwelles in sensual delights,' II.xii.1–3). The subtext for the whole is Odysseus' victory over the feminine enticements and enchantments of Circe, pointedly, in that dilated and dilatory text, with his sword; and the victory which in the *Odyssey* only proleptically prefigures the homecoming or closure of the entire narrative is here only too easily converted into a figure for this canto's ending, the coming to a point of another strikingly dilated text.

This association of the dilation of romance narrative with the figure or body of a female enchantress is, moreover, extended in the debate over romance itself as a Circean, female (or even effeminate) form, particularly in the later stages of the Renaissance. Thomas Nashe's *Anatomy of Absurdity* (1589), for instance, combined a satire on women and those who praised them with an attack on the authors of romance. Both were conceived of as potentially corrupting, or leading astray, the will, as making it into a kind of Prodigal Son who might never return to his father.[4] The very popularity of the story of the Prodigal Son in Elizabethan England—of his errancy and prodigality but also of his eventual, repentant return—became, as Richard Helgerson points out, a chief exemplum for the potential vagrancy of the literary activity itself, and of the suspect effeminacy of poets. When Sir Philip Sidney replies to the attacks on romance, as on poetry, in his celebrated *Defence*, by saying that 'he knows men that even with the reading of *Amadis de gaule* . . . have found their hearts moved to the exercise of courtesie, liberalitie, and especially courage,' he uses the word 'men' pointedly as a counter to the attackers' association of poetry with the feminine.[5] The polemic against the Italianization of Englishmen in the work of one of these opponents of romance— Roger Ascham's *The Schoolmaster* (1570), which follows the model of Vives in its attack and characterizes romances as nothing but bold bawdry—is, in fact, inseparable from a polemic against the romance's corrupting and enervating effect, with the implication that the reader of such texts is cast as an endangered Odysseus whose only moly is a humanist countertraining in virtue and in more canonical reading—the preoccupation, precisely, of the schoolmaster.

Certainly it is this plot of reformation or return from such enchantments—or a turning away from them to something higher or more serious—which is the burden of the figure of the Prodigal Son in which one Elizabethan reader casts himself. John Harington, translator of Ariosto's *Orlando furioso*, first finds in Ariosto's portrayal of Rogero's enticement by the Circe-like Alcina (a source for Spenser's Acrasia) 'the very picture of the Prodigal Son spoken of in the scripture, given over to all unthriftiness, all looseness of life and conversation,' and then discerns a link between such prodigal vagrancy and his own pursuits. He writes as follows of coming to the place in his translation of the *Furioso* where Melissa reproves Rogero for his dalliance with Alcina (for which the model is Mercury's reproof of Aeneas for his dalliance with Dido rather than getting on with the higher task of establishing the Roman empire): 'straight I began to think that my tutor, a grave and learned man, and one of very austere life, might say to me in like sort, "Was it for this that I read Aristotle and Plato to you and instructed you so carefully both in Greek and Latin, to have you now become a translator of Italian toys?" '[6] Such indulgence in romance was a form of dilatoriness or dalliance, preventing all such latter-day Aeneases from getting on with the business more proper to them.

Just as important a preface to our subject—and to the role of particular dilated female bodies in particular Renaissance texts—are a number of influential subtexts that a Renaissance poet or playwright would have inherited for the narrative topos of overcoming a female enchantress or obstacle en route to completion and ending. Here, where such female figures are linked with a threat to the execution of closure or accomplishment, the appropriate motto would seem to be not *Cherchez la femme*—or a certain way of understanding the question 'Is there a woman in this text?'—but rather what we might dub *Ecrasez la femme*, ways of mastering or controlling the implicitly female, and perhaps hence wayward, body of the text itself.[7] The first of these subtexts—already suggested in the opening reference to Rahab, the redeemed harlot whose name is *dilatio* and who stands as a figure for the dilated space of deferred judgment and ending—is the Bible, which is filled with figures for the space and time of such extension (the forty-day space between the announcement of judgment and its execution in the stories of Noah's Flood or Jonah's mission to Nineveh; the space of respite or temporary reprieve from death granted to Hezekiah; the holding back of time itself in the staying of the sun in Joshua, and so on). The reprieve granted to Adam and Eve, the 'remnant' of Noah and his family after the almost final closure of the Flood—these and other such reprieves extend both text and time, widening or increasing the space between beginning and end which in Genesis threatens to be very contracted indeed. A structure of deferral inhabits even the Bible's own end or last word, the Book of Apocalypse or Revelation. There, ending is linked to the stripping or overcoming of a female figure, the Whore of Babylon, by the now at last returned Master, Christ. But the final lines end in the still-deferred and still-anticipatory mode of an apostrophe, invocation, or vocative, 'Even so, come, Lord Jesus' (Revelation 22), a retreat from a vision of Ending into the ambiguous space before that ending (the model, perhaps, of a similar retreat at the end of Spenser's *Faerie Queene*). What looks like *the* end is, in this quintessential book of endings, presented as still put off or deferred, still yet to come. The New Testament, like the Old, however, is filled with warnings that this deferral of ending must not lull its hearers into the assumption that the promised end will never come. The crucial thing about deferral in its biblical context, then, is that its days are finally numbered, that all time is ultimately borrowed time. The structure of deferred ending remains resolutely teleological—waiting for the return of a delayed but finally coming Master.

The second major subtext for the association of specifically female figures with such dilation or delay is the *Odyssey* already referred to, where Calypso, the enchantress at whose dwelling we first glimpse the latent hero, has a name which means 'covering,' the very opposite of apocalypse or uncovering, and where Odysseus' mastery of Circe with his sword may be by implication a sort of narratively retroactive liberation from the covering and latency of Calypso's cave, just as it is an anticipation of homecoming to Penelope.[8] Penelope herself, keeping her suitors suspended by the stratagem of weaving and unweaving, while the suitors act like swine, is clearly a subtler or displaced counterpart of Circe, whose spells turn men *into* swine. It is perhaps no accident, then, that subsequent tradition tended to conflate or confuse these three female figures—Calypso, Circe, Penelope—since bringing the story to its ending here involves overcoming the implicitly female body of the romance narrative itself. We might remember, by way of parenthesis, that in Roland Barthes the properly narrative desire to reach an ending and the properly hermeneutic desire to penetrate a text's meaning are countered by the desire to linger or dilate. In Ariosto's *Orlando furioso*, a Renaissance text remarkable for its metafictional sophistication in these matters, one of the principal figures for ending is the overcoming of an enchantress who recalls both Circe and the Whore of Babylon; stripping her bare is termed 'reading her pages' in the way they should be read.[9]

It is easy to move from this second subtext to the third—Virgil's influential *Aeneid*—because it is the latter's combination of Odyssean or romance dilatoriness with Iliadic or epic haste which makes it the progenitor of so many Renaissance hybrids, or epic-romances. Virgil's poem, moreover, seems almost to be commenting, in what we would now call self-reflexive fashion, on the differing tendencies and gender associations of both epic and romance: the resolutely teleological drive of epic in its repeated injunctions to 'break off delay' (*rumpe moras*) and the Odyssean or romance delaying tactics which make it the long poem it is and which disrupt or postpone the end promised from the beginning. Once again, it is the female figures—Dido, Allecto, Amata, Juno (and their agents)—who are the chief perpetrators of delay and even of obstructionism in relation to the master or imperial project of the completion of the text. Jupiter, the text's meta-authorial presence, is also the guarantor or at least the Olympic patron of ultimate closure. By making the *Aeneid* a principal subtext of his romance *Cymbeline*, Shakespeare provides an implicit reading of Virgil's poem in precisely such terms. In *Cymbeline* the Queen, like Juno in the *Aeneid*, can delay the fated ending but cannot indefinitely forestall or finally alter it; and a character representing Jupiter descends from the meta-authorial skies in that play's final act to announce why the promised ending has been so long deferred, which is to say, in view of this romance play's massively complicated movement to its own point of revelation or recognition scene, why the play itself has lasted as long as it has.

These influential texts—and their female obstructors—already, then, forge a link between such female figures and the extension or dilation of the text in order to defer its end or 'point.' But the even more specific link we need to explore before moving on to particular dilated *bodies* in a number of Renaissance and other texts is the rhetorical tradition of the dilation of discourse, and specifically its dilation through 'partition,' through the multiplication of partitions or rhetorical dividing walls. It is this towards which we need to turn before focusing on the identification of such dilation with corpulent bodies of various kinds, and the significance of their appearance in particular texts.

Erasmus's *De Copia* is here the readiest source not just for this rhetorical tradition but for its dual concerns. The preoccupation of this massively influential text is not only how to expand a discourse—to make its 'matter' or *materia* respond to the rhetorical counterpart of the command to Adam and Eve to 'increase and multiply'—but also how to control that expansion, to keep dilation from getting out of bounds, a concern repeated in the countless Renaissance rhetorical handbooks which both teach their pupils how to amplify and repeatedly warn them against the intimately related vice of 'Excesse' (the same name, we might remember, as Spenser's dilating 'Dame'). Dilation, then, is always something to be kept within the horizon of ending, mastery, and control, and the 'matter' is always to be varied within certain formal guidelines or rules.

The rhetorical figure of walls or partitions, from that part of Cicero's *Topics* where a discussion of physical 'walls' is juxtaposed with a definition of oratorical 'partition,' involves the dividing of a discourse, like a body, into 'members'—a tradition which Shakespeare reveals he knows only too well when, in the Pyramus and Thisbe play of *A Midsummer Night's Dream*, he has Demetrius punningly call the mechanical playing the character of Wall the 'wittiest partition that ever I heard discourse' (V.i.161–8).[10] In the related art of preaching, the principal method of proceeding was to divide and open up a closed or difficult scriptural text so that it might 'increase and multiply,' be dilated upon by the preacher so as to dilate and spread abroad the Word. In the words of Donne, summing up the entire tradition of the *ars praedicandi*, 'Through partition or division, the Word of God is made a Sermon, that is, a Text is dilated, diffused into a Sermon.' And this rhetorical dilation by partition was to be used by preachers of the Word in precisely that period of the 'dilation of Christendome' before Apocalypse, before the final apocalyptic end both of that 'wall of partition' spoken of in Ephesians (2:14) and of discourse itself.[11]

This tradition of rhetorical *dilatio*—with its references to the 'swelling' style or its relation to the verbal 'interlarding' produced through an excessive application of the principle of 'increase'—provides its own links between fat bodies and discoursing 'at large,' between the size of a discourse and the question of body size. Ascham's *Schoolmaster* treats of the use of 'epitome' in reducing the inflated bulk of an oration through the example of the need to put an 'overfat' and 'fleshy' style on a diet, as Cicero himself did in order to rid himself of 'grossness.' Though fat is not gendered as female in this passage from Ascham, it most definitely is in anti-Ciceronian contrastings of a more effeminate Ciceronian or Asiatic style—linked with 'bignesse' as well as prodigality—to the more virile Attic. Erasmus's *Ciceronianus* (1528) speaks of seeking in vain in Ciceronian eloquence for something 'masculine' and of his own desire for a 'more masculine' style. Ciceronian copia in these discussions is both effeminate and the style of a more prodigal youth, to be outgrown once one had become a man: 'I used to imitate [Cicero],' writes Lipsius; 'but I have become a man, and my tastes have changed. Asiatic feasts have ceased to please me; I prefer the Attic.' A similar contrast, with the appropriate shift of symbolic locus, informs the opposition of fat and effeminating Egypt to lean and virile Rome in Shakespeare's *Antony and Cleopatra*.[12]

This specifically rhetorical tradition of amplified textuality and dilated middles is joined by and easily combined with a whole host of other resonances of 'dilation' in the Renaissance, which we can only briefly touch on here, but must at least mention, since they too figure frequently in the imaging of postponed ending or 'increase' in the texts of our exemplary fat ladies. One is the Neoplatonic tradition of *dilatio* as the dilation or Emanation of Being, its procession out from and its crucial return to the Source or One. For not only is this one Western example among many of what Derrida repeatedly wants to distinguish from 'différance' (since deferral or dilation in this tradition is contained within the horizon of ending, a simple detour between Origin and End); it also provides Spenser with the crucial authority for the final 'putting downe' of the upstart Goddess Mutabilitie (as well as the specter of endlessness, perhaps) by Jupiter's female agent Nature, who has clearly been reading her Ficino. A second, related meaning is as a synonym for temporality, for the mediate or earthly as distinguished from the eternal, simultaneous, or immediate—hence the easy identification of dilation, as of the female, with the body of both time and the world, or creation itself. A third is the sense of dilation as the puffing up of pride, as in the warning in an English translation of Erasmus's *Adages* that 'we dylate not our selves beyond our condition and state,' or the 'dilation' of Satan, progenitor of sin, in Milton's *Paradise Lost* ('Collecting all his might dilated stood'; IV.986).[13]

Still another use of 'dilation' occurs in the context of propagation or generation, the postponing of death through natural increase, one of the principal arguments against the premature closure of virginity and a meaning crucial to the potential identification of the rhetorical tradition of 'increase and multiply' with the more fruitful dilation of another kind of 'fat lady'—the pregnant female body, promising even as it contains and postpones the appearance of an 'issue.' The generational joins the rhetorical and hermeneutic here through the fact that the command to 'increase and multiply' which stands behind this kind of dilation ('Two joyned can themselves dilate') has its rhetorical counterpart in the tradition of the copia of discourse. Augustine in the *Confessions* has a whole chapter devoted to 'increase and multiply' (XIII.xxiv) in the sense of the interpreter's opening and fruitful extension of a closed or hermetic scriptural text, what the rhetorical tradition would call 'dilating or enlarging of a matter by interpretation.' But this 'matter' and its enlarging also easily joined with *mater*. Obstetrical descriptions in the Renaissance frequently start with a reminder of the divine command to 'increase and multiply' and see the 'mouth' of the *matrix* or womb as 'an orifice at the entrance into the which may be dilated and shut.' Dilation as the 'opening' of a closed text to make it 'increase and multiply' and to transform its brevity into a discourse 'at large,' then, joins dilation as both sexual and obstetrical 'opening' and the production of generational increase.[14]

There are, to complete this Renaissance catalogue, two other signal contexts for dilation, which in fact often appear together as figures for the postponed ending of a text. The first is the judicial one—the tradition of Essoins or 'dilatory pleas' which Hamlet, in a play very much concerned with postponement or deferral, calls 'the law's delay,' a means of putting off judgment or execution. Hamlet's complaint against the 'law's delay' comes in the middle of the very soliloquy of hesitation or doubt ('To be or not to be'), with both its 'consummation / Devoutly to be wish'd' and its hesitation to rush to that conclusion. And 'dilatory pleas' as a means of putting off an ending easily participate in a crossing of legal with other contexts of judgment or consummation. At the end of Chaucer's *Canterbury Tales*, for example, the Parson, speaking of the apocalyptic 'day of doom,' describes it as that one 'juggement' before which 'there availeth noon essoin,' a reminder that, in the biblical tradition out of which he speaks, dilation as delay is circumscribed finally by a telos, that the putting off of ending here is finally only temporary. The appearance of such a reference in the Parson's Tale (which has been frequently described as the *Tales'* culminating Book of Apocalypse or Revelation) may suggest retrospectively that all of the impressive *copia* or 'God's plenty' of The *Canterbury*

Tales up to that ending has been a form of 'essoin' or 'dilatory plea,' including the text of that female figure, the Wife of Bath, whose copious discourse or dilated textual body puts off the Parson's concluding text, who announces 'My joly *body* shall a tale tell,' whose motto is 'increase and multiply,' and who herself turns to her own quite different purposes the sermon art of the dilation of discourse. As one recent reading of this excessive 'Dame' puts it, Alisoun of Bath ameliorates the harsh polarizations of apocalyptic judgment and eschatology and opens up a space of dilation in which what we have come to call literature can have its place. Her 'increase,' however, is verbal rather than generational, and from this more judgmental perspective, as a form of sterility or fruitless activity, it is finally preempted by the teleological framework in which there is no—or no longer—'essoin.'[15]

The final context for 'dilation' is an erotic one within a specific masculinist tradition—the putting off of coitus or consummation which Andreas Capellanus describes as a feminine strategy in the art of love, a purportedly female plot in which holding a suitor at a distance creates the tension of a space between as well as an intervening time. By the time of Eve's 'sweet reluctant amorous delay' in Book IV of *Paradise Lost*, 'dilation' in this sense was almost a *terminus technicus* for the erotics of prolongation, a tradition still current in Addison's reference to 'women of dilatory Tempers, who are for spinning out the Time of Courtship.' Its focus on the hymen as a dividing wall or partition, moreover, made it easily conflatable with both the rhetorical tradition of the dilation of discourse by 'partition' and the intervening 'partition wall' of Ephesians 2. This amorous dilation is a frequent part of the plot of wooing or courtship in Shakespeare, in examples almost too numerous to name. But this plot of feminine dilation or delay is rarely linked, by critics of Shakespeare, with the temporal and rhetorical dilation of the plays themselves, though in *A Midsummer Night's Dream* (to take just one example) the erotic consummation promised in the play's opening scene is deferred for a time and space which coincides with that of the play as a whole and which is achieved only when a 'partition' or wall associated both with the hymen and with the rhetorical 'partition of discourse' is finally put 'down,'[16] just as in *The Comedy of Errors* the wall of partition which prolongs the play's various romance-like 'errors' by delaying the final recognition scene is associated with the intervening body of a much-dilated female.

*   *   *

Gail Kern Paster, *The Body Embarrassed: Drama and the Disciplines of Shame in Early Modern England* (Ithaca, New York: Cornell University Press, 1993), pp. 23–63.

The incontinence on which this [essay] focuses is not the relatively comfortable subject of sexual incontinence in women but its much less comfortable analogue—bladder incontinence. In particular, I want to discuss the two odd occasions in Jacobean city comedy which represent women needing or failing to relieve themselves. The first occurs in Ben Jonson's *Bartholomew Fair* when the urgent need for a chamber pot brings Win Littlewit and Mrs. Overdo to Ursula's booth, the second in Thomas Middleton's *Chaste Maid in Cheapside* when the gossips at the Allwit christening wet the floor beneath their stools. Though both plays have received a goodly share of critical discussion over the years, neither of these episodes has provoked sustained comment. It is easy to understand why. Even now, when so much intellectual attention is directed toward the social formation of the historicized body and its literary representations, the cultural inhibitions that are part of the body's history have made sex easier to discuss than excretion. The bedroom is a discursive site as the bathroom or—to be less anachronistic—the chamber pot and the privy are not, because we are the silenced inheritors of what Keith Thomas has called 'the cult of decorum.'[1] Norbert Elias, acknowledging that 'in considering this process of civilization, we cannot avoid arousing feelings of discomfort and embarrass-ment,' counters that 'it is valuable to be aware of them.'[2] However protected by the historical distance and impersonal mediation provided by a scholarly focus upon seventeenth-century comedy, in writing about women excreting I take the risk of evoking embarrassment or distaste.

But criticism should be wary of marginalizing the literary reproduction of any behavior, especially an everyday behavior mentioned so rarely in literary discourse, let alone represented onstage. To the charge that there is little in the physical needs of Win Littlewit or Dame Overdo to write about in the form of historical argument, I would point out the sheer gratuity of staging biological need as engendered joke in the first place. In spite of the recent television appearances of elderly but still attractive female stars delicately promoting the virtues of reinforced underclothing for adults (assumed to be mostly female) who want to get back 'into the swim' of vigorous physical activity, the bladder incontinence at the source of Middleton's joke against the gossips is still protected by the taboo of silence.[3] Far from being beneath our critical notice, the two scenes in *Bartholomew Fair* and *A Chaste Maid in Cheapside* constitute important and by no means isolated instances of early modern English culture's complex articulation of gender—the weaker vessel as leaky vessel.

At these moments onstage two affective formations are at work. One involves that sig-nifying practice we call 'manners'; the other a culturally familiar discourse about the female body, an anxious symptomatological discourse to be found in a variety of other texts including Renaissance medical texts, iconography, and the proverbs of oral culture. This discourse inscribes women as leaky vessels by isolating one element of the female body's material expressiveness—its production of fluids—as excessive, hence either disturbing or shameful. It also characteristically links this liquid expressiveness to excessive verbal fluency. In both forma-tions, the issue is women's bodily self-control or, more precisely, the representation of a particular kind of uncontrol as a function of gender.[4] This ascription of uncontrol is further naturalized by means of the complex classification of bodily fluids to which Galenic humoral-ism was committed both in theory and in practice. Thus the conventional Renaissance associ-ation of women and water is used not only to insinuate womanly unreliability but also to define the female body even when it is chaste, even when it is *virgo intacta*, as a crucial problematic in the social formations of capitalism—an instance of corporeal waste of the female body, representing, in Julia Kristeva's phrase, 'the objective frailty of symbolic order.'[5]

Natalie Zemon Davis has argued that the deepening subjection of women in the early modern period can be understood as a 'streamlining' of the patriarchal family for the economic efficiency required by emerging capitalist modes of production.[6] Representations of the female body as a leaking vessel display that body as beyond the control of the female subject, and thus as threatening the acquisitive goals of the family and its maintenance of status and power. The crucial problematic was whether women as a group could be counted on to manage their behaviors in response to historically emergent demands of bodily self-rule.

[. . .] [T]he question of bodily control took on a new interest and urgency in early modern European culture, legible from the publication in 1530 and frequent reprintings thereafter of Erasmus's treatise *De civilitate morum puerilium*. The bodily controls Erasmus begins to enjoin upon upper-class boys more often concern table manners and bodily carriage than the 'natural' functions I concentrate on here. Even so, the new injunctions against urinating or defecating in public, for example, though frequently ignored in practice even by upper-class males, begin to inscribe what Lacan calls 'the laws of urinary segregation'—laws employing gender norms to compel restraint and, more important, to distinguish between the norms of restraint for men and women.[7] The modesty that is an ethical norm for women governs not only their own expression of excretory functions but also what men may or may not do in the presence of women. Elias quotes from German court regulations of 1570 calling those who would relieve themselves in front of ladies 'rustics who have not been to court or lived among refined and honorable people.'[8]

The advance of the shame threshold affects discourses of the body no less than behavior in ways that begin to clarify differences of both class and gender. One proof of Erasmus's success in inscribing greater shame in the boys he addresses is that, unlike later writers on manners, he does not seem reluctant to mention the behavior he is trying to refashion.[9] This growing delicacy, especially as displayed by those imitating without sufficient warrant the more refined behavior of their social superiors, becomes a powerful signifier of class identification and newly drawn boundaries. In *The Winter's Tale*, for example, Autolycus employs euphemism to establish a firm social distance between himself and Perdita's shepherd family. [. . .]

What is at stake here is a semiology of excretion in which an ostensibly natural behavior becomes thoroughly implicated in a complex structure of class and gender differences. [. . .] In *Bartholomew Fair*, both Win Littlewit and Mrs. Overdo display much greater reluctance to acknowledge their urgent bladders than did Autolycus, perhaps because they really do need, as it were, to relieve themselves, whereas Autolycus is only pretending a need in the body in order to accomplish other social tasks. Finding herself among a group of strangers at Ursula's booth, Dame Overdo must 'entreat a courtesy' of Captain Whit, but she cannot reply to his expansive offer to 'shpeak out' and 'entreat a hundred' because—'with modesty' (4. 4.185–87)—the courtesy she requires can only be un-spoken.[10]

Win's reluctance is even more noticeable. Leaving Ursula's booth with her husband, she resists his entreaty to see more of the fair together, saying 'I know not what to do. . . . For a thing, I am asham'd to tell you, i'faith, and 'tis too far to go home' (3.6.113, 115–16). Her evident desperation depends upon a recognized need for privacy which cannot be met merely by turning away or—until their discovery of Ursula's chamber pot—by any measure short of an actual return home.[11] But Win reacts indignantly to the assumption that her embarrassment is caused by the presence onstage of Leatherhead, the puppet-seller: 'Hang him, base bobchin, I scorn him' (120). The sensation of shame is a function of social structure. In hierarchical societies, one does not feel the same bodily shame before inferiors as before equals or superiors. By such logic, Win has no reason to feel ashamed, has no social cause for verbal squeamishness if she, like Autolycus, feels superior or at least equal to her companions onstage.

But the vehemence of her response may tell us more than her word. Poor Win is experiencing a redundancy of shame, here the social shame of *feeling ashamed* to acknowledge urgent bodily need not to an inferior but merely in his presence. In this instance, the operative distinctions helping to constitute an embarrassment based on the laws of urinary segregation are those of gender and class and also those of urban or rural identification. Unlike Harington's country maids, the city wife has no woods to cover her retreat and prevent her exposure. She is trapped by the relentless copresence of the crowded metropolis, her sense of respectability, and the lower thresholds of offensiveness characteristic of urban life. If we accept what she says, then her husband's presence or even the otherwise unacknowledged presence of an audience has molded Win's confusion, has called forth a redundancy of euphemism: 'I have very great what sha'call'um, John' (3.6.120–21).

If Win's problem is more cultural than physical, so too is its solution. Ursula's booth—the fair's central locus—is usually associated with the body as part of the play's apparent cele-bration of Carnival. Thus, in Jonathan Haynes's Bakhtinian representation of the booth's symbolic functions, 'the material bodily principle is magnificently embodied in the enormous flesh of the pig-woman Ursula and in her booth, which caters to all the body's needs (eating, drinking, defecating, fornicating).'[12] Here, as so often, the call of culture is mistaken for the call of nature, and a generic body, like Leatherhead's puppets lacking sex or gender, stands in for concealed cultural norms that distinguish sharply between the bodily 'needs' of men and women. No character in *Barthomolew Fair* is known to defecate offstage in Ursu-la's booth. And only female characters are shown to need and want Ursula's chamber pot—in actuality 'the bottom of an old bottle' (4.4.203)—because, unlike Autolycus or any other male character in this period who needs to urinate, they cannot merely 'look upon' the nearest stage property hedge but are tied by the invisible leading strings of culture to a concealed receptacle. Thus is Malvolio's verbal trespass constituted; 'Thus makes she her great P's.'

As Haynes suggests, Jonson may well intend Ursula's booth to situate his festive advocacy of 'the material bodily principle,' and Ursula, by virtue of her office, may represent at one level a de-idealized version of the goddess Nature. Such a symbolic placement is itself fully conventional in binary Renaissance constructions of gender whereby man is associated with culture and woman with nature.[13] We ought to notice that Ursula describes herself as an archetypal representation of woman because, in standing over the hot fire, she becomes a vessel leaking and melting, to be known by her loss of corporeal being—loss of content, form, and integral identity—and marked like Olivia by the liquid letters she makes: 'I shall e'en melt away to the first woman, a rib, again, I am afraid. I do water the ground in knots as I go, like a great garden-pot; you may follow me by the S's I make' (2.2.50–53). She and her booth are mutually identifying—in Overdo's words, 'the very womb and bed of enormity! gross, as herself' (2.2.107–8). Yet, as proprietor of the booth and supplier of the chamber pot, Ursula crosses over the boundaries of gender to become the agent of culture, the instrument of patriarchy, for the cultural norms constraining Win Littlewit and Mrs. Overdo to seek out the booth as privy function to keep them there as prostitutes. That is, because the booth is the central locus of desire in the fair, it serves prevailing cultural requirements in transforming the women from subjects to objects. The chamber pot has become a bawd, the 'jordan' a seller of flesh literalized in Jordan Knockem, the horse-corser. Perhaps Ursula herself senses some of the ideological contradictions in her function, for she objects to helping Mrs. Overdo to a jordan and tells Whit to find Captain Jordan instead: 'I bring her! Hang her,' she tells Whit furiously, 'heart, must I find a common pot for every punk i'your purlieus? . . . Let her sell her hood, and buy a sponge' (4.4.198–201).

Behind Ursula's rejoinder is a specific linkage between whores and urine, which also surfaces in *The Alchemist* (2.1.43–45) when Surly imagines self-punishment to take the form of a whore pissing out his eyes. [. . .] It was thought that whores used urination immediately after copulation both as a form of contraception and as a preventative against venereal disease.[14] If business at the fair was good—and the attempted recruitment of Win and Mrs. Overdo certainly contributes to that impression—then the whores' demand for Ursula's chamber pot would have been great and her resistance reasonable enough. This semiotic connection between whores and the chamber pot suggests why the wives' desire to use the chamber pot is found to be so compromising and how a bodily behavior so commonplace among fairgoers then and now could become the groundplot of a final, humiliating exposure.

But as far as Win Littlewit's putative transformation from wife to whore is concerned, a wonderful irony is at work. In persuading the pregnant Win to pretend a 'longing' to eat Bartholomew pig, John Littlewit had caused his wife to manifest one of the conventional weaknesses of women—the bizarrely irrational cravings of pregnancy, which had to be satisfied in order to prevent harm to mother and unborn baby.[15] If visiting the fair is an act of irrational appetite, the proctor will sanction and justify his weakness by displacing it onto his wife and, through her, women at large. It is Littlewit who acts most powerfully to make his wife into an emblem of female desire: 'You may long to see, as well as to taste, Win: how did the 'pothecary's wife, Win, that long'd to see the anatomy, Win? Or the lady, Win, that desir'd to spit i'the great lawyer's mouth, after an eloquent pleading? I assure you they long'd, Win; good Win, go in, and long' (3.6.12–16). Similarly, it is Win who publicly confesses to having 'very great what sha'call'um,' but later the proctor seems to have it too. Ursula tells Whit that 'an honest proctor and his wife are *at it*, within' (4.4.204–5, emphasis mine), thus forcing poor Mrs. Overdo to wait to use the bottle. But given the multiple functions of Ursula's booth, we should also notice here the multiple significations of her phrase, the sexual suggestion in 'at it.' [. . .]

Ursula's pun makes physiological sense because Galenic humoralism proposed a structural homology among all forms of evacuation, including the bodily release of male and female 'seed' in sexual climax. (Indeed, it is the Galenic image of female ejaculation of seed that makes phallogocentric sense of the upward displacement of genital desire in the lady longing to spit into the eloquent mouth of the great lawyer.) For Win and Mrs. Overdo to express literally unspeakable desires for the bodily release of urination is to bring them within the overall humoral logic of bodily repletion, a logic of the lower bodily stratum in which the sensory differences between excretion and copulation blur and lose distinction. It can hardly be coincidental that once Littlewit has abandoned his wife at Ursula's booth in order to see how his puppet show is going forward, other conventional uses of her and Mrs. Overdo can be culturally sanctioned—and made intelligible to a modern reader. As Ursula tells Knockem, 'persuade this between you two, to become a bird o'the game, while I work the velvet woman within (as you call her)' (4.5.17–19).

How and why these two women find themselves at Ursula's booth, therefore, is just as revealing of gender norms as what happens to them afterward. The chamber pot is bawd indeed. It is not that Ursula confuses the two city wives with Ramping Alice or any of the other

Bartholomew birds but rather that she and Knockem merely act upon the implication of the wives' presence, without male escort, at her booth. [. . .] [S]o here unlawful access to otherwise inaccessible women is made possible by the odd but crucial mediation of the chamber pot: it discloses their vulnerability, announces an occasion of physical and social permeability, hints at the outermost horizon of their desires.[16]

But even beyond the linkage established by Jonson's play between the whore and the city wife [. . .] there are other connections between bodily fluids and the contemporary constructions of woman. That women's bodies were moister than men's and cyclically controlled by that watery planet, the moon, was a given of contemporary scientific theory. Their bodies were notable for the production of liquids—breast milk, menstrual blood, tears, and great P's. Both popular and medical discourse, moreover, conceptualized all these fluids as related forms of the same essential substance. Breast milk was the purified form of menstrual blood, 'none other thing than blood made white.'[17] It changed color according to function by means of a process that occurred in two veins—'occult passages'—which carried the fluid back and forth between the breast and the womb.[18] And to judge from the discursive evidence of one proverb —'Let her cry, she'll piss the less'—tears and urine also may have seemed interrelated in nature and function, flow from one orifice drawing off flow in another.[19]

But the proverb's permissive '*let* her cry' suggests another way of thinking about the matter of women's great pees—as occasions of patriarchal control and intervention, with the apparently desirable goal of making women 'piss the less.' Early modern culture was preoccupied with the quality and quantity of bodily evacuations as a crucial index of the body's solubility. Humoral medicine's nosology of evacuations constructed a complex symbology in which social differences were given objective verification and natural authority. In humoral medicine, urine was an evacuation of great epistemological potential. As with other signifying properties of the body, urine participates in a powerful hermeneutic circularity in which social distinctions govern both what is sought and what is found in the physical world. The attributes of sexual and other forms of difference were thought to be readily discernible in the body's liquids.

One of the things urine signified—and confirmed—was the nature of women. Thus most advocates of uroscopy were convinced that age and sex functioned materially in the taxonomy of urines along with other key determinants such as color, temperature, quantity, smell, taste, 'substance,' and 'contents.' In his 1623 treatise on urine, for example, John Fletcher cites recognized medical authority in insisting that 'distinctione between men and womens urine is easily knowne by often comparing [the urines] together. *Fernel*.'[20] From men of the ideal, sanguine temperament came the standard urines by which all others were to be measured: in color 'palew [*sic*], light saffron'; 'meane' or moderate in substance and quantity; 'in contents} equall, white, light'; 'not stinking'; and produced 'in due time without} paine, heat, cold.'[21] Most women, being of colder temperament, were supposed to have urines lighter in color and greater in quantity than those of healthy adult males. [. . .]

The categorical complexity of traditional uroscopy is likely to amaze the modern reader who moves without preamble into its discursive precincts. It is hard for us to recognize how a bodily fluid with which we, too, are intimately (if less professionally) familiar can differ so vividly and complexly from itself and can seem so deeply infused with historical particularity and social significance. But the physicians who read urines did not see themselves as fantasists. They were eager to distinguish their own practice in assessing the true signifying potential in urine from the grander claims of uromancers—those who read samples of urine to tell fortunes—or even from the practice of those empirics, women healers, and other lay practitioners who judged urines apart from other bodily signs and often diagnosed disease without examining the patient.[22] Physicians inspecting urines believed themselves engaged in the scientific recovery and classification of bodily signs that were objectively *there*. To the trained uroscopist, urines came in a rainbow of twenty or twenty-one colors ranging from several shades of white at the pale end of the spectrum through saffrons, reds, greens, blacks. These variations gave rise to conventional descriptions of great particularity and even beauty. We find urine 'nygh as yelowe as saffron of the garden' or 'reed as a brennynge cole,' 'redde as it were the lyver of a beast,' 'grene as wortes,' 'blacke & shinyng as a Ravens fether.'[23] [. . .]

In terms of the history of women's bodies, however, female leakiness was not just a purely illusory construct of Galenic humoralism. It was a real physical condition more or less peculiar to women, the inevitable result of primitive obstetrical techniques and the reproductive practices of the upper and aspirant classes. Dorothy McLaren has persuasively demonstrated the correlation between the extremely high fertility rates among rich women and their abandonment of breast-feeding, arguing that 'the choice for wives during their teeming years in preindustrial England was an infant in the womb or at the breast.'[24] That this choice may have been dictated largely by class norms is less important to my argument than the possibility that women, whether suckling infants or suppressing the flow of milk after annual childbirth, must often have seemed ready to overflow at the breast or leak down below. In some circumstances, the two thresholds were interchangeable. Joubert devotes an entire chapter to the question of 'whether it is true that a woman who has just delivered is able to piss milk' and decides that it is, 'as is the case when the parturient woman does not nurse.'[25] Early gynecologists believed that women who had never been pregnant could have milk in their breasts, that 'marriageable virgins full of juice and seed' could have as much breast milk as wet nurses.[26]

The cultural association of women and liquids was so deeply inscribed that it required little empirical support, as we see in the case of the milk-laden virgins. Given the intractability of gynecological disease in the period and the incessant childbearing of an important female minority, evidence for an iconology of women as leaky vessels must have seemed undeniable. Obstetrical instruments did in fact leave women mangled after difficult or protracted labors, threatening them with urinary incontinence.[27] And even among women who gave birth more easily, the frequency of childbearing must have severely weakened control of the urinary musculature. Or as another of Tilley's proverbs puts it, 'Like an old woman's breech, at no certainty.'[28] [. . .]

Far more than even the leaking women of *Bartholomew Fair*, the female characters of *A Chaste Maid in Cheapside* reproduce a virtual symptomatology of women, which insists on the female body's moisture, secretions, and productions as shameful tokens of uncontrol. [. . .] The play's symptomatological discourse of women is perhaps most striking in the christening scene. [. . .]

The christening in early modern Europe was an occasion that typically called for much eating and drinking, even when celebrated in Lent, as this one is.[29] The signal feature of this christening, however, is less the communal carnivalism than a demarcation of gender even sharper than what we have seen in *Bartholomew Fair*, as the men band together in vocal disgust at the women's gluttony, drunkenness, reeking wet kisses, and finally incontinence. 'They have drunk so hard in plate,' comments Allwit to his manservant, 'that some of them had need of other vessels' (3.2.171–72).

Allwit's male anxiety at the christening scene could not be clearer or more representative of patriarchal feelings, even though they issue from a man whose apparent desire to give over his rights to his wife's body to the man who can keep them both in material comfort seems at first glance to invert the patriarchal ethos. [. . .]

For Allwit, the threat posed by a collective, hence Amazonian female appetite and female fertility is so catastrophic that it supplants the male rivalry, virtually normative in plays of the period, which Middleton's city comedies, with their obsessive feuding of merchant and gallant, usually lay bare. Indeed, what mitigates our sense of Allwit's gender anomalousness in giving up his wife's sexual services is that he so clearly defines them rather as sexual demands—costly ones. Her latest pregnancy is marked by a longing for 'pickled cucumbers'— a sexually suggestive longing far more anxiety-provoking than anything other pregnant women of the stage, such as Win Littlewit or even the Duchess of Malfi, manifest. Allwit hopes the cucumbers will 'hold [his] wife in pleasure / Till the knight come himself' (1.2.9–10). Mrs. Allwit's appetites can be satisfied only by dint of a sexual, financial, and psychological effort and expense that Allwit has craftily transferred to Sir Walter. It is Allwit, not his cuckolder, who congratulates himself on his escape from the alienated labor of sexual performance and the attendant anxieties of sexual possession:

> These torments stand I free of; I am as clear
> From jealousy of a wife as from the charge:
> O, two miraculous blessings! 'Tis the knight
> Hath took that labour all out of my hands:
> I may sit still and play; he's jealous for me,
> Watches her steps, sets spies; I live at ease,
> He has both the cost and torment.
>   (1.2.48–54)

Here the enemy of middle-class conservation of wealth is women. 'They never think of payment,' complains Allwit (3.2.79) to the man who does offer payment for sexual privileges in the house, as they flee the room together. Here then, uniquely, cuckoldry becomes wittoldry. Erstwhile male rivals become partners in arms, banding together to conserve for themselves and the variously fathered offspring whom they feel obliged to support an economic and sexual substance that the appetite of woman and her conspicuous lack of self-control threaten to destroy.

[T]he leaky women of Middleton's Cheapside cannot by themselves keep their barrels full or their holes plugged. Attempting such impossible tasks becomes the self-imposed responsibility of the patriarchal order. In this play, moreover, the tasks themselves offer patriarchy the distinct advantage of prompting unusually stable male alliances [. . .] to get the job done. Although the play seems to suggest that these male alliances are forged by necessity—a necessity occasioned by female unreliability and appetite—we can perceive in the construction of women as leaky vessels the powerful interests of patriarchal ideology. At the end, the leaky vessels of Cheapside have been contained, perhaps because they, unlike Win Littlewit or Mrs. Overdo, have not ventured into the free space of a fairground to follow mother Ursula and find the public chamber pot. Ursula's revenge.

*   *   *

Louis Montrose, 'The work of gender in the discourse of discovery', *Representations* 33 (1991), 6.

Michel de Certeau reproduces the engraving of Vespucci's discovery of [an embodied, feminised] America as the frontispiece of his book *The Writing of History*. As he explains in his preface, to him this image is emblematic of the inception of a distinctively modern discursive practice of historical and cultural knowledge; this historiography [. . .] ruptures the continuum 'between a subject and an object of the operation, between a *will to write* and a *written body* (or a body to be written).' For de Certeau, the history of this modern writing of history begins in the sixteenth century with 'the "ethnographical" organization of writing in its relation with "primitive", "savage", "traditional", or "popular" orality that it establishes as its other.' Thus, for him, the tableau of Vespucci and America is

> an inaugural scene [. . .]. The conqueror will write the body of the other and trace there his own history. From her he will make a historied body—a blazon—of his labors and phantasms [. . .].
>
> What is really initiated here is a colonization of the body by the discourse of power. This is *writing that conquers*. It will use the New World as if it were a blank, 'savage' page on which Western desire will be written.[1]

*   *   *

Jonathan Dollimore, *Sex, Literature and Censorship* (Polity: Cambridge, 2001), pp. 50–1.

And then there is the new 'body theory'. The body has become a fashionable topic: athletes work out; cultural theorists 'work on' the body, and with a tenacious abstraction which suggests to me evasion if not aversion. [. . .] Here's an exchange between an older and a younger academic, overheard at a cocktail party (you'll know which is which):

> 'So what do you work on?'
> 'The Body.'
> 'The body—how interesting; [longish pause in which both sip drinks] in what sense exactly?'
> 'I see the body as an effect of repressive discursive constructions and in particular the site of the inscription of power.'
> 'Right. So this is a body in chains, as it were?'
> 'Well, yes and no: I also theorize the body as the site of subversion and subjugated knowledges.'
> 'Interesting.'

· ·

QUESTIONS

- To what extent do the above writers see the body as material and in what ways do they 'read' the body through text and discourse?
- What are the implications for the history of women of the representations of the female body analysed above?
- What is Dollimore's objection to new theories of the body and what critical force does it have?

3 | Theorizing the body: desire and transformation

Richmond Barbour, 'Britain and the Great Beyond: *The Masque of Blackness* at Whitehall', in John Gillies and Virginia Mason Vaughan (eds.), *Playing the Globe: Genre and Geography in English Renaissance Drama* (London: Associated University Presses, 1998), pp. 139–41.

Thus Dudley Carleton describes [. . .] Anna of Denmark] and her ladies [in Jonson's *Masque of Blackness*]:

> Their Apparell was rich, but too light and Curtizan-like for such great ones. Instead of Vizzards, their Faces, and Arms up to the Elbows, were painted black, which was Disguise sufficient, for they were hard to be known; but it became them nothing so well as their red and white, and you cannot imagine a more ugly Sight, then a Troop of lean-cheek'd Moors.[1]

[W]hat strikes most readers today is the racist edge to Carleton's mislike. For he finds the costumes 'Curtizan-like,' [. . .] not because they are too revealing, but because they reveal black skin. [. . .] Carleton's 1605 antipathies spring [. . .] from an equation of blackness with unbridled sexuality. That women should embody this linkage only heightens his unease: racial fears combine with patriarchal anxieties about female lust and generativity. Because black women may be fantasized to erase white paternity in their children, Boose suggests, to represent black women in Jacobean England is a queasy matter. Particularly as objects of desire: 'Theyre black faces, and hands wch were painted and bare up to the elbowes, was a very lothsome sight,' Carleton writes again, 'and I am sorry that strangers should see owr court so strangely disguised.'[2]

The terms of Carleton's critique, however, indicate a specifically theatrical provocation as well: The women are 'strangely disguised.' [. . .] Arguing that it 'became them none so well as their red and white', Carleton mocks the new cosmetics. 'Instead of Vizzards, their faces' were shown, looking perhaps more 'lean-cheek'd' than with a mask. Moreover, the masque gave him sound occasion to protest. For if their blackness had been effected with the usual gloves and masks (they wore full-length dresses), the nymphs' transformation into [white] daughters of Albion should have been achievable within a few seconds. The look of verisimilar skin, probably an item of Inigo Jones's illusionistic agenda, called for painting that obscured the fiction's central conceit.

Thus, the novel means of representation exacerbates racial and sexual anxiety: what troubles Carleton is that [. . .] the masquers' skin is indelibly black.

* * *

Peter Stallybrass, 'Tranvestism and the body beneath: speculating on the boy actor', in Susan Zimmerman (ed.), *Erotic Politics: Desire on the Renaissance Stage* (London and New York: Routledge, 1992), pp. 77–80.

The interplay between clothing and undressing on the Renaissance stage organized gender around a process of fetishizing, which is conceived *both* as a process of fixation *and* as indeterminable. If the Renaissance stage demands that we '*see*' particular body parts (the breast, the penis, the naked body), it also reveals that such fixations are inevitably unstable. The actor is both boy and woman, and he/she embodies the fact that sexual fixations are not the product of any categorical fixity of gender. Indeed, all attempts to fix gender are necessarily *prosthetic:* that is, they suggest the attempt to supply an imagined deficiency by the exchange of male clothes for female clothes or of female clothes for male clothes; by displacement from male to female space or from female to male space; by the replacement of male with female tasks or of female with male tasks. But all elaborations of the prosthesis which will supply the 'deficiency' can secure no essence. On the contrary, they suggest that gender itself is a fetish, the production of an identity through the fixation upon specific 'parts'. The imagined 'truth' of gender which a post-Renaissance culture would later construct is dependent upon the disavowal of the fetishism of gender, the disavowal of gender as fetish. In its place, it would put a fantasized biology of the 'real'.

But it is this notion of the 'real' which seems to be dramatically undone in undressing scenes, as in *Othello* when Desdemona/the boy actor is unpinned. Lynda Boose has demonstrated how the play itself demands both concealment (of the sexual scene, of the bed and its burden which 'poisons sight') and exposure (the stimulated desire that we should *see*, should 'grossly gape'). But [. . .] *what* we should see is radically uncertain. It is not so much a moment of indeterminacy as of contradictory fixations. On the one hand, the clothes themselves—the marks of Desdemona's gender and status—are held up to our attention; on the other, we teeter on the brink of seeing the boy's breastless but 'pinned' body revealed. It is as if, at the moments of greatest dramatic tension, the Renaissance theatre stages its own transvestism.

Contradictory fixations, though, are precisely what mobilize *Othello*. Think, for instance, of how Iago constructs the narrative of Desdemona's betrayal so that Othello can approach the 'grossly gaping' of her being 'topp'd'. He does it by casting *himself* in the role of Desdemona:

> I lay with *Cassio* lately . . .
> In sleepe I heard him say, sweet *Desdemona*,
> Let us be wary, let us hide our Loves,
> And then (Sir) would he gripe, and wring my hand:
> Cry, oh sweet Creature: then kisse me hard,
> As if he pluckt up kisses by the rootes,
> That grew upon my lippes, laid his Leg ore my Thigh,
> And sigh, and kisse . . .

> (1623: 3.3.419–31)

It is these contradictory fixations (Desdemona and/as the boy actor, Desdemona and/as Iago) which a later theatre would attempt to erase, precisely because the *site* of the audience's sexual fixation is so uncertain.

This uncertainty is, paradoxically, most powerfully felt by anti-theatrical writers. They oscillate between seeing the boy actor as woman, as neither woman nor man, as alluring boy, as male prostitute (or 'dogge', to use Rainolds' term). Prynne, for instance, incorporates Cyprian's account of how the theatre taught 'how a man might be effeminated into a female, how their sex might be changed by Art' (1633: 169). But he can also think of actors as those who, 'by unchaste infections of their members, effeminate their manly nature, being both effeminate men and women, yea, being neither men nor women' (ibid.). Yet the uncertainty of *what* anti-theatricalists saw in no way inhibited the fascinated fixity of their (imaginary) gaze. What they gazed at was a theatre imagined *as a bedroom*, a bedroom which spills off the stage and into the lives of players and audience alike:

> O . . . that thou couldest in that sublime watch-tower insinuate thine eyes into these *Players secrets; or set open the closed dores of their bed-chambers, and bring all their innermost hidden Cels unto the conscience of thine eyes. . . . [M]en rush on men with outragious lusts.*

> (Prynne 1633: 135)

So writes Prynne, translating Cyprian. And Phillip Stubbes sees the actors as contaminating the spectators so that, 'these goodly pageants being done, every mate sorts to his mate . . . and in their secret conclaves (covertly) they play *the Sodomits*, or worse' (Stubbes 1583: 144–5). But *what* anti-theatricalists saw in the 'secret conclaves' of the theatrical bedroom constantly shifted, thus mimicking the shifting perspectives of the Renaissance stage itself.

For the bed scenes and undressing scenes with which I have been concerned produce moments of dizzying indeterminacy. It was such moments that Freud attempted to describe in his essay on 'Fetishism', where the fetish stands in for and mediates between the marks of sexual difference.[1] Freud writes:

> In very subtle instances both the disavowal and the affirmation of the castration (of woman) have found their way into the construction of the fetish itself. This was so in the case of a man whose fetish was an athletic support-belt which could also be worn as bathing drawers. This piece of clothing covered up the genitals entirely and concealed the distinction between them. Analysis showed that it signified that women were castrated *and* that they were not castrated; and it also allowed of the hypothesis than men were castrated, for all these possibilities could equally well be concealed under the belt. . . .

The athletic support-belt, through its concealments, supports contradictory hypotheses. But for Freud, all those hypotheses must be grounded in the fantasy of castration. Why? Because Freud needs to find a fixed point (and a *male* point) outside the play of fetishism, a point to which all other fetishes will teleologically point. The fetishist is, Freud suggests, someone whose interest '*comes to a halt half-way, as it were*' (my emphasis). 'Thus the foot or shoe owes its preference as a fetish—or a part of it—to the circumstance that the inquisitive boy peered at the woman's genitals from below, from her legs up.' The fetish is, for Freud, but part of the larger category of perversions. 'Perversions', he writes in the 'Three essays on the theory of sexuality':

> are sexual activities which either a) *extend*, in an anatomical sense, beyond the regions of the body that are designed for sexual union, or b) *linger*, over the intermediate relations to the sexual object which should normally be traversed rapidly on the path towards the sexual aim.
>
> (Freud 1905: 62)

The very notion of the perverse, like that of the fetish, can only emerge in relation to a) the parts of the body which are 'naturally' sexual and b) a teleological path towards the genitals. The transvestite theatre of the Renaissance, though, does not allow for any such distinction between the 'perverse' and the normal teleological path.

From a Freudian perspective, it 'comes to a halt half-way, as it were'. It does so because it resists the sexual and narrative teleologies which would be developed in the eighteenth and nineteenth centuries. But that resistance is, I believe, less a matter of indeterminacy than of the production of contradictory fixations: the imagined body of a woman, the staged body of a boy actor, the material presence of clothes. Freud's brilliant insight was to see that the 'real person' was itself a displacement of fetishism:

> The progressive concealment of the body which goes along with civilization keeps sexual curiosity awake. This curiosity seeks to complete the sexual object by revealing its hidden parts. It can, however, be diverted ('sublimated') in the direction of art, if its interest can be shifted away from the genitals on to the shape of the body as a whole.
>
> (Freud 1905: 69)

'The body as a whole', then, is itself a fantasy, a sublimation. But for Freud, the real tends to reappear *behind* or *beneath* that fantasy, a real which always tends towards the formation of sexual difference. In the 'mingle–mangle', the 'hodge–podge', the 'gallimaufry' of Renaissance tragedy, though, contradictory fetishisms (body parts, costumes, handkerchiefs, sheets) are staged not in the play of pure difference but in the play between indeterminacy and fixation.

*   *   *

Valerie Traub, *The Renaissance of Lesbianism in Early Modern England* (Cambridge: Cambridge University Press, 2002), pp. 197–8, 203, 204–28.

Just as the 'birth' of the *lesbian* is not a discrete social occurrence, the emergence of anatomy as a field of knowledge production is not a singular scientific phenomenon. Rather, anatomy as a separate epistemology was consolidated in concert with the development of other domains of knowledge, and it was enabled by the ability of anatomists and popularizers of medical texts to appropriate and reformulate the knowledges of other genres, including natural histories, herbals, Latin commentary on Greek and Roman literature, and travel narratives. Early modern travel accounts, in particular, contribute significantly to the construction of the contours and meanings of the early modern body. Generated at the same historical moment and governed by similar tropes of exploration and discovery, anatomies and travel narratives share a common imperative to chart, catalogue, and colonize the body.[1] Both genres synthesize received authority, observation, and invention as they commit highly inter-pretative acts under the guise of disinterested description.[2] Their narrative strategies and cultural functions are allied closely: both are dedicated to rendering intelligible and distinct that which appears chaotic, primitive, or previously unknown by employing strategies of description, nomination, and classification. Metaphorically, anatomical texts act as a discourse of travel, visually traversing the body in order to 'touch' and reveal a cosmically ordained corporeal whole, while travel narratives observe and dissect peoples and countries, interrogat-ing and reaffirming their place in the cosmic order. Together, their exploratory gazes create the possibility of looking 'inward' and 'outward,' as they formulate the contours of bodily, social, and geographical boundaries.[3] Their processes fashion two sides of the same coin: whereas the dissection of the corpse and its textual reconstitution create a normative, abstracted body whose singularity encompasses and signifies all others, travel accounts compose an exoticized body which often, though not inevitably, reveals the antithesis of (Western) normativity. Locating bodies within prevailing epistemic hierarchies by charting corporeal cartographies, anatomies and travel narratives not only function as colonialist discourses but urge colonialism into being.[4]

Whether primarily concerned with commerce or conquest, Western European travelers to foreign lands chart a cultural anthropology that functions like a physical geography. Describing the New World, Africa, and the East, narrators obsessively remark upon those cultural practices that distinguish native inhabitants from Europeans, often employing rhetorics of gender and sexuality as explanatory tropes.[5] Marriage rituals, dowries, divorce, and polygamy excite Western curiosity and provide travelers to Africa and Arabia, in particular, a means of deploying the sexual status of indigenous women as a primary marker of cultural definition and civility.[6] A spatial geography of erotic behavior constructs women (and by implication, the nation) as beautiful and chaste (for instance, Persians) or hideous and loose (black Africans). The assumption of female lasciviousness gains self-evident power through the structure of a cross-cultural polarity: whereas the partial nudity of women in various African nations authorizes readings of female incontinence, the practice of Muslim purdah constructs the woman whose body is hidden as a highly desirable (and also desiring) object. Although same-gender female eroticism rarely is mentioned in these accounts (unlike charges of male sodomy), its presence routinely is associated with certain locales. Travelers to Turkey, in par-ticular, curious about Muslim attitudes toward cleanliness and intrigued by the Ottoman segregation of women, typically relay rumors about women pleasuring one another—or themselves—within all-female spaces.[7] [. . .]

[P]rotocolonialist imperatives of travel narratives ultimately contribute to the erotic represen-tation of Englishwomen. Jane Sharp alludes to the dissemination of travel accounts as she describes clitoral enlargement in *The Midwives Book* (1671): sometimes the clitoris 'grows so long that it hangs forth at the slit like a Yard, and will swell and stand stiff if it be provoked, and some lewd women have endeavoured to use it as men do theirs.'[8] 'In the *Indies*, and *Egypt*,' she says, such incidents 'are frequent'; but she goes on to assert that illicit contact among women occurs primarily beyond England's borders: 'I never heard but of one in this Country.' She then concludes with the ambiguous statement, 'if there be any they will do what they can for shame to keep it close,' an admonition that, in conflating the enlarged clitoris with the use to which it could be put, could refer either to keeping genitals hidden or illicit erotic practices secret.[9] [. . .]

[T]he incorporation of the clitoris within the domain of scientific knowledge gave female erotic pleasure a new, albeit ambivalent, articulation. With that articulation, I now want to suggest, came a representational crisis. This crisis stemmed less from the rancorous disputes among anatomists regarding the clitoris's existence than from the fact that anatomical representation of the clitoris became a focal point for the expression of anxieties about the cultural meanings of the female body. As anatomical plates and texts from Italy, France, Spain, and Germany made their way into England, as English physicians and midwives contributed their own methods of textually communicating the 'new science' of anatomy, strategies of accommodation—of, quite literally, in-corporation—were developed. The trajectory of these strategies suggests that this clitoral 'age of discovery' was a pivotal moment in the cultural history of English women, of their embodiment and eroticism. Over the next century, as information about this 'new' anatomical organ was incorporated into, and helped to refigure, an old corporeal framework, a discourse evolved that increasingly fixed on the clitoris as the disturbing emblem of female erotic transgression.

We need only [read] Crooke's conclusion of his description of the clitoris in *Microcosmographia* to recognize the contours of this crisis. When he says, for instance, that it is an enlarged clitoris that 'those wicked women doe abuse called *Tribades* (often mentioned by many authors, and in some states worthily punished) to their mutuall and unnaturall lustes,' and then marginally glosses his text with '*Tribades odiosae feminae*,'[10] Crooke draws from prior authority, citing Caelius Aurelianus (a fifth-century Latin translator of Soranus) and Leo Africanus. When Falloppia laid claim to his discovery of this organ in 1561, he likewise had referred back to the authority of classical and Arabic writers:

> Avicenna makes mention of a certain member situated in the female genitalia which he calls *virga* or *albathara*. Albucasis calls this *tentigo*, which sometimes will increase to such a great size that women, while in this condition, have sex with each other just as if they were men. The Greeks call this member *clitoris*, from which the obscene word *clitorize* is derived. Our anatomical writers have completely neglected this and do not even have a word for it.[11]

Intent on proclaiming the existence of this organ, Falloppia focused on its nomenclature and only vaguely described the practices to which it could be put. Later in the sixteenth century, André Du Laurens, however, used the name for the women who, so endowed, engaged in libidinous behavior: 'I have become aware of the use of this, whereby after being rubbed all over it excites the sluggish faculty. It increases in some people to such an inappropriate extent that it hangs outside the fissure the same as a penis; women then often engage in mutual rubbing, such women accordingly called *tribades* or *fricatrices*.'[12] Jacques Daléchamps, professor of medicine at the University of Montpellier, describes in his 1570 *Chirurgie françoise* a troublesome large 'nymphe,' pervasive among Egyptian women as well as 'some of ours, so that when they find themselves in the company of other women, or their clothes rub them while they walk, or their husbands wish to approach them, it erects like a male penis, and indeed they use it to play with other women, as their husbands would do.'[13] If here the surgeon reproduces the medieval confusion about whether it is the clitoris or the labia that enlarge, he nonetheless connects hypertrophy to tribadism. As Katharine Park notes in her examination of Daléchamps' sources, 'Daléchamps seems to have fabricated the connection between clitoral hypertrophy and female homoeroticism by consolidating what were in fact two separate topics in his ancient texts and then to have authorized his construction by projecting it back onto those texts. The amalgamation of these two separate ideas became standard in French.'[14] Indeed, this conflation became definitive in English texts as well.

Drawing from previous authorities to bolster his claims of knowledge, Crooke makes specific use of both medical and 'anthropological' texts. And yet something crucial changes as we move from travel narration to anatomical treatise: none of the travel writers of the late sixteenth century mention the 'abuse' of a particular body part. Though the words *tribade*, *fricatrice*, and *Sahacat* are used, and cucumbers and public baths loom large, no enlarged clitoris haunts their accounts; rather, there is simply a boundless, deceitful desire of which all foreign, non-Christian women presumably are suspected. As anatomical descriptions of the clitoris absorb and revise the representations of travel accounts, however, the site of transgressive female eroticism subtly shifts away from the behavioral excesses of Mediterranean climes to the excessive endowment of female bodies.

This is not to suggest that the strategies of travel literature and anatomical texts are all that different. Indeed, the anatomical articulation of clitoral hypertrophy carries with it lineages from medieval accounts of 'marvels' and 'wonders,' a genre from which travel literature itself evolved. As Mary Campbell notes,

> The 'wonders' are the most extreme and exquisite projections of European cultural fantasy: it is against their iconographic background of grotesque similes that a responsible literature of travel will develop, and it is among their images that Europe will find nourishment for its notions of 'monstrous' savagery. The model (which finds its authority, though not its origins, in Pliny) of a world normal at its (European) center and monstrous at its (Asian and African) margins is easy to see as the self-image of a culture quite literally scared of its own shadow.[15]

Campbell further remarks, '[t]he features of the organic marvels manifest characteristically grotesque principles: hyperbolic dimensions, multiplication of body parts, and fusions of species.'[16] Likewise, 'The marvelous is marginal, biologically and culturally, although it may be used as a figure for central and interior desire. The marvelous is also, in part, a rhetorical phenomenon. A brief enough description, especially when communicated as a distortion of the familiar rather than as something *essentially* different, produces a marvel.'[17]

The tribade is not literally a marvel or wonder of nature. Although her behavior regularly was described in moral terms as monstrous and *contra naturam*, in ontological terms her being was not *praeter naturam*, outside the ordinary course of nature. She does not appear in the medieval typologies of the monstrous races derived from the natural history of Pliny or the geography of Strabo, although she is included, at least initially, in Paré's discussion of monsters and marvels (alongside hermaphrodites and sex transformations).[18] Once expelled from Paré's subsequent editions, however, the tribade demonstrates that her relation to a discourse of teratology is moral rather than ontological, and thus a matter of continuing negotiation. To take up Campbell's terms, the tribade is a marvelous 'distortion of the familiar,' produced rhetorically as a marker of gender and erotic norms. She may not *be* a marvel, but, with her hyperbolic clitoris and allegedly grotesque efforts at coupling, she functions *like* a marvel. Indeed, it is through a diffusion of the rhetorical operations of the marvelous into anatomy that the tribade, as a phenomenon knowable to modern science, was discursively born.[19] [. . .]

By the early seventeenth century, under the auspices of anatomical research, a paradigm of women's boundless *desire* present in travel literature is transmuted into a paradigm of discrete and empirically verifiable bodily *structure*. In the emerging terms of early modern medicine, it is not the tribade's inconstant mind or sinful soul, but her uniquely female yet masculinized *morphology* that either propels her to engage in, or is itself the effect of, her illicit behavior. Clitoral hypertrophy is posited as one cause of early modern tribadism, but perhaps more importantly, early modern tribadism increasingly is inconceivable without clitoral hypertrophy. Anatomy provides a map of this connection.

The early modern mapping of the tribade's body produces and is produced by an anatomical essentialism—the riveting of body part to behavior—that continues to underpin modern discourses of sexuality. Such essentialism is the result not of empirical fact, but of a strategy to organize and make intelligible the plurality of corporeal structures and behaviors within the conceptual confines of Renaissance cosmological and earthly hierarchies. [. . .]

Despite the confident descriptions of a range of classical, medieval, and Renaissance authorities; despite the precise discriminations of crime and punishment achieved by forensic theologians like Sinistrari; and despite the insertion of local color by Thomas Bartholin, no one knew what caused tribadism—and that, precisely, was the trouble. Every woman possessed the necessary clitoral equipment as well as a predisposition to immoderate lust. Given the inherent instability of the humors and the capriciousness of female desire, then, any woman's genitals might grow to monstrous proportions. In contrast to later periods, when a woman's lust for another woman signified primarily a deviation of gender (and thus was intelligible within a paradigm of inversion), in the early modern period, despite the imitative masculinity ascribed to the tribade, her behavior was a logical extension—indeed, a confirmation—of femininity in all its heavenly ordained intemperance.

The implications of this nexus of gender are important to our understanding of the various interpretative matrices imposed on early modern eroticism. One might have thought that the tribade's clitoral hypertrophy—described as a long-term somatic condition correlated with a specific erotic predisposition—would confer upon her a coherent erotic identity. Foucault, after all, described the 'nineteenth-century homosexual' as 'a type of life, a life form, and a morphology, with an indiscreet anatomy and possibly a mysterious physiology.' The anatomy of the early modern tribade was nothing if not indiscreet; her body was, above all, defined as an excessive morphology. But even as the tribade was understood in such minoritarian terms, she always was in danger of being universalized. In the absence of an unambiguous boundary between the size of a 'normal' clitoris and the size of a tribade's, in the absence of scientific measurements that could adjudicate between a 'commonly small' organ and one the length of a man's finger, clitoral hypertrophy threatened, at the level of unspoken ideology, to become hyper*typic*.

Anatomists hid their confusion regarding causality behind the standard correlation of quantity of lust with size of the genitals. Medical and theological authority represented women as more vulnerable to lust than men, yet, within the contradictory Renaissance logic of sex transformation [. . .], a woman's excessive lust paradoxically threatens to make her into a man. Physical metamorphosis, in other words, provided a satisfying cultural narrative that massaged the links between anatomy and gender, and both of these to erotic desire. But as medical science became more committed to empiricism, and as disbelief about the viability of spontaneous sex transformation grew over the seventeenth century, the (putatively cohesive and transparent) logic of anatomy, gender, and eroticism previously expressed through narratives of metamorphosis sought an alternative mode of articulation.

It was found in the fantasy of the enlarged clitoris. Belief in the possibility of women metamorphosing into men initially was contested and pressured by the anatomical possibility of genuine hermaphroditism [. . .]. Nonetheless, the *coup de grâce* of sex transformation was the construction of the tribade. For a long time, the hermaphrodite (the person with ambiguous or doubled genitalia) and the tribade (the woman who used her enlarged clitoris to penetrate other women) were confused and conflated. But whereas the medical controversy over the distinction between tribadism and hermaphroditism continued into the eighteenth century, the concept of sex transformation died out. It is not that cultural fears about the mutability of gender altered, or that anatomy's role as adjudicator of such fears lessened. Rather, such fears of gender instability and transgression, previously articulated through concepts of sex difference, began to be refracted through a tendentious description of erotic practices. From Crooke to Sinistrari, the tribade is what disrupts the prior model. Sinistrari is adamant in his disbelief about sex transformation:

> Now, unsexing [sex transformation] is utterly impossible, seeing that the generative organs are so widely different in make, shape, substance and situation in males from the organs of females, as those with even a very slight knowledge of anatomical experiments are aware. Therefore the girls looked upon as changed into males were those whose clitoris, as we have said, broke out; and it is owing to this transformation in their sex [the enlargement of their clitoris] that persons unacquainted with anatomy thought they had turned males . . . An accident of this kind happened to a nun in her fourteenth year's profession, in the Convent of the Passion, at San Feliz de los Galegos; in the diocese of Ciudad. She consulted Barbosa about her case. But I suppose he had not read this doctrine on the clitoris. Because if he had glanced over what modern Anatomists write about it, he would have boldly asserted that this nun was not at all unsexed [transformed into a man]; that she was consequently bound to keep her vows and cloister, but that care should be taken to prevent her from being able to carry on any obscene practices with the nuns.[20]

Unlike the woman who spontaneously transforms into a man, the creature endowed with ambiguous genitalia fails to provide a reassuring cultural narrative. To the contrary: she exposes the strains in the linkages among erotic practices, gender identity, and anatomical sex. In the body of the tribade, gender is perceived less as a function of anatomical sex than as an effect of an erotic behavior authorized by a particular anatomy. In the historically contingent and mutually constitutive triad of anatomy, gender, and eroticism, the accent increasingly falls on the latter term; eroticism becomes the primary diacritical marker, the thing that matters most.

The seriousness with which anatomists took the tribade's behavioral 'imitation' of men is evinced in the rhetorical linkages forged in their work between anatomy, eroticism, and surgery. Since the narrative trajectory of these texts monotonously moves from a description of normative genitalia to a discussion of clitoral hypertrophy, and from there to censure of the tribade, it perhaps comes as no surprise that the narrative often ends with a recommendation of genital amputation. Paré, who in his early discussion of tribadism confuses the clitoris with the labia, recommends labial amputation;[21] and Bartholin approvingly cites the practice of female circumcision of ancient and Eastern nations. Culpeper goes one step further in his *Fourth Book of Practical Physick* (published in 1662 after his death with his best-selling *A Directory for Mid-wives*), providing precise if erroneous instructions for how to excise both the enlarged clitoris and the labia.[22] *The Chyrurgeons Store-house* (1674), an English translation of *Wundarztneyishes Zeughaufs* (1665), a surgical textbook by Johannes Scultetus, includes a pictorial depiction of an adult clitoridectomy as a treatment for 'the unprofitable increasing of a Clitoris.'[23] Whereas none of these writers explicitly recommends eradicating the social phenomenon of tribadism through clitoridectomy, the narrative logic of their entries makes clear that, if clitoral hypertrophy causes problems, surgical intervention is available.[24] Within this hypertropic discourse, whether the clitoris or the labia are cut off, what is excised *ideologically* is an agency and a pleasure that grow beyond their own abjection.[25] [. . .]

[T]he increased circulation of discourses about the tribade was in part a function of an intensifying social investment in the erotic desire of the conjugal couple or, as I call this ideological formation, *domestic heterosexuality*. Yet, heterosexual desire did not assume its new significance alone. It is partly through women's common clitoral inheritance—an inheritance that is as much historical as biological—that the oppositional dyads of modernity (homo/hetero) develop. If the clitoris comes into representation accompanied by the tribade, and the tribade only takes up residence in England when endowed with an enlarged clitoris, and the clitoris must be threatened with removal whenever the tribade appears, then these associations provide some of the raw material out of which modern erotic identity categories would begin to be constructed. The inauguration of 'the heterosexual' as the original, normative, essential mode of erotic behavior is haunted, from its first recognizably modern articulation, by an embodiment and practice that call the conceptual priority of heterosexuality into question. In historical terms, *lesbianism* is not, as Freud's developmental narrative would have it, the preoedipal embryo of an adult heterosexuality, but rather the troubling potential that accompanies and threatens to disrupt heterosexuality. In the psychomorphology that our clitoral inheritance inaugurates, *lesbianism* is less an alternative to female heterosexuality than its transgressive twin, 'born' into modern discourse at the same ambivalent cultural moment. [. . .]

Although late nineteenth-century psychoanalysis, sexology, anthropology, and criminology solidified erotic identities, the critical tendency to subsume early modern eroticism under modern categories obscures the indebtedness of modern discourses to prior discourses and conflicts. This presentist tendency thwarts inquiry both into the construction of the homo/hetero divide and the regulatory function of identity. The early modern reinvention of the tribade demonstrates that several aspects of the modern formation of *lesbianism*—in particular, its anatomical essentialism and colonial imaginary—are not original to the Enlightenment regime of 'the subject'; rather, they predate and help to constitute such modern formations.[26] That is, under the auspices of protocolonialist discourses a new nexus of modern knowledge about female bodies was produced. Within the logic of this emerging epistemology were some of the primary terms by which certain female bodies subsequently would be pleasured as reproductive capital, while others would be condemned for their usurpation of masculine prerogatives and their pursuit of autonomous pleasures. If the regimes of Enlightenment knowledge inaugurated the category of 'the subject' out of which a *lesbian* identity would be generated (by Freud among others), then such epistemologies inherited from early modern travel narratives and anatomies the bodily contours of that subject.

Inherited, but not without significant change. Tribades were not *lesbians*; tribades were constructed out of an anatomy, physiology, and epistemology of desire that only inter-mittently and incoherently map on to contemporary understandings. And, whereas the early modern mapping of the tribade's body provides a means of understanding historical ante-cedents to modern identities, it does not reinscribe such identities as historically invariable or self-evidently knowable. How is the tribade *not* like a contemporary *lesbian*? Or more precisely: how does the early modern discourse about tribades differ from dominant (and thus, often homophobic) discourses about *lesbians*? *Lesbians* today are not assumed to be marked by an anatomical deviation. (Such marking, rather, is reserved for a discourse of intersexuality.) Their erotic practices are not assumed primarily to take the form of vaginal penetration. (Quite the contrary; oral sex is widely assumed to be 'what *lesbians* do.') Nor are *lesbians* believed to be more lustful than heterosexual women. (Even within the *lesbian* community, jokes about 'lesbian bed death' abound.) Most importantly, according to the logic of modern homophobia, *lesbians* hate (or fear) men; in contrast, according to the Renaissance psychomorphology of the clitoris, the tribade enacted that sincerest form of flattery: emulation.[27] [. . .]

The modern psychoanalytic discourse of *lesbianism* recuperates and refigures the seven-teenth-century psychomorphology of the clitoris, accepting the analogy between penis and clitoris, yet reading that analogy through the developmental narrative of castration. The indebtedness of modern discourses to preexisting corporeal maps, then, impels us not only to question the provenance of definitional tautologies ('lesbianism as we know it'), but to query the adequacy of the trope of metonymy to organize our understanding of the relation between bodies, identities, and desires. If the psychomorphology of the clitoris demonstrates the extent to which the clitoris and the *lesbian* are mutually constituted by a colonialist and patriarchal dynamic (which represses as much as it reveals same-gender female desire), then perhaps we can recognize the impact of this history on our attempts to think beyond the pathologies inscribed by Freud. In particular, we can trace the lineages of this occluded history in current feminist strategies to displace the phallus by a female corporeal imaginary; for, as important as this displacement of the phallus by the labia has been in refiguring female sexuality as something other than lack, the theoretical recourse to female genitals tends to reiterate the logic of metonymy through which same-gender female desire has been anatomized and colonized.

The problem with such feminist strategies extends beyond the inability to conceive of the pleasures for *lesbians* of vaginal penetration (by fingers, penis, tongue, or dildo) or the possibility of a non-phallocentric heterosexuality—although these are crucial issues as well.[28] In her attempt to counter the intense vaginal focus of modern discourses, Paula Bennett, for instance, recognizes that female sexuality is not limited to clitoral stimulation; and yet she concludes her essay on clitoral imagery in nineteenth-century poetry by asserting that '[w]ithout the clitoris, theorists have no physical site in which to locate an autonomous sense of female sexual agency . . . With the clitoris, theorists can construct female sexuality in such a way that women become sexual subjects in their own right . . . No longer married . . . to the penis or the law, they can become . . . by themselves healthy and whole.'[29] Locating the possibilities of psychic health, wholeness, and agency in the clitoris seems a lot to ask of any one organ, particularly if women's embodied experience of desire, pleasure, and orgasm is, according to many testimonies, more fragmented and diffuse than unitary. But more is at issue here than the humanist basis of such claims: for the elevation of the clitoris (or labia) as the *sine qua non* of *lesbian* sexuality not only overvalues the genitals as a source of pleasure, but overestimates the power of bodily metonymy to represent that pleasure.

In 1611, the lexicographer Randle Cotgrave defined the clitoris as 'a womens Privities,' thus making explicit the metonymic logic animating early modern thinking about the female genitals.[30] If the clitoris stands, as it were, for the privities, then it functions not only as 'the seat of women's delight,' the residence or site of woman's erotic pleasure, but also as the synecdochal part for the genital whole. Oddly enough, the assertion of metonymy advanced by Cotgrave continues to exert such a stranglehold on feminist thinking that we can trace its impact among a diverse set of feminist theorists and critics. The radical feminist critique of patriarchy promulgated by Andrea Dworkin and Catherine MacKinnon, for instance, posits a seamless equation between male domination and heterosexuality; their critique of female subordination extends outwards in many directions to encompass almost all aspects of contemporary life, and yet the source of subordination is found to reside in the genitals, with the opposition of phallic violence to vaginal vulnerability condensed by Dworkin in the term *intercourse*.[31] The critique of compulsory heterosexuality advanced by Audre Lorde and Adrienne Rich focuses less on women's victimization than the ability to reclaim the female body as a source of self-knowledge, authenticity, and power, but this reversal nonetheless operates by way of a metonymic logic that results in an idealization of the *lesbian* body as a privileged locus on the continuum of female identification and bonding.[32] More recently, the tendency to spatialize the female body through a logic of metonymy underpins Ruth Vanita's focus on genital metaphors (mainly gems and flowers) in her quest for 'sapphic' representations in nineteenth-century British literature.[33]

But by far the most sophisticated expression of a metonymical mode of interpretation is that of Luce Irigaray. By situating a mechanics of fluids against the specular economy of the phallus and mobilizing a labial logic characterized by multiplicity, movement, fluidity, and tactility, Irigaray challenges the humanist tradition of phallomorphic logic, with its emphasis on singularity, unity, and visibility. Irigaray's invocation of vaginal and facial 'lips' that 'speak together' disperses the singularity of the signifier into a plurality of pleasures, zones, and sites of articulation:

[W]oman's pleasure does not have to choose between clitoral activity and vaginal passivity . . . The pleasure of the vaginal caress does not have to be substituted for that of the clitoral caress. They each contribute, irreplaceably, to woman's pleasure . . . Among other caresses . . . [f]ondling the breasts, touching the vulva, spreading the lips, stroking the posterior wall of the vagina, brushing against the mouth of the uterus, and so on . . . *[W]oman has sex organs more or less everywhere.*[34]

Supplementing the clitoris with the labia, the vagina, and the breasts, Irigaray charts a 'geography of feminine pleasure' which would seem to bypass and subvert the history of analogies between penis and clitoris that I have been tracing.[35]

Or does it? Does Irigaray's 'vulvomorphic geography' actually sustain the deconstructive project she announces in *This Sex Which Is Not One*? Or does Irigaray's labial morphology reenact the anatomical essentialism that links body part(s) to erotic desire, and then enforces this link through the identification (and abjection or celebration) of a social type? I submit that the metonymic association of female bodily organs (no matter how plural) with an erotic identity (no matter how 'deviant') does not so much refigure female desire as reproduce the contours of the colonialist geographies and anatomies out of which *lesbian* identity emerged.

To respond to Irigaray in this way is not simply to rehash the problems of essentialism and referentiality that have dominated the reception of this theorist's work in the North American academy.[36] As Diana Fuss and Jane Gallop have argued persuasively, Irigaray's bodily aesthetic can be read as a strategic *composition*, a *poiesis*, rather than a referential *reflection* of the female body.[37] Nonetheless, this strategy of reading Irigaray rhetorically and performatively fails to take into account the extent to which the terms of that (re)composition carry with them a particular history. This ignorance of historical terms is evinced by Gallop: 'Vulvomorphic logic, by *newly* metaphorizing the body, sets it free, if only momentarily.' Although Gallop recognizes that 'as soon as the metaphor becomes a proper noun, we no longer have creation, we have paternity,' she nonetheless asserts: 'Metaphor heals.'[38]

I propose to read Irigaray's bodily poetics, not from the perspective of philosophy, but from the angle of genealogy. Lineages of a colonialist history of embodiment become evident if we recognize *This Sex Which Is Not One* as an effort to articulate not only a specifically 'feminine' voice and desire, but also a *lesbian* subject. This subject is brought into being by a textual progression of chapters within *This Sex Which Is Not One* that asserts the commensurability of body part(s) to erotic identity under the guiding auspices of metonymy. To read Irigaray genealogically, in other words, means to move from the problem of ontology (the task of defining what a woman 'is') and mimesis (the adequacy of the signifier to denote the real) to the problem of metonymy and synecdoche (the adequacy of the part to stand for the whole). It is metonymy that enables Irigaray's valorization of a tactile over a visual economy, that allows her to envision the possibility of a touch unmediated by culture and bodily difference. And it is metonymy that enables, over the course of her text, the supplanting of the category 'woman' by the category '*lesbian*.' In chapter 2, 'This Sex Which Is Not One,' the two lips that cannot be parted (except through phallic violence) represent the inherent autoeroticism and self-sufficiency of the female body—and this image functions as her central metaphor throughout. Which makes it all the more striking that in chapter 11, 'When Our Lips Speak Together,' the two lips become the lips of (at least two) women erotically pleasuring one another. What began as an assertion of bodily self-sufficiency ('she touches herself in and of herself without any need for mediation'[39]) ends in a poetics of female merger: 'You? I? That's still saying too much. Dividing too sharply between us: all.'[40] In a move reminiscent of Rich's *lesbian* continuum but devoid of Rich's acknowledgment of differences along that spectrum, Irigaray slides from celebrating a unique female positivity to lauding the special effects of homoerotic desire. Negating the difference between one and two (bodies, subjects, erotic practices), Irigaray collapses the labia, the female voice, and *lesbian(s)* into a unified expression of feminine *jouissance*. If Irigaray's strategic 'concentrism' is a reversal and displacement of phallocentrism, it nonetheless constructs *lesbianism* through the terms bequeathed by phallocentric models of the subject: preoedipal desire for the mother, autoeroticism, and narcissism. As if she is performing her own thematics of merger, Irigaray conflates these psychic affects and desires, in the name of an Imaginary plenitude which is both prior to and beyond the Symbolic.[41]

Where this correlation positions women who are not *lesbian*,[42] just where the exteriority of *lesbianism* is located, how *lesbians* may relate psychoanalytically to their mothers, and the extent to which *lesbians* may not enact a transgressive politics, are questions left unanswered by Irigaray's bodily composition. But, more importantly for my argument, Irigaray's conflation of body part(s) and erotic identity maintains the psychomorphology of the clitoris by positing body part(s) as a sufficient sign of desire, and desire as adequately expressed through the rubric of (constructed) identity.[43] Although the specific terms of embodiment have changed, the logic of metonymic equivalence still holds: if not penis = clitoris = *lesbian*, then labia = *lesbian* desire = *lesbian* identity. My point is not to dispute the connection between body parts and erotic pleasure, but to highlight the extent to which body parts and pleasures are employed to anchor erotic identity. Despite the erasure of phallomorphism from the equation, the underlying structure of commensurability secured by the phallus remains: body part = embodied desire = erotic identity. The phallus remains secure because this metonymic logic enacts and reinforces the power and propriety of naming. Indeed, one reason the relational structure I have described is so resistant to alteration is that it functions as a meta-narrative of legitimation.[44] Although the clitoris is no longer posited as an equivalent to the penis, female genitals are still invested with the power conventionally attributed to the phallus: they serve as the authorizing signature, the 'proper name' of erotic desires, practices, and identities.

The problem with these bodily metonymies, then, is the synecdochal presumption that a part *can* stand for a whole, and that there is in fact a whole to be represented. I do not mean to imply that bodily metonymy invariably is colonialist. As a performative strategy, metonymy may be as good a strategy as any: one continually is in the process of narrativizing one's own body, and the more rhetorical figures at one's disposal the better.[45] (Such was the case [. . .] for Queen Elizabeth.) However, the particular metonymies that organize the *lesbian* body have functioned hegemonically as a master narrative that occludes not only its own historical construction, but the (anatomical) emergence of the body it purports to represent. My genealogy thus confirms, and in some ways departs from, certain of the theoretical arguments advanced by Judith Butler. Her contention that the abject 'is the excluded and illegible domain that haunts' intelligibility, 'the spectre of its own impossibility, the very limit to intelligibility, its constitutive outside,' could have been written about the early modern tribade.[46] However, although Butler recognizes that 'regulatory schemas are not timeless structures, but historically revisable criteria,' her work, albeit genealogically motivated, is written more with an eye toward the future than the past.[47] In this, she reiterates the predisposition of much feminist theory which, regardless of important differences among its central terms—patriarchy (Dworkin and MacKinnon), compulsory heterosexuality (Rich), phallocentrism (Irigaray), the heterosexual matrix (Butler)—tends to avoid submitting these structures to historical investigation. This indifference to history is of particular concern in regard to Butler's astute analysis of 'the lesbian phallus and the morphological imaginary.' She argues that *lesbians*' appropriation of the phallus not only exposes 'the synecdochal logic by which the phallus is installed as the privileged signifier' but, through its detachability and transferability, could be deployed in the service of a new sexual imaginary.[48] Her greatest advance is in recognizing that the detachability of the phallus could release the body from the logic of identity altogether. As much as I applaud this utopian project, my genealogy interjects a caution: even as the tribade challenged patriarchal edicts, performing through her 'prosthetic' bodily acts a fair amount of gender trouble, insofar as her appropriation of the phallus was interpreted through the rubric of masculine imitation, it comprised part of a colonial, patriarchal history of abjection that helped give rise to the very logic of erotic identity that Butler would deconstruct.

As long as this metonymic logic of legitimation holds steady, female—female desire will be caught within the coordinates of a colonialist and patriarchal history. What finally is most troubling about the strategy to refigure the *lesbian* as a body composed of multiple lips or (to a lesser extent) the celebration of the *lesbian* phallus, is the way it allows us to forget the centuries-long material processes that have pathologized those female psyches and bodies that desire other women. Insofar as Irigaray is working within the terms of a psychoanalytic paradigm that elides history in the name of the psyche, she cannot help but reiterate these material processes; insofar as Butler's appeal for a different morphological imaginary is a response to Irigaray, it pushes against, yet to a certain extent remains caught within, some of these prior terms. The reason for their imprisonment, my genealogy has tried to show, is this: the very intelligibility of *lesbianism* has devolved from the recitation of a past that exerts its power precisely because it is so rarely self-consciously cited.

Our task now is not to revise or reject the psychoanalytic narrative of *lesbian* pathology; these and other scholars already have done so brilliantly.[49] Rather, in order to resist the overdeterminations of history, we need to acknowledge the force of the psychomorphology that contributed not only to the psychoanalytic narrative of *lesbian* pathology, but to the feminist counter-narrative of *lesbian* identity, health, and wholeness. As two sides of the same identity coin, both narratives offer the *lesbian* body as the diacritical marker of female subjectivity, even though the values they confer on that body differ dramatically. As someone who is called, interpellated, identified by that name, I protest: *lesbianism* neither *is* the problem of female desire nor *solves* the problem of female desire. Rather than simply repudiate or disavow that version of *lesbianism* (a strategy that remains caught within an oscillating prison of identification/disidentification) I suggest that we pry apart the terms—the equation of body part and embodied desire, of embodied desire and erotic identity—through which the metonymic logic of anatomical essentialism continues to delineate, define, and discipline erotic possibility. Only by disarticulating these links can we extend the meanings of same-gender erotic desires beyond the geographies and anatomies that would circumscribe them; only by articulating the incommensurability of desires, bodies, and identities can we move beyond the history from whence, inscribed, abjected, and unintelligible to ourselves, 'we' came.

··

QUESTIONS

- How is desire related to the body in the above extracts?
- What scope for bodily transformation emerges here?
- How do you assess Valerie Traub's claim that desire should not be constrained by the body?

4 | Theorizing material culture

Margreta de Grazia, Maureen Quilligan and Peter Stallybrass (eds.), *Subject and Object in Renaissance Culture* (Cambridge: Cambridge University Press, 1996), 'Introduction', pp. 1–5.

There are no subjects in seventeenth-century *vanitas* still-lifes. Only objects. Or more accurately, their subjects are objects: books, pens, hats, purses, coins, jewelry, pipes, bottles. The great novelty of these early still-lifes is that objects have evicted the subject.[1] Only a memory of one remains—the *memento mori* or skull, now an object among objects. And with the subject goes its world. The window space that receded behind the Renaissance subject gives way to the wall or virtual wall that drops behind the object. With such a foreshortening of space comes the standing still of time. While the subject of a painted narrative or history moves through time, objects of a still-life exist in inert stasis. Spatially and temporally secluded, *vanitas* objects appear to have a (still) life of their own. There is no need for a musician to play, a reader to read, a smoker to smoke: flute, book, pipe exist without makers, owners, buyers, users.

Yet the purpose of *vanitas* paintings is to urge the dispensability not of subjects but of objects—the vanity of all the things of this world. By their title (*vanitas vanitatum*, Eccles. 1.2) and by the symbolic encoding of the things represented (signs of transience and mortality), they exhort subjects to renounce objects. But can such a sequestering hold? [. . .]

The viewer too testifies to their attachment. While the skull repels sight, the other objects attract it with their opulent splendor. While bringing to mind the passing of things, the paintings also give those things the permanence of art. In effect, they perform the opposite of what they profess, richly and fully embodying things rather than emptying them out.[2] While their *vanitas* moral would make the objects null and void, the lustre of paint enhances their irresistibility. In addition, reproduction increases their store, so that there are more purses, jewels, books than ever before. Among their number, the *vanitas* paintings themselves must be counted, for they become what they renounce: objects to augment the subject's prestige and wealth, additional earthly things to be coveted, purchased—often at great price—and displayed as ornament. (In later *vanitas* still-lifes, paintings themselves appear among the depicted vanities.)[3]

Renaissance studies have slighted the objects that are the subject of these paintings.[4] It is as if we had listened to their renunciatory moral without seeing their sumptuous allure. For in the main we have proceeded as if it were both possible and desirable for subjects to cut themselves off from objects. The essays collected here aim to address this bias with a basic question:

in the period that has from its inception been identified with the emergence of the subject, *where is the object?* This is not to say that the sovereignty of the subject has gone unquestioned in Renaissance studies, especially in recent decades. Indeed the various tauto-logical self-reflexives once thought so characteristic of the Renaissance have lost their trans-parency as the subject has been seen increasingly to be constructed from the outside.[5] Yet even in recent critiques of Renaissance autonomy, the focus has remained the same: the subject at center and the object beyond the pale. What happens, we wish to ask, once the object is brought into view? What new configurations will emerge when subject and object are kept in relation?

At the outset of this inquiry, it may be useful to turn to an account that, like the *vanitas* still-lifes, questions the viability of separating subject and object. In the 'Lordship and Bondage' section of Hegel's *Phenomenology of Spirit*, they are inextricable. The subject passes into the object, the object slides into the subject, in the activity by which each becomes itself. Hegel's dramatization of this complex dialectic goes something like this:

> A subject desired verification that he was in truth a subject, more particularly, that he was free of all dependencies on objects. Verification could come only from another subject (in an act of mutual recognition), but how could one subject know the truth of the other any more than of himself? A situation was needed that required the subject to risk all objects—a fight-to-the-death. But a fight-to-the-death could only end in impasse. Though one contestant would be triumphant (unless the struggle resulted in death for both), he would never attain the recognition he desired. For the other contestant, if alive, would be reduced to an enslaved object—disqualified, therefore, as witness to the subject's truth.[6]

Hegel's zero-sum contest seems worth recounting because it so forcibly dramatizes the interrelation of subject and object. It is precisely this interrelation that drops out of the history which has done most to periodize the Renaissance. Jacob Burckhardt's *The Civilization of the Renaissance in Italy* posits an individual as free-standing as the statue of the con-dottiere Colleoni on the cover of its illustrated English edition.[7] It is only *after* the subject emerges in its individuality that it puts itself in relation to objects. In this respect, the Renaissance subject begins with just that full consciousness of itself that is the ultimate (though hardly assured) end of the Hegelian dialectic of the subject/object or lord/bondsman. What in Hegel the subject would give up its life to know is in Burckhardt the ready-given of individuality that, when not quelled by a restrictive church or state, will run its fulfilling course.

Self-consciousness for Burckhardt comes about epiphanically rather than agonistically, as the result of revelation rather than struggle. When benighting illusions are stripped away—when the medieval 'veil melted into air'—Renaissance consciousness could turn both inward and outward, in both 'subjective' consideration of itself and 'objective' consideration 'of the State and of all things of this world.'[8] Burckhardt's 'uomo singolare' or 'uomo unico' stands before and apart from the object of his attention, confident of his ability to make the object compliant with his political or scientific or artistic will.[9] As Ernst Cassirer maintains in *The Individual and the Cosmos in Renaissance Philosophy*—the philosophical study intended to supplement Burckhardt's cultural history—the subject's relation to the object was that of mastery or would-be mastery: the mind trained and positioned to understand and overcome the object of its interest.[10]

Marx seems to offer a similar narrative of separation in accounting for the rise of capitalism. His recurrent focus on alienation also appears to sever subject and object. The capitalist mode of production estranges the worker from both the product of the worker's labor and the entire material world that is the aggregate of such products. Insofar as the two could be said to conjoin, it seems to be in the unhappy process of commodification: the object comes to overpower the subject, mysteriously incorporating the latter's labor into itself—so that the subject's activity looks like a property of the produced object itself. The mastery of Burckhardt's subject is inverted in this capitalist configuration: commodities come to hold sway over their producers.

The hostility, even violence, of these subject/object relations inflects a whole series of terms which speak to their connection in the negative. To treat a subject like an object is to *reify, objectify*. To treat an object like a subject is to *idolize*, to *fetishize*. In the modern idiom, the substitution of one term for the other is a theoretical and political problem—a category mistake of the highest order. Might the problem lie in the artificiality of the categories themselves?—that is, in their enforced opposition as binaries? Another look at Marx suggests the interdependency of the two. For it is not only the subject that is lost in commodification: the object too is lost. In the process of converting it to purely quantitative exchange value, commodification depletes the object of its qualities. If 100 paper cups = 5 plastic plates = 30 boxes of matches, the particular qualities of cup, plate, and match evaporate. Commodification is thus not only the vanishing point of the subject into the commodified object but also of the object into pure exchangeability.[11]

Let us return to the lordship and bondage narrative, and continue it by tracing the object, not as Hegel in fact did but as Marx might have.[12] If we situate the bondsman in some imaginary realm outside existing modes of production, we may see her or him in relation not to the lord but to the object she or he is working upon in what Marx terms 'a human manner.'[13] The object made then takes on inestimable value. For, in working upon it, the bondsman comes to recognize her or his identity as 'an objective being' or 'objective personality' – that is, a being in need of outside objects and in need of being an outside object to another.[14] The consciousness that comes into formation looks very different from the masterful Renaissance individual. In the experiencing of its double 'objectivity,' the subject recognizes itself as 'a suffering, conditioned and limited creature.'[15] Quite unexpectedly, the subject's agency turns out to lie in suffering, in feeling its own corporeal and sensual receptivity as it intently plies its object: '*Passion* is the essential *force* of man energetically bent on its object.'[16]

If we allow Hegel's (working) bondsman to stand for the object-as-position and Marx's (uncommodified) product to stand for the object-as-thing, it may be possible to break open what can seem a long and monotonous history of the sovereignty of the subject. In highlighting the subject, Renaissance studies have prodded this history on, for, from its Burckhardtian inception, the period has been identified as 'the beginning of the modern era' – what we now term the Early Modern.[17] Once the Modern era is seen to start with the emergence of the subject, the course is set for all of its extensions into the future, from Early Modern through postmodern. We are stuck then with what Foucault has described as 'the continuous history [that] is the indispensable correlative of the founding function of the subject.' Such a protracted history provides a 'citadel' or 'privileged shelter for the sovereignty of conscious-ness' protecting it from displacement and preemption. According to Foucault, this history begins to be written (by Burckhardt, for example) in the nineteenth century, in nervous response to the extensive epistemological mutations (of Marx, for example) that were shaking the subject at its foundations.[18] A long anthropomorphic or humanistic history was then forged to 'shelter' the beleaguered subject from dispersal and hold out the promise of its eventual reinstatement. If Foucault is right, Renaissance studies have been doubly instrumental in sustaining this obsessive teleological history: by keeping the subject out of touch with the object and by staging this exclusion as the beginning of the Modern, an exclusion rehearsed all the way through the Modern and the late Modern and the postmodern. [. . .]

Indeed, the tendency has increasingly been to reconceptualize the subject in less subjective terms: as a construct responding to changing historical structures, as an effect issuing from the reproduction of an ideological system, as a site caught in the always short-changing play of signifiers. Yet the role of the object here too has been negligible, except to mark and remark the position of the dominated or oppressed term. From the moment of its mid-nineteenth-century inception as subject-oriented, the Renaissance as Early Modern has given short and limited shrift to the object. In the wake of such a tradition, the recent tendency to periodize around the concept of the 'Colonial' rather than the 'Modern' seems an improve-ment. The period division 'Early Colonial' at least assumes the presence of colonized as well as colonizer, object as well as subject.

The purpose [here] is not to efface the subject but to offset it by insisting that the object be taken into account. With such a shift, it is hoped that new relations between subject (as position, as person) and object (as position, as thing) may emerge and familiar relations change. If, for example, we do not assume the unidirectional power relationship from top to bottom, then the linkages of subject to object may differ from those of subversion or containment. The proposed shift might also reveal the linkages to be historical; that is, they may change over time, and asymmetrically in relation to each other.

The very ambiguity of the word 'ob-ject,' that which is *thrown before*, suggests a more dynamic status for the object. Reading 'ob' as 'before' allows us to assign the object a prior status, suggesting its temporal, spatial, and even causal *coming before*. The word could thus be made to designate the potential priority of the object. So defined, the term renders more apparent the way material things—land, clothes, tools—might constitute subjects who in turn own, use, and transform them. The form/matter relation of Aristotelian metaphysics is thereby provisionally reversed: it is the material object that impresses its texture and contour upon the noumenal subject. And this reversal is curiously upheld by the ambiguity of the word 'sub-ject,' that which is *thrown under*, in this case—in order to receive an imprint.

*   *   *

Jerry Brotton, *The Renaissance Bazaar* (Oxford: Oxford University Press, 2002), pp. 172–3.

By 1502, the first major phase of seaborne travel had reached its climax. Ptolemy's world picture had been shattered and a recognisably modern image of the world had started to emerge. The Portuguese had rounded Africa, reached India, accidentally discovered Brazil [. . .] and were pushing on to Malacca (1511), Hormuz (1513), China (1514), and Japan (1543). To the west Columbus' three voyages to the Americas had established a thriving trade in gold, silver, and slaves. In four voyages undertaken between 1497 and 1502 Amerigo Vespucci conclusively proved that Columbus had discovered a new continent. [. . .]

   With the revision of the European geographical imagination came a transformation of the texture of everyday life. The spices that flowed back into Europe affected what and how people ate, as did the influx of coconuts, oranges, yams and bananas (from the east) and pineapples, groundnuts, papayas, and potatoes (from the Americas). The term 'spices' could also refer to a dizzying array of drugs (including opium, camphor, and cannabis) [. . .] sugar, waxes, and cosmetics. Silk, cotton, and velvet changed what people wore, and musk and civet altered the way they smelt. Dyes like indigo, vermilion, lac, saffron, and alum made Europe a brighter place, while porcelain, amber, ebony, sandalwood, ivory, bamboo, and lacquered wood all transformed the public and private domestic interiors of wealthy individuals. Tulips, parrots, rhinoceroses, chess sets, sexual appliances, and tobacco were just some of the more esoteric but significant goods that reached Europe from east and west. Lisbon itself was transformed into one of Europe's wealthiest cities: here it was possible to buy virtually anything and marvel at the monuments to the discoveries that drew on African and Indian motifs to create a beautiful hybrid architectural style. Princes displayed jewels, armour, statues, paintings, bezoar stones, and even parrots, monkeys, and horses in cabinets of curiosity, and Albrecht Dürer enthusiastically listed his acquisition of African salt cellars, Chinese porcelain, sandalwood, parrots, and Indian coconuts and feathers. If anything characterises the nature of the English Renaissance, it is this complete transformation of all aspects of life to such an extent that it is almost impossible to appreciate today.

                                        *   *   *

Jonathan Gil Harris, 'Shakespeare's hair: staging the object of material culture', *Shakespeare Quarterly* 52.4 (2001), 479–91.

   Why is Time such a niggard of hair, being (as it is) so plentiful an excrement?
                                        (*The Comedy of Errors*, 2.2.77–8)[1]

Renaissance historicism has witnessed something of a sea change in recent years. If the new historicism of the 1980s was preoccupied primarily with the fashioning of early modern *subjects*, the growing tendency at the millennium, evidenced in the recent turn to 'material culture,' is to engage with *objects*. This new preoccupation has been showcased in a pair of anthologies that offer readers wonder-cabinets of material goods in Shakespeare's culture: *Subject and Object in Renaissance Culture* includes essays on a variety of early modern objects, including feathers, textiles, and communion wafers; and *Renaissance Culture and the Everyday* boasts an even more extensive catalogue of items such as 'mirrors, books, horses, everyday speech, money, laundry baskets, graffiti, embroidery, and food preparation.'[2] For a growing number of Renaissance and Shakespeare scholars, then, the play is no longer the thing: the *thing* is the thing.

   The turn to objects best exemplifies, perhaps, what Hugh Grady has memorably dubbed the 'new-antiquarian' potential of recent historicism.[3] Grady's somewhat derogatory epithet makes a certain amount of sense given Renaissance historicists' seeming fascination with the dull weight of evidentiary material, a weight constituted now as much by physical materials as by archival minutiae. Yet to damn object criticism as lamentably and even fetishistically invested in mere things repeats rather than corrects one of that criticism's ongoing problems: even as the new object scholarship has situated itself within a broadly materialist tradition of historicist criticism, the 'material' of 'material culture' has remained largely untheorized.

What exactly, then, *is* the material object? This essay takes as its starting point a mundane item that could be comfortably housed in any of the recent anthologies devoted to Renaissance things. Yet this item also begs the hairy question of how we are to understand its materiality. In attempting to tease out an answer to that question, I will suggest—perhaps perversely—that if the 'new antiquarianism' is to theorize more comprehensively the *material* of 'material culture,' it needs to become, if anything, *more* antiquarian. For all that the antiquarians of the eighteenth and nineteenth centuries placed a naive faith in objects as the unmediated residua of the past, they were nonetheless attentive to a dimension of materiality that object criticism has all too frequently overlooked: the diachronic trajectories of things through time and space.

I

I begin with a curio—or more accurately, perhaps, a relic. In 1999 the Folger Shakespeare Library acquired a strange object: a single, auburn hair, short and slightly curly. Mounted on a card and encased in mylar, the hair is accompanied by a nineteenth-century inscription that identifies it as 'Shakespeare's Hair.' The same inscription also tells us that the hair entered the sphere of public circulation in an undated letter sent by Samuel Ireland, presumably around 1800, to Mr. Bindley, commissioner of the Stamp Office in London. It was subsequently auctioned by a Mr. Evans on Tuesday, 8 August 1820; either then or at some later point it passed into the possession of one J. E. H. Taylor, Esq., who donated it to the collector W. J. Bernhard Smith on 24 August 1866. The card on which the hair is mounted seeks to vouch for the authenticity of these transactions and hence, perhaps, of the Shakespearean relic itself. The inscription is accompanied by Bernhard Smith's autograph and Taylor's stamped signature, which is annotated by a somewhat eyebrow-raising note from a certain 'VMT'—presumably Taylor's son or daughter—asking us to 'Kindly Accept / The aboue is my Fathers handwriting.'[4]

What exactly is Shakespeare's Hair? At one level, the question is easy to answer: it is almost certainly a fake. Tellingly, the trajectory of exchanges recorded by the card starts with Samuel Ireland, the infamous eighteenth-century travel painter, antiquarian, and Bardolater. Ireland's name was sullied by a scandal surrounding his publication in 1796 of a volume containing allegedly newly discovered Shakespearean 'papers,' including part of a manuscript of *Hamlet*, a whole *Lear* manuscript, and a 'lost' Shakespeare play, *Vortigern and Rowena*.[5] All these documents were quickly exposed as forgeries. Although full responsibility for fabricating them was taken by Samuel's son, William Henry Ireland, the elder Ireland also fell under a cloud of suspicion—where he still remains, thanks in large part to his having earlier dabbled in the burgeoning eighteenth-century market for false Shakespeare relics.[6] On a visit to Stratford in the 1780s he allegedly bought a number of such artifacts, including Shakespeare's Chair and Shakespeare's Purse; perhaps his acquisition of Shakespeare's Hair dates to this visit.[7] Alternatively, the hair may be a strand from a tuft originally affixed to another William Henry Ireland forgery—an effusive love letter from William Shakespeare to 'Dearesste Anna'

Hathaway.[8] That this 'plentiful excrement' should reach us in the etiolated form of a single strand perhaps only serves to confirm Antipholus of Syracuse's conviction that Time is 'such a niggard of hair.'

But its status as a fake doesn't answer the question: in what does the materiality of Shakespeare's Hair consist? The card on which it is mounted offers two quite different answers. On the one hand, the card literally demands that the hair be viewed as a remarkable relic, an excrescence that synecdochically stands in for a missing bodily whole, regardless of whether the hair was ever actually attached to that body (never mind to which part). In this view the humble material object gestures invitingly to a larger, supramaterial plenitude that transcends it yet also transposes its mundanity into something magical, alluring, desirable. On the other hand, the card's inscriptions also allow us to view the hair as something altogether less magical—as a commodity whose reliquary synecdochical value has been and continues to be produced by means of its passage through multiple modes and sites of exchange, whether as auctionable item, gentlemanly gift, or scholarly curio. The material object encodes not a supramaterial plenitude beyond it, then, but the ongoing processes of location and dislocation, exchange and enclavement that produce and reproduce its 'magical' signifying power.

The inscriptions accompanying Shakespeare's Hair highlight how these two differing modes of materiality are implicated in two very different conceptions of history. The hair serves as the point of entry into a synchronic totality historically remote from us—it promises to be a wardrobe affording access to the Narnia of the early modern epoch. But in a fashion that typifies the nineteenth-century antiquarian obsession with the provenance of objects, the card on which the hair is mounted also records a diachronic economic history that spans several centuries, leading from Samuel Ireland to its twenty-first-century owners and consumers. Although the history of exchange detailed by the card's inscription stops at 1866, that history obviously continues into the present. When the Folger first acquired the hair, it was the object of some considerable voyeuristic excitement on the part of scholars then studying at the library, including me; in hankering for a glimpse of a hair that may or may not have been once attached to Shakespeare's body, my colleagues and I participated in the ongoing reproduction of its reliquary value.[9]

The diachronic history recorded on the card, however, works in one sense to erase itself. The hair's trajectory of location and dislocation is documented in antiquarian fashion not to divert attention to the dynamics of cultural or economic production through time, of course, but to legitimize the hair's status as the residue—authentic or forged—of an unchanging, phantom plenitude: the Bard. The curio *is* called Shakespeare's Hair, after all, and it is hard not to hear in that name 'Shakespeare's HERE!'

I wish to suggest that Shakespeare's Hair can help to illuminate the ways in which objects have functioned in recent writing about early modern English material culture. Not only short and curly auburn locks but all manner of other mundane yet magical things have been seized upon by recent scholars in attempts to conjure up the ghost of a seemingly 'authentic' past. This is not to suggest that such objects are, like Samuel Ireland's Hair of the Bard, forgeries. What they share with the latter curio, though, are elusive histories of production, exchange, and dislocation which have tended to be suppressed even as they have enabled these objects to function in the present as synecdoches for a past plenitude—suppressed histories that have allowed us, in other words, to conclude: 'Early Modern Culture's HERE!' I will first consider how *Subject and Object in Renaissance Culture* constitutes the object within a synchronic economy of the historical 'moment'; then I will sketch ways in which we might theorize the all-too-frequently suppressed diachronic dimensions of materiality. Finally, I shall argue that the props of the Renaissance stage highlight the material object's simultaneous participation in the synchronic and the diachronic, the aesthetic and the temporal.

II

Opening their preface with a discussion of seventeenth-century *vanitas* paintings, the editors of *Subject and Object in Renaissance Culture* observe:

> Renaissance studies have slighted the objects that are the subjects of these paintings. It is if we had listened to their renunciatory moral without seeing their sumptuous allure. For in the main we have proceeded as if it were both possible and desirable for subjects to cut themselves off from objects. The essays collected here aim to address that bias with a basic question: in the period that has from its inception been identified with the emergence of the subject, *where is the object?*[10]

The question is a fair one, given the overwhelming preoccupation of earlier generations of historicists with issues of Renaissance identity and interiority. But the 'where's Waldo?' approach to the object that the above passage advocates assumes that scholars of material culture already know with some certainty what Waldo looks like. By figuring the modern critic's relation to objects in the terms of the *vanitas* painting's choice between 'renunciation' and 'allure,' the editors of *Subject and Object* imply that, when it comes to the world of Renaissance goods, critics—like early-modern subjects—are confronted with a simple, albeit agonizing, decision: should or shouldn't seemingly vain objects be deemed worthy of serious attention? This 'choice' conceals, however, the extent to which the nature of the object has already been predetermined by the religio-economic discourse within which the choice is framed. Whether repudiated or succumbed to, disdained or celebrated, the object remains a thing whose very objecthood is registered in the *present instant* of the early modern subject's or the postmodern critic's struggle with her desire. The object is apprehended, therefore, as a static entity, immobilized like the goods of the *vanitas* painting in the freeze-frame tableau of a historical 'moment.'

Rather than ask *where* is the object, however, we might instead wonder: *what* is the object? Can it be reduced, as it is in the above passage, to a physical item preserved in the amber of an epochal instant? Or, as the instance of Shakespeare's Hair suggests, does the object also possess a more dynamic, diachronic dimension? We might additionally ask, then: *how* is the object constituted as it passes historically through multiple stages of discursive and economic production?

A long tradition of materialist philosophy has insisted on the diachronic dimension of matter. In *De Anima*, Aristotle drew a critical distinction between 'form' and 'matter,' according to which 'form is actuality' and 'matter is potentiality [*dynameos*].'[11] In other words, Aristotle understood matter as a synonym not for physical presence but for dynamic process; matter, in his writing, is always *worked upon*. Marx attributed the same meaning to matter in his 'Theses on Feuerbach,' in which he criticized Feuerbach for conceiving matter 'only in the *form* of the object.'[12] Marx understood the materiality of objects to belong to the domain of labor and *praxis*, and thus to entail diachronic temporality; as Judith Butler has trenchantly observed, Marx conceived of matter 'as a principle of *transformation*, presuming and inducing a future.'[13] In the case of Shakespeare's Hair, one might add that matter also presumes and induces a past—a past that we can understand not as a static moment, but as a continuum of material transformations.

Although the recent turn to 'material culture' might suggest a continuing engagement with Marxist tradition, the word *material* has come to signify something quite different from what it meant for Marx. Indeed, scholarship on early modern 'material culture' has tended to entail study of what Marx or Aristotle would have regarded as 'formal culture'—that is, the study of 'actual' objects within the synchronic framework of a cultural formation or system. The diachronic, transformative aspect of objects has remained largely ignored and hence untheorized, as *Subject and Object's* static model of the *vanitas* painting makes clear. How, then, might we rematerialize 'material culture' in its Aristotelian or Marxist sense and thereby restore to it an understanding of materiality as *process*?

One apparent answer has been provided by the anthropologist Arjun Appadurai. In the introduction to his important edited collection *The Social Life of Things* (1986), Appadurai attempts a radical retheorization of objects that provides an illuminating alternative to the synchronic formalisms of recent work on material culture. For Appadurai objects are not to be understood in terms of their synchronic contexts; far more importantly, he argues, objects possess 'life histories' or 'careers' that invest them with social significance and cultural value. According to Appadurai, the present value of any given object thus derives diachronically from its differential relations to its known (or assumed) past and future contexts. In order to read the significance of any object, then, it becomes necessary to trace its 'cultural biography' as it 'moves through different hands, contexts, and uses.'[14] Appadurai's approach moves beyond any understanding of objects as spatially or temporally static entities; instead, he argues with a suggestive turn of phrase, we need to pay more heed to 'things-in-motion.'[15]

Appadurai's collection of essays analyzes objects foreign to English Renaissance culture—textiles in post-Raj India, the circulation of the *qat* plant in colonial North Africa. But his investment in 'things-in-motion' might have a particular resonance for the scholar of early modern drama, for Shakespeare uses the very same phrase in *Troilus and Cressida*. As part of his strategy to stir the Greeks' best warrior into action, Ulysses tells Achilles that 'things in motion sooner catch the eye / [Than] what stirs not' (3.3.183–84). Ulysses speaks here of subjects rather than objects—of Ajax and his (supposed) popularity as a result of his dynamic feats in battle, which contrast with those of the motionless Achilles, sulking in his tent. But Ulysses's argument about 'things in motion' is illustrated particularly well by one of the play's stage properties. At his parting from Cressida, Troilus gives her a sleeve as a love-token. Its value shifts—as does Cressida's own—when she relinquishes it to Diomedes: in the space of less than a hundred lines it degenerates from a 'pretty pledge' (5.2.77), nominally enclaved as a sacred object, to a 'greasy relic' (l. 159) that has entered the sphere of commodity exchange.[16] Having seen the sleeve pass from Cressida to Diomedes, Troilus famously exclaims: 'This is, and is not, Cressid' (l. 146). The anamorphic disjunction embodied in this line arguably conveys not only his struggle to understand Cressida's new identity as Diomedes's lover but also his perception of the sleeve's difference from itself. Troilus thus registers the garment less in terms of its physical form than as diachronic matter; rather than a 'thing' that 'stirs not,' it is for him a profane 'thing in motion.'

In fact *Troilus and Cressida* provides two models for a dynamic, diachronic materialism grounded in 'things in motion.' If the first is offered by the sleeve, the second is evident in the play's extensive pathological vocabulary. Throughout *Troilus and Cressida*, diseases are under-stood less as *synchronic states* of humoral imbalance (the conventional Galenic view) than as *mobile entities* that move from body to body, and from nation to nation. The affliction of 'suppeago' (i.e., serpigo), a skin condition referred to by Thersites (2.3.74), provides a notable case in point. *Suppeago*'s etymological root—the Latin *serpere*, meaning 'to creep'—helps figure the disease as an affliction that migrates, both *in* the body and *from* body to body.[17] With Thersites's reference to suppeago, Shakespeare hints at the impact of new ontological conceptions of disease proposed in the sixteenth century by the Continental physicians Girolamo Fracastoro and Paracelsus. The latter pair separately argued that disease is transmitted by a determinate *semina* or seed that invades the body through its orifices. By reimagining disease as a migratory entity, both Fracastoro and Paracelsus endeavored to explain the spread of epidemic diseases in semi-empirical terms, although Fracastoro's theory of the infectious *semina* may also have owed a debt to Lucretius's *De Rerum Natura* and its materialist vision of atoms in motion.[18] In any case, these emergent conceptions of disease proved particularly useful for explaining that comparatively new European illness, syphilis, which more than any other affliction tested the humoral assumption that disease was an internally derived state.[19] Syphilis's customary names in England—Spanish pox, *morbus gallicus* or the French sickness, the Neapolitan disease—make clear how it was understood to derive from *elsewhere*, to reside in and be transmitted by foreign bodies that had infiltrated English bodies politic and natural. This view was shared on the Continent. The Spanish physician Ruy Díaz de Isla remarks in his *Tractado contra el Mal Serpentino* that

> The French called it the *Disease of Naples*. And the Italians and Neapolitans, as they had never been acquainted with such a disease, called it the *French Disease*. From that time on as it continued to spread, they gave it a name, each one according to his opinion as to how the disease had its origin. In Castilia they called it *Bubas*, and in Portugal the *Castilian Disease*, and in Portuguese India the Indians called it the *Portuguese Disease*.[20]

Throughout Europe, therefore, the pox in all its nomenclatural guises was over-whelmingly understood to be matter in motion, possessed of a pathological version of what Appadurai would term a 'biography' or 'career.' And indeed, the perception of syphilis as matter in transnational motion is powerfully present in *Troilus and Cressida*: Thersites anachronistically refers to it as 'the Neapolitan bone-ache' (2.3.18–19) and 'diseases of the south' (5.1.18), and Pandarus's concluding reference to the Winchester goose (5.10.54), a colloquial name for the pustules of syphilitic infection, notably figures the disease not only as an organism but also as migratory—an illness one might 'bequeath,' to use his term (l.56).[21]

In other words, *Troilus and Cressida*'s 'things in motion' strongly suggests that we should look beyond the model of the *vanitas* painting if we wish to broaden our understanding of early modern conceptions of materiality and the object. The play's migratory stage properties and epidemic diseases are at odds with the static presences that populate *vanitas* paintings and much—though certainly not all—scholarship on Renaissance material culture.[22] But is it enough simply to replace a static model of the object with a dynamic one? Or does a critically nuanced theory of the object need to find some way of theorizing how it partakes of *both* the synchronic and the diachronic?

III

As its reliquary power makes clear, Shakespeare's Hair does not transparently lay bare its material-cultural biography in the manner of *Troilus and Cressida's* sleeve or its epidemic diseases. Instead the hair functions as a reversible turnstile between commercial history and Bardic timelessness, between matter and form, between hair and Hair; that is, it does not point *unidirectionally* from the synchronic to the diachronic. To this extent it cannot be understood simply in the temporal terms of Appadurai's anthropological account of objects. Its vacillation between matter and form is more adequately illuminated, perhaps, by Walter Benjamin's comments about the allegorical object of baroque German *Trauerspiel*, or mourning-drama.[23] For Benjamin, the allegorical object occupies the cusp between history and transcendence. It *aspires* to timeless signification, yet it cannot entirely shed its historical markings, including those inscribed upon it by the processes that have made it available for allegorical use. It is thus located at the junction between the synchronic and the diachronic, the allegorical and the historical, the formal and the material.

To theorize this turnstile quality of objects, we could do worse than turn once more to the materials of the early modern stage. (And in this regard it is notable that Benjamin's analysis of the allegorical object also pivots on the disjunctions of what he terms the 'fatal stage property' of the *Trauerspiel*.[24]) Take, for example, the Spanish suit that Abel Drugger borrows from a playing company in Ben Jonson's *The Alchemist*, first performed by the King's Men in 1610. Face informs the audience that this costume consists of 'Hieronimo's old cloak, ruff, and hat';[25] even as it is incorporated into the narrative of the play, therefore, the costume's previous theatrical life in Kyd's *Spanish Tragedy* is made prominently visible—and perhaps all the more so for *The Alchemist*'s original audiences in light of the possibility that Jonson had himself played the part of Hieronimo. The Spanish suit thus possesses a deliberately anamorphic quality: Face foregrounds its simultaneous status as form (as a synchronic object that is a timeless property of the play) and as matter (as a diachronic 'thing in motion,' the historical property of the playing company).

The Alchemist's Spanish suit suggests how early modern stage costumes not only migrated from play to play but could also even disclose these histories of migration. One might think of Gloriana's skull in *The Revenger's Tragedy*, another play in the King's Men's repertory; given this stage property's prominent place in a work that consistently exposes its own parasitic relation to *Hamlet*, it becomes hard to avoid the conclusion that the skull had in all likelihood previously starred as Yorick.[26] Shakespeare's own drama also offers potential disclosures of its costumes' material histories. When, for example, Petruchio derides Katherina's dress in *The Taming of the Shrew* as 'masquing stuff' (4.3.87), we are offered a metatheatrical glimpse of the forms of exchange that may have constituted the dress's social life. As Natasha Korda has argued, the costume may well have been purchased by Shakespeare's company from the Office of the Revels, which discarded many of its theatrical garments after they had been used in court masques, believing them to be soiled or profaned.[27] Petruchio's remark thus invites an audience to pay heed not only to the costume's function within the illusion of the drama but also to its material history of transformation outside of it—including the very transformation that may have made it available for use by Shakespeare's company.

The extent to which stage properties potentially disrupt even as they foster theatrical illusion is made clear in a review by William Hazlitt of an 1818 performance of *A Midsummer Night's Dream*:

> All that is fine in the play, was lost in the representation. The spirit was evaporated, the genius was fled; but the spectacle was fine: it was that which saved the play. Oh, ye scene-shifters, ye scene-painters, ye machinists and dress-makers, ye manufacturers of moon and stars that give no light . . . rejoice! This is your triumph; it is not ours. . . . Poetry and the stage do not agree together. The attempt to reconcile them fails not only of effect, but of decorum. The *ideal* has no place on the stage, which is a picture without perspective; every thing there is in the foreground. That which is merely an airy shape, a dream, a passing thought, immediately becomes an unmanageable reality. . . . Thus Bottom's head in the play is a fantastic illusion, produced by magic spells: on the stage it is an ass's head, and nothing more; certainly a very strange costume for a gentleman to appear in.[28]

Hazlitt's extended complaint betrays a deep-rooted hostility to the economic dimensions of theatrical production. The 'spirit' or 'airy shape' of his cherished '*ideal*' play has been punctured by the contrivances of mere 'manufacturers' such as 'scene-shifters,' 'scene-painters,' 'machinists,' and 'dress-makers,' an uncanny repetition of the play's own sub-ordination of fairy spirits to the carnivalesque misrule of so-called rude mechanicals. As his remarks about the still-ruder 'manufacturers' make quite clear, what Hazlitt sees in the objects of the stage is not just their physical forms but also their pre-stage histories. These point decisively away from the 'fantastic illusion' of the play: artifice presumes artificers and hence narratives of mechanical labor that compete with the sublime 'dreams' of the poet. It is such narratives, I would argue, that constitute the 'unmanageable reality' Hazlitt complains of. The phrase suggestively captures something of the refractory nature of stage properties. Like Snout's crude 'rough-cast' wall in the play of Pyramus and Thisbe (5.1.161), theatrical objects always potentially refuse to be subordinated to the *logos* of the play in which they appear and instead make visible, by virtue of their conspicuous fabricatedness, alternate biographies of manufacture. Like Shakespeare's Hair, then, the props of the early modern stage can draw explicit attention to their twin citizenship in a timeless world of formal illusion and a diachronic universe of material labor and transformation.

I would suggest that to understand the oscillation of objects between matter and form, the temporal and the aesthetic, we need first and foremost to understand their staged quality. I use *staged* in its double sense—both as a performative term designating synchronic pro-duction (on a stage) and as a temporal term designating diachronic sequence (in stages). Shakespeare's Hair, or any object used to decorate the 'stage' we call Renaissance material culture, can be read not just in terms of its signifying power within the synchronic drama for which it has been co-opted. It can be understood also in terms of what it might tell us about its ongoing, diachronic histories of production—the various 'stages' of its social life. The antidote to the formalist tendencies of the so-called new antiquarianism, then, may be to become *more* rather than *less* antiquarian—if by *antiquarian* we mean a more thoroughgoing sensitivity to the locations and dislocations of objects through space and time. In this respect, at least, antiquarians more than present-day scholars of material culture might be inclined to recognize Benjamin's insistence that 'the word "history" stands written on the countenance of nature in the characters of transience.'[29] Time may be a niggard of hair, in Antipholus of Syracuse's words. But hair need not be a niggard of Time, at least not in the narratives of material culture.

*   *   *

Eric Wilson, 'Abel Drugger's sign and the fetishes of material culture', in Carla Mazzio and Douglas Trevor (eds.), *Historicism, Psychoanalysis and Early Modern Culture* (London and New York: Routledge, 2000), pp. 122–4.

At the alchemist's shop, the fetishized object par excellence is the philosopher's stone, the object that itself promises to transvalue all others. It never appears, of course, beyond the words of its conjuring, its fantasmatic 'projection.' Its material essence is precisely, exclusively its presence as a means of linking the various characters and their needs, a fabled construct that sutures their quilt of fantastic value. The missing object is, in fact, the most valuable one, a precocious nod to the Lacanian principle that desire is structured through Lack, as well as an ironic inversion of the Marxian commodity, in which the fetishized object is here obscured and overwhelmed by the insistent transactions through which it will be made to have never appeared. For Jonson, the most cutting irony is that the phantom philosopher's stone is *only* what is made of it, the social relations that conjure its value, that structure its economy. The dialectic between presence and emptiness, figured in both Drugger's sign and Mammon's stone, finds another pertinent echo in Lacan's 'Fable of the Pot and the Vase,' in which he moves beyond the distinction between the vase's 'use as a utensil and its signifying function' to suggest that 'if it really is a signifier, and the first of such signifiers fashioned by the human hand, it is in its signifying essence a signifier of nothing other than signifying as such, or, in other words, of no particular signified.'[1] The pot emerges as a profound emblem in repositioning a long philosophical tradition negotiating between 'matter' and 'nothing'; when considering the vase

> as an object made to represent the existence of the emptiness at the center of the real that is called the Thing, this emptiness as represented in the representation presents itself as a *nihil*, as nothing. And that is why the potter, just like you to whom I am speaking, creates the vase with his hand around this emptiness, creates it, just like the mythical creator, *ex nihilo*, starting with a hole. (121)

Reading Jonson's play as a critique of these basic problems of materialist encounter, we might well wonder about our own attempts to claim the missing objects of the past, the ones we will into existence, into an intelligibility or value that may be, if not laughable, then perhaps more illusory than we care to think.

Like the psychic formations that would apprehend them, all material objects—whether playbooks or tobacco pipes—are overdetermined, subject to a variety of appropriations, uses, frames, and descriptions. What I'm calling the historical fetish—like its psychoanalytic counterpart—is best understood not as the fantastic object of singular value but as a signifier in a matrix of overlapping, at times contradictory relations. Anchored in a history of displaced origins, the fetishized objects of historical materialism emerge at the point where an empirical historicism crosses into the alchemy of historical fantasy, coordinate with the desires, distinctions, and delusions of our own cultural imagination. In working to 'discover the *various* uses of things' that Marx described as the work of history, the study of material culture stands to complement the rewards of specificity with the multiple contingencies of value. Sometimes a cigar may just be a cigar, but sometimes it just might also point to Abel Drugger's shop. And no sooner do we puff away in self-assurance, than René Magritte reminds us, 'This is not a pipe,' that the figurative and the material may collapse before our very eyes. Such depth of vision may further help to survey in ever more peculiar detail, the shifting relations between 'the pastness of the things we seek to understand and the presentness of our seeking to understand them.' To continue in Gary Tomlinson's lyrical phrasings, '[A] new historical goal emerges: not to recreate a docile past "the way it really was" but to build a past that resists our intellectual attempts to occupy it even while it takes its shape from us—and moreover, takes only the shape we give it. We build into our histories a keen responsiveness to the evidence of the historical traces we (for our own reasons) select.'[2]

* * *

Dympna Callaghan, 'Body problems', *Shakespeare Studies* 29 (2001), 70–1.

To posit the brute facticity of matter is not materialism (though it is widely believed to be so) but reification. This is so because wherever we attribute brute facticity to anything, we make it seem as if it stands beyond its interactions with human consciousness and therefore beyond history in any meaningful sense. We are guilty of a sort of historicist idolatry. [. . .] To say that human consciousness and its intercourse with the material environment is the dynamic force of human history sounds antimaterialist only because Marx's own complex theorization of dialectical materialism has been ignored in favour of the profoundly erroneous belief that matter has a life of its own and that human consciousness is irrelevant to the course of human history. Such views constitute what I regard as the political misuse of materialism; so that analysis of any old dead matter [. . .] gets paraded as 'materialist' analysis in a manner that is by no means allayed by the qualification that the object of inquiry is 'discourses about' lights, livers, and entrails, for example, as distinct from the organs themselves. [. . .]

Perhaps unfortunately for us, who live in what is arguably the most visual culture that has ever existed, early moderns were more interested in things unseen than in matter visible, in which they simply did not share our faith. [. . .] No matter how well-informed he may have been of the new developments of his era, when Donne implores God to batter his heart, he is not worried about his circulation but is rather concerned to grasp the concrete reality of the divine presence. [. . .]

My final gripe about [the study of the body and material culture] as it is manifested in Renaissance literary criticism is that it is not much concerned with literature at all. [. . .] I believe [. . .] that commitment to literature is politically distinct from merely privileging literature, and that now, more than ever, in a world where the humanities are increasingly regarded as irrelevant, we need such a commitment. [. . .] When I read yet another essay on the early modern body, I fear we have abandoned our political commitment to literature in favor of medical texts and an ahistorical literalism that constitutes those aspects of knowledge that our own world deems more valuable and less troublesome than poetry. Call me old-fashioned, but I'd rather spend my time with Leander and Adonis.

. . . .

QUESTIONS

- How does the critical recovery of the object affect theories of the subject and how do the above writers characterize the relationship between the material and non-material?
- To what extent is the object a political category?
- What are the advantages and limitations of criticism orientated towards materiality? What do you think is the way forward?

SUGGESTED FURTHER READING

Breitenberg, Mark, *Anxious Masculinity in Early Modern England* (Cambridge: Cambridge University Press, 1996)

Foucault, Michel, *Discipline and Punish: The Birth of the Prison*, trans. by Alan Sheridan (London: Penguin, 1991)

Fumerton, Patricia, *Cultural Aesthetics: Renaissance Literature and the Practice of Social Ornament* (Chicago and London: University of Chicago Press, 1991)

Hillman, David and Mazzio, Carla (eds.), *The Body in Parts: Fantasies of Corporeality in Early Modern Europe* (New York and London: Routledge, 1997)

Jardine, Lisa, *Worldly Goods* (London: Macmillan, 1996)

Jones, Ann Rosalind and Stallybrass, Peter, *Renaissance Clothing and the Materials of Memory* (Cambridge: Cambridge University Press, 2000)

Kerwin, William, *Beyond the Body: The Boundaries of Medicine and English Renaissance Drama* (Amherst: University of Massachussetts Press, 2004)

Kantorowicz, Ernst W. *The King's Two Bodies: A Study in Medieval Political Theology* (Princeton, NJ: Princeton University Press, 1981)

Laqueur, Thomas, *Making Sex: Body and Gender from the Greeks to Freud* (Cambridge, MA, and London: Harvard University Press, 1990)

Schoenbaum, Samuel, *Shakespeare's Lives*, 2nd edition (Oxford: Clarendon Press, 1991)

Schoenfeldt, Michael C., *Bodies and Selves in Early Modern England: Physiology and Inwardness in Spenser, Shakespeare, Herbert and Milton* (Cambridge: Cambridge University Press, 1999)

Orgel, Stephen, *Impersonations: The Performance of Gender in Shakespeare's England* (Cambridge: Cambridge University Press, 1996)

Warner, Marina, *Monuments and Maidens: The Allegory of the Female Form* (London: Weidenfeld & Nicolson, 1985)

NOTES

Vickers, Diana described

1. Elizabeth Cropper, 'On beautiful women: Parmigianino, *Petrarchism*, and the vernacular style', *Art Bulletin* 58 (1976), 374–94.

2. On enumeration and the descriptive text, see Roland Barthes, *S/Z* (Paris: Éditions du Seuil, 1970), pp. 120–2.

3. Robert Durling, 'Petrarch's *Giovene donna sotto un verde Lauro*', *Modern Language Notes* 86 (1971), 1–20, and John Freccero, 'The fig tree and the laurel: Petrarch's poetics', *Diacritics* 5 (1975), 34–40.

4. James V. Mirollo, 'In praise of "*La Bella Mano*": aspects of late Renaissance lyricism', *Comparative Literature Studies* 9 (1972), 31–43. See also James Villas, 'The Petrarchan topos "Bel piede": generative footsteps', *Romance Notes* 11 (1969), 167–73.

Parker, Literary fat ladies

1. On Rahab in the Hebrew Bible, see Judith Baskin, 'The rabbinic transformations of Rahab the Harlot,' *Notre Dame English Journal*, 11, 2 (April 1979), pp. 141–57.

2. For Rahab as *dilatio*, see Jean Daniélou, *From Shadows to Reality: Studies in the Biblical Typology of the Fathers*, trans. Dom Wulstan Hibberd (London, 1960), pp. 250 ff. For the 'dilation of Christendome,' see St Thomas More, *Comfort against Tribulation* (1529), III, weeks 1213/2. And, for 'différance,' see Jacques Derrida, *Marges de la philosphie* (Paris, 1972), pp. 1–29; trans. Alan Bass as *Margins of Philosophy* (Chicago, 1982), pp. 1–27. The Donne sonnet cited is Holy Sonnet 179. On women's spreading of the word, see Lee W. Patterson, ' "For the Wyves love of Bathe": feminine rhetoric and poetic resolution in the *Roman de la Rose* and the *Canterbury Tales*,' *Speculum*, 58, 3 (1983), p. 664, citing the *Liber Lamentationum Matheoluli*. Unless otherwise noted, all italicization in the text is mine.

3. In *Inescapable Romance: Studies in the Poetics of a Mode* (Princeton, NJ, 1979), esp. pp. 54 ff. For Hamlet's 'mother' and 'matter,' below, see Margaret W. Ferguson, '*Hamlet*: letters and spirits,' in Patricia Parker and Geoffrey Hartman (eds.), *Shakespeare and the Question of Theory* (New York and London, 1985), p. 295.

4. St Jerome, who repented of his own attraction towards rhetoric, interpreted the swine's food in the Parable of the Prodigal Son as 'the song of the poets, prophane philosophy, and the verbal pomp of the rhetoricians.' On Jerome and other patristic commentary on the Prodigal Son parable, see Bernard Blumenkranz, 'Siliquae Porcorum: L'exégèse médiévale et les sciences profanes,' *Mélanges d'histoire du Moyen Age dédiés à la mémoire de Louis Halphen* (Paris, 1951), pp. 11–17, and Richard Helgerson, *The Elizabethan Prodigals* (Berkeley and Los Angeles, 1976), p. 55, together with Helgerson's overall discussion of the importance of the parable for Renaissance English literary men.

5. On Sidney and the attack on poetry as not fit for men, see Walter J. Ong, SJ, 'Latin language study as a Renaissance puberty rite,' in his *Rhetoric, Romance, and Technology* (Ithaca, NY, 1971), pp. 130 ff. The text used in all subsequent citations from Ascham is *The Schoolmaster* (1570), ed. Laurence V. Ryan (Ithaca, 1967).

6. See Sir John Harington (trans.), *Orlando furioso* (1591), sig. Mm iii and sig. ¶ viii-viii^v (UMEES, Reel 194), with Helgerson, *Elizabethan Prodigals*, pp. 38–9.

7. See Mary Jacobus, 'Is there a woman in this text?,' *New Literary History*, 14, 1 (Autumn 1982), pp. 117–41. I use 'subtext' here in the sense of an informing predecessor text. See Thomas M. Greene, *The Light in Troy: Imitation and Discovery in Renaissance Poetry* (New Haven and London, 1982), pp. 18–31.

8. I am, of course, aware that Calypso comes chronologically later than Circe in the homecoming journey of Odysseus. But the *narrative* order moves from Calypso, and an initial latency, to the victory over Circe. The *Odyssey* is traditionally characterized as a romance or *romanzo* in Renaissance discussions of the form.

9. See Ariosto, *Orlando furioso*, VII.74.1–4; Parker, *Inescapable Romance*, pp. 30–1; and Roland Barthes, *S/Z: Essai* (Paris, 1970). There is clearly an important difference between closural forms in the Bible, even with its open-ended ending, and the *Odyssey*, where we are told within the text that Odysseus, after reaching home and Penelope, will one day set out again. But the conflation within later literary, and specifically romance, tradition of temptress figures from both texts suggests the perceived links between the trajectory of 'homecoming' in both.

10. See Desiderius Erasmus, *De Copia*, in *Collected Works of Erasmus*, vol. 24, ed. Craig R. Thompson (Toronto, 1978); the warnings against 'Excesse' in, for example, Henry Peacham's *The Garden of Eloquence* (1593 edn), ed. William G. Crane (Gainesville, Florida, 1954). For the 'wall' or *paries* and Cicero's *Topics*, see T. W. Baldwin, *William Shakspere's Small Latine and Lesse Greeke*, 2 vols (Urbana, 1944), vol. II, p. 110. The link between weaving and the dilation of discourse, as of the play, in *A Midsummer Night's Dream*, might be most succinctly conveyed through the fact that the name of 'Bottom' the 'Weaver' comes from that 'bottom' of thread which Francis Bacon, in *The Advancement of Learning* (II.xviii.8), has recourse to as a figure for 'rhetoric' as having to do with discoursing 'at large,' and the attendant need to avoid 'prolixity' ('as skeins or bottoms of thread, to be unwinded at large when they come to be used'). Though the relation between Bottom's name and the play's constant playing on the dilation and partition of discourse has not been discussed, the link with 'bottom of thread' both in relation to weaving and in relation to phallic 'point' has. See Wolfgang Franke, 'The logic of *Double Entendre* in *A Midsummer-Night's Dream*,' *Philological Quarterly*, 58 (1979), pp. 284, 287 ff.

11. See *The Sermons of John Donne*, ed. George R. Potter and Evelyn M. Simpson, 10 vols., Vol. V (Berkeley and Los Angeles, 1959), p. 56; and the discussion of the *ars praedicandi* tradition in John S. Chamberlin, *Increase and Multiply* (Chapel Hill, NC, 1976), and Patterson, ' "For the Wyves love of Bathe", ' p. 675.

12. See Ascham, *The Schoolmaster*, pp. 106–14; Erasmus, Epistle 899, quoted in Izora Scott, *Controversies over the Imitation of Cicero* (New York, 1910), Vol. II, p. 84, and, for the reference to 'bignesse,' Cornwallis's essay 'Of vanity' (1601), both cited in George Williamson, *The Senecan Amble* (Chicago, 1951), pp. 19 and 106. For Lipsius, see Morris W. Croll, ' "Attic Prose" in the seventeenth century,' *Studies in Philology*, 18 (April 1921), p. 98.

13. See, respectively, Ficino's use of *dilatio* in his translation of Plotinus' Fifth *Ennead*, with his translation of *Enneads*, 6:7.2,3; *De immortalitate animorum*, I.iii;v.x; and *De vita coelitus comparanda*, ch. 1; John Erskine Hankins, *Source and Meaning in Spenser's Allegory* (Oxford, 1971), p. 291; Parker, *Inescapable Romance*, pp. 54–6; Hugh Latimer's sermon of 1552 on the Lord's Prayer, where he remarks that heaven, unlike earth, is a place where God's will is done 'without dilation'; Richard Taverner's 1539 English translation of the *Adages* of Erasmus; and Milton, *Paradise Lost*, IV.986.

14. See Herbert of Cherbury's 'Ode upon a Question Mov'd' ('So when one wing can make no way / Two joyned can themselves dilate, / So can two persons propagate'). For the obstetrical tradition, as well as the use of the term 'dilation' for the sexual opening of a woman, see *The Works of Aristotle, the Famous Philosopher*, in the reprint edition by Arno Press (New York, 1974), pp. 10, 81. For 'dilating or enlarging of a matter by interpretation,' see John Smith's *Mysterie of Rhetorique Unvail'd* (1657), under 'Paradiastole or *distinctio*.' Audrey Eccles' *Obstetrics and Gynaecology in Tudor and Stuart England* (Kent, Ohio, 1982), pp. 28 and 40, also cites passages on the 'opening of the cervix in Copulation . . . and in childbirth.'

15. The language of legal 'dilation' still continues in Hobbes's *Leviathan* (I.xiv: 'the not decreeing Execution, is a decree of Dilation,' its 'deferring till another time'). I am indebted here to the reading of the ordering of the *Canterbury Tales*, of the Wife of Bath as putting off the Parson's Tale, and of the link with literature in Lee Patterson's ' "For the Wyves love of Bath",' pp. 676 ff.

16. For the tradition of erotic dilation or putting off, see Andreas Capellanus, *De Arte Honeste Amandi*; and Addison, *Spectator*, 89 (1711), with Patterson, ' "For the Wyves love of Bath",' p. 671n. on Andreas's substitution of *dilatio* for the *mora* of Ovid's *Ars amatoria*. The 'Wall' between the lovers which must be 'down' in the play of Pyramus and Thisbe in *A Midsummer Night's Dream* is linked by a series of obscene double entendres to the hymeneal wall, and the imagery there draws on the traditional typological assimilation of Ephesians' 'wall of partition' to the 'wall' of Canticles 2:9. For this assimilation see, for example, *The Sermons of John Donne*, ed. Potter and Simpson, Vol. II (Berkeley and Los Angeles, 1955), pp. 108, 110–11. In *A Midsummer Night's Dream*, Hippolyta is identified with the erotic delay: C. L. Barber, in *Shakespeare's Festive Comedy* (Princeton, NJ, 1959), p. 125, provides a formulation indicative of the continuance of this gendered tradition: 'Theseus looks towards the hour with masculine impatience, Hippolyta with a woman's happy willingness to dream away the time.' The edition

used for all citations from Shakespeare is *The Riverside Shakespeare*, ed. G. Blakemore Evans (Boston, Mass., 1974).

Paster, The Body Embarrassed

1. Keith Thomas, 'The place of laughter in Tudor and Stuart England,' *TLS*, 21 January 1977, p. 80.

2. Norbert Elias, *The History of Manners* (1939), Vol. 1 of *The Civilizing Process*, trans. Edmund Jephcott (New York: Pantheon, 1978), p. 59.

3. A recent story in the *Washington Post* explores the ferocity of that silence in relation to the unavailing attempts by Johns Hopkins University Press to secure publicity for *Staying Dry: A Practical Guide to Bladder Control*, written by Kathryn L. Burgio, K. Lynette Pearce, and Angelo J. Lucco, two doctors and a nurse specializing in geriatric urology (Baltimore, 1990). None of the morning talk or news shows expressed willingness to feature the authors; none of the major book chains would feature the book until the press inserted a letter about the book in an Ann Landers column. At that point, requests for the book outpaced the press's ability to keep it in print. Urinary incontinence most affects the elderly, causing 'humiliation and anxiety in many, many people,' the *Post*'s article quotes Burgio as saying, but it also affects 'women in their forties and fifties who have had several children' (*Washington Post*, 27 September 1990, p. C1). Recently Camille Paglia has broken the taboo, praising the efficiency of male urination and its 'arc of transcendence' as a 'genre of self-expression women will never master' because they, 'like female dogs, are earthbound squatters.' See *Sexual Personae: Art and Decadence from Nefertiti to Emily Dickinson* (New Haven: Yale University Press, 1990), p. 21. Such a binarism between urinating male as culture and urinating female as nature is, I will argue, both simplistic and ahistorical.

4. On the relationship between corporeal openness and garrulousness in women, see Peter Stallybrass, 'Patriarchal territories: the body enclosed,' in *Rewriting the Renaissance: The Discourses of Sexual Difference in Early Modern Europe*, ed. Margaret W. Ferguson, Maureen Quilligan, and Nancy J. Vickers (Chicago: University of Chicago Press, 1986), pp. 123–42.

5. Julia Kristeva, *Powers of Horror: An Essay on Abjection*, trans. Leon S. Roudiez (New York: Columbia University Press, 1982), p. 70.

6. Natalie Zemon Davis, *Society and Culture in Early Modern France: Eight Essays* (Stanford: Stanford University Press, 1975), p. 126.

7. Jacques Lacan, 'The agency of the letter in the unconscious, or reason since Freud,' [1957] in *Ecrits: A Selection*, ed. and trans. Alan Sheridan (New York: Norton, 1977), p. 151.

8. Elias, *History of Manners*, p. 131.

9. Ibid., p. 58.

10. I quote from the Revels editions of Ben Jonson, *Bartholomew Fair*, ed. E. A. Horsman, and *The Alchemist*, ed. F. H. Mares (Cambridge, Mass: Harvard University Press, 1960 and 1967).

11. One might extrapolate from this evidence that the pissing alleys we know to have been numerous in London may have been frequented only or primarily by men. Thanks are due here to Peter Blayney, not only for his rediscovery of Pissing Alley behind the bookshops of Paternoster Row but for the benefit of countless conversations on this lowly archaeological topic.

12. Jonathan Haynes, 'Festivity and the dramatic economy of Jonson's *Bartholomew Fair*,' *ELH* 51 (1984), 647.

13. See Ian Maclean, *The Renaissance Notion of Woman: A Study in the Fortunes of Scholasticism and Medical Science in European Intellectual Life* (Cambridge: Cambridge University Press, 1980), pp. 2–4 and passim.

14. See James T. Henke, *Gutter Life and Language in the Early 'Street' Literature of England: A Glossary of Terms and Topics Chiefly of the Sixteenth and Seventeenth Centuries* (West Cornwall, Conn.: Locust Hill Press, 1988), sub *pissing after copulation*, p. 192; also E. J. Burford, *Bawds and Lodgings: A History of the London Bankside Brothels, c. 100–1675* (London: Owen, 1976), p. 173. Interestingly, in connection with *Bartholomew Fair*, which takes place at the fair in

August, Henke also cites the phrase, 'as wholesome as a whore in dog-days,' as quasi-proverbial (p. 286).

15. Audrey Eccles, *Obstetrics and Gynaecology in Tudor and Stuart England* (Kent, Ohio: Kent State University Press, 1982), p. 64.

16. See Stallybrass on the contrasting signs of the chaste woman—silence, the closed mouth—and the whore—'her linguistic "fullness" ' and her open mouth—in 'Patriarchal territories,' pp. 126–7.

17. Ambroise Paré, *The Workes of that Famous Chirurgion Ambroise Parey*, trans. Thomas Johnson (London, 1634; STC 19189), p. 947, quoted in Patricia Crawford, 'Attitudes to menstruation in seventeenth-century England,' *Past and Present* 91 (1981), 51.

18. Eccles, *Obstetrics and Gynaecology*, p. 52.

19. Morris Palmer Tilley, *A Dictionary of Proverbs in England in the Sixteenth and Seventeenth Centuries* (Ann Arbor: University of Michigan Press, 1950), G443, p. 237. Empirical interest in women's tears has not flagged, if the evidence of a 1987 Ann Landers column is any indication. Landers reprints a scientific report, submitted by a reader, that claims to prove a hormonal basis for women's teariness: 'Research has shown that the hormone prolactin, which stimulates lactation, also stimulates the tear glands. Women have 60% more prolactin in their blood than men do. It is Frey's theory that weeping is the body's way of excreting substances produced by the body in response to stress.' See *Washington Post*, 31 October 1987, p. D16.

20. John Fletcher, *The Differences, Causes, and Judgements of Urine* (London, 1623; STC 11063), p. 8.

21. Ibid., p. 107.

22. On the historical context for this controversy, see Harold J. Cook, *The Decline of the Old Medical Regime in Stuart London* (Ithaca: Cornell University Press, 1986), chap. 1. Heywood's *Wise Woman of Hogsdon* contains a scene of uromancy (2.1.7–21), in which the wise woman pretends to find in a country wife's urine the symptoms she draws from the woman's simple husband in conversation. See *The Dramatic Works of Thomas Heywood*, Vol. 5 (London: Russell, 1964), p. 292. This scene is quoted and the play discussed by Jean E. Howard in 'Scripts and/versus playhouses: ideological production and the Renaissance public stage,' *Renaissance Drama* n.s. 20 (1989), 41–7.

23. I quote from *The Seeing of Urines* (London, 1562; STC 22161), sigs. Ai^v–Aiii^r; but the colors are repeated virtually verbatim in the other vernacular treatises on urine.

24. Dorothy McLaren, 'Marital fertility and lactation, 1570–1720,' in *Women in English Society, 1500–1800*, ed. Mary Prior (London: Methuen, 1985), p. 46.

25. Joubert, *Popular Errors*, trans. and ed. Gregory David de Rocher (Tuscaloosa: University of Alabama Press, 1989), p. 188.

26. See Eccles, *Obstetrics and Gynaecology*, p. 53, for several references to this belief. Here she is paraphrasing Ambroise Paré.

27. Michael MacDonald cites one such case in *Mystical Bedlam: Madness, Anxiety, and Healing in Seventeenth-Century England* (Cambridge: Cambridge University Press, 1981), p. 273n.

28. Tilley, *Dictionary of the Proverbs*, W667, p. 744.

29. Peter Burke, *Popular Culture in Early Modern Europe* (London: Temple Smith, 1978), pp. 191–9.

Montrose, The work of gender

1. Michel de Certeau, *Writing of History* (New York: Columbia University Press, 1988), xxv–xxvi.

Barbour, Britain and the Great Beyond

1. C. H. Herford and Percy and Evelyn Simpson (eds.), *Ben Jonson* (Oxford: Clarendon Press, 1925–52), 10: 448.

2. Herford and Simpson, *Ben Jonson*, 10: 449. [. . .] Lynda Boose, ' "The getting of a lawful race": racial discourse in early modern England and the unrepresentable black woman', in Margo Hendricks and Patricia Parker (eds.), *Women, 'Race,' and Writing in the Early Modern Period* (London and New York: Routledge, 1994), pp. 35–54, 46.

Stallybrass, Transvestism and the body beneath

1. My account of fetishism is deeply indebted to Marjorie Garber, 'Fetish envy', paper given at the Modern Languages Association, New Orleans in 1989. See also her fine, wide-ranging study, *Vested Interests: Cross-dressing and Cultural Anxiety* (New York and London: Routledge, 1991).

Traub, Renaissance of Lesbianism

1. I explore the relations between anatomy, travel narration, and cartography in constructing a normative body in 'Gendering mortality in early modern anatomies,' in *Feminist Readings of Early Modern Culture*, ed. Valerie Traub, Lindsay Kaplan, and Dympna Callaghan (Cambridge: Cambridge University Press, 1996) pp. 44–92, and 'Mapping the global body,' in *Early Modern Visual Culture*, ed. Peter Erickson and Clark Hulse (Philadelphia: University of Pennsylvania Press, 2000), pp. 44–92. Anthony Pagden, *European Encounters with the New World: From Renaissance to Romanticism* (New Haven: Yale University Press, 1993), provides a provocative account of the way in which tropes of 'discovery' govern early modern science and, by implication, link anatomy to travel narratives: 'The discoverer carries out with him his lexicon of names, his repertoire of classifications, his knowledge of the invisible isolines and parallels which link him to home. He returns with samples, exhibits, slaves. This itinerary, which is always invariable, is, as Descartes may have been the first to recognize, the same "journey" which every scientist must make,' pp. 30–1. Patricia Parker links anatomies and travel narratives, provocatively reading Renaissance discourses of the body through the racialized discourse of colonialism in 'Fantasies of "race" and "gender": Africa, *Othello*, and bringing to light,' in *Women, 'Race' & Writing in the Early Modern Period*, eds. Margo Hendricks and Patricia Parker (London: Routledge, 1994), pp. 84–100.

2. The generic instability of both anatomy and travel writing is worth underscoring. What Mary Campbell, *The Witness and the Other World: Exotic European Travel Writing, 400–1600* (Ithaca, NY: Cornell University Press, 1988), says of early travel literature is equally true of early anatomy: 'Knowledge was scarce, reverenced, and largely inseparable from the particular texts that transmitted it. At the same time, texts themselves were fluid: plagiarized, misquoted, mistranslated, interpolated upon, bowdlerized, epitomized, transformed, and transformable at every stage of their complex dissemination' (p. 140).

3. In this respect, Greenblatt's question, 'What is the origin of boundaries that enable us to speak of "within" and "without"?' is crucial. See his meditation on the early modern construction of such boundaries, *Marvelous Possessions: The Wonder of the New World* (Chicago: University of Chicago Press, 1991), p. 121. Margaret Hodgen, *Early Anthropology in the Sixteenth and Seventeenth Centuries* (Philadelphia: University of Pennsylvania Press, 1964), describes cosmographers and compilers of travel narrators thus: 'they were all in some degree geographers, absorbed in the minutiae of the distribution of man and his cultures on every continent and island of the world. All were conners of maps, disposed to think of the array of strange rituals, creeds, and theologies in spatial terms; as associated with certain already located peoples; as distributed geographically' (p. 218).

4. Denise Albanese, *New Science, New World* (Durham, NC: Duke University Press, 1996).

5. As Louis Montrose has noted, the identification of territory with the female virginal body provided explorers of the New World powerful justifications for their right to conquer and subject native inhabitants, while simultaneously providing an image of one's own nation as inviolable; see 'The work of gender in the discourse of discovery,' *Representations* 33 (1991): 1–41. Likewise, in *Sodometries*, Goldberg shows how the discourse of sodomy could be manipulated to rationalize European ascriptions of bestiality onto South American tribes, while occluding the very desires that constitute the colonial imaginary.

6. Kim F. Hall, *Things of Darkness: Economies of Racial Difference in Early Modern England* (Ithaca, NY: Cornell University Press, 1995).

7. The Western fascination with the seraglio is explained by Mohja Kahf, in *Western Representations of the Muslim Woman: From Termagant to Odalisque* (Austin: University of Texas Press, 1999), as a historically specific phenomenon linked to political, socio-economic, and cultural developments in the seventeenth century such as discourses of monarchical absolutism and the emergence of a division between public and private spheres.

8. Jane Sharp, *The Midwives Book, or the Whole Art of Midwifry Discovered* (London, 1671), p. 45.

9. Ibid.

10. Helkiah Crooke, *Microcosmographia: A Description of the Body of Man* (London, 1615), p. 238. In 1610, Jacques Ferrand, *Laurie Maladie d'amour, ou mélancholie érotique* (The Disease of Love, or Erotic Melancholy), trans. as *A Treatise on Lovesickness* (1610/1623), ed. Donald A. Beecher and Massimo Ciavolella (Syracuse, NY: Syracuse University Press, 1990), similarly asserted that the clitoris could be enlarged through passion and that it is 'known to many other women who unhappily abuse this part called *fricatrices* by the Latins, *tribades* by the Greeks and *ribaudes* by the French—among whom Sudas and Muret place the learned Sappho' (pp. 230–1).

11. This translation of Falloppia's Paris edition of 1562 is that of Harriette Andreadis, 'Sappho in Early Modern England,' p. 114. The first edition of *Observationes anatomicae* was published in Venice in 1561.

12. André Du Laurens (Andreas Laurentius), *Historia anatomica humani corporis et singularum eius partium multis* (Paris: 1595); translated by Andreadis, 'Sappho in Early Modern England,' pp. 114–15.

13. Cited by Katharine Park, 'The Rediscovery of the Clitoris: French Medicine and the Tribade, 1570–1620', in *The Body in Parts*: *Fantasies of Corporeality in Early Modern Europe*, ed. D. Hillman and C. Mazzio (New York and London: Routledge, 1997), pp. 171–93, p. 175.

14. Ibid., p. 176.

15. Mary Campbell, *The Witness and the Other World: Exotic European Travel Writing, 400–1600* (Ithaca, NY: Cornell University Press, 1988), p. 8.

16. Ibid., p. 71.

17. Ibid., p. 249.

18. [R]eferences to the tribade (drawn from Leo Africanus) added to the second edition of Ambroise Paré's *Des Monstres et Prodiges* (1575) were excised from the third edition (1579) due to harassment by the Faculty of Medicine. Paré was forced to replace his discussion of Leo Africanus with a much briefer citation about a recent sodomy conviction of two women set down by the jurist Jean Papon; eventually he removed the entire passage about female genitalia (*Des Monstres et Prodiges*, ed. Jean Céard, Geneva: Droz, 1971, pp. 162–3). Park notes that Paré 'had reassured his critics in the Faculty of Medicine that the deformity that allowed a woman to have sex with another woman was extremely rare—so much so, he wrote, "that for every woman that has it, there are ten thousand who don't." His successors had no such consolation' ('The Rediscovery of the Clitoris,' p. 178). Paré's original discussion of genital enlargement concerns the labia, not the clitoris: 'The Greeks call them nimphes, which hang and, in some women, fall outside the neck of the womb; and they lengthen and shorten like the comb of a turkey cock, principally when they desire coitus, and, when their husbands want to approach them, they grow erect like the male rod, so much that they can take pleasure from them, with other women.' (Translation of Céard's edition provided by Adriane Stewart.)

19. Although medieval accounts of marvels regularly feature various monsters and amazons, none list tribades in their classifications. See John Block Friedman, *The Monstrous Races in Medieval Art and Thought* (Cambridge, MA and London: Harvard University Press, 1981); and Lorraine Daston and Katharine Park, *Wonders and the Order of Nature, 1150–1750* (New York: Zone Books, 1998).

20. Friar Ludovico Maria Sinistrari, *De Delictis et Poenis* (1700), trans. as *Peccatum Mutum* (The Secret Sin), ed. M. Summers (Paris: 1958), items 17 and 18, pp. 43 and 45.

21. In his first edition of *Des Monstres et Prodiges*, Paré describes labial excision as a remedy to

women's abuse with other women: 'Thus they make them very shameful and deformed being seen naked, and with such women one must tie and cut that which is superfluous, because they can misuse them, giving that the surgeon is careful not to cut too deeply for fear of a great flow of blood, or of cutting the neck of the bladder, for then afterward they will not be able to pass urine, but it would trickle out drop by drop.' (Translated of Céard's edition by Adriane Stewart.) After this passage he refers to the 'memorable story drawn from the *History of Africa*.' Likewise, Crooke (who did recognize a difference between the clitoris and labia) discusses labial (but not clitoral) amputation:

Sometimes, they grow to so great a length on one side, more rarely on both; and not so ordinarily in maidens as in women . . . what through the affluence of humours, what through attrectation, that for the trouble and shame (being in many Countryes a notable argument of petulancie & immodesty) they neede the Chirurgions helpe to cut them off (although they bleed much and are hardly cicatrised) especially among the Egyptians, amongst whom this accident (as Galen saith) is very familiar. Wherefore in Maidens before they grow too long they cut them off, and before they marry.

This passage is printed with the marginal gloss: 'The Egyptian women lascivious' (*Microcosmographia*, p. 237).

22. The entire passage from *The Fourth Book of Practical Physick* (London: 1662) reads:

The *Aloe* or wings in the privities of a woman, are of soft spongy flesh, like a Cocks-comb in shape and colour; the part at the top is hard and nervous, and swells like a Yard in Venery, with much Spirit. This part sometimes is as big as a mans Yard, and such women were thought to be turned into men.
It is from too much nourishment of the part, from the loosness of it by often handling.
It is not safe to cut it off presently: but first use driers and discussers, with things that a little astringe; then gentle Causticks without causing pain, as burnt Allum, Ægyptiacum.
Take *Ægyptiacum, Oyl of Mastich, Roses, Wax, each half an ounce.* If these will not do, then cut it off, or tie it with a Ligature of Silk or Horse-hair, till it mortifie.
Ætitus teacheth the way of amputation, he cals it the *Nympha* or *Clitoris*, between both the wings: but take heed you cause not pain or inflammation. After cutting, wash with Wine, with Myrtles, Bays, Roses, Pomegranate flowers boyled in it, and Cypress-nuts, and lay on an astringent Pouder.
Some excrescenses grow like a tail, and fill the privities: they differ from a Clitoris: for the desire of Venery is increased in that, and the rubbing of the cloaths upon it, cause lust, but in an Excrescence of flesh, they cannot for pain endure copulation, but you may cut off this better than a Clitoris, because it is all superfluous. (pp. 3–4)

According to the *OED*, a 'discusser' is a medicine that disperses humors.

23. E. B., *The Chyrurgeons Store-house* (London: 1674), a translation of Johannes Scultetus, *Wundarztneyishes Zeughaufs* (Frankfurt: 1655 and 1666). The illustration of Figure 1 of Table XLI (p. 194) 'teacheth how *Hierom. Fabritius ab Aquapendente*, with an instrument made for a Polypus, cuts off the unprofitable increasing of a Clitoris, which is a common disease amongst the Ægyptians and Arabians. A shews the Clitoris laied hold of with the pincers: B shews the body of the Clitoris cut off, and placed beyond the pincers' (p. 195).

24. In *Making Sex*, Laqueur argues that clitoridectomy was neither advocated nor practiced in England until the eighteenth century. This view is contradicted at the level of advice, if not at the level of surgical practice, by Paré, Bartholin, and Culpeper. The historical and ideological relationship between ritual circumcision and Western surgical practices is confused. Western genital amputation is not identical to culturally sanctioned ritual circumcision. But many Western authors use ritual practices to authorize their descriptions of tribades and the need for surgery, and such surgery would attempt to achieve some of the same ends: forcibly imposing, and thereby affirming, cultural sameness, constancy, and homogeneity.

25. Historicizing the production of anatomical essentialism provides a means of challenging modern regimes of identity formation which demand that people 'choose' one of only two

erotic 'orientations' or seek to find the origin of such 'choices' in biology. Indeed, the historical development of anatomical essentialism provides a perspective from which to view the current debate over genetic origins of homosexuality. That such debates do have a history seems to me to help dispel utopian visions of redemption through biology (whether figured through a belief that an appeal to genetics will herald an end to homophobia or an end to homosexuals). Rather than authorizing modern quests for a 'gay gene,' early modern anatomies provide a cautionary tale: insofar as the 'cure' of clitoral hypertrophy was genital mutilation, and the punishment for tribadism (at least in some countries) was burning at the stake, the discourse of anatomy sounds from the distance of centuries a warning about the liberatory promises of bio-genetics.

26. For sophisticated readings of this problem, see Jonathan Goldberg's Introduction and Margaret Hunt's Afterword to Goldberg (ed.), *Queering the Renaissance*. As Hunt points out, the definition of the 'subject' has hardly been available to women on the same terms that it has been to men.

27. I would argue that the psychomorphology of the tribade has more in common with current discourses of transgender and intersexuality than with butch affect and style. For the relationship between transgender and butch affect, see Halberstam, *Female Masculinities*. On intersexuality, see Anne Fausto-Sterling, *Myths of Gender: Biological Theories about Women and Men* (New York: Basic Books, 1985); and Alice Domurat Dreger, *Hermaphrodites and the Medical Invention of Sex* (Cambridge, MA and London: Harvard University Press, 1998), and ed., *Intersex in the Age of Ethics* (Hagerstown, MD: University Publishing Group, 1999). See also Sandy Stone, 'The Empire strikes back: a posttranssexual manifesto,' in Epstein and Straub (eds.), *Bodyguards*, pp. 280–304; and Julia Epstein, 'Either/Or—Neither/Both: sexual ambiguity and the ideology of gender,' *Genders* 7 (1990): 99–142.

28. The need to reassert the pleasures of the vagina and penetration is advocated by Jane Gallop in *Thinking Through the Body* (New York: Columbia University Press, 1988).

29. Paula Bennett, 'Critical clitoridectomy: female sexual imagery and feminist psychoanalytic theory,' *Signs: Journal of Women in Culture and Society* 18 (1993): 235–59; citation pp. 256–7.

30. Cotgrave, *A Dictionary of the French and English Tongues* (1611).

31. Andrea Dworkin, *Intercourse* (New York: Macmillan, 1987); Catharine MacKinnon, *Feminism Unmodified: Discourses on Life and Law* (Cambridge and London: Harvard University Press, 1987).

32. Rich, 'Compulsory heterosexuality and lesbian existence'; Audre Lorde, 'Uses of the erotic: the erotic as power,' in *Sister Outsider* (New York: Crossing Press, 1984), pp. 53–9.

33. Vanita, *Sappho and the Virgin Mary: Same-Sex Love and the English Literary Imagination* (New York: Columbia University Press, 1996).

34. Luce Irigaray, *This Sex Which Is Not One*, trans. C. Porter and C. Burke (Ithaca: Cornell University Press, 1985), p. 28. See also *Speculum of the Other Woman*, trans. Gillian G. Gill (Ithaca, NY: Cornell University Press, 1985).

35. Irigaray, *This Sex Which Is Not One*, p. 90.

36. Critiques of Irigaray are legion, for the essentialism with which she was associated comprised a crucible for feminist theory in the 1980s. For two early influential critiques of Irigaray's essentialism, see Ann Rosalind Jones, 'Writing the body: toward an understanding of *l'Écriture féminine*,' in *The New Feminist Criticism: Essays on Women, Literature, and Theory*, ed. Elaine Showalter (New York: Pantheon, 1985), pp. 361–77; and Toril Moi, *Sexual/Textual Politics: Feminist Literary Theory* (London and New York: Methuen, 1985).

37. Diana Fuss, *Essentially Speaking: Feminism, Nature, and Difference* (London: Routledge, 1989). Fuss's reassessment of essentialism as a strategy that one risks in order to advance certain political claims, as well as her analysis of the mutually implicated dynamic between essentialism and anti-essentialism, are helpful in reading Irigaray. Jane Gallop, 'Lip Service,' in *Thinking Through the Body* (New York: Columbia University Press, 1985), pp. 92–9, is particularly good at demonstrating how Irigaray's *poiesis* of female sexuality 'is always

figurative, can never be simply taken as the thing itself' (p. 98). For defenses of Irigaray, see Margaret Whitford, *Luce Irigaray: Philosophy in the Feminine* (New York: Routledge, 1991); and Carolyn Burke, Naomi Schor, and Margaret Whitford (eds.), *Engaging With Irigaray: Feminist Philosophy and Modern European Thought* (New York: Columbia University Press, 1994), particularly Carolyn Burke, 'Irigaray Through the Looking Glass' (pp. 37–56), and Naomi Schor, 'This essentialism which is not one: coming to grips with Irigaray' (pp. 57–78).

38. Gallop, *Thinking Through the Body*, p. 96, emphasis mine.

39. Irigaray, *This Sex Which Is Not One*, p. 24.

40. Ibid., p. 218.

41. This is the basis of an important critique by Annamarie Jagose, 'Irigaray and the lesbian body: remedy and poison,' *Genders* 13 (1992): 30–42, who argues that Irigaray problematically relies 'on a concept of *exteriority* . . . *as the very condition of female homosexuality*' (p. 33). According to Jagose, Irigaray's construction of femininity is even more insidious than this, for its ultimate goal is not the elaboration of a *lesbian* politics, but a 'renegotiation of an emancipated heterosexuality across the repressed and unrepresentable body of the female homosexual' (p. 38). In 'The hetero and the homo: the sexual ethics of Luce Irigaray,' in *Engaging With Irigaray*, pp. 335–50, Elizabeth Grosz offers a more generous reading of Irigaray's advocacy of a '*tactical homosexuality* modeled on the corporeal relations of the preoedipal daughter to her mother' (p. 338); what is crucial is Irigaray's commitment to '*the right to choose for oneself*' (p. 339). Grosz thus deems Irigaray less a *lesbian* theorist—a position which Grosz seems to equate with a prescriptive morality—than someone maintaining a critical difference 'from all existing modes of sexual relation' (p. 335).

42. On feminist heterosexuality, see Joan Cocks, 'Power, desire, and the meaning of the body,' in *The Oppositional Imagination: Feminism, Critique, and Political Theory* (London and New York: Routledge, 1989). Investigating feminist alternatives to a wholesale condemnation of heterosexual relationships, Cocks demonstrates the lack of fit between subjective desire and ideology, and imagines a range of possible subject and power positions within sexual relations.

43. I would argue that it is her reliance on metonymy that authorizes Irigaray's by now notoriously problematic conflation of male homosexuality and male patriarchal homosociality as 'an economy of the same' in her coinage 'hom(m)osexuality.' See Fuss, *Essentially Speaking*, p. 111; Jagose, 'Irigaray and the lesbian body,' pp. 36–7; and Craig Owens, 'Outlaws: gay men in feminism,' in *Men in Feminism*, eds. Alice Jardine and Paul Smith (London and New York: Routledge, 1987), pp. 219–32.

44. My thinking about legitimation as a metanarrative has been enhanced by Roof's 'Lesbians and Lyotard: legitimation and the politics of the name,' in Doan (ed.), *The Lesbian Postmodern*, pp. 47–66.

45. Interestingly, Fuss praises Irigaray's logic of metonymy because it displaces conventional linguistic hierarchies that privilege metaphor over metonymy. While I agree that metonymy might, at certain historical moments, have some advantages over metaphor, it is not clear to me that this has been the case historically with the *lesbian* body.

46. Judith Butler, *Bodies that Matter: On the Discursive Limits of Sex* (London and New York: Routledge, 1993), p. xi.

47. Ibid., p. 14.

48. Ibid., p. 81.

49. See, in addition to Irigaray and Butler, Judith Roof, *The Lure of Knowledge: Lesbian Sexuality and Theory* (New York: Columbia University Press, 1991); and Fuss, *Identification Papers* (New York and London: Routledge, 1995).

de Grazia, Quilligan, Stallybrass (eds.), Subject and Object

1. For a discussion of the still-life's 'assault on the prestige of the human subject,' see Norman Bryson, *Looking at the Overlooked: Four Essays on Still Life Painting* (Cambridge, Mass., 1990), p. 61.

2. Bryson discusses the inherently contradictory nature of the *vanitas* still-life, ibid. p. 115.

3. See, for example, David Bailly's 'Still Life,' which includes reproductions of Bailly's own paintings, as well as a self-portrait and personal memorabilia, discussed by Svetlana Alpers, *The Art of Describing: Dutch Art in the Seventeenth Century* (Chicago, 1983), pp. 106–7, color plate 1.

4. Recent exceptions include: Patricia Fumerton, *Cultural Aesthetics: Renaissance Literature and the Practice of Social Ornament* (Chicago and London, 1991); Douglas Bruster, *Drama and the Market in the Age of Shakespeare* (Cambridge, 1992); and Jeffrey Knapp, *An Empire Nowhere: England, America, and Literature from 'Utopia' to 'The Tempest'* (Berkeley, 1992).

5. For a wide-ranging list of Renaissance self-reflexives, see William Kerrigan and Gordon Braden, *The Idea of the Renaissance* (Baltimore and London, 1989), pp. 221–2, n.20. For Montaigne's reflexivity, see Terence Cave, *The Cornucopian Text: Problems of Writing in the French Renaissance* (New York, 1979), p. 274.

6. For Hegel's account, see *Phenomenology of Spirit*, trans. A. V. Miller (Oxford, New York, Toronto, Melbourne, 1977), pp. 111–19.

7. 2 vols., trans. S. G. C. Middlemore (New York, 1959), vol. I, p. 39.

8. Ibid., vol. I, p. 143.

9. On Burckhardt's emphatically male gendering of this individual, see the Introduction to Margaret W. Ferguson, Maureen Quilligan, and Nancy J. Vickers (eds.), *Rewriting the Renaissance: The Discourses of Sexual Difference in Early Modern Europe* (Chicago and London, 1986), p. xv.

10. *The Individual and the Cosmos in Renaissance Philosophy*, trans. Mario Domandi (New York, 1963). See also Kerrigan and Braden, *The Idea of the Renaissance*, pp. 73–81.

11. *Capital*, vol. I, ch. 1, 'Commodities,' in *The Marx-Engels Reader*, ed. Robert C. Tucker (2nd edn, New York and London, 1978), pp. 302–29.

12. For a Marxist extension of Hegel's dialectic, see Alexandre Kojève, *Introduction to the Reading of Hegel*, ed. Allan Bloom, trans. James H. Nichols, Jr. (Ithaca and London, 1980), ch. 1, pp. 3–30.

13. *On James Mill*, in *Karl Marx: Selected Writings*, ed. David McLellan, (Oxford, 1977), pp. 114–23.

14. 'An unobjective being is a *nullity*—an *un-being*,' Marx, *Economic and Philosophic Manuscripts of 1844*, in *Reader*, p. 116.

15. Ibid., p. 115.

16. Ibid., p. 116. For another account of the intimate relation between subject and object, maker and artifact, see Elaine Scarry, 'The interior structure of the artifact,' in her *The Body in Pain: The Making and Unmaking of the World* (New York and Oxford, 1985), pp. 278–326. For Scarry, however, subjects are necessarily prior to objects, for it is through artifacts that the body extends and projects itself.

17. Felix Gilbert has counted some thirty passages in which Burckhardt identifies the Renaissance with the 'modern age,' the Renaissance individual with 'modern man.' *History: Politics or Culture? Reflections on Ranke and Burckhardt* (Princeton, 1990), p. 61.

18. Michael Foucault, *The Archaeology of Knowledge and The Discourse on Language*, trans. A. M. Sheridan (New York, 1972), p. 12.

Harris, Shakespeare's hair

1. All quotations from Shakespeare's works follow *The Riverside Shakespeare*, ed. G. Blakemore Evans et al., 2nd edn (Boston: Houghton Mifflin, 1997).

2. See Margreta de Grazia, Maureen Quilligan, and Peter Stallybrass (eds.), *Subject and Object in Renaissance Culture* (Cambridge: Cambridge UP, 1996); and Patricia Fumerton and Simon Hunt (eds.), *Renaissance Culture and the Everyday* (Philadelphia: U of Pennsylvania P, 1999). Two other studies that attend specifically to early modern material culture are Lisa Jardine, *Worldly Goods: A New History of the Renaissance* (New York: Nan A. Talese, 1996); and Lena Cowen Orlin (ed.), *Material London, ca. 1600* (Philadelphia: U of Pennsylvania P, 2000). For a powerful critique of such studies' understanding of the 'material,' see Douglas Bruster, 'The

new materialism in Renaissance Studies' in *Material Culture and Cultural Materialism in the Middle Ages and the Renaissance*, ed. Curtis Perry (Turnhout, Belgium: Brepols, 2000), 220–38. For a useful overview of critical approaches to twentieth-century material culture, see Tim Dant, *Material Culture in the Social World: Values, Activities, Lifestyles* (Buckingham, UK: Open UP, 1999). The recent scholarly turn to objects has attracted attention even from the mainstream US press; see Emily Eakins, 'Screwdriver scholars and pencil punditry,' *The New York Times*, 24 February 2001, pp. B7 and B9. In referring to 'wonder-cabinets,' I am alluding, of course, to Steven Mullaney's discussion of the *Wunderkammer*, or wonder-cabinet, in *The Place of the Stage: License, Play, and Power in Renaissance England* (Chicago: University of Chicago Press, 1988). I analyze how Mullaney's account of the wonder-cabinet resonates with Renaissance historicism's epistemology of the object in 'The new new historicism's *Wunderkammer* of objects,' *European Journal of English Studies* 4 (2000), 125–39.

3. Hugh Grady, *Shakespeare's Universal Wolf: Studies in Early Modern Reification* (Oxford: Clarendon Press, 1996), 24.

4. 'Shakespeare's Hair,' Folger Art Cabinet No. 2. The inscriptions on the card have been transcribed for me by Heather Wolfe, Curator of Manuscripts at the Folger Shakespeare Library.

5. Samuel Ireland published these documents as *Miscellaneous Papers and Legal Instruments under the Hand and Seal of William Shakespeare: Including the Tragedy of King Lear, and a Small Fragment of Hamlet: from the Original Mss. in the Possession of Samuel Ireland of Norfolk Street* (London, 1796). Subsequent to Edmond Malone's exposé of Ireland *père*, William Henry Ireland accepted sole responsibility for the forgeries in *An Authentic Account of the Shakesperian Manuscripts, &c* (London, 1796). For a useful account of William Henry Ireland's career, see Paul S. Collins, *Banvard's Folly: Tales of Renowned Obscurity, Famous Anonymity, and Rotten Luck* (New York: Picador, 2001).

6. On this industry, see Ivor Brown and George Fearon, *Amazing Monument: A Short History of the Shakespeare Industry* (London and Toronto: William Heinemann, 1939); and, more recently, Graham Holderness, 'Bardolatry: or, The cultural materialist's guide to Stratford-upon-Avon' in *The Shakespeare Myth*, ed. Graham Holderness (Manchester, UK: Manchester UP, 1988), 2–15, esp. 3–5; and Tricia Lootens, *Lost Saints: Silence, Gender, and Victorian Literary Canonization* (Charlottesville and London: University Press of Virginia, 1996), esp. 1–115.

7. See Timothy Murray, 'Forging a collection: William Henry Ireland and the Shakespeare fabrications,' Special Collections Department, University of Delaware Library, http://www.lib.udel.edu/ud/spec/exhibits/forgery/ireland.htm (28 November 2001).

8. The love letter and lock of hair are in the Folger Shakespeare Library, in a specially bound volume (Folger MS W.b. 496) that interleaves pages of *Miscellaneous Papers* with William Henry Ireland's original forgeries. Bruce R. Smith discusses this document in *Roasting The Swan of Avon: Shakespeare's Redoubtable Enemies and Dubious Friends* (Washington, DC: Folger Shakespeare Library, 1984), 34–5.

9. One might recall in this context John Keat's and Leigh Hunt's awestruck responses to seeing a lock of John Milton's hair. Aaron Santesso discusses the 'inescapable material dimension' of the two poets' search for 'the "real" Milton' in his unpublished essay, 'The birth of the birthplace: Bread Street and literary tourism before Stratford.' I thank Dr Santesso for sharing a copy of his essay with me.

10. De Grazia, Quilligan, and Stallybrass (eds.), 1–13, esp. 2.

11. Aristotle, *De Anima* in *The Basic Works of Aristotle*, trans. Richard McKeon, 2 vols. (New York: Random House, 1941), 2:555; see also Henry S. Turner, 'Nashe's red herring: epistemologies of the commodity in *Lenten Stuffe*,' forthcoming in *ELH*. Through extraordinarily insightful readings of Thomas Nashe, Karl Marx, and Michel Foucault, Turner teases out a strain of Aristotelian hylomorphism in Western conceptions of the material that, in its emphasis on the discursively constituted nature of objects, contrasts with the static formalism of 'material culture.' I thank Dr Turner for sharing a copy of his paper with me in advance of its publication.

12. Karl Marx, *Writings of the Young Karl Marx on Philosophy and Society*, trans. Lloyd D. Easton and Kurt H. Guddat (New York: Doubleday, 1967), 400, emphasis added.

13. Judith Butler, *Bodies That Matter: On the Discursive Limits of Sex* (New York and London: Routledge, 1993), 31. For an excellent discussion of the temporality of matter, see Jean-François Lyotard, *The Inhuman: Reflections on Time*, trans. Geoffrey Bennington and Rachel Bowlby (Stanford, CA: Stanford UP, 1991), 8–21.

14. Arjun Appadurai, 'Introduction: commodities and the politics of value' in *The Social Life of Things: Commodities in Cultural Perspective*, ed. Arjun Appadurai (Cambridge: Cambridge UP, 1986), 3–63, esp. 34.

15. Appadurai, 5.

16. For an invaluable discussion that touches on the materiality of Troilus' sleeve, see Peter Stallybrass and Ann Rosalind Jones, 'Fetishizing the glove in Renaissance Europe,' *Critical Inquiry* 28 (2001): 114–32.

17. Perhaps Shakespeare unconsciously picks up on suppeago's etymology when he has Hector speak about the fever of emulousness that afflicts the Greek army: 'Their great general slept, / Whilst emulation in the army *crept*' (2.2.211–12, emphasis added). For a more extensive discussion of the play's pathological imagery, see my essay ' "The enterprise is sick": pathologies of value and transnationality in *Troilus and Cressida*,' *Renaissance Drama* 28 (2000): 3–37.

18. On the emergence of protomicrobiological or 'ontological' notions of disease, see Walter Pagel, *Paracelsus: An Introduction to Philosophical Medicine in the Era of the Renaissance* (Basel and New York: S. Karger, 1958), 134–40; Vivian Nutton, 'The seeds of disease: an explanation of contagion and infection from the Greeks to the Romans,' *Medical History* 27 (1983): 1–34; and Jonathan Gil Harris, *Foreign Bodies and the Body Politic: Discourses of Social Pathology in Early Modern England* (Cambridge: Cambridge UP, 1998), 22–30.

19. See Greg W. Bentley, *Shakespeare and the New Disease: The Dramatic Function of Syphilis in* Troilus and Cressida, Measure for Measure, *and* Timon of Athens (New York: Peter Lang, 1989); and Johannes Fabricius, *Syphilis in Shakespeare's England* (London and Bristol, PA: Jessica Kingsley, 1994).

20. Ruy Díaz de Isla, *Tractado contra el Mal Serpentino: que vulgarmente en España es llamado Bubas* (Seville, 1539), 180–1; English language translation here quoted from Fabricius, 6–7, esp. 7. Compare Claude Quétel, *History of Syphilis*, trans. Judith Braddock and Brian Pike (Baltimore: Johns Hopkins UP, 1990): 'the Muscovites referred to it as the Polish sickness, the Poles as the German sickness, and the Germans as the French sickness—a term of which the English also approved (*French pox*) as did the Italians. . . . The Flemish and Dutch called it "the Spanish sickness," as did the inhabitants of North-West Africa. The Portuguese called it "the Castillian sickness," whilst the Japanese and the people of the East Indies came to call it "the Portuguese sickness" ' (19).

21. Although Shakespeare's editors tend to gloss 'goose of Winchester' as 'prostitute' (Blakemore Evans, for example, notes that the phrase means 'prostitute [so called because the brothels in Southwark were under the jurisdiction of the Bishop of Winchester]' [5.10.54n]), the term had a specifically pathological application. In *The Nomenclator, or Remembrance of Adrianus Junius* (London, 1585) a 'bubo' is defined as 'a sore in the grine or yard, which if it come by lecherie, it is called a Winchester goose, or botch' (439). Similarly, John Taylor refers in his 'Praise of Cleane Linnen' to 'A Groyne Bumpe, or a Goose from *Winchester*' (*All the Workes of Iohn Taylor The Water Poet* [London, 1630], sig. Pp2ᵛ).

22. See, for example, Stephen Greenblatt's famous essay on *King Lear*, 'Shakespeare and the Exorcists' in *Shakespearean Negotiations: The Circulation of Social Energy in Renaissance England* ([Berkeley and Los Angeles, CA: U of California P, 1988], 94–128), in which he discusses the transmigration of props from the vestry to the tiring house. Some of the recent scholarship on early modern objects has been alert to this diachronic countertradition in the older new historicism; see, most notably, Peter Stallybrass, 'Worn worlds: clothes and identity on the Renaissance stage' (in de Grazia, Quilligan, and Stallybrass (eds.), 289–320), which examines the transmigrations of costumes between the institutions of the church and the theater in light of Greenblatt's essay.

23. Walter Benjamin, *The Origin of German Tragic Drama*, trans. John Osborne (London: New Left Books, 1977), passim.

24. Benjamin, 132.

25. Ben Jonson, *The Alchemist*, ed. Peter Bement (London: Methuen, 1987), 125 (4.7.71).

26. For a discussion of the skull in *Hamlet* and *The Revenger's Tragedy*, see Andrew Sofer, 'The skull on the Renaissance stage: imagination and the erotic life of props,' *English Literary Renaissance* 28 (1998): 47–75.

27. Natasha Korda, 'How many joint stools had Lady Macbeth?' in *Household Stuff: Shakespeare's Domestic Economies* (Philadelphia, U of Pennsylvania P, 2002). I thank Dr Korda for allowing me to see her manuscript in advance of its publication.

28. William Hazlitt, *A View of the English Stage; or, A Series of Dramatic Criticisms* (London: Robert Stodart, 1818), 220 and 223.

29. Benjamin, 177.

Wilson, Abel Drugger's sign

1. *The Seminar of Jacques Lacan. Book VII: The Ethics of Psychoanalysis* (1959–60), ed. J. A. Miller, trans. Dennis Porter (New York: Norton, 1992), pp. 119–21. Lacan's critique here attempts to forge a synthetic understanding of 'the Thing,' taking up the classic paradigms offered by Freud and Heidegger (whose heuristic 'thing' also takes the form of a jug, in *Poetry, Language, Thought*. trans. Albert Hofstadter [New York: Harper and Row, 1971], pp. 165–86).

2. Gary Tomlinson, 'Unlearning the Aztec *Cantares*: preliminaries to a post-colonial history,' in M. de Grazia, M. Quilligan and P. Stallybrass (eds.), *Subject and Object in Renaissance Culture* (Cambridge: Cambridge University Press, 1996), p. 261.

REFERENCES

Andreadis, Harriet, 'Sappho in early modern England', in *Re-reading Sappho: Reception and Transmission*, ed. Ellen Greene (Berkeley: University of California Press, 1996), pp. 105–21.

Doan, Laura (ed.), Robyn Wiegman (introd.), *The Lesbian Postmodern* (New York: Columbia University Press, 1994)

Epstein, J. and K. Straub (eds.), *Bodyguards: The Cultural Politics of Gender Ambiguity* (New York and London: Routledge, 1991)

Freud, Sigmund, 'Three essays on the theory of sexuality', in *On Sexuality*, trans. James Strachey, ed. James Strachey and Angela Richards (1905; Harmondsworth: Penguin, 1977), pp. 33–204.

Goldberg, Jonathan, *Sodometries: Renaissance Texts, Modern Sexualities* (Stanford: Stanford University Press, 1992)

—— (ed.), *Queering the Renaissance* (Durham, NC: Duke University Press, 1994)

Laqueur, Thomas, *Making Sex: Body and Gender from the Greeks to Freud* (Cambridge, MA, and London: Harvard University Press, 1990)

Prynne, William, *Histrio-Mastix; or, The Player Whipped* (London, 1633)

Rich, Adrienne, 'Compulsory Heterosexuality and Lesbian Existence', *Signs: Journal of Women in Culture and Society* 5 (1990), 631–60.

Shakespeare, William, *Othello*, in C. Hinman (ed.), *The First Folio of Shakespeare: The Norton Facsimile* (1623; New York: Norton, 1968)

Stubbes, Philip, *The Anatomie of Abuses*, ed. F. J. Furnivall, New Shakespere Society (1583; London: Trübner, 1877–9)

7

Values

EWAN FERNIE

Many of the insights considered in the General Introduction and represented in the preceding sections of this volume have had a profound, even devastating, effect on traditional notions of value and judgement in criticism. The deconstruction of fixed and autonomous authors and texts has deprived critics of anything solid and distinct enough to evaluate. Moreover, if everything is relative and changing, then absolute standards of literary merit and achievement—such as 'beauty' and 'truth'—no longer apply. Indeed, it has been widely recognized that, in spite of their apparent neutrality, such standards often entail oppressive politics. Elaine Hobby asserts bluntly that 'our ideas about what makes for "good writing" are connected to and help support many of the values of the "establishment": of white, heterosexual, middle-class men'.[1]

As a result of this kind of scepticism, much recent attention devoted to value in literature and criticism has taken the form of negative critique. We have seen throughout *Reconceiving the Renaissance* that literature is typically regarded in contemporary critical thought as part of the general cultural continuum. Where context has become indispensable, Coleridge's timehonoured criterion of 'organic unity' for the work of art cannot be sustained. Samuel Johnson's mimetic gold-standard of 'just representations of a general nature' fares scarcely better, since, for contemporary critics, language is an artificial and historically conditioned system, reality is seen as predominantly cultural, and generalizing is avoided as suspiciously unresponsive to context and contingency. What emerges from recent writing on issues of value is a principled hostility to the abstract standards that have enabled evaluative discriminations in the past in favour of a democratic and unprejudiced openness to cultural diversity and difference. 'Beauty', 'goodness'

---

[1] Elaine Hobby, *Virtue of Necessity: English Women's Writing 1646–1688* (London: Virago, 1988), p. 25.

and 'truth' have excluded a vast range of phenomena, which offers itself as a fresh field for current criticism.

But if the fundamentals of literary value have been discredited in this way, the question arises—why go on reading? Some critics have answered by characterizing criticism in terms of continuing warfare with the values of domination and exclusion enshrined in the traditional canon. They have successfully opened up curricula and reading-lists to writers who had previously been excluded, read canonical authors such as Shakespeare against the grain of orthodox interpretation, and cultivated a form of reading that exposes and thrives on the open 'undecidability' of texts. All this deconstructs what T. S. Eliot saw as the 'ideal order' of literary tradition. It is an oppositional mode of criticism but, as Catherine Connor has suggested, its practitioners may also be seen positively as connoisseurs of chaos, just like contemporary scientists.[2]

The political implications of assailing order are clear enough but in some Renaissance scholarship the traditional critical priority of aesthetics over politics has been explicitly reversed. Stripped of a spurious reputation for transcendent loveliness, literature is recognized as thoroughly involved in social and historical struggle, and some present-day interventions are primarily intended as political acts. Radical critics like Terence Hawkes have argued that, instead of inhering in the text, value is conferred upon it by interpretation, which is always politically interested. The business of criticism is therefore to contest conservative readings in order to further and realize the values of the Left.[3] Since political change is hard to bring about, Alan Sinfield prefers to speak below not of subversion but of dissidence and 'dissident reading', which reserves its potential for continued critique even while the current regime remains standing.

The resultant rejection or subordination of the value and distinctiveness of art has not been universally welcomed. In a notable and popular book extracted below, Jonathan Bate elegantly reformulates an essentially Keatsian notion of the 'genius of Shakespeare'. Bate's work is imbued with a liberal inclusiveness not altogether at odds with postmodern values of diversity and change, unlike Harold Bloom's more reactionary gestures (most notably in *The Western Canon* (1994) and *Shakespeare: The Invention of the Human* (1998)) which sweep away at a stroke all the reconceiving represented in this volume. The recent emergence of an edited anthology titled *The New Aestheticism* (2003) augurs better for the fusion of aesthetic and political values in developing critical thought.[4] Inspired especially by Frankfurt-school Marxist theorists such as Theodor Adorno, this book, which features chapters on Shakespeare and the Renaissance, argues that art, as an end in itself and by disclosing utopian truths, resists the omnipotence of postmodern capitalism.

---

[2] Catherine Connor, 'Postmodernism *avant la lettre*: the case of early modern Spanish drama', *Gestos* 9. 17 (1994), 43–59.

[3] See Terence Hawkes, *Meaning by Shakespeare* (London and New York: Routledge, 1992).

[4] See John J. Joughin and Simon Malpas (eds.), *The New Aestheticism* (Manchester and New York: Manchester University Press, 2003). Joughin on the aesthetic is featured below.

The resurgence of the aesthetic has usefully drawn new attention to the question of value, for one potential problem for recent Renaissance criticism is the apparent contradiction between its committed ethical and political values and its equally committed relativism. Historical and cultural relativism allow for the hope of justice in a transformed world but justice is itself an absolute which undermines this philosophy. One way out of this double-bind which has emerged from post-structuralist ethics is to recast justice not as a fixed, unchanging standard but in relative terms of responsibility to whatever is 'other'. As this anthology has already borne out, much of the critical energy of recent years can be seen as working in favour of various others: women, homosexuals, different races, etc. Michel de Certeau argues that our period more or less invented 'the Other'—as new peoples were encountered in the New World, as Catholic divided from Protestant, as Counter-Reformation mysticism testified to the sheer foreignness of God.[5] In one of the longer extracts below, writing partly under the influence of Certeau and using the discovery of the Americas as his major example, Stephen Greenblatt nominates 'wonder' as the passion of overwhelming recognition of the Other. 'Wonder' has been welcomed as offering a favourable basis for reconceiving the value of literature, although arguably it still objectifies the Other as the source of the subject's fascination and delight. The most important contemporary philosopher of difference, Jacques Derrida, argues in this volume and elsewhere that responsibility to the Other encompasses not just human others but also other times—including the past, with which historical criticism is necessarily concerned, and the future, which politically progressive critics are striving to improve. Around this idea of the Other values of openness and egalitarianism, in opposition to exclusion, established power and prejudice, have crystallized in recent debates.

But if the common denominators of emergent political, aesthetic and ethical values in recent criticism are plurality, difference and change, these values have also given rise to problems, doubts and disagreements. One concern is that the valorization of diversity in criticism, for all its radical political ambition, may be related to the commodification of ideas and the commercialization of the academy. There is also a discernible tension between the theoretical elaboration of ideas of diversity and change and a more empirical dedication to particular concrete differences and to what recalcitrantly resists transformation, which can be related to Jacques Lacan's notion of a pre-symbolic 'Real' that both underlies and under-mines culture. An embarrassment specific to Renaissance studies is that the pro-motion of diversity has resulted in the disruption of Shakespeare's domination of questions of literary value only to a limited extent, although this is also because the Bard's 'cultural capital' is such that a 'dissident reading' of him is certain to be more effective. In recent years, Slavoj Žižek and Alain Badiou have challenged postmodern pluralism by suggesting that, in spite of its progressive rhetoric, it is totalitarian, because it debars any commitment to any one thing above others,

---

[5] See Michel de Certeau, *The Certeau Reader*, ed. Graham Ward (Oxford and Malden, MA: Blackwell, 2000) and *The Possession at Loudon*, trans. Michael B. Smith (Chicago and London: University of Chicago Press, 2000).

as well as complacently conservative, because only such a commitment and a refunctioned notion of 'truth' can enable a revolutionary break with the status quo.[6] It remains to be seen how such an initiative might affect new conceptions of the Renaissance. The issue of value in Renaissance studies remains intriguingly open.

1 | Reflections on literary value

Cary Nelson, 'Against English', *Profession* 87 (1987), pp. 49–50

When a curriculum requires a course in Shakespeare but not a course in black literature, what message does it give students about black or hispanic people, what message about the cultural traditions that are valuable and those that are expendable? [. . .] What does it mean that the experiences of most of the world's peoples are obliterated in the 'humanism' of the English curriculum? As the authors of *Rewriting English* put it: 'Beneath the disinterested procedures of literary judgement and discrimination can be discerned the outlines of other, harsher words: exclusion, subordination, dispossession'.[1]

*   *   *

Kim F. Hall, 'These bastard signs of fair: literary whiteness in Shakespeare's Sonnets', in *Post-Colonial Shakespeares*, edited by Ania Loomba and Martin Orkin (London and New York: Routledge, 1998), pp. 64–84.

> More white then whitest Lillies far,
> Or Snow, or whitest Swans you are:
> More white then are the Whitest Creams,
> Or Moone-light tinselling the streames:
> More white then *Pearls* or *Juno's* thigh;
> Or *Pelops* Arme of *Yvorie*.
> True, I confesse; such Whites as these
> May me delight, not fully please:
> Till, like *Ixion's* Cloud you be
> White, warme, and soft to lye with me.
> > Robert Herrick, 'To Electra'

Whiteness is currently enjoying a certain vogue, particularly in American studies. Invigorated by Toni Morrison's call in *Playing in the Dark* to 'discover, through a close look at literary "blackness," the nature—even the cause—of literary "whiteness" ' (Morrison 1992: 9),

---

[6] See, for instance, Alain Badiou, *Ethics: An Essay on the Understanding of Evil*, trans. Peter Hallward (London and New York: Verso, 2001) and Slavoj Žižek, *The Fragile Absolute: or, Why is the Christian Legacy Worth Fighting For?* (London and New York: Verso, 2000) as well as *On Belief* (London and New York: Routledge, 2001).

scholars have been examining the ways in which an Africanist presence in the texts of American culture has been used to create white subjects. Likewise, some post-colonial theorists suggest how gender relations and cultural interactions dominated by the West are shaped by the need both to establish white hegemony and to deflect attention from whiteness as a source of power. However, despite liberal borrowing from other theoretical schools and periods, the study of whiteness *per se* has generally not been part of early modern scholarship.[1] On the one hand, there are logical reasons for this: the study of race has only belatedly reached the period and most work on whiteness in other arenas has pointed out that the most salient quality of whiteness is that it tends to be rendered invisible through being 'naturalized in dominant ideologies' (Mercer 1991). On the other hand, since neither 'race' nor white supremacy are dominant ideologies at this time, whiteness should in fact be more visible and open to analysis than it has been in early modern scholarship.[2] While not much is known about the presence of certain ethnic and religious minorities in England, one can say with some certainty and (only slightly facetiously) that England was inhabited by a large population that came to be seen as 'white' and yet we have not uncovered ways of discussing this as a factor in English identity formation. Even as scholars examine the social, political and imaginative construction of whiteness, whiteness still becomes normative so long as we assume that its viability as a racial signifier is self-evident. More bluntly, they do not address the more basic question: why is whiteness the mark of racial privilege at all?

The poem I cited above from Robert Herrick's *Hesperides* (1648) demonstrates an excess that is typical of evocations of whiteness in the period and thus is a vivid reminder that whiteness is an ubiquitous albeit little noted facet of early modern lyric and beauty culture. Through excessive comparisons the poet strains to find a 'white' that fulfills his poetic needs and desires as much as he anticipates that his beloved's body will. In this he is not alone, such idealized figures are almost always characterized by 'blondness' and sparkling whiteness (Vickers 1982: 96). For example, Imogen in Shakespeare's *Cymbeline* is white on white: a 'fresh lily, / And whiter than the sheets!' (II. ii. 15).[3] While the praise of white beauty is by no means new in the early modern period and can be seen in classical and medieval verse (Ogle 1965), I am drawing on Roland Greene's recent assertion that the 'Petrarchan subjectivity' related to lyric whiteness is an important adjunct to European colonialist practices (Greene 1995: 130–3).

Whiteness often appears in hyperbolic comparison, as seen in Herrick, and in juxtaposition with references to African blackness. For example, in *A Winter's Tale*, Florizel claims that Perdita's hand is 'As soft as dove's down and as white as it, / Or Ethiopian's tooth, or the fann'd snow that's bolted / By th' Northern blasts twice o'er' (IV. iv. 362–5). Just as it interrupts the ongoing simile, the use of 'Ethiope' 'interrupts' or perhaps energizes a poetic tradition that was increasingly being satirized. (Polixenes mockingly comments 'How prettily th' young swain seems to wash / The hand that was fair before!' (366–7)). This Africanist presence becomes a crucial part of a larger economy of whiteness in early modern England.[4] Color is one of the categories much pressured as the result of European colonialism (Greene 1995: 148) and the signs of this economy can be seen in the many 'eruptions of whiteness' that occur in early modern texts. So too, the appearance of references to African blackness suggests that the sense of whiteness is being reconfigured by England's expanding trade and colonial ambitions.

Importantly, the linkage of white/fairness with these economic practices make lyric whiteness a key component of white supremacy. The desirability and overvaluation of a seemingly abstract whiteness in conjunction with images linking blood, family and property interests then has material effects in that it upholds a system of power which increasingly licenses the exploitation of people perceived as nonwhite.

Critical practice has also tended to make early modern whiteness even more impervious to critique because most of the earliest terms employed to avoid the anachronism (or the politics) of the term 'race' all tend to refer to people of color (a phrase that also normalizes white people). The 'exotic,' the 'outsider,' the 'other' and 'the stranger' all shift attention away from the center that uses these strategies and categories to establish dominance (see Fiedler 1972; Hunter 1978).[5] Like the general focus on Africans, Indians and other non-Europeans, such discursive practices assume that 'race' somehow only accrues to minoritized peoples. More importantly, they provide no conceptual clues for thinking about whiteness as a developing identity with potentially racialized meanings. If whiteness buries itself in dominant ideologies, then theoretically at least, looking at whiteness in texts produced while those ideologies are in flux should give us a better idea of how 'race' becomes part of a social heritage.

Herrick's poem should demonstrate that Shakespeare's sonnets are not the privileged site of whiteness in the culture. However, they do seem an obvious choice for such an investigation; they have for a long time now been haunted by the specter of a possible Africanist presence (the dark lady)[6] and they begin with a recognition of a dominant sexual ideology articulated in relation to a 'fair' beauty.[7] The poetic sequence foregrounds the contrast of dark and light that Winthrop Jordan sees as a crucial pre-text for modern racial ideologies (Jordan 1968; Hall 1995).

This essay offers, first, a broader discussion of how fairness is racialized in Elizabethan culture, then, a look at the sonnets rooted in a reading of fairness as an emergent ideology of white supremacy. It will end by considering the larger question of why whiteness is such a transferable trope of privilege. My discussion of fairness rests on the assumption that the young man's beauty performs (albeit in a more muted way) as whiteness does in the dialectic described by Morrison in which 'images of blinding whiteness seem to function as both the antidote for and a meditation on the shadow that is the companion to whiteness' (Morrison 1992: 33). I have argued elsewhere that in the later sonnets the poet strives to make darkness 'fair,' thereby demonstrating his poetic prowess (Hall 1995: 66–7). However, the early young man sonnets reveal an equally difficult task—maintaining fairness as a stable and pure linguistic and social quality. This view of fairness does not have to rely on any particular narrative sequence of reading, although it does depend on certain gender assumptions (that there is a triangle featuring the poet, a young man and the dark lady). I am trying here to look merely at the workings of 'fairness,' particularly in the sonnets that urge procreation. These are the poems that, as Bruce Smith terms it, 'argue Elizabethan orthodoxy' (Smith 1991: 251) and it is in such moments that whiteness both lies hidden and produces itself.

I

Looking at white/fairness in other locations might help contextualize the sonnets even as they reveal the problems of fairness. In his 1589 *Arte of English Poesie*, George Puttenham offers as an example of *Antiphrasis* or the 'Broad floute,' the following:

Or when we deride by plaine and flat contradiction, as he that saw a dwarfe go in the streete said to his companion that walked with him: See yonder gyant: and to a Negro or woman blackemoore, in good sooth ye are a faire one . . .

(Puttenham 1589: 201)

In a larger sense the contradiction is obvious—the putative black woman is meant to be the opposite of 'fair'; however, a close look reveals that what Puttenham posits as a 'plaine and flat contradiction' is not so plain after all. Here, the 'Negro or woman blackemoore' is in a way quite concrete. We can locate this instance of an Africanist presence within a range of historical meanings associated with African peoples in England even if we disagree about its specific valences. Rhetorically, 'Negro or woman blackmoore' leaves almost no room for the customary doubt about the blackness of the 'Moores' who inhabit Elizabethan texts. Conversely, the phrase 'ye are a faire one' is frustratingly elusive—it has no 'moorings'—no specific gender or cultural connotations. It presents itself as obvious and in that sense impenetrable. Most certainly, 'faire' here relies on its primary meaning, 'beautiful,' and is meant to mock the black woman as ugly; however, its binary context also makes it a somatic reference. Even if 'complexion' and 'race' do not refer so obviously to a visual regime as they do now, whiteness becomes in such instances a term of what we know as complexion. In addition, as I note elsewhere, 'fair,' another ubiquitous term in praise of female beauty that is closely associated with white, becomes a term of referring to skin color (Hall 1994: 178–9).

Puttenham's text is an excellent example of how 'faire' can escape its racial codings in modern readings. Like 'whiteness,' it avoids particularity, and like whiteness, it is represented as 'plain,' obvious and curiously opaque. This example also shows the 'drift' that occurs in representations of whiteness: our attention is almost inevitably drawn to the Africanist presence and away from fairness/literary whiteness which is presented as normative.

Although the language of fairness is key to lyric praise throughout Europe, it becomes highly resonant when thinking more politically about Elizabethan culture. Peter Erickson succinctly reiterates a point made originally by Winthrop Jordan when he reminds us that representations of blacks and blackness in this time 'were played out against a spectacle of whiteness, most prominently figured in the cosmetically enhanced and poetically celebrated version presented by Queen Elizabeth I' (Jordan 1968: 4–11; Erickson 1993a: 517). If, as art historian Roy Strong notes, later paintings of Elizabeth reflect a certain 'imperialist, messianic' cult that presented Elizabeth as an almost magical and divine icon of England, then the fairness that was so reveled in was also a significant part of that imperial fervor (Strong 1987: 133). In the Armada and Ditchley portraits, for example, a dark/light dichotomy plays out in the background which obviously shows Elizabeth/England as key to a larger, cosmic triumph of good over evil (Strong 1986:45). As John Hodge argues, this type of dualist thinking plays a key role in racial oppression (Hodge 1990: 96). With this in mind, what may seem like a simple replay of the good/evil dichotomy is explicitly connected to Elizabeth's queenly physical presence and evocations of nation. Elizabeth herself is extremely white in these portraits, and if that whiteness reflects her virgin purity and Christian grace, it also, through association of Elizabeth with the kingdom (Strong 1987: 136), represents England as white—as powerful and favored by the forces of good and a Christian God (see Hodge 1990: 94).[8] That whiteness becomes a specific attribute of Englishness becomes more obvious in the Armada portrait, which frames Anglo-Spanish enmity within a cosmic struggle of good over evil in which Elizabeth's enhanced whiteness reigns supreme.

In another context, Richard Dyer notes how lighting works to associate certain film stars with whiteness in a way that identifies them as morally and aesthetically superior. These portraits of Elizabeth likewise make her 'the source of light,' and stress the 'intrinsic transcendent superiority of the colour white' (Dyer 1993: 2) while not grafted on to biological accounts of racial difference, this whiteness is melded onto a projection of national solidarity and superiority that portends such future associations. Although I do not have space to go into this here, this representation of fairness as a specific attribute of Elizabeth's Englishness takes place in other ways as well, most notably in the literal denigration of other 'European' cultures, such as the Irish and the Spanish, as 'black.'[9]

The examples of Puttenham and Elizabeth demonstrate how fairness and whiteness become racialized in connection with ideologies of nationhood and physical beauty. On the surface, physical beauty is the focus of the earlier sonnets. Sonnet 1 opens:

> From fairest creatures we desire increase,
> That thereby beauty's rose shall never die,
> But as the riper should by time decease
> His tender heir might bear his memory:

The young man is—at least initially—what we recognize as the 'good, the pure, the beautiful in Western aesthetics' (Mercer 1991). In her perceptive reading of the sonnets, Eve Sedgwick notes that fairness is the young man's principal attribute: 'The male who is paired with/against this female, has, at the most, one trait (if fair means beautiful here and not just coloured) and no energy' (Sedgwick 1985: 32). While looking at the juxtaposition of black and white that occurs with the introduction of the dark lady can help us think about the ways in which whiteness acquires racial overtones, we can also assess the value of fairness and its potentially racialized meanings by looking at possible threats to whiteness. At first, the procreation sonnets easily allow a modern reader to equate fairness merely with an abstracted ideal of beauty since its primary threats are old age and death, as indicated by lines such as 'That thereby beauty's rose shall never die' (1.2) or 'O carve not with thy hours my love's fair brow' (19.9).[10] However, in the later sonnets, female painting becomes a significant threat. The poet's solutions to these possible threats—reproduction and poetry itself—in different ways evoke issues of 'race' in multiple senses of the term.

If the cult of Elizabeth made a virtue of necessity by turning anxieties over the Queen's non-reproductive state into a celebration and revaluing of virgin purity and whiteness, then the opening exhortation of the sonnets: 'From fairest creatures we desire increase' (1.1) reverses that dynamic—revealing fairness as a social quality so valuable that it demands reproduction (de Grazia 1993: 44–5). The young man, like Elizabeth in the paintings I discussed earlier, is placed within a dualist framework in which he is associated with the moral force of the good. As Sedgwick notes, 'the sonnets' poetic goes to almost any length to treat the youth as a moral monolith; while the very definition of the lady seems to be doubleness and deceit' (Sedgwick 1985: 41; see also Fineman 1986: 175–7). This is most obvious in Sonnet 144:

> Two loves I have of comfort and despair,
> Which like two spirits do suggest me still;
> The better angel is a man right fair,
> The worser spirit is a woman coloured ill.

The exhortation to 'increase' in the sonnets is consonant with other Shakespearean texts that more explicitly use whiteness as a prime characteristic for identifying desirable reproductive pairings. Erickson identifies in the comedies a regime of color which uses blackness to place women outside of the social world of the plays—and hence as outside of the marital/reproductive imperatives of the genre (Erickson 1993a: 516–19). For example, in *Much Ado About Nothing*, Claudio, in recompense for his wrongs, promises to marry Leontes' niece. His promise, 'I'll hold my mind were she an Ethiope' (V. iv. 38), uses the sense that black women are outside of reproductive/social boundaries to suggest his resoluteness. So, too, the Nurse in *Titus Andronicus* inextricably links fair complexion with reproduction when she brings in Aaron's son, proclaiming: 'Here is the babe, as loathsome as a toad / Amongst the fair-fac'd breeders of our clime' (IV. ii. 66–7). Within this circulation of meanings, the conjunction of fairness with breeding in the sonnets seems more credibly racialized. In a recent essay, Margreta de Grazia likewise notes the critical avoidance of 'the ideological force' (de Grazia 1993: 44) of the sonnet's opening lines and reminds us that '*fair* is the distinguishing attribute of the dominant class' (ibid.: 45) in a way that nicely shows how class intersects with race within the troping of fairness.

Véronique Nahoum-Grappe argues that beauty becomes 'a gift, an identifying characteristic as objective as wealth or education' (Nahoum-Grappe 1993: 86). The young man's beauty has just such material force. It is a kind of currency which the poet encourages the young man to spend wisely in Sonnet 4:

> Unthrifty loveliness, why dost thou spend
> Upon thyself thy beauty's legacy?
> Nature's bequest gives nothing but doth lend,
> And being frank she lends to those are free.
> Then beauteous niggard why dost thou abuse
> The bounteous lárgesse given thee to give?
> Profitless usurer, why dost thou use
> So great a sum of sums yet canst thou not live?
> For having traffic with thyself alone,
> Thou of thyself thy sweet self dost deceive.
> Then how when nature calls thee to be gone,
> What ácceptable audit canst thou leave?
>   Thy unused beauty must be tombed with thee,
>   Which usèd lives th'executor to be.

Paradoxically, the young man is both 'unthrifty loveliness' (1) and 'beauteous niggard' (5), a liberal spender and a miser. The poem's series of repeated pairs ('Upon *thy*self *thy* beauty's legacy?' [2]; 'bounteous lárgesse *given* thee to *give*' [6]; emphasis mine) mimics the young man's self-absorption. The repetition also reinforces a paradoxical sense that, linguistically, one can both spend freely (with endless repetition) and withhold (the repetition means that no new words are being used). The opening lines, ' . . . why dost thou spend / Upon thyself thy beauty's legacy?' introduce a metaphor of inheritance which makes beauty part of a very specific economy. Despite the use of 'Profitless usurer' (7) and 'acceptable audit' (12), this is not the economy of the marketplace, but a more insular economy of inheritance based on bloodlines.

That these concerns are specific to the land-owning classes is reinforced by the many references to and images of inheritance and housekeeping in the poems (de Grazia 1993: 44–6).[11] As early as Sonnet 2, the poet introduces the argument for reproduction:

> How much more praise deserved thy beauty's use,
> If thou couldst answer, 'This fair child of mine
> Shall sum my count and make my old excuse'
> Proving his beauty by succession thine.
>
> (10–12)

Again, this reproductive argument is linked to the young man's 'thrift' which may interrupt an orderly pattern of inheritance. Maintaining an estate that demonstrates one's class status and producing a male heir who does likewise are of particular concern to the gentry for whom 'the individual is seen as standing at the apex of a double helix intertwining land and blood' (Heal and Holmes 1994: 22; see also Stone and Stone 1984).[12] Sonnet 3 gives us an inkling of this, as well as some insight into gender concerns when the poet proclaims, 'For where is she so fair whose uneared womb / Disdains the tillage of thy husbandry?' (5–6). Thomas Greene notes that in this line

> an ad hoc meaning 'marriage' joins the traditional meanings of 'thrift' and 'estate management' in the word 'husband' and again when the word is picked up in Sonnet 13, 'Who lets so fair a house fall to decay / Which husbandry in honor might uphold'
>
> (Greene 1995: 22)

In both of these poems, the accusation 'of a dereliction of those responsibilities incumbent on the landowning class', is accomplished with the joining of 'fair' with management/ marriage. Thus 'fair house' refers both to the young man's body and to his family line which must be perpetuated in a kind of masculine perfection (Greene 1995: 232; de Grazia 1993: 45).[13]

Greene's astute analysis also leaves room to question the relationship between early modern definitions of the word 'race,' and a color politics which might resemble more modern racial attitudes rooted in presumably inherited physical and 'cultural' characteristics. In articulating the dominant class's interest in property and inheritance, the earlier poems link the young man to 'race' in its more dominant usage in the period. As Tessie Liu notes, 'The *OED* makes clear that ideas about descent, blood ties, or common substance are basic to the notion of "race." It is striking that "house," "family," and "kindred" are synonyms for race' (Liu 1995: 565; see also Hendricks 1992: 183–5). This period of obsessive concern over the legitimacy and continuation of elite status (Stone and Stone 1984: 7) combined with the poem's insistence that physical appearance, termed as beauty or fairness, significantly marks that status, suggests that this older usage of race has a visual component as well.

Whiteness and tropings of color may be in fact what links these two equally virulent forms of 'race.' Sara Matthews Grieco notes that the white aesthetic was class-based as well as gendered:

> White was the color associated with purity, chastity, and femininity. It was the color of the 'female' heavenly body, the moon, as distinct from the more vibrant hues of the 'masculine' sun. A white complexion was also the privilege of the leisured city dweller as distinct from the sunburnt skin of the peasant.
>
> (Grieco 1993: 62)

Just as the idea of 'sunburnt skin' comes to have racial overtones during English colonization (see Hall 1995: 92–106), 'color' itself is 'one of the most semantically weighted categories in European writing about the New World' (Greene 1995: 148) and whiteness acquires such resonance when non-aristocratic European men begin defining themselves as 'white' against those they perceive as tawny or black. In doing so, they borrow a semantic distinction that already invests them with entitlement. What began as a visible sign of class—particularly of leisure and ownership of property—is a crucial precondition for whiteness as a mark of racial privilege when it later in America becomes a compensatory measure that designated and linked property-owners with those 'free' men who could not be made property (Dubois 1977: 700–1; Roediger 1991: 55–60; Allen 1994: 21).

Jonathan Goldberg points out the necessary masculinity of the young man's beauty: 'the young man who seems to have a patent on beauty that the sonneteer cannot imagine located anywhere but in him and a progeny of young men who will duplicate and keep forever in circulation his unmatchable beauty' (Goldberg 1994: 224). It is an interesting observation given Grieco's argument that whiteness is usually marked on the bodies of aristocratic women: she suggests that in Renaissance paintings men were consistently given a 'darker, more "virile" complexion': 'White was more feminine, more delicate, more beautiful. Dark was more robust, more masculine, more tenebrous' (Grieco 1993: 62). If Grieco is correct, then the reversal of that dynamic in the sonnets—the marking of fairness on the male body—is worth further attention as it contributes to a certain gender ambiguity that I will comment upon later. Male fairness may also be consistent with the need for the aristocracy to reproduce itself; the idea of the young man's self-reproduction evokes the scientifically outmoded but still ideologically useful Aristotelian trope of reproduction in which men transmit the most important heritable characteristics (here including 'fairness' / skin color) and women's 'uneared womb[s]' (3:5) are merely vessels for male seed. In the sonnets, this dynamic comes close to what Lynda Boose has described as the 'patriarchal fantasy of male parthenogenesis' (Boose 1993: 45). Such a view of procreation requires a 'fair' male and suggests that fairness in the sonnets is a desirable and transmissible characteristic.[14]

II

> A woman's face, with nature's own hand painted,
> Hast thou, the master mistress of my passion—
> A woman's gentle heart, but not acquainted
> With shifting change, as is false women's fashion;
>
> (20: 1–4)

The young man's beauty is also striking in that it is very specifically gendered. Not just fairness, but male fairness is praised throughout. Female fairness is merely an abstraction since the only woman in the sequence is deliberately made not fair, but black. Women, in fact, become a threat to 'true' fairness. The threat of women and the gendering of fairness become quite obvious in Sonnets 20 and 21, poems whose gender instability has occasioned reams of comment.[15] If the early poems all insist on the uniqueness of the young man's fairness, these sonnets create his singularity by insisting on its difference from (and superiority to) the fairness of women. Moreover, by 'othering' female fairness, Sonnet 20 manages to make the young man's fairness both extraordinary and natural. The conceit of Nature as artist in its first line, 'A woman's face, with nature's own hand painted,' suggests that the fairness of the man is noteworthy, in distinct contrast with women who are commonly 'painted' in a more debased way—through cosmetics.

Sonnet 20, with its extreme ambiguity and complex gender slippages, is a definite turning point in the sequence; it is here that the poet gives up the argument for physical reproduction and concentrates on the powers of poetry. An attention to color imagery in the poem reveals that the gender ambiguity is undergirded by a less transgressive politics of color. Gregory Bredbeck argues that the cognate pun 'own/owne' acts as a structural trope which connects this sonnet to 127 ('In the old age black was not counted fair') and thus works to recirculate and unfix homo- and hetero-erotic desire in the sequence: 'the resurfacing of the hands of nature collapses the linearity of the cycle and draws us back to the "master mistris" even as it pushes us ahead to the mistress' (Bredbeck 1991: 178–9). However, that intertextual connection and recirculation of erotic energy does not destabilize the politics of color in the sequence; in fact, it brings into play the dark/fair binarism and reiterates the bias against female fairness. In his praise of blackness in 127, the poet argues that black has become 'beauty's successive heir' (3) precisely because fairness is debased by cosmetics:

> For since each hand hath put on nature's pow'r,
> Fairing the foul with art's false borrowed face,
> Sweet beauty hath no name, no holy bow'r,
> But is profaned, if not lives in disgrace.
>
> (5–8)

In both cases, the association with cosmetics reinforces an understanding of fairness as white complexion[16] and reiterates the undesirability of female fairness and poems that would praise it.

The instability of fairness becomes in Sonnet 20 linked to the duplicity of femininity, a duplicity which is the cornerstone of the dark lady sonnets. The sexual pun in the lines: 'A woman's gentle heart, but not acquainted— / With shifting change, as is false women's fashion' (4) further joins traditional fears of women's uncontrolled sexual appetites with anticosmetic and misogynist discourses: 'false women's fashion.' In contrast with the chaos suggested by women, the young man evokes mastery: he is 'A man in hue all hues in his controlling' (20). The doubled use of 'hue' suggests an homology of form and color. The line would seem to imply that men—or at least this particular man—has a power over both forms/bodies and color; it gives his fairness a stability and power specifically not accorded it in other arenas (a power, I might add, that women seem to be able to achieve only with cosmetics).[17]

Tellingly, Stephen Booth suggests that one meaning of the line is that the young man has power over other complexions in that he causes people to flush or grow pale' (Booth 1977: 164, n.7). Both blushing and turning pale often come to be seen as the property of whiteness. As late as *Oroonoko* (1688), Aphra Behn feels compelled to repudiate this:

> 'tis a very great error in those who laugh when one says, A Negro can change colour, for I have seen 'em as frequently blush and look pale, and that as visibly as ever I saw in the most beautiful white.
>
> (Behn 1994 [1688]: 17)

Sonnet 20 suggests that the young man has a superior control over emotions; in this case the lines might then be read as an interesting obverse of Aaron's mocking and proverbial condemnation of white / fairness in *Titus Andronicus*: 'Fie treacherous hue, that will betray with blushing / The close enacts and counsels of thy heart!' (IV. ii. 116–17) and his praise of blackness which 'is better than another hue, / In that it scorns to bear another hue' (IV. ii. 99–100). All of these examples have at their heart concerns over bodily control and suggest the primacy of reason and rationality.

If Sonnet 20 brings to the fore an homoerotic love of the poet for the young man, then Sonnet 21 complements that gesture by suggesting that the more common heteroerotic tradition of epideictic praise, which is generally a praise of female beauty, is inadequate because it cannot create a fairness that transcends material notions of value. This sonnet also announces a link to the 'dark lady' poems, this time through anti-Petrarchism. It duplicates the equation of female beauty with 'painting' and, more specifically, worries how one can find a language of praise suitable for the young man when popular praise has become devalued by its focus on possibly adulterate female beauty: 'So it is not with me as with that muse / Stirred by a painted beauty to his verse' (21: 1).

The competition between these types of fairness is rhetorically suggested by the repetition of 'fair' in line 4: 'and every fair with his fair doth rehearse' which also ironically points out the poet's dilemma. In even making this gesture of rejection he himself 'rehearses' fairness, stubbornly holding on to it six lines later: 'And then believe me, my love is as fair / As any mother's child' (10–11). Throughout the poem, he replaces the allegedly strained couplings of the beloved with objects in epideictic praise with his own punning and repetitive couplings which self-referentially connect the beloved to the intangible or the sanctified. This simile in particular ('as fair as any mother's child'), replaces the earlier urgings to procreate in Sonnet 2 'this fair child of mine / Shall sum my account and make my old excuse' (10–11) with his own creation of the young man as a 'fair' child. However, as Bredbeck notes, the completion of that thought, 'though not so bright / As those gold candles fixed in heaven's air' (21: 11–12), even as it mocks the gestures of otherworldliness in lyric, suggests that there is an absolute source of truth, the transcendent light of heaven's heir.[18] The pun on air/heir suggests that the poet finds refuge (as whiteness) often does, in religious allegory and notions of transcendence. This transcendence is placed within a black / white schema when the poet in Sonnet 70 proclaims, 'The ornament of beauty is suspect, / A crow that flies in heaven's sweetest air' (3–4).

Sonnet 21's desire 'O let me be true in love but truly write' (9), complements this belief in a transcendent 'fairness' with a need for a pure language which I have argued elsewhere is a driving force behind paradoxical praise. To 'truly write' and to be truly 'right' argue a need for a language that transparently represents the young man's pure beauty without somehow marring it. This sonnet thus seems to initiate what becomes a recurring anxiety—that the young man's fairness is such that the poet's words can never convey it. This theme is also linked to what I have argued is an overwhelming drive/desire for a language that can represent without marring or blotting. Sonnet 83 is an excellent example of this dynamic: unlike the rival poet who damages as he praises, our poet prefers silence: 'For I impair not beauty, being mute, / When others would give life and bring a tomb' (11–12).

So too, Sonnet 68's nostalgic decrying of 'bastard signs of fair' articulates the fear of a deadening, overused language of praise:

> Thus is his check the map of days outworn,
> When beauty lived and died as flow'rs do now,
> Before these bastard signs of fair were borne,
> Or durst inhabit on a living brow—
> Before the golden tresses of the dead,
> The right of sepulchers, were shorn away,
> To live a second life on second head—
>
> (1–7)

The imitation of the dominant aesthetic—evoked here by the image of the blond wig made from the hair of the dead—makes preserving the validity and purity of the young man's fairness a central project. In a larger sense, however, the 'bastard signs' that are linked to the 'bastard' beauty in Sonnet 127 connect this anti-cosmetic sentiment to rampant anxieties over birth and legitimacy at the same time as it reiterates poetic fears about language. Bastardy also connotes patriarchal fears over bloodlines, usually in the context of inheritance. The image of the young man as map, repeated twice in Sonnet 68 ('And him as for a map doth nature store / To show false art what beauty was of yore' (13–14)) and nowhere else in the sequence, reinforces the sense of property interests and establishes a connection between fair skin and the land in a way that is reminiscent of the Ditchley portrait. That his body is somehow a map of the past ('his cheek the map of days outworn') may evoke the new interest in maps that are key ground for articulations of Elizabethan colonialism and nationhood accompanied by an interest in English antiquity (see Helgerson 1992: 108–24).

Although the poet in the procreation sonnets has asserted a certain value for the young man's fairness in economic terms, he now wishes to withhold the young man's fairness from the devalued marketplace: 'I will not praise that purpose not to sell' (21: 12).[19] This replicates an interesting dynamic in the earlier poems. 'Fair beauty' is established as the highest quality across a number of explicitly social registers. The economic, the juridical and the religious all come into play. This happens as early as Sonnet 2:

> How much more praise deserved the beauty's use,
> If thou could answer, 'This fair child of mine
> Shall sum my count and make my old excuse'—
> Proving his beauty by succession thine.
>
> (9–11)

However, this 'economic' imperative to reproduce is both a hedge against nature which causes decay and is made to seem completely 'natural' through the use of pastoral metaphor. This movement between the social and the natural suggests that the poems attempt both to circulate a valuable fairness within culture and to insist that it has a value beyond culture. Like the paintings of Elizabeth I, the young man sonnets struggle to produce the 'intrinsic transcendent superiority of the colour white' (Dyer 1993: 2). Heterosexual social order is literally re/produced in a context that responds to new social pressures that force fairness/ whiteness into visibility. The poems strive for transcendence even as they reveal fairness as constructed, and not inherently valuable. The dual movement suggests to me that fairness is in fact not hegemonic, that its signification and value have been contested, possibly by increased social mobility, anxiety over gender roles, and colonial encounters.

III

The seemingly abstract descriptions of beauty are a key quality of the sonnets and are one of the factors that would immediately forestall one from thinking about race in the sequence. His beauty is described in terms of Christian transcendence: it has no 'holy bower.' It can be 'profaned.' He is a 'better angel' and 'a saint' (Sonnet 144) who is seemingly beyond the physicality that is a crucial part of more modern racial categories. How can we say that they are racially coded when we are not even sure what the young man looks like, other than that he is generically beautiful?

For my answer, I turn again to Toni Morrison. I was thinking about this issue of transcendence and race while teaching *The Bluest Eye*. This novel is in part an extended meditation on the force of the Western beauty aesthetic and I was particularly struck by her description of a certain class of aspiring bourgeois black women:

> They go to land grant colleges, normal schools, and learn how to do the white man's work with refinement: home economics to prepare his food; teacher education to instruct black children in obedience; music to soothe the weary master and entertain his blunted soul. Here they learn the rest of the lesson begun in those soft houses with porch swings and pots of bleeding heart: how to behave. The careful development of thrift, patience, high morals and good manners. In short how to get rid of the funkiness. The dreadful funkiness of passion, the funkiness of nature, the funkiness of the wide range of human emotions.
>
> Wherever it erupts, this Funk, they wipe it away; where it crusts, they dissolve it;

wherever it drips, flowers or clings, they find it and fight it until it dies. They fight this battle all the way to the grave. The laugh that is a little too loud; the enunciation a little too round; the gesture a little too generous. They hold their behind in fear of a sway too free; when they wear lipstick, they never cover the entire mouth for fear of lips too thick, and they worry, worry, worry about the edges of their hair.

(Morrison 1972: 6)

Morrison describes here the result of a particular form of mental colonization—the exaltation of the mind, spirit and reason at the expense of the body and its passions. She demonstrates how this mind/body split is inflected through gender, class and race. The passage also allows us to see another facet of literary blackness. Black women have more reason to fear 'funk' because blackness and femaleness are so connected to devalued discourses of the body. In early modern England, blackness becomes the mark of bodies—be they female, African, Welsh, Jewish, Irish or lower class—that escape, deny or just cannot be contained by certain cultural boundaries. Eruptions of 'Funk' disrupt the surveillance and discipline of the idealized classical body which is created in lyric by the eruptions of whiteness with which I began this essay.

Such praise of the beautiful white body also implies a certain transcendence of the body and its 'funk' in that it draws attention to certain disciplinary codes of cleanliness and sweetness (Grieco 1993: 47–52). While it may have originated in class differentiation, the very real social, political and emotional effects that Morrison demonstrates in *The Bluest Eye* make it impossible to see transcendent fairness as anything but a contributing factor to white supremacy. The accompanying emphasis on property, wealth and lineage that is so pronounced in the sonnets is also linked to 'race' in its earliest usage and runs throughout discourses of beauty in the period. Moreover, the ideology of white beauty is a 'racial formation,' in that it helps construct a visual regime that uses human bodies and their signification to determine access to political, social and economic power (Omi and Winant 1994: 55–6). The eruptions of whiteness with which I began this essay are part of an aesthetic system that identifies certain bodies as desirable—as entitled to wealth, land and power—and others as dangerous to that entitlement. Certainly in this way they must be seen as a form of colonization as potent as economic imperialism. When we insist on attempting to protect Shakespeare and his works by reading Shakespeare's poems (and Shakespeare himself) as 'universal' and merely as praise of an abstract 'beauty' (male or female) rather than as specific cultural productions that manage fairness, modern teachers and critics produce the invisibility that fuels white hegemony.

* * *

Stephen Greenblatt, *Hamlet in Purgatory* (Princeton: Princeton University Press, 2001), p. 4.

It seems a bit odd to bear witness to the intensity of *Hamlet*; but my profession has become so oddly diffident and even phobic about literary power, so suspicious and tense, that it risks losing sight of—at least failing to articulate—the whole reason anyone bothers with the enterprise in the first place.

. . . .

QUESTIONS

- What do Cary Nelson's and Kim F. Hall's texts suggest about the meaning, construction and operation of literary value?
- In the light of these critiques, how do you assess Stephen Greenblatt's recalcitrant 'witness' to Shakespeare's 'literary power'?

2 | Deconstructing literature and literary value

Derek Attridge, *Peculiar Language: Literature as Difference from the Renaissance to James Joyce* (London: Methuen, 1988), pp. 18–19, 21–2, 24–40.

The text I use to exemplify the Renaissance's posing of the question of literary difference is George Puttenham's *Arte of English Poesie*, first published in 1589.[1] This treatise, often regarded as a charming but unsophisticated and inconsistent potpourri of Renaissance commonplaces,[2] may be read as a quite strenuous attempt to articulate crucial problems having to do with the status of poetic language within a specific linguistic and cultural framework. Not only does it show clearly the parameters of Renaissance discourse in regard to this issue, but it also offers a clearer view than a more recent text might do of the tacit boundaries to our own confrontations with related questions. In particular, to the degree that it appears fissured or self-contradictory it may reveal conceptual inconsistencies or blind spots over which the passage of later intellectual history has laid down a veneer, but which are still present in our own thinking. Puttenham's treatise is especially useful in this respect because it does not exercise to the full the rhetorical and persuasive powers that are, in part, its subject—unlike, for instance, Sidney's roughly contemporary *Apologie for Poetrie*, where tensions and contradictions tend to disappear under the immaculate surface of courtly *sprezzatura*.[3] [. . .]

Nature appears in Renaissance writing and in the classical texts upon which that writing drew as both the principle of perfection and the principle of imperfection—and so does art, in a contrary or complementary relationship. How are we to characterize such an unstable and apparently self-contradictory distinction? Is it sufficient to refer to the changeableness and variety of opinion and to attempt to extract some compromise 'balance' between nature and art as representing the best possible Renaissance position on the matter? Or is radical instability in some way intrinsic to the distinction and to its function within the discourse of the period?[4] [. . .]

The opposition of nature and art is, of course, related to several other divisions typical of Western thought, among them the literal versus the figurative, wisdom versus eloquence, dialectic (or logic) versus rhetoric, object versus sign (or representation), speech versus writing, and nature itself versus nurture, or convention, or culture. Jacques Derrida, in discussing several of these dualisms as they occur in a variety of texts, literary and philosophical, from Plato to Ponge, has sought to show that they do not and cannot function as stable, given, mutually exclusive oppositions of which one member is primary and self-sufficient and the other secondary, exterior, and dependent. [. . .]

The decorous art of English poetry

The stability and mutual exclusiveness of the opposition between nature and art seems to be a necessary foundation for Puttenham's enterprise, which is the composition of a manual setting out in detail what can be said about English poetry as an art of language. At first sight the distinction, as it operated for an Elizabethan, seems solid enough: 'nature' refers to that which occurs *naturally*, or by *kind*, by virtue of what a thing is in all its fullness and self-sufficiency, 'art' to that which is contrived by an *artificer* working upon the given materials of nature. Every object or specimen of behavior which is not natural is artificial (or 'artful'), and vice versa. Human beings behave naturally by following *instinct* and artificially by learning and following the *rules* of the art in question. The connection between art and rules is always very close. Puttenham gives as the accepted definition of art 'a certain order of rules prescribed by reason and gathered by experience,' and he states that poetry was not an art 'until by studious persons fashioned and reduced into a method of rules and precepts' ([Puttenham 1936:] 5).[5] [. . .] An art is therefore by definition *teachable*, and an 'Art' of English poetry is designed to teach (and to further) that art by setting out its rules and precepts. The first of the three books of Puttenham's *Arte*, entitled 'Of Poets and Poesie,' is not strictly speaking of this kind; it is partly a defense, partly a description and a history of poetry. But Book Two, 'Of Proportion,' and Book Three, 'Of Ornament,' which together account for more than three-quarters of the work, set out without stinting on detail the two methods by which natural language is altered by the art, or artifice, of the poet—by being organized into lines of regular verse and stanzas, and by being enriched with rhetorical figures. [. . .]

Again and again Puttenham stresses the artificiality of art and its distance from nature. [. . .] Puttenham's poetics seem to represent a view of art as something defined *against* nature, which would tend to be associated with the instinctive, the savage, the uncivil, the ignorant— a view for which there is a great deal of evidence in his time and which retained at least a degree of force until the later eighteenth century, when art begins to claim for itself those 'natural' qualities, renaming them 'spontaneity,' 'sincerity,' 'innocence,' and so forth. But to read Puttenham only as a representative of this Renaissance commonplace is to ignore much that is present in his text, and it is worth pausing on a few of the places at which something more complex—and much less easy to describe—is happening.

In the title to the second chapter of Book One Puttenham announces in general terms the position that the entire work is going to defend and elaborate: 'That There May Be an Art of Our English Poesie, Aswell as There is of the Latine and Greeke' (5). In substantiating this claim, Puttenham is faced with the same problem that faced all defenders of vernacular poetry in the Renaissance: the prosody of the modern-language verse traditions, as far as it was understood, seemed to lack the intense degree of organization of Latin and Greek verse, by which every syllable was weighed and measured and given an appropriate place in the line. One response, repeated all over Europe throughout the sixteenth century, was to attempt to create similar metrical forms in the vernacular. The other was to look for organizing principles of equivalent intricacy and reliability in the vernacular tradition itself. It is typical of

Puttenham's open enacting of the contradictions within the intellectual fabric of his age that he attempts both, scarcely making an effort to reconcile the two radically different solutions and unintentionally providing evidence both for the impossibility of a quantitative system of meter in English and for the prevailing lack of insight into the structures of English verse.[6]

But the problem goes deeper, for it is one aspect of a more generalized dilemma that lies at the heart of the humanist program of *imitation*. The only goal vernacular verse can set itself, given the controlling assumptions of humanism, is to match its model, classical verse; yet because that model is taken to be the absolute standard, the perfect exemplar, vernacular verse is necessarily condemned always to fall short.[7] This is our first example—one we need not dwell on—of the problematic of the supplement: vernacular verse necessarily is only an addition to the already complete and fully realized body of classical verse, and if it appears to be making claims to be an improvement on, or a substitute for, classical verse, which it must do to escape perpetual secondariness, it constitutes a threat to the latter's exemplary status and therefore to its own raison d'être. Any assertion of the merits of modern as compared with classical verse, therefore, must somehow involve at the same time a counterassertion, or the humanist program will disintegrate.

In his attempt to deal with this issue early in Book One, Puttenham calls on the opposition between nature and art to argue that English versification is quite different from, and as good as (but, significantly, not better than), that of Latin and Greek. The argument is that the English rhyming type of verse, to judge from historical evidence and reports of travelers, is 'the first and most ancient Poesie, and the most universall', which two points do otherwise give to all humane inventions and affaires no small credit.' So, Puttenham can boast, 'our maner of vulgar Poesie is more ancient than the artificiall of the Greeks and Latines, ours comming by instinct of nature, which was before Art or observation' (10). At the very beginning of his art of English poetry, Puttenham seems to be privileging nature over art, instinct over rules. Not surprisingly, he quickly adds a qualification, that such priority is only priority in *time*, like the priority of the naked over the clothed or the ignorant over the learned. This addition seems to go to the opposite extreme, demolishing the case for the vernacular by associating it with the naked and the ignorant, but Puttenham is reluctant to let the earlier argument go and attempts a highly unstable compromise: 'The naturall Poesie therefore being aided and amended by Art, and not utterly altered or obscured, but some signe left of it, (as the Greekes and Latines have left none) is no lesse to be allowed and commended than theirs' (10). Naturalness manages to be both an inherent advantage and, in a metaphor at least as old as Aristotle, a weakness in need of the aid and amendment of art. [. . .]

In a later chapter of Book One, Puttenham firmly reasserts the slightly shaken superiority of the artificial over the natural, sharpening the criticism of his own appeal to nature and its twin associates, universality and antiquity. Poetry is praiseworthy not only 'because I said it was a metricall speach used by the first men, but because it is a metricall speach corrected and reformed by discreet judgements, and with no lesse cunning and curiositie than the Greeke and Latine Poesie, and by Art bewtified and adorned, and brought far from the primitive rudenesse of the first inventors, otherwise it might be sayd to me that *Adam* and *Eves* apernes were the gayest garmentes, because they were the first, and the shepheardes tente or pavillion, the best housing, because it was the most auncient and most universall' (23). But now the whole argument in favor of English versification is threatened, and nature has to be reintroduced in another attempt to reconcile the irreconcileable: 'It is not my meaning but that Art and cunning concurring with nature, antiquitie and universalitie, in things indifferent, and not evill, doe make them more laudable' (23). Art, it seems, must in some way agree with nature even though it is defined against nature. And lest this requirement should seem to throw the ball entirely back into nature's court, there is the important qualification 'in things indifferent, and not evill.' The role of the artist is to identify what is evil in nature and therefore not to be followed. In this way nature is 'corrected and reformed by discreet judgements.' Poetry is modeled on nature yet some-how perfects nature (in the same way that, in the example of supplementarity noted earlier, modern poetry is both modeled on and yet perfects classical poetry). The concept of nature is self-divided (and is therefore not strictly a concept): it stands both for that which is itself, in total self-sufficiency, and that which is necessarily incomplete and in need of repair.

But there is a further difficulty. Insofar as art departs from nature itself (and not just flawed nature) and is constituted as art by that departure, it is in some sense essentially *un*natural. The figures of rhetoric have always been defined as transgressions of the norms of what Putten-ham, like many of his successors through to the present day, calls 'ordinary' language. In his chapter 'Of Figures and Figurative Speaches,' Puttenham is perfectly explicit about this: 'As figures be the instruments of ornament in every language, so be they also in a sorte abuses or rather trespasses in speach, because they passe the ordinary limits of common utterance, and be occupied of purpose to deceive the eare and also the minde, drawing it from plainnesse and simplicitie to a certaine doublenesse, whereby our talke is the more guilefull and abusing' (154). Paradoxically, that which is unnatural and deceitful is able to cure nature of its faults—in a specific context. Most of these vices, says Puttenham, can in poetry be transformed into virtues, and they occur as such in his lengthy list. Even some of the deviations that he lists unambiguously as vices can on some occasions become virtues, if they are handled in a particular manner by the poet.

What is it that defines the delicate—yet crucial—balance between virtue and vice? What is the source of the 'discreet judgments' whereby nature is 'corrected and reformed' by art and not further depraved? To answer these questions Puttenham invokes a completely independent standard, which he calls by a plethora of different names, their proliferation suggesting the importance of this moment within the argument as well as its elusiveness as a stable concept. Its titles include *decorum* (which I shall arbitrarily favor), *decency, discretion, seemliness, comeliness, agreeableness, seasonableness, well-temperedness, apt-ness, fittingness, good grace, conformity, proportion*, and *conveniency*.[8] And in a tight corner this notion is always available to be appealed to, by one or another of its names. If the argument seems to be heading toward a point where virtue and vice, good art and bad art, become indistinguishable—and the whole of Puttenham's enterprise threatens to collapse—decorum can step in to make the vital decision [. . .] Decorum is the principle whereby any given poetic device can be judged, according to all the specific, perhaps unique, configur-ations of its individual situation. Clearly it is by far the most important rule in the poet's handbook; without it, he might as well not begin to write. Yet what emerges with surprising clarity from Puttenham's text is that *there is no such rule, and there could not possibly be one.* Decorum is precisely that aspect of the poet's art which is not reducible to rule. And human activity that is not reducible to rule is usually called 'natural.'

 Puttenham does not shy away from this conclusion. When he begins his full and direct treatment of decorum in the third-to-last chapter (having availed himself somewhat surreptitiously of its aid throughout the treatise), he stresses both its central importance and its unamenability to rules: 'In all things to use decencie, is it onely that giveth every thing his good grace and without which nothing in mans speach could seeme good or gracious, in so much as many times it makes a bewtiful figure fall into a deformitie, and on th'other side a vicious speach seeme pleasaunt and bewtifull: this decencie is therfore the line and levell for al good makers to do their busines by. But herein resteth the difficultie, to know what this good grace is, and wherein it consisteth, for peradventure it be easier to conceave than to expresse' (261). Puttenham's way of expressing it is by means of an analogy between mind and senses: as, for instance, a sound that is 'too loude or too low or otherwise confuse' is displeasing to the ear, so a 'mental object' (Puttenham's phrase), if it is disproportioned, can be displeasing to the mind. And whence is this immediate and apparently instinctive response derived? 'This lovely conformitie, or proportion, or conveniencie betweene the sence and the sensible hath nature her selfe first most carefully observed in all her owne workes, then also by kinde graft it in the appetites of every creature working by intelligence to covet and desire: and in their actions to imitate and performe: and of man chiefly before any other creature aswell in his speaches as in every other part of his behaviour' (262). To counteract the side effects of art's distance from nature—its potential viciousness, ridiculousness, and duplicity—a principle operating in the name of nature must be reintroduced. [. . .]

It follows that the products of art and those of nature can be very difficult to tell apart. In praising two of his favorite speakers in Parliament and the Star Chamber, Puttenham observes that it 'maketh no matter whether the same eloquence be naturall to them or artificiall (though I thinke rather naturall) yet were they knowen to be learned and not unskilfull of th'arte, when they were yonger men' (139–40). He does not really know which it is—and it matters perhaps a little more to him than he admits. Similarly, discussing the question of style, he notes that a certain manner of writing is 'many times naturall to the writer, many times his peculier by election and arte, and such as either he keepeth by skill, or holdeth on by ignorance, and will not or peradventure cannot easily alter into any other' (148).

But the naturalness of art reaches even further, for an artful principle, it seems, is already present in nature. In discussing 'feete of three times,' Puttenham notes that apart from the dactyl 'they have not hitherto bene made artificiall [that is, not been admitted into the art of English poetry], yet nowe by more curious observation they might be. Since all artes grew first by observation of natures proceedings and custome' (128). And toward the end of the work Puttenham even blurs the distinction to the extent of tracing the figures of rhetoric—those 'trespasses in speach'—back to nature itself: 'All your figures Poeticall or Rhethoricall, are but observations of strange speeches, and such as without any arte at al we should use, and commonly do, even by very nature without discipline' (298). Here he is perhaps going too far, because art seems now to have disappeared entirely, and he quickly adds, after noting that different people use these 'strange speeches' to differing extents and in differing ways, 'so as we may conclude, that nature her selfe suggesteth the figure in this or that forme: but arte aydeth the judgement of his use and application' (298). However, we know by now that the art in question, which makes judgments in specific situations—that is, the art of decorum—is in some way a natural rather than an artificial principle. [. . .]

The politics of nature

We need to scrutinize this return of nature a little more closely, however. [. . .] What has actually happened in the course of the argument is not that great creating nature, having been excluded by art, is allowed back in the form of decorum to control art; rather, a surrogate that is more acceptable to Puttenham and his courtly readers has taken over nature's role as a final determinant of art. Although the natural judgment of decorum is said to be equivalent to the ear's dislike of a harsh sound, it turns out not to be as universal a human capacity as aural sensitivity to unpleasant noise. [. . .] The recurrent problem with decorum—and Puttenham sees this as clearly as anyone before or since—is that, because a final appeal to rule is by definition impossible, the 'correctness' of the judgment to be made is ultimately a matter of the authority of the judge. 'It may be a question,' he notes, 'who shal have the determination of such controversie as may arise whether this or that action or speach be decent or indecent: and verely it seemes to go all by discretion, not perchaunce of every one, but by a learned and experienced discretion, for otherwise seemes the *decorum* to a weake and ignorant judgment, than it doth to one of better knowledge and experience' (263).[9] Decorum, in other words, is what comes 'naturally' not to all humanity but to an elite, and members of that elite can be identified by their 'natural' sense of decorum. Bourdieu, writing of the main twentieth-century descendant of decorous judgment, puts it thus: 'Taste classifies, and it classifies the classifier. Social subjects, classified by their classifications, distinguish themselves by the distinctions they make, between the beautiful and the ugly, the distinguished and the vulgar' (*Distinction*, 6). What comes naturally to the majority, who are ignorant and inexperienced, is not *truly* natural.

This contradiction is something Puttenham simply does not notice, as is evident from his well-known discussion of the proper variety of language for the poet to use. He defines this linguistic paradigm extremely narrowly: 'that which is spoken in the kings Court, or in the good townes and Cities within the land' (144). Even that geographical generosity shrinks, at least in the case of England, to 'the shires lying about London within 1x. myles, and not much above' (145). On what grounds is the poet to favor the language of a tiny minority of English speakers? It is, says Puttenham, 'naturall, pure, and the most usuall of all his countrey' (144). 'Usual,' which is clearly nonsense in statistical terms, suggests that Puttenham is able to assimilate the notion of universality to a politically less troublesome notion of cultural superiority. So the appeal to 'a learned and experienced discretion,' which sounds like a democratic appeal to merit and effort, marks a prior exclusion of that class which has no access to learning or to the kind of courtly experience Puttenham has in mind.[10] Hence the 'naturalness' of decorum is at a distant remove from universal human nature or instincts; it is an ideological product, a sixteenth-century equivalent of one of Barthes's modern myths, whereby a historically specific class attitude is promoted and perceived as 'natural.'[11] [. . .]

The problem for Puttenham at this point is that he is writing a *manual* whose only conceivable user is the individual who does *not* possess the natural decorum of the few: the would-be poet, who is eager to acquire the necessary learning and experience.[12] But if there are no rules to be adduced as to the essential distinction between successful and unsuccessful poetry, how is Puttenham to pursue his aim as an instructor? His solution to the problem is a lengthy catalog of examples of decorum in action amounting to over a tenth of the book, drawn not from literature but from incidents in court life (264–98).[13] [. . .] The neophyte poet is expected to acquire from these vividly depicted exempla a sense of decorum then to be applied to writing; Puttenham has no qualms about making a direct link between the modes of behavior which sustain political power and the graces of poetry. But his unwillingness to draw up rules of decorum, even though he has no hesitation in saying that rules can be deduced by the close observation of nature in its more general sense, points to a wider dilemma: if art—whether the art of poetry or the art of courtly conduct—were reconcilable to rule, it would be available to all who were willing to make the effort. As the existence of poetry, like the power of the court, is predicated upon exclusiveness, such a conclusion is unthinkable. Puttenham must therefore produce a manual designed to fail.[14]

We have not finished with the dangerous supplement of art, however; it is not to be so easily controlled by being embedded in a social and political context and granted the status of a pseudo-nature. The threat of the supplement is that, because it belies its own secondariness in making good what is lacking in the nature that it supplements, it constantly endangers nature's primariness. [. . .]

The source of the problem becomes clearer if we ask what purposes the term 'nature' in its most general sense is being asked to fulfill within the discursive system that makes possible Puttenham's writing. 'Nature' is called upon to stand for a notion of self-sufficiency, wholeness, and plenitude, that which is, and is itself, without self-division or self-consciousness and without dependence on anything exterior to itself—like the past (in such forms as memory and history), the future (goals, for instance), and rules or codes that would preexist and predetermine it. This notion is powerfully operative even (or especially) within Puritan or Neoplatonic emphases on the fallenness or secondariness of the nature we experience: fallen nature is, precisely, fallen from its true self, from what it should have been.[15] But any attempt to ground this notion empirically, or even to give it theoretical or imaginative substance, necessarily fails, caught up as our existence, our language, our thought is in the operation of difference, loss, mediation, desire, secondariness, instability, deferral, and all the other features of our experience whose inescapability gives rise to our yearning for what we call (among other things) 'nature.' Art, which is a reaching after or an echo of that oneness and self-sufficiency which is nature's alone by right, and which constitutes nature, is called upon at the same time to *produce* the oneness and self-sufficiency of nature by virtue of its own healing and perfecting powers. However, to accept fully that art has this central function, that the apparent supplement has a primary role and not a merely supplementary one, would be to allow the founding notion of nature, of a principle of plenitude and transcendence, to collapse, and with it much of the enabling intellectual (and political/religious) discourse of the time. In the *Apologie*, Sidney comes close to articulating this view by arguing that art is the only means of attaining, in a fallen world, a glimpse of prelapsarian perfection. He half withdraws the claim as soon as he has made it, however: 'But these arguments will by fewe be understood, and by fewer granted' (157); – a strangely uncomfortable moment in the easy assurance of his rhetoric. [. . .]

The danger that art will supplant nature becomes most acute when art ceases to be distinguishable by its distance from nature and takes on the appearance of nature itself (as threatens to happen, for example, in the Bower of Bliss [in Spenser's *The Faerie Queene*])[16]. Puttenham has accepted that art can come naturally, as does Sidney in the famous passage in the *Apologie* about the 'smally learned Courtier' who, 'following that which by practise hee findeth fittest to nature, therein (though he know it not) doth according to Art, though not by Art' (203). But if art can come by nature, can nature come by art? The whole discussion of decorum tends in this direction, and is prevented from reaching this conclusion only by the insistence that decorum is not reducible to rules of art: *natural* art can come only by means of a natural principle. But at the end of his book, after a concluding summary of the whole treatise, Puttenham admits—in what can only be called a supplement—that art does have the power to disguise itself as nature. This assertion is, of course, as old as the notion of art itself; it appears as the classical *ars est celare artem* [art is to conceal art] and the courtly accomplishment of *sprezzatura*, the ability to present the artificial *as* the natural, but it must always constitute an uneasy place in the discussion of the crucial distinction between art and nature.[17] Puttenham's belated treatment of it is no exception—that belatedness itself being one sign of its potential disruptiveness. In closing the final book, he says he will offer a 'principall good lesson for al good makers to beare continually in mind,' the lesson of the courtier, 'which is in plaine termes, cunningly to be able to dissemble' (299). He states it in plain terms, because *he* is not going to dissemble in presenting us with this unpleasant fact, whose unpleasantness he stresses by going on to quote several unsavory examples of courtly duplicity. But the poet or at least 'our English maker' is an honest man and not a hypocrite (Puttenham forgets that he has described *all* figurative language as deceitful) and is allowed only one form of deception: 'When he is most artificiall, so to disguise and cloake it as it may not appeare, nor seeme to proceede from him by any studie or trade of rules, *but to be his naturall*' (302, my emphasis). At this point art, kept in check throughout the book by the operations of nature, breaks loose. If there is an *art* of behaving and writing naturally—and this more than anything else seems to constitute the arts of poetry and courtliness—the supplement has indeed put itself in nature's place.

. . . .

QUESTIONS

• What difficulties of defining literary value emerge from Attridge's analysis of Puttenham?

• What are the implications for current criticism?

3 | Reading the subversive potential of texts

Thomas Healy, *New Latitudes: Theory and English Renaissance Texts* (London, Melbourne and Auckland: Edward Arnold), pp. 54–5.

We are increasingly becoming aware of the interaction between high and popular culture, and how the Renaissance does not exclusively separate the two. [. . .] We can no longer smugly claim that literary criticism is concerned only with 'the best' expression of the period, because what is best is dependent on a host of preconceptions about what we wish to learn about Renaissance writing. An Collin's expression of self-effacing humility is *better* than Herbert's in the sense that Collin's humility is paramount where Herbert is maintaining a strong concept of self and, indeed, self-applause. We return to the need to make the questions we ask of Renaissance literature distinct. If we claim our interest is to focus on the writing produced only by a sophisticated elite, and that we determine the best literature is that which, in terms of generic structure, subject, and eloquent rhetoric, concerns itself with the preoccupation of males who have a high social and political standing, then the traditional canon will serve the majority of our needs. But if our interests are increasingly focused on different types of expression across a wide social framework, for instance if we are concerned to pursue the dissemination of vernacular innovation across the whole social spectrum, then our previous canon will prove inadequate. Bauthumley's or Trapnel's literary sophistication is limited, yet their writings as cultural documents are as important as Herbert's. The resistance to Bauthumley or Trapnel as figures worthy of study is part of an institutional assumption that literary study in higher education should force a separation between the elite and the popular, the sophisticated and simplistic.

*   *   *

Catherine Belsey, 'Disrupting sexual difference: meaning and gender in the Comedies', in *Alternative Shakespeares*, ed. John Drakakis (London: Methuen, 1985), pp. 166–7.

Meaning, Saussure argued, is an effect of difference. And if poststructuralism has moved beyond Saussure's diagrams, which seemed to imply a single meaning for every unit of language, every signifier, it has not abandoned the most radical principle of Saussurean theory, that meaning depends not on the referent, not on intention, but only on the relations of difference between one term and another within the language. Subsequently we have come to see meaning as unfixed, always in process, always plural. This is a result first of the analysis of language itself as the location of distinct discourses (or knowledges), sets of terms and relations between terms in which a specific understanding of the world is inscribed. And secondly it takes account of the argument that meaning is never fully present in any individual utterance but is always deferred, always provisional, precisely because it is dependent on the relations of difference between *this* term and all the other terms which constitute the language and which are by definition absent.

The problem with the meanings that we learn—and learn to produce—is that they seem to define and delimit what is thinkable, imaginable, possible. To fix meaning, to arrest its process and deny its plurality, is in effect to confine what is possible to what *is*. Conversely, to disrupt this fixity is to glimpse alternative possibilities. A conservative criticism reads in quest of familiar, obvious, common-sense meanings, and thus reaffirms what we already know. A radical criticism, however, is concerned to produce readings which challenge that knowledge by revealing alternative meanings, disrupting the system of differences which legitimates the perpetuation of things as they are. The project of such a criticism is not to replace one authoritative interpretation of a text with another, but to suggest a plurality of ways in which texts might be read in the interests of extending the reach of what is thinkable, imaginable or possible.

*   *   *

Patricia Parker, *Shakespeare from the Margins: Language, Culture, Context* (Chicago: University of Chicago Press, 1996), pp. 1–19.

This is [. . .] about the contemporary contexts and historical resonances of Shakespearean wordplay. But it is also about what in Shakespeare has been marginalized or overlooked, and the edification from the margins (to borrow from *Hamlet*) that can be gained by attending to what might appear the simply inconsequential. Wordplay itself has frequently been reduced to the purely decorative 'quibble,' treated with the same sense of dismissal as Johnson's of Shakespeare's 'fatal Cleopatra,' an eighteenth-century prejudice that still lingers in powerful forms. But it is the argument [here] that both comic wordplay and what Kenneth Muir called the 'uncomic pun' lead us to linkages operating not only within but between Shakespeare's plays, across the often arbitrary boundaries of genre. And it is its broader contention that the terms of this wordplay make possible glimpses into the relation between the plays and their contemporary culture, in a period when English was not yet standardized into a fixed orthography, obscuring on the printed page the homophonic networks possible before such boundaries were solidified.[1] In this sense, the approach to language here has affinities with what Leo Spitzer called 'historical semantics' and opposed to the dehistoricizing tendencies of the New Critics. But it is also an attempt to respond to what Catherine Belsey describes as the need to link feminist and literary criticism to a more historically grounded study of language and culture, one that takes seriously the 'matter' of language as part of the 'material Shakespeare.'[2] And it addresses questions about the status of wordplay in the collaborative context of the Shakespearean theater, together with ways of thinking about variant texts that differ from editorial or critical practices that assume the singularity of an 'authentic' Shakespeare.

The analysis here of the language of particular plays and its embedding in various contexts in the early modern period starts, then, from its historical dimensions, including interconnections difficult to recognize without an awareness of resonances lost on modern ears—terms such as *preposterous, conveyance, translation, delation/dilation, construction, joinery*, or *matter* itself. In its sense of the importance of words to the relation between culture, society, and history, this study has been inspired by the examples of Raymond Williams and Kenneth Burke: the former for his articulation of the importance of language to cultural and historical studies, including the notion of key words; the latter for his repeated emphasis on the inseparability of language, rhetoric, and discourse from political and social issues and for his failure (as a figure marginal to the academy) to observe the decorum of a more restricted kind of literary criticism.[3]

To these influences on what follows, however, need to be added the explosion of recent work on Shakespeare—one of the most vibrant developments in literary and cultural studies— and researches in feminist and gender studies: in particular, the dedication of materialist feminist criticism to the historical study of gender, race, and class, and recent writing on homoeroticism and the construction of sexuality that reminds us that modern preoccupations frequently import binaries and boundaries that do not fit the complexities of early modern gendering or erotic play.[4] Judith Newton and Deborah Rosenfelt, in their introduction to *Feminist Criticism and Social Change: Sex, Class, and Race in Literature and Culture*, speak of the need for a 'double work shift' that would include 'work on the power relations implied by gender and simultaneously on those implied by class, race and sexual identification,' one where 'an analysis of literature' would be part of a broader sense of culture itself as a material practice.[5] I share both in this and in the conviction, outlined in Valerie Wayne's introduction and Catherine Belsey's afterword to *The Matter of Difference*, of the necessity of focusing on language and culture in their historical specificity as an important 'matter' for criticism, as well as the sense of *matter* or *materia* that in this period linked various 'rude' or unruly matters characterized as needing to be shaped or ruled. [. . .] I concur as well [. . .] with the sense (represented by anthologies such as *Queering the Renaissance*) of the need to move criticism of Shakespeare (and the implications of Shakespearean wordplay) away from its heterosexist bias and from assumptions about the erotic that reflect modern preoccupations rather than early modern ones.

The most accurate description, then, of the approach taken here might be to adapt the title of Judith Butler's recent *Bodies That Matter* into a sense of words (as well as bodies) that matter, and of language itself not just as mattering but as providing a crucial aspect of what a materialist criticism (or editing the 'material Shakespeare') might attend to.[6] The present study resists, therefore, the trivialization of language and wordplay as secondary or accessory, in the recognition that this very reduction to the ornamental was itself a historical process, one frequently associated with the relegating of women and other marginal subjects to the status of the secondary or accessory. For poets and playwrights, of course, words do matter, in the more concrete sense that they are the material, or part of the material, with which they work. [. . .] In *Othello*, for example, the links that operate, beyond the bounds of logic or the supposed origins of etymology, between *monstrous, show, hideous*, and *hid* become part (as Michael Neill has taught us) of a suggestibility the play itself demonstrates in its tragically momentous consequences.[7] But even this is not remarked here in order to bracket the language of Shakespeare, in some historically anachronistic fashion, from its contemporary culture, as a realm of the aesthetic cordoned off from other uses and practices. On the contrary, the assumption [. . .] is that words not only 'matter' but function in relation to a larger field of discourse—or conflicting discourses—in this period, in ways that involve not only language but institutions, practices, and laws.

My argument here, as elsewhere, is that discourse in Shakespeare—whether the 'smooth discourse' (*3 Henry VI*, III.iii.88) that attempts in the histories to smooth over the fault lines of lineal succession or the ordered 'chain' that Theseus refers to in *A Midsummer Night's Dream* (V.i.125)—is inseparable from the social and political. This, together with the attempt to suggest larger interpretative frameworks for Shakespeare's plays, distinguishes the approach taken in what follows from that, for example, of Keir Elam or other more formalist approaches to Shakespearean language or wordplay in particular.[8] Among contemporary uses of the term *discourse*, the analysis here may at times suggest the several (and by no means self-consistent) senses of discourse articulated in the work of Foucault. But [. . .] this study resists the stalled subversion-containment model that is part of the Foucauldian inheritance of an early strain of new historicism.[9] Much of what follows has to do with the exposure in the plays of discourse *as* discourse, as well as its naturalization into something that attempts to efface its own con- struction—in the discussion of the language of 'fair sequence and succession' in the history plays; in the highlighting of the disjunction of discourses within *The Comedy of Errors;* in the exposure, by 'rude mechanicals,' of the joints and seams of the joinery on which order and rule depend. At several points here, similarly, Lacan's 'discourse of the Other' (or its extensions in postcolonial theory) may seem to come closest among modern formulations to the extra- ordinary sense of occupation, or being occupied by another's discourse, that is such a chilling feature of *Othello;* but the play itself also gives us its own language for this tragic loading/ lodging (the alternate textual variants of its closing lines), in its 'uncomic' puns on lieu- tenantry and its reference to 'Othello's occupation,' an ambiguous combination of active and passive that makes it difficult to know, finally, what it might mean in this context to be possessed of agency or to be a speaking subject. In this as in other instances, the argument here is that the plays themselves provide a language with which to approach such questions, a historically more concrete and grounded language, finally, than importations from con- temporary literary or cultural theory, however helpful the latter might be heuristically at different times.

Several examples may help to suggest why I think a simultaneously more concrete and more detailed study of the 'matter' of Shakespeare's language is critical at this juncture, especially in relation to the 'double work shift' counseled in the now-classic essay of Newton and Rosenfelt. The association of 'Moor' and 'more,' for instance, in the lines on the pregnant female Moor from *The Merchant of Venice* (III.v.37–42), is reduced to a mere linguistic 'jingle' in the Vari- orum Shakespeare notes and by the Arden editor to speculation that the entire passage is introduced 'simply for the sake of an elaborate pun on Moor/more.' But as Kim F. Hall has observed, this reduction to mere quibble or jingle (a telling instance of the racial as well as gender overtones of Shakespeare's 'fatal Cleopatra,' even apart from its assumptions about the 'merely verbal') makes an already invisible black female figure disappear even more effect- ively from these lines—a technique that parallels the effacing of any sense of coloring from Morocco's 'complexion' elsewhere in the play.[10] The common early modern linking of *Moor* and *more*, however, is an important part of the assumption of disruptive excess behind Eliza- beth's proclamation in 1601 banishing 'Negars and Blackamoors' from England on the grounds of their 'great numbers' (a perception that Hall cogently argues had very little to do with their actual numbers) or the sense of sexual excess in the description of Othello as a 'lascivious Moor.' It involves associations still being chronicled by contemporary writers on race such as Patricia Hill Collins or Angela Davis, words powerful in their effect (or the work they do in the world) despite their contradiction by documentable facts or statistics.[11] The more/Moor link, then—even apart from the possibility of a topical reference in these lines on a pregnant female Moor—is part of a set of associations that, far from being reducible to a trivializing sense of the merely verbal, have influenced laws and social practices. Such instances query not only what the 'merely verbal' in this regard might even mean, but also what is being accomplished by such dismissive reductions.

To take another instance cited here, *barber* and *Barbary* are associated in the plays with a common, tainted, or effeminizing sexuality—in the lines of *All's Well* that link a sexually ambiguous Helen with a common 'barber's chair' (II.ii.16) and in the description of Antony as 'barber'd ten times o'er' (*AC*, II.ii.224), lines that suggest his barbering (with its implications of castration or effeminacy) as well as his subjection to a 'barbarous' queen (one who evokes the barbarous associations of the transvestite stage in her evocation of the actor who will 'boy' her greatness). The link between a barbarous or common sexuality and the sexual tainting of a 'white,' echoed in the ironic naming of Bianca in *Othello*, associates Desdemona—accused of having 'contaminated' the marriage bed (IV.i.208) and thus pronounced to be 'begrim'd and black' (III.iii.387–88)—with a 'Maid of Barbary,' in a play that begins with Venetians evoking not only an 'erring barbarian' but the specter of adulteration as the mixing of kinds. The language, then, of contaminating, sullying, or mixing is part of a series of distinctions already in place before *miscegenation* (literally 'mixing') became the historically later term for the adulterating or sullying of 'white.' And it is bound up in this period [. . .] with the matter of adultery, intermarriage, and cross-class breeding.[12] [. . .]

The methodological assumption here that it is important to read the language of Shakespeare's plays with an awareness of crucial historical resonances also extends to the broader reading of early modern culture. Perhaps one example among many will suffice. Medical and other texts of the period, in treating of the controversial phenomenon of changes of gender, frequently repeat the orthodoxy (outlined by Thomas Laqueur and Stephen Greenblatt) that such changes occur in one direction only—from female to male. George Sandys, for instance, in citing the anecdote of Marie Germain from Paré and Montaigne in his commentary on Ovid's story of Iphis's transformation from female to male (a story echoed in Lyly's *Gallathea*, an acknowledged subtext for *A Midsummer Night's Dream*), writes that 'it is without example that a man at any time became a woman,' since it is 'preposterous in Nature, which ever aimes at perfection, when men degenerate into effeminacy.'[13] Without closer inspection of the terms of this iteration of the orthodox teleology, Sandys's statement might be extracted as a simple declarative instance of a Renaissance, as opposed to a later, understanding of changes of gender.[14] But the fact that it is the term 'preposterous' that appears in Sandys's repetition of this familiar assertion complicates this iteration of the orthodox teleology with the specter of its reverse, making it a much less straightforward utterance than it might otherwise appear. For *preposterous* was the term that appeared in contemporary denunciations of sodomy such as Etienne Dolet's *In praepostere venere utentes* and the Latin translated by Sir Thomas Browne, in his discussion of the 'double sex' of hares, as the danger of 'unnatural venery and degenerous effemination' in the species of 'man'.[15] Reading historically, with the resources not just of literary or dramatic texts but of a full range of early modern discourses, is in such instances a way of avoiding taking the iteration of a particular orthodoxy at face value rather than interrogating what might be motivating its insistent repetition. We can, in other words, receive through such terms (often in the interstices of the orthodox pronouncements themselves) an edification from the margins important for historians of gender and culture as well as for literary critics.

This leads us, then, into differences between the methodological assumptions here and particular forms of new historicist analysis. The field of early modern studies owes a tremendous debt to the charting of new directions (and the turn from a narrower and predominantly ahistorical formalism) initiated, over a decade ago, by the work of Stephen Greenblatt and others. My own sense of the need to read Shakespeare historically is in part the product of a continuing engagement (as well as critical disagreement) with this work, though my sense of the fault lines of apparently orthodox utterances is closer to the assumptions of the cultural materialism inspired by Raymond Williams and others than the subversion-containment model of a now largely abandoned form of new historicism or the tendency in the early work of Greenblatt in particular to idealize (or identify with) the operations and the ends of power.[16]

I concur, therefore, with the critiques mounted by feminist and cultural critics of the tendency in earlier new historicist writing to marginalize women and other groups (in its focus on elites or on the exceptional female monarch Elizabeth) or to repeat the gender or class investments of the text and phenomena it describes, in ways that often resembled the conclusions of an older historicism more explicitly conservative in its aims. Critics as various as Walter Cohen, Lisa Jardine, Annabel Patterson, Michael Bristol, Valerie Wayne, Marguerite Waller, Carol Thomas Neely, Lynda E. Boose, and Ania Loomba—to provide only a partial listing—have contributed in the past decade to a critique of the assumptions of such strains within new historicism, even as it was experiencing an impressively broad (if also, increasingly, mechanically reproduced) prestige within and beyond the American academy. Scholars and cultural critics themselves identified with new historicism (Louis Montrose, Leah Marcus, Karen Newman, Steven Mullaney, Patricia Fumerton, and others) have, moreover, contributed important extensions and modifications of the subversion-containment model or the marginalization of women and other groups that respond to these critiques even as they themselves have offered finely nuanced analyses of early modern subjects.[17]

The approach to Shakespearean wordplay here resists the conclusions represented by Greenblatt's famous study of the Henriad in particular and its statement that 'actions that should have the effect of radically undermining authority turn out to be the props of that authority,' conclusions that David Scott Kastan has described as 'suspect on historical grounds alone.' In the now familiar debate over this particular model, Kastan himself contended that 'the Elizabethan theatre and especially the history play, which critics as different as E. M. W. Tillyard and Stephen Greenblatt agree effectively served the interests of royal power, seem . . . to be at least as effective as a subversion of that authority' and argued that representation (including theatrical representation) could in the period be 'powerful and dangerous,' its subversions not 'as easily contained or co-opted as the New Historicists would suggest.'[18] [. . .] Robert Weimann, in his classic study of the contemporary stage, has demonstrated the ways in which the shifting of the action between upstage locus and downstage platea literally displaced the dominant aristocratic ideology, submitting 'aristocratic postures and assumptions' to the interrogation of commoners and clowns, even as it thrust the action itself 'into the space of the audience.'[19] The assumption in the approach to wordplay and its mockeries here is that it performs a similar dislocation on the terms and preoccupations of the language and contexts it repeats.

Subversion in the period of the plays could operate at the verbal as well as the visual level, transmitted sotto voce in a wordplay that could be taken several ways at once.[20] The methodological presupposition [. . .] is that Shakespearean wordplay—far from the inconsequentiality to which it has been reduced not only by the influence of neoclassicism but by continuing critical assumptions about the transparency (or unimportance) of the langauge of the plays involves a network whose linkages expose (even as the plays themselves may appear simply to iterate or rehearse) the orthodoxies and ideologies of the texts they evoke. Holding up to 'show'—the phrase used repeatedly here for such exposure—frequently involves demonstrating the workings of a particular language or discursive form, exposing the mechanics of its joints and seams, in ways that move in very different directions from the totalizing or unifying that would [. . .] make all 'one.' [. . . We should consider, for example,] the 'forged process' (counterfeit as well as constructed) by which Claudius forges his own succession. To become aware of the contemporary resonances of *forged* as well as of *processe* ('narrative,' but also 'legal proceeding') is to apprehend not just the broader implications of forgery in *Hamlet* (or the power of narrative and judicial 'process' in *Othello*) but also the links between narrative 'processe,' judicial proceeding, and royal processional in a play like *Henry VIII*, in ways that suggest not a displaying of power that merely iterates that power's interests but power on display in ways that expose or hold it up to show. Sir Henry Wotton's complaint, then, that the latter made greatness familiar may apprehend this exposure more shrewdly than critical arguments that read this or other late Shakespearean plays as a simple reflection of the interests of Jacobean power.[21]

The sense, similarly, of an edification from the margins that cannot be interrogated at a more explicit level (or assigned to a particular intention) subtends the discussion here of various forms of government and rule—in relation, for example, to the scrambling of proper punctuation, partition, or 'pointing' by the rude mechanicals of the *Dream* or the undermining from the margins of the apparently straightforward 'march' of *Henry V*. The shadowing of Henry's own language of right by this play's exploitation of the histories' preposterous ordering or its evocation of breaches, 'countermines,' and 'leeks' escapes, finally, both the interpreter's and the censor's claim to certainty, like the comparison, from the mouth (or Monmouth) of an ostensibly faithful Welsh deputy, of Henry himself to 'Alexander the Pig.' Annabel Patterson's argument, in *Censorship and Interpretation*, that it was both more common and wiser for sixteenth- and early seventeenth-century dramatists to employ ambiguity rather than a readily identifiable one-to-one correspondence in their reference, along with the strategy that Pierre Bourdieu designates as 'making use of indeterminacy,' are closer to the sense here of Shakespearean wordplay in relation to attempts at containment that the plays both foreground and expose.[22]

To recall in this context the subversion-containment model of an earlier new historicism is not therefore to rehearse once again a familiar debate but rather to suggest the dramatization of the very problem of containment within the plays themselves, both more generally and in the Henriad in particular. [. . .] The Henriad, for example, undoes the kind of historical punctuation or pointing that would enable the former Prince Hal, as the newly renovated Henry V, to cordon off his reign from contaminating 'base companions' (not just the thieveries of the tavern world but the other histories in the series). And it undermines the certainty of Henry's (and English) dominion through wordplay on *leeks* and *leaks* that contaminates the very symbol of Welsh fidelity with the possibility of a containment only too vulnerable to breaching. It also provides, in the frequently marginalized *2 Henry IV*, a place to begin to examine the relation between the impossibility of containing or controlling the associations of words and other forms of boundary-drawing—in its discussion of the problem of preserving words like the formerly honest *occupy* (an 'excellent good word before it was ill sorted,' *2H4*, II.iv.149–50) from 'base companions,' or the wordplay on continents and continence that has explicitly to do with what can (or cannot) be contained.[23] The Henriad itself—the focus of the earlier subversion-containment debate—thus already dramatizes the attempt at containment and what (ambiguously) escapes or exceeds such comprehension or control. And the argument here in relation to other plays—including the botched constructions of the so-called rude mechanicals that make possible a doubled perspective on the ending of *A Midsummer Night's Dream* or the repetition of the language of 'fair sequence and succession' in other Shakespearean contexts—is that what often appears in the plays as a rehearsal or replaying of such closural procedures is frequently closer to the contemporary sense of *parodia* as an iterative reproduction, a repetition that simultaneously dislocates or displaces what is being shown, without necessarily enabling a particular deciphering.

The emphasis on the marginal [. . .] in part evokes what has often been too readily forgotten about a cultural icon as central as William Shakespeare. This includes what Jean Howard, Louis Montrose, Steven Mullaney, and others have described as the marginal or liminal position of the Shakespearean theater itself, located in a so-called Liberty (outside and inside the City at once) and featuring players who if upwardly mobile came from the socially or geographically marginal, elevated (in cases like Shakespeare's) to the position of gentlemen forged or made but also ranged among 'mechanics' and cited in the statute that included vagabonds and other placeless men. The popular theater in particular—as the last decade of scholarship has taught us—was a threateningly liminal space, whose 'mingling of kings and clowns' (in the famous phrase of Sidney) blurred a whole range of distinctions, evoking the specter of adulterating, crossbreeding, and hybridity.[24]

Edification from the margins—in Horatio's 'I knew you must be edified by the margent ere you had done' (*Hamlet* V.ii.155)—further evokes early modern texts such as the Geneva Bible, which facilitated translation into plainer English through their marginal glosses. But glossing in the period in its broader translative sense also opened up the possibility of 'damnable iteration' (*1H4*, I.ii.90) and more ambiguous forms of *glozing*, like the ones evoked in the legal context of the Salic law speech of *Henry V* (I.ii.40) or in *Richard II* (II.i.9). 'Margent'—the early modern spelling from the Second Quarto text of *Hamlet*—enables, moreover, apprehension of its associations with *marchant* or *merchant*, resonances that would be even more suggestive for the links [. . .] between margins and merchants, translation and trade, the pejorative sense of glozing that surrounds the figure of the trader/traitor, and the crossings between margins, *marges*, and marches or borderlands that haunt the borders of Shakespeare's histories with the specter of insurrection from the margins and the rival earls of March. [. . .]

There is, surprisingly, so much in the plays attributed to Shakespeare that has been either marginalized or ignored that we need, in this regard, to be wary of Jonathan Culler's advice to abandon interpretation altogether, however much sympathy we might otherwise have for impatience with 'readings' as a form of academic reproduction.[25] Apparently minor scenes or passages of the plays are often the very ones lopped off not only in theatrical production but by our reading practices—though they are often the sites of the dismantling of what only looks whole without them. [. . .]

Wordplay itself, of course, already complicates the certainties of characterological integrity or the assigning of a particular speaker's intent, operating as it does in ways often independent of any given character's control. This is one of the similarities between the present study and recent work on the editing of the 'material Shakespeare' that has recalled our attention to the inconsistency of Shakespearean speech-prefixes, undermining the stability of dramatic character, in either the eighteenth-century or the Bradleian sense. [. . .]

Close attention to language, and in particular to terms that function (not necessarily at the center of attention) as key words, is (as Evelyn Fox Keller and others have argued recently in relation to the documents of early modern science) an important tool for cultural and historical studies, providing edification from the margins, so to speak, even of texts we thought we knew. The preliminary tools for this historical investigation are not hard to find. There are contemporary interlingual dictionaries and manuals of language (Barret's *Alvearie*, Cotgrave's *Dictionarie*, Minsheu's *Ductor in Linguas*, Florio's *Worlde of Wordes* [. . .]), texts that record the importance of interlingual crossings in a culture not as dominantly monolingual as later periods or as fixed in its sense of the boundaries between words. The *OED* is useful in certain instances, in spite of its obvious biases and critical omissions, as are recent dictionaries of Shakespeare's sexual puns or available concordances, often products of the unsung labor of marginalized scholars, including women. But it is primarily reading itself, across a broad interdisciplinary range of documents and texts and without a map in advance of what there is to find (difficult as it would be to patent as a reproducible method), that is the basic tool of a craft whose joinery is often that of the *bricoleuse*.

Until recently, part of the problem in early modern or other historical studies has been the anachronistic division into academic disciplines that obscured the range of interlinking interests, discourses, and practices in the period. Thanks largely to the advent of new historicism, cultural studies, and historical researches on sexuality and gender, we are now more aware of the connections, for example, that made it possible for an upwardly mobile figure such as Thomas Wilson to produce a tract against usury as well as influential treatments of rhetoric and logic; or Francis Bacon to be at once formative in the articulation of early modern science (in texts that employed metaphors of other-world discovery), a prominent jurist, proponent of torture, and spy, as well as a writer of essays, an influence on the reform of language, and a public figure whose sexual relations with men were part of a contemporary open secret. Crossing boundaries that are in any case anachronistically irrelevant to an era like the early modern is as important as the recognition, for historians of economics (a field that in its present American form appears very little interested in history or in its own discursive or ideological constitution), that Adam Smith lectured on language and rhetoric as well as writing *The Wealth of Nations*. The present study proceeds on the assumption that in order to read the language of early modern culture as well as the plays attributed to Shakespeare, we need to apprehend the implications of its terms from a full range of contemporary discourses and texts. [. . .] We need not repeat the boundedness of an editor's rejection of the accusatory overtones of judicial 'delation' in the 'close dilations' of *Othello* on the grounds that there was no evidence for its use in this sense in Shakespeare's day, while a prominent modern historian was working on the 'delations and informations' connected with the growing accusatory network of informers and spies in that very period.

[. . .] As with the acquisition of any language, there is no shortcut, finally, to the process of immersion. The lateral workings of verbal networks also at times defy the conventions of linear structuring or argument—forms of linearity often parodied in Shakespeare [. . .] or revealed in their limitations within the plays themselves. Circling, backtracking, or revisiting from another perspective is therefore integral to treating the accretive associations through which Shakespearean wordplay works, just as direct quotation (rather than paraphrase) is unavoidable in any attempt to trace its density. [. . .] Difficult as it is to counsel one's students, particularly in the present academic context where everything, including the pressure to publish, is so grotesquely speeded up, to read widely and without a foreclosing sense in advance of what is to be found, this is, in my experience, what often does enable us to stumble upon links that may have been obvious to early modern subjects, writers, playgoers, or readers, but that are anything but obvious, at least at the outset, to those of us approaching this period from across such a broad historical and cultural gap.

* * *

Alan Sinfield, *Faultlines: Cultural Materialism and the Politics of Dissident Reading* (Oxford: Clarendon Press, 1992), pp. 49–51.

I have generally used the term *dissident* rather than *subversive*, since the latter may seem to imply achievement—that something *was subverted*—and hence (since mostly the government did not fall, patriarchy did not crumble) that containment must have occurred. 'Dissidence' I take to imply refusal of an aspect of the dominant, without prejudging an outcome. This may sound like a weaker claim, but I believe it is actually stronger insofar as it posits a field necessarily open to continuing contest, in which at some conjunctures the dominant will lose ground while at others the subordinate will scarcely maintain its position. As Jonathan Dollimore has said, dissidence may provoke brutal repression, and that shows not that it was all a ruse of power to consolidate itself, but that 'the challenge really *was* unsettling'.[1]

[. . .] Formal textual analysis cannot determine whether a text is subversive or contained. The historical conditions in which it is being deployed are decisive. 'Nothing can be intrinsically or essentially subversive in the sense that prior to the event subversiveness can be more than potential; in other words it cannot be guaranteed a priori, independent of articulation, context and reception,' Dollimore observes.[2] Nor, independently of context, can anything be said to be safely contained. This prospect scandalizes literary criticism, because it means that meaning is not adequately deducible from the text-on-the-page. The text is always a site of cultural contest, but it is never a self-sufficient site.

It is a key proposition of cultural materialism that the specific historical conditions in which institutions and formations organize and are organized by textualities must be addressed. That is what Raymond Williams was showing us for thirty years. The entrapment model is suspiciously convenient for literary criticism, because it means that little would be gained by investigating the specific historical effectivity of texts. [. . .] Cultural materialism calls for modes of knowledge that literary criticism scarcely possesses, or even knows how to discover—modes, indeed, that hitherto have been cultivated distinctively within that alien other of essentialist humanism, Marxism. These knowledges are in part the provinces of history and other social sciences—and, of course, they bring in their train questions of historiography and epistemology that require theory more complex than the tidy post-structuralist formula that everything, after all, is a text (or that everything is theater). This prospect is valuable in direct proportion to its difficulty for, as Foucault maintains, the boundaries of disciplines effect a policing of discourses, and their erosion may, in itself, help to 'detach the power of truth from the forms of hegemony (social, economic and cultural) within which it operates at the present time' in order to constitute 'a new politics of truth.'[3]

Shakespearean plays are themselves powerful stories. They contribute to the perpetual contest of stories that constitutes culture: its representations, and our critical accounts of them, reinforce or challenge prevailing notions of what the world is like, of how it might be. 'The detailed and substantial *performance of a known model* of "people like this, relations like this", is in fact the real achievement of most serious novels and plays,' Raymond Williams observes;[4] by appealing to the reader's sense of how the world *is*, the text affirms the validity of the model it invokes. Among other things, *Othello* invites *recognition* that this is how people are, how the world goes. That is why the criteria of plausibility are political. This effect is not countered, as essentialist-humanists have long supposed, by literary quality; the more persuasive the writing, the greater its potential for political intervention.

The quintessential traditional critical activity was always interpretive, getting the text to make sense. Hence the speculation about character motivation, image patterns, thematic integration, structure: the task always was *to help the text into coherence*. And the discovery of coherence was taken as the demonstration of quality. However, such practice may feed into a reactionary politics. The easiest way to make *Othello* plausible in Britain is to rely on the lurking racism, sexism, and superstition in British culture. Why does Othello, who has considerable experience of people, fall so conveniently for Iago's stories? We can make his gullibility plausible by suggesting that black people are generally of a rather simple disposition. To explain why Desdemona elopes with Othello and then becomes so submissive, we might appeal to a supposedly fundamental silliness and passivity of women. Baffled in the attempt to find motive for Iago's malignancy, we can resort to the devil, or the consequence of skepticism towards conventional morality, or homosexuality. Such interpretations might be plausible; might 'work,' as theater people say; but only because they activate regressive aspects of our cultural formation.

Actually, coherence is a chimera, as my earlier arguments should suggest. No story can contain all the possibilities it brings into play; coherence is always selection. And the range of feasible readings depends not only on the text but on the conceptual framework within which we address it. Literary criticism tells its own stories. It is, in effect, a subculture, asserting its own distinctive criteria of plausibility. Education has taken as its brief the socialization of students into these criteria, while masking this project as the achievement by talented individuals (for it is in the program that most should fail) of a just and true reading of texts that are just and true. A cultural materialist practice will review the institutions that retell the Shakespeare stories, and will attempt also a self-consciousness about its own situation within those institutions. We need not just to produce different readings but to shift the criteria of plausibility.

....

QUESTIONS

• What different ways of releasing the subversive potential of literature are proposed or described in these extracts?

• In what ways do the writers depart from traditional notions of aesthetic value?

4 | A new aestheticism?

Jonathan Bate, *The Genius of Shakespeare* (London: Picador, 1997), pp. 327–35.

'Shakespeare' may be thought of as a vast collection of games. Games in which the oldest and most enduring stories—children coming to terms with their parents; men and women falling in love, fearing infidelity, seeking power, renouncing power, growing old, dying well—are made new. Games in which public is pitched against private, young against old, female against male, inheritance against environment; games of yearning and loss, of will and revenge, of sobriety and wit. And, in a bewildering spiral, games which are resolved by games within the game—by cross-dressing and dressing up, disguising and play-acting. Each play-world has its own particular rules—you can make moves in Arden that you can't make in Rome—but I think that we can discern two laws which all the plays obey.

The first law is that truth is not singular. Formal recognition of what may be called 'the aspectuality of truth' is a key feature of many different twentieth-century cultural fields. Albert Einstein perceived it in atomic physics, William Empson in literary criticism. Wittgenstein perceived it in his later philosophy when he used the idea of 'aspects'. He meditated upon a famous drawing in a work of *Gestalt* psychology:

This is a drawing of a duck. This is a drawing of a rabbit. Now you see a duck; now you see a rabbit. Both the duck aspect and the rabbit aspect are 'true', but try as you might you cannot see them both at one and the same time.

Long before the twentieth century, Shakespeare's genius was attuned to aspectuality. Both the Hal aspect (call it the rule of providence) and the Falstaff aspect (call it the rule of the body) are truths of the *Henry* plays, but you cannot see them both at one and the same time.[1] Both the Prospero aspect and the Caliban aspect are truths of *The Tempest*, but you cannot see them both at one and the same time. Again, inherent in the conception of desire performed by many of the plays and sonnets is the truth that, as Empson put it, 'the notion of what you want involves the notion that you must not take it, and this again involves the "opposite defined by your context," that you want something different in another part of your mind.'[2][. . .]

The formal origin of Shakespeare's ambidextrousness was the rhetorical training he received in school. The main purpose of an Elizabethan grammar school education in the arts of rhetoric was the preparation of future public and private servants. By developing a persuasive way with words, one was readying young men to argue a case in secretarial correspondence, council, diplomatic exchange, or law-court. Essential to the training was the ability to argue either side of a case with equal force. This is still a staple in the education of lawyers. Good oratory is thus like good acting: by deploying a full range of suasive linguistic effects, orator and actor make their audience believe—make them feel—the truth of the 'voice' they are animating. It is essential to the effect that the voice is *performed*. Intonation, pitch, pause, and gesture contribute to the emotive effect as much as argument, figurative device, and image. That is the key link between rhetoric and Renaissance drama.

Sixteenth-century educational theory also proposed that active virtue could be learnt through the study of the classic texts of ancient Greece and Rome: read about the noble Aeneas and you will become a little noble yourself. In this respect, the theatre was an advance on the schoolroom. Educational practice was confined to the formal analysis and imitation of vocabulary, syntax, and grammar. The theatre allowed for full rhetorical performance of a kind which could have a far greater effect than any mere philological exercise. In his *Apology for Actors*, Thomas Heywood defended the theatre from its Puritan antagonists by just such an argument.

But the Puritans had a case—a case, indeed, as old as Plato. Granted, the theatre presents to the public virtuous personae who are voiced so powerfully that one is moved to wish to be like them. But the well-trained dramatist and actor will, with equal force, give voice to vicious personae. In the theatre, we will see alluring Cleopatras and scheming Iagos as well as sturdy Caesars and noble Othellos. What is to stop us being moved to wish to be like the sirens and machiavels? In practice, audiences do tend to be more stirred by the voices of Richard III and Edmund the Bastard than those of the virtuous Richmond and Edgar. When we go to the theatre, we are more interested in characters who appeal to theatricality than those who appeal to morality.

As far as Renaissance humanist theory was concerned, this was a place where ideals and pragmatics fell apart. Ideally, a humanist education should have been a stirring to virtue. Pragmatically, it was technical, not moral—what the state needed were men of linguistic skill, never mind to what end those skills were deployed. The art of arguing both sides with equal conviction was a two-edged sword.

In the long term, it was Shakespeare's mastery of the art of making so many different voices persuasive that led to his renewability. Good rhetoric means having an effect on your audience; what I have called the Shakespeare Effect has been so strong, so varied, and so persuasive because Shakespeare was such a good rhetorician. By rhetoric I mean the full art of animating a voice, not the narrower technical sense of mastering tropes and schemes—the latter were but a part of the art of voicing. Since the eighteenth century, Shakespeare has been admired above all for two things: the range of his characters and the inventiveness of his language. The two go closely together, for it was by investing so many of his dramatic persons with memorable language that Shakespeare animated more voices than did any of his contemporaries. And because he animated so many opposing voices, he has been able to speak to many later dispositions.

Prior to the new way of thinking which became possible with such twentieth-century developments as *Gestalt* psychology and quantum physics, the person who came nearest to an understanding of Shakespeare's aspectuality was John Keats, writing under the influence of William Hazlitt. For Hazlitt, the key to Shakespeare's genius was his open-mindedness, his lack of egotism, and freedom from bias, his capacity to see both sides of a question and to empathize equally with all:

> The striking peculiarity of Shakspeare's mind was its generic quality, its power of com-
> munication with all other minds—so that it contained a universe of thought and feeling
> within itself, and had no one peculiar bias, or exclusive excellence more than another.
> He was just like any other man, but that he was like all other men. He was the least of an
> egotist that it was possible to be. He was nothing in himself; but he was all that others
> were, or that they could become. He not only had in himself the germs of every faculty
> and feeling, but he could follow them by anticipation, intuitively, into all their conceivable
> ramifications, through every change of fortune or conflict of passion, or turn of thought.
> He had 'a mind reflecting ages past,' and present:—all the people that ever lived are
> there. There was no respect of persons with him. His genius shone equally on the evil and
> on the good, on the wise and the foolish, the monarch and the beggar.[3]

Keats heard Hazlitt lecture to this effect and concluded that the true poet must be a chameleon, must take 'as much delight in conceiving an Iago as an Imogen'. Shakespeare refuses to swear allegiance either to the principle of reflection (call it Hamlet-in-soliloquy) or to that of improvisation (call it Iago). He was the supreme exemplar of what Keats called *negative capability*: a willingness to be content with 'half knowledge', to remain in uncertainty and doubt 'without any irritable reaching after fact and reason'. Keats regarded this quality as the necessary condition of all great art.[4]

Negative capability is a brilliant formulation because it holds together a negative and a positive term in the exact manner of Heisenberg's 'uncertainty principle'. How can negativity be a capability, how can uncertainty be a principle? Since Keats lived in a Newtonian universe of 'fact and reason', he could only articulate negative capability as a form of scepticism which he opposed to scientific truth; he had to leave Shakespeare undecided between two possi-bilities. In the quantum universe, we have discovered that undecidability is the condition of scientific truth and that contraries are equally true. Light has both wave and particle aspects, though wave and particle equations are incompatible with one another; an electron has both momentum and coordinates, but both cannot be specified at the same time. Undecidability, as Empson perceived in that crucial passage of *Seven Types*, is a condition of nature, not a fallibility or predilection of the interpreting mind. In an aspectual world, *Negative capability* becomes comprehensible as a law rather than a mystery. The sonnets can be understood as both autobiographical and fictive, Hamlet can be seen as both iconic and elusive.

To simplify, we may say that 'negative' corresponds to the rabbit/Falstaff/Caliban, 'capability' to the duck/Hal/Prospero. But if we do so, we must recognize that this is indeed a simplification. The duck-rabbit is a neat icon of aspectuality, but it only has two aspects. Each of Shakespeare's plays has many more than two. Every character has a point of view, while more and more aspects are revealed through the unfolding of the action. The duck-rabbit is experienced in a moment on the page, whereas the Shakespearean drama is experienced through time in the theatre.

The law of aspectuality governs many dramatic and poetic worlds; in itself, it does not make Shakespeare unique. What is it, then, that sets Shakespeare apart from even his most talented contemporaries, that gives him his unique capacity to be reperformed again and again through history? [. . .]

[T]he key gift which belonged to Shakespeare, but not to Christopher Marlowe, was experience as an actor. Faustus and Hamlet endure because each of them seems to be both himself and Everyman, both intensely individualized and an embodiment of the restless intellectual activity that is the unique mark of our species. But Faustus cuts an awkward figure when horsing around on stage; Hamlet's extra dimension is the adept role-playing which goes with his love of theatre. Marlowe's heroes never quite recognize that Everyman is a player; that is their pathos and their limitation. Shakespeare's most memorable characters are irresistibly drawn to game-playing—Richard of Gloucester's wooing of Lady Anne, Rosalind's dressing-up, Falstaff's play extempore, Hamlet's 'Mousetrap', Cleopatra's celerity in dying, and so the list goes on. That is their glory and their mobility. [. . .]

[T]he peculiar power of Shakespearean characterization stems from the way in which the motivations that drive his source-narratives are removed. Instead of being predetermined, identity is performed through action. At the same time, a vacuum is created in the space which belongs to motive; spectators and readers rush in to fill that vacuum, thus performing their own versions of the play. A greater variety of greatly different performances is thus possible than is the case with, say, the plays of Ben Jonson, which tend to be pre-scripted by character 'type'. Volpone is by nature cunning, whereas Falstaff is no single thing by nature but potentially everything by performance.

This suggests that the second law of the Shakespeare world is the idea of performativity itself. [. . .]

There are other dramatists among his contemporaries who wrote extraordinary poetry and brought an astonishing range of human experience to the stage. There are precedents in early Tudor dramatic 'interludes' for the idea of the play within the play; there are precedents in Lyly for the cross-dressing of the boy actor. But no other successful poet of the period was an actor through almost all his working life. No other dramatist among his English contemporaries combined so many manifestations of the figure of 'the theatre of the world'. No other writer returned so obsessively to what Borges in his fable 'Everything and Nothing' called 'the fundamental identity of existing, dreaming and acting'.

*   *   *

Kiernan Ryan, *Shakespeare*, 3rd edn (Palgrave: Basingstoke and New York, 2002), p. 33.

Shakespeare's polyphony makes it impossible to invest any of the currently competing world views with exclusive legitimacy or self-evident sovereignty. Their mutual interrogation generates instead a synoptic vision, which overrides the imperatives of division and domination. The plays' roving impulse to displace the perspective across a spectrum of identities and attitudes creates their structural identification with the common impulses of our kind rather than with one sector of society at the expense of the rest. It is a way of seeing which neither precedes, nor survives abstraction from, the total complex of dramatized acts and statements, in whose unfolding alone Shakespeare's vision is discovered and articulated.

*   *   *

John J. Joughin, 'Shakespeare, modernity and the aesthetic: art, truth and judgement in *The Winter's Tale*', in *Shakespeare and Modernity: Early Modern to Millennium*, ed. Hugh Grady (London and New York: Routledge, 2000), pp. 61–7, 73.

Any discussion of the literary or artistic merit of Shakespeare's plays is almost bound to arouse suspicion. For most radical critics, aesthetics still tends to be discarded as part of the 'problem' rather than part of the 'solution', all too reminiscent of a brand of outdated idealism which privileged notions of refined sensibility and the immutability of 'literary value'. As a consequence, contemporary political and historicist criticism has tended to regard a 'commitment to the literary' as 'one of the major limitations' of traditionalist approaches to the playwright's work (Hawkes 1996: 11). Yet more recently, the emergence in a British context of a critical formation, sometimes pejoratively labelled 'new aestheticist' in its orientation, has foregrounded the need to give some further consideration to the transformative potential of the aesthetic.

In the course of resituating some of the assumptions of poststructuralist thought in relation to the philosophical analysis of modernity offered by the Frankfurt School tradition of Critical Theory, philosophers like Jay Bernstein (1992), Andrew Bowie (1990; 1997a), Howard Caygill (1989) and Peter Dews (1987; 1995) have enabled a reconsideration of key issues concerning aesthetic validity which were often neglected in the first stage development of literary theory.[1] I want to argue that this work has also indirectly paved the way to the revival of the aesthetic as a politically critical category in English studies. Rather than ceding the question of aesthetic value as the exclusive preserve of the political Right, this [extract] aims to demonstrate that the time is now ripe for a re-examination of the idea of the aesthetic in materialist criticism.

Of course the danger of a return to an old-style aestheticism in Shakespeare studies remains a constant threat, as Harold Bloom's (1999) celebration of 'Shakespeare's universalism' testifies. Bloom complains that, in relying on 'ideologically imposed contextualization', recent critical approaches like cultural materialism and new historicism tend to 'value theory over the literature itself'. For these critics, Bloom reflects sadly, 'the aesthetic stance is itself an ideology' (Bloom 1999: 9). But in some sense, even as he is prone to overstate the case, Bloom is partly right. Cultural materialism usefully draws our attention to the fact that the question of aesthetic value is a politically loaded issue and not a neutral one. Yet while the deployment of Shakespeare is clearly open to 'ideological misuse', surely Bloom also has a point when he implies that the endurance of Shakespeare's texts cannot be reduced solely to the question of their ideological function in any given period.

Nor, I might add (and this is where Bloom partly misses the point himself), is this necessarily a position which recent critical approaches would wholly resist: after all, as the bulk of recent work on the cultural production and reception of Shakespeare's plays has demonstrated, historically speaking at least, the striking thing about the playwright's texts is their continued refusal to be exhausted by their continued appropriation and counter-appropriation in an endless variety of contexts (see e.g. G. Taylor 1991; Marsden 1991). This is not to say that the playwright's work is somehow of 'timeless' significance, nor is it to deny the value of work which has revealed the playwright's involvement in securing regimes which have deployed Shakespeare for their own oppressive ideological ends. There can be no doubt that the revival of certain plays, at specific moments, in particular contexts, usefully alerts us to the manipulation of Shakespeare as an instrument of social control. Yet the enduring longevity of the dramatist's work is also clearly related to its ability to sustain interpretations which are often contestable or diametrically opposed. Cultural materialism allows for precisely this type of contestation, yet as Andrew Bowie observes:

> the failure [of radical criticism] to engage with the most powerful works of bourgeois culture . . . beyond revealing their indisputable relations to barbarism, means we do not understand why such works are enduringly powerful in ways which cannot finally be grasped by the category of ideology and which cannot be merely a function of their roots in barbarism.
>
> (Bowie 1997a: 7)

Bowie offers us a more nuanced and effective defence of the aesthetic than Bloom can possibly muster, yet his point also implicitly echoes Bloom's complaint, that one of the limitations of ideology critique is that it fails satisfactorily to explain why it is that, in most circumstances, even once they are demythologized or problematized, outside of their immediate ideological function, certain canonical texts like Shakespeare's continue to remain meaningful and authoritative.

For Bloom the 'ultimate use' of Shakespeare is in teaching us 'whatever truth you can sustain without perishing' (Bloom 1999: 10). Yet paradoxically, as I have already implied, it appears as if Shakespeare's very survival as a literary text is less a product of the type of meaningful repleteness Bloom alludes to than a result of its resistance to ever being clearly understood (cf. Bowie 1997a: 11). [. . .]

Traditionalist viewpoints which uncritically endorse the 'superior validity' of Shakespeare's plays, to the exclusion of all other considerations, often claim that they are politically neutral. Excepting the qualifications I have outlined above, the major contribution of ideology critique in Shakespeare studies has been in unmasking this stance of polite disinterestedness, and in revealing the extent to which it effectively conceals a series of tendentious presumptions concerning the 'truth' of the human condition, the overall tenor of which Terence Hawkes helpfully summarizes in the following fashion:

> That, in short, Shakespeare's plays present us with nothing less than the truth, the whole truth and nothing but the truth about the most fundamental matters of human existence: birth, death and the life that comes between.
>
> (Hawkes 1996: 9)

For all its self-evident transparency this 'common sense' view of literature actually secretes its own theoretical agenda, underpinning an approach to interpretation which Catherine Belsey helpfully characterizes as 'expressive realist' in its overall connotation:

> expressive realism . . . is the theory that literature reflects the *reality* of experience as it is

perceived by one (especially gifted) individual, who *expresses* it in a discourse which enables other individuals to recognise it as true.

(Belsey 1980: 7, Belsey's emphasis)

As Belsey argues, this apparently 'natural way of reading' actually presupposes a rather fixed understanding of the value of literary texts and their claim to authenticity.

Crucially, 'expressive realism' presumes a practice of reading literature which is founded on what philosophers would categorize as a *correspondence model of truth*. In other words, literature's relationship to the world is conceived in terms of a naive mimeticism which posits the truth of an anterior or predetermined ideal reality, of which literature is correspondingly a 'true' re-presentation. Furthermore, as Belsey's statement implies, empirical-idealist variants of lit. crit. locate their premise on the assumption that the origination, reception and knowledge of these 'truths' is generally accessible to experience and self-evident—although more so to some than others, and especially to the more refined sensibilities of 'high and solitary minds'. In effect, literary texts are treated as if they were physical phenomena whose very existence serves to verify clear and testable ideas. In the case of its neo-classical variants, literary criticism reimposes an understanding of art as corresponding with the pre-existent uniformity of nature itself.

As Belsey, Hawkes, and a host of other critics have demonstrated, recent developments in literary theory have revealed just how restrictive these 'rational' truth claims actually are. Materialist approaches to the plays demonstrate that the 'meaning' of a text is historically determined and is dependent on its cultural context. In turn, a poststructuralist critique of metaphysics has produced a healthy climate of hermeneutic suspicion, both in disclosing the complicity between truth, reason and domination, and in revealing language itself to be 'perpetually in process' and productive of a potential plurality of meanings (cf. Belsey 1980: 19–20). Yet, in taking an exclusively linguistic and culturalist turn, recent criticism also runs the risk of excluding from its consideration the distinctively qualitative aspects of literary meaning. In short, as Bowie observes, *literary* theorists are often effectively in danger of being 'without a valid way of talking about "literature" ' (Bowie 1997a: 5). While poststructuralism usefully focuses on the reader's role in the constitution of meaning and allows for the possibility that texts are open to a number of interpretations, it tends to neglect the truth-potential of the particular transformation wrought by the aesthetic experience itself. For new aestheticists like Bowie, our understanding of the relationship between art, truth and interpretation is not merely dependent on an openness to the fact that literary texts transform meaning, but is also equally concerned with asking precisely *how* this revelation is to be construed (Bowie 1997a: 5). Understood in relation to more conventional truth claims, the distinctive articulation of truth in works of art—in being truer than empirical or mimetic 'truth'—underpins what Bowie terms a 'disclosive' literary distinction, which he characterizes in the following terms:

> rather than truth being the revelation of a pre-existing reality, it [art's truth status] is in fact a creative process of 'disclosure'. Art-works, in this view, reveal aspects of the world which would not emerge if there were no such disclosure: truth 'happens'—it does not imitate or represent.

(Bowie 1992: 33)

Such moments could conceivably be construed purely in formal or 'linguistic terms', in relation to overturning conventional expectations or in breaking with existing rules. Yet the revelatory potential of aesthetic disclosure suggests that it also needs to be understood as a more participatory and consensual event, in the course of which, as Bowie puts it, in defamiliarizing habitual perceptions: 'something comes to be seen as something in a new way' (Bowie 1997a: 301).

Crucially, the relationship between the 'happening' of aesthetic disclosure and the interplay by which we understand it to 'be' a distinctively *literary* happening throws a new light on the question of interpretation and enables us to retain a sense of the creative and evaluative dimension which informs judgement (aesthetic or otherwise), without then merely lapsing back into the restrictions which obtain to the more traditionalist truth claims of essentialism or empiricism. Instead, in developing a Heideggerian sense of the disclosive capacity of the aesthetic (without wanting to restrict 'disclosure' to uncovering 'some kind of already present essence'), Bowie persuasively locates 'seeing as' as a constitutive experience which effectively: ' "discloses" the world in new ways . . . rather than copying or representing what is known to be already there' (Bowie 1997a: 5, 301). [. . .]

In its qualitative independence, autonomous art resists subsumption within the instrumentalist logic of capital production and offers an enclave for the articulation of alternative values. In this form, aesthetics is not a rejection of reason; indeed, as Andrew Bowie observes: 'it becomes the location in which what has been repressed by a limited conception of reason can be articulated' (Bowie 1990: 4). The appearance of a separate aesthetic domain during the eighteenth century proceeds to provide a compensatory site for the evaluation of our experience of those sensuous particulars, which are now also increasingly denied to us in our newly 'alienated' modern condition. And in this respect, the survival of canonical texts like Shakespeare continue to confirm their significance in manifesting the potential to play a crucial role in reconfiguring our understanding of modern society. Tied to actuality, in ways that cannot be reduced to the empirical, the emergence of literature serves as a type of 'non-empirical record', which allows for the creation of 'possible-worlds' (Bowie 1997a: 16–27) beyond but also within the regulated sphere of its 'new' bourgeois confinement.

. . . .

QUESTIONS

- In what ways do the writers in this subsection attempt to recover an understanding of the central aesthetic value of Shakespeare in particular and literature in general?

- How successful are they?

- How applicable are such cases to more obscure women writers such as those mentioned by Healy above?

5 | Ethics of the other

Don E. Wayne, 'New Historicism', in *Encyclopedia of Literature and Criticism*, ed. Martin Coyle, Peter Garside, Malcolm Kelsall and John Peck (London and New York: Routledge, 1990), p. 803.

What some of these critics sense is the need for an ethics based on the acknowledgement of difference, but also on the principle of relationship.

* * *

Stephen Greenblatt, *Marvelous Possessions: The Wonder of the New World* (Chicago: University of Chicago Press, 1991), pp. 14–24.

Nil admirari, the ancient maxim taught. But, in the presence of the New World, the classical model of mature, balanced detachment seemed at once inappropriate and impossible. Columbus's voyage initiated a century of intense wonder. European culture experienced something like the 'startle reflex' one can observe in infants: eyes widened, arms outstretched, breathing stilled, the whole body momentarily convulsed. But what does it mean to experience wonder? What are its origins, its uses, and its limits? Is it closer to pleasure or pain, longing or horror? Is it a sign and an agent of renunciation or possession? The ambiguities of wonder in the New World may be suggested by a passage from Jean de Léry's great *History of a Voyage to the Land of Brazil*. A Huguenot pastor, Léry lived for several months in 1557 among the Tupinamba in the Bay of Rio. During this stay he and two other Frenchmen (one of them a Norman interpreter) had occasion, he writes, to witness a solemn religious assembly of the natives. What he saw and heard amazed and frightened him:

> While we were having our breakfast, with no idea as yet of what they intended to do, we began to hear in the men's house (not thirty feet from where we stood) a very low murmur, like the muttering of someone reciting his hours. Upon hearing this, the women (about two hundred of them) all stood up and clustered together, listening intently. The men little by little raised their voices and were distinctly heard singing all together and repeating this syllable of exhortation, *He, he, he, he*; the women, to our amazement, answered them from their side, and with a trembling voice; reiterating that same interjection *He, he, he, he*, let out such cries, for more than a quarter of an hour, that as we watched them we were utterly disconcerted. Not only did they howl, but also, leaping violently into the air, they made their breasts shake and they foamed at the mouth—in fact, some, like those who have the falling-sickness over here, fell in a dead faint; I can only believe that the devil entered their body and that they fell into a fit of madness.[1]

For Léry the spectacle is the very embodiment of what his culture views not only as otherness but as evil: the intimations of bestiality and madness merge with an overarching, explanatory image of demonic possession. The reference to the devil is not a metaphor; it is the deep truth of the natives' condition: 'the Americans are visibly and actually tormented by evil spirits' (p. 138). This torment is deeply significant, for in Léry's view the natives' religious fear and suffering is both a divine punishment—proof that 'even in this world there are devils to torment those who deny God and his power'—and justification for their future damnation: 'one can see that this fear they have of Him whom they refuse to acknowledge will render them utterly without excuse' (p. 139). In the Kafka-like logic of this argument, the Tupinamba will be justly condemned through all eternity precisely because they fear the one true God whom they do not and cannot know and whom for this reason they refuse to acknowledge. Léry reports, as the most vivid example of this refusal, that he and his fellows chose the natives' intense fear of thunder as an opportunity to evangelize: 'Adapting ourselves to their crudeness,' he writes, 'we would seize the occasion to say to them that this was the very God of whom we were speaking, who to show his grandeur and power made heavens and earth tremble; their resolution and response was that since he frightened them in that way, he was good for nothing' (p. 135)

Such a response, in Léry's view, condemns the Tupinamba to fear, credulity, and superstition. It is not an accident that the Protestant Léry thought that the low chanting from the men's house sounded at first 'like the muttering of someone reciting his hours' (p. 141); [he condemned] the Catholic Mass as cannibalism.[2] For Léry, whose *History of a Voyage* was published in Calvinist Geneva, Catholic rituals are occasions in which the devil is doing his work, and he invites his readers to interpret the Tupinamba ceremony in the light of that Mass: in both the experience of wonder is linked to a violation of all that is most holy.

In the 1585 edition of the *History of a Voyage*, Léry added to his account a description taken from Jean Bodin's *De la démonomanie des sorciers* (1578) of a witches' sabbath. Bodin was one of the most learned, influential, and uncompromisingly punitive of the Renaissance witchmongers, the most articulate of those who insisted that the devil was literally present in what appeared to be fantastic and imaginary claims. Léry evidently felt he had found in Bodin's account the European ritual that most closely resembled the astonishing scene he had witnessed more than twenty years earlier, a resemblance that transcended the immense cultural and geographical distance he himself continually remarks: 'I have concluded,' Léry writes, 'that they have the same master: that is, the Brazilian women and the witches over here were guided by the same spirit of Satan; neither the distance between the places nor the long passage over the sea keeps the father of lies from working both here and there on those who are handed over to him by the just judgment of God.'[3]

What Léry has seen in Brazil then is nothing less than the active and literal manifestation of Satan, and like Bodin he insists that those who would take this manifestation as a delusion, imagination, or metaphor are 'atheist dogs,' 'worse than the devils themselves' (p. 139). And yet it is precisely here, at the moment in which the wonder aroused by the religious assembly is fully disclosed as a justifiable shudder of revulsion, a prelude to flight, that the mood shifts radically:

Although I had been among the savages for more than half a year and was already fairly well used to their ways, nonetheless (to be frank) being somewhat frightened and not knowing how the game might turn out, I wished I were back at our fort. However, after these chaotic noises and howls had ended and the men had taken a short pause (the women and children were now silent), we heard them once again singing and making their voices resound in a harmony so marvelous that you would hardly have needed to ask whether, since I was now somewhat easier in my mind at hearing such sweet and gracious sounds, I wished to watch them from nearby. (p. 141)

Avoidance is transformed into approach, as Léry and his fellows draw nearer to the dancing, singing men:

At the beginning of this witches' sabbath, when I was in the women's house, I had been somewhat afraid; now I received in recompense such joy, hearing the measured harmonies of such a multitude, and especially in the cadence and refrain of the song, when at every verse all of them would let their voices trail, saying *Heu, heuaure, heura, heuraure, heura, heura, oueh*—I stood there transported with delight [*tout ravi*]. Whenever I remember it, my heart trembles, and it seems their voices are still in my ears. (pp. 142–4)

Wonder is now not the sign of revulsion but of ravishment, an ecstatic joy that can be experienced anew even twenty years later through an act of remembrance. The authenticity of the recovery is confirmed in Léry's body itself, in the trembling of his heart, for this trembling is the authentic sign of wonder, proof that the marvelous Tupinamba voices are still in his ears: wonder, as Albertus Magnus wrote, is like 'a systole of the heart'.[4] As Albertus' brilliant figure and Léry's experience make clear, the marvelous gestures toward the world by registering an overpowering intensity of response. Someone witnesses something amazing, but what most matters takes place not 'out there' or along the receptive surfaces of the body where the self encounters the world, but deep within, at the vital, emotional center of the witness. This inward response cannot be marginalized or denied, any more than a constriction of the heart in terror can be denied; wonder is absolutely exigent, a primary or radical passion.

But what is the meaning of this passion for Léry? What is the relation between the experience of exquisite beauty and the horror of satanic evil? It would be possible to reconcile the two by reminding the reader, as Renaissance clerics frequently did, that the angel of darkness disguised himself as an angel of light. The beauty of the music would be revealed then to be a lure. But, though he can be an alert and even relentless moralist, Léry does not interpret his experience as a temptation; he seems eager to provide not a warning but a reflection of his own intense pleasure. Thus in later editions of his *History of a Voyage* he even includes musical notation for the Tupinamba chant, as if he longed for his reader actually to hear the music and share his ravishment. Nor does he quite turn this ravishment, as he elsewhere does, into a lesson for atheists, a sign that even the benighted savages have some higher vision, some practice of religious adoration. He does, to be sure, learn from the Norman interpreter that the songs he has just heard mingle laments for the dead and threats against enemies with something else: a tale of a flood in ancient times that had covered the world and drowned everyone except their ancestors who climbed to safety in the highest trees. Not surprisingly, Léry believes that this tale is a corrupt oral version of the biblical Flood—'being altogether deprived of writing, it is hard for them to retain things in their purity' (p. 144)—but the scriptural echo is not what gives the chant its power, for it had ravished his senses before he knew its meaning.

Léry presents his appreciation of the beauty of the savage music as a triumph over his own panic fear in the presence of the demonic. Perhaps we should interpret his response then as a version of the aesthetic recoding by means of which medieval Christians neutralized the images of the ancient pagan deities. In Michael Camille's account of this recoding, 'the aesthetic anesthetizes': medieval admiration for the wonders of pagan art, he writes, 'was really a phenomenon of distancing, a taking out of context.'[5] It is certainly true that Léry's ravishment takes the ceremony—which he has identified as a witches' sabbath—out of context, but his response does not seem to be the same as distancing: on the contrary, he takes it out of context—any context, including his own beliefs—in order to approach more closely, to draw it into himself, to remember it in the very beating of his heart. The experience of wonder seems to resist recuperation, containment, ideological incorporation; it sits strangely apart from everything that gives coherence to Léry's universe, apart and yet utterly compelling. This passage in the *History of a Voyage*, Michel de Certeau writes, is 'a stolen instant, a purloined memory beyond the text.' The fact that Léry does not securely attach a meaning to his experience—and that we cannot do so for him—is the source of its mysterious power: 'An absence of meaning,' de Certeau remarks, 'opens a rift in time.'[6]

This rift, this cracking apart of contextual understanding in an elusive and ambiguous experience of wonder, is a central recurring feature in the early discourse of the New World. It is the feature that most decisively links this discourse, stylistically unambitious and conceptually muddled though much of it is, to both philosophical and aesthetic discourse. For wonder plays a decisive role in the period's philosophy and art, theorized by the former as a principal cause and by the latter as a principal effect. That is, philosophy (as Socrates had already formulated it) begins in wonder, while the purpose of poetry (as innumerable poets said) was to produce the marvelous. This theoretical conceptualization of the marvelous was already under way before the discourse of the New World, but it was by no means fully articulated. It is not, in other words, only or even primarily as an intellectual background to Columbus and other early voyagers that I find discussions of the marvelous important. Something like the reverse is also the case: the frequency and intensity of the appeal to wonder in the wake of the great geographical discoveries of the late fifteenth and early sixteenth centuries helped (along with many other factors) to provoke its conceptualization.[7]

This conceptualization can be read back into the discourse of travel in order to explicate some of its most persistent and puzzling features. According to Descartes—to choose the philosopher who marks the endpoint of the mental world of the early modern voyagers and the inception of a different and more familiar world—wonder is not, as Albertus had thought, registered in the heart and blood; unlike the other passions that have good or evil as their objects and hence involve the heart, wonder has only knowledge as its object and thus occurs strictly in the brain. This relocation would seem to detach wonder from the source of its somatic authority—the experience of something very much like a heart attack—but Descartes too insists on its immense strength, a strength that derives from the element of surprise, 'the sudden and unexpected arrival of this impression.'[8] This surprise does not cause the heart to contract, in Descartes's view, but at its most extreme it causes a drastic alteration in the spirits of the brain which rush, as it were, to bear witness to the object of wonder:

> And this surprise has so much power in causing the spirits which are in the cavities of the brain to take their way from thence to the place where is the impression of the object which we wonder at, that it sometimes thrusts them all there, . . . and this causes the

whole body to remain as immobile as a statue, and prevents our perceiving more of the object than the first face which is presented, or consequently of acquiring a more particular knowledge of it. This is what we commonly call being astonished, and astonishment is an excess of wonder which can never be otherwise than bad. (pp. 363–4)

A moderate measure of wonder is useful in that it calls attention to that which is 'new or very different from what we formerly knew, or from what we supposed that it ought to be' and fixes it in the memory, but an excess of wonder is harmful, Decartes thought, for it freezes the individual in the face of objects whose moral character, whose capacity to do good or evil, has not yet been determined. That is, wonder precedes, even escapes, moral categories. When we wonder, we do not yet know if we love or hate the object at which we are marveling; we do not yet know if we should embrace it or flee from it. For this reason wonder, Descartes argues, 'has no opposite and is the first of all the passions.' Similarly for Spinoza—in whose account wonder was not, strictly speaking, a passion at all, but rather a mode of conception (*imaginatio*)—wonder depends upon a suspension or failure of categories and is a kind of paralysis, a stilling of the normal associative restlessness of the mind. In wonder, 'the mind comes to a stand, because the particular concept in question has no connection with other concepts.'[9] The object that arouses wonder is so new that for a moment at least it is alone, unsystematized, an utterly detached object of rapt attention.

Wonder—thrilling, potentially dangerous, momentarily immobilizing, charged at once with desire, ignorance, and fear—is the quintessential human response to what Decartes calls a 'first encounter' (p. 358). Such terms, which recur in philosophy from Aristotle through the seventeenth century, made wonder an almost inevitable component of the discourse of discovery, for by definition wonder is an instinctive recognition of difference, the sign of a heightened attention, 'a sudden surprise of the soul,' as Descartes puts it (p. 362), in the face of the new. The expression of wonder stands for all that cannot be understood, that can scarcely be believed. It calls attention to the problem of credibility and at the same time insists upon the undeniability, the exigency of the experience.

It is in this spirit that Milton invokes wonder when he describes the rebel angels shrinking themselves in scale in order to enter the council chamber of Pandemonium:

> Behold a wonder! they but now who seemed
> In bigness to surpass Earth's giant sons
> Now less than smallest dwarfs, in narrow room
> Throng numberless, like that pygmean race
> Beyond the Indian mount, or faerie elves,
> Whose midnight revels, by a forest-side
> Or fountain some belated peasant sees,
> Or dreams he sees, while overhead the moon
> Sits arbitress, and nearer to the earth
> Wheels her pale course, they on their mirth and dance
> Intent, with jocund music charm his ear;
> At once with joy and fear his heart rebounds.
> *(Paradise Lost* 1.777–88)[10]

The transformation of the rebel angels is at once unbelievable and true—hence a wonder, akin to the marvelous beings, giants and pygmies, long associated with voyages to the Indies. The experience of beholding such a wonder is, in Milton's account, profoundly ambiguous: the exalted spectacle of radical evil is likened to a belated peasant's hallucinatory encounter with fairies, likened then to moon-struck Bottom who tells his mates, 'I am to discourse wonders; but ask me not what' (*Midsummer Night's Dream* v. ii. 29–30). For a moment epic is confounded with comedy, as are giant with dwarf, torment with mirth, demonic with harmless, what lies outside the mind with what lies within. Magical charms, compelling and dangerous, are fleetingly lodged within the pleasures of art, as the fairies 'charm his ear' with their music. The whole experience produces the somatic effect that is, as we have seen, the hallmark of wonder: 'At once with joy and fear his heart rebounds.'

With this rebounding of the heart we are back to Jean de Léry and the wonder of Tupinamba music and dance. Experiences such as those he wishes to describe pose a serious rhetorical problem, a problem akin to that Milton faced in describing events in Heaven and Hell. At the beginning of his account, Léry asks how his French readers can be made to 'believe what can only be seen two thousand leagues from where they live: things never known (much less written about) by the Ancients; things so marvelous that experience itself can scarcely engrave them upon the understanding even of those who have in fact seen them?' (p. lx). The skepticism that educated Europeans have developed must somehow be suspended; they must be made to revise their sense of what is possible and what is only fabulous.

In Guiana in the 1590s Sir Walter Ralegh hears of a people who 'are reported to have their eyes in their shoulders, and their mouths in the middle of their breasts.' Ralegh knows that this 'may be thought a meere fable,' precisely the kind of report that had given Mandeville—who writes of 'foul men of figure without heads, and they have eyes in either shoulder one, and their mouths are round shaped like a horseshoe, y-midst their breasts' (p. 142)—a reputation for lying. But for Ralegh it is skepticism rather than credulity that is likely to be misleading: 'Such a nation was written of by Mandevile, whose reports were holden for fables many yeeres, and yet since the East Indies were discovered, we find his relations true of such things as heretofore were held incredible.'[11] Similarly, Léry writes, with a sarcastic glance at his great enemy Friar Thevet, 'I do not endorse the fabulous tales found in the books of certain people who, trusting to hearsay, have written things that are completely false,' but, he goes on to declare, 'I am not ashamed to confess that since I have been in this land of America, where everything to be seen—the way of life of its inhabitants, the form of the animals, what the earth produces—is so unlike what we have in Europe, Asia, and Africa that it may very well be called a "New World" with respect to us, I have revised the opinion that I formerly had of Pliny and others when they describe foreign lands, because I have seen things as fantastic and prodigious as any of those—once thought incredible—that they mention' (pp. lx–lxi).

The discovery of the New World at once discredits the Ancients who did not know of these lands and, by raising the possibility that what had seemed gross exaggerations and lies were in fact sober accounts of radical otherness, gives classical accounts of prodigies a new life. Léry's text depends for its authority precisely on its claim to sober accuracy ('simply to declare what I have myself experienced, seen, heard, and observed'), on its refusal of the lies, hearsay, and exaggerations of Thevet; but at the same time, he is writing not in testimony to the ordinariness and familiarity of Brazil but to its utter strangeness, the strangeness of 'lands completely unknown to the Ancients' (p. 3). His work can only be believed if he arouses in his readers something of the wonder that he himself has felt, for that wonder will link whatever is out there with inward conviction. For the early voyagers, wonder not only marked the new but mediated between outside and inside (Milton's 'sees/Or dreams he sees'). Hence the ease with which the very words *marvel* and *wonder* shift between the designation of a material object and the designation of a response to the object, between intense, almost phantasmagorical inward states and thoroughly externalized objects that can, after the initial moments of astonishment have passed, be touched, cataloged, inventoried, possessed.

The marvelous is a central feature then in the whole complex system of representation, verbal and visual, philosophical and aesthetic, intellectual and emotional, through which people in the late Middle Ages and the Renaissance apprehended, and thence possessed or discarded, the unfamiliar, the alien, the terrible, the desirable, and the hateful. By a 'system of representation,' I do not mean to suggest that there was a single, perfectly integrated mimetic practice. In this period, as in many others, philosophy and art are distinct and often opposed— the former seeking to pass through the wonder that the latter seeks to enhance—and each is in turn distinct from discourses like history, theology, natural history, and law. Each of the discursive regimes has its own characteristic concerns, intellectual and procedural boundaries, specialized languages. But each of these also touches and interacts with the others in a loose but powerful association, an association driven by certain mimetic assumptions, shared metaphors, operational practices, root perceptions.

Interpreters of literature are trained to analyze the imagination at play; in most early European accounts of the New World we are dealing instead with the imagination at work. It would be foolish to conflate the two modes and to proceed as if interpretive practice could be the same with both; I am painfully aware of all of the ways in which a literary critic is ill-equipped to deal with a text such as Columbus's letter to Santangel. But the European encounter with the New World, with its radical displacement of routines, brought close to the surface of non-literary texts imaginative operations that are normally buried deep below their surface (unlike works of literature where these operations are prominently displayed). Consequently, it may be possible to use some of the concerns of literary criticism to illuminate texts written with anything but literary ambitions and actions performed with anything but theatrical intentions—texts and actions that register not the pleasures of the fictive but the compelling powers of the real.

Let me try to be clear: I am not identifying an overarching Renaissance ideology, a single way of making and remaking the world. Any of the individual national cultures of early modern Europe, let alone the fantastically complex whole, had so many different and conflicting ways of seeing and describing the world that any attempt to posit a unified perceptual field will prove a gross distortion. But the variety is not infinite, and in the face of the New World—the epitome of Descartes's 'sudden and unexpected arrival'—the differing responses disclose shared assumptions and techniques. Struggling to grasp hold of the immense realms newly encountered, Europeans deployed a lumbering, jerry-built, but immensely powerful mimetic machinery, the inescapable mediating agent not only of possession but of simple contact with the other. For this reason, the early modern discourse of discovery [. . .] is a superbly powerful register of the characteristic claims and limits of European representational practice.

The qualities that gave wonder its centrality to this practice also gave it its ideological malleability. For the perception in Descartes or Spinoza that wonder precedes recognitions of good and evil, like the perception in Aristotle or Albertus Magnus that it precedes knowledge, conferred upon the marvelous a striking indeterminacy and made it—like the imagination to which it is closely linked—the object of a range of sharply differing uses. [. . .] I do not think that this possessive use of the marvelous is decisive or final: [. . .] the experience of wonder continually reminds us that our grasp of the world is incomplete.

The most palpable sign of this incompleteness for the early voyagers was an inability to understand or be understood. Such language difference perhaps always has some element of the marvelous. (A Tuscan farmer once told me he could not quite get past his astonishment that *pane* was not called *pane* in English; all other words might possibly differ, but *pane*?) Europeans were particularly struck by encountering peoples who spoke languages, as one observer put it, 'neither knowen nor understood of any.' [. . .] [T]he early discourse of the New World is, among other things, a record of the colonizing of the marvelous. [. . .] But an historical trajectory is not a theoretical necessity. [. . .] I return to the marvelous as a sign of the eyewitness's surprising recognition of the other in himself, himself in the other. [. . .]

This is the utopian moment of travel: when you realize that what seems most unattainably marvelous, most desirable, is what you almost already have, what you could have—if you could only strip away the banality and corruption of the everyday—at home.

*   *   *

Jacques Derrida, *Specters of Marx: The State of the Debt, The Work of Mourning, and The New International*, trans. Peggy Kamuf (New York and London: Routledge, 1994), p. xix.

If I am getting ready to speak at length about ghosts, inheritance, and generations, generations of ghosts, which is to say about certain *others* who are not present, not presently living, either to us, in us, or outside us, it is in the name of *justice*. [. . .] It is necessary to speak *of the* ghost, indeed *to the* ghost and *with* it, from the moment that no ethics, no politics, whether revolutionary or not, seems possible and thinkable and *just* that does not recognize in its principle the respect for those others who are no longer or for those others who are not yet *there*, presently living, whether they are already dead or not yet born. No justice [. . .] seems possible or thinkable without the principle of some *responsibility* [. . .] before the ghosts of those who are not yet born or who are already dead, be they victims of wars, political or other kinds of violence, nationalist, racist, colonialist, sexist, or other kinds of exterminations, victims of the oppressions of capitalist imperialism or any of the forms of totalitarianism. Without this *non-contemporaneity with itself of the living present*, without that which secretly unhinges it, without this responsibility and this respect for justice concerning those who *are not there*, of those who are no longer or who are not yet *present and living*, what sense would there be to ask the question 'where?' 'where tomorrow?' 'whither?'

. . . .

QUESTIONS

- How far does Greenblatt's distinctive comprehension of 'wonder', as the delight in and an acknowledgement of otherness, unite aesthetic and ethical value?

- To what extent can an ethics of wonder fulfil what Wayne calls 'the principle of relationship?
- Do Derrida's *Hamlet*-inspired reflections supply an acceptable rationale for historical critcism?

6 | Qualifying recent theory

David Scott Kastan, *Shakespeare after Theory* (New York and London: Routledge, 1999), p. 42.

'Texts are worldly,' Edward Said has written, 'to some degree they are events, and even when they appear to deny it, they are nevertheless a part of the social world, human life and of course the historical moments in which they are located and interpreted'.[1] It is, however, only by turning to history from theory that this can be shown to be true and meaningful, that the particular forms and particular effects of a text's 'worldliness' can be discovered and demonstrated. A recognition of the historicity of the play—as book and as performance—a focus on the specific conditions of its production and reception, returns it to the world in which and to which it is alive; increasingly literary criticism is learning that what it attends to are the marks of this worldliness. Reading those marks, recognizing that a play's materializations, in the printing house and in the playhouse, *are* the play's meanings rather than passive and sometimes embarrassing conveyors of them, is what I take to be the almost inevitable practice of Shakespeare after theory, no longer *chasing* after it but working powerfully and productively in its wake.

* * *

Bruce R. Smith, *Shakespeare and Masculinity* (Oxford: Oxford University Press, 2000), pp. 131–3.

Constructionism is one of the basic propositions by which new historicism [. . .] has distinguished itself from humanism. Where humanism assumes a core essence that unites people otherwise separated in time and social circumstances new historicism insists on cultural differences. *Deconstruction* likewise needs constructionism [. . .]

And yet the case of Lear himself points up the limits of the essentialist/constructionist dichotomy. Reduced to fragments of speech on the heath, his identity literally deconstructed, the once self-possessed autocrat awakes from madness with a more circumspect sense of who he is: 'Pray do not mock. / I am a very foolish, fond old man'. His sense of self-identity, as he realizes, is contingent on those around him. No longer a king, he acknowledges first the simple fact of his manhood, then his fatherhood: 'For *as I am a man*, I think this lady / To be my child, Cordelia' (*The Tragedy of King Lear*, 4.6.52–3, 62–3, emphasis added). Lear's new-found identity is neither the essence he thought it was at the beginning of the play nor the empty nothing it seemed to be after deconstruction on the heath but an *evolving* phenomenon. Michel Serres catches this dynamic state of affairs when he recalls that the word *subject* was originally not a noun but an adjective ('In a state of subjection or dependence; under the control, rule, or influence of something; subordinate', *OED* I.2). The sense of 'subject' as 'the thinking or cognizing agent, the self or ego', dates only from the end of the seventeenth century (*OED* II.9). 'Who am I as a subject?' Serres insists on a qualified answer: 'No, I am not a problem: literally, I am a solution. And I would tolerate writing titles on my visiting card on condition that the title comprise the diverse relations of the substances dissolved in it, their density in the alloy. Who am I? A fusion of alloys, more coalescent than coalesced.'[1] [. . .] Where *essence* is a state of being (from Latin *esse*, 'to be'), *coalescence* is a process (from Latin *co*, 'with, together', + *alescere*, 'to begin growing'). *Colaescence* recognizes the multiple identities that a protagonist like Lear embraces. [. . .] It recognizes that those identities can be successive or simultaneous or both. It recognizes, not the 'one-and-the-sameness' that the word *identity* denotes, but self-understanding across time, under changing circumstances. As such, *coalescence* offers a way to avoid the impasse between essentialism and constructionism [. . .].'

* * *

Jonathan Dollimore, 'Shakespeare and Theory', in *Post-Colonial Shakespeares*, edited by Ania Loomba and Martin Orkin (London and New York: Routledge, 1998), pp. 267–70, 275–6.

At its worst [wishful theory] is the kind of theorizing that gestures towards difference yet from a perspective that remains intellectually totalizing and reductive; which is self-empowering in a politically spurious way, and which, despite its ostentatious performance of a high sophistication, tends to erase the psychic, social and historical complexities of the cultural life it addresses. Critical theory originally sought to integrate theory with praxis. But what did that mean, exactly? For some of the Frankfurt School it entailed a commitment to emancipation inseparable from painful and difficult historical analysis—praxis as the pursuit of philosophy by other means.[1] Marx had said, famously, that hitherto philosophers had sought only to understand the world; now they were to change it too. But, if anything, this effort to change the world itself required an even greater effort of understanding. To change in the direction of emancipation meant above all that one had to understand the ideological conditions that prevented change. Whatever we may now think of the Frankfurt School, its sustained analysis of the historical conditions that prevented change has to be respected. Arguably, those who now completely reject Marxism have abandoned not only any serious intention of changing, but also the serious commitment to understanding. Certainly an aspect of the tradition of cultural critique has been lost: the effort to understand the historical real as we inherit it—in Marx's words, those historical conditions we don't choose and which profoundly affect the choices we do make.

Let me be more specific. There is a particular model of social struggle which has been influential in recent theory. Very briefly, it concentrates on the instabilities within the dominant, identifying, for instance, ways in which the marginal is subversive of the dominant, especially at those points where the dominant is already rendered unstable by contradictions intrinsic to it and which include the fact (disavowed by the dominant yet apparent within the subordinate) that the two are connected in complex ways. If this model originates with Hegel, its modern form has been deeply influenced by, among other movements, Marxism, psychoanalysis and deconstruction. It's because I've been influenced by this account of social struggle, and remain persuaded by it, that I can't subscribe to what I regard as a wishful theoretical deployment of it most pronounced in some strands of post-modernism. Bits and pieces from all sorts of different theoretical sources are expertly spliced together, often with the aim of demonstrating a repressive dominant always allegedly on the edge of its own ruin and about to be precipitated over the edge by the marginal, the other or the different. The marginal is first appropriated, then theoretically reworked as radical, subversive, avant-garde or whatever.

The result of such theoretical reworking is not so much a demonstration of the intrinsic instability of the social order, or its effective subversion by forces within or adjacent to it, but an abstract, highly wrought re-presentation of it—a theoretical narrative whose plausibility is often in inverse proportion to the degree to which it makes its proponents feel better. To that extent, wishful theory is also feel-good theory. It is also a theory in which human freedom is emphatically denied, only to be endlessly replayed in intellectual fantasies of subversion. And this same 'sublimation' of freedom is apparent in the way that so much theoretical denial of freedom is strangely written from a masterful, omniscient subject position.

The contrived narratives of wishful theory insulate their adherents from social reality by filtering it, and this in the very act of fantasising its subversion. So much so that in some contemporary theory, the very concept of subversion has become a form of disavowal. Theory is deployed in a way that is usually self-exonerating, hardly at all in a way that is self-questioning. This kind of theory can be so quickly updated because it is so tenuously connected with the real. Drop this bit of theory, splice in that, and the whole thing can be updated to correspond to intellectual fashion. What is disappearing from theory is the intellectual commitment to engage with the cultural real in all its stubborn contingency, surprising complexity and—in Brecht's phrase, terrible contradictions—that which makes change necessary but which also makes it terribly difficult and likely to exact a terrible cost. Nor does scepticism about such theory imply a disregard for that which is so often its subject—the marginal, otherness, difference; on the contrary, I believe that such scepticism is now the precondition for a more thoughtful (but not necessarily uncritical) encounter with them.

And what of instabilities in the dominant? Those who pretend that deconstruction is *only* about the undecidability of texts, or about reducing everything to the status of a text, are just wrong. But in the context of literary criticism, a certain use of it has encouraged a tendency to move too quickly from spotting a tension, an instability or inconsistency in dominant formations to speculating that here the text, and the culture being represented by the text, were in crisis. We discern an instability or a contradiction in gender domination, sexual difference or masculinity—but so what? I mean: what follows, exactly? Especially if we always bear in mind the materialist commonplace that dominant ideologies not only mask contradictions and instabilities but also mobilize them, and that it is when ideology is pushed nearly to incoherence that such instabilities and contradictions may be most brutally and most effectively mobilised. What price then some local disruption within sexual difference—whose *frisson* is this anyway? One of the wishful aspects of some queer theory is the assumption (hope?) that heterosexual masculinity is so riven with contradictions and insecurities it will any day now collapse into itself—or better still, collapse into the homosexuality which is its constitutive repression.

A more thoughtful encounter with both the dominant and the dissident has for some time been an aspect of social history. Some years ago we argued that theory was becoming too self-referential and remained far too contemporary. We argued for a critical practice in which we could use history, especially social history, to read theory, as well as vice versa.[2] Now I feel more than ever that theory, or at least some strands of post-modern theory, needs history. And if social history remains as important as ever, I would now stress the importance of intellectual history as well. Post-modernism desperately needs both kinds of history. [. . .]

This is not—I repeat not—an argument for the wholesale rejection of theory, nor even of post-modernism. It's rather to insist that we need a theory that embodies a greater effort of historical understanding; a theory adequate to understand, challenge and maybe even change those complex cultural realities that we inherit. An effort of understanding which knows that we always risk misrecognizing the real structure of the 'terrible contradictions' we live, and the struggles they imply, and that going back into the past via intellectual history is one way of reducing that risk. For this purpose the materialist concepts of contra-diction and dialectic remain, for me, imperative. Arguably they remain significant too for any cultural politics prepared to confront and not evade the complexities of our cultural histories, and which knows, *contra* post-modernism, the importance of the traditions of intellectual history and even philosophical anthropology; which knows, in short, that there is so much more to be learned from the past than either the current reactionary defenders of tradition, or their post-modern critics, allow. The cultural politics that matters is the kind which strives to understand the contradictions we live and which, after making that effort, does not lack the courage to risk truth claims about the real; a cultural politics that knows the difference between human agency and human essence and that recognizes that the feeble relativism of post-modernism is only viable because it's never tested. For all its cosmopolitan affect, much post-modernism thrives on a new parochialism—that self-absorbed, inward-looking and relatively insulated existence characteristic of intellectual urban life, and which reminds us once again that material conditions profoundly influence not only the direction of our thought but the very structure of what it includes and excludes, of what is thinkable and what is not. A cultural politics, then, that knows we have to believe in what we write but also that we might well be wrong; which is, in a word, and in the broadest sense of that word: ethical.

....

QUESTIONS

- To what extent does the historical 'Real' emerge here as a category resistant to post-modern relativity?

- In what different ways, and for what different reasons, do Smith and Dollimore qualify recent critical values of plurality and change?

- Can you imagine any new alternatives to the critical values that have been revealed in this book?

SUGGESTED FURTHER READING

Bloom, H., *Shakespeare: The Invention of the Human* (New York: Penguin Putnam, 1999)

Bruster, Douglas, *Shakespeare and the Question of Culture: Early Modern Literature and the Cultural Turn* (Basingstoke and New York: Palgrave, 2003)

Dollimore, Jonathan and Sinfield, Alan (eds.), *Political Shakespeare: New Essays in Cultural Materialism* (Manchester and New York: Manchester University Press, 1985)

Grady, Hugh, *The Modernist Shakespeare: Critical Texts in a Material World* (Oxford and New York: Clarendon Press, 1991)

Hawkes, Terence, *Shakespeare in the Present* (London and New York: Routledge, 2002)

Hobby, Elaine, *Virtue of Necessity: English Women's Writing 1646–1688* (London: Virago, 1988)

Joughin, John J. and Malpas, Simon (eds.), *The New Aestheticism* (Manchester and New York: Manchester University Press, 2003)

Mousley, Andy, *Renaissance Drama and Contemporary Literary Theory* (Basingstoke: Macmillan, 2000)

Reynolds, Bryan, *Performing Transversally: Reimagining Shakespeare and the Critical Future* (Basingstoke and New York: Palgrave, 2003)

Vickers, Brian, *Appropriating Shakespeare: Contemporary Critical Quarrels* (New Haven and London: Yale University Press, 1993)

NOTES

Nelson, 'Against English'

1. Janet Batsleer, Tony Davies, Rebecca O'Rourke, and Chris Weedon, *Rewriting English: Cultural Politics of Gender and Class* (New York: Methuen, 1985).

Hall, 'These bastard signs of fair'

1. Peter Erickson's series of essays on whiteness is a notable exception to this (1993a; 1993b; 1996), as is Barbara Bowen's work on Aemilia Lanier (1998).

2. For more specific discussions on the varied meanings of the term 'race' and the instability of the concept of race, see the essays in *Women, 'Race' and Writing in the Early Modern Period* (Hendricks and Parker 1994). Lynda E. Boose's essay in that same anthology begins by querying the differences between early modern and contemporary notions of race (Boose 1993: 35–7).

3. All references to Shakespeare's plays are from *The Riverside Shakespeare*, ed. G. Blakemore Evans (1974).

4. My use of 'Africanist' is drawn from Toni Morrison, who uses 'Africanism' 'as a term for the denotative and connotative blackness African peoples have come to signify, as well as the entire range of views, assumptions, readings, and misreadings that accompany Eurocentric learning about these people' (Morrison 1992: 7).

5. For an astute analysis of the problem of 'race,' see Erickson (1993a: 500–3). See also bell hooks's critique of how the use of the term 'ethnicity' can be used to efface political action (hooks 1990: 52).

6. For an overview (albeit dismissive) of how the question of race and the dark lady was addressed (or not) by leading critics from the nineteenth and early twentieth centuries, see Appendix IX of Shakespeare (1944).

7. The poems individually may have acquired this valence. If, as Patricia Fumerton (1991), has argued, sonnets and jewels circulated in the same rhetorical/social system, we might similarly see these sonnets being read amidst an Africanist presence in visual culture. Thus, a poem

celebrating the young man's fairness might be held in the same cabinet as one of the popular cameos featuring an African face.

8. My reading of the Ditchley portrait slightly adjusts Richard Helgerson's sense that the portrait, in sublimating the map to the monarch, resists the developing meaning of maps, which 'strengthened the sense of both local and national identity at the expense of an identity based on dynastic loyalty' (Helgerson 1992: 114). Whiteness as a characteristic is not purely dynastic, but is in portraits a quality ceded to a powerful elite. The joining of land and ruler then allows for a different configuration.

9. We can also see this operating in tandem with both narrative and political exclusions of blacks and blackness from the nation. Citing the welfare of her own 'natural' subjects, Elizabeth expels 'Negars and Blackamoores' from England in 1596 and 1601; as I noted in *Things of Darkness*, George Best's now-infamous description of a marriage between an 'Ethiopian blacke as a cole' and 'a faire English woman' works to make blackness and Englishness mutually exclusive (Hall 1995: 11–12).

10. All references to the sonnets are from *Shakespeare's Sonnets*, ed. Stephen Booth (Shakespeare 1977).

11. For example, the extended perfuming conceit in Sonnet 5 ('Then were not summer's distillation left / liquid pris'ner pent in walls of glass / Beauty's effect with beauty were bereft,' (9–11)); the use of scents on the clothes and body was a sign of wealth and the manufacture of those scents was characteristic mainly of aristocratic households.

12. They continue: 'Lineage also creates a web both of privileges and of duties. The latter are to friends, neighbours, tenants, servants—but pre-eminently to lineage itself' (Heal and Holmes 1994: 22). See in the writings of Sir John Oglander: 'Oglander insists that the key responsibility is to the continuation of the lineage, or "house" as he calls it, of which the current holder of the estate is representative and beneficiary' (ibid.: 22).

13. Wendy Wall's (1996) discussion of 'national husbandry' is illuminating on this point and suggestive of the way in which the concerns of husbandry are being disrupted by class as well as national agendas. Unlike Markham, Shakespeare seems to be tying husbandry to a particular class in ways that may have nationalist implications. This difference may also be related to the difference of print technology, which Wall sees as key to Markham's publication of a national husbandry.

14. As de Grazia notes, this orderly fantasy is disrupted by the obsession with the dark lady's reproductive body (de Grazia 1993).

15. For discussion of this, see de Grazia (1993); and on Sonnet 20 specifically, see Stallybrass (1993a: esp. pp. 94–6).

16. Characteristically, Sonnet 127, with its monetary language ('beauty's successive heir') raises the specter of reproduction seen in the earlier sonnets ('Proving his beauty by succession thine' (2: 12)).

17. I disagree here with Margreta de Grazia's claim that the young man 'is described as a paragon of both masculine and feminine beauty' (de Grazia 1993: 41) as well as with her tendency to reduplicate the binary grid of fair/man, dark/woman. There is an important degree of gender play within the category fair and less absolute hegemony than her reading indicates.

18. Although I absolutely agree with Bredbeck's deconstructive point that 'the continually irreducible punningness of the poem makes poetry itself an other to fixed meaning' (Bredbeck 1991: 170), I take the desire for transcendence at face value. Fineman helpfully sees such images, 'of an idealizing, clarifying light, transparent even in its burnishing luminosity' (Fineman 1986: 68) as highly visual and referring to both the thing seen and the way of seeing.

19. This line is in some ways extremely typical as the poet attempts to remove the fair beloved from the marketplace of praise.

Attridge, Peculiar Language

1. I use the edition by Gladys Doidge Willcock and Alice Walker (which includes a long

introduction on such problematic matters as authorship and dating—matters that have no direct bearing on my argument here). Page references are given in the text.

2. The first published reference to it, by Sir John Harington in 'A Brief Apology for Poetry' (1591), was derogatory; Harington remarks that 'the poore gentleman laboreth greatly to prove, or rather to make Poetrie an art' and compares him pointedly with 'M. *Sidney* and all the learneder sort that have written of it' (G. Gregory Smith, *Elizabethan Critical Essays*, 2:196–7). The note of condescension (as well as the unfavorable comparison with Sidney) has been echoed by many later commentators. Smith in his introduction to *Elizabethan Critical Essays*, after praising Sidney and Daniel, includes Puttenham's work among 'essays of less sustained power' (lxx). Baxter Hathaway opens his introduction to a modern facsimile of Arber's 1906 reprint with a warning that 'one must shut one's eyes to the book's many shortcomings' and later complains about the work's 'flippancy, its popularization and watering-down of theory for court consumption,' applauding it rather faintly as a 'more than adequate summation of a traditional approach to poetics' and a 'synthesis of commonplaces' (v, xxiii–xxiv). W. K. Wimsatt and Cleanth Brooks refer to Puttenham's 'uneven collection of jokes and conceits and the theoretical hints which he musters to introduce them' (*Literary Criticism*, 234). The 'accuracy' of such assessments is not the issue; more important is what kind of reading such attitudes produce and are produced by.

3. Two readings of the *Apologie* which highlight some of these contradictory processes are those by Margaret W. Ferguson in *Trials of Desire*, chap. 4, and Ronald Levao in *Renaissance Minds and Their Fictions*, chap. 5. On Sidney's *sprezzatura*, see also Daniel Javitch, 'The impure motives of Elizabethan poetry.'

4. Tayler's emphasis is not so much on the contradictoriness as on a reading that will minimize it. Thus he writes of the classical authors mentioned: 'There are passages open to primitivistic or "naturalistic" interpretation, but the balance in all of these minds falls finally against Nature in the sense of the spontaneous and unreflective' (51). J. W. H. Atkins, in *English Literary Criticism: The Renascence*, comes to a different conclusion about the same texts, finding that nature (or reason) is the final court of appeal. Thus he quotes from a passage by Quintilian (*Institutionis Oratoriae* 9.4.120) in which the writer is advised in matters of rhythm to take nature for a guide (166)—but he omits the last part of Quintilian's sentence, which reads 'none the less there will always be some principle of art underlying the promptings of nature' (Loeb edn). Madeleine Doran is another who seeks a principle of 'balance' to reconcile contradictions, in her discussion of 'Art *vs.* Nature' in Renaissance writing (*Endeavors of Art*, 54–70), while Edwin M. Duval, discussing a similar inconsistency in Montaigne's 'Des Cannibales,' explains it as a deliberate demonstration of the mutability of human judgment ('Lessons of the New World'). It is perhaps Longinus who achieves the most skillful accommodation between the two terms: after giving several reasons why effects of the sublime in literature require art as well as nature, he comments, 'Most important of all, the very fact that some things in literature depend on nature alone can itself be learned only from art' (*On Sublimity*, 463).

5. On the importance of rules in Elizabethan conceptions of art, see my *Well-weighed Syllables* (138–43 and passim). Puttenham's association of rules with *reason* marks another dimension of the question which it is not possible to broach here (though it is implicated, as I suggested earlier, in the very procedures we are using). I simply note that reason can appear on the side of either nature or art, depending on whether the latter is seen as perverter or perfecter of the former (see Tayler, 27–30 and passim, and Duval, 103).

6. See Attridge, *Well-weighed Syllables*, 217–19. The disparity between the two arguments is usually taken as an indication that they were written at different times (see Willcock and Walker's Introduction to Puttenham's *Arte*, xliv–liii). If this view is accepted, we still have to account for the fact that Puttenham did not correct the earlier argument but merely added the latter one—as a supplement.

7. The tensions within the Renaissance program of imitation have been ably brought out by several scholars, notably Thomas M. Greene, *The Light in Troy*; Terence Cave, *The Cornucopian Text*, especially chap. 2; Margaret Ferguson, *Trials of Desire*, especially chap. 2; and David Quint, *Origin and Originality in Renaissance Literature*.

8. Decorum in one guise or another has been a recurrent (and indispensable) element in the tradition of classical and postclassical literary criticism until this century. It is usually presented as a neutral critical term, referring to the proper matching of the various aspects of a text, so that its style is appropriate to the speaker, the theme, the time and place, the audience, and so forth: see, for instance, Smith, *Essays*, xli–xlvi; Rosemond Tuve, *Elizabethan and Metaphysical Imagery*, chap. 9 and passim; and Annabel M. Patterson, *Hermogenes and the Renaissance*, chap. 1. For a useful survey of the notion of decorum in classical, medieval, and Renaissance writing, see Thomas Kranidas, *The Fierce Equation*, chap. 1. [The Romantics transformed the idea of decorum] and in this century Valéry remains wholly, and typically, within this tradition when, having defined the writer of literature as a 'maker of *deviations*,' he adds that it is a question only of 'the deviations that enrich' ('The poet's rights over language,' in *The Art of Poetry*, 172). Literary structuralism can be understood as an attempt to abolish the appeal to any such unformulatable principle by standing outside it and giving an objective account of it.

9. Decorum became notorious as a defense that writers (or their apologists) could take advantage of to justify an apparent lapse of taste by pointing to the unique demands of the particular text; Chaucer, for instance, is a past master at disarming criticism by appealing to the authority of decorum to allow low language in the depiction of lewd and villainous characters. Defined by the absence of a permanent or rational reference-point, the concept of decorum—like its modern equivalents—is empty of content, allowing whoever has authority over the discourse to fill it. It is not surprising that modern commentators, while recognizing its centrality, find it difficult to pin down as a critical tool; Kranidas, for instance, talks of its 'ubiquity and instability' in Elizabethan criticism (39). He adverts to the source of decorum's power as a social weapon, though without realizing its significance, when he comments: 'No matter how central decorum is to the work of art, no matter how long the tradition of its importance, it is applied anew to every piece of discourse, it adapts constantly to the environment'(18). It is because it is freshly invoked each time that it remains in the hands of those who have the power to enforce their own interpretation of it. The ethical equivalent is the virtue of prudence; see Victoria Kahn, *Rhetoric, Prudence, and Skepticism*.

10. It would be possible to represent the dividedness within Puttenham's formulations as a tension between the humanist ideology (with its belief in human perfectibility and its program of education) and that of the courtier (with its strictly political criteria and its emphasis on advancement and power); G. K. Hunter has written well in 'Humanism and Courtship' of this clash of attitudes. But both of these ideologies are inconsistent within themselves, claiming as each one does to be based on universal values but endorsing actions that serve narrower ends.

11. See Roland Barthes, *Mythologies*, especially the essay 'Myth Today.'

12. Or the would-be courtier, as some studies of Puttenham have emphasized; see, for instance, Daniel Javitch, *Poetry and Courtliness*; Heinrich Plett, 'Aesthetic Constituents'; and Louis Adrian Montrose, 'Gentlemen and Shepherds.' That the *Arte of English Poesie* can be read as a courtesy handbook does not, of course, diminish its importance as a poetic handbook; what it does do is to bring out the close relation between aesthetic and political questions. Montrose observes that—as 'itself a courtly performance, an open bid for royal preferment'—'the most subtle irony of Puttenham's text is that it constitutes, in effect, a *meta*courtly discourse: it simultaneously exemplifies and anatomizes the art it purports to describe' (442). We should not, given our own institutional context, be too surprised that a scholarly book can at the same time be a bid for personal promotion, even if its subject is, in part, the art of getting promoted.

13. Puttenham also mentions a book of his, now lost, entitled *De decoro* (277), which no doubt contained many more exempla of this kind. On Puttenham's preference for examples over theory, see Victoria Kahn, 'Humanism and the resistance to theory.'

14. These are, in fact, the terms used against Puttenham by Harington, who remarks cuttingly of the former's theory of poetry that 'he doth prove nothing more plainly than that . . . it is a gift and not an art' because 'he sheweth himselfe so slender a gift in it' (Smith, *Essays*, 2:197). Puttenham is not, for Sir John, a member of the natural elite, and therefore no amount of effort

will allow him to succeed in his aim. Bourdieu describes essentially the same aim and the same difficulty as Puttenham's:

> Above all—and this is why aesthetes so abhor pedagogues and pedagogy—the rational teaching of art provides substitutes for direct experience, it offers short cuts on the long path of familiarization, it makes possible practices which are the product of concepts and rules instead of springing from the supposed spontaneity of taste, thereby offering a solution to those who hope to make up for lost time. . . . The embarrassment of academic minds, indebted and committed to acquisition, surfaces whenever it is a question of the adequate approach to a work of art and the right way to acquire it; and the contradiction is at the heart of all their aesthetic theories, not to mention their attempts to establish a pedagogy of art. The ideology of natural gifts is too potent, even within the educational system, for an expression of faith in the powers of a rational pedagogy aimed at reducing the practical schemes of familiarity to codified rules. (68,74).

15. Compare Derrida's comment: 'The speech that Rousseau raised above writing is speech as it should be or rather as it *should have been*' (*Grammatology*, 141). Empson writes interestingly on the particular melancholy induced by Milton's presentation of Edenic nature before the Fall, in *Some Versions of Pastoral*, 152–3.

16. The surface praise of the garden's inseparable blend of nature and art is sternly qualified by such words as 'wantonesse,' 'repine,' and 'undermine':

> One would have thought, (so cunningly, the rude,
> And scorned parts were mingled with the fine,)
> That nature had for wantonesse ensude
> Art, and that Art at nature did repine;
> So striving each th'other to undermine,
> Each did the others worke more beautifie. (2.12 st. 59)

17. In 'Interpretation at court' Frank Whigham discusses the social importance in the Renaissance court of learning how to behave as if one had not learned how to behave (626). The belief—or the pretense—that courtly speech and behavior were a natural endowment was, of course, a denial of their institutional determination; to the extent that this *was* a belief (and part of a wider assumption about speech and human activity), it formed one constituent of an ideology that is still powerful today.

Parker, Shakespeare from the Margins

1. See Kenneth Muir, 'The uncomic pun,' *Cambridge Journal* 3 (1950): 472–85; and Margreta de Grazia's 'Homonyms before and after lexical standardization,' *Deutsche Shakespeare-Gesellschaft West Jahrbuch* (1990), 143–56. De Grazia argues that the term *pun* is anachronistic in relation to this kind of homophony, since it implies the joining of words more completely separated than they in fact were in the period. *Pun* is thus used here only as a shorthand, without the implication of these more modern boundaries.

2. See Leo Spitzer, *Representative Essays*, ed. Alban K. Forcione et al. (Stanford, Calif.: Stanford University Press, 1988); Catherine Belsey, afterword to *The Matter of Difference: Materialist Feminist Criticism of Shakespeare*, ed. Valerie Wayne (Ithaca, N.Y.: Cornell University Press, 1991), 257–70.

3. See, for example, Raymond Williams, *Keywords: A Vocabulary of Culture and Society*, rev. edn (London: Oxford University Press, 1983); and among other work on Burke, Hayden White and Margaret Brose (eds.), *Representing Kenneth Burke* (Baltimore: Johns Hopkins University Press, 1982). The chapters that follow also bear the imprint of the attention to language in William Empson's *Structure of Complex Words* and *Seven Types of Ambiguity*, along with the conviction that careful or close reading is not the preserve of the ahistorical or apolitical. Evelyn Fox Keller's *Secrets of Life, Secrets of Death:* (New York: Routledge, 1992), esp. 56–72, also suggests the importance of close reading and of Williams's notion of keywords to historians of science as well as of culture. The present study attempts therefore to employ not only historical

semantics (though in different forms from Spitzer's) and the resources of 'close reading' (referring, in the process, to the best of analyses of Shakespearean punning and wordplay, including the work of such critics as Stephen Booth, Joel Fineman, and Harry Berger Jr.) but also the insights of poststructuralism, in the interest of a more historical feminism and gender study and a materialist analysis that takes seriously Raymond Williams's sense (in contrast to some subsequent developments within cultural studies) of the crucial importance of language and words.

4. See the essays, for example, in Jonathan Goldberg (ed.), *Queering the Renaissance* (Durham, N.C.: Duke University Press, 1994), many of which acknowledge the influence of Eve Kosofsky Sedgwick's *Between Men* (New York: Columbia University Press, 1985) and *Epistemology of the Closet* (Berkeley and Los Angeles: University of California Press, 1990), as well as engagements with Alan Bray's *Homo-sexuality in Renaissance England* (London: Gay Men's Press, 1982) and Judith Butler's *Gender Trouble* (New York: Routledge, 1990).

5. See Judith Newton and Deborah Rosenfelt (eds.), 'Introduction: toward a materialist-feminist criticism,' *Feminist Criticism and Social Change* (New York: Methuen, 1985), xv–xxxix. See also the intersections foregrounded in Dympna Callaghan, Lorraine Helms and Jyotsna Singh. *The Weyward Sisters: Shakespeare and Feminist Politics* (Oxford: Blackwell, 1994).

6. See Judith Butler, *Bodies That Matter* (New York: Routledge, 1993). See also Judith H. Anderson: *Words that Matter: Linguistic Perception in Renaissance English* (Stanford, CA: Stanford University Press, 1996).

7. See Michael Neill, 'Unproper beds: race, adultery, and the hideous in *Othello*,' *Shakespeare Quarterly* 40 (1989): 383–412.

8. See Keir Elam, *Shakespeare's Universe of Discourse* (Cambridge: Cambridge University Press, 1984); and M. M. Mahood's *Shakespeare's Wordplay* (London: Methuen, 1957); with the critiques of Elam in, for example, Bridget Gellert Lyons, 'Shakespeare's wordplay,' *Raritan* 4 (1986), esp. 150, 153; and Harry Berger Jr., 'What did the king know and when did he know it? Shakespearean discourses and psychoanalysis,' *South Atlantic Quarterly* 88 (1989): 811–62, esp. 828–9, which also cites Catherine Belsey's description of any 'domain of language-use' as a social construction, from her *Critical Practice* (London: Methuen, 1980), 3. 'Faultlines' here is meant to summon not only Alan Sinfield and Jonathan Dollimore's term used in Sinfield's *Faultlines: Cultural Materialism and the Politics of Dissident Reading* (Berkeley and Los Angeles: University of California Press, 1992) but also the pervasive Shakespearean wordplay on cracks and 'faults' examined in several chapters here. Lorna Hutson, in *Thomas Nashe in Context* (Oxford: Clarendon Press, 1989), develops linkages between language, rhetoric, economics, and contemporary social transformations in England that go beyond formalism in fascinating and important ways.

9. The term 'stalled subversion-containment model'—a now familiar critique of earlier versions of new historicism—comes from Linda Charnes's *Notorious Identity: Materializing the Subject in Shakespeare* (Cambridge, Mass.: Harvard University Press, 1993), 18.

10. See the Arden edition of *The Merchant of Venice*, ed. John Russell Brown (London: Methuen, 1977), 99 n. 35; and the Variorum *Merchant of Venice*, ed. Horace Howard Furness (1888; rpt. New York: Dover Publications, 1964); with Kim Hall's 'Reading what isn't there: "Black" studies in early modern England,' *Stanford Humanities Review* 3, no. 1 (1993): 23–33, esp. 28–9.

11. See Hall, 'Reading what isn't there,' 26–7, on Elizabeth's proclamation, cited from James Walvin, *The Black Presence: A Documentary History of the Negro in England, 1550–1860* (New York: Schocken Books, 1972), 65; Patricia Hill Collins, *Black Feminist Thought: Knowledge, Consciousness, and the Politics of Empowerment* (Boston: Unwin Hyman, 1990), 76–7, and Angela Davis, 'Racism, birth control, and reproductive rights,' in *Women, 'Race,' and Class* (New York: Vintage, 1981). Wordplay on 'more' and 'Moor' is joined in the early modern period by the association (through Latin *mora*) of female Moors with mulberries that turn (in the Pyramus and Thisbe story) from white to dark, and (through Latin *morus*) of the mulberry tree with the ass or fool. Ovid's Pyramus and Thisbe narrative—so important for *A Midsummer Night's Dream* (as for *Romeo and Juliet*)—also puns in Latin on *mora* as 'delay' as well as 'mulberries' (echoed in the 'tarrying in mulberry shade' in *MND*), as well as on the *moriens* (or dying) Pyramus whose passion turns the mulberries from white to dark. (The *Ovide moralisé*

tradition famously conflates this passion with the tree of Christ's sacrifice.) Erasmus famously puns on *moria* (folly) and the name of Thomas More, in the *Encomium Moriae*, while early modern emblem books contain verses on the *morus* or mulberry tree that play on the fruit that is not foolish because of its delay (*mora*) in putting forth its fruit. And the turning of mulberries (*mora*) from light to dark enables the association in the period between mulberries and female Moors via climatological theories of the origin of blackness (as the consequence of being 'too much i' the sun,' as Hamlet puts it). We might, therefore, in relation to these already exploited contemporary linkages, reconsider *A Midsummer Night's Dream*, with its references to 'Ethiope' and its contrasting of 'fair' and 'dark,' its *morus* or fool, and the curious fact that it transfers reference to the mulberry of the Pyramus and Thisbe story (set in Babylon or the East) and its turning from white to dark to the lines on the love-juice in the scene that contains both allusion to the 'imperial votaress' (Elizabeth) and the Indian votaress described in relation to evocations of contemporary voyaging to other worlds. We might also in this regard revisit its allusions to the 'morris' and the puzzling 'Now is the morall downe' in the Pyramus and Thisbe play-within-a-play.

12. [. . .] The historical study of language also matters in relation to distinctions that prepared for the later development of a fullfledged racism based on skin color or characteristics measured against the standard of 'white.' This language (with its implications for gender and class as well as for the 'black Irish' and others) may be seen at work in Shakespeare's plays even in contexts that appear to be less immediately relevant to racial questions than *Othello, Titus Andronicus, The Tempest*, or *The Merchant of Venice*. When, for example, Hal exclaims, 'Why then your brown bastard is your only drink! for look you, Francis, your white canvas doublet will sully. In Barbary, sir, it cannot come to so much'—in the scene with the lower-class drawer Francis in *1 Henry IV* (II.iv.73–75)—'Barbary' appears to allude simply to a location in the north of Africa already associated with the sullying of 'white.' But this English history—geographically removed from that Barbary (in a series in which 'Barbary,' however, is also the name of the horse who bears both Richard and Bolingbroke)—also activates the complex (traced in chaps. 5 and 6) of contemporary associations of illegitimacy or bastardy (product of adultery) with adulteration or sullying, and 'Barbary' with the taint of the 'barbarous license' (*H5* I.ii.271) with which a usurper's son is stained. The sense of the staining or sullying of the white (attached to a figure, like Hamlet, too much in the sun/son) is already, therefore, linked with the complex of bastardy, illegitimacy, adultery, and adulterating that operates within the Henriad itself, including the history of domestic English infidelities and treacheries expressed in the language of the 'infidel,' following this usurper's conveyance of the crown and the counterfeiting of 'true' kingship. On race as a category in the early modern period, see Hall, 'Reading what isn't there,' 23; and the Introduction and essays by Margo Hendricks, Verena Stolcke, Kim Hall, Ania Loomba, and Lynda E. Boose, and others in *Women, 'Race,' and Writing in the Early Modern Period*, ed. Margo Hendricks and Patricia Parker (London: Routledge, 1994). For another instance of 'barbarous' and 'barbering,' see *Titus Andronicus* V.i.92–97.

13. See Thomas Laqueur, 'Orgasm, generation, and the politics of reproductive biology,' *Representations* 14 (1986), esp. 13, and the opening chapters of his *Making Sex* (Cambridge, Mass.: Harvard University Press, 1990); Stephen Greenblatt, 'Fiction and Friction,' in *Shakespearean Negotiations* (Berkeley and Los Angeles: University of California Press, 1988), esp. 80–81; George Sandys, *Ovid's Metamorphosis Englished, Mythologized and Represented in Figures* (London, 1640), 184; and my critique of unidirectional models in 'Gender ideology, gender change: the case of Marie Germain,' *Critical Inquiry* 19 (1993): 337–64.

14. See the conclusions, for example, in Greenblatt, 'Fiction and Friction,' 88.

15. See Etienne Dolet, *Carmina* 2:32, *Carminum Libri Quatuor* (Lyon, 1538); and Browne, *Pseudodoxia Epidemica*, 'Of hares,' 227, lines that translate the 'sed etiam praeposterae libidinis' of Petro Castellanus's *De Esu Carnium* 3.5 (1626), one of Browne's principal sources.

16. On British cultural materialism and American new historicism, see, among others, Paul Werstine's review of Jonathan Dollimore's *Radical Tragedy* in *Shakespeare Quarterly* 38, no. 4 (1987): 522–4, esp. 523; with Dollimore's introduction to *Political Shakespeare*, ed. Jonathan Dollimore and Alan Sinfield (Manchester: Manchester University Press, 1985), 2–17, and 'Shakespeare, cultural materialism, feminism, and Marxist humanism,' *New Literary History* 21 (1990): 471–93.

17. In addition to Wayne's introduction and essays by Ann Thompson and others in *The Matter of Difference*, see, among others, the essays by Walter Cohen and Don E. Wayne in *Shakespeare Reproduced*, ed. Jean Howard and Marion O'Connor (London: Methuen, 1987); Annabel Patterson, *Shakespeare and the Popular Voice* (Oxford: Basil Blackwell, 1989); Michael D. Bristol, *Carnival and Theater* (New York: Routledge, 1985) and *Shakespeare's America, America's Shakespeare* (London: Routledge, 1990), 203–9; Lisa Jardine, ' "Why should he call her whore?" Defamation and Desdemona's case,' in *Addressing Frank Kermode: Essays in Criticism and Interpretation*, ed. Margaret Tudeau-Clayton and Martin Warner (Urbana: University of Illinois Press, 1991), 124–53; Catherine Belsey, 'Towards cultural history—in theory and practice,' *Textual Practice* 3, no. 3 (1989): 159–72; Marguerite Waller, 'Academic Tootsie: the denial of difference and the difference it makes,' *Diacritics* 17 (1987): 2–20; Graham Bradshaw, *Misrepresentations* (Ithaca: Cornell University Press, 1993), ch. I; Peter Erickson, 'Rewriting the Renaissance, rewriting ourselves,' *Shakespeare Quarterly* 38 (1987): 327–37; Carol Thomas Neely, 'Constructing the subject: feminist practice and the New Renaissance discourses,' *English Literary Renaissance* 18 (1988): 5–18; Lynda E. Boose, 'The family in Shakespearean Studies; or—Studies in the family of Shakespeareans; or—The politics of politics,' *Renaissance Quarterly* 40 (1987): 707–42; Louis A. Montrose, 'Renaissance literary studies and the subject of history,' and Jean E. Howard, 'The new historicism in Renaissance Studies,' both in *English Literary Renaissance*, 16, no. 1 (1986): 5–12 and 13–43; Ania Loomba, 'The color of patriarchy,' in Hendricks and Parker, *Women, 'Race,' and Writing*; Kumkum Sangari, 'Patrolling the borders: feminist historiography and the new historicism,' *Radical History Review* 43 (1989): 23–43; Judith Newton, 'Family fortunes: "new history" and "new historicism," ' *Radical History Review* 43 (1989): 5–42; Carolyn Porter, 'Are we being historical yet,' *South Atlantic Quarterly* 87 (1988): 743–87; and 'History "after the new criticism," ' *New Literary History* 21 (1990): 253–81; Franco Moretti, ' "A huge eclipse": tragic form and the deconsecration of sovereignty,' in *The Power of Forms in the English Renaissance*, ed. Stephen Greenblatt (Norman, Okla: Pilgrim Books, 1982), 7–40; and H. Aram Veeser (ed.), *The New Historicism* (New York: Routledge, 1989). Stephen Greenblatt and Catherine Gallagher have also produced a book on new historicism that addresses these objections. Greenblatt himself has abandoned the subversion-containment model of his earlier work.

18. See David Scott Kastan, 'Proud Majesty made a subject: Shakespeare and the spectacle of rule', *Shakespeare Quarterly* 37 (1986): 460, 472–3, which also warns against the temptation of idealizing representation's subversive power; E. M. W. Tillyard, *Shakespeare's History Plays* (London: Chatto and Windus, 1944); Stephen Greenblatt, 'Invisible bullets,' in *Shakespearean Negotiations*, chap. 2; and E. K. Chambers (ed.), *The Elizabethan Stage*, 4 vols. (Oxford: Clarendon Press, 1923), 4:247, on Henry Crosse's complaint, for example, after James's accession, that 'there is no passion wherwith the king, the soveraigne maiestie of the Realme was possesst, but is amplified, and openly sported with, and made a May-game to all the beholders.'

19. Kastan, 'Proud Majesty,' 467–8; Weimann, *Shakespeare and the Popular Tradition in the Theatre*, ed. Robert Schwartz (Baltimore: Johns Hopkins University Press, 1978), 208–52.

20. See also in this regard Kastan, 'Proud Majesty,' 460; and Steven Mullaney's *The Place of the Stage* (Chicago: University of Chicago Press, 1988), chap. 5.

21. See, for example, Leonard Tennenhouse's *Power on Display* (New York: Methuen, 1986), 96–99 and 153–54.

22. Annabel Patterson, *Censorship and Interpretation* (Madison: University of Wisconsin Press, 1984); Pierre Bourdieu, *Outline of a Theory of Practice*, trans. Richard A. Nice (Cambridge: Cambridge University Press, 1977), chap. 3.

23. See, for example, the description of Falstaff as a 'globe of sinful continents' (*2H4*, II.iv.285) [. . .]. The question of the limits of wordplay itself [. . .] might be addressed not only through the contemporary dictionaries and surrounding discourses cited throughout this book but also through such constraints as a passage's own dramatic context, which may activate (or not) the various resonances of a given word. A polyvalent early modern term like *excrement*, for instance, may be limited to its general sense of 'outgrowth' when it appears in the discussion of hair in *The Comedy of Errors* (II.ii.78). But its more specifically lower-bodily associations are

clearly summoned in the scene of *Love's Labor's Lost* (V.i) where Armado's reference to the king's 'royal finger' dallying 'with my excrement' (103–4) is linked not only with hair ('my mustachio') but also with surrounding references to '*ad dunghill*, at the fingers' ends' (77–8), to the 'posterior of the day' (91)—a phrase described as 'well cull'd' (93)—and to letting 'pass' what is 'inward' (97) [. . .].

24. See, among others, Montrose's pioneering 'The purpose of playing: reflections on a Shakespearean anthropology', *Helios* 7 (1980): 51–74; Mullaney, *Place of the Stage*; Kastan, 'Proud Majesty,' 474, on the theater's 'oddly liminal' status; Jean Howard, 'Renaissance antitheatricality and the politics of gender and rank in *Much Ado about Nothing*,' in *Shakespeare Reproduced*, ed. Jean E. Howard and Marion F. O'Connor (New York: Routledge, 1987), 116–40, and more recently *The Stage and Social Struggle in Early Modern England* (New York: Routledge, 1994), Leeds Barroll, *Politics, Plague, and Shakespeare's Theater* (Ithaca: Cornell University Press, 1991), esp. chap. 1.

25. See Jonathan Culler, *The Pursuit of Signs* (Ithaca, N.Y.: Cornell University Press, 1981).

Sinfield, Faultlines

1. Jonathan Dollimore, 'Shakespeare, cultural materialism, feminism and Marxist humanism', *New Literary History*, 21 (1990), pp. 471–93 (p. 482). See also James Holstun, 'Ranting at the new historicism', *English Literary Renaissance*, 19 (1989), pp. 189–225.

2. Jonathan Dollimore and Alan Sinfield (eds.), *Political Shakespeare* (Manchester: Manchester University Press; Ithaca, NY: Cornell University Press, 1985), p. 13; discussed in Jonathan Dollimore and Alan Sinfield, 'Culture and textuality: debating cultural materialism', *Textual Practice*, 4/1 (1990), pp. 91–100. See also Alan Liu's argument that we need to consider not only subject and representation, but action: Alan Liu, 'The power of formalism: the new historicism', *English Literary History*, 56 (1989), pp. 721–77 (pp. 734–5).

3. 'The political function of the intellectual', trans. Colin Gordon, *Radical Philosophy*, 17 (1977), pp. 12–15 (p. 14); see Eve Tavor Bannet, *Structuralism and the Logic of Dissent* (London: Macmillan, 1989), pp. 170–83.

4. Raymond Williams, *Marxism and Literature* (Oxford: Oxford University Press, 1977), p. 209.

Bate, The Genius of Shakespeare

1. In *Shakespeare and the Problem of Meaning* (Chicago, 1981), Norman Rabkin offers a duck-rabbit reading of Henry V, but without reference to Wittgenstein.

2. *Seven Types of Ambiguity* (London: Chatto & Windus, 1930), p. 246.

3. William Hazlitt, 'On Shakspeare and Milton', in Jonathan Bate (ed.), *The Romantics on Shakespeare* (Harmondsworth: Penguin, 1992), p. 181.

4. Letters to Richard Woodhouse, 27 October 1818 ('What shocks the virtuous Philosopher delights the chameleon Poet'), and to George and Tom Keats, 21–7 December 1817 ('at once it struck me, what quality went to form a Man of Achievement especially in Literature & which Shakespeare possessed so enormously—I mean *Negative Capability*'). *The Letters of John Keats*, ed. Hyder Edward Rollins, 2 vols. (Cambridge, MA: Harvard University Press, 1958).

Joughin, Shakespeare, modernity and the aesthetic

1. My indebtedness to these thinkers will be evident throughout, but I am particularly grateful to Bowie, on whom I draw heavily here and below, and whose exploration of the philosophical origins of literary theory has proved especially informative (see esp. Bowie 1997a: 1–27). For more on the emergent debate surrounding 'new aestheticism' in its British context see Beech and Roberts (1996), Bernstein (1997) and Bowie (1997b).

Greenblatt, Marvelous possessions

1. Jean de Léry, *History of a Voyage to the Land of Brazil, Otherwise Called America*, trans. Janet Whatley (Berkeley: University of California Press, 1990) p. 141. Léry voyaged to Brazil in 1556–8,

but he did not publish the first edition of the *History* until 1578; five other editions, with substantial additions and revisions, appeared during his lifetime. See Frank Lestringant, 'L'Excursion brésilienne: Note sur les trois premières éditions de l'*Histoire d'un voyage* de Jean de Léry,' in *Mélanges sur la littérature de la Renaissance à la mémoire de V.-L. Saulnier* (Geneva: Droz, 1984), 53–72. Lestringant has published a series of astute and learned studies of Léry to which I am indebted.

2. He remarks similarly that the 'false prophets' whom the Tupinamba call *caraïbes* go from village to village 'like popish indulgence-bearers' (p. 140), bearing in each hand a maraca or rattle like 'the bell-ringers that accompany those impostors who, exploiting the credulity of our simple folk over here, carry from place to place the reliquaries of Saint Anthony or Saint Bernard, and other such instruments of idolatry' (p. 142).

3. Quoted by Whatley in Jean de Léry, *History of a Voyage*, 248.

4. Albertus Magnus, *Opera Omnia*, ed. Augustus Borguet (Paris, 1890), vi, 30*a*–31*a*; trans. in J. V. Cunningham, *Woe and Wonder* (Denver: Denver University Press, 1951), 79. See Chap. 2, pp. 16 ff.

5. Michael Camille, *The Gothic Idol: Ideology and Image-Making in Medieval Art* (Cambridge: Cambridge University Press, 1989), 78–81.

6. Michael de Certeau, *The Writing of History*, trans. Tom Conley (New York: Columbia University Press, 1988), 213.

7. In the Middle Ages, Jacques Le Goff has observed, there are endless references in both popular and learned writing to 'marvels' (*mirabilia*) but little or no discussion of 'the marvelous' as a category (Jacques Le Goff, *L'Imaginaire médiéval* [Paris: Gallimard, 1985], 18 ff.). Le Goff argues that this is because there is something disturbing to the dominant ideology about marvels, something unpredictable and alien, as if the proliferation of wonders bespoke a tacit, unorganized, but tenacious resistance to Christian orthodoxy, an atavistic survival of the old pagan marvels and the belief in a plurality of spiritual forces. Gradually, through the concept of the miraculous, supernatural and strictly Christian elements are separated out: in the Christian marvelous, there is only one author, one source of all spiritual power. Thus the Church was able to make predictable, to legitimate, and to colonize some of the old marvels, while at the same time pushing what remained toward the domain of magic. Le Goff suggests that in the later Middle Ages there were other strategies for containing the marvels, including what he calls its 'aestheticization.' In Columbus we [. . .] find further strategies for Christianizing and colonizing the marvelous in the very place—the East—that had long been its great reservoir.

8. Descartes, *Philosophical Works*, trans. Elizabeth Haldane and G. R. T. Ross, 2 vols. (Cambridge: Cambridge University Press, 1911), i. 363.

9. Baruch Spinoza, *Chief Works*, trans. R. H. M. Elwes, 2 vols. (London: George Bell & Sons, 1884), ii. 174. 'The thought of an unusual thing, considered in itself, is of the same nature as other thoughts, and for this reason I do not count wonder among the emotions; nor do I see why I should do so, since this distraction of the mind arises from no positive cause that distracts it from other things, but only from the lack of a cause for determining the mind, from the contemplation of one thing, to think of other things' (Baruch Spinoza, *The Ethics and Selected Letters*, trans. Samuel Shirley, ed. Seymour Feldman [Indianapolis: Hackett, 1982], 143). Unlike Descartes, Spinoza thought that wonder does have an opposite: contempt.

10. In *The Poems of John Milton*, ed. John Carey and Alastair Fowler (London: Longman, 1968). David Quint kindly called my attention to the relevance of this passage. Milton is, at least by implication, a brilliant reader of the discourse of discovery and the uses of wonder. See, for example, the passage in which Satan, on the lowest stair of heaven, 'Looks down with wonder at the sudden view / Of all this world at once':

> As when a scout,
> Through dark and desert ways with peril gone
> All night; at last by break of cheerful dawn
> Obtains the brow of some high-climbing hill,

> Which to his eye discovers unaware
> The goodly prospect of some foreign land
> First-seen, or some renowned metropolis
> With glistering spires and pinnacles adorned,
> Which now the rising sun gilds with his beams.
> Such wonder seized, though after heaven seen,
> The spirit malign, but much more envy seized,
> At sight of all this world beheld so fair.
>
> (*PL* 3. 542–54)

11. Sir Walter Ralegh, *The Discoverie of the Large, Rich, and Beautifull Empire of Guiana*, in Richard Hakluyt, *The Principal Navigations, Voyages, Traffiques and Discoveries of the English Nation*, 12 vols (Glasgow: J. MacLehose & Sons, 1903–5), x. 406.

Kastan, Shakespeare after Theory

1. Edward Said, *The World, the Text, and the Critic* (Cambridge, MA: Harvard Unversity Press, 1985), p. 4.

Smith, Shakespeare and Masculinity

1. Michel Serres, *The Troubadour of Knowledge*, trans. Sheila Faria Glaser and William Paulson (Ann Arbor: University of Michigan Press, 1997), p. 147.

Dollimore, Shakespeare and Theory

1. [The standard study of the Frankfurt School is Martin Jay's *The Dialectical Imagination: A History of the Frankfurt School and the Institute of Social Research 1923–50* (Berkeley, CA: University of California Press, 1996).]
2. [See especially Jonathan Dollimore, *Radical Tragedy: Religion, Ideology and Power in the Drama of Shakespeare and his Contemporaries*, 3rd edn (Basingstoke and New York: Palgrave, 2004) and Jonathan Dollimore and Alan Sinfield (eds.), *Political Shakespeare* (Manchester and Ithaca, NY: Manchester University Press, Cornell University Press, 1985).]

REFERENCES

Allen, T., *The Invention of the White Race*, Vol. I: *Racial Oppression and Social Control* (London and New York: Verso, 1994)

Atkins, J. W. H., *English Literary Criticism: The Renascence*, 2nd edn (London: Methuen, 1951)

Attridge, Derek, *Well-weighed Syllables: Elizabethan Verse in Classical Metres* (Cambridge: Cambridge University Press, 1974)

Barker, F. and Hulme, P., ' "Nymphs and reapers heavily vanish": the discursive contexts of *The Tempest*', in J. Drakakis (ed.), *Alternative Shakespeares* (London: Methuen, 1985)

Barthes, Roland, *Mythologies*, selected and translated by Annette Lavers and Colin Smith (London: Cape, 1967)

Beech, D. and Roberts, J., 'Spectres of the aesthetic', *New Left Review*, 218, pp. 102–27

Behn, A., *Oroonoko, and Other Writings*, ed. Paul Salzman (1688; New York: Oxford University Press, 1994)

Belsey, C., *Critical Practice* (London: Methuen, 1980)

Bennett, A. and Royle, N., *An Introduction to Literature, Criticism and Theory* (Hemel Hempstead: Prentice Hall Europe, 1999)

Bernstein, J. M., 'Introduction' to T. Adorno, *The Culture Industry* (London: Routledge, 1991)

—— *The Fate of Art: Aesthetic Alienation from Kant to Derrida and Adorno* (Oxford: Polity Press, 1992)

—— 'Against voluptuous bodies: of satiation without happiness', *New Left Review*, 225 (1997), pp. 89–104.

Boose, Lynda, ' "The getting of a lawful race": racial discourse in early modern England and the unrepresentable black woman', in M. Hendricks and B. Parker (eds.), *Women, 'Race' and Writing in the Early Modern Period* (London: Routledge, 1993)

Booth, Stephen (ed.), *Shakespeare's Sonnets* (New Haven: Yale University Press, 1977)

Bourdieu, Pierre, *Distinction: A Social Critique of the Judgement of Taste*, trans. Richard Nice (London: Routledge, 1984)

Bowie, A., *Aesthetics and Subjectivity: From Kant to Nietzsche* (Manchester: Manchester University Press, 1990)

—— 'Aesthetic autonomy', in D. Cooper, J. Margolis and C. Sartwell (eds.), *A Companion to Aesthetics* (Oxford: Blackwell, 1992)

—— *From Romanticism to Critical Theory: The Philosophy of German Literary Theory* (London: Routledge, 1997a)

—— 'Confessions of a "new aesthete": a response to the "new philistines" ', *New Left Review*, 225 (1997b), pp. 105–26.

Bredbeck, G. W., *Sodomy and Interpretation: Marlowe to Milton* (Ithaca, NY: Cornell University Press, 1991)

Bloom, Harold, *Shakespeare: The Invention of the Human* (New York: Riverhead, 1998)

Cave, Terence, *The Cornucopian Text: The Problems of Writing in the French Renaissance* (Oxford: Oxford University Press, 1979)

Caygill, H., *The Art of Judgement* (Oxford: Blackwell, 1989)

de Grazia, M., 'The scandal of Shakespeare's sonnets', *Shakespeare Survey*, 41 (1993), pp. 35–50.

Derrida, Jacques, *Of Grammatology*, translated by Gayatri Chakravorty Spivak (Baltimore: Johns Hopkins University Press, 1976)

Dews, P., *Logics of Disintegration: Post-Structuralist Thought and the Claims of Critical Theory* (London: Verso, 1987)

—— *The Limits of Disenchantment: Essays on Contemporary European Philosophy* (London: Verso, 1995)

Doran, Madeleine, *Endeavours of Art: A Study of Form in Elizabethan Drama* (Madison: University of Wisconsin Press, 1954)

Dubois, W. E. B., *Black Reconstruction in the United States, 1860–1880* (1935; New York: Kraus-Thomson, 1977)

Duval, Edwin M., 'Lessons of the New World: Design and Meaning in Montaigne's "Des cannibales" and "Des Coches" ', *Yale French Studies*, 64 (1983), pp. 95–112.

Dyer, R., 'The colour of virtue: Lillian Gish, whiteness and femininity', in Pam Cook and Philip Dodd (eds.), *Women in Film: A Sight and Sound Reader* (Philadelphia: Temple University Press, 1993), pp. 1–9.

Empson, William, *Some Versions of Pastoral* (London, 1935; Harmondsworth: Penguin, 1966)

Erickson, P., 'Representations of blacks and blackness in the Renaissance', *Criticism*, 35 (1993), pp. 499–528.

—— 'Profiles in whiteness', *Stanford Humanities Review*, 3 (1993), pp. 98–111.

—— 'Seeing white', *Transition*, 67 (1996), pp. 166–87.

Ferguson, Margaret W., *Trials of Desire: Renaissance Defences of Poetry* (New Haven: Yale University Press, 1983)

Fiedler, L., *The Stranger in Shakespeare* (New York: Stern & Day, 1972)

Fineman, J., *Shakespeare's Perjured: The Invention of Poetic Subjectivity in the Sonnets* (Berkeley: University of California Press, 1986)

Fumerton, P., *Cultural Aesthetics: Renaissance Literature and the Practice of Social Ornament* (Chicago: University of Chicago Press, 1991)

Goldberg, J., '*Romeo and Juliet's* open Rs', in J. Goldberg (ed.), *Queering the Renaissance* (Durham, NC: Duke University Press, 1994), pp. 218–35.

Greene, R., 'Petrarchism among the discourses of imperialism', in Karen Ordahl Kupperman (ed.), *America in European Consciousness 1493–1750* (Chapel Hill: University of N. Carolina Press, 1995), pp. 130–65.

Greene, T. M., 'Pitiful thrivers: failed husbandry in *The Sonnets*', in P. Parker and G. Hartman (eds.), *Shakespeare and the Question of Theory* (London: Methuen, 1985), pp. 230–44.

—— *The Light in Troy: Imitation and Discovery in Renaissance Poetry* (New Haven: Yale University Press, 1982)

Grieco, S. F., 'The body, appearance and sexuality', in Natalie Zemon Davis and Arlette Farge (eds.), *A History of Women in the West: Renaissance and Enlightenment Paradoxes* (Cambridge, MA and London: Harvard University Press, 1993), pp. 46–84.

Hall, K. F., ' "I rather would wish to be a blackamoor": race, rank and beauty in Lady Mary Wroth's *Urania*', in M. Hendricks and P. Parker (eds.), *Women, 'Race' and Writing* (London: Routledge, 1994), pp. 178–94.

—— *Things of Darkness: Economies of Race and Gender in Early Modern England* (New York and London: Cornell University Press, 1995)

Hathaway, Baxter, Introduction to *The Art of English Poesie* by George Puttenham (Kent: Kent State University Press, 1970)

Hawkes, Terence, Introduction, T. Hawkes (ed.), *Alternative Shakespeares*, Vol. 2 (London: Routledge, 1996)

Heal, F. and Homes, C., *The Gentry in England and Wales, 1500–1700* (Stanford: Stanford University Press, 1994)

Helgerson, R., *Forms of Nationhood: The Elizabethan Writing of England* (Chicago: University of Chicago Press, 1992)

Hendricks, Margo, 'Managing the barbarian: *The Tragedy of Dido, Queen of Carthage*', *Renaissance Drama*, 23 (1992), pp. 165–88.

—— and Parker, Patricia (eds.), *Women, 'Race' and Writing in the Early Modern Period* (London: Routledge, 1994)

Herrick, Robert, *Poems*, ed. L. C. Martin (New York: Oxford University Press, 1965)

Hodge, J., 'Equality: beyond dualism and oppression', in D. T. Goldberg (ed.), *Anatomy of Racism* (Minneapolis: University of Minnesota Press, 1990), pp. 89–107.

hooks, bell, *Yearning: Race, Gender and Cultural Politics* (Boston: South End Press, 1990)

Hunter, G. K., 'Humanism and courtship', in Paul Alpers (ed.), *Elizabethan Poetry: Modern Essays in Criticism* (New York: Oxford University Press, 1967), pp. 3–40.

—— *Dramatic Identities and Cultural Tradition: Studies on Shakespeare and His Contemporaries* (New York: Harper, 1978)

Javitch, Daniel, 'The impure motives of Elizabethan poetry', *Genre*, 15 (1982), pp. 225–38.

—— *Poetry and Courtliness in Renaissance England* (Princeton: Princeton University Press, 1978)

Jordan, W., *White over Black: American Attitudes toward the Negro, 1550–1812* (Chapel Hill: University of N. Carolina Press, 1968)

Kahn, Victoria, *Rhetoric, Prudence, and Skepticism in the Renaissance* (Ithaca, NY: Cornell University Press, 1985)

—— 'Humanism and the Resistance to Theory', in Patricia Parker and David Quint (eds.), *Literary Theory/ Renaissance Texts* (Baltimore: Johns Hopkins University Press, 1986), pp. 373–96.

Kranidas, Thomas, *The Fierce Equation: A Study of Milton's Decorum* (The Hague: Mouton, 1965)

Levao, Ronald, *Renaissance Minds and Their Fictions: Cusanus, Sidney, Shakespeare* (Berkeley: University of California Press, 1985)

Liu, T., 'Teaching the differences among women from an historical perspective', *Women's Studies International Forum*, 14/4 (1991), pp. 265–76.

—— 'Race', in R. Wrightman Fox and J. T. Kloppenberg (eds.), *A Companion to American Thought* (Oxford: Blackwell, 1995), pp. 564–7.

Longinus, *On Sublimity*, trans. D. A. Russell, in D. A. Russell and M. Winterbottom (eds.), *Ancient Literary Criticism* (Oxford: Oxford University Press, 1972), pp. 460–503.

Marsden, J. I. (ed.), *The Appropriation of Shakespeare: Post-Renaissance Reconstructions of the Works and the Myth* (Hemel Hempstead: Harvester Wheatsheaf, 1991)

Mercer, K., 'Skin head sex thing: racial difference and the homoerotic imaginary', in Bad Object-Choices (ed.), *How Do I Look: Queer Film and Video* (Seattle: Bay Press, 1991), pp. 211–22.

Montrose, Louis Adrian, 'Gentleman and shepherds: the politics of Elizabethan pastory form', *ELH*, 50 (1983), pp. 415–59.

Morrison, T., *The Bluest Eye* (New York: Washington Square Press, 1972)

—— *Playing in the Dark: Whiteness and the Literary Imagination* (Cambridge, MA: Harvard University Press, 1992)

Nahoum-Grappe, V., 'The beautiful woman', trans. Arthur Goldhammer, in Natalie Zemon and Arlette Farge (eds.), *A History of Women in the West: Renaissance and Enlightenment Paradoxes* (Cambridge MA and London: Harvard University Press, 1993), pp. 85–100.

Ogle, M. B., 'The Classical Origin and Tradition of Literary Conceits', *American Journal of Philology* 34.2 (1965), 125–52.

Omi, M. and Winant, H., *Racial Formation in the United States: From the 1960s to the 1990s* (New York: Routledge, 1994)

Patterson, Annabel M., *Hermongenes and the Renaissance: Seven Ideas of Style* (Princeton: Princeton University Press, 1970)

Plett, Heinrich, 'Aesthetic constituents in the courtly culture of Renaissance England', *New Literary History* 14 (1983), 597–621.

Puttenham, George, *The Arte of English Poesie; Continued into Three Bookes: the first of Poets and Poesie, the Second of Proportion, the Third of Ornament* (London, 1589)

—— *The Arte of English Poesie*, ed. Gladys Doidge Wilcock and Alice Walker (Cambridge: Cambridge University Press, 1936)

Quint, David, *Origin and Originality in Renaissance Literature: Versions of the Source* (New Haven: Yale University Press, 1983)

Quintilian, *Institutionis Oratoriae*, trans. H. E. Butler (Cambridge: Harvard University Press, 1920)

Roediger, D., *The Wages of Whiteness: Race and the Making of the American Working Class* (New York and London: Verso, 1991)

Sedgwick, E. K., *Between Men: English Literature and Male Homosocial Desire* (New York: Columbia University Press, 1985)

Shakespeare, William, *A New Variorum Edition of Shakespeare: The Sonnets*, ed. Hyder Edward Rollins, 2 vols. (Philadelphia and London: Lippincott, 1944)

—— *The Riverside Shakespeare*, ed. G. Blakemore Evans (New York: Houghton Mifflin, 1974)

—— *Shakespeare's Sonnets*, ed. Stephen Booth (New Haven and London: Yale University Press, 1977)

Sidney, Sir Philip, *An Apologie for Poetrie*, in G. Gregory Smith (ed.), *Elizabethan Critical Essays*, vol. 1, pp. 148–207.

Smith, B., *Homosexual Desire in Shakespeare's England: A Cultural Poetics* (Chicago: University of Chicago Press, 1991)

Smith, G. Gregory (ed.), *Elizabeth Critical Essays*, 2 vols. (London: Oxford University Press, 1904)

Spenser, Edmund, *The Faerie Queene*, ed. J. Smith (Oxford: Oxford University Press, 1909)

Stallybrass, P., 'Editing as cultural formation: the sexing of Shakespeare's sonnets', *Modern Language Quarterly*, 54/1 (1993), pp. 91–103.

Stone, L. and Stone, J. C. *An Open Elite? England, 1540–1880* (New York: Oxford University Press, 1984)

Strong, R., *The Cult of Elizabeth* (Berkeley: University of California Press, 1986)

—— *Gloriana: The Portraits of Elizabeth I* (London: Thames & Hudson, 1987)

Tayler, Edward William, *Nature and Art in Renaissance Literature* (New York: Columbia University Press, 1964)

Taylor, C., *Sources of the Self: The Making of the Modern Identity* (Cambridge, MA: Harvard University Press, 1989)

Taylor, G., *Reinventing Shakespeare: A Cultural History from the Restoration to the Present* (Oxford: Oxford University Press, 1991)

Tuve, Rosamund, *Elizabethan and Metaphysical Imagery* (Chicago: University of Chicago Press, 1947)

Valéry, Paul, *The Art of Poetry*, trans. Denise Folliot, Vol. 7 of *The Collected Works of Paul Valéry*, ed. Jackson Matthews (Princeton: Princeton University Press, 1958)

Vickers, Nancy, 'Diana described: scattered women and scattered rhyme', in Elizabeth Abel (ed.), *Writing and Sexual Difference* (Chicago: University of Chicago Press, 1982), pp. 98–110.

Wall, W. 'Renaissance national husbandry: Gervase Markham and the publication of England', *Sixteenth Century Journal*, 27/3 (1996), pp. 767–85.

Weimann, R. 'A divided heritage: conflicting appropriations of Shakespeare in (East) Germany', in J. J. Joughin (ed.), *Shakespeare and National Culture* (Mancester: Manchester University Press, 1997)

Whigham, Frank, 'Interpretation at court: courtesy and the performer-audience dialectic', *New Literary History*, 14 (1983), pp. 623–39.

Willcock, G. D. and Walker, A., see under Puttenham, George

Wimsatt, W. K. and Brooks, Cleanth, *Literary Criticism: A Short History* (London: Routledge, 1957)

Acknowledgements of Sources

Textuality

Ramona Wray

Margreta de Grazia and Peter Stallybrass, 'The materiality of the Shakespeare text', *Shakespeare Quarterly*, 44 (1993), 280–2.

Peter W. M. Blayney, 'The publication of playbooks', in John D. Cox and David Scott Kastan (eds.), *A New History of Early English Drama* (New York: Columbia University Press, 1997), pp. 383–422.

Leah Marcus, *Unediting the Renaissance: Shakespeare, Marlowe, Milton* (London and New York: Routledge, 1996), pp. 225–6.

Lukas Erne, *Shakespeare as Literary Dramatist* (Cambridge: Cambridge University Press, 2003), pp. 234–44.

Jeffrey Masten, *Textual Intercourse: Collaboration, Authorship, and Sexualities in Renaissance Drama* (Cambridge: Cambridge University Press, 1997), pp. 14–15, 19–27.

Margaret W. Ferguson, 'Renaissance concepts of the "woman writer"', in Helen Wilcox (ed.), *Women and Literature in Britain, 1500–1700* (Cambridge: Cambridge University Press, 1996), p. 145.

Annabel Patterson, *Censorship and Interpretation: The Conditions of Writing and Reading in Early Modern England* (Madison: University of Wisconsin Press, 1984), pp. 10–11.

Arthur F. Marotti, 'Malleable and fixed texts: manuscript and printed miscellanies and the transmission of lyric poetry in the English Renaissance', in W. Speed Hill (ed.), *New Ways of Looking at Old Texts* (Binghamton, New York: Medieval and Renaissance Texts and Studies, 1993), pp. 170–2.

Jonathan Goldberg, *Shakespeare's Hand* (Minneapolis and London: University of Minnesota Press, 2003), pp. 253–67, 270.

Stephen Orgel, 'What is a text?', in David Scott Kastan and Peter Stallybrass (eds.), *Staging the Renaissance: Interpretations of Elizabethan and Jacobean Drama* (London and New York: Routledge, 1991), pp. 86–7.

Andrew Murphy, 'Texts and textualities: a Shakespearean history', in Andrew Murphy (ed.), *The Renaissance Text: Theory, Editing, Textuality* (Manchester and New York: Manchester University Press, 2000), pp. 197–205.

Gary Taylor, 'The Renaissance and the end of editing', in George Bornstein and Ralph G. Williams (eds.), *Palimpsest: Editorial Theory in the Humanities* (Ann Arbor: The University of Michigan Press, 1993), pp. 142–3.

Suzanne Gossett, 'Introduction', in *'Pericles': The Arden Shakespeare* (London: Thomson, 2004), pp. 46–54.

Ann Thompson, 'Teena Rochfort Smith, Frederick Furnivall, and the New Shakspere Society's Four-Text Edition of *Hamlet*', *Shakespeare Quarterly*, 49 (1998), 138.

David Scott Kastan, *Shakespeare and the Book* (Cambridge: Cambridge University Press, 2001), pp. 123–31.

Leah Marcus, Janel Mueller and Mary Beth Rose, 'Preface', in Leah Marcus, Janel Mueller and Mary Beth Rose (eds.), *Elizabeth I: Collected Works* (Chicago and London: University of Chicago Press, 2000), pp. xviii–xxii.

Histories

Mark Thornton Burnett and Ramona Wray

Jean Howard, 'The New Historicism and Renaissance Studies', *English Literary Renaissance*, 16 (1986), 24–30.

Frances E. Dolan, *Whores of Babylon: Catholicism, Gender and Seventeenth-Century Print Culture* (Ithaca and London: Cornell University Press, 1999), pp. 2–3.

Louis Montrose, 'New historicisms', in Stephen Greenblatt and Giles Gunn (eds.), *Redrawing the Boundaries: The Transformation of English and American Literary Studies* (New York: MLA, 1992), pp. 400–6.

Tina Krontiris, *Oppositional Voices: Women as Writers and Translators of Literature in the English Renaissance* (London and New York: Routledge, 1992), pp. 21–3.

Stephen Greenblatt, *Renaissance Self-Fashioning: From More to Shakespeare* (Chicago and London: University of Chicago Press, 1980), pp. 193–200.

Christopher Highley, *Shakespeare, Spenser, and the Crisis in Ireland* (Cambridge: Cambridge University Press, 1997), pp. 89–90.

Dympna Callaghan, 'Re-reading Elizabeth Cary's *The Tragedie of Mariam, Faire Queene of Jewry*', in Margo Hendricks and Patricia Parker (eds.), *Women, 'Race', and Writing in the Early Modern Period* (London and New York: Routledge, 1994), pp. 167–77.

Mark Thornton Burnett, *Constructing 'Monsters' in Shakespearean Drama and Early Modern Culture* (Basingstoke: Macmillan, 2002), pp. 11–12.

Catherine Gallagher and Stephen Greenblatt, *Practicing New Historicism* (Chicago and London: University of Chicago Press, 2000), pp. 14–16.

Mary Fuller, *Voyages in Print: English Travel to America, 1576–1624* (Cambridge: Cambridge University Press, 1995), pp. 58–65.

Bruce R. Smith, *Homosexual Desire in Shakespeare's England: A Cultural Poetics* (Chicago and London: University of Chicago Press, 1991), pp. 6–7.

Adam Fox, *Oral and Literate Culture in England 1500–1700* (Oxford: Oxford University Press, 2000), pp. 325–34.

Patricia Fumerton, 'Introduction: A New New Historicism', in Patricia Fumerton and Simon Hunt (eds.), *Renaissance Culture and the Everyday* (Philadelphia: University of Pennsylvania Press, 1999), pp. 3–4.

David Scott Kastan, *Shakespeare after Theory* (New York and London: Routledge, 1999), pp. 17–18.

Kim Hall, *Things of Darkness: Economies of Race and Gender in Early Modern England* (Ithaca and London: Cornell University Press, 1995), pp. 215–26.

Juliet Fleming, *Graffiti and the Writing Arts of Early Modern England* (Philadelphia: University of Pennsylvania Press, 2001), pp. 60–7.

Appropriation

Mark Thornton Burnett

Daniel Fischlin and Mark Fortier, 'General Introduction', in Daniel Fischlin and Mark Fortier (eds.), *Adaptations of Shakespeare: A Critical Anthology of Plays from the Seventeenth Century to the Present* (London and New York: Routledge, 2000), p. 1.

Samuel Schoenbaum, *Shakespeare's Lives* (Oxford: Clarendon, 1991), pp. 550–9.

Barbara Hodgdon, *The Shakespeare Trade: Performances & Appropriations* (Philadelphia: University of Pennsylvania Press, 1998), pp. 232–4.

Michael Anderegg, *Orson Welles, Shakespeare, and Popular Culture* (New York: Columbia University Press, 1999), pp. 61–73.

Michael Bristol, *Big-Time Shakespeare* (London: Routledge, 1996), pp. 5, 91.

Courtney Lehmann, *Shakespeare Remains: Theatre to Film, Early Modern to Postmodern* (Ithaca and London: Cornell University Press, 2002), pp. 165–6, 168–9, 170, 175–6, 176–7, 180–8.

Heidi Hutner, *Colonial Women: Race and Culture in Stuart Drama* (Oxford: Oxford University Press, 2001), pp. 45–6.

Michael Dobson and Nicola J. Watson, *England's Elizabeth: An Afterlife in Fame and Fantasy* (Oxford: Oxford University Press, 2002), pp. 217–18, 255–6, 257–9, 262–7.

Lawrence Normand, '*Edward II*, Derek Jarman, and the state of England', in J. A. Downie and J. T. Parnell (eds.), *Constructing Christopher Marlowe* (Cambridge: Cambridge University Press, 2000), pp. 177, 180–3, 189–93.

Sarah Werner, *Shakespeare and Feminist Performance: Ideology on Stage* (London and New York: Routledge, 2001), pp. 77–87.

Dennis Kennedy, 'Afterword: Shakespearean Orientalism', in Dennis Kennedy (ed.), *Foreign Shakespeare: Contemporary Performance* (Cambridge: Cambridge University Press, 1993), p. 301.

Ania Loomba, 'Local manufacture made-in-India Othello fellows', in Ania Loomba and Martin Orkin (eds.), *Post-Colonial Shakespeares* (London: Routledge, 1998), pp. 151–63.

Lawrence W. Levine, *Highbrow/Lowbrow: The Emergence of Cultural Hierarchy in America* (Cambridge, Mass.: Harvard University Press, 1988), pp. 20–1, 23.

Francesca T. Royster, *Becoming Cleopatra: The Shifting Image of an Icon* (New York: Palgrave, 2003), pp. 9–17.

Richard Burt, '*Shakespeare in Love* and the end of the Shakespearean: academic and mass culture constructions of literary authorship', in Mark Thornton Burnett and Ramona Wray (eds.), *Shakespeare, Film, Fin de Siècle* (Basingstoke: Macmillan, 2000), pp. 226–7.

John Russell Brown, *New Sites for Shakespeare: Theatre, the Audience and Asia* (London and Routledge, 1999), pp. 191–2, 193, 197.

Identities

Clare McManus

Alan Sinfield, *Faultlines: Cultural Materialism and the Politics of Dissident Reading* (Oxford: Clarendon Press, 1992), pp. 52–4.

Lorna Hutson, 'Why the lady's eyes are nothing like the sun', in Clare Brant and Diane Purkiss (eds.), *Women, Texts and Histories 1575–1760* (London and New York: Routledge, 1992), pp. 17–18.

Douglas Trevor, 'George Herbert and the scene of writing', in Carla Mazzio and Douglas Trevor (eds.), *Historicism, Psychoanalysis and Early Modern Culture* (London and New York: Routledge, 2000), pp. 228, 229–35, 251–2.

Ania Loomba, 'Shakespeare and cultural difference', in Terence Hawkes (ed.), *Alternative Shakespeares Vol. 2* (London and New York: Routledge, 1996), pp. 172–3.

Katharine Eisaman Maus, *Inwardness and Theater in the English Renaissance* (Chicago and London: University of Chicago Press, 1995), pp. 26–30.

Diane Purkiss, 'Material girls: the seventeenth-century woman debate', in Clare Brant and Diane Purkiss (eds.), *Women, Texts and Histories 1575–1760* (London and New York: Routledge, 1992), pp. 69–70.

Joyce Green MacDonald, 'The disappearing African woman: Imoinda in *Oronooko* after Behn', *English Literary History*, 66 (1999), 77–8.

Margo Hendricks, 'Civility, barbarism, and Aphra Behn's *The Widow Ranter*', in Margo Hendricks and Patricia Parker (eds.), *Women, 'Race,' and Writing in the Early Modern Period* (London and New York: Routledge, 1994), pp. 225–6, 227–9, 234–9.

David Scott Kastan, 'Is there a class in this (Shakespearean) text?', *Renaissance Drama*, 25 (1993), 101–7, 114.

Thomas Healy, 'Selves, states, and sectarianism in early modern England', *English*, 44 (1995), 195, 198–9.

Alan Bray, 'Homosexuality and the signs of male friendship in Elizabethan England', *History Workshop*, 29 (1990), 2–3.

Valerie Traub, *Desire and Anxiety: Circulations of Sexuality in Shakespearean Drama* (London and New York: Routledge, 1992), pp. 94–116.

Ania Loomba and Martin Orkin (eds.), 'Introduction: Shakespeare and the post-colonial question', in *Post-Colonial Shakespeares* (London and New York: Routledge, 1998), p. 4.

Paul Brown, ' "This thing of darkness I acknowledge mine": *The Tempest* and the Discourse of Colonialism', in Jonathan Dollimore and Alan Sinfield (eds.), *Political Shakespeare: Essays in Cultural Materialism* (Manchester: Manchester University Press, 1985), pp. 49–51.

Stephen Greenblatt, *Renaissance Self-Fashioning: From More to Shakespeare* (London and Chicago: University of Chicago Press, 1980), pp. 179–92.

Jonathan Dollimore, *Death, Desire and Loss in Western Culture* (London: Allen Lane, Penguin Press, 1998), pp. 84–5, 90–3.

Erica Fudge, *Perceiving Animals: Humans and Beasts in Early Modern English Culture* (Basingstoke: Macmillan, 2000), pp. 1–8.

Materiality

Ewan Fernie and Clare McManus

Francis Barker, *The Tremulous Private Body: Essays on Subjection* (London and New York: Methuen, 1984), pp. 1–25.

Jonathan Sawday, *The Body Emblazoned: Dissection and the Human Body in Renaissance Culture* (London and New York: Routledge, 1995), pp. 4–5.

Terry Eagleton, *The Ideology of the Aesthetic* (Oxford: Blackwell, 1990), p. 7.

Nancy Vickers, 'Diana described: scattered woman and scattered rhyme', *Critical Inquiry*, 8 (1981), 265–6.

Patricia Parker, *Literary Fat Ladies: Rhetoric, Gender, Property* (London and New York: Methuen, 1987), pp. 8–17.

Gail Kern Paster, *The Body Embarrassed: Drama and the Disciplines of Shame in Early Modern England* (Ithaca, New York: Cornell University Press, 1993), pp. 23–63.

Louis Montrose, 'The work of gender in the discourse of discovery', *Representations*, 33 (1991), 6.

Jonathan Dollimore, *Sex, Literature and Censorship* (Polity: Cambridge, 2001), pp. 50–1.

Richmond Barbour, 'Britain and the Great Beyond: *The Masque of Blackness* at Whitehall', in John Gillies and Virginia Mason Vaughan (eds.), *Playing the Globe: Genre and Geography in English Renaissance Drama* (London: Associated University Presses, 1998), pp. 139–41.

Peter Stallybrass, 'Tranvestism and the body beneath: speculating on the boy actor', in Susan Zimmerman (ed.), *Erotic Politics: Desire on the Renaissance Stage* (London and New York: Routledge, 1992), pp. 77–80.

Valerie Traub, *The Renaissance of Lesbianism in Early Modern England* (Cambridge: Cambridge University Press, 2002), pp. 197–8, 203, 204–28.

Margreta de Grazia, Maureen Quilligan and Peter Stallybrass (eds.), *Subject and Object in Renaissance Culture* (Cambridge: Cambridge University Press, 1996), 'Introduction', pp. 1–5.

Jerry Brotton, *The Renaissance Bazaar* (Oxford: Oxford University Press, 2002), pp. 172–3.

Jonathan Gil Harris, 'Shakespeare's hair: staging the object of material culture', *Shakespeare Quarterly*, 52.4 (2001), 479–91.

Eric Wilson, 'Abel Drugger's sign and the fetishes of material culture', in Carla Mazzio and Douglas Trevor (eds.), *Historicism, Psychoanalysis and Early Modern Culture* (London and New York: Routledge, 2000), pp. 122–4.

Dympna Callaghan, 'Body problems', *Shakespeare Studies*, 29 (2001), 70–1.

Values

Ewan Fernie

Cary Nelson, 'Against English', *Profession*, 87 (1987), 49–50.

Kim F. Hall, 'These bastard signs of fair: literary whiteness in Shakespeare's Sonnets', in Ania Loomba and Martin Orkin (eds.), *Post-Colonial Shakespeares* (London and New York: Routledge, 1998), pp. 64–84.

Stephen Greenblatt, *Hamlet in Purgatory* (Princeton: Princeton University Press, 2001), p. 4.

Derek Attridge, *Peculiar Language: Literature as Difference from the Renaissance to James Joyce* (London: Methuen, 1988), pp. 18–19, 21–2, 24–40.

Thomas Healy, *New Latitudes: Theory and English Renaissance Texts* (London, Melbourne and Auckland: Edward Arnold), pp. 54–5.

Catherine Belsey, 'Disrupting sexual difference: meaning and gender in the Comedies', in John Drakakis (ed.), *Alternative Shakespeares* (London: Methuen, 1985), pp. 166–7.

Patricia Parker, *Shakespeare from the Margins: Language, Culture, Context* (Chicago: University of Chicago Press, 1996), pp. 1–19.

Alan Sinfield, *Faultlines: Cultural Materialism and the Politics of Dissident Reading* (Oxford: Clarendon Press, 1992), pp. 49–51.

Jonathan Bate, *The Genius of Shakespeare* (London: Picador, 1997), pp. 327–35.

Kiernan Ryan, *Shakespeare*, 3rd edn (Palgrave: Basingstoke and New York, 2002), p. 33.

John J. Joughin, 'Shakespeare, modernity and the aesthetic: art, truth and judgement in *The Winter's Tale*', in Hugh Grady (ed.), *Shakespeare and Modernity: Early Modern to Millennium* (London and New York: Routledge, 2000), pp. 61–7, 73.

Don E. Wayne, 'New Historicism', in Martin Coyle, Peter Garside, Malcolm Kelsall and John Peck (eds.), *Encyclopedia of Literature and Criticism* (London and New York: Routledge, 1990), p. 803.

Stephen Greenblatt, *Marvelous Possessions: The Wonder of the New World* (Chicago: University of Chicago Press, 1991), pp. 14–24.

Jacques Derrida, *Specters of Marx: The State of the Debt, The Work of Mourning, and The New International*, trans. Peggy Kamuf (New York and London: Routledge, 1994), p. xix.

David Scott Kastan, *Shakespeare after Theory* (New York and London: Routledge, 1999), p. 42.

Bruce R. Smith, *Shakespeare and Masculinity* (Oxford: Oxford University Press, 2000), pp. 131–3.

Jonathan Dollimore, 'Shakespeare and Theory', in Ania Loomba and Martin Orkin (eds.), *Post-Colonial Shakespeares* (London and New York: Routledge, 1998), pp. 267–70, 275–6.

Efforts have been made to trace and contact copyright holders prior to printing. Oxford University Press apologizes for any errors or omissions in this list and, if notified, will be pleased to make corrections at the earliest opportunity.

Index

DATE DUE

Demco, Inc. 38-293